The Female Trickster: The Mask That Reveals

"Ricki Tannen, like one of her postmodern detectives, displays irreverence, persistence and verve as she goes about exposing the lack of recognition that attends the female trickster in our culture. This is a delightful work of rescue. Its combination of sociological polemic and therapeutic amplification slips sexism into a double bind and sets the reader's soul free to laugh and breathe and argue."
John Beebe, founding editor, *The San Francisco Jung Institute Library Journal*.

"A stunning tour de force, *The Female Trickster* unites depth psychology, mythology, cultural theory, feminism, and literature in an incisive revelation of the feminine in a postmodern age. The analysis of the fictional female detective as trickster is a startling and valuable contribution to gender research. Tannen is to be congratulated on a book important for students of the humanities and clinicians alike."
Dr Susan Rowland, Reader in English and Jungian Studies, University of Greenwich, Chair: International Association for Jungian Studies 2003–6.

"Reading this amazing book puts one at the heart of that rare event – a major, discernible shift in human culture and behaviour. *The Female Trickster* is a really new take on women in Western society, shattering, in fine Trickster style, not only the turgid and neat gender binaries we all know and hate, but also the (by now) equally safe attempts to proclaim the binaries dead and buried. Entertaining, informative, inspiring, frightening, freaky! Essential reading for academy and clinic alike."
Andrew Samuels, Professor of Analytical Psychology, University of Essex

The Female Trickster presents a post-Jungian postmodern perspective regarding the role of women in contemporary Western society by investigating the re-emergence of female Trickster energy in all aspects of popular culture.

Ricki Stefanie Tannen explores the psychological aspects of what happened when women's imagination was legally and psychologically enclosed millennia ago and demonstrates how the re-emergence of Trickster energy through the female imagination has the radical potential to effect a transformation of western consciousness. Examples are drawn from a diverse range of sources, from Jane Austen, and female sleuth narratives, to Madonna and *Sex and the City*, illustrating how Trickster energy is used not to maintain power and control but to integrate and unite the paradoxical through humor. Subjects covered include:

- Imagination and metaphor
- The traditional Trickster
- Law and the imagination
- Humor: Eros using Logos
- The postmodern female Trickster

This highly original perspective on women's role in contemporary culture will offer readers a new vision of how humor psychologically operates as a healthy adaptation to trauma and adversity. It will be of great interest to all analytical psychologists and psychoanalysts as well as those in women's, cultural, legal and literary studies.

Ricki Stefanie Tannen, LLM, PhD is an analytical psychologist, attorney, author, artist and former professor of women's studies, law and rhetoric. She has published and lectured internationally on the subjects of gender bias, depth psychology and constitutional law.

The Female Trickster: The Mask That Reveals

Post-Jungian and postmodern psychological perspectives on women in contemporary culture

Ricki Stefanie Tannen

Routledge
Taylor & Francis Group

LONDON AND NEW YORK

First published 2007 by Routledge
27 Church Road, Hove, East Sussex BN3 2FA

Simultaneously published in the USA and Canada
by Taylor & Francis Inc
270 Madison Avenue, New York, NY 10016

Routledge is an imprint of the Taylor & Francis Group, an informa business

© 2007 Ricki Stefanie Tannen

Typeset in Times by Garfield Morgan, Swansea, West Glamorgan
Printed and bound in Great Britain by T J International Ltd, Padstow,
Cornwall
Paperback cover design by Sandra Heath

British Library Cataloguing in Publication Data
A catalogue record for this book is available from the British Library

Library of Congress Cataloging in Publication Data
Tannen, Ricki Stefanie.
   The female trickster: the mask that reveals: post-Jungian and postmodern
psychological perspectives on women in contemporary culture / Ricki
Stefanie Tannen.
      p. cm.
   Includes bibliographical references.
   ISBN 0-415-38530-X (hbk) – ISBN 0-415-38531-8 (pbk) 1. Women in
popular culture–History. 2. Women in literature. 3. Women and literature.
4. Tricksters. 5. Tricksters in literature. 6. Wit and humor–Social aspects.
7. Jungian psychology. 8. Feminist criticism. I. Title.
   HQ1122.T36 2007
   305.42–dc22

                                                              2006024860

ISBN 978-0-415-38530-5 hbk
ISBN 978-0-415-38531-2 pbk

To Laine and Adam

Contents

Preface   xi
Acknowledgments   xiii

PART I
Introducing the female Trickster   1

1   Introduction   3
Definitions 4
*What is a Trickster and is the female Trickster
    really different? 7*
How Trickster energy transforms culture through art 9
The fictive female sleuth as postmodern female Trickster 9
Notes 11

2   Meetings with remarkable women   12
Introduction 12
Jung and I: captured by a literary manifestation 12
Me and the girls 13
The postmodern female Trickster appears 23
Conclusion 26
Notes 26

3   Location, location, location   30
Introduction 30
*Texts written by women and a feminist approach to text are
    not the same 30*
Psychological considerations: research on the feminine 34
Jungian and post-Jungian perspectives on the feminine 41
Summary 50
Notes 51

PART II
Calling upon the ancestors   57

4   **Imagination and metaphor**   59
    Introduction 59
    Imagination and recovered memory: the numinous process of
        remembering 59
    Shape-shifting and transformation in the imaginal realm 60
    Imagination 61
    What has women's imagination produced? 66
    Summary 70
    Notes 71

5   **Where have all the virgins gone?**   72
    Introduction 72
    Mnemosyne, mistress of Eleutherian Hills 72
    The pre-patriarchal virgin and today's virginal feminine
        presence 73
    The pre-patriarchal virgin energy and Jungian feminism 75
    Summary 75
    Notes 76

6   **Law and the imagination**   78
    Introduction 78
    The enclosure 78
    The importance of being: ancient Athens 79
    The crumbling of the enclosure 82
    Can law produce a new archetype? 93
    Summary 94
    Notes 94

7   **From the madwomen in the attic to mainstream and**
    mysterious: a brief and highly selective history of
    literature and literary theory as it relates to the
    female Trickster   97
    Introduction 97
    The novel form and early women's literature in England and
        the United States 97
    The importance of developments in the mid to late
        nineteenth century 105
    The importance of being single and mysterious 107
    The 1970s and women's literature 113
    Jungian approaches to popular cultural forms 115

The psychological and the aesthetic attitudes 115
Problems with traditional Jungian literary criticism 118
Summary 119
Notes 119

PART III
Honoring the traditions   121

8   The traditional Trickster   123
Introduction 123
Traditional Trickster myths 124
Traditional Trickster as individuation myth 129
Other voices on the meaning of Trickster 130
Trickster as taboo transgressor 133
Enter Hermes 134
Conclusion: Trickster is humor 135
Notes 137

9   Humor: Eros using Logos   138
Introduction 138
Deep play 138
How and when in the developmental sequence does
   humor develop? 140
Psychoanalytic approaches to humor 145
A brief gallop through humor's pasture 148
Summary 151
Notes 152

PART IV
Re/storation   153

10 Women *are* funny   155
Introduction: is there a female sense of humor? 155
An example of a postmodern female Trickster 155
Differences between male and female humor 156
What is a feminist comic sensibility? 161
Psychological considerations 162
A woman with a sense of humor is dangerous 163
Anger 167
Women writing redux: women writing funny 167
Conclusion 173
Notes 174

11 The postmodern female Trickster   176
Introduction 176
Reconsidering what Trickster signifies 177
Refusal to be a victim 179
The postmodern female Trickster as social worker 181
Status within a culture 187
Sex and pro/creativity 188
Kinsey as quintessential Trickster or how to deal with the
*   tough stuff through humor 192*
Ethics and the postmodern female Trickster 196
Summary 200
Notes 201

12 Blanche White, re/storation agent   203
Introduction 203
Introducing Blanche White: re/storation agent 204
Blanche's ancestry 219
Conclusion 223
Notes 223

13 New sightings, *Sex and the City*   225
Introduction 225
Sex and the City *225*
The serious nature of being: Sex and the City *233*
Other Trickster sightings 237
Conclusion 238
Notes 239

14 Conclusion: the divine comedy of being   240
Introduction 240
Individuation 241
Does literature have the radical potential to change imagination
*   into reality? 244*
Is mainstream culture capable of adopting the humor
*   sassitude found in out-group humor? 245*
Ethics and the postmodern female Trickster 246
Recent sightings or just another first wave? 249
Conclusion 251
Notes 252

Bibliography   253
Index   268

Preface

This book elaborates my discovery of a major shift in western consciousness regarding the emergence of an intentional and acknowledged feminine energy which has been held inchoate within the collective unconscious for a millennium. I discovered this energy, which I call the female Trickster, during my dissertation investigation as an archetypal energy which could be manifested only by women writing about women for women. In this work I explicate and illustrate from a post-Jungian psychological perspective how the re-emergence of Trickster energy through the female imagination contains nothing less than the revolutionary possibility of a complete transformation of the consciousness of the world in which we live.

As a young girl, I was a voracious reader captivated by (though I didn't know it then) the transformative energy of Hermes. I was fascinated by these tales of Zeus' messenger who staked a claim at the crossroads and used the substance of the status quo to make magic. I was enamored by those tales of slippery words and deeds where the high and mighty became the fool while the perennially foolish prevailed. I was intrigued that transformation could be triggered by the pleasant medicines of comedy. Yet, I was forever wondering, where were the female Tricksters?

As an adult I became aware of a particular genre of detective stories which had a female sleuth in the lead role. My dissertation advisor/mentor at Pacifica Graduate Institute, Helene Lorenz, encouraged me to find out what it was that I loved about these characters, to map the energy which had darted in and out of my unconscious for so many years. I started on this exploration without any idea of what I might find, all I knew was that I had to follow the leads I was given and to name what I was drawn to and to feed it not corn but the possibility of possibility.

It was during this investigation that I discovered that these sleuths which I was drawn to represented contemporary manifestations of archetypal energies originating in the collective unconscious previously imagined through the male imagination but which were now emerging for recognition and integration into the collective consciousness through the female imagination. As I continued my research this Trickster energy compelled me to recognize and acknowledge her capacity to transform the collective consciousness.

The Trickster in female form has been with us as long as archetypal energies have manifested on the temporal plane of human existence, but they were not called tricksters. Why had the female been excluded from occupying the named and mapped terrain of Trickster? What was it about Trickster embodiment in a female form that rendered trickster energy unnameable? Was there even a Trickster essence to discover and did it matter if the generating mechanism, i.e., the imagination within a sexed body, was male or female? In other words, was there a difference in the manifestation of the archetypal energy of Trickster when filtered through a female imagination rather than a male one?

This book attempts to answer the question of why this Trickster energy when manifested in a female body were not called Tricksters and why, in the postmodern western world, they could be named as that which they were. It traces the female Trickster's re-emergence in the last 400 years in the manifestations of female imaginations from Jane Austen to the fictive female sleuths of the last quarter of the twentieth century, and from Madonna, and other female artists and drag queens to the worldwide hit television series, *Sex and the City*.

I have identified the commonalities of this female Trickster throughout the ages as movement, aimed at disruption of and through the status quo, embodied in the opening acts of postmodernity as a refusal to be a victim. Postmodern in its whimsy, humor is at the center of its fusion of the Trickster and the feminine. Embodiment is in the female form, transformation of the culture is her game, and Trickster is her name.

In this exploratory exegesis I review the inter- and cross-disciplinary literature, and while extensive and comprehensive, I make no claim that I have exhausted the sources or lines of inquiry, in this work, I offer what I have found in my investigations into the major critical lines of thought and theory regarding the Trickster energy and its re-emergence in the postmodern world and invite you, dear reader, to join me in what for me has been a exhilarating journey.

Acknowledgments

So many people have talked with me over the years about this idea that they all deserve to be first on this list. To the women in my life who have shown me that the only way to live in this life is with humor, I salute you all. First and foremost, I thank my mother, for all of her funny stories and laughter in the face of tragedy. To my dearest friends, Cheyenne Chernov, Carol Lerner, and Sandra Layton, without your constant reassurances and emotional support for many of my ludicrous ideas I would never have had the courage to write this book. To the women of the Inner Work Program; Dee, Carol, Genie, Joan, Desmond, Libby, Joyce, Trudy, Ellie, Judy, Myriam, Barbara, and Randy, and all my individual clients over the years, I am grateful that I had the opportunity to discover the fragility and kindness of the human heart in the company of such wonderful women. Your stories, support, and love given with much generosity enriched me more than I can express.

There have been teachers who have appeared when most needed, including my dear guides at Temple Adath Or: Shoni and Phil Labowitz, Florence Ross, and the Women's Spirituality Group. Thank you for giving my strange ideas the space to be heard and worked through in an atmosphere of love and connection. To Carol Gilligan, I offer gratitude for opening my ears to another voice, and to Martha Minow, who insisted I get it into print, it's been a long time, but I haven't forgotten! To John Beebe, this book could not have been written in the absence of your wonderful ear and heart; without Mona Lisa's smile, I would still be where I was. To Andrew Samuels, thanks for believing in the female Trickster, and thanks for perceiving that V.I. Warshawski was one. To Marion Woodman, you showed up when most needed and inspired me to emulate your vision of Conscious Femininity as I continued my work. To Helene Lorenz, who dared me to go and find out why it was that I loved the sleuths, many thanks for hanging in there with me and supplying so many critical theoretical leads over the years it took to complete the work. To the Center for Jungian Studies of South Florida, thank you for teaching me the craft of listening, especially my wonderful friends and colleagues, Brenda Astor, Ann Lynch, and Madonna Basilici, who listened to me endlessly.

Thanks to my special pals, Dee Fuller and Ed Baur, who actually read the manuscript and offered critical suggestions and encouragement when I was too tired to think or write another word. To Mike and Leoni Denney, whose doors were always open for food and stimulating dialogue, I never left without appreciating your support and encouragement.

To those who have put up with me the longest, my wonderful daughter and son, Laine and Adam, thanks for hanging in there, I know it was hard to be supportive through so many revisions of my life. Without Laine, my dissertation would have been lost in the flood waters and my deepest appreciation and love goes out to her, she has saved me with her wit and humor, more times than I can recall.

Responsibility for the ideas in this book are mine, of course, as well as all the errors. If I have forgotten to thank anyone, I am sorry.

Part I

Introducing the female Trickster

Chapter 1

Introduction

A pile of rocks ceases to be a rockpile
when someone contemplates it with the
idea of a cathedral in mind.
Anonymous

A female Trickster is among us. She stands, visible, at the crossroads of feminism, humor, depth psychology and postmodernism, ready for us to unpack her bag of multiple meanings. This postmodern female Trickster possesses the characteristics which define all Tricksters. She manifests the capacity to transform both an individual life and the collective consciousness of the culture she becomes visible to. She appears at the crossroads in a culture's psychic development, always cloaked in the appropriate drag. As with all Tricksters, she is not recognized as the transformative shape-shifter of the unconscious she is. Like all Tricksters, she makes us laugh.

Trickster energy is the archetypal energy of individuation – for a culture as well as an individual – and can not be ignored, yet like all Tricksters, this female Trickster is not recognized as the shape-shifter of the unconscious that she is. Like all Tricksters, humor is the energy which propels her movement through the collective consciousness yet unlike previous Tricksters she is embodied as a female who refuses to be a victim of a collective consciousness which restricts female psychological authority, bodily autonomy, and physical agency. Like all archetypal energies, this Trickster is a new incarnation of an eternal verity but this female Trickster brings revolution and not the revolt of previous Trickster incarnations.

In this book, I investigate the mystery of what happened 4,000 years ago to this female Trickster when she was legally and socially excluded from the western collective consciousness, and what has occurred in the last 400 years which has triggered the appearance of the female Trickster in western collective culture. In Part I, "Introducing the female Trickster," I explore the synergistic phenomena of female sleuth literature and the simultaneous emergence of critical discourses in feminism, ethnicity, gender and postcolonial studies. In Part II, "Calling upon the ancestors," I investigate the ways in which women's imaginal realms were enclosed within patriarchal consciousness 4,000 years ago. I analyze what happens when the imagination is legally enclosed, and what is necessary from a psychological perspective for a flowering of the autonomous psyche through the imaginal realms and metaphor. In Part III, "Honoring the traditions," I dissect the variations of traditional Trickster manifestation demonstrating how Trickster utilizes the erotic energy of humor to integrate the dark and disassociated aspects of culture. In Part IV, "Re/ storation," I focus on women's humor, and recent sightings of the female Trickster in other media as an example of Trickster's constellation as the divine comedy of being.

Definitions

Throughout this book I use words as terms of art and for those readers who do not have a Jungian psychoanalytic background, I offer the following definitions as guides.

Archetype

Jung in *Man and his Symbols* found an archetype to be a "tendency" to form representations from a motif "that can vary in great details without losing their basic pattern." (Jung and Franz 1964: 67). Marion Woodman's articulation of archetypal energy captures the essence of my use:

> If we accept, as Jung believed, that there are what he called "arche-types" in our unconscious, then we can read myths and fairy tales with an open mind. If we do not accept the existence of archetypes, then we have no way of explaining the superhuman surges of energy that magnetize us toward someone or something – or repel us. The word does not matter. What matters is our recognition of the power of these energy fields in our unconscious; they can dictate our destruction (if our ego is weak) or they can be our greatest gift in life . . . we project images onto these energy fields. The goddess may be the Virgin Mary, eclipsed by Lilith, eclipsed by Julia Roberts.
>
> (Woodman and Dickson 1996: 126)

Archetypes as I use the term are images from the unconscious that energize the individual and the collective, and can be found in any imaginative cultural artifact such as stories, myths, films, and cultural pop icons.

Reading as active imagination

Reading is a process of *active imagination* which is capable of changing how an individual's imagination functions, thus it has the capacity to transform consciousness. The active imaginal reading process is a dialogic relationship between text and reader which can transform both the surface and the deep structural levels of the psyche.

Psyche

When I refer to *psyche* I am speaking about the "totality of all psychic processes, conscious as well as unconscious" (Jung *Collected Works (CW)* 6: par 797).[1] Psyche thus includes the entire continuum of psychological activities and processes; in the individual it can be glimpsed from the way the soul manifests itself in conscious personality (ego) to the deepest unconscious realms where numinous energy resides.[2] In the collective culture, psyche manifests itself in cultural artifacts and historical movements. Jung thought that the psyche was a self-regulating mechanism which sought to keep itself in balance. When the psyche, whether individual or world, is out of balance another corresponding energy will be constellated for integration, thus restoring balance to the psyche.

Liminality

Limen is Latin for threshold. Victor Turner described liminality as the psychic space where new energies could manifest before being transported into the consciousness of a community (Turner 1967: 106). Murray Stein elaborated upon Turner's thesis, explaining that liminality represents

> a cultural, social psychological interstitial space between fixed identities and "locations" which predominates during transitional periods in the life-cycle.
>
> (Stein 1980: 2)

John Beebe elaborates upon the concept in relation to the Trickster:

> Archetypalists speak of a love of inhabiting spaces between psycho social regions established by convention as "liminality" and "liminality" is a hallmark of the Trickster.
>
> (Beebe 1981: 34)

Trickster makes her appearance, whether as female sleuth, pop icon, court jester, or clown in places and spaces which are unattended to by mainstream culture.

Authority, autonomy and agency

Authority

Authority is not related to the concept of power as over or against another. Authority means that an individual is the genuine creator of imagery produced within that individual's own imaginal realms. Authority is synonymous with psychological health in terms of being able to maintain a stable identity while inhabiting a liminal terrain. The word authority has the same root as authentic and author (aut); the Greek word *authentikos* was a derivative of the Greek noun *authentes*, the doer or master which was formed from *autos* meaning self and the base *hentes*, worker or doer. The word shows itself to be a Trickster, as the dictionary definition of authority *shape-shifted* from its "original meaning of 'authoritative' to its current sense of 'genuine' in the late 18th century" (Ayto 1991: 44).

Autonomy

The word autonomy has the same root as authority (aut) and having bodily autonomy means feeling free to choose your intentional behavior. This sense of self-determination and self-governance is a psychological condition precedent to successful identity formation. For women, this requires abso-lute control over their procreative capacities. "Expressing and supporting one's decisions with responsible action, ethical values, and clear language is a skill that can be developed only through conscious understanding and effort," says Polly Young-Eisendrath, (1999: 186) and I agree. Marion Woodman agrees that autonomy and authority are condition precedents to successful identity formation:

> We know we can change ourselves when we are not dependent on how we feel, nor on how others feel about us, nor on what the situation is around us. The values we hold, the choices we make within ourselves and for ourselves remain our prerogative. In most situations, if we begin to change, to do our inner work, to accept our own darkness and work towards consciousness, the situation will change. We begin to emanate a different energy, one that exudes a sense of autonomy and authenticity.
> (Woodman and Dickson 1996: 66)

This "different energy" Woodman refers to which "exudes" autonomy and authority is the energy of a woman's psyche that is not identified with any relationship nor confined by any bond. "She infuses an intrinsic sense of self-worth, of autonomy, into the role of virgin and mother and gives the woman strength to stand to her own creative experience" (Woodman 1996: 134). This is the kind of autonomy which (some fortunate) women can develop in the twenty-first century because their creativity is not tied exclusively to their procreative role. While Woodman talks of the mother, the virgin and the crone, the female Trickster as shape-shifter can appear in any and all of these forms or none at all.

Agency

The word *agency* comes from the Greek root *gen* meaning potent, convincing and compelling, as in a co*gen*t argument. Agency is used in its sense of potency, as a mode of action and as the means to employ a mode of action (Moore and Moore 1997a: 6). Agency is based in the sense of movement as action and also as being capable of acting on others' behalf, as in how a detective agency is a business or service authorized to act for others. Inherent in this use of agency is the presumption that one who has agency also has the power and freedom of physical and psychological movement within their culture.

What is a Trickster and is the female Trickster really different?

Traditional scholarship has consistently employed similar descriptive terms when discussing archetypal Trickster energy: individuality, satire, irony, magic, indeterminacy, open-endedness, ambiguity, sexuality, chance, disruption and reconciliation, betrayal and loyalty, closure and disclosure, mediation and unity of opposing forces (e.g., Gates 1988: 6). Tricksters preside over moments of passage, rupture, and transformation. Tricksters appear to model change and possibilities. Jung found in Trickster the self, the individuation process and the collective unconscious:

> (1) Mercurius consists of all conceivable opposites. He is thus quite obviously a duality, but is named a unity in spite of the fact that his innumerable inner contradictions can dramatically fly apart into an equal number of disparate and apparently independent figures.
> (2) He is both material and spiritual.
> (3) He is the process by which the lower and material is transformed into the higher and spiritual, and vice versa.
> (4) He is the devil, a redeeming psychopomp, an evasive Trickster, and God's reflection in physical nature.
> (5) He is also the reflection of a mystical experience of the artifex that coincides with the *opus alchymicum.*
> (6) As such, he represents on the one hand the self and on the other the individuation process and, because of the limitless number of his names, also the collective unconscious.[3]
>
> (Jung *CW* 13: par 284)

The postmodern female Trickster is different from the traditional Trickster

The most significant difference can be seen in the postmodern embodiment of the archetypal Trickster energy in a female body with psychological authority, physical agency, and bodily autonomy. Another major difference in the postmodern female Trickster is how humor and irony are deployed as strategic subversive and transformative devices aimed at revolution and not just revolt. Another important aspect of the postmodern female Trickster is how her cultural and psychological revolution is accomplished through social work which takes place concomitantly with the construction of an identity which refuses to be a victim. These differences in characteristics between the way that Trickster has been imagined in the past and in postmodernity are directly attributable to the imagination of women imagining and sharing with other women images of women with authority, agency and autonomy.

The body

If traditionally Trickster has been said to include all the possibilities, then what could be different about the female Trickster other than her embodiment in a female body? The imagery and narrative of the Trickster has always mirrored the culture within which the energy manifests. Traditional cultural norms overemphasize sexual determinants of birth and underemphasize the process of identity formation. Traditionally, identity has been fixed and stable, depending upon what body your psyche happened to be embodied within. In traditional narratives, Tricksters' refusal to recognize the power over paradigm has meant that Trickster energy manifested with a bodily fluidity called shape-shifting, but images embedded in traditional narratives, even if they might shape-shift from one to another, always ended up being male in the final image. This was because only the elite male body was permitted legal freedom of movement. Now our Trickster narratives and imagery can be embodied in a female, because females are no longer (in western civilization and democratic societies) legally restricted from physical movement. Postmodernity has brought us a dawning consciousness where the cultural body and the physical embodiments of consciousness can exhibit the fluidity that was found in the Trickster of the Winnebago cycle (see Radin 1972; Hynes and Doty 1993), but now the body can be imaged as strong, self-reliant, and *female*. This embodiment in the female is precisely the point because previously a female body, by definition, excluded the possibilities of movement which was one of the defining characteristics of Trickster. Yet, the definition itself of Trickster, as Henry Louis Gates posited correctly, represents the "indeterminacy even of one's inscribed fate" (Gates 1988: 28). What could be more attractive as a marker, symbol, and metaphor in this postmodern age of ambiguity than an image which confirms the possible indeterminacy of your inscribed fate regardless of how your psyche is embodied? This is a major evolutionary step in our collective western consciousness.

Irony and humor

Another major distinction in the postmodern female Trickster can be seen in how humor and irony are deployed as strategic subversive and transformative devices. Humor and irony have always been central to the Trickster energy and of course, it is not that women haven't always been funny.[4] The postmodern trick is that this use of humor and irony is now embodied in a female and humor is recognized as part of her attraction thereby reinscribing the traditional assumption that "wit in women is apt to have bad consequences" (Stibbs 1992: 247).

Refusal to be a victim

The single most significant aspect of the postmodern female Trickster is the integral role that social work plays in their behavior. This is part of the transformed ethical orientation in the postmodern female Trickster which results in the construction of an identity which refuses to be a victim.

How Trickster energy transforms culture through art

In the arts, archetypal energy manifests through an individual imagination as the conduit of transformation for the greater cultural collective. Initially, the artist's imaginal realm is manifested in a tangible art form in a particular culture's physical world; a painting, literature, or an idea contains the irrepresentable archetypal energy in the culturally inflected form. If an artifact is influential or popular then the archetypal energies represented through the artifact *can* be integrated into many aspects of the culture. This integrative process can occur whether the process is conscious or not. If you see an image or an idea often enough, it will sink down into the unconscious and reappear as a *sue sponte* thought. Advertising and its derivative, propaganda, are just as much a culturally inflected manifestation of this Trickster energy as high art is. This is why popular literature and other forms of pop culture, such as music, film and television, have the radical potency to turn imagination into reality.

The fictive female sleuth as postmodern female Trickster

This book is the result of my investigation into the question of why I was drawn like a magnet to certain fictive female sleuths while others, considered more classic or literary, left me cold. Certain sleuths transformed my consciousness and others did not, therefore I have focused upon those which were most influential in my own transformation of consciousness. V.I. Warshawski, Kinsey Millhone, Kate Shugak, and Blanche White are the exemplars of how popular literature has the potency to turn imagination into reality, thereby transforming both collective and individual consciousness. These four women are not representative of characters usually found in traditional detective literature, whether male or female, white or black, cop or private eye. These characters have not only transformed the genre, but also accomplished their task by coming in the cracks unattended by the canon. These fictive female sleuths in their manifestation as female Tricksters have strategically subverted and transformed Anglo-American collective consciousness related to the female by transforming the detective genre itself.

This female Trickster must be attended to because she has begun the work of bridging the troubled waters of feminism, depth psychology, and postmodernism through humor. Her trick is postmodern because her bridge building encourages communication across difference and diversity. Like Hermes, her Greek cousin, she creates an encouraging terrain for messages to be sent and received across previously seeming uncrossable chasms. Humor is the energy, movement is the process and embodiment is in a female image who refuses to be a victim of the collective consciousness which restricts feminine energies manifesting psychological authority, bodily autonomy and physical agency.

If it is true that the traditional Trickster constellates in a culture in order to combat the adversity and hostility of that culture to certain archetypal energies, then the fictive female sleuth as constellated in the late twentieth century in North American culture is a postmodern Trickster appearing to have come not to combat but to make a new relationship with the historical adversity and hostility found in western consciousness toward females manifesting autonomy, agency, and authenticity as single, fulfilled, physically strong, and psychologically whole individuals. This is a revolution not a revolt. That this energy has appeared in the metaphoric image of female detectives as the agents of this revelation is the traditional Trickster energy at work, using an accepted literary genre to subvert and transform not only the genre but also the larger collective consciousness.

It is significant that several of the fictional characters I have chosen to focus upon, Sara Paretsky's V.I. Warshawski, Sue Grafton's Kinsey Millhone, and Dana Stabenow's Kate Shugak, are fictively embodied as private investigators with detective agencies of their own. This energy reveals itself as a psycholinguistic Trickster as well. For these women, their own detective *agency* is not merely a physical location where they work but situated in psyche's realm as well; these women have agency in the sense of psychological identity. They have autonomy and authority which can constellate because they are the agents of physical and psychological movement in their own lives. They do not have to manipulate or convince others to act on their behalf; these women act on their own. Before we proceed any further, it is now time to meet these women and the others who are prime examples of how the archetypal energy of the Trickster is manifesting through the culturally inflected imagery of the postmodern female Trickster.

Notes

1 Jung found the attempt to formulate a comprehensive theory of the psyche doomed to failure because:

> The premises are always too simple. The psyche is the starting point of all human experience, and all the knowledge we have gained eventually leads us back to it. The psyche is the beginning and end of all cognition. . . . At one moment it finds itself in the vicinity of instinct, and falls under its influence; another it slides along to the other end where spirit predominates and even assimilates the instinctual processes most opposed to it.
>
> (*CW* 8: pars 408 and 261)

> There is also a relationship between psyche and the body which does not "involve the psyche as based on, derived from, analogous to or correlated with body but as a partner with it" (Samuels et al. 1986: 116)

2 My use of the word soul is meant to emphasize attention to depth and intensity, and is not analogous to the use of the word soul in the Christian sense.

3 Hence the designation of Mercurius as *mare nostrum*.

4 Regina Barreca's (1991, 1996) body of work amply demonstrates the fallacy in that presumption.

Chapter 2

Meetings with remarkable women

Introduction

The fictional female detectives, V.I. Warshawski, Kinsey Millhone, Kate Shugak, and Blanche White, were my introduction to the re-emergence in the collective consciousness of female Trickster energy. These women, demonstrating psychological authority, bodily autonomy and physical agency, were revolutionary when imagined in the late twentieth century and were representative of a major shift occurring throughout western collective culture. This chapter explores how an enlarged consciousness can be triggered when an individual or collective psyche is captured by a literary manifestation.

Jung and I: captured by a literary manifestation

In 1980, there were only 13 fictive female sleuths in the 166 mystery novels written by Anglo-American female mystery writers. Fifteen years later Anglo-American women had written over 1,200 mystery novels featuring an amazing 366 fictive female sleuths and the numbers are still increasing (Walton and Jones 1999: 28). Booksellers report that these books about female sleuths literally walk out of the bookstores as fast as they arrive. Why did these texts become so important to so many women?

Kohut's (1971) concept of the selfobject provides illumination for this phenomenon. Kohut defines self-objects as objects which we experience as parts of our selves (Kohut, 1971: xiv). Christopher Bollas elaborates on the idea and concludes that we use "evocative" objects to "express the self that we are." But what we select can also be a "type of self-utterance" for aspects of the self that may have gone unexpressed (Bollas 1992: 30, 36). Jung selected a literary manifestation as a selfobject when he inscribed "Philemon's Sanctuary, Faust's Atonement" over the entrance to Bollingen Tower in Switzerland. According to Wolfgang Giegerich:

> An inscription over the threshold to one's home is like a motto under which one's entire life and thought are placed. By placing his spiritual

existence under a motto taken from the world of Goethe's Faust, Jung declares that what happened there was personally significant for him.

(Giegerich 1984: 61)

Giegerich explicates how a psychological appreciation of literature can influence an individual psyche so that it transforms the whole of one's personal perspective:

> We all want to see the works of poets and writers only as "literature" and therefore approach them only with a literary, aesthetic, and historical frame of mind. Jung shows us, however, that a poetic work can also make personal demands on our lives. This happens whenever and wherever there is an awareness of psychological reality. Such an awareness is nothing but faith in the reality of the psychological, in the reality of the soul and its activities. When we read a work of literature psychologically, the world and events portrayed there begin to take on the character of a reality around us, as it were, from outside, much as do economic or meteorological realities. In this sense, then, Jung, wrote in 1942 that it shocked him to realize he had assumed Faust as his inheritance, specifically as the advocate and avenger of Philemon and Baucis.
>
> (Giegerich 1984: 61–62)

Me and the girls

My own identification with an evocative selfobject occurred as I savored the original Nancy Drew Mystery Series where Nancy was clever and independent.[1] Riding along with Nancy in her convertible with her hair blowing freely in the wind gave me the chance to imagine being the center of an adventure where my wits were necessary for more than cooking and sewing. Nancy was left behind as a part of my girlhood as I became surrounded by the images and texts promoted in the teen magazines that my friends and I devoured. I started to think more about not beating the boys at tennis and less about how to create an adventurous life of my own filled with movement, agency and authority.

It was not until I met V.I. Warshawski almost twenty years later in Sara Paretsky's *Indemnity Only* (1982) that I experienced the same sensation of adventure and joy in reading that I had as a girl reading Nancy Drew. Paretsky's body of work featuring the detective V.I. Warshawski has social work, one of the markers for the female Trickster as a central focus. The first novel, *Indemnity Only* (1982), concerned fraud in the insurance industry.[2] *In Deadlock* (1984) V.I. investigates corruption in the Great Lakes shipping industry; in *Killing Orders* (1985) it is institutional fraud in the Catholic Church; *Bitter Medicine* (1987) dealt with fraud and corruption in the hospital industry. In *Bloodshot* (1989) V.I. investigates corruption in local politics.[3] The homeless situation in Chicago and its losing battle with institutional corruption is under the microscope in *Burn Marks* (1990), which was followed by *Guardian Angel* (1992) which investigated how gentrification and elderly abuse can go hand in hand. In *Tunnel Vision* (1994) the reader learns about domestic violence, child abuse in the upper classes, and how a city of the homeless can exist in an urban underground. In *Hard Times* (1999) corruption in the world of private security, prison services, and the entertainment industry is probed. *Total Recall* (2001) explores an international insurance conspiracy involving the denial of reparations for Jews and African Americans, *Blacklist* (2004) gives the reader insight into the discrepancies inherent in how the criminal justice systems deals with diversity from the Blacklists of the McCarthy era through to the current Patriot Act and in *Fire Sale* (2006) big-box type stores are revealed for not paying a living wage, while gangbangers, fundamentalists, and teenage mothers in postmodern culture are scrutinized.

V.I. captured my imagination because she had been trained and practiced as a lawyer like I did, and when she found the practice of law disappointing, she found a way to use her talents for social work while maintaining her sense of humor and her independence. She provided me with a role model of how to construct an ethical life with psychological authority, bodily autonomy and physical agency. She establishes this authority, autonomy, and agency in the first pages of *Indemnity Only*. Written in 1980, but rejected by many publishers and not published until 1982,[4] it went on to become a bestseller:

> My voice was husky with anger. . . . don't waste my time like this. I don't need to argue you into hiring my services. . . .
> I'm not questioning your honesty, he said quickly. Look, I'm not trying to get your goat. But you are a girl and things may get heavy.
> I'm a woman . . . and I can look out for myself. If I couldn't, I wouldn't be in this kind of business. If things get heavy, I'll figure out a way to handle them – or go down trying. That's my problem not yours. Now, you want to tell me about your son, or can I go home where I can turn on the air conditioner?
>
> (Paretsky 1982: 5)

In 1982, V.I. was an unusual protagonist, a white woman who valued her professional life on equal par with her personal life, thus placing her at the crossroads of attitudes towards women; her sexuality and creativity were not bound to the work of raising a family (hers or someone else's) thus she provided the reader with an opportunity to imagine sexuality which could be vulnerable without false bravado:

conscious vulnerability

> It had been a long time since I had anyone up to my apartment and I suddenly felt shy and vulnerable. I'd been overexposed to men today and wasn't ready to do it again in bed.
>
> (Paretsky 1982: 77)

In the passage above V.I. illustrates what Marion Woodman calls a mature virgin, "confident enough to be consciously vulnerable" (Woodman 1985: 85). Conscious vulnerability requires an autonomous, authoritative psyche which can reflect upon the tensions inherent in choices made, while continuing to participate in social work, with agency and humor. An example of how the female Trickster manifests fluidity of psychological movement is seen in this excerpt where V.I. is speaking with Bobby, her deceased father's closest friend on the police force, about violence towards women and the institution of marriage:

> Bobby Mallory: You know, if Tony had turned you over his knee more often instead of spoiling you rotten, you'd be a happy housewife now, instead of playing at detective and making it harder for us to get our job done.
>
> V.I.: But I am a happy detective, Bobby, and I made a lousy housewife. That was true. My brief foray into marriage eight years ago had ended in an acrimonious divorce after fourteen months: some men can only admire independent women at a distance.
>
> (Paretsky 1982: 28)

V.I. again deals with the issue of domestic violence 12 years later, this time concerning how insidious abuse can be and how even those charged with a duty to protect may repress the obvious telltale signs. In the following excerpt V.I. has been called in to investigate Emily, a runaway who she suspects was being abused. V.I. is questioning Emily's teacher:

> You know she's disappeared – I'm concerned about her. And I feel some responsibility. Perhaps she wouldn't have run off if I hadn't told her on Saturday that there were places of refuge for girls like her. . . . When you're a child you think what happens in your house is normal . . . . If she doesn't have friends she may not know other kinds of households exist: She might not talk about it. But I've seen Fabian in action. Believe me he's a wild man.

Emily's teacher is surprised at V.I.'s assessment:

> Is he? I've never noticed that. Perhaps . . . well, autocratic. But we see a fair amount of that: the parents here often are in positions of considerable authority and are used to deference.

V.I.'s psychological reflections encourage the reader to enlarge their own imagination regarding the insidious nature of abuse; the discrepancy between the charm in public and the horror in private:

> My lips tightened bitterly. Fabian exuding witty charm with his guests last Wednesday, displaying heartbreaking distress over his lost daughter last night – his public personality persuaded a shrewd cop like Terry Finchley. Why not a high school teacher as well? If I hadn't returned for my coat last week and seen him in action would I have believed he could be violent? Instead of trying to persuade Cottingham of Fabian's sadistic side, I asked what had precipitated Emily's flight.
> (Paretsky 1994: 145–146)

Ethics as psychological awareness of and movement between seemingly disparate positions is one of V.I.'s postmodern Trickster characteristics. In this excerpt from *Settled Score*, a short story contained in the collection *Windy City Blues* (Paretsky 1996a), V.I. is talking with her surrogate mother Lotty Herschel, a physician, who is arguing that a parent's attitudes can cause a death as much as swallowing oven cleaner can and should be recognized by the legal system:

> "I put it to you, Victoria: you're a lawyer. Would you not agree?"
> "I agree that the law defines responsibility differently than we do when we're talking about social or moral relations." I said carefully, "No state's attorney is going to get Mrs. Hampton arrested, but does that. . . ."
> Lotty forced herself to smile. "Paul, you think you develop a veneer after thirty years as a doctor. You think you see people in all their pain and that your professionalism protects you from too much feeling. But that girl was fifteen. She had her life in front of her. She didn't want to have a baby. And her mother wanted her to. Not for religious reasons, even – she's English with all her contempt for Catholicism. But because she hoped to continue to control her daughter's life. Claudia felt overwhelmed by her mother's pressure and swallowed a jar of oven cleaner. Now don't tell me the mother is not responsible. I do not give one damn if no court would try her: to me, she caused her daughter's death as surely as if she had poured the poison into her."

The Trickster move in the text encourages the reader to imagine a seemingly opposing ethical perspective, thus opening the psyche to integration of both positions:

Servino ignored another slight head shake from Lotty's niece. "It's a tragedy. But a tragedy for the mother, too. You don't think she meant her daughter to kill herself, do you, Lotty?

(Paretsky 1995: 244–245)

The female Trickster's social worker aspect as refusal to be anyone's victim is demonstrated in *Total Recall* (2001) through the issue of reparations for slavery as well as Holocaust victims, and in *Blacklist* (2004) where V.I. has her records at the library tagged by the Patriot Act as she tries to protect an Egyptian adolescent from government terrorist hunters. All of this is accomplished, like all Tricksters, with a healthy dose of humor about bodily functions, here as V.I.'s hunger occupies center stage:

It was almost three; I hadn't eaten since my yogurt at eight this morning. Maybe the situation would seem less depressing if I had some food. I passed a strip mall on my way to the expressway and bought a slice of cheese pizza. The crust was gooey, the surface glistened with oil, but I ate every bite with gusto. When I got out of my car at the office I realized I'd dropped oil down the front of my rose silk sweater. Warshawski zero, visitors five, at this point. At least I didn't have any business meetings this afternoon.

(Paretsky 2001: 56)

Kinsey Millhone, Sue Grafton's fictive female sleuth, became a friend from the moment my assistant slapped *"A" is for Alibi* (Grafton 1982) down on my desk and said, "Read this tonight."[5] Sue Grafton, an award-winning television writer whose father was a mystery writer as well, uses the alphabet as her calling card for titles, Grafton published *"A" is for Alibi* (1982), *"B" is for Burglar* (1985), *"C" is for Corpse* (1986), *"D" is for Deadbeat* (1987), *"E" is for Evidence* (1988), *"F" is for Fugitive* (1989), *"G" is for Gumshoe* (1990), *"H" is for Homicide* (1991), *"I" is for Innocent* (1992), *"J" is for Judgement* (1993), *"K" is for Killer* (1994), *"L" is for Lawless* (1995), *"M" is for Malice* (1996), *"N" is for Noose* (1998), *"O" is for Outlaw* (1999), *"P" is for Peril* (2001), *"Q" is for Quarry* (2002), *"R" is for Ricochet* (2004) and *"S" is for Silence* (2005). Kinsey lives and works in a thinly disguised Santa Barbara, California, fictionalized as Santa Teresa. From her first case to her latest investigation, Kinsey demonstrates an ironic, sarcastic, Tricksterish deconstructive psychological attitude towards the rich and powerful for the reader to ponder and integrate:

Horton Ravine, where I was headed, is a moneyed enclave, carved out by land grant and deed, whereby successive California governors rewarded military leaders for killing people really, really, well. The resulting three thousand acres were passed from rich man to richer, until the first in a line, a sheep rancher named Tobias Horton, had the good sense to subdivide the land into saleable lots, thus making a killing of another kind.

(Grafton 1982: 105–106)

Kinsey liked small, enclosed spaces, lived on sandwiches, cut her own hair, and owned a single dress. Her costume was jeans and a turtleneck, and when she donned them she became the ironic truth-telling Trickster, in this excerpt linking detective work to its cultural twin, traditional feminine work:

I did a couple of personal errands and then went home. It had not been a very satisfying day but then most of my days are the same: checking and cross-checking, filling in blanks, detail work that was absolutely essential to the job but scarcely dramatic stuff. The basic characteristics of any good investigator are a plodding nature and infinite patience. Society has been inadvertently grooming women to this end for years.

(Grafton 1982: 27)

Kinsey – as woman and Trickster – recognizes that she has sexual and relational needs but she refuses to subordinate her psychological health:

I dumped the first and the second one dumped me. With both I did my share of suffering, when I look back on it, I can't understand why I endured it for so long. It was dumb. It was a waste of time and cost me a lot.

(Grafton 1987: 52)

Another aspect of Kinsey as ethical female Trickster is her riff on the nature of justice, tinged with irony. The following occurs after she drives by a state mental hospital:

I've heard that there is less tendency to violence among the institutionalized insane than there is in the citizenry at large and I believe that. . . . Somehow I was more offended by the minor crimes of a Marcia Threadgill who tried for less, without any motivation at all beyond greed. I wonder if Marcia was the new standard of morality against which I would now judge all other sins. Hatred, I could understand – the need for revenge, the payment of old debts. That's what the notion of "justice" was all about anyway: settling up.

(Grafton 1982: 192)

Ten years later, Kinsey continues her justice riff, prodding the reader to integrate the paradoxical nature within themselves:

He was the obvious suspect, with the means, the motive, and the opportunity to have killed her, but murder is an aberrant deed, often born of passions distorted by obsessiveness and torment. Emotion doesn't travel in a straight line. Like water, our feelings trickle down through cracks and crevices, seeking out the little pockets of neediness and neglect, the hairline fractures in our character usually hidden from public view. Beware the dark pool at the bottom of our hearts.

(Grafton 1992: 202)

Ten years after Kinsey and V.I. were born, Alaska native Dana Stabenow created Kate Shugak.[6] Having left her job as star investigator for the Anchorage District Attorney's office, Shugak was homesteading land 25 miles north of her native Aleut village in the Alaskan Bush. She lived with a half-husky, half-wolf named Mutt which she compares favorably to her grandmother, the tribal leader Ekaterina. Kate demonstrates a Trickster's fluidity, crossing easily between species and characteristics:

Mutt's eyes were wide and wise, as wise as Ekaterina's. She stood three feet at the shoulder and weighed in at 140 pounds, all of it muscle. There was Husky in her solid torso; her long legs and her smarts were all wolf. Proving it, she nosed Kate under the arm again. "All right, all right, don't get pushy."

(Stabenow 1996: 24)

Kate was attractive at 5 feet, 120 pounds, and could crab and fish with anyone in the Bering Straits. Like a Trickster, she lived alone, 25 miles from the nearest village:

Usually, Kate was comfortable with silence. It was why she lived alone on a homestead in the middle of a twenty-million acre federal park, twenty-five miles from the nearest village over a road that was impassable to anything but snow machines in the winter and to anything but the sturdiest trucks in the summer.

(Stabenow 2001: 46)

Kate as a social worker Trickster is demonstrated in this excerpt where she shares with the reader how prejudicial attitudes can exist within any population, even her own indigenous Native American tribe. In the following selection Kate is having a talk with her grandmother Ekaterina, the tribal leader:

At last she said, "We invent so many prejudices on our own. Do we really need to impose new ones from the top down?" Ekaterina said nothing, and Kate said slowly, feeling her way, "Emma, someday you are going to have to drag yourself kicking and screaming, if necessary, into this century. You want to keep the family at home, keep the tribe together and make the old values what they were."

She leaned forward, her fists on the table, and spoke earnestly, looking straight into the eyes that were so very much like her own. "It's not going to happen. We have too much now, too many snow machines, too many prefabs, too many satellite dishes bringing in too many television channels, showing the kids what they don't have. There's no going back. We've got to go forward, bringing up what we can of the past with us, yes, but we've got to go forward. It's the only way we're going to survive."

(Stabenow 1992: 47)

Kate as ethical Trickster is forever balancing the conflict between personal autonomy and her leadership obligations. This drama is played out between Kate and her grandmother Ekaterina, the current tribal leader. Both are strong women, both are leaders, yet they see things quite differently:

Every time she says it, Katya, she says it in that voice of doom. I see fifty generations of Aleuts lined up behind her, glaring at me. Every time she says it, she's telling me I betrayed her and my family and the village and my culture and my entire race by running away . . . and now she believes I've betrayed myself by running back . . . and I live in a log cabin five miles from my closest neighbor and twenty-five miles from the nearest village. I'm shipping Xenia off to town, but I can't bear to go in myself.

(Stabenow 1992: 195)

Being pulled like a rubber band in many directions at once is what many people – no matter their ethnicity, sexual orientation, color, or other signifier – confront on a daily basis. By setting this narrative in a culture to which most North Americans have had no information about, the reader is exposed to a community which reveals commonalities across diversity focusing upon patterns of relationship rather than essential differences. The ability to be in flux, to move between cultures and remain in a healthy psychological state of mind illuminates for the reader how the Trickster energy of nomadic identity operates.

Recently, I have become an enamored fan of Blanche White,[7] who is a largish, middle-aged African American domestic worker without apology. Created by BarbaraNeely,[8] Blanche solves crimes while wryly and incisively commenting on what it is like to be a woman of color in a white world. In the following excerpt we see her Tricksterish ability to protect her bodily autonomy:

Blanche had learned long ago that signs of pleasant stupidity in household help made some employers feel more comfortable, as though their wallets, their car keys, and their ideas about themselves were all safe. Putting on a dumb act was something many black people considered unacceptable, but she sometimes found it a useful place to hide. She also got a secret pleasure from fooling people who assumed they were smarter than she was by virtue of the way she looked and made her living.

(Neely 1993: 16)

Blanche is a Trickster here when she uses the ruse of playing dumb as a strategic move against white oppression. This move allows Blanche to use her subjugated knowledge (knowledge that is temporarily suspended) to resist and transgress thus nourishing her location in that liminal terrain betwixt and between dominant ideologies. She does not need to confront because her own values are not in conflict; thus her Trickster energy is ethical. In *Blanche among the Talented Tenth* (1994) Blanche demonstrates another aspect of Trickster energy to the reader for integration when she must navigate the psychological terrain when both the oppressive and subjugated communities come together at the exclusively African American upper-class vacation community, Amber Cove. In this intra-racial situation, it is Blanche who is worried about *her* values being infringed:

She was still fighting the irritation left over from her encounter at the check-in desk. She felt like she was paying dearly to be someplace she wasn't going to like. She wasn't one for dismissing her feelings, she always got into trouble when she did. Like the way she's tried to ignore the Republican vibes Malik and Taifa were bringing into her house. Now she had to do something about it. At least she'd be able to use this time to get some information. She wanted to see Taifa and Malik on their friends' turf. She wanted a glimpse of how and why being among people who had everything could make a child or a fool look down on those who didn't have a pot. She wanted to see how Taifa and Malik behaved towards her on her friends' turf. Then maybe she could figure out what to do.

(Neely 1994: 18)

Blanche's fluidity in negotiating the terrain of being a perennial outsider (as an African American) in her own physical territory (born in America) while surviving and prospering through her embeddedness within her own community makes Blanche a central focus of this work and the subject of Chapter 12 on Re/storation later in this book. She gives me, an off-white reader,[9] insight into just how bigoted this United States of America still is and how (paradoxically) African Americans can be complacent in their enclosures just like the rest of us:

> Blanche had never suffered from what she called Darkie's Disease. There was a woman among the regular riders on the bus she often rode home from work who had a serious dose of the disease. Blanche actually cringed when the woman began talking in her bus-inclusive voice about old Mr. Stanley, who said she was more like a daughter to him than his own child, and how little Edna often slipped and called her Mama. That women and everyone else on the bus knew what would happen to all that close family feeling if she told Mr. Stanley, or little Edna's Mama, that instead of scrubbing the kitchen floor she was going to sit down with a cup of coffee and make some phone calls.
>   Loving the people for whom you worked might make it easier to wipe old Mr. Stanley's shitty behind and take young Edna's smart-ass rich-kid remarks. And, of course, it was hard not to love children, or to overlook the failings of the old and infirm. They were not yet responsible in the first case and beyond it in the other. What she didn't understand was how you convinced yourself that you were actually loved by the people who paid you the lowest possible wages; who never offered you the use of one of their cars, their cottage by the lake, or even their swimming pool; who gave you handkerchiefs and sachets for holiday gifts and gave their children stocks and bonds. It seemed to her that this was the real danger in looking at customers through love-tinted glasses. You had to pretend that obvious facts – facts that were like fences round your relationships – were not true.
>
> (Neely 1994: 48)

Yet when it comes to the enclosure of marriage, Blanche has no problems with recognizing commonality across differences:

> But all the married women she knew worked hard in someone else's house, field, or plant and came home to take care of a full grown man and a houseful of kids who seemed to think her labor was their due. Blanche had other ideas.
>
> (Neely 1994: 11)

Noticed at the crossroads

These four women and those like them brought a fresh discourse to mystery fiction in the last quarter of the twentieth century. When Kinsey Millhone was created in 1982, the reviewers called her "the best new private eye" in the business,[10] describing her energy as "feisty".[11] V.I. was recognized as a genre-changing "gumshoe for modern times,"[12] whose "name always

makes the top of the list when people talk about the new female opera-
tive."[13] This Trickster energy of the female sleuth represented by Kinsey
Millhone and V.I. Warshawski created a liminal imaginal terrain so that ten
years later, Blanche White could make the scene as "a heroine-detective
who is a real woman: middle-aged, African American, working class,
plump, feisty, funny, feminist! What a delight!"[14] Kate Shugak could be
described as "compelling, brutal and true,"[15] and be embodied believably
as a woman. In just ten years, what had initially seemed like a fantasy
became a reality, the autonomous women with her own agency literally and
fictionally. She had taken up residence in the North American collective
consciousness and was making the bestseller list her home.

The postmodern female Trickster appears

The overwhelming proliferation of female sleuths' texts during the last
quarter of the twentieth century is undeniable, but is this proliferation
merely attributable to the genre itself? That is, mysteries have always been
among the most popular of reading material, and today mystery fiction is
considered to be the most popular type of reading material shared by men
and women. Crime fiction is the most popular form of reading nowadays,
accounting for over a quarter of all books sold in the United States
(Schroeder 2002). In 2002, 175,000 books were published in the United
States. Seven years earlier there were only 55,000 books published.[16] However, within the last 20 years of the twentieth century, there was a seismic
wave of change in the mystery fiction field as women consumers, writers,
and publishers began to dominate the genre and fictive female sleuths took
center stage. Women have come to dominate the mystery field.[17] Female
sleuths put mystery on the map – by attracting women looking for good
reads to a once mostly male bastion (Frederick 2000: 12). Bantam editor
Kate Miciak notes that mystery lists are "composed almost entirely of
women" because women writers are "more interested in the psychology of
the crime than in the action, something she didn't find in many manuscripts
from men." Jim Huang, editor of the *Drood Review*, concluded that women
"found success by breaking the mold from which most mysteries came . . .
the settings were different, the people were different and the concerns were
different" (Dyer 2001: 1).

Of course, there are dissenting opinions about the phenomenon.[18] Yet
even so, male editors report that "that women readers are more gender
oriented than men" calling the phenomenon "literary affirmative action."
Whether it is an underground affirmative action campaign or not, editor
Marian Wood at Putnam, who has published Sue Grafton's Kinsey
Millhone series since she bought *"A" is for Alibi* (1982) on the basis of 60
pages of text, says "Sue is writing about the real tension that's going on
between men and women in precinct houses and in actual investigative

work." Natalee Rosenstein of the Berkeley Press thinks "that the successful female protagonists now reflect a more realistic view of the contemporary woman." Part of that new view is the appearance of more and more diversity within the genre. Susan O'Connor at Crown points out that the Blanche White character "redefines the meaning of an iron fist in a velvet glove" (Dyer 2001: 1–4).

Developments in the last quarter of the twentieth century

Over the short course of its history, the fictive female sleuth phenomenon has grown increasingly more inclusive of the diversity found in Anglo-American culture. Since the early 1980s an exponentially increasing number of sexually, ethnically, and socially diverse fictive female sleuths have made their appearance. They have materialized parallel to critical discourses in feminism, ethnicity, gender, and postcolonial studies within Anglo-American culture.

The compendium *Detecting Women* (Heising 2000) notes not only 225 new women authors but also a total of 815 mystery series being written by women.[19] Although not all of these serializations feature a female sleuth, what I find significant is the breadth of backgrounds and occupations which these newest female sleuths give to the reader's imagination. The following is a highly selective list meant to give my readers a sampling of the still emerging phenomenon of the fictive female sleuth. (In parentheses is the date the series started and the number of volumes in each series at time of writing.)

There is Alison Kane, the lesbian leather cop created by Kate Allen (1993, four); Lucia Ramos, a Chicano lesbian police detective created by Mary Morell (1991, two); Eve Dallas, a twenty-first-century New York Police Department lieutenant created by J.D. Robb (1995, eight); Ella Clah, a Navajo FBI agent created by Aimee Thurlo (1995, five); Carlotta Caryle, a 6'1" cab-driving ex-cop private investigator created by Linda Barnes (1987, seven); Mali Anderson, a black ex-cop in Harlem created by Grace Edwards (1997, two); Molly Bearpaw, a Cherokee civil rights investigator created by Jean Hager (1992, four); Holly-Jean Ho, an Anglo-Chinese bisexual investigator created by Irene Lin-Chandler (1995, three) to name just a few. Some of the more unusual occupations which have recently made an appearance to the reader through a fictive female sleuth are Letty Campbell, a lesbian chicken farmer created by Alma Fritchley (1997, three); Glynis Tryon, an 1860s librarian suffragette created by Miriam Monfredo (1992, six); Bonnie Indermill, a tap dancing Manhattan office temp (1987, seven); and Ariel Gold, an amnesiac TV news magazine producer (1996, three). There is now an entire subcategory within the genre called *Environment and Wilderness Background Types* (Heising 2000: 308) where we find such fictive female sleuths as Em Hanse, an oil company geologist created by Sarah Andrews (1994, four); Anna Pigeon, a park ranger created by Nevada Barr (1993, seven); Gar, a Neanderthal shaman created by Sandy Dengler (1998, two); Texana Jones, a desert trading post owner created by Allana Martin (1996, three) and Lauren Maxwell, a wildlife investigator created by Elizabeth Quinn (1993, four).

More than 500 new mystery titles written by women were published in 1998–1999 and there seems to be no end in sight to this phenomenon, according to those in the know.[20] One of the noteworthy expansions of the genre for psychological purposes are the *historical* sleuths. There is even a series out with Jane Austen as the protagonist.[21] Even though these *historicals* are scorned for their popularity in much the same way as Nathaniel Hawthorne scorned the popular (female) novelists of the nineteenth century as "scribbling women," there is a revisioning going on that cannot be ignored by trivializing or restricting the import of these novels because they belong to a genre category.[22] The Elizabethan period offers the paradox of the powerful Queen Bess along with a female sleuth, and the reader gets gender conflict and fancy costumes. Masquerades through costuming are a perennial in Tricksters' tool box which places reason off guard so that Trickster energy may manifest. The psychic dynamism involved in the continuing proliferation of boundary crossing texts is a convincing argument against those who want to box the fictive female sleuth born in the last quarter of the twentieth century into merely being part of the overall mystery fiction genre written by women.

The sheer proliferation of these texts is a credible clue that these current fictive female sleuths are not merely representative of a second golden age, simply following in the pathways hacked out of the forest by those first golden agers,[23] Agatha Christie, Dorothy L. Sayers, and Ngaio Marsh (Dilley 1998: xi). However, my concern here is more relational and circular, that is, I wonder whether this first "golden age" of women's mystery writers shared a reciprocal energy with the first wave of feminism.[24] If the first golden age of women's mystery writers reciprocated energy with first wave feminism, then did the proliferation of texts in the 1980s and 1990s mark a similar reciprocity with second wave feminism?[25] Assuming for the moment that this is correct, then what can be said about the influence of third wave feminism upon the genre? This is where the *historicals* come into play. Third wave feminism cannot be reflected upon yet, since we are still in that stage, however these *historicals* represent a postmodern time-traveling cyborg-type consciousness in how they revision canonical history. Donna Haraway, writing in *Simians, Cyborgs, and Women: The Reinvention of Women* (1991) and "A Manifesto for Cyborgs" (1985), makes an "argument for pleasure in the confusion of boundaries and for responsibility in their construction" (Leitch et al. 2001: 2270). Haraway's argument that the cyborg imagery represents an opportunity for jettisoning the myth of original unity in favor of "partiality, irony, intimacy and perversity"

(Leitch et al. 2001: 2270) applies to all female Tricksters, whether sleuth, cyborg or media icon.[26]

Conclusion

The female Trickster, whether embodied fictionally as sleuth, cyborg or time-traveling feminista, are messengers charged with informing the collective consciousness about how identity and subjectivity can be constructed in postmodernity. These new energies, now available for integration, could not have been imagined without the rupture of energies wrought by World War II. After the war, as new questions were asked on academic campuses, the art of detection itself transformed. Now the *other* was also increasingly at the table for discussion. The white Eurocentric male canon in literary studies, sociology, psychology, and history, as in all academia, was critiqued, attacked, defended, and then revised to include feminist, African American, and other ethnicities and religious orientations as well as postcolonial perspectives. The imaginal realms where our fictional characters now roam freely have been immeasurably enriched by the cross-pollination between hitherto separate fields of study. The following example from my own education illustrates how much has changed, literally and metaphorically.

When I was an undergraduate at the University of Florida (UF) in the early 1970s there was no Women's Studies Department and the African American students were protesting daily on campus about not having office space for the Black Student Union. Their request for space at the student union[27] was denied because the Pan-Hellenic Council, *the Greeks*, occupied all the available student office space at the union. When asked to share their space, the Greeks said no – they had always had this space and saw no reason to change.[28] When I enrolled my daughter at UF in 2000 I found the student union space building radically changed. The huge Pan-Hellenic Office Suite which had greeted me in 1970 as I ascended the stairs was no longer there. Instead of the purple and gold royal Pan-Hellenic banner across the door, there was a simply lettered sign which said "*Student Organizations*" and listed groups (alphabetically) such as the African American Student Union, The Gay and Lesbian Student Center, The Islamic Student Center, The Young Republicans, *and* the Pan-Hellenic Council along with a plethora of other organizations which I am sure did not ask for space on campus in the early 1970s because they had not been imagined yet.[29]

Notes

1 Edward Stratemeyer is usually credited with writing the series, which after his death in 1930 his daughter Harriet Adams officially took over. However, according to Davidson, the first series was actually written by Mildred Wirt Benson, who "made Nancy independent and capable." Davidson comments on

the change in Nancy as the years went by: "Later writers who revised the originals and who are still turning out the Nancy Drew Files series have made the teenage detective a pretty figure around who the action happens, taking away much of her cleverness and independent spirit" (Davidson and Wagner-Martin 1995: 597).

2 The author Sara Paretsky had worked in the insurance industry for years.

3 The book was published in Great Britain as *Toxic Shock*, and won the British Crime Writers' Silver Dagger Award in 1988.

4 Sara Paretsky (1982) writes of her many rejections, which called *Indemnity Only* a "derivative story" that was "too talky," as making her feel that "my stories were a sign of the sickness afflicting the woman in the play, and that true love would cure me as it did her, for I grew up in a time and place where little girls were destined to be wives and mothers." Thus for years she kept her stories to herself (p. x). Marcia Mueller, who began the Sharon McCone series with her first publication in 1978, reports that she had trouble getting her work published (quoted in Dilley 1998: 7).

5 In 1982, I was representing the *Ft. Lauderdale News and Sun Sentinel*, a major metropolitan daily. My secretary and assistant Sandy gave me the book.

6 Dana Stabenow's works included in this book, although not her entire collection, are *A Cold Day for Murder* (1992a), *A Fatal Thaw* (1992b), *Dead in the Water* (1993), *A Cold-Blooded Business* (1994), *Play with Fire* (1995), *Blood Will Tell* (1996), *Breakup* (1997), *Killing Grounds* (1998), *Hunter's Moon* (1999), *Midnight Comes Again* (2000), and *The Singing of the Dead* (2001).

7 BarbaraNeely has created the "Blanche" series, which includes *Blanche on the Lam* (1993), *Blanche among the Talented Tenth* (1994), *Blanche Cleans Up* (1998), and *Blanche Passes Go* (2000).

8 The blending of the first and last name is not a typo, BarbaraNeely spells her name this way.

9 Karen Brodkin's *How Jews Became White Folks* (1998) uses the term "off-white" to refer to Jewish Americans of Semitic descent.

10 Reviewer comment by *The Detroit News* on the back cover of Grafton's *"A" is for Alibi* (1982).

11 Reviewer comment by *Kirkus Reviews* on the back cover of Grafton's *"A" is for Alibi* (1982).

12 Reviewer comment by *People* on the back cover of Paretsky's *Burn Marks* (1990).

13 Reviewer comment by *The New York Times Book Review* on back cover of Paretsky's *Bloodshot* (1989).

14 Reviewer comment by Robin Morgan, author of *The Demon Lover*, on the back cover of Neely's *Blanche Passes Go* (2000).

15 Reviewer comment by the *Boston Globe* on the back cover of Stabenow's *Breakup* (1997).

16 Chicago Book Expo on C-Span, Book TV, June 5, 2004.

17 According to editor Susan Corcoran, one of the most obvious trends "is the rise and continued dominance of women writers in the genre." While Carolyn Marino, editor at HarperCollins, agrees, editor Sessalee Hensley opines that "female sleuths actually put mystery on the map – by attracting women looking for good reads to a once mostly male bastion" (Frederick 2000: 12). How these women writers put mystery on the map and continue to keep it on the map was addressed by *Publisher's Weekly* (Dyer 2001) in its annual review of the mystery genre. Best-selling author Sue Grafton (2001) offered the opinion that "women brought a fresh sensibility" (quoted in Dyer 2001: 1). What are the elements of

this fresh sensibility that editors and authors alike identify? Editor Kate Miciak says that the reason that mystery lists began to be "composed almost entirely of women" is that women writers were "more interested in the psychology of the crime than in the action, something she didn't find in many manuscripts from men" (quoted in Dyer 2001: 1). Jim Huang, editor of the *Drood Review*, concludes that women "found success by breaking the mold from which most mysteries came – the settings were different, the people were different and the concerns were different" (quoted in Dyer 2001: 1–2).

18 I found that male editors, like John Cunningham, argue that "any correlation between an author or protagonist's gender and sales" (quoted in Dyer 2001: 2) is misguided.

19 It is important to note that these series include fictional characters which are both male and female.

20 I attended several Mystery Conferences and talked with authors and publishers during the period of research spanning 1999–2002. I visited quite a number of bookstores throughout the United States, more than a few devoted to mystery fiction. I also participated in an online research forum devoted to the scholarly study of mystery fiction. This is the consensus from my unscientific anecdotal experiences in the genre while researching this project.

21 Written by Stephanie Barron, which is the pseudonym of Colorado author and former CIA intelligence analyst Francine (Stephanie) Mathews. Six novels have been written in the series which have been described as "a Jane Austen for the 1990s complete with a blunt and ardent feminism" (*Booklist Review*, in Heising 2000: 28).

22 Now that the "contemporary female sleuth [is] so commonplace these days," the once exciting fictive domain of them struggling for acceptance in a male dominated world isn't quite as captivating as it once was, so we find them being the Trickster by restoring women's imaginative manifestations to other historical time periods. "So there it is, you get your female sleuth, you keep your gender conflict, and as a bonus, you get fancy costumes." According to Ott (1999: 61), "A new trend has been born . . . with Queen Elizabeth and Mary Queen of Scots" walking "down these mean streets."

23 The Golden Age is the term used to describe British Mystery Fiction written after World War I to the period immediately preceding the outbreak of World War II (1920–1937). It is characterized by the puzzle plot, the manor house, and a generally closed system. Agatha Christie was the acknowledged master of this form.

24 First wave feminism was concerned with being *equal to*, while second wave feminism can be said to focus on being *different from and free from*. The norm, a white, male property owner, remained the same. First wave feminism is also considered to be the movement to gain the vote for women in many countries.

25 Second wave feminism was concerned with retrieving women's lost history and making new history through the investigation of concerns exclusive to women in all fields of study.

26 While Haraway convincingly argues that traditional psychoanalysis is dependent upon a perceived need to separate from the mother as a prelude to the need for individuation, I do not agree that all psychology is based upon this notion, although reading Freud and Lacan might lead one there. Jungian psychology offers a way to go beyond the adolescent hero myth which has dominated both traditional and depth psychology to a new integration based on the plethora of imaginative manifestations – which are presented by the female sleuth image rather than just a limited selection as representative of a norm for the entire

human race. Each and every imaginative manifestation reveals possibilities unimaginable from some other vantage point. I agree with Haraway that single vision produces worse illusions than "double-vision or many headed monsters" (quoted in Leitch et al. 2001: 2275). I do not see the difference between talking of the single vision of the ego-dominated psyche or the single vision of the ego-dominated cultural consciousness. It is the unitary vision leading to the single explanation which has been the problem in theoretical inquiry. Haraway suggests building a coalition that "actually manages to hold together witches, engineers, elders, perverts, Christians, mothers, and Leninists long enough to disarm the state." This statement is one that V.I., Kinsey, Kate, and Blanche can agree with. Haraway's work is radical in that she asks us not to view the cyborg as "the final appropriation of woman's bodies in a masculinist orgy of war" or "about the final imposition of a grid of control on the planet" but rather from

> another perspective a cyborg world might be about lived social and bodily realities in which people are not afraid of their joint kinship with animals and machines, not afraid of permanently partial identities and contradictory viewpoints. The political struggle is to see from both perspectives at once and I would add that this is the psyche's struggle as well, to integrate and see from many perspectives within the particular embodiment one finds oneself.
>
> (quoted in Leitch et al. 2001: 2275)

The fictive female sleuth narratives are a place "where characters refuse the reader's search for innocent wholeness while granting the wish for heroic quests, exuberant eroticism, and serious politics" (quoted in Leitch et al. 2001: 2297).

27 The J. Wayne Reitz Union housed all "officially" recognized student organizations, a bowling alley and game area, a cafeteria, a movie and art theater, and a variety of services for students living on campus and off, like copying, a computer lab (complete with punch cards) and the such. It was the place to meet, to sit on the lawn outside and hear a concert and generally the center of campus life.

28 Similar *Greeks* around the nation occupied the spatial field in many colleges during the 1960s and early 1970s, not only literally in terms of office space in student unions but also having prime real estate on campus with which to house their members.

29 Although representatives from these groups may have been enrolled on campus in the early 1970s, they did not have the voice or presence that I experienced in the fall of 2000.

Chapter 3

Location, location, location

Introduction

The issue of location – where one is located and where others are located – is, like the issues related to the meaning of words like feminine, feminist, and Feminine are constantly evolving. These terms have never been stable and that is why this chapter is necessary before going any further. The reader should be aware of how these words are used throughout the remainder of this work as well as the current research, from a scientific standpoint and then from the post-Jungian perspective, which informs the use of these terms.

Texts written by women and a feminist approach to text are not the same

Literary cultural artifacts infuse the culture of their birth with a constant source of new imagery which is evidence of an enlarging consciousness, yet for most of recorded history women's voices have been marginalized at best and silenced at worst and thus the repository of cultural artifacts from which we draw the "human" experience is myopic. Yet, simply because a text is written by a woman it does not mean that it is a *feminist* text. Because the two are frequently conflated, differentiation is necessary. The analysis of a text written by a female can be made from a historical, cultural, or theoretical perspective, and this would include considerations of postmodernity, poststructuralism, and critical literary theory. The key point is that it is a *text* written by a woman which is under consideration, thus the interpretation then can be done by either male or female, for it is the *text* itself which is under investigation. This type of analysis, which was initiated primarily by women, has reinterpreted and revalued much of what was written in the eighteenth, nineteenth, and twentieth centuries by women. This is not the type of analysis I have engaged in.[1]

My technique is a feminist approach to textual materials and such a feminist approach can be done by either a man or a woman. A feminist approach to a text, any text (including all mystery fiction), necessitates situating oneself and the text in accord with the politics of location as well as explicitly engaging in the deconstruction of implicit and explicit phallocentric power structures which are found in the text. Telling a woman's story or moving women to center focus is not sufficient for what I am calling a feminist approach to the text; a feminist approach would require at the very least an explicit demonstration of sensitivities to the differences that affect the writer, the reader, and the culture they are embedded within, including an analysis of the impact of these contexts upon the writing. A feminist perspective, no matter whether utilized by a male or female, requires a sensitivity to the author's and investigator's situation, location, and an awareness of the politics involved in occupying such locations at the particular point in time and terrain when the text was written. The feminist approach to literary analysis asks the same questions that feminists across all fields ask: What perception of reality do the great books of our time offer the reader? Whose perception is offered to the reader? Who is the implied reader of the work? Who evaluates and selects the texts for the literary canon? Why is it that when we think of great books, male authors come primarily to mind? What sort of images of women are presented to us in texts produced by the male imagination? What values and ideals are represented in literary masterpieces?

Women writing about feminism may not be feminist writing even though women are at center focus. The following quotation from Adrienne Rich's essay "Notes toward a Politics of Location" (1984) illustrates how using a feminist lens changes content:

> I wrote a sentence just now and x'd it out. In it I said that women have always understood the struggle against free-floating abstraction even when they were intimidated by abstract ideas. I don't want to write that kind of sentence now, the sentence that begins "Women have always . . ." We started by rejecting the sentences that began "Women have always had an instinct for mothering" or "Women have always and everywhere been in subjugation to men." If we have learned anything in these years of late twentieth-century feminism, it's that "always" blots out what we really need to know: When, where, and under what conditions has the statement been true?
>
> (Rich, quoted in Eagleton 1996: 208–209)

Contemporary theoretical discourse must support a theory of recognition of the multiple differences that exist among women and other persons, not just feminist discourse.[2] Specifying location recognizes the epistemological danger associated in writing without explicitly situating oneself and one's perspective clearly to the reader.

Where is feminism located in a postmodern postcolonial world?

Feminism is at the core of my personal narrative as well as this book. The term feminism and its derivative, feminist, has encompassed many concepts since its inception thus manifesting a shape-shifting Trickster energy. When I was in undergraduate school in the early 1970s, the bumper sticker on my car stated that *feminism is the radical notion that women are people*. At that time, and now, I find that to be an adequate definition.

When I was in high school in the late 1960s, being a feminist meant asserting a right to take shop classes instead of home economics (which meant cooking and sewing) and to wear pants instead of the required dresses. When I was teaching and coaching high school in the mid-to-late 1970s, being a feminist meant getting funds for the girls' tennis team to travel (only the boys' team got to travel then). Both of these feminisms shared a commonality which centered on being entitled to those rights which men *seemed* to have. The concept of being equal to the elite white male norm was at the core of first wave feminism.[3]

Second wave feminism is traced within the critical literary world to the publication of Simone de Beauvoir's classic *The Second Sex* (1953) after World War II. De Beauvoir's radical reformulation of feminism shifted the focus from equality to freedom; from getting the vote (equality) to women's psychological liberation. Women, according to de Beauvoir, had to choose to liberate themselves; this is why this second wave is termed women's liberation in differentiation from the suffragette or getting the vote movement.

Many types of female liberation movements have developed in the wake of this second wave of feminism.[4] While the categories within feminist theory which have developed, for example, just to name a few, radical, liberal, and materialistic feminism, can be perceived as rather discrete entities, I have found that these seemingly static categories are actually quite fluid and indeterminate. While it is accurate to say that the movement between the first wave of feminism and subsequent waves focuses on the differentiation between equality of opportunity and equality of value, these categories overlap depending on who are members of the group or the particular issue being discussed. Onto this stage of multiple personalities vying for attention comes those who challenge the very notion of the term "woman" in postmodernity.[5]

African American theorists and other women of color representing the developing world and postcolonial geographies have added another discourse to the mix. While second wave theorists might have focused on the differences between men and women, women of color are focusing on differences between women, thereby incorporating the most recent research findings that there are about greater variations within each sexual grouping than between the sexual groupings. These women of color who contend that what has been written so far about the "commonality" of women only reflect the themes relevant to white, privileged Anglo-North American women pose questions that go to the heart of this book, as many women are the subaltern other not only in relationship to the patriarchal symbolic order but also in relationship to privileged women. My own experiences as "the other," whether as an off-white woman,[6] or as a Jew, does not give me the standing to assert that what I perceive is true for anyone other than myself. My job here though is not to come up with another theory or even to enter this discourse because there are (too) many contemporary theorists who are hard at work on this project.[7]

My focus is how the female Trickster is a product of the confluence of all the waves of feminism, including the womanist perspective through my exploration of the African American Blanche White and a Native American perspective through my exploration of Kate Shugak. These two women, in addition to the two white sleuths I have chosen, neither of which fits the stereotype of the privileged white elite woman, touch upon many contact points in the developing web of feminism, such as equality, liberation, and the refusal to be a victim, which are emblematic of third wave feminism. In refusing to be a victim, the female Trickster energy in a contemporary woman is manifested trangressively using humor and irony while constructing a life replete with agency, autonomy, and authority. These values and ideals traverse the web and are inclusive of all women and men.

Postmodernism and feminism

Postmodernism and feminist epistemologies are wrestling with similar questions of postcolonialism and poststructuralism, including: Who said it, for what purpose was it said, in what historical period was it spoken, and to advance what theory? While the questions may be the same, in postmodernism the focus is not primarily on women's position in relation to the patriarchal symbolic order, rather it is upon "the very criteria by which claims to knowledge are legitimized" (Nicholson 1990: 3).[8]

Early feminist theoreticians developed many theories to account for the (almost) total worldwide situation of female subordination. The problem with many of these theories is that they suffered from the same infirmity that modernism's theories did, no sensitivity to diversity or historicity. But when we place these founding mothers of feminist theory in their own contextual locations I find that they did not propose theories which purported to be ultimate truth so much as they were positing possible reasons for their own subordinate situations. Why not extend the lamp which precedes discovery to women and others before we conclude that we no longer need the light. Enfranchising the previously disenfranchised was a laudatory goal of the first wave of feminism and there is no need to jettison it prematurely until we are all the implied reader. This is the crux of the problem as many postmodernist theoretical assumptions are born of a context which excludes awareness of the politics of location and includes an implicit agenda which marginalizes those who are not the implied reader. When the *implied reader* of a text is not identified with sensitivity to those who are not the *implied* reader, it breeds alienation as bell hooks cogently summarizes:[9]

> it is sadly ironic that the contemporary discourse which talks the most about heterogeneity, the de-centered subject, declaring breakthroughs that allow recognition of the Otherness, still directs its critical voice primarily to a specialized audience sharing a common language rooted in the very master narratives it claims to challenge.
>
> (hooks 1990, quoted in Leitch et al. 2001: 2480)

hooks criticizes postmodernism's discourse as threatening feminist discourse of all kinds because it asks "the other" to close down identity formation before the identity has been formed and I agree with her that this is but a new variant of colonization of the mind (hooks 2002).[10] Another problem I have discovered is that postmodern writers today are fearful of describing or identifying any *commonality* – no matter the category (cultural, historical, or literary) – because it might open the door to a new variant of essentialism and binary opposition which results in rampant self-censorship regarding commonalities. Postmodernism thus falls into the binary trap it attempts to deconstruct.

Rather than conceptualizing my work as binary opposition, i.e., the female Tricksters are either conservative or disruptive, Tricksters or mainstream dupes, I prefer to occupy Turner's liminal zone with its sense of radical openness to new forms of being. This liminal state of being is aware that while decentering the traditional male norm is a significant aspect of the postmodernist project, there is no need for a new grand theory with a feminist normative center. What I am interested in is mapping a dialogic feminism that appreciates the differences between people yet remains united in the struggle for equal rights for all people on this planet.[11] This is a primary reason Trickster energy is implicated; when Trickster appears in a cultural context, energy is transformed from the static into a dynamic state of movement.[12] Yet I am painfully aware that there are cultures who have yet to write their *texts* and therefore postmodernism's strategic move to abandon the *text* before it is written is myopic, and this concern is at the heart of the feminist and postcolonial critique of the postmodern perspective.[13] Perhaps there are remnants of the modern that may ameliorate this discord?[14]

Psychological considerations: research on the feminine

Are there any commonalities that can be identified in the concept of the feminine that might form the basis for a consensus definition of the term?

That is what I propose to do in the last section of this chapter and while I do agree with Judith Butler (1990, 1997) that the term feminine will always be somewhat context dependent, there is research which does explicate the former contexts in which our ideas and subsequent ideals of the *feminine* in the symbolic order developed and some suggestions for a redefinition of the term which I have found helpful and which informs the use of the term feminine in the remainder of this work.

Eleanor Maccoby in *The Two Sexes: Growing Up Apart, Coming Together* (1998) developed an elegant template within which to view psychological considerations attendant to sex and gender role stratifications and separations based upon her lifetime of work in the area. Maccoby differentiates three distinct categories of femininity and masculinity: social/anthropological, socialization, and psychological.

The social/anthropological model

Maccoby's sociological/anthropological perspective differentiates the characteristics a culture determines to be masculine or feminine. For example, the concept of nurturance is one that is associated with women cross-culturally; in western culture a feminine woman is nurturant while a masculine man is successful in the competitive world of work. In many subsistence cultures women do most of the heavy work as a nurturing activity, despite the greater upper body strength of the male. Another example occurs when a woman enters the public competitive realm – she will not be considered feminine, despite how she feels internally about herself, unless she also demonstrates behavior which is perceived in her culture as nurturant. This characteristic can be manifested in a variety of ways, but those behaviors or attitudes will all support the larger concept of nurturance. This perspective underlies such statements as, a man doing X is considered assertive, while a woman doing the same activity is considered aggressive. This is because their behavior is being judged against a different norm; the male against a cultural norm of masculinity and the female against a cultural norm of femininity.

This concept of femininity is extremely hard to change because it is based upon that most powerful of psychological archetypes, *The Great Mother* (Neumann 1963). This type of femininity is also represented by Jung's anima, although split off from the mother in many ways, it remains the archetypal template through which women have been associated because of the limited knowledge about men and women's reproductive biology. In the twenty-first century however, the biological basis of this archetype has changed dramatically because of new reproductive technologies. More has changed for women in this area since the 1950s than in the previous 5,000 years from a reproductive standpoint, at least in western cultures. But that is not to say that femininity will no longer be associated with nurturance, it will, but we may tend to see it manifesting in the ways Samuels (2000) has suggested, in environmental awareness and leadership; what I have named the social worker aspect of the postmodern Trickster, the woman who nurtures the community rather than an individual child.

The socialization model

Maccoby's second category of femininity and masculinity concerns socialization. Normed socialization patterns within a particular culture require a child be socialized within a same-sex grouping and this occurs between 19 and 42 months of age. The gender distinctions which many cultures have introjected as sexual differences arise mainly from the dynamics and interactions which occur when the sexes play with same-sex partners in pairs or groups. All male or all female groups differ widely from mixed group configurations in how they operate, yet no difference was found in the actual observed social behavior of boys and girls when the sex of the partner was disregarded and scores for behavior of a given sex are averaged across partner conditions.

According to Maccoby (1998), "it is only when one compares same-sex with mixed sex dyads that the importance of gender springs into bold relief." Thus, "the acquisition of masculine versus feminine traits turns out to be essentially irrelevant to gender differentiation that depends on social context" (Maccoby 1998: 12). Maccoby concluded that these distinctions were embedded by the child's third year and from that time forward social avoidance of the other sex becomes progressively stronger from pre-school through grade school. This finding has been replicated in all settings (Maccoby 1998: 288).

Another, perhaps more important finding from the research is that same-sex boy groups achieve more autonomy and group cohesion, despite higher levels of conflict within the group than girl groups. This is important because it may help us understand why girls and women tend to feel uncomfortable in groups where power is the dominant characteristic and also may explain why girls do not report dreams of forming corporations or large organizations. Boy groups talk about the sexual attributes of girls and female bodies in general more than girl groups do about boys which accounts for the variations between what each sexually segregated group finds humorous. But this may be changing, as I show in my discussion of the television hit *Sex and the City* in Chapter 13.

The research concluded that the young male style of rough and tumble play is the single and most significant influence on gender segregation because girls avoid rough group play. It is important to realize that this style of rough and tumble play does not dominate or play a role when an individual girl or boy's play style is under consideration, it occurs only in sexually segregated group play. Maccoby offers the suggestion that rough sexually segregate play is "better understood as a male response to girls' lack of interest in the kind of play boys seek" (Maccoby 1998: 290). Thus, girls refuse to play the way boys do in groups of other boys, but if a boy is alone and wants to play with a girl, they will change their style of play in order to keep playing.

Having played separately throughout childhood, when the sexes are reunited for procreation and other sexual possibilities, the socialized roles are recreated in parenting and thus the segregated settings in which the sexes grow up are replicated over and over through the generations. The word sex then becomes synonymous with gender, which actually means the social construction of your sex role. The word gender is not a synonym for sex, although it has now passed into wide usage incorrectly as a synonym for sex. The socialization model is always in flux dependent upon the cultural milieu and the data available regarding sex differences. Until the middle of the nineteenth century women were considered to be merely an empty vessel until impregnated with the male sperm; now we know that it takes both male sperm and female egg to make a baby and a woman is not an empty vessel. Data about girls and women is just starting to be collected and compared to the male norm; after all it is sobering to realize that Carol Gilligan's landmark work *In a Different Voice* was published the same year as the V.I. series started, in 1982. As the data about female behavior, psychology and physiology comes in, behaviors previously thought to be absolute markers of femininity are being revised as they are recognized to be the products of socialization. The fact that girls tend to play differently on the playground or engage in different forms of humor does not establish that these quantifiable behaviors are a cross-cultural marker of femininity.

The psychological model

Maccoby's (1998) third category is the *psychological model underlying individual identity*. Behaviors which are strongly associated with femininity can cause intra-psychic identity problems when they are not naturally exhibited by a particular woman or are exhibited naturally by a man. In most cultures a masculine or feminine person is one who exemplifies explicit examples of the behavior which has come to be associated with the differentiation between the sexes that predominate in that particular culture. Women stay in a domestic realm and nurture, men hunt. A feminine woman is expected to behave in a particular fashion in order to support, for example, the general cultural value of nurturance which has been defined by the male projective imagination as the female role in the patriarchal symbolic order. When (elite) mothers were expected by traditional value systems to stay within the domestic realm a panoply of behaviors became associated with the domestic realm and were perceived as intrinsically feminine; the joy of cooking, cleaning and sewing. Women who deviated from this view, by, for example, writing about the domestic realm or who entered into political discussions were shunned by the mainstream, and in many cultural contexts, still are. During World War II middle-class women in the United States were expected to be Rosie the Riveter and then were quickly told to transform themselves back into domestic workers, which many followed. This behavior can be seen as nurturing the body politic when needed, but then was willingly given up when the resumption of more traditional notions of femininity and nurturance were necessitated when the men came back from war. However, the energy of psychological health associated with working outside the home proved irresistible for some women, and through that small opening, women started to enter the public domains in ever increasing numbers. Women's natural adaptative behavior become fused with the concept of femininity and much of the classical Jungian model, including the anima and animus are based upon the larger concept of traditional nurturance as the exclusive psychological and creative energy output for the female.

Another example has to do with more specific behaviors that become fused from a popular cultural standpoint with femininity. For example, when elite women wore intricate and extravagant hairdos and didn't want to get their hair wet, women took baths and men took showers. It was a feminine thing to do to bathe while a man in the bathtub or wearing a bathrobe was used for comedic effect such as we find in the humor of Milton Berle or Benny Hill. Advertisements buttressed the model. When I was growing up I recall all those commercials where women were bathing their cares away with various images of these feminine products (either that or the images were of women obsessed with cleaning). If a woman preferred showers or hated cleaning, she was deviating from the norm and thus her innate intra-psychic identity was not mirrored in her culture. But now that many women wash their hair every day, that has changed, and taking a shower is not a marker for femininity.

Another fluid example is what type of clothing is considered appropriate. George Sand wore pants because she found them more practical than the long sweeping skirts she was supposed to wear, which picked up all kinds of dirt and litter from the Parisian streets, but she was ostracized for it. Today there are schools where skirts for girls are prohibited, although one could say that watching football on television is still a masculine marker. Identifying girls as feminine because they play with dolls has always been problematic; this behavior raises a child's score on the femininity continuum of psychological measurements, but what is a G.I. Joe but a doll even though it's named an action figure?

The procreation/evolutionary model

Maccoby's (1998) final category is based upon *proceation/evolutionary* considerations. A feminine woman is one who strives to be attractive to men and a masculine man is one who is attractive to women. This perspective on femininity and masculinity is the basis of studies in the field of evolutionary psychology. In a woman this femininity would show up as the unconscious desire to be a good listener, one who flirts with a man, and works to make herself sexy and good-looking in order to procreate. This view looks at the behaviors exhibited by the sexes as instinctual in the survival of the fittest sense. What is considered flirting behavior or what ideals there are for being considered good-looking or sexy have considerable fluidity across cultures and this is where drag and camp come into play as disguise. What one culture may consider feminine may be abhorrent in another; the evolutionary perspective accepts that ideals of physical beauty vary not only by culture but also by time and space. For example, scarification has multiple meanings around the globe, signifying everything from disfigurement to ultimate beauty. The hourglass figure popular at the turn of the nineteenth century gave way to the boyish figure of the roaring 1920s. The anorexic look of Twiggy of the 1960s has given way to the athletic well-toned look found in *Sex and the City*, the turn of the twentieth century's mass media blockbuster about four sexually adventurous women which is explored in depth in Chapter 13.

The evolutionary model does have psychological implications and is the basis for the femininity we find being challenged and reinscribed in Haraway's (1985) description of cyborg consciousness and in the campy drag world of exaggeration and burlesque. Evolutionary psychology contends that the reason for segregated same-sex play groups is biological, in that boys' style of play prepares them, first, for in-group dominance hierarchies which regulate male aggression and socialize boys for cooperation with other males, and second, is a social mechanism which minimizes in-breeding in small cultural groupings. However, there is a wide divergence in male parenting in simians and humans; cross-culturally these primate groups are flexible in what they invest in fatherhood thus permitting adaptation to a variety of social conditions.

Fatherhood, as Luigi Zoja (2001) argues, is a conscious choice for every male and fatherhood must to be differentiated from the sexual act which impregnates a fertile female. Research has demonstrated that when androgens are prenatally introduced into female monkeys their play styles change to more of a rough and tumble style. Androgen antagonists introduced to male monkeys delayed their move away from adults and into male peer groups. These types of biological predispositions do not manifest until there is a triggering event, which may be the social structure already in place as boys see other boys playing just with boys and girls see the same and thus a predisposition for same-sex segregation occurs. Genetic predispositions have not been found to explain the distinctive interaction styles which develop within same-sex groupings. The differences which have been replicated in research demonstrate that the differences are between the style of play and the content of play, as "play themes that children enact in their same-sex groups do differ considerably with time and place and cultural gender roles" (Maccoby 1998: 292). If we observe that a child of either sex goes to the mother for comfort and the father for fun and games does that have any impact on why that occurs? Are boys and girls trained by their parents to adopt different play styles that lead to childhood segregation? Is fun removed from the purview of girls at an early age and encouraged in boys, since *boys will be boys*. Both parents play rougher with boys and talk more about feelings with girls: is this because girls' cognitive abilities develop at a different rate than boys resulting in earlier language acquisition? As a middle school teacher it was plain to me that most of the girls were almost grown up and the boys were still little boys for the most part.

In those cultures where boys have a higher status because they are valued differently than girls, they are encouraged to avoid contact with lower status girls and women. The status power dynamic of adult over children is replicated with boys over girls and then men over women as well as the hierarchies which are encouraged to develop in same-sex male groups. Research demonstrates that boys tend to ignore suggestions made by girls, which may account for the male rejection of female humor, while girls respond more equally to humor, listening to peers of either group, so women can find male or female humor funny, while men tend to reject women's humor as not humorous.

In conclusion, three themes emerge from replicated research about the differences between boys and girls: the tendency to separate, the divergence in interaction styles and the balance of power between the groups. Societal gender rules are flexible but are still influenced by the childhood segregation patterns (Maccoby 1998: 305). Can these be changed and is it even desirable to try to modify single-sex groups in childhood, especially boys' groups, which lead to sexist adult behaviors? It may actually be more trouble than it's worth in terms of the time involved in adequate adult supervision to counterbalance the natural tendencies and which may lead to a loss of spontaneous activity which is the marker for being a child of either sex in western culture.

Encouraging cross-sex cooperation instead of encouraging same-sex cooperation may be a more beneficial way to ameliorate the social construction of sex into gender roles. Coeducational institutions are the least sexist institutions in our culture. But when all-boy clubs are opened to girls the research found that the girls emulate the boys in terms of joining gangs and exhibiting toughness and other forms of macho behavior and if that is not permissible within the cultural group, then the girls hang around as auxiliaries on the fringes of the male groups, like cheerleaders (Maccoby 1998: 308). The research regarding all-girl groupings such as clubs and schools is that they empower girls to demand and achieve greater equality in their interactions with males, so this finding supports all-girls schools as an ameliorative strategy which works with as opposed to children's own tendency towards sex segregation.

Jungian and post-Jungian perspectives on the feminine

The feminist Jungian analyst Polly Young-Eisendrath has cited Carolyn Heilbrun's *Writing a Woman's Life* (1988) for the proposition that women have no narrative, no plot, no paradigm for the life of a strong adventurous women. At the start of the twenty-first century women do have access to narratives of authoritative, autonomous women with agency which encourages other women to manifest their own imaginative cultural artifacts. In the previous section I discussed the terms feminine and masculine based upon recent replicated research, concluding that there were very few actual differences between the sexes that cannot be accounted for by socialization in its various cultural inflections. Connie Zweig recommends that the word *feminine* (in the lower case) be used to refer to the adjective derived from *Latin femina* for woman and should be defined as the characteristics associated with the *patriarchal woman* – receptive, nurturant, quiet, docile (Zweig 1990: 8). The Feminine, signified through the use of the upper-case capital, connotes the archetypal energy which is not restricted to any sex. The Masculine can be treated similarly, with the lower-case masculine denoting a relationship to the patriarchal symbolic order while capitalizing the M in Masculine gives it an archetypal cast. I will use these differentiations through the remainder of this work, but it is important to further differentiate the feminine of the patriarchal epoch and the archetypal Feminine when manifested through the female imagination as being different than the Feminine manifested through the male imagination.

Marion Woodman agrees that we have confused patriarchal power over dynamics with the Masculine and submissiveness with the Feminine (Woodman 1990: 241). Woodman suggests that what she has been seeing in her clinical practice and workshops is the emergence of Dark Goddess imagery (Woodman and Dickson 1996). As an image coming from women, it is significant for that reason alone, but also this image of darkness as newly available creative energy is a significant reinscription as the color black was first associated with the wise one and the black arts were the wisdom arts. Woodman and Dickson (1996) see black as rooted in suffering but remaining lusty while singing the tragedy. This is a perfect description of Blanche White, one of my quaternity of fictive female sleuths, who represents the postmodern female Trickster energy in the collective culture. Being lustful and full of song are Trickster modalities so let's remember it was Hermes who gave the world music and laughter.

The ascendancy of linear progressive history as exemplified by the hero mythology which dominates western consciousness occurred by 1500 BCE. The adoption of the hero mythology repressed the cyclical patterns of women causing the collective culture to become disassociated from the cyclical patterns of nature. Disassociation is the splitting of the psyche into different parts which are walled off from each other. In the sense Woodman (1990) is using disassociation, she is not talking about an individual psyche but the patriarchal culture which has disassociated itself from itself. To Woodman, disassociation is a psycho-neurotic reaction in which a portion of experience is split off, or isolated from conscious awareness. A person or a culture disassociates in order to avoid anxiety and disassociation can provide protection from threatening impulses, but it also allows the acting out of impulses without having to bear any responsibility for the actions thereby avoiding both anxiety and guilt. In the patriarchal symbolic order collective, the disassociation from the Feminine cyclical nature resulted in the invention of a phallic mother. The Feminine became not totally disassociated, but it is only available to the patriarchal symbolic order in its distorted form just as Masculinity is distorted as well.

According to Betty D. Meador (1990), the years from 3500 BCE to 1500 BCE saw the previous abundance of female imagery giving way to an abundance of male imagery (Singer 2000: 50). The Age of Pisces was in ascendancy during the past 2,000 years in which we have this abundant imagery of the dualisms, signified by Gemini, the twin fishes. The Age of Aquarius is just beginning in the twenty-first century. As Jung said in Aion (*CW*, 9II) the collective consciousness is at the beginning of another great age of transition where the sharp splits of the past 2,000 years will be integrated into a unified whole. This integration will be as significant as that which occurred during the Axial Age (800–200 BCE), which produced monotheism. According to Karen Armstrong writing in *A History of God*:

> There was a new prosperity that led to the rise of a merchant class. Power was shifting from king and priest, temple and palace, to the marketplace. . . . Each region developed a distinctive ideology to address these problems and concerns, Taoism and Confucianism in China, Hinduism and Buddhism in India and Philosophical rationalism in Europe. The Middle East did not produce a uniform solution, but in Iran and Israel Zoraster and the Hebrew prophets respectively evolved different versions of Monotheism. Strange as it may seem, the idea of "God" like the other great religious insights of the period, developed in a market economy in the spirit of aggressive capitalism.
>
> (Armstrong 1993: 37)

Significantly, women were not included in any of the imagery of God developed during this period, since the Catholic Church as we know it today did not even come into the consciousness of the Roman World until Constantine in the fourth century AD. This cult of monotheism, which still possesses much of the world psyche, is one based upon the early development of the male as projected onto the world as market. The rules from the playground were shifted onto the larger scene of the world and we have yet to recover from it.

Masculinity forced through the conduit of patriarchal consciousness is grounded in a tragic world view, a *but for this* all would be fine, so let's get rid of the irritant through dominance and hierarchal structures, then we can have the illusion of certainty and order. This is a delusion which has captured the male imagination for millennia, the disassociative state Woodman refers to. The comedic world view that Trickster is part of accepts that what is, is – with humor and wit as the adaptive process. The patriarchal world view does not recognize any image of the Feminine which is not related to the dominant imagery of woman as womb-like receptacle or the maintenance of what came from that womb, but in doing so the patriarchal symbolic order repressed the tremendous energy of the Feminine which occurs as a part of the birthing process and which is the antithesis of the submissive feminine mandated by patriarchal consciousness. While it is true that the feminine does receive and provide the womb, at the right moment, it pushes with great force towards birth. How could this energy ever have been imagined by the male in the same way it is experienced by a female? Perhaps this is an aspect of Masculine energy inherent in the female which has no counterpart in the male. Can this behavior be reinscribed as an act of ejaculation in terms of male psychology?

This type of reinscription is already occurring. Genia Pauli Haddon (1990), in "The Personal and Cultural Emergence of Yang-Femininity," agrees that if our ideas about femininity were based upon the pushing of the womb, positive feminine traits would include being pushy – as in being the initiator of life – by moving the child from the inside of the womb into the outside world. This movement of creation from interior to exterior world is missing entirely from the characteristics of the Feminine within patriarchal consciousness; rather it has been assigned as a function of Masculine energy to remove the (male) child from the domestic inside space and socialize the (male) child into the outside space of the public domain, thereby splitting off how the child came into the world, which only occurs through the tremendous exertions of Feminine force. Our ideas about masculinity and femininity are based on a false dichotomy which is only awareness of half of the story, and this is the problem in Jungian psychology; it only represents the phallic side of masculine and femininity. This may be why thoughtful Jungians have expressed the view that the anima and animus delineations should be forgotten in favor of a more sophisticated view towards the Feminine and Masculine.[15] I am not making the argument that the thrusting force of phallic masculinity is the same as the exertions of the Feminine, what I am saying is that the thrusting force acts towards a focused goal whereas the Feminine exertive energy acts only within a specific context and thus can be differentiated from thrusting energy. Haddon suggests a framework of yin and yang femininity and masculinity which breaks up the pie into quarters rather than into the dichotomies we are more familiar with:

> In terms of this analogy, we might say that the Masculine is like the mountain, having both yang and yin sides; the Feminine like the river, also both yang and yin. These four modes of human experience correspond metaphorically to the penis/phallus (yang-masculine), testicles (yin-masculine), gestating womb (yin-feminine), and exertive womb (yang-feminine).
>
> (Haddon 1990: 247)

This metaphorical way of dividing the pie does not depend upon a woman actually giving birth, it is dependent upon the energies which reside in the body and psyche which can be manifested. Being a father is a choice, and being a mother is also becoming a choice, but the energies of exertion are inherent in both the male and female body. What psychological shift occurs if we recognize that there may be a pushy attitude in women which is necessary for the creative birthing process? Can this "pushy" behavior be reinscribed by asking what purposes it serves rather than assuming it to be a negative quality when found in a female body. Offering a Feminine perspective through the female imagination using a case from her clinical Jungian practice Haddon asks what:

> Different meanings emerge, however, if we ask what *birthing value* [emphasis in original] Marcia's bitchiness might serve. The man at whom she tended to bitch was stuck in procrastination, a negative expression of poorly integrated testicular masculinity. At its best, testicular masculinity gives one the capacity to "hang in there," hence steadfastness, patience and stability. In exaggerated form this becomes stagnation. In this context, the image of busting open the balls suggests not castration but opening the way for the seeds of creation to come forth. Marcia could see that her task was not to eliminate her feminine force but to become more and more conscious in exercising its birthing function.
>
> (Haddon 1990: 248)

So we have a reinscription of the ball-busting bitch into the initiator of the birth process, whatever may be in the process of being born:

> The woman (or anima) whose exertive yang-feminine side develops wholesomely will know when to push herself and others toward new life in harmony with organic processes of transformation. Her style will be to *move with* [emphasis in original] the birthing processes in ongoing affirmation of herself and others through the throes of change.
>
> (Haddon 1990: 248)

As in all psychological processes, this reinscription of the Feminine and the Masculine has a shadow aspect which must be recognized if we are to move beyond yet integrate the gains of the patriarchal epoch:

> If yang-femininity becomes overcharged (either directly or through compensatory buildup) a woman's style becomes "forced." She pushes prematurely, demanding untimely changes of herself and others, rejecting old patterns without respect for the purposes they may serve, often abandoning tender new potentialities before they mature enough to survive.
>
> (Haddon 1990: 249)

In another clinical vignette Haddon offers, we find out that a woman who is running a non-profit agency has come to realize that emergencies are part of the process in her agency, yet she cannot get rid of the feeling of inadequacy when the emergencies arise, although she handles them with equanimity. Haddon's analysis inverts the patriarchal masculine's reading of emergency as a threat to control and order to reinscribe emergency as an emergence of the masculinity found in the female psyche. Within the context of this woman's non-profit agency, emergencies are a routine and regular part of the context, not a threat to her control. In patriarchal consciousness only the gestative is related to the culturally appropriate ideal of femininity and so the push has been virtually ignored as part of a woman's natural state of being. The male imagination has idealized the gestating womb from which they come into the world out of existence without acknowledging that without the push nothing could be born.

The dark side of such goddesses as Hecate and Cali is revisioned by Haddon to be good, the dramatic assertion of a women's femininity; actively delivering a lost side of herself which has no counterpart in the male, because men do not have a womb. She points out that in *The Frog Prince*, the transformation comes about not through kissing the frog, it is by throwing him against the wall that he is transformed into the prince. The frog hidden deep in the well is the unconscious shadow of the patriarchal conscious culture represented by the King. This type of unconsciousness can be very primitive like the frog but no matter how it's dressed up, it too becomes a masquerade, a put on. And it is not the idealized feminine warmth which produces the transformation it is the "fiery feminine thrust" (Haddon 1990: 250).

Haddon concludes that equating yang energy only with the phallus leaves women with only an impotent fake penis, forcing her to adopt a phallic masculinity. Women get angry because they cannot express their inner masculinity through the exertion of the womb like energies and when this happens the shadow may appear as an inner tyrant, recreating the patriarchal melodrama. An example of this would occur when a women with natural yang-masculinity is confronted with the old feminine stereotypes. In an effort to distance herself from and reject the old patriarchal ideals, she exhibits an ego driven intensity filled with shoulds and oughts. These misplaced yang energies will be applied without compassion to herself and others. Haddon concludes that when phallic masculinity is "substituted for the woman's exertive-womb energy, the phallic animus fixates an abstract, unreachable goal that, although irrelevant to the real concerns of the women's life, become her taskmaster" (Haddon 1990: 251).

How does the Feminine know when to exert and when to wait? Isn't the patriarchal pregnancy over yet? Women are finished with being held within the enclosure of the male imagination which only gave them the role of passive gestation. Women are ready to push the margins and stop the worldwide enslavement of women which has developed wherever the patriarchal symbolic order has taken root. Yet, women push differently than men do and according to Haddon, it is marked by the humor women bring to the table:

> One hallmark of yang-masculine consciousness is the ability to cut through irrelevancies and get straight to the goal. Commonly this gift is exercised with an attitude of mastering and overpowering obstacles. With the emergence of yang-femininity, this phallic talent is found to operate with *humor, lightness and laughter* [emphasis added] rather than aggressiveness.
>
> (Haddon 1990: 251)

Haddon points out that the oughts of the shadow yang-masculinity is "replaced by a compassionate demand for authenticity rooted in the actual context of each situation" (Haddon 1990: 254). This is what happens on the playground with little girls; when a problem develops it is handled individually, with compassion rather than competitiveness. If the game or play is not appreciated by some members, then the game is changed. Haddon's work is Trickster scholarship because it demonstrates that when women vision the exertive or yang-feminine it is not seen either as a put down or as aggressive behavior, it is a totally different perspective that is brought to bear on Feminine actions. But can women reinscribe the Feminine without the cooperation of men? We are past, at least in the west, the period of trying to become equal to the male norm. We are in a period which requires that the masculine and feminine norms be reinscribed because our notions of the Feminine and the Masculine are incomplete. If the shadow of the patriarchal symbolic order is aggression and control, how is it to be handled so that we can cooperate instead of dominate? According to Maccoby (1998) what is needed is equal status interaction even if separate spheres remain. The rapid social changes we have been witnessing most especially in the last quarter of the twentieth century are evidence of the ability and capacity of human cultures and institutions to change what has been perceived as deep-seated differences between the sexes. But it has been slow and uneven, especially in child rearing. This is where Trickster moves the stalled patriarchal symbolic order which has fixated on the abstract, unreachable goal of worldwide hegemony based upon a dichotomous power over dynamic.

The dichotomous model ignores critical variances because the model itself does not take into account the nuances of adaptation. It's like the economic model which has no method of calculating the value of an old growth forest until it is cut and made into board lumber. When each individual element (currently or in the future) perceived as possible and relevant is accounted for, only a few variants between the sexes emerge. The bulk of the research to date supports the conclusion that there is more variance within each sex's characteristics than between them. But the culture, based on the model of the undeveloped masculine of early childhood, has focused on the extreme end of each linear continuum as its definition of the Feminine and Masculine, ignoring the vast overlap. The linear model cannot take into account all the variations in the web of life. The logic that has been produced from these underdeveloped Masculine characteristics has skewed the world into a disaster waiting to occur, and in fact is occurring through drastic global changes in the weather patterns, genocide, ethnic cleansing, domestic violence, poverty and worldwide starvation.

The same linear logic which excluded that which was not easily factored into the equation was used to segregate the sexes at a stage of development preceding full development. The conditional was made the absolute and then codified first by the clans, then tribes and finally in the law. A single theoretical perspective was placed upon the wide range of human behaviors for both sexes. When women exhibit yang-masculinity or other innate behaviors which have been determined to occur exclusively in the male, the female questions herself intra-psychically about the discordance between her desire and her culture's definition of femininity. If women exhibit the taboo behaviors they are usually shunned, the most powerful form of punishment for an animal designed to live in culture with others. I am not talking about physical shunning, although that occurs when women are forced into wearing restrictive clothing or are kept indoors, but a psychological shunning which is introjected regarding innate behaviors. Why did this develop, since the overwhelming research conclusion is that girls and boys are more alike than different, that is except for a few little differences in prenatal androgen washes and regulation of impulse control at differing ages because of different development in the pre-frontal lobes (Maccoby 1998). Research demonstrates that girls develop impulse control at an earlier age which means they are able to regulate their behavior even in the face of impulses earlier than boys are able to. This cognitive gift is turned against girls and women, who may be using their natural gifted ability for adaptation, therefore yielding to the more frenetic, demanding energy of the less developed male child. And because girls use the strategy of avoidance to boys' rough and tumble and space dominating play, girls vacate both geographical and psychological terrain to the boys who build forts and make war. Patriarchy is just the chronological aging of this model, played out not by 5 year olds but 25 year olds. Keep in mind that until the medical advances of the twentieth century, many women died in childbirth before the age of 30 and most men were considered old if they reached the age of 30. It is only in the twentieth century that the life expectancy rose above age 50 for the first time in human history. To continue to use the model of the male from age 3 to 13 to design a cultural system is just plain ridiculous. We now live longer and can almost expect a tripling of the life span; why do we continue to use the model of young male children on the playground to order our world affairs? Boys' rough and tumble group form of play may sound humorous because of the constant laughter and teasing but this form of humor, which we find in the imagery of the traditional Trickster, is a relatively undeveloped variant of humor. Perhaps that's why I have never found a woman who likes The Three Stooges or other forms of slapstick; it's just too childish a form of humor but it does remind me of what small boys do on a playground. Wit and irony are more developed forms of humor and are found throughout the literature of women and other marginalized groups. Slapstick and patriarchal competitiveness are reciprocal energies which the collective must evolve beyond or we are – simply put – doomed as a species on this planet.

From all areas of research, from Gottman's (1994) finding that men resist the influence of their wives, even though to do so is one of the prime markers of a happy marriage and fulfilling lifelong relationship, to little boys refusing to listen to girls' voices at a young childhood age – these are not biological but sociological and therefore can be changed, just as there have been major transformations in consciousness before in the world as the outside contexts change. Of course, this development is not going to happen worldwide at the same time, but just as slavery was considered a natural part of the order of human society, nowhere is that accepted as natural anymore. Whether it is practiced or not, it is not considered acceptable and is a shadow practice where it still occurs. Whether we can extend the idea that slavery is inappropriate in all its contexts then we may have to let the animals free as well, but that is another story yet to be written. Boys do grow up, but by the time they develop impulse control and can regulate their androgen extreme mood swings, they are already encased in a male peer model that specifically discourages further psychological development. This keeps them locked through peer dominance and hierarchal constraints into continuing their play with forms of play toys which really do maim and kill. It is these deep models which Maccoby's (1998) work dramatically exposes and then sifts the assumptive ideas regarding what is nurture and what is nature through the latest scientific neurology, biology, and sociology, finding that very little actually separates the sexes, and that it is the exaggeration of these differences which are at the root of our gender stereotypes, which vary dramatically cross-culturally. It reminds me of "natural law" theories, which held that all we do is discover the law that is already there.

Peggy Sanday's (1981, 1990) work establishes that sex segregation and dominance are primary processes in cultures which have scarce natural resources. In these cultures the natural competitiveness of the developing male model becomes an aggressive way of life as survival tactic. In cultures of prosperity, negotiation and cooperation are more highly valued than aggressiveness and dominance. Cultures of scarcity have come to dominate the prosperous cultures of this earth. What can a culture do that is different than what an individual can do? If you are living peacefully and a new neighbor moves in who plays music so bassy your walls vibrate, and they fill their yard with rotting vehicles, what can you do if you are not violently inclined? Do you figure out a way to adapt to the ever present nuisance of noise and garbage or do you move away? Either way, you haven't changed the neighbor's behavior so what do you do? If you are a man who has been raised in patriarchal culture, you fight for dominance. If you are a woman, more than likely if you have been raised in a traditional cultural milieu you yield, find ways to adapt – wearing earplugs, being away from home more, or sending pies over when you want them to lower the speaker – but more than likely if you are a woman you will not plan to blow up their stereo or puncture their tires, unless of course you have introjected the under-developed male template as the appropriate masculine response. Or you might deal with it humorously, as many who cannot escape from their tormentors have done.

Later in this book, specifically Part IV which deals with Re/storation, I give examples of how women have adopted the subversive strategy of deploying humor as psychological adaptation. As women have developed new strategies, men seem to be drawing lines and standing their ground, for example, it can be seen in the skewed dependence on male reviewers as arbiter of mainstream opinion and awards. There is even evidence of a resurgence in idealization of the housewife and stigmatization of the independent women among the elite college student in the United States. The research done in "Understanding the Structure of Stereotypes of Women: Virtue and Agency as Dimensions Distinguishing Female Sub-groups" (DeWall et al. 2005) was an attempt to expand and replicate earlier findings which found that the stereotypes "professional women, housewives and sex objects could be distinguished from each other based on two dimensions; agency (a combination of power and competence) and virtue (both sexual and moral)" (DeWall et al. 2005: 2).[16] The study found that it was power, not competence, that was oppositional to a perception of warmth in a woman. The group who was the subject of this research is significant because they are current undergraduates at the University of Chicago, an elite university in the United States. In the group, 50 percent were male, 61 percent identified themselves as European American or Caucasian, 13 percent African American, 13 percent Asian/Indian, 6 percent Latino/Latina and 7 percent other. The sample is slightly over-weighted in the Caucasian category and underweighted in the Latino/ Latina category, but it is a distributive sampling of those who are currently attending a school from which the policy makers of Anglo-American culture will be drawn. The final conclusion of the study found that:

> whereas competence was strongly correlated with (and thus to some degree redundant with) virtue, power was relatively independent of virtue. Power – defined as the capacity to influence others and to resist their influence – may play a more important role than competence in maintaining status differences between groups because of its direct association with self-determination.
>
> (DeWall et al. 2005: 10)

Power in a woman was not correlated positively with virtue among this group of undergraduates and female beauty was found to still hold the trump card of virtue (DeWall et al. 2005: 9). While this study did not find agency and virtue to be polar opposites, it did find that agency in a woman is not rated as highly as beauty or homemaking. Recalling that 40 percent of the sample were young women, it is amazing that they, as well as the young men, still prize beauty and homemaking rather than competence and power in a woman. Obviously, Trickster has more work to do!

Summary

The differences between the sexes are quite small and have been exaggerated into social constructions of gender. Girls tend to avoid groups of boys who are engaged in rough and tumble play. The reliance upon under-developed male attributes has frozen concepts of the masculine and the feminine into archaic patterns when the life span was a third of what it is today. Yet, these stereotypes regarding what is virtuous in a women can be found on the campuses of the United States' most elite universities. Women's pushing abilities have been ignored while their womb-like receptivity and holding have been exaggerated as the only biological marker for femininity, both in the general culture and within Jungian psychology.

In 1929 Joan Riviere suggested in "Womanliness as a Masquerade" that genuine womanliness and masquerade are one and the same, that is, there is a performative aspect to the assumption of normal masculine and feminine subjectivity to some extent. Patriarchal femininity and masculinity are masquerades in which both sexes adopt a role which covers over the ambivalence and anxiety of subjectivity and sexual identity. To some, there is no need for masking because they fit into the natural ebb and flow of the collective unconscious which is consciously experienced as normality. Judith Butler (1990, 1997) questions all categories of identity asking why do we need a stable feminine identity for feminine theory. For Butler it is not inner capacities, attributes and identities but a set of repeated performances that conceals the true self, or if you repeat the lie often enough it's hard to tell what is true or real; that's the masquerade or performance. We are all performers in our own lives. On stage, off stage, persona, ego, id. Fragile human beings trying desperately to understand the mystery of our own and other's lives. Females become women within their own social class, history, fields and contexts. De Beauvoir's "woman is not born but made" is also "man is not born but made." Both men and women are not born but made in their cultures. Male and female are sexual attributes usually attendant at birth. Masculine and Feminine concerns the unconscious psychic life of a male or female; how the images of the unconscious archetypes manifest. The postmodern female Trickster, through her representation in the fictive female sleuth and as pop culture icons such as Madonna and Carrie Bradshaw of *Sex and the City*, gives the collective consciousness additional data, another set of attributes for feminine identity, to add to the variety of imaginative manifestation of the Feminine now being manifest in the collective.

Notes

1 Representative examples are Tillie Olsen's *Silences* (1978), Elaine Showalter's *A Literature of their Own* (1977) and Sandra Gilbert and Susan Gubar's *The Madwoman in the Attic: The Woman Writer and the Nineteenth-Century Literary Imagination* (1979b).

2 Attention to the situated as opposed to the universalistic is implicit in how Audre Lorde challenges the reader to come into relationship with her and her work through her revelation of location, "I am a Black feminist lesbian warrior poet mother doing my work. Who are you and how are you doing yours?" (Lorde, in de Lauretis 1993: 402). Gloria Anzaldúa also accomplishes this critical task of locating herself for the reader through allegorical imagistic descriptions:

> I am a wind-swayed bridge, a crossroads inhabited by whirlwinds. . . . You say my name as ambivalence? Think of me as Shiva, a many-armed and legged body with one foot on brown soil, one on white, one in straight society, one in the gay world, the man's world, the women's, one limb in the literary world, another in the working class, the socialist, and the occult worlds. A sort of spider woman hanging by one thin strand of web. Who, me confused? Ambivalent? Not so. Only your labels split me.
>
> (Anzaldúa 1987: 205)

Rosi Braidotti would argue that woman's writing which is not located in it's own contextual realm is suspect because in "feminist theory the only consistent way of making general theoretical points is to be aware that one is actually located somewhere specific" (Braidotti 1994, in Eagleton 1996: 238).

3 First wave feminism occurred in North America after the Civil War and covers the period surrounding the establishment of the right to vote for North American women.

4 Radical feminism in the 1970s focused on sexuality but rejected the idea that there was anything immutable about the nature of women's sexuality. Radical feminists agree with de Beauvoir that a woman is not born but made. Liberal feminism was next up. One way to tell the difference between a radical and a liberal feminist is to ask the question, why are women subordinate in society? A radical answer would focus on women as a subordinated class that needs to act collectively to achieve liberation. A liberal feminist would focus on the social construction of what we (mistakenly) think are innate sex roles based on differences between the sexes, arguing for the amelioration of those roles into an androgynous ideal which has full equality before the law. While all forms of feminism are concerned with the normative symbolic order called patriarchy, socialist feminism, now frequently called Materialist Feminism extends the traditional Marxist analysis from the means of production to the means of reproduction as the situs of women's oppression. Socialist Marxist or material feminism views the worldwide oppression of women as arising from capitalism, patriarchy and racism. See, for example, *Materialist Feminism: A Reader in Class, Difference, and Women's Lives* (Hennessy and Ingraham 1997).

5 It is precisely this type of writing – that a woman writing is writing from a feminist perspective – which has been attacked by African American writers such as Alice Walker, who coined the term *womanist* in order to set herself (and other female African American writers) apart from the all inclusive terminology of feminism dominated by white women from which Walker felt excluded (Walker 1983: xi). Walker's work, *In Search of our Mothers' Gardens* (1983) as well as the work of Bonnie Zimmerman, "What Has Never Been: An Overview of Lesbian Feminist Literary Criticism" (1981) (white, lesbian feminist), Paula Gunn Allen, *The Sacred Hoop: Recovering the Feminine in American Indian Traditions* (1986) (Native American feminist), and Gloria Anzaldúa, *Borderlands: The New Mestiza* (1987) (developing world feminist) all rely in part on the work of Barbara Smith (1977) who published "Toward a Black Feminist Criticism" challenging the literary world with her statement that "All segments of the literary world – whether establishment, progressive, Black, female, or lesbian – do not know, or at least act as if they do not know, that Black women writers and Black lesbian writers exist" (Smith 1977: 165). Smith's rereading of Morrison's *Sula* (1973) from a lesbian perspective was groundbreaking work.

6 Here I adopt Karen Brodkin's definition in *How Jews Became White Folks* (1998).

7 I would suggest as a beginning the writing of Maria C. Lugones and Elizabeth V. Spelman, "Have We Got a Theory for You! Feminist Theory, Cultural Imperialism and the Demand for the Women's Voice" (1983), Hélène Cixous, "The Laugh of the Medusa" (1976), bell hooks, *Feminist Theory: From Margin to Center* (1984), Sandra Bartky, *Foucault, Femininity and the Modernization of Patriarchal Power* (1988), and Marilyn Pearsall, *Women and Values: Readings in Recent Feminist Philosophy* (1999).

8 Linda Nicholson points out in *Feminism/Postmodernism* (1990) that postmodernism replicated the same "universalizing moves found in the particular schools of thought to which their work was most closely allied." Nicholson sees the fundamental problem as "a failure, common to many forms of academic

scholarship, to recognize the embeddedness of its own assumptions within a specific historical context" (Nicholson 1990: 1–2).

9 The writer bell hooks chooses to spell her first and last name using all lower case letters.

10 bell hooks' interview on C-Span, May 5, 2002. See also Thomas J. Cottle's *Black Children, White Dreams* (1974). While agreeing with hooks, I also have to give credit to those who awakened my own awareness that all canonical works must be questioned, and so I bow to postmodernist philosophers such as Derrida and Foucault. These men were the "other" in their own French communities; Derrida was a Jew brought up in Algeria (like Hélène Cixous) and thus was never really considered French. Foucault was gay and thus never fit into mainstream French culture either.

11 For further discussion of dialogic feminism see Lídia Puigvert, "Dialogic Feminism: 'Other Women's' Contributions to the Social Transformation of Gender Relations" in Butler, Beck-Gernsheim, and Puigvert, *Women and Social Transformation* (2001).

12 This approach encourages me to honor work such as Foucault's masterwork on the birth of the prison in western civilization, *Discipline and Punish: The Birth of Prison* (1979). Foucault's basic theory is that discourse orders knowledge which produces an individual open to the manifestation of power in their lives. This power is operationalized through daily routines which produce the docile body upon which the power operates implicitly.

13 Key early texts which demonstrate the emergence of postcolonial criticism out of the colonial experience are Aimé Césaire, *Discourse and Colonialism* (1950); Frantz Fanon, *Black Skin, White Masks* (1952) and Ngugi wa Thiong'o, *Homecoming Essays* (1972). Academic discourse was opened up by Edward Said's *Orientalism* (1978) and Gayatri Chakravorty Spivak's *In Other Worlds: Essays in Cultural Politics* (1987) which also makes a significant addition to feminist theory through its weaving of Marxism and feminism into postcolonial studies. Homi K. Bhabha's *The Location of Culture* (1994) is notable for its poststructural approach employing Derridean deconstruction. Representative readers include *Edward Said: A Critical Reader* (Sprinkler 1992), which utilizes a poststructural approach through a Foucauldian lens and *The Spivak Reader: Selected Works of Gayatri Chakravorty Spivak*, edited by Landry and Maclean (1996). For an earlier treatment, *"Race", Writing and Difference* (1986) edited by Henry Louis Gates is excellent. El San Juan Jr's *Beyond Postcolonial Theory* (1997) takes issue with Bhabha and Spivak, arguing against theory and for political action.

14 Perhaps we should consider the "unfinished project of modernism" (with its focus on the individual dignity of the human and fundamental rights attendant to birth). Jurgen Habermas (1967) implores contemporary academic discourse to allow humanist modernism a chance to finish up its work before we throw it out. As I understand Habermas, his major point is that reason hasn't yet been constellated in the actual practice of politics. This is why he argues for an *ideal speech situation* as a condition precedent to communicative action while he questions the postmodernist's stance which seeks to place the blame upon *reason* as the dominant ideology which excluded, denigrated and silence opposition. For Habermas modernity cannot be said to be finished until there is a re-evaluation of what a free and just society guided by "reason" would be in actuality and this is where Habermas departs from Derrida and Foucault. Habermas is interested in actualities of constitutional representative government whereas the postmodernists as exemplified by Derrida and Foucault are theoretically oriented

and have never (as far as I am aware) written on how to achieve the ideal. Habermas' work theorizes the necessity of a "speech situation" where all parties get a chance not only to speak but also to be heard. In this view he shares theoretical space with Paulo Freire (1972) and David Bohm's work (Bohm and Nichol 1996) on how to get people to speak to each other in ways that trigger social change, yet Habermas goes further and insists that there are commonalities and that a consensus can be reached about terms we use. Judith Butler questions whether Habermas or anyone who advocates such consensus over terms as the condition precedent to the ideal speech situation, "in which no one's speech disables or silences another's speech" is possible (Butler 1997: 86). If mutual understanding is dependent on a consensus about the meaning of words, Butler asks:

> But are we, whoever "we" are, the kind of community in which such meanings could be established for once and for all? Is there not a permanent diversity within the semantic field that constitutes an irreversible situation for political theorizing? Who stands above the interpretative fray in a position to "assign" the same utterances the same meanings? And why is it that a threat posed by such an authority is deemed less serious than the one posed by equivocal interpretation left unconstrained?
>
> (Butler 1997: 86–87)

Butler correctly points out that utterances may have multiple meanings depending upon the context within which it is uttered and thus "the very words which seek to injure might well miss their mark and produce an effect counter to the one intended" (Butler 1997: 87). Butler is onto what I describe as the Trickster project of reinscription; her work focuses on previously hateful words while mine focuses on women's agency, autonomy and authority, but the process is the same one of resignification or reinscription. We see it today with Rap music and the resignified use of the "N" word among African Americans. One can never know how another is interpreting utterances unless it is revealed through the dialogic process which Bohm suggests. Butler utilizes a hermeneutical Trickster like sensitivity when she realizes that some words, which were meant to be universal, such as those found in the United States Constitution, can mean one thing in a particular time period and quite another in another. If the Constitution guarantees freedom of speech and equality before the law, then hate speech stands outside the Constitutional guarantees and is, a priori, unlawful, thus no law needs to be passed outlawing hate speech. Butler suggests the adoption of a Trickster strategy in the semantic context of hate speech which I find fully applicable to the analysis of images and the fictive female sleuth narratives:

> We begin by noting that hate speech calls into question linguistic survival, that being called a name can be the site of injury, and conclude by noting that this name-calling may be the initiating moment of a counter mobilization. The name one is called both subordinates and enables, producing a scene of agency from ambivalence, a set of effects that exceed the animating intentions of the call. To take up the name that one is called is no simple submission to prior authority, for the name is already unmoored from prior context, and entered into the labor of self-definition. The word that wounds becomes an instrument of resistance in the deployment that destroys the prior territory of its operation. Such a deployment means speaking words without prior authorization and putting into risk the security of linguistic life, the sense of one's place in language, that one's words do as one says. That risk, however,

has already arrived with injurious language as it calls into question the linguistic survival of the one addressed. Insurrectionary speech becomes the necessary response to injurious language, a risk taken in response to being put at risk, a repetition in language that forces change.

(Butler 1997: 163)

Is there any value then to commonality? Or are we collectively caught in the liminal zone between and betwixt the traditional false objectivity called consensus and that which is yet to come but is not yet imaginable? The process Butler explicates in playing Trickster with speech that hurts is taken up throughout this work, as I show how Trickster has manifested at this point in our collective history in order to offer aid and assistance in the strategic redeployment of words and thoughts regarding the proper role of women in culture. My focus however is on the use of humor in this strategic redeployment of words. As Butler concludes, "insurrectionary speech becomes the necessary response to injurious language, a risk taken in response to being put at risk, a repetition in language that forces change" (Butler 1997: 163). I would add that not only speech may be used but imagery and narrative as well.

So here I sit writing this section, wanting to embrace and hesitating to identify myself as a liberal humanist, but the lawyer in me knows that only through basic dignity and equality before the law can we start a more authentic journey towards *integrity*. I agree with Habermas (1967) that we are "still the contemporaries of that kind of aesthetic modernity which first appeared in the midst of the nineteenth century" and while the wars and dismantling of the colonial system in the twentieth century may have "shattered this optimism" I support Habermas' humanist project which implores the western world, "to hold onto the *intentions* [emphasis in original] of the Enlightenment, feeble as they may be, or should we declare the entire project of modernity a lost cause?" (Habermas 1967: 1749–1754). I do not think the intentions of the Enlightenment were feeble – perhaps too narrowly focused at the time – but I consider it grand in its ideals and a polestar to which humanity can still move toward. Liberal humanism is, at the core, a belief in the dignity and freedom of an individual as a condition of birth. While it may have started out only applying to a narrow population, the idea itself has grown to become more and more inclusive of diversity and should not be jettisoned.

15 See, for example, the work of Claire Douglas (1990).
16 All page citations are to the Internet edition.

Part II

Calling upon the ancestors

Chapter 4

Imagination and metaphor

In certain favorable moods, memories – what one has forgotten – come to the top. Now if this is so, is it not possible – I often wonder – that things we have felt with great intensity have an existence independent of our minds; are in fact still in existence? And if so, will it not be possible, in time, that some device will be invented by which we can tap them? I see it – the past – as an avenue lying behind; a long ribbon of scenes, emotions.

Virginia Woolf[1]

Introduction

There was a time when women were honored and valued and the mystery of giving life captured the imagination of the collective consciousness. Then a time came when the reverence for women as life givers was trampled under the harsh light of the Middle Eastern and Greek sun as the illusion of certainty replaced the certainty of illusion. The archetypal energies which were constellated in the collective culture were concentrated upon elevating a false objectivity supported by a logos/centric patriarchal hegemony which rested upon collective acceptance of the illusion of certainty as a universal concept.[2] This time of honoring women is in the archaic past and we must re/member this time in order to bring the energy from its inchoate state into a state of dynamic energy. This can occur, and I am contending this is occurring, through the reception of potent remembered new imagery of women as imagined by women.

Imagination and recovered memory: the numinous process of remembering

When I first read the fictive female sleuth narratives I felt as Virginia Woolf (1882–1941) described in her essay "A Sketch of the Past" (1939), an excerpt from which opened this chapter. Is Woolf describing one of Bachelard's secret rooms, perhaps where Proust believed memories hid? Eva Brann

(1991) described this experience of remembering as a kind of "recognition, a recall, even a return. It is an epiphany of something long waiting to appear, an evocation of something expecting to be called" (Brann 1991: 737). When one reads as active imagination, there is a type of "spatial-temporal magic that comes about wherever a place draws the past into present" (Brann 1991: 751). This is not a concrete present, as if we were trying to bring Artemis or Hera into the room on the temporal plane. This is not a process of catching an energy which is already embodied in some form. What I am speaking about here is a quality of memory that is not tangible and cannot be made tangible except through an evocative image. This quality of memory is what the postmodern female Trickster has tapped into.

Shape-shifting and transformation in the imaginal realm

> Transformative images are engaging and even arresting metaphors. To live through the transformational process they often engender is a special experience. From the moment these images appear, they take possession of one's consciousness and, at least temporarily, change it, sometimes dramatically. . . . Over time, they become irreversible. This is because these images reflect psychological content that is emerging in a person's life and give it shape.
>
> (Stein 1993: 41)

How does the imagination produce new metaphoric imagery which if grasped, has the potential to both trick and transform? Eliade (1987) and Ricoeur (1977) concur that *grasping* the metaphor is a process of shape-shifting psychological cognition much like working a dream or being witty. To enter into this type of psychological dialogic with the narrative and characters a liminal field called the imaginal zone must be constellated. This space occurs when the unconscious slightly emerges from its depths and the ego puts aside its controller role and through dialogic relationship joins with the unconscious in constellating a zone, a terrain where metaphor is nourished into temporal existence. The way the integration of a shape-shifting metaphor expands consciousness is as follows. An image or verbal narrative evoking an image is juxtaposed against existing schemata in the brain. It is similar to a pegboard, once you put a hook in there are lots of possibilities, but if there are no holes or hooks or not the right kind, the pegboard becomes useless. The more pegs and holes in the psyche, the more incoming imagery can be manipulated among the various possibilities of meaning.

The Trickster aspect is the movement between the pegs, thus the "doubling" nature inherent in the archetypal origin of metaphor. Being able to oscillate between the "double" brings us beyond the initial image to something more complex – even contradictory – and sometimes paradoxically true. This represents not a tension of the opposites so much as an ability to move between seemingly disparate poles and the more poles you have the richer the metaphoric possibilities. That's why it is important to have cultural artifacts which represent the imaginations of the entire population, otherwise too many possibilities are lost because there are not enough pegs and holes. The word metaphor means *to go beyond* and it is in this sense that I envision the metaphoric image of the female Trickster offering the opportunity for and encouragement of consciousness to move beyond the present boundaries of spirit, society, geography, species, and gender; those structural components with which we order our contemporary perceptual world. Shape-shifting metaphors reside most comfortably in the imaginative realm because of their "always undecidedly double and contradictory" nature (Young 1999: 896). This is the place where the tension of the opposites resides as well, and is a fluid zone with no fixed meaning. It is the land of the Trickster. Hierarchical rules and regulations are ridiculous down the rabbit hole.

The transformational potential of metaphoric fluidity inherent in a shape-shifting image relies partially upon the concept of imagination which "was to become a main source of early dynamic psychiatry" (Ellenberger 1970: 194). The other concept of the imaginal realm I incorporate is the concept of imagination as recovered memory in the Jungian sense of memory expressing itself in symbolic form.[3] This dual sense of imagination, metaphor and recovered memory is what fuels the female Trickster's shape-shifting travel. Her image embodies energies which have long been dormant in the feminine psyche. It is with this awareness of the dual power for making and informing the world which metaphoric imagery possesses that I use the word *imagination*.

Imagination

Imagination as shape-shifting metaphoric imagery originated in the Renaissance (Kugler 1997) after the black plague (1347–1361) annihilated half of Europe's population:

> Survivors of the plague, finding themselves neither destroyed nor improved, could discover no divine purpose in the pain they suffered. God's purposes were usually mysterious, but this scourge had been too terrible to be accepted without questioning. If a disaster of such magnitude, the most lethal ever known, was a mere wanton act of God or perhaps not God's work at all, then the absolutes of a fixed order were loosed from their moorings. Minds that opened to admit these questions could never be shut. Once people envisioned the possibility of change in a fixed order, the end of the age of submission came in sight,

the turn to individual conscience lay ahead. To that extent the Black Death may have been the unrecognized beginning of modern man.

(Tuchman 1978: 123)

For Descartes and other rationalists, the mind could not have played a role in the body which had betrayed them and their populations; as a consequence of this conceptualization, they developed a "control over" metaphysics, a master–slave relationship which permitted no dialogic relationship between body and psyche. Those that adhered to a relational perspective between mind and body could be cleansed such as occurred with the cleansing of witches which decimated the wise women of Europe. Yet, we can see in the work of artists like Dante, Cervantes and Shakespeare a redeployment of binary oppositions which triggered an evolution in metaphoric imagery away from revelations of divine agency to those of individual revelation and agency. It was this shift to "individual revelation" which was later incorporated in Jung's work on the imagination (Eliade 1987: 108). Was this move from divine to personal revelation a compensatory stage in our psychological evolution? Jung posits a dialectical relationship between art and consciousness, explaining that "works of art illuminate and compensate for the one-sidedness of the spirit of the times . . . [concluding that] art represents a process of self-regulation in the life of nations and epochs" (*CW* 15: par 131). How then are the emerging images of the postmodern female Trickster transformative works of art within this dialectical relationship Jung says exists between art and consciousness?

If previous psychological evolution is signified by a shift in the arts from the divine to personal revelation, whose psychological shift are we examining? The evolution in Renaissance art was from the imaginal realm of the male divine image to male images of individuation as projected almost exclusively from the male imagination. As (male) individual revelation is to (male) divine revelation, female revelation is to male revelation and perhaps out of this dialectic will come some idealized evolutionary synthesis of unity. This would be the logical outcome of Jung's grand theory that the collective unconscious and the individual psyche are self-regulatory towards wholeness and unity as the realization of innate human (not male or female) possibilities. These innate possibilities, our original skin so to speak, are a goal we never reach according to Jung, but which the entire collective strives for through the agency of the individual creator as compensation for that which has *not* been developed in the collective consciousness. What is developed in compensation are new metaphorical images.

The "function of a metaphor is to instruct by suddenly combining elements that have not been put together before" (Ricoeur 1977: 190). It is through this combining of previously unlike elements that our psychological perceptions become enlarged through a relationship with a new culturally inflected archetypal image. This description applies to the process of wit as well. Thinking in a witty fashion is an enlargement of consciousness. It is done internally, as opposed to the comic which is found in the "other." Ricoeur's formulation of the significance of how new metaphoric images trigger psychic evolution was, in the opinion of Mircea Eliade, a significant contribution to imaginal theory because it refocused attention upon "metaphor as exemplifying the creative dynamics of imagination" (Eliade 1987: 108). What Ricoeur and Eliade are describing is the *process*, the dynamic which the imagination engages in – it connotes an active imaginal dialogue. Appreciating these emergent archetypal energies when they appear in popular cultural forms, such as novels, is critical for psychological evolution:

> Currents of thought succeed each other; what was valuable for one period often becomes valueless for the next. Seen in psychological terms, this would mean that changing archetypal ideas attain validity and develop into the cultural canon of an era. Out of all possible modes of human existence those which best lend themselves to coping with existing conditions are unconsciously selected. Views which help us come to terms with the greatest variety of encountered conditions and which, at the same time, produce meaningful relations, constitute the valid prototypes of the collective consciousness.
>
> (Jacoby 1992: 66)

Jung recognized the importance of certain types of literature to psychological investigation, especially the popular cultural phenomenon of mystery fiction:

> There is a fundamental difference of attitude between the psychologist's approach to a literary work and that of a literary critic. What is of decisive importance and value for the latter may be quite irrelevant for the former. Indeed, literary products of highly dubious merit are often of the greatest interest to the psychologist. The so-called "psychological novel" is by no means as rewarding for the psychologist as the literary-minded suppose. Considered as a self-contained whole, such a novel explains itself. It has done its own work of psychological interpretation, and the psychologist can at most criticize or enlarge upon this.
>
> In general it is this non-psychological novel that offers the richest opportunities for psychological elucidation. Here the author, having no intentions of this sort, does not show his character in a psychological light and thus leaves room for analysis and interpretation, or even invites it by his unprejudiced mode of presentation. Good examples of such novels are . . . as well as that most popular of literary mass-production, the detective story, first exploited by Conan Doyle. . . . An

exciting narrative that is apparently quite devoid of psychological intention is just what interests the psychologist most of all.

(Jung *CW* 15: pars 136–137)

Jung realizes the unique contribution popular cultural forms such as the detective novel can make as "prototypes" of the collective consciousness. If Jung was correct that the collective as well as the personal psyche strives inextricably for full realization of its innate possibilities, then when an especially potent force appears in popular culture, its force in the cultural consciousness occurs because the metaphoric image is evidence of an archetypal energy which has emerged into the foreground of consciousness rather than remaining dormant in the collective unconscious. That it is upsetting or marginalized is not the point. It is the slamming together of imagery previously separated which causes psychological growth. Eliade (1987) describes this integration of duality through duality as a process where new images and metaphors "can both resonate with the cherished vestiges of dormant aspects of our past and delight us with the vibrancy of unexplored dimensions, that as human beings, we have not yet even begun to grasp" (Eliade 1987: 108). Thus the relevant metaphoric image encourages the psyche to "grasp" through apperception and integration of duality what has not yet been grasped. A critical condition precedent to this "grasping" is that the collective must appreciate the relevancy of an especially apt metaphor when it does appear in consciousness. Samuels et al. (1986) conclude that Jung's psychology is "based on the supposition that the psyche reasons imagistically and that the closest rational equivalent is analogy or metaphor." The process is fluid and dual encouraging the ego to open to the "psychic message, while the psyche can re-orient itself by way of an enlarged image in consciousness" (Samuels et al. 1986: 93, 94). The process described is a relational and reciprocal dynamic where the energy manifested through a relevant metaphoric image fuels a changed perception about any subjectivity. This energy is reciprocated through the relationship developed between the ego's perception of the metaphoric image and its integration into the unconscious, which then projects itself as new culturally inflected archetypal imagery, which is what the postmodern female Trickster is.

James Hillman places emphasis on the importance of popular cultural icons as archetypal images when he advises that "an archetypal image is a rich image, even though its surface shows only a can of beer in a Chevy at the curb" (Hillman 1977: 80). As Hillman instructs, it is through *working* the image which the culture (any culture) has produced that we "ennoble or empower the image with the widest, richest, and deepest possible significance" (Hillman 1977: 82). For Hillman, the image has to be worked and it is only when we work the image by means of metaphorical analogies that hidden connections are revealed. This is how one gets to the soul of an image. I agree whole-heartedly with Hillman about the need to work the image. And the image that appears before me as I write this is the image of the postmodern questioner – who now asks, *who has worked our images* and thus *whose soul has been revealed*?

Part of the postmodern epistemological revolution is the cognitive awareness that objectivity is a reflection of the observing eye. Thus an awareness of whose images are presented and who serves as interpreter is critical. The previous investigations into imagination done by scholars such as Jung, Hillman, and Kugler are concerned almost exclusively with the imaginative manifestations of men. Admittedly wonderful art, music, and ideas abound from the male embodied psyche, but here I am asking for an awareness of *whose* imaginal manifestations we are referring to when we speak of art and literature and philosophy. Hillman and Jung's theoretical constructs about the significance of emergent imagery encourage broader application. If Hillman prods us to work the images, this should include "working" the images from women's imaginations, such as the female sleuth and other popular cultural imagery, for their relationship with identity/subjectivity formation. As Jung said, "imagination is a primary and autonomous psychic activity in all humanity" (Jung *CW* 11: par 845); however, it is my contention throughout this work that *in order to imagine one has to be subject of their own life*. In the following passage Jung uses the word fantasy rather than imagination, however he correctly describes how imagination's role is implicated in the creation of identity:

> This autonomous activity of the psyche, which can be explained neither as a reflex action to sensory stimuli nor as the executive organ of eternal ideas, is, like every vital process, a continually creative act. The psyche creates reality every day. The only expression I can use for this activity is fantasy. Fantasy is just as much feeling as thinking; as much intuition as sensation. There is no psychic function that, through fantasy, is not inextricably bound up with the other psychic functions. Sometimes it appears in primordial form, sometimes it is the ultimate and boldest product of all our faculties combined. Fantasy, therefore, seems to me the clearest expression of the specific activity of the psyche. *It is, preeminently, the creative activity from which the answers to all answerable questions come; it is the mother of all possibilities, where, like all psychological opposites, the inner and outer worlds are joined together in living union* [emphasis added]. Fantasy it was and ever is which fashions the bridge between the irreconcilable claims of subject and object, introversion and extroversion. In fantasy alone both mechanisms are united.
>
> (Jung *CW* 6: par 78)

This quotation leads inextricably to the question, what happens to the imaginative capacities of those who are legally enclosed within the projections of another? Where do their "answers to all the questions come?" Mary Lynn Kittelson explains in *The Soul of Popular Culture* that "an accurate sense of reality requires an interplay of dreaming, fantasy, some play of the imaginative field to be reliable" (Kittelson 1998: 6). Women's sense of reality has always been questioned throughout the hegemony of patriarchal consciousness. Jane Wagner writes humorously in her play *The Search for Signs of Intelligent Life in the Universe*, which Lily Tomlin has performed throughout the world:

> I refuse to be intimidated by reality anymore. After all, what is reality anyway? Nothin' but a collective hunch. My space chums think reality was once a primitive method of crowd control that got out of hand. In my view, it's absurdity dressed up in a three piece suit.
>
> (Wagner 1986: 18)

Whose hunches have we been playing collectively? It is no wonder that Jung, writing in the introduction to Esther Harding's *The Way of All Women* (1961), concluded that while it was true that men "understand nothing of women's psychology as it actually is" it was even more "astonishing to find that women do not know for themselves" (Harding 1961: xv). How could women know for themselves who they were if they could not imagine a place where they could play in their own imaginative fields as the subject of their own lives. ·

What has women's imagination produced?

Does women's imagination produce different archetypal images and cultural artifacts than men? This question is imperative in Jungian studies for although Jung championed a flexible, dynamic approach to psychological materials, he also set up rigid dichotomies which have bootstrapped the application of his theories in a wider context. While this may have occurred in that first generation after Jung was codified and thus can be considered provisional, it is time for a revision and this work is taking place and this book is an example. Estella Lauter, the author of a landmark study of visual imagery by women, asks specifically whether "the archetypal images Jung described as characteristics of female development appear in the works of visual art by women?" (Lauter and Rupprecht 1985: 46). Lauter's study was the first to "assess the relationship between images created by professional women artists and existing theory regarding female development", concluding that women's imaginations produce different imagery than male imaginations do about the female. The problem with classical Jungian theories about the female is that they did not question the assumption that women find their creativity primarily through their relationships (to men) and daily living, not in the "objective language of visual art."

Looking at the Jungian concepts of mother, animus and the independent woman (the Amazon) through the work of women artists, that is, through the female imagination, Lauter concludes, concerning the mother archetype, that the pattern described by Jung and Neumann is

> not the pattern of the good and terrible mother who either cares for or restrains her child, but of the vulnerable mother whose great capacities are for sheltering, nurturing, protecting supporting, caring, liberating, and reflecting the other (child or adult) cannot ensure her success.
> (Lauter and Rupprecht 1985: 59)

Her findings regarding other "archetypal" imagery which has come through the male imagination are similarly illuminating.

The domestic realm

When women began to paint, they painted domestic scenes because these were the ones considered appropriate for women, just as when women began to write they wrote domestic novels. In paintings, Lauter found that men tend towards an idealization of the role of mother and child while women's paintings of the same subject were more realistic. When the domestic realm was left behind as subject a major difference in conceptualization of the feminine was discovered. Niki de Saint Phalle's (b. 1930) sculpture *Hon* was an enormous woman, "positioned on her back with her legs spread and bent, her vaginal canal open to serve as the entrance for her visitors." Lauter interprets the sculpture as:

> a celebration of Neumann's Great Mother, and a demonstration of how she is defiled in modern life. The image of the mother was positive in the sense that it became the ground against which technology was negatively evaluated. But her prone position and ridiculously small head called attention to the least pleasant aspects of the archetype – the mother's assumed passivity, her supposedly slight intelligence, her acceptance of all who enter her without regard for her own feelings.
> (Lauter and Rupprecht 1985: 54)

Lauter concluded that the female imagination "also merged the images of the good mother and the seductress in a way Neumann didn't foresee, demonstrating on and in the body how the desire to enter a woman is linked to the desire to return to the mother" (Lauter and Rupprecht 1985: 54–55). This doubling of the imagistic is also found in the work of Frida Kahlo, which Lauter concludes offers a new perspective on the myth of Demeter and Persephone:

Her work casts the issues of mother-child differently than either Neumann or Wolff do, in terms of the inevitable gap between two persons who must be separate from each other no matter how much they desire union. Perhaps this is the central meaning of the Demeter-Persephone story, focused for so long by the business with Hades. The issue addressed in both is not the adequacy of nurturance or its continuation beyond its appropriate time, but a complex range of needs and desires of both parties that cannot be met in this relationship.

(Lauter and Rupprecht 1985: 55)

Lauter emphasizes how women artists' pieces are "full of paradoxes" both inviting and empty, using the art of African American Camille Billops (b. 1933), especially her piece *Mother* (1971) as an example. *Mother* is a ceramic chair in the form of a women's body. After analyzing a variety of images produced by women, Lauter concludes that mother imagery produced by women's imaginations demonstrates that:

The mother may be stronger than Jungians have thought without being "terrible," and also more vulnerable, not just in her relationship to children whom she must lose one way or the other, but in her own body, particularly the so-called "mysteries" of menstruation, parturition and lactation.

(Lauter and Rupprecht 1985: 56)

Lauter argues that the mother, as imagined by women infuses the basic archetype with a different energy, concluding that "it is the reification of Renaissance, Romantic, and Victorian ideologies of the mother that we need to protest, not the archetype of the mother." She resolves that "we need to revise our descriptions of the archetype [mother] to accord with images created by women" (Lauter and Rupprecht 1985: 72).

The animus

On the issue of the animus, Lauter finds no support in visual art by women for the concept of the animus. She bases this conclusion on the available historical sources on visual arts by women, finding that "men have not been so important to women as subjects for art as women have been for men . . . similarly women do not seem to have seized upon portraits of men as a means of representing their own inner lives." After reviewing a plethora of visual imagery she concludes that "the history of visual art by women does not document the existence of the animus." While she acknowledges that there may be several reasons for the historical dearth of visual arts due to several factors, such as a male lack of desire to own paintings "reflective of a woman's animus," or these works may have passed "into oblivion, as many other works have done," or she examines the possibility that they "exist but are not yet known" and finally she considers that such images did exist in the female imagination "but were inhibited by convention from ever being realized in paint or sculpture" (Lauter and Rupprecht 1985: 65–66). Lauter acknowledges that these difficulties have been "somewhat diminished" in the late twentieth century, yet she still can identify "only a tiny handful of works" which could "be described as animus images; that is to represent the masculine within the female and credit it with spiritual powers."

Lauter emphasizes three points about the lack of animus imagery in female art, "first there is the problem of scarcity, men do not appear as subjects in art as frequently as do other subjects, and they appear even less frequently as psychological subjects." On this issue she concludes that "women do not often present images of the self as masculine" thus the animus concept does not relate to any particular patterns she could identify. Second, Lauter found that when men did appear in women's art, "they are not well explained by the concept of animus" as an internal spiritual guide comparable to the anima. Men do not appear very much in women's art at all and when they do there is a "tendency to form images of men as oppressive and dangerous" or to make satires of the "military persona." If the imagery of men is either satiric or angry, she asks "why would anger toward men derive from a masculine source in the woman's self?" Instead of struggling with the ill-fitting concept of the animus, she asks whether it:

> would it not be more productive to examine all the images of men and the masculine in works by women to see whether any substantial pattern exist. . . . It is even possible that men are not often numinous for women, instrumental as they may in women's entry into society.
>
> (Lauter and Rupprecht 1985: 72)

Finally Lauter found when she abandoned looking for the animus in women's art she discovered "Other patterns that are potentially just as pervasive and charged with feeling." One of these concerns male frailty which she concludes "may document a tendency to form images of men based on empathy as well as anger" (Lauter and Rupprecht 1985: 70–72).

The independent woman

Lauter agrees that it is not possible to "subsume all aspects of the feminine under the archetype of the Great Mother." Acknowledging Toni Wolff's (1934) contention that the medial woman could be relevant for the women artist, she finds little support for Wolff's theory, concluding that she did not "doubt that such a figure exists" but Lauter finds that Wolff's medial woman "correlates better with well-known images of the muse who inspires others than with the images of women who are themselves inspired or otherwise empowered to act" (Lauter and Rupprecht 1985: 74). Here, Lauter is noting the vital component of agency and autonomy in a woman's life as condition precedents to producing independent artwork. This leads Lauter to investigating the image of the Amazon as a possibility for analogy to the autonomous authoritative woman with agency, but she finds that even Toni Wolff's description of the positive Amazon is found wanting when placed against the data: "neither her qualifiers nor her lists of roles correspond to the realities presented in works of art by women." The problem she identifies in the archetypal description of Amazon is that "as soon as the female's independence threatens her personal relationships, it becomes negative" (Lauter and Rupprecht 1985: 74–75). In reviewing works by women artists, Lauter concludes that their works demonstrate "declarations of psychological strength rather than more convention-bound statements of accomplishments" (Lauter and Rupprecht 1985: 73).

The virgin

Lauter's approach to the independent women rests upon the foundation "suggested by the new developments in archetypal psychology" identifying Esther Harding's work on the virgin as "the precursor of this approach; in describing the goddess as one unto herself." Lauter speculates on the goddess imagery of archaic cultures and wonders whether the image of a whole independent woman was split and fractured "as they were assimilated by patriarchal religions." Still she argues that the presence of such episodes "in our cultural mythology suggests that post-medieval images of female independence are not aberrations in the course of female evolution" (Lauter and Rupprecht 1985: 76). The type of revisioning that Lauter recommends was a revolutionary idea in Jungian circles when it was introduced during a panel titled "Women and Psychology" at the University of Notre Dame's annual C.G. Jung Conference in 1976. The panel "asserted that his [Jung's] highly reputed reverence for the feminine, though certainly valuable, involved only recognition and support for the feminine principle in men and did not value the actual experiences of women themselves" (Lauter and Rupprecht 1985: 7). Lauter published her ground-breaking essay in 1985, at the beginning of the period which I have reviewed throughout this work and which certainly lends credible support to my contention that the female imagination produces different imagery and narrative than feminine aspects of the male imagination.

Summary

I opened this chapter saying that there was a time when women were honored and valued and the mystery of giving life captured the imagination of the collective consciousness, upon what evidential support do I make these statements? Am I describing a reality or a fantasy or a bit of both? Does it matter to our collective psychological evolution whether it was imagination or actual history if it is a sacred narrative, much as the patriarchal symbolic order perceives the Bible or the Koran? From a post-modern perspective, evolution is about increasing variety not about cloning past historical documents. Thelma Shinn, author of *Women Shapeshifters: Transforming the Contemporary Novel* (1996), beautifully locates the place of sacred narratives within a psychological terrain of equal value to the historical:

> Human patterns of actions reflected in sacred narratives can help us understand the relevance of the Past to our lives; the literary artist provides the words that select and interpret those actions and make them available as our "other" history. Read as romantic imaginings, these narratives may even reveal hidden historical truths, offering a more complete re-visioning of reality than available from historical records. At the same time, they shift our focus to what is often dismissed as the emotional but may also be the spiritual or moral context of that moment which reflects our ideologies and motivates human actions. The historical record, in fact, may prove less reliable than the art of song and tale which reveals in process the "whole story."[4]

In the next chapters I investigate what the ancestors of the fictive female sleuths have produced as cultural artifact ready for integration as a sacred narrative of the past into the collective consciousness.

Notes

1 Woolf (1939: 67).
2 The certainty of the Greeks changed it all, starting with adding vowel sounds to the alphabet in order to make words more certain and less susceptible to the shape-shifting inherent in Semitic languages such as Hebrew, where there are only consonants and the vowel sounds used give and change the utterances' meaning (Abram 1996); see Robert Graves' work, *The White Goddess: A Historical Grammar of Poetic Myth* (1966) for its revelation of the connection between shape-shifting and artistic creativity.
3 Bachofen taught Jung to decipher the meaning of symbols through a recovery of memory which included an awareness of how archaic "memory expresses itself in symbolic form" (Ellenberger 1970: 729).
4 The quote is from "Patterns of Possibility in Doris Lessing's Space Fiction" by Thelma Shinn Richard, Ph.D., Professor of English and Women's Studies, Arizona State University, Tempe, AZ, USA, http://www.gwiep.net/site/dlessing.htm.

Chapter 5

Where have all the virgins gone?

> As I understand the virgin archetype, it is that aspect of the feminine, in man or woman, that has the courage to Be and the flexibility to be always Becoming.
>
> (Woodman 1985: 78)

Introduction

There was a time when the archetypal energies of authority, autonomy, and agency were available for integration into a woman's psyche. She was called the woman unto herself and known as a virgin. This virginal energy was repressed and disassociated from identification with women during the emergence of institutionalized patriarchy over 4,000 years ago, but it is now re-emerging through the archetypal energy of the postmodern female Trickster. This Trickster energy can be accessed by women through the act of reading or through participation in ritual activities, such as rock concerts, where the archaic archetypal memory is constellated as "an epiphany of something long waiting to appear, an evocation of something expecting to be called" (Brann 1991: 737). It is through the imaginative cognitive act of remembering the virgin archetypal energy that this energy of the women unto herself is being resurrected in the guise of the postmodern female Trickster.

Mnemosyne, mistress of Eleutherian Hills

Memory is critical to the psyche's healthy dynamic and storytelling is the strategic imaginative method of implanting memory. The power of memory was recognized in Ancient Greece by the goddess Mnemosyne who ruled over the Elysian Fields. The nine daughters of Mnemosyne and Zeus are the muses,[1] with Thalia, the muse of comedy imaged with a Trickster's mask as she playfully composed comedy and ironic poetry. The muses were women unto themselves. According to the myth, upon death a person makes a choice to either drink from the River Lethe or the spring of memory. If you drink from Lethe you forget your pain and all the lessons of your life and are reborn again on earth. Those who choose to drink from the spring of memory go to the Elysian Fields, where there is no strife or pain. The myth tells us that the path to psychological integration comes from a willingness to value and interact with memory. Those that repress memory are doomed to repeat it, over and over again. This is what has happened in the symbolic patriarchal order, the repression of disassociation along with its grim reaper; war, slavery and destruction of the natural world.

It does not matter whether a memory is based upon temporal phenomena and lived experience or from the imaginal realms to impact a person's daily existence. Whether one experiences phenomena through the five senses or through the imagination, it can be nearly the same experience because "neurobiology and art meet" in the psyche (Ackerman 2004: 68). Conscious memory is stored in the hippocampus while unconscious memories are stored in the amygdala or unconscious reptilian brain stem.[2] Memory retrieval from the conscious hippocampus must be alchemically mixed with those memories resident and accessible to unconsciousness for the kind of memories which, if constellated, can compensate for a dangerously unbalanced epoch.[3] Memory, thus, has two ancestral lines, one stretching into the temporal past proper and the other into a depth that is both felt and named by analogy to that past. The imagination has the power of joining these two tributaries into a popular cultural flow that can rebalance the dangerously one sided epoch called patriarchy.[4]

The pre-patriarchal virgin and today's virginal feminine presence

The pre-patriarchal virgin, the feminine archetypal energy as *woman unto herself* is an inner attitude of a woman's psyche which has no counterpart in the male psyche. This is the energy found in the fictive female sleuths I have already discussed, along with other postmodern virginal women, such as Madonna, Cyndi Lauper, and Carrie Bradshaw of *Sex and the City*:

> In the same way the woman who is virgin, one-in-herself, does what she does – not because of any desire to please, not to be liked, or to be approved, even by herself; not because of any desire to gain power over another, to catch his interest or love, but because what she does is true. Her actions may, indeed, be unconventional. She may have to say no, when it would be easier, as well as more adapted, conventionally speaking, to say yes. But as virgin she is not influenced by the considerations that make the non-virgin woman, whether married or not, trim her sails and adapt herself to expediency. I say whether married or not, for in using this term virgin in its psychological connotations, it refers not to external circumstances but to an inner attitude.

A woman who has a psychological attitude to life which makes her dependent on what other people think, which makes her do and say things she really does not approve, is no virgin in this meaning of the term. She is not one-in-herself but acts always as female counterpart or synergy to some male. This "male" may be an actual man, her father, or husband, or some man whose opinion she esteems very highly, or it may be some quite abstract idea of what people think, or an even more remote opinion, formulating itself as "one must do this to be liked," or "a girl should act thus and so if she wants to get married." These ideas and opinions are manifestations of the male within her, her own animus, and she is related to this psychological male in much the same way as many married women are related to their husbands. A woman with such an attitude is not one-in-herself, she is dependent upon someone or something outside her own psyche. Her qualities and characteristics are determined by that other, just as the characteristics of the Egyptian goddess Nut were dependent on those of her syzygy Nu, or the Latin Fauna on Faunus. The woman who is psychologically virgin is not dependent in this way. She is what she is because that is what she is.

(Harding 1955: 125–126)

Jungian theorist and analyst Marion Woodman brings the "emerging archetype of the virgin" into postmodernity with her examples of Cyndi Lauper and Madonna, who "does what she does . . . because what she does is true." Woodman's description of Cyndi Lauper as "auto-eroticism . . . gypsy garb . . . manic energy and gentle sensitivity . . . the outsider" reveals her Trickster nature as does Madonna's "playing the paradox for all its worth" employing a "boy-toy." Woodman sees Lauper and Madonna "playing a decisive role in constellating millions of unconscious virgins, male and female . . . they are concretized versions of an archetype . . . still in the process of becoming conscious in the culture as a whole." Emphasizing their role in carrying and releasing new energy into the culture for integration, Woodman calls them the "virgin forever pregnant with new possibilities" (Woodman 1985: 76). There it is, a definition of the female Trickster brought to the world through a female imagination. The sexuality is there as well as the performance through the spectacle of theater but humor is in the foreground.[5]

These women are not con artist Tricksters, although some thought Madonna was one, but a con artist does not have a sense of humor pervading their persona and both Madonna and Lauper exude a Trickster-like humor about what they are doing,[6] and in so doing initiate change by asking questions and encouraging others to ask questions about their own lives. V.I., Kinsey, Kate, and Blanche, along with Trickster artists such as Lauper and Madonna, provide "an example of how an old myth grows into contemporary relevance through the imagination of the individual expressing the unconscious need of their time" (Luke 1986: 51).

The pre-patriarchal virgin energy and Jungian feminism

There is a strong tradition within Jungian psychology of using archaic goddess myths to heal and empower the feminine. These stories, from so many differing sources, can be used as divination tools which encourage women to use their own imaginations to heal themselves. It is the images and stories of these goddesses in their very human actualities; as depressives, as raging, as fearful but active in the world anyway, that inspires. Susan Rowland in *Jung: A Feminist Revision* (2002) agrees that Jungian goddess feminism can be seen in a "more postmodern way . . . as a kind of experiment in the imagination" rather than as some grand theory (Rowland 2002: 48). Rowland's work is significant because she has differentiated anima-animus, Eros and goddess feminism within the Jungian orientation,[7] but it is her perspective of how a reconnection with the goddesses of memory can heal which is synonymous to my perspective regarding the virgin energy returning to the postmodern world in the guise of the female Trickster:

> Jungian goddess feminists reject the unifying energy posited in the self archetype and latch onto its plurality, including that of gender. . . . In goddess feminism, the metaphysical feminine principle is mapped onto pre-Christian mythologies in order to seek out non-patriarchal narratives and ways of thinking. Such feminists remain Jungian when they stay within the Jungian paradigm of theory-into-myth: psychic imagery, theorized as archetypal, is identified with a traditional mythology and vice versa. Jungian feminists of this creed are not advocating literal goddess worship. Their divine beings live in the human imagination in the unconscious. A transcendent existence of goddesses actually "out there" is not considered.
>
> (Rowland 2002: 61)[8]

Summary

The energy of the pre-patriarchal virgin – as woman unto herself – was exiled and repressed from patriarchal consciousness millennia ago. The memory of this kind of feminine energy has been held inchoate, but always waiting to be recalled and re/membered. Sometimes the route back is through the archaic mythological images routinely used in analysis and sometimes it is through a relevant new metaphor from popular culture. Both are routes of healing which transit through the imaginal realms gaining energy which can be expended in terrains where bodily autonomy, physical agency and psychological authority embodied in a female form, can roam freely.

Notes

1 The nine muses are Clio, the muse of history, Urania of astronomy, Melpomene of tragedy, Thalia of comedy, Terpsichore of the dance, Calliope of epic poetry, Erato of love poetry, Poluhynia of songs to the gods and Euterpe of lyric poetry.

2 There is the semantic memory of long strings of facts about sensory perceptions of things – the template of houses and individual rooms – which are then filled with a specific memory, like furniture. Episodic memory contains the specifics of a particular event while declarative memory is a combination of the semantic and the episodic.

3 Jung said in *Modern Man in Search of a Soul*: "an epoch is like an individual, it has its own limitations of conscious outlook, and therefore requires a compensatory adjustment" (Jung 1933: 166). To Jung it was not important that the adjustment should result in good or evil. The healing of the epoch or its destruction was irrelevant to the psychological collective process of compensation.

4 Nancy Chodorow (1978) has emphasized how patriarchy has repressed the trauma of the break from the past and therefore repressed the memory of a feminine past in order for men to beget men. Freud and others who speak about pre-Oedipal situations obscure how critical that period is to the development of a healthy psyche. Freud thought that the pre-Oedipal was as great a discovery as realizing that the foundation for Greek culture was to be found in the Minoan and Mycenaean cultures. From a feminist perspective patriarchy is a traumatic rupture with autonomous self creation with separation and independence as the inducement for serving patriarchal and capitalistic values and imperatives. Masculinity from the view of the pre-patriarchal virgin is reactionary and incredibly fragile as Martha Nussbaum's *The Fragility of Goodness: Luck and Ethics in Greek Tragedy and Philosophy* (1986) elegantly demonstrates. The compensation for the deferred gratification of patriarchal logos is an Eros of violence, not against the structure itself of patriarchy but against new growth, as symbolized by a son, whether it be Laros against Oedipus, Abraham against Isaac or Christianity's God the Father against Jesus.

5 Woodman (1985) also explicates how rock concerts (like carnival and Mardi Gras) can be ritual performance spaces where transformation occurs. She sees the process of transformation inherent in the image of the pregnant virgin as dependent upon ritual but not the kind of ritual we are familiar with in religious observance; Woodman illustrates with reference to rock concerts and the "accouterments of ritual" that are there, such as "masks, jewelry, tattooing, ritual garments, suggestive symbols, dance – all these held together by the insistence of the musical beat and the shriek of heavily amplified guitars" (Woodman 1985: 75).

6 In an interview (*New York Times Magazine*, p. 14, April 16, 2006) Lauper says that her megahit "Girls Just Want to Have Fun" was not a backlash: "It's a song about entitlement. Why can't women have fun?"

7 Those who have reinvigorated anima-animus theory includes Esther Harding (1955, 1961), Emma Jung (1957), Linda Fierz-David (1988), Irene Claremont de Castillejo (1973), Marion Woodman (1982), Polly Young-Eisendrath (1984, 1987), and Claire Douglas (1990). Rowland (2002) finds that this group of female Jungian theorists have through extension and revision dealt (successfully) with

Jung's problematic concept of animus and anima. She applauds these women writers who, working "from Jung's depiction of the animus as plural and negative," have "produced a revised version of an animus capable of being unitary and positive" (Rowland 2002: 50). On the role of Eros in Jungian feminism Rowland places those who have used amplification to extend Jung's work on Eros and the feminine principle. She finds that this "mainstream direction in Jungian feminism serves to accentuate the binary approach to gender while allowing for cultural influences in the lives of actual women and men" (Rowland 2002: 54). Rowland finds areas within the Eros sub-grouping to both praise and criticize:

> Despite the theoretical severing of sex and gender from the archetypal principles, most writers see women as likely to be more attuned to the feminine principle, men to the masculine. On the other hand, embracing the binary approach of the feminine principle does allow for profound critiques of masculine-dominated corporate capitalist existence on a social level. It permits attacks upon the limitations of Christianity as over-masculine and predatory upon a nature defined as feminine.
>
> (Rowland 2002: 55)

Rowland (2002) includes in this Eros/feminine principle school the work of Toni Wolff (1934), Erich Neumann (1963, 1994), June Singer (1973, 1976), and E.C. Whitmont and S.B. Perera (1989).

8 In this group Rowland places Ginette Paris (1992), Sylvia Brinton Perera (1981), Christine Downing (1984), Linda Schierse Leonard (1982, 1993) and Nancy Qualls-Corbett (1988). These theorists have been influential in my own work, in the way they have resurrected the images and narratives of the goddesses and thereby have encouraged women and men to think differently about the feminine then how it has been imaged and interpreted throughout the hegemony of patriarchal consciousness. Their work is a bridge to revisioning the feminine in the same way that the fictive female sleuth is in the following ways. Paris's (1992) work "demonstrates the feminist potential of using a non-Christian narrative to structure thinking on a deeply contentious personal, political, and social issue," that of abortion. Perera's (1981) retelling of the Innana myth in her *Descent to the Goddess* "provides an alternative to viewing dark, repressed feminine pain as an abyss of inferiority . . . thus reshaping depressive mental states as potentially empowering women" (Rowland 2002: 62). Christine Downing's (1984) work "shows the potential of pagan narratives to produce more plural and active forms of feminine imagery than Jung's apparently more static images" (Rowland 2002: 63). Linda Schierse Leonard "takes the demeaning stereotype of the deviant crazy female and uses it as an image of psychic empowerment. It becomes a way of understanding female rage within patriarchy" (Rowland 2002: 64). Nancy Qualls-Corbett's *The Sacred Prostitute* (1988) "allows men and women to imagine more plural forms of sexual practice and social codification contained in the tales of the goddesses" (Rowland 2001: 64). These Jungian writers serve up inspiration which supports my view that modern myth can re-imagine the feminine as much as archaic goddess energy can.

Law and the imagination

Introduction

Four thousand years ago women's physical autonomy was legally enclosed by patriarchal consciousness. This legal enclosure excluded women's imaginative manifestations from the public domain and caused a concomitant enclosure of women's imaginal realms. Only unmarried women retained any degree of legal capacity as marriage legally extinguished a woman's identity.

The enclosure

The Code of Urakagina of Summer (approximately 2415 BCE) is the first evidence of a western culture restricting women to an exclusively procreative role within marriage by restricting her sexuality to a single man, her husband. These new laws were a radical departure from the previous clan-based communal matrilineal residence and descent systems. One of the most salient arguments for this change in women's status is complicity out of necessity. During the later Bronze Age and beginning Iron Age (2000 BCE to approximately 1200 BCE) the need for increased population triggered the creation of a patriarchal system dependent upon women producing the maximum number of children they could while they were alive and men inheriting the family's wealth:

> Consequently, it should not be surprising that the elders of any ancient tribal group were males, since a greater proportion of males would have survived into the chronological seniority which was at the basis of political seniority and leadership. It is no wonder that ancient biologists, Aristotle among them, proclaimed that the male of all species live longer than females. It is a relatively modern phenomenon that the converse is true for humans. Women in antiquity were a class of humanity in short supply.
>
> (Meyers 1978: 33)

Unfortunately, later legal restrictions were not solely related to these issues of retaining assets in those persons who were most likely to survive longest. The rationale of population necessity was forgotten and the enclosure of women became "natural" and was utilized as the explanation which supported the exclusion of women in newly emerging public arenas.

Six hundred years later Hammurabi's Code illustrates the trajectory of diminished autonomous status with a heightened focus upon women and children as property:

> If when a seignior was taken captive and there was not sufficient to live on in his house, his wife has then entered the house of another before his [return] and has borne children, and later her husband has returned and has reached his city, that woman shall return to her first husband, while the children shall go with their father.
>
> (Tannen 1990a: 169–170)

The use of force against women who disagreed with their designated role was also sanctioned:

> apart from the penalties for a seignior's wife which were prescribed on the tablet, when she deserved it, a seignior could pull out the hair of his wife, mutilate or twist her ears, with no liability attaching to him.
>
> (Tannen 1990a: 173)

Children of both sexes socialized into this type of family accepted violence against women to ensure their subordination as the norm.

The importance of being: ancient Athens

Ancient Athens produced a plethora of imaginative popular cultural artifacts which formed much of the foundation for western civilization, yet women in fifth-century BCE Athens were not legally permitted to appear in public spaces without a chaperone. Literature, philosophy, and dramatic arts were only available to them through their status relationships to men:

> creative, public cultural expression was severely restricted for women. Women could excel in dance, music or song: achievements aimed to please men, performed often by courtesans and slaves at entertainments to which only men were admitted.
>
> (Buck 1992: 5)

When women do make an appearance in the ancient texts it is only in relationship to or in a derivative status dependent upon a male. Women do not appear on any list of citizens from ancient Athens because a woman's citizenship consisted *only* in the capacity to give birth to male citizens. A woman's "consent was not required" in marriage, "since she was not a party to a contract but an object of it" (Sealey 1990: 21, 33). The references that we do find about women's roles in Ancient Athens concern their limited attendance at religious festivals and in a few situations where they took part in a public occasion as a wife or mother of a citizen. It must be remembered that despite these appearances, women were without any independent legal capacity. The law explicitly forbade a child or a woman to contract for the disposal of anything of a value above one *medimnos* of barley, thus limiting women's opportunities of self-expression to easily disposable movable property.

The references we see to women's public activities, especially the giving of gifts as participants in cults such as Athena, Artemis or Askelpios, must be viewed in light of the law which restricted women's independent possessions to relatively small sums or to items women had exclusive use of, such as jewelry and clothing. But it must be emphasized that behind the scenes influence or engagement in religious functions and rituals is not the same as imaginative manifestations which are recognized by the collective consciousness as cultural artifact. It is an arrogant devaluation to presume that there was symmetry between these dissimilarities. While recent scholarly work in areas sensitive to women's contributions have reclaimed and revalued much that was excluded from the historical record the focus here is upon what could not be permitted to be imagined by women much less be manifested and accepted as cultural artifact.

The distinction between religious functions and public functions is significant when we consider that women were not legally permitted to play any kind of a public role. Not present in public except in limited sexual roles, women were likewise not present during the transition in ancient Athens from public debate to dramatic interpretation. There is absolutely no evidence to support the inference that women attended events such as plays in the amphitheaters or went to the Olympic games, either as participants or as spectators (Woeller and Cassiday 1988: 9). Who then was encouraged to utilize their imaginations at the plays of Aeschylus, Sophocles, and Euripides? Whose imaginal realms were encouraged to seek a critical and self-evaluating perspective on the world through consideration of the issues presented in the 14,000-seat amphitheater built into the side of the hill at Epidarus where plays went on from dawn to dusk for several days? No argument can be made as to the elegance of imaginative expression that was presented in the amphitheater, but what effect did the complete exclusion of women's imaginative manifestations have upon what has been considered by much of the west to be universal archetypal energies? There simply is no data upon which to draw conclusions,[1] thus it is perilous to make any universal generalizing claims for archetypal energies when more than one half of the population is excluded. Therefore we enter treacherous presumptive territory unless we are always cognizant that our current attitudes are just that, current and not correct for other women and other persons, in other locations, at other times and places. And though we have fragments of Sappho's writing and portions of Plato's dialogues refer to Diotima's perspectives:

> it must be admitted that the real women of everyday Athens are inaccessible to historical research. None of their utterances have survived. The inscriptions on their tombstones were carved by men, and the vases which show their everyday activities were painted by men.
>
> (Sealey 1990: 4)

By the fifth century BCE women had become enclosed within the imaginations of men as illustrated by the Homeric Hymn to Pythian Apollo, "when the son of Cronos himself/was giving birth to glorious Athena in his head" (Young 1994: 171).

Homer's women

While much commentary has focused on the nature of the women in the Homeric epics, even ascribing female origination to the poems themselves, several of the narratives which have been interpreted as supportive of autonomous and authoritative feminine energies are actually more supportive of an interpretation that Homer's women – especially Helen, Clytemnestra, and Penelope – did not and could not demonstrate autonomy, authority, or agency. For example, Homer's Helen of Troy is a woman of relative passivity who takes no initiative and exhibits no autonomous behavior;[2] rather what happens to her is exclusively determined by her relationships to men. Helen derives her status from her successive consorts.[3] Penelope, that "most loyal of women," is constantly misread as a woman of agency according to legal scholar Ralph Sealey, who interprets her as "relatively passive" by making the argument that Penelope's initiative was undercut by the play itself:

> The initiative which she took on setting the contest with the bow was crucial and essential to the course of the action. The poets adopted two devices to diminish the impact of this female initiative on the audience. The first is poetic delay. Toward the end of book 19 Penelope tells the disguised Odysseus that she will set the contest (19.571-81). She sets it at the beginning of book 21. Book 20 intervenes between book 19 and book 21, and book 20 moves slowly; in it a series of people do unimportant things. Thus the audience is given time to reconcile itself to the prospect of female initiative. The other device is presented in book 24, when the ghost of Amphimedon, speaking for the suitors, tells

Agamemnon their story. Amphimedon says that Odysseus, disguised as a beggar, came to the palace and told Penelope to set the contest (24.167-69). This version of the story is not true. Indeed it is impossible, for as long as Odysseus had not made himself known to Penelope, he lacked authority to give her instructions. By suppressing Penelope's initiative Amphimedon's version enabled the Panathenaic audience who listened to the Odyssey to go away without feeling shocked.

(Sealey 1990: 145–146)

An audience made up exclusively of men would understandably be shocked by a woman demonstrating agency and authority since women had been deprived of legal agency (initiative) and autonomy for at least a millennium by the time the play was staged.

Philosophy suffered the same malady of inadequate imaginal data input from women as we find in early drama. Even when a woman was acknowledged to be a philosopher, what was recorded were her sexual predilections, not her philosophy. Diogenes mentions Hipparchia in *Life of the Philosophers* (second century AD) but all the information we get is that she was a cross-dresser infatuated with her teacher and later husband Crates with whom she had "unusual sexual habits" (Hawley 1992: 6).[4] Post-Jungian Andrew Samuels notes that one must have some kind of metaphoric imagining which enlarges the psychic field in order to trigger an enlarged image in consciousness (Samuels et al. 1986: 93–94).[5] What images and narratives did the female psyche in ancient Athens have that would trigger the kind of enlarged consciousness Samuels speaks of?

The crumbling of the enclosure

Scholars date the western modern world as starting approximately in 1500 AD,[6] when the printing press was in its infancy and agriculture was still the main occupation as it had been since humanity moved from a nomadic existence to settlements. The majority of men were still involved in farming their own or another's land and were not yet in factories or working in town. The separate spheres approach developed in ancient civilizations continued between the aristocracy and the peasant classes in Europe as well as generally between the sexes. This separate spheres approach of the peasant classes (those who were directly involved in manual labor) was certainly encouraged by the philosophy of Christianity which was not only the primary religion in Europe at the start of the modern world but also the dominant political system. Inherent in Christianity is a subordination of the female and an inflation of the male role and this approach can be contrasted with what had developed throughout the pendency of Roman law, where over the course of the Republic and the Empire women were given more legal rights in the private law realm. Private law has to do with those areas that were not covered by the public laws regarding the state apparatus such as family relationships, real estate and other private transactions, thus women were still restricted from participation in public life but did have more legal status as to their children and property brought into the marriage. By the beginning of the Roman Empire, women could alienate their own property as well as participate in decisions regarding the custody of their children (Robinson 1988: 47). With the acceptance of Christianity and the development of the Catholic Church into a state apparatus superseding the individual sovereigns on the European continent, Roman law was transformed into clerical law and medieval jurists reversed the liberalizing influence of Rome as to the private legal rights and responsibilities of women. As the feudal system took over and there was no overall authority to provide guidance, local sovereignties increased the restrictions on a married woman's capacity to act on her own behalf and on the behalf of others, thus "the progress woman had made in Roman private law was utterly lost" (Robinson 1988: 55). Robinson concludes that up until the last century:

> the primary legal distinction in the law of persons has not been between men and women, but between, on the one hand, men and unmarried women, particularly widows and on the other hand, married women.
>
> (Robinson 1988: 55)

If unmarried women retained some degree of legal capacity as compared to married women, then unmarried women also retained more access to imaginative capacity than married women could. This explains the development of a Trickster imagination in Jane Austen (1775–1817), *who never married*. Having some legal capacity as compared with a married woman encouraged Austen to cast an (imaginatively) observing critical eye towards an institution she had no personal stake in justifying. She was a brilliant Trickster detective of marital politics. Those who married were held to the standard set by William Blackstone, whose *Commentaries on the Laws of England* (1765) formed the basis of the legal system in the American colonies:

> By marriage, the husband and wife are one person in law, that the very being or legal existence of the woman is suspended during the marriage, or at least is incorporated and consolidated into that of the husband under whose wing, protection and cover she performs everything. Although our law in general considers man and wife as one person, yet there are some instances in which she is separately considered as inferior to him . . . these are the chief legal effects of marriage during coverture upon which we may observe, that even the disabilities, which the wife lies under, are for the most part intended for her protection and benefit. So great a favorite is the female sex of the laws of England.
>
> (Blackstone 1979: 430)

A married woman, Abigail Adams, the wife of John Adams, the second President of the United States, warned her husband that the continuing exclusion of women from participation in governmental affairs "would lead to the fermenting of a rebellion . . . [since women] will not hold ourselves bound by any laws in which we have no voice or representation" (Rossi 1973: 10). Less than 100 years later Lucretia Mott and Elizabeth Cady Stanton would adopt Abigail's philosophy, modeling the Declaration of Rights and Sentiments upon the United States' Declaration of Independence.

Between the wars

Between the Revolutionary and Civil Wars production increasingly moved out of the home to the factory. Elite white women were "advised" to adopt a positive attitude towards the "sedative . . . duties which the home involves" to which they were confined (Lindgren and Taub 1993: 12). Such sedation could be counted on to subdue even those with imagination and spirit. The early-nineteenth-century women of the upper classes, like their counterparts in ancient Greece, had to find their place within the enclosure of marriage. Those women who advocated for innate equality between the sexes, such as Mary Wollstonecraft, were condemned as "semi-women, mental hermaphrodites" (Lindgren and Taub 1993: 12). Under such cultural pressure, is it any surprise that elite women's imaginative manifestations focused, as Lee Edwards tells us in *Psyche as Hero* on "how to catch a man" (Edwards 1984: 27)?

Enmeshed in an interracial hierarchal web in the south and in the cult of domesticity in the north, any change in women's status within this hierarchal system was seen, then as now, as threatening family values. This system enclosed all women, of color or white, upper or middle class, slave or free, in north or south, from developing economic autonomy. For example, women who had been encouraged (in the north at least) to work in the emerging textile and other manufacturing sectors of the new industrial economy were now discouraged. In the census figures of 1860 it was estimated that less than 15 percent of American women were engaged in paid labor. While these figures did not include slave women, who were not paid of course, the figures are still illuminating:

> Although many women supplanted their family income by taking in boarders, doing laundry for others and performing other work at home, approximately half of the female population would never work outside the home and for two thirds of the remaining half, work stopped at marriage. Only those compelled by economic necessity engaged in paid labor outside the home.
>
> (Lindgren and Taub 1993: 19)

The Industrial Revolution rather than liberating women's imaginations because of economic self-sufficiency had resulted in intensifying the legal ideology of separate spheres, not only for men and women but also for white and black and the upper and lower classes. But this separate sphere of legal and philosophical ideology had unintended benefits for women as well when you consider that women had a certain degree of autonomy within their own (separate) sphere of influence. As Taub and Schneider tell us in "Women's Subordination and the Role of Law" this occurred because:

> It gave them the opportunity to organize extensively into religious and secular welfare associations, afforded access to education, and provided them with a basis for uniting with other women.
>
> (Taub and Schneider 1990: 125–126)

When the first fictional female Tricksters appear before the turn of the nineteenth century, most women stayed at home and those who had to work or supplement their families' income did so through domestic activities. These working women had no legal agency of their own, yet they gained access to education even as emerging scientific theories buttressed the view that women were the lesser of the two sexes. Women's acknowledged strengths in intuition and perception were seen as "characteristics of the lower races, and therefore of a past and lower state of civilization" (Darwin 1981 [1871]: 326–327). Darwin's view is in sharp contrast to those of Jung, Pauli, and Goswani, who argue that the intuitive sense is akin to quantum consciousness.[7]

Before, during and after the Civil War

Whereas women had previously worked within the separate spheres ideology to gain educational and other opportunities, women's activities in the Abolitionist Movement enlarged their consciousness to the point where direct confrontation regarding legal status became imaginable. After Lucretia Mott and Elizabeth Cady Stanton, who had worked tirelessly on the Abolitionist Movement in the United States, were refused a seat at the 1840 Anti-Slavery Convention in London and told to sit in the balcony, they came back to the United States determined to change women's legal status. Modeling their Declaration of Rights and Sentiments on the Declaration of Independence, where men had asserted their legal rights on the basis of their inherent humanness, the Declaration of Sentiments, was presented to a convention of women in Seneca Falls on July 19, 1848 and is considered the most significant document in women's legal emancipation in the United States. The Declaration is an illustration of the depth psychological perspective that reciprocal and familiar images spark new imaginings which then enlarge consciousness. The Women's Rights Convention in

1848 was soon eclipsed by the American Civil War with women suspending their political challenges, assuming that the Fourteenth and Fifteenth Amendments would rectify their legal status. However, the Fourteenth Amendment deliberately excluded women from its provisions by specifying that only male citizens would count in the census for congressional representation,[8] and the Fifteenth Amendment did not add sex to race, color, or previous condition of servitude for voting purposes.[9] When those who had sacrificed for the benefit of the Abolitionist cause were abandoned in its moment of triumph, Stanton prophesied what was needed and (though she didn't know it) called for the (re)membering of the female pre-patriarchal virgin:

> Thus far women have been the mere echoes of men. Our laws and constitutions, our credo and codes, and the customs of social life are all of masculine origin. The true woman is as yet a dream of the future.
>
> (Gilbert and Gubar 1988: 47)

Lack of legal recognition

After the Civil War married women still could not own property or contract in their own names. The situation for African American women was worse than it had been under slavery:

> The hopes that she held for a better life after Emancipation were quickly dashed. The Black Codes that were passed after the Civil War virtually re-enslaved many blacks. State legislatures passed bills that made it impossible for freed men and women to go into commercial fields or work as artisans, to protect themselves and their families, or to achieve justice in Southern courts. They gave the white employers enormous control over all activities of their workers. They allowed the arrest of blacks under loose vagrancy and idleness statutes, and then authorized white landowners to force them to work off their sentences in their employ. They forbade blacks from holding office, voting, from serving on juries, or testifying in court against whites. These laws effectively put Negroes in a more vulnerable position than did slavery.
>
> (Dance 1998: 458)

While the first Married Women's Property Act was passed in Mississippi in 1839 it was passed in order to permit a woman a right to inherit if there was no male heir, and not for the purpose of permitting a woman to hold and have control over her own property during the marriage. Immediately preceding the outbreak of the Civil War each jurisdiction, north and south, free and slave, had different laws regarding a woman's right to her own wages, to devise any property she brought into the marriage and her rights regarding the guardianship of her own children. By the end of the Civil War 29 states had passed Married Women's Property Acts, which some thought would lead to "a nightmare vision of misrule in which men are confined to the domestic sphere by autocratic female authorities" (Gilbert and Gubar 1988: 49).[10] The underlying rationale for the Acts differed from north to south, with the northern wives having obtained more redress from their traditional legal disabilities than southern women, but no woman could actively protest anything in the law courts except through a male voice, since women were absolutely barred from participating in the legal profession.

Onto this stage comes Myra Bradwell, who was the founder and editor of the *Chicago Legal News*, a well-regarded legal periodical who had special legislation passed in her favor so that she could own and contract on behalf of the legal newspaper she had started. In 1869 she passed the Illinois Bar Exam but was denied permission to practice by the Illinois Supreme Court on the ground that females were not legally eligible to practice law. Myra Bradwell pressed her case to the United States Supreme Court, which upheld the Illinois Supreme Court decision, denying her the right to practice law. Justice Bradley's opinion correctly sums up the legal ground upon which women stood in 1873 in the United States:

> the civil law, as well as nature herself has always recognized a wide difference in the respective spheres and destinies of man and woman. Man is, or should be, woman's protector and defender. The natural and proper timidity and delicacy which belongs to the female sex evidently is unfit for many of the occupations of civil life. The constitution of the family organization, which is founded in the divine ordinance, as well as in the nature of things, indicates the domestic sphere as that which properly belongs to the domain and functions of womanhood. The harmony, not to say identity, of interests and views which belong, or should belong, to the family institution is repugnant to the idea of a woman adopting a distinct and independent career from that of her husband. So firmly fixed was this sentiment in the founders of the common law that it became a maxim of that system of jurisprudence that a woman had no legal existence separate from her husband, who was regarded as her head and representative in the social state; and, notwithstanding some recent modifications of this civil status, many of the special rules of law flowing from and dependent upon this cardinal principle still exist in full force in most States.
>
> One of these is, that a married woman is incapable, without her husband's consent, of making contracts which shall be binding on her or him. This very incapacity was one circumstance which the Supreme Court of Illinois deemed important in rendering a married woman incompetent fully to perform the duties and trusts that belong to the

office of an attorney and counselor. It is true that many women are unmarried and not affected by any of the duties, complications, and incapacities arising out of the married state, but these are exceptions to the general rule. The paramount destiny and mission of woman are to fulfil the noble and benign offices of wife and mother. This is the law of the Creator. And the rules of civil society must be adapted to the general constitution of things, and cannot be based upon exceptional cases.

(Minor v. Happersett, US Supreme Court 1885)

After rejecting Myra Bradwell's claim for legitimacy as a lawyer, the United States Supreme Court in 1885 found that while women were considered to be citizens, that citizenship did not imply a right to vote.[11] After the Supreme Court denied women the right to vote, the emergent women's movement focused primarily on voting as the only way to alleviate the disabilities which still faced them in owning property, contracting, joining occupations, and controlling their wages. However, the suffrage movement (feminism's first wave), which was successful in gaining the vote in 1920 in the United States, did not turn out to be the panacea hoped for.[12]

Between another set of wars

The years between the two world wars were years of role confusion for many women. On one hand there was the "flapper" who smoked, drank and wore deconstructed clothing, but on the other hand most women were still enclosed by marriage, family, and home. Women were marrying at younger ages and for the first time since they were able, the number of women who entered the professions, obtained graduate degrees or used their degrees at all declined. A new cult of domesticity, accompanied by psychoanalytic notions about the nature of woman and media promotion of consumption aimed at housewives, reinforced the traditional ideology of the home and motherhood as woman's exclusive sphere (Becker et al. 1994: 16). Thus, when women started entering the workforce in significant numbers as they did during the Depression and World War II, they were confronted with serious discrimination. Women continued to work in sex segregated jobs and were paid much less than men. During the 1920s and 1930s over 40 percent of all women in manufacturing were in textiles and more than 75 percent of the women professionals were either teachers or nurses (Becker et al. 1994: 14, n. 52). Many industries simply did not hire women, at least until their labor was required to replace the men who were drafted after Japan attacked the US forces at Pearl Harbor. When the veterans returned, Rosie the Riveter was ousted and those that remained in the workforce settled for lesser jobs. Women of color throughout this period continued to be confined to the most marginal jobs. The economic independence which was seen by the early wave of reformers as a logical extension of women being able to keep their wages did not materialize for a variety of factors. Many of the significant changes which American women now take for granted really did not occur until after 1971 when the United States Supreme Court held for the first time that there could be *sexual discrimination* in the law.

In 1971 the Court held for the first time that an employer who refused to hire mothers with preschool children but not fathers, violated Title VIII of the Civil Rights Act,[13] and that it was unconstitutional to prefer men as executors of estates.[14] Until then, all sex-specific cases had been upheld. For example, in 1948, the Supreme Court upheld a state statute prohibiting women from working as bartenders unless the bar was owned by a husband or father.[15] In 1961 the United States Supreme Court upheld a statute which automatically placed men on juror rolls, but included only women who specifically made the request.[16] Other laws on the books included setting a lower age of majority for men than women, differing minimum ages for marriage, prostitution laws which criminalized only the conduct of women, sex-segregated education, differential sentencing provisions for the same criminal offense, exemption from military service and then exclusion from governmental preferences for veterans and firing women who had pregnancy-related disabilities while covering men who had male-related disabilities. Restrictions were upheld on women's employment opportunities by barring them from certain occupations, limiting their access to others, imposing maximum working hours as protection and prohibiting night work for women.

The cumulative effect of these and like measures was to inhibit the participation of women in the public life of the community and to confine them, for the most part, to a dependent role in the family. These laws were upheld based upon what has been termed *natural* law, that is, based on the presumption that because of a woman's biological nature she could do nothing else but engage in maternal functions. The feudal idea of coverture, that man and woman upon marriage were merged into the one being of the husband, was still such a powerful ideal that it was seen as a legally sufficient reason to enforce sexual discrimination throughout the nineteenth and much of the twentieth centuries.

Sexual discrimination cut both ways, as can be demonstrated when we look at laws which gave preferences to women over men, but these laws were still built upon a presumption that women's natural and exclusive function was in the maternal role. One example is the *best interests of the child* presumption which vested child custody in the mother when the children were of tender years since they were especially in need of her natural maternal nurturing. Other laws which seemed to prefer women over men were those which assumed that a wife had no agency of her own and thus she was incapable of criminal activity. Often the presumption was made that if a woman was involved in criminal activity, she had been coerced into it by her husband or another man. The Florida Supreme Court Gender Bias Commission, of which I was the reporter and a commissioner, found that this was true but only for women involved in the commission of violent crimes. In the economic arena women were not presumed to be coerced by men they were in relationship with and therefore they experienced the full force of the law when they wrote bad checks to cover child care and food expenses (Tannen 1990b).

In places where women's legal identity was merged into their husband's upon marriage, laws forbade women to have an independent legal domicile. Most of us are familiar with presumptive laws which automatically changed a woman's family name to her husband's when married and giving the husband's family name to the children whether he was involved in their raising or not. In community property states, laws gave the husband control of the property during the marriage. There were laws which allowed a man but not a woman to sue for loss of consortium. In other states, laws gave overwhelming presumption as to division of the marital assets to men and despite the Married Women's Property Acts there were laws which limited the wife's ability to convey her own real property as well. Grounds for divorce were often different for men and women; for example, several states allowed a husband to divorce a wife if she was not a virgin at the time of the marriage. Other laws made divorce for adultery easier for men to obtain than for women. After the decisions made by the United States Supreme Court in 1971, all laws based on differential treatment because of sex became slightly suspect. But please keep in mind it is 1971 and not a moment earlier. While some areas of the law had changed in the time between colonial times and the 1970s, such as women owning property, voting and becoming lawyers, in many respects their legal status was only marginally different from the situation Abigail Adams found herself in in 1776.

It was not until the second wave of feminism, the movement not for equality with men but for women's liberation and freedom, occurred that women's enclosure was recognized as the psychological impairment it was. Simone de Beauvoir (1953) was among the first to recognize the problem as one of psychological misidentification. In the United States, Betty Friedan in *The Feminine Mystique* (1963) called the lack of psychological authority, physical agency and bodily autonomy *the problem that has no name*:

> The problem lay buried, unspoken, for many years in the minds of American women. It was a strange stirring, a sense of dissatisfaction, a yearning women suffered in the middle of the twentieth century in the United States . . . she was afraid to ask of herself the silent question – "Is this all?"
>
> (Friedan 1963: 11)

Naming is a precondition to social recognition of a problem in society. This critical first step identifies a discrete entity which is then capable of being spoken about; the naming of the feminine mystique gave women a way to perceive their own psychological infirmities. The second step is the statement of the grievance, i.e. blaming. The final step is the initiation of a dispute, or "claiming." At one time, though a "standard practice" throughout parts of the United States, slavery was not viewed by the symbolic order as a "problem." Hindsight allows us to see that slavery was always a "problem" albeit not named as such. Slavery, by not being "named" a problem," was socially constructed as normal and so those who called slavery a problem deviated from the collective norm. The dominant discourse was thus able to marginalize discussions relating to the "problem" of slavery, but only until slavery was named as a social problem. The power of naming is different from coercive or violent power, but it is a power in that it defines what knowledge is.[17]

The power of naming a problem as such – the legal and imaginative enclosure women had been put in throughout the past thousands of years – was brilliantly articulated by the California Supreme Court in a case which initially struck down a law restricting women from becoming bartenders:

> Laws which disable women from full participation in the political, business and economic arenas are often characterized as protective and beneficial. Those same laws applied to racial or ethnic minorities would readily be recognized as invidious and impermissible. The pedestal upon which women have been placed has all too often, upon closer inspection, been revealed to be a cage.[18]

As women streamed into the legal profession in the 1970s and 1980s, they were the ones who could not avert their eyes from the legal enclosure women found themselves in and thus led in pushing through the cases which challenged sex-based discrimination. One of those leaders now sits on the United States Supreme Court, but let's not forget that when Ruth Bader Ginsburg (and Sandra Day O'Connor) graduated from law school they both had a problem finding work as lawyers.

Bringing it up to date

In 1982, the same year that Kinsey Millhone and V.I. Warshawski were created, the New Jersey State Supreme Court initiated the first Gender Bias Study Commission. The disturbing findings launched a national gender bias task force movement within the US legal system. The first state to issue a formal report was New York, which stated unequivocally that as of 1986, "gender bias against women litigants, attorneys and court employees is a pervasive problem with grave consequences. Women are often denied equal justice, equal treatment and equal opportunity" (Schafran 1990: 186). Lynn Hecht Schafran, the Director of the National Judicial Education to Promote Equality for Women and Men in the Courts, commented that for most gender bias task force members, the investigation process was a transformative experience. She found that while many are initially skeptical, if not hostile to the idea that there is a gender bias problem in the United States, after months of listening to judges, lawyers, experts, service providers, and individual litigants testify; after reviewing the answers to surveys and hypotheticals; after reading transcripts, decisions, and studies; most participants "conclude that there is a very serious problem out there, and no one knows about it" (Schafran 1990: 202).[19] One male judge was especially insightful when he commented upon the effect that such long-term gender bias had upon women. In the following excerpt he is speaking about his own courtroom in the early 1980s but he is summarizing quite eloquently what has occurred psychologically to women kept within a legal and imaginative enclosure:

> My first impression was that the mothers who were in [the courtroom] had come into court maybe up to twenty times and they just kind of sat there and they had been there and heard somebody fuss at somebody and nothing happened and they left and they still didn't get any money. And they really had kind of the look of a prisoner of war. It reminded me of some of the pictures you see of the hopeless people hanging on to the barbed wire in Auschwitz [sic] and places like that. They just had this hollow look about them. Then after they began to see that something was really happening, I could see a spark in their eye and they were ready to stand up and fight for what they needed and what they were entitled to.
>
> (Schafran 1990: 206)

Task force and commission members emphasized how critical and sobering it was for them to hear these stories directly from women unmediated by anyone else's perspective (Schafran 1990: 206). The critical distinction in changing the legal system, according to those who had responsibility for implementing such change, was hearing women telling their own stories. Women's voices, not silenced, not held within the enclosure that refused them a public voice are what constellated the energy field within which transformation occurred. It had taken many millennia to correct the situation which occurred when women were first placed within a legal and imaginative enclosure which denied them a voice about their own lives. Please keep in mind that I am discussing the changes which occurred in the 1980s. I cannot stress this time frame enough because it is critical to the argument I am making about why the female Trickster, in the guise initially of such fictive women as Kinsey Millhone and V.I. Warshawski, could not have been born until these legal transformations occurred.

Can law produce a new archetype?

Can the law give birth to a new archetype? Jungian Peter Rutter claims that it can and provides proof with the case of Ellison v. Brady, where the Court adopted "the perspective of the reasonable woman primarily because we believe that a sex-blind reasonable person standard tends to be male biased and tends to systematically ignore the experiences of women." The Ellison Court was sensitive that women were psychologically, economically and socially diverse, "as a group" yet held "women as a group did share some common concerns which were different from men" which a reasonable person standard would not appreciate. The Court reasoned that since women are disproportionately victims of rape and sexual assault, they have a stronger incentive to be concerned with sexual behavior, thus women who are victims of mild forms of sexual harassment may understandably worry whether a harasser's conduct is merely a prelude to violent sexual assault. Men, who are rarely victims of sexual assault, may not appreciate the underlying threat of violence that a woman may perceive. The Court captured the law's capacity for triggering transformation by recognizing that "conduct considered harmless by many today may be considered discriminatory in the future" (Singer 2000: 245).[20] Rutter concludes that the case "brought into stable form the first archetypal image of gender equality in the history of our culture."[21] Focusing on the archetypal nature of the decision, Rutter emphasized that "for millennia, indeed until only recently, the political and civic life of the culture would not contain and hold in stable form the notion of gender equality." He sees this as a paradigm shift illustrating the dynamic nature of the psyche in interaction with the world:

> But the psyche did not give up. No matter how oppressed by even the most monstrous political inequities – female infanticide, legalized rape, genocide, conquer and whole slaughter of defeated peoples, slavery, persecutions based on difference of color, gender, religious or political belief – the undaunted psyche, meaning countless undaunted individual women and men, kept "dreaming" of possible political and social forms that did not exist, and in fact had never existed.
>
> (Singer 2000: 246)

I would add that Trickster energy helped open the way for this revisioning which Rutter points out can happen when the law recognizes an archetypal idea, such as equality. While Rutter focuses on the reasons why people who are in power should cede their power to previously disenfranchised groups, I would argue that Trickster is at work. What Rutter calls the archetype of equality I might call the ideal of liberalism, but it is true that once "elevated to a politically articulated ideal" it became more inclusive as time progressed. This illustrates my previous argument on the power of naming and while we haven't reached Habermas' ideal speech situation, it is inspiring to trace the evolutionary framework; from slavery on to women's suffrage, then to the organization of workers through unionization to the 1955 decision in Brown v. Board of Education rejecting the separate but equal American national standard onto the civil rights movement and the women's movement. This is the evolutionary framework within the law which has resulted in this new archetype of "equality" through a sexual harassment case which differentiated the psychological imaginal realms between a reasonable woman and a reasonable man.

Summary

Women's imaginal realms were enclosed during the time when the earth was being populated. Limiting women, through law, to a procreative role originated through necessity, but evolved into a rigid exclusion of women's imaginal manifestations from the public domain of patriarchal cultures. Men and women raised into these cultures believed that women were naturally limited to their procreative role and it is not until the 1970s that this enclosure of women's imaginations is demolished. In the next chapter the trajectory of women's imaginative manifestations in the literary world is mapped.

Notes

1 The only work we have are the fragments of Sappho's work, "the only woman whose poetry has come down to us from antiquity." And even though Sappho "sings not of work and war, not of the instrumentalizing of the body" what else do we have that represents not the male imagination on the nature of women, but women's imagination on the nature of women from antiquity? See du Bois (1998: 11).
2 From Homer's *The Iliad* (date unknown).
3 On the subject of lack of feminine initiative in the works of Homer, Sealey tells us that, "Although Agamemnon and Menelaos attribute a share of the responsibility to Klytaimestra, it is a subordinate share, contingent upon external character which she acquires as consort of Aigisthos. Klytaimestra, like Helen, does not take initiative" (Sealey 1990: 144).
4 According to Hawley it is hard to say whether the philosophy of the women loosely defined as Pythagorean women actually wrote what is attributed to them as well. Hawley posits this because the philosophy of those described as Pythagorean women was firmly restricted to acceptable themes for women, this is why it is hard to say for certain that any of the other women identified as *Pythagorean women* actually wrote the works attributed to them (Sealey 1990: 6).
5 Andrew Samuels tells us that for Hillman and Giegerich, "the imagination and the imaginal" are "some way opposed to consciousness" (Samuels 1985: 77).

Samuels (1985: 78) cites Plaut (1973) as advancing the idea that the ego is an essential precondition for imagination, where imagination is seen as distinct from phantasy; phantasy as the expression of frustrated wishes not imagines. If Hillman is correct that the "heroic ego" is "inherently hostile to the imagination" whose imagination would it be most hostile to then? Plaut's view that the ego is no opponent of the imagination but is a "prerequisite for the development of the imagination" would seem to buttress my investigations into imagination as being in reciprocal relationship to the ego (Samuels 1985: 76–79).

6 The modern world is distinguished from the modernistic aesthetic movement which occurred after World War I.

7 Darwin's theory is discussed by Elaine Showalter in *The Female Malady: Women, Madness, and English Culture, 1830–1980* (Showalter 1985: 122).

8 The Fourteenth Amendment reads (in pertinent part) as follows:

> Section 1. All persons born or naturalized in the United States, and subject to the jurisdiction thereof, are citizens of the United States and of the State wherein they reside. No State shall make or enforce any law which shall abridge the privileges or immunities of citizens of the United States; nor shall any State deprive any person of life, liberty, or property, without due process of law; nor deny to any person within its jurisdiction the equal protection of the laws.
>
> Section 2. Representatives shall be apportioned among the several States according to their respective numbers, counting the whole number of persons in each State, excluding Indians not taxed. But when the right to vote at any election for the choice of electors for President and Vice President of the United States, Representatives in Congress, the Executive and Judicial officers of a State, or the members of the Legislature thereof, is denied to any of the male inhabitants of such State, being twenty-one years of age, (See Note 15) and citizens of the United States, or in any way abridged, except for participation in rebellion, or other crime, the basis of representation therein shall be reduced in the proportion which the number of such male citizens shall bear to the whole number of male citizens twenty-one years of age in such State.
>
> Proposal and Ratification: The fourteenth amendment to the Constitution of the United States was proposed to the legislatures of the several States by the Thirty-ninth Congress, on the 13th of June, 1866. Ratification was completed on July 9, 1868. http://www.nps.gov/malu/documents/amend14.htm

9 "Section 1. The right of citizens of the United States to vote shall not be denied or abridged by the United States or by any State on account of race, color, or previous condition of servitude."

10 Interesting that men thought that women would institute the same kinds of autocratic restrictive rules that they had done so towards women. See, for example, Walter Besant's *The Revolt of Man* (1896).

11 The Court held that if the framers of the Constitution had intended to make all citizens of the United States voters, the framers of the Constitution would not have left it to implication.

12 Newly enfranchised women did not turn out to vote in massive numbers and no power block developed after the passage of the Nineteenth Amendment.

13 Phillips v. Martin Marietta Corp (US Supreme Court 1971).

14 Reed v. Reed (US Supreme Court 1971).

15 Gossert v. Cleary (US Supreme Court 1948).

16 Hoyt v. Florida (US Supreme Court 1961).

17 Foucault's work focuses on the power of naming and categorization to define knowledge and the very structure of society. On the power of naming as a precondition to social recognition of a problem in society, see Felstiner et al. (1980–1981: 631). See also Mather and Yngvesson (1980–1981: 775). Carol Smart (1990) applies the Foucauldian view to knowledge and the law (Smart 1990: 194).
18 Sailer Inn, Inc. v. Kirby (California Supreme Court 1971).
19 Writing in a 1990 article "Gender and Justice: Florida and the Nation," Schafran goes on to point out that women such as Hillary Rodham Clinton, an Arkansas attorney at the time she chaired the American Bar Association Commission on Women in the Profession, has expressed her own surprise at the extent of the problems the ABA Commission identified and the status of the women who testified about these problems (Schafran 1990: 203).
20 The judge writing for the Court was a Reagan Republican conservative appointee on the Ninth Circuit Court of Appeals, which hears cases from the western portion of the United States.
21 Rutter emphasizes that the culture he is referring to is European-North American civilization which does not have any images of gender equality, although he leaves open whether they might exist in other cultures (Singer 2000: 245).

Chapter 7

From the madwomen in the attic to mainstream and mysterious

A brief and highly selective history of literature and literary theory as it relates to the female Trickster

Introduction

> For three centuries women novelists have been gathering us around the campfires . . . where they have dug the goddess out of the ruins and cleansed the debris from her face, casting aside the gynophobic masks that have obscured her beauty, her power, and her beneficence. In so doing they have made of the women's novel a pathway to the authentic self, to the roots of our selves beneath consciousness of self and our innermost being.
>
> (Pratt 1981: 178)

This chapter is a weave of historical antecedents from early Anglo- and North-American women's writing which support my perspective that the postmodern female Trickster's lineage is traceable through those pioneer women writers who opened up new terrains of the imaginal realms to their women readers. In Chapter 3, a distinction was made between writing by a woman and a feminist approach to writing. This distinction is important for understanding the context of this chapter, as some of the works I cite herein have been criticized for conflating writing by a woman and the feminist approach to writing,[1] yet I have included these analyses of women's writing because they were germinal in beginning the revaluing of women's imaginal manifestations. My treatment excludes consideration of narrative imaginal manifestations from women in other cultures and backgrounds which manifested during the same time frame as the work reviewed herein since it is outside the scope of this work.

The novel form and early women's literature in England and the United States

> But there is another reason why women writers should have gravitated to the novel. It was a new form, not known in antiquity. Therefore,

there were really no classical models nor critical rules that one would have to know in order to practice its writing.

(Donovan 1990: 445–448)

Timing is never coincidental. The birth of the novel as an art form and women's access to education were synchronous events occurring in early modernity. For the first time in western culture those who were previously considered to be *other*, which included elite white British and Anglo-American women, were able to produce cultural artifacts from their imaginal realms which contained seeds of transformation awaiting reception by women as the implied reader. Before the birth of the novel it was almost impossible to even imagine a woman producing cultural artifacts from her imaginal realm. Virginia Woolf imagined what might have happened if Shakespeare had had a more gifted sister named Judith:

> it would have been impossible, completely and entirely, for any woman to have written the plays of Shakespeare in the age of Shakespeare.
>
> Let me imagine, since facts are so hard to come by, what would have happened had Shakespeare had a wonderfully gifted sister, called Judith, let us say. Shakespeare himself went, very probably – his mother was an heiress – to the grammar, where he may have learnt Latin – Ovid Virgil and Horace – and elements of grammar and logic. . . . He had, it seems, a taste for the theatre; he began by holding horses at the stage door. Very soon he got work in the theatre, became a successful actor, and lived at the hub of the universe, meeting everybody, knowing everybody, practicing his art on the boards, exercising his wits in the streets, and even getting access to the palace of the queen.
>
> Meanwhile, his extraordinarily gifted sister, let us suppose, remained at home. She was as adventurous, as imaginative, as agog to see the world as he was. But she was not sent to school. She had no chance of learning grammar and logic, let alone of reading Horace and Virgil. She picked up a book now and then, one of her brother's perhaps, and read a few pages. But then her parents came in and told her to mend the stockings or mind the stew and not moon about with books and papers. They would have spoken sharply but kindly, for they were substantial people who knew the conditions of life for a woman and loved their daughter – indeed, more likely than not she was the apple of her father's eye. Perhaps she scribbled some pages up in an apple loft on the sly, but was careful to hide them or set fire to them. Soon, however, before she was out of her teens, she was to be betrothed to the son of a neighboring wool-stapler. She cried out that marriage was hateful to her, and for that she was severely beaten by her father. Then he ceased to scold her. He begged her instead not to hurt him, not to shame him in this matter of her marriage. He would give her a chain of

beads or a fine petticoat, he said; and there were tears in his eyes. How could she disobey him? How could she break his heart? The force of her own gift alone drove her to it. She made up a small parcel of her belongings, let herself down by a rope one summer's night and took the road to London. She was not seventeen. The birds that sang in the hedge were not more musical than she was. She had the quickest fancy, a gift like her brother's, for the tune of words. Like him, she had a taste for the theatre. She stood at the stage door; she wanted to act, she said. Men laughed in her face. The manager – a fat, loose-lipped man – guffawed. He bellowed something about poodles dancing and women acting – no woman, he said; could possibly be an actress. He hinted – you can imagine what. She could get no training in her craft. Could she even seek her dinner in a tavern or roam the streets at midnight? Yet her genius was for fiction and lusted to feed abundantly upon the lives of men and women and the study of their ways. At last – for she was very young, oddly like Shakespeare the poet in her face, with the same grey eyes and rounded brows – at last Nick Greene the actor-manager took pity on her; she found herself with child by that gentleman and so – who shall measure the heat and violence of the poet's heart when caught and tangled in a woman's body? – killed herself one winter's night and lies buried at some cross-roads where the omnibuses now stop outside the Elephant and Castle.

(Woolf 1929: 46–48)

Shakespeare's works were the popular culture of their day. Nonetheless, works written during Shakespeare's time and not performed were circulated in manuscript form among the British upper classes. Any women writing during this time frame had to be extremely privileged in relation to material and ideological determinants such as money, education, status, genre and conduct to have her imaginal realms even come near pen and paper. When a woman did write she was seen as an exception, a maverick figure, bold enough to follow her own temperament and typology, yet she was not psychologically mirrored in her culture. It was not until 300 years after Shakespeare died that "it was openly thinkable that women could participate in the literary pursuits that were part of both the post-feudal patronage economy and the capitalist trade in words and print" (Wiseman 1992: 11). Yet, only 11 percent of the female population in the United States was literate during the seventeenth century, so reading and writing remained a primarily upper-class activity, for both men and women. Even when both sexes were educated, they were educated differently. An upper-class girl's education emphasized domestic arts rather than philosophy, languages, and exposition. Even after the Reformation of Henry VIII the focus remained on "the education and training of women to fulfill the social functions becoming to their station," leading to the development of "a

growing body of literature on the socially appropriate conduct of women"
(Wiseman 1992: 13). Women who wrote imaginally were condemned. Anne
Finch (1661–1720), Countess of Winchelsea, used humor to make her
invective in *The Introduction*:

> Did I my lines intend for public view,
> How many censures would their faults pursue
>
> . . .
>
> True judges might condemn their want of wit,
> And all might say, they're by a woman writ.
> Alas a woman that attempts the pen,
> Such an intruder on the rights of men,
> Such a presumptuous creature is esteemed,
> The fault can by no virtue be redeemed.
> They tell us, we mistake our sex and way;
> Good breeding, fashion, dancing, dressing, play
> Are the accomplishments we should desire;
> To write, or read, or think, or to enquire,
>
> Would cloud our beauty, and exhaust our time,
> Whilst the dull manage of a servile house
> Is held by some, our utmost art, and use.
>
> . . .
>
> How are we fallen, fallen by mistaken rules?
> And education's more than Nature's fool,
> Debarred from all improvements of the mind
> And to be dull, expected and designed;
> And if someone would soar above the rest,
> With warmer fancy and ambition pressed,
> So strong, th' opposing faction still appears,
> The hopes to thrive can never outweigh the fears;
> Be cautioned then, my Muse, and still retired;
> Nor be despised, aiming to be admired;
> Conscious of wants, still with contracted wing,
> To some few friends, and to thy sorrows sing;
> For groves of laurel thou wert never meant;
> Be dark enough thy shades, and be thou there content.
> (quoted in Barreca 1996: 204–206)

Anne Finch, who wrote in the early 1700s, was among the very first
women in western culture who could contemplate offering their imaginal
manifestations in popular culture. While Charlotte Brontë (1816–1855) is
reported to have been told that writing could not be the business of a
woman's life, many women began to rely upon their imaginal realms to

produce novels which were received appreciatively in popular culture while disparaged by mainstream critics:

> it's a melancholy fact that the group of female authors is becoming every year more multitudinous and more successful. Women write the best novels, the best travels, the best reviews, the best leaders and the best cookery books. . . . Wherever we carry our skillful pens, we find the place preoccupied by a woman.
>
> (Burlinson 1992: 22)

What questions were being asked by elite white women writers?

According to Elaine Showalter, author of *A Literature of their Own: British Women Novelists from Brontë to Lessing* (1977), the literature of white, upper-class women can be grouped into three stages, the feminine, the feminist and the female, with placement within any category being dependent upon the focus and subject of the narrative. Lee Edwards (1984) tracks the progression of questions raised in elite white women's fiction as movement from the query of how to catch a man (the feminine stage), to the feminist question of how to avoid matrimony, and finally arriving at the stage where the questions themselves are no longer focused on a woman's status in relation to the male elements in her external world (like a husband or son) but focused more on her relationship to herself and the world. Showalter's *end/female* stage is the landscape within which the female sleuths as female Tricksters introduced in Chapter 2 were born. Tricksterish activities during this first traditional feminine stage of writing which, according to Showalter (1977), encompassed the majority of the nineteenth century, can be seen in how women took male names or showcased their married titles in order to get published and (hopefully) read. Thus we had two Georges, George Sand (1804–1876) and George Eliot (1819–1880), and none of the Brontë sisters originally published in their own names. The narratives they imagined did confront cultural expectations, but they worked within women's traditional statuses and role expectations to manifest their Trickster energies. Emily Brontë's (1818–1848) character of Cathy in *Wuthering Heights* (1847) transgresses when she dares to consider marriage with someone who captures her soul but who (unfortunately and tragically) is a mismatch in terms of social class. Even though she must die in order to cross the boundary of class and marriage, the tension in her struggle is transgressive, inherently humorous and thus Tricksterish:

> "Why canst thou not always be a good lass, Cathy?".
> And she turned her face up to his, and laughed, and answered –
> "Why cannot you always be a good man, father?"
>
> (quoted in Barreca 1996: 127)

The story encourages us – through the use of humor – to question our complacency which represents a significant aspect of Trickster energy. According to John Beebe, "we know the Trickster is present in an art work when it has . . . the ability . . . to create paradoxical, even contradictory, emotions in an audience" (Beebe 1981: 30). We can see the contradictory energy of the Trickster who shocks us out of our complacency in the works of Jane Austen (1775–1817). In *Mansfield Park* (1814) there is an undeniable transgressive energy in Fanny's character when she astounds everyone by demanding to be the subject of her own life even if it costs her the ultimate patriarchal prize of marriage. Fanny also demonstrates autonomy by manifesting initiative – exposing the slavery drawings – those shadows of *Mansfield Park* which had to be kept secret. Revelation is transformative. The trick here is in how the revelation heals.

Charlotte Brontë's *Jane Eyre* (1847) gave us the first plain hero in a novel and for this act alone it is transgressive, but humor is abundantly present in the novel as well:

> "What tale do you like best to hear?"
> "Oh! I have not much choice! They generally run the same theme – courtship; and promise to end in the same catastrophe – marriage."
> . . .
> "Do you doubt me, Jane?"
> "Entirely."
> "You have no faith in me?"
> "Not a whit."
>
> (quoted in Barreca 1996: 117–118)

The madwomen writer

A fascinating image in *Jane Eyre* alongside the Trickster quality of humor is the direct confrontation of the excluded wife in the attic who sets fire to the house. This has been a longstanding tradition in women's literature, adopting the role of the madwoman as a way out of the collective enclosure. Sandra Gilbert and Susan Gubar's study, *The Madwoman in the Attic: The Woman Writer and the Nineteenth-Century Literary Imagination* (1979b), considers the fictive device of the madwoman in *Jane Eyre* and other early women's novels as having a dual energy, that of a deeper, secret text submerged within the surface structure of orthodox plotting:

> By projecting their rebellious impulses not into their heroines but into mad and monstrous women (who are suitably punished in the course of the novel or poem) female authors dramatize their own self division, their desire both to accept the structures of patriarchal society and to reject them.
>
> (Gilbert and Gubar 1979b: 77–78)

While Gilbert and Gubar (1979b) are describing a split-off kind of energy fueling the characterization (and this view is correct) I want to focus on the madwoman in the attic who sets fire to the house as a transgressive act because of the autonomy, agency, and authority it demonstrates. The wife in *Jane Eyre* directly confronts the enclosure, even though she, like Cathy in *Wuthering Heights*, must die in order to make her point. That the madwoman/wife's violence in *Jane Eyre* still shocks demonstrates how deeply our patriarchal introjections remain regarding women's natural behaviors. Women are still not supposed to be violent. Linda Leonard, a Jungian theorist, argues persuasively about this madwomen energy in *Witness to the Fire: Creativity and the Veil of Addiction* (1990) concluding that this deviant stereotype of the crazy women, which I suggest projects authority and agency, can also symbolize empowerment. Leonard's re-imagining of this negative energy as a means of psychological transformation is valuable from an archetypal perspective:

> Because we refuse to accept the energy of the Madwoman, we are unable to see the creative wisdom inherent in her madness. Other cultures honor the creativity of dark goddesses, like Kali, Hecate, Ereshkigal, Oya – and find exotic colors in the chaos. The challenge is to lean to recognize the Madwoman and to integrate and value the dark, chaotic, creative energy that she represents. Through doing so, we can transform the energy of the Madwoman into that of the Priestess who has the intoxicating gift of divine prophecy and the intuitive knowledge of the dark moon mysteries that inspire cosmic renewal.
>
> (Leonard 1990: 117)

Of course, there is not much humor in the madwoman, nor do we find much humor in Kali or Ereshkigal as they have been imagined through a male imagination. This is one of the female Trickster's postmodern tricks; she is able to harness the rage and anger through channeling the same kind of shadow energy we find in the madwoman or dark feminine goddesses of world culture into humor. Tragedy has been said to become comedy with enough time, but what provides the energy for that transformation is in the repressed shadow.

Luckily, those women who managed to write had outlets in popular culture created by the spaces opened up by the invention of the printing press and its progeny, magazines and newspapers, and new publishing businesses and lending libraries. In the United States, where there were fewer publishing houses than in England, newspapers and magazines became the significant outlets for women's writing and the demand for reading material increased with the increased literacy of the American colonists. This is not unlike what occurred in ancient Athens: when romances came into being as popular literature they "tended to be in codex [early book] form, rather than on the papyrus rolls which were still used for high literature" (Williamson 1986: 32). Popular culture always appears in forms most readily available to the mass population. Television is like that in postmodernity; it is ubiquitous and the main source of information for the mainstream masses. Newspapers and magazines along with serialization were the television of the eighteenth and nineteenth centuries. Pulp fiction in the form of serialized novels and multivolume Gothic and sentimental literature kept readers and writers busy. Yet pay was abysmal and even the few that supported their families by their writing had to get by on small sums. It was reported in the *Cornhill Magazine* of 1868 that the bookseller Tom Lowndes, "the dullest rude niggardly fellow the muses ever made to sell their works," was reported at his death in 1784 never to have given more for a novel than one guinea. (Todd 1987: 1).

The importance of revolutionary times

The first American novels were published in the late eighteenth century and were immediately successful with those women who had access to them. Libraries had always made written forms of literature available to more than just the upper classes.[2] The lending library, which was available in the smallest frontier communities, made the novel available to women who would then read aloud from a popular novel to other women who could not read, or to a community of those who embroidered or quilted together. This made the cost minimal while encouraging a weaving of the plots of novels into women's everyday lives through communal dialogue. Novels were also circulated in newspapers as serializations called dime novels which, because of their low price and easy availability, became a prime factor in mystery fiction becoming such a popular cultural phenomenon (Davidson and Wagner-Martin 1995: 635–636).

These easily accessible narratives were available to many social classes. The upper classes, the educated, and the middle classes enjoyed the images and narratives relating to the lives of the working classes, as did the working classes themselves. These popular narratives examined social issues and human psychology. The female imaginings emanating from popular culture encouraged more nuanced representations of social problems than would be found in a political tract. Another attraction of the novel form was the array of characters available to the author to image social change. For these reasons recent immigrants from a variety of cultural backgrounds found the novel to be an accessible form for investigating the impact of culture shock, assimilation, and resistance. The internal dialogues found in these early novels are antecedents of the internal dialogues found in the fictive female sleuths. Early American women novelists, like the pioneers from Britain discussed above, were investigating or figuring out what could be imagined (by observing events and reflecting upon them through internal dialogue). These narrative dialogues became hugely popular and incurred the wrath of the canonical literary establishment. Samuel Johnson, in an essay of 1753, emphasized how natural laws gave the pen to the men:

> the pen like the sword, was consigned by nature to the hands of men . . . the revolution of the years has now produced a generation of Amazons of the pen, who with the spirit of their predecessors have set masculine tyranny at defiance.
>
> (Todd 1987: 1)

The work of women authors such as Susanna Haswell Rowson's *Charlotte Temple* (1791) and Hannah Webster Foster's *The Coquette* (1797) were popular bestsellers before the turn of the eighteenth century, yet, as novelists their work was routinely minimalized by the (male) literary canon. The term *scribbling women*, originally coined by Nathaniel Hawthorne in 1855 in a letter to his publisher, came to mean "those [women] who refuse to be silenced by critical standards that trivialize the subjects of women's lives, and who write with energy, intelligence, and commitment" (quoted in Davidson and Wagner-Martin 1995: 784). Hawthorne lamented that his publisher would not see his manuscripts for some time since:

> America is now wholly given over to a mob of scribbling women, and I should have no chance of success while the public taste is occupied with their trash – and should be ashamed of myself if I did succeed.
>
> (quoted in Davidson and Wagner-Martin 1995: 784)

The message, despite women's overwhelming popularity among readers in novels such as Harriet Beecher Stowe's *Uncle Tom's Cabin* and a plethora of other bestsellers, was that they were not to be taken seriously. This is the same attack made against popular contemporary mystery authors like Sue Grafton and Sara Paretsky. If women read it and write it then it can't have any literary merit, even though socially relevant images are integrated and cultural consciousness is transformed, as was the case in *Uncle Tom's Cabin*.

The importance of developments in the mid to late nineteenth century

It is at mid-century that we can begin to see the sketchy imprint of a different energy manifesting itself in women's writing as characters and plots begin to focus on women confronting prevailing social norms. Two strands develop which are significant for the subsequent development of the female Trickster: the businesswoman novel, and the social protest novel, which I will discuss first.

The social protest novel

Harriet Beecher Stowe's (1811–1896) *Uncle Tom's Cabin* (1852) – arguably the most influential North American popular novel ever written – is the prototypical forerunner of the direct social protest novel. Another fine example which influenced both cultural consciousness and literary sensibilities was Rebecca Harding Davis' (1831–1910) masterwork, *Life in the Iron Mills or The Korl Woman* (1861). The best Anglo-North American women's writings during this period have a numinous energy generated by the revelation of the shadow of the American dream. For example, Harriet Beecher Stowe revealed the repressed and silenced social reality of slave culture upon which economic progress in the southern part of the United States had been based. The bringing to consciousness of the unconscious shadow side of culture had been repressed since *progress* had been idealized millennia before. How often did the great classical works upon which most of western literature was built reveal that slaves outnumbered citizens in both ancient Athens and Rome? I do not recall much in Aristotle, Plato, Ovid, or Virgil that touched on basic inequities imposed upon human beings because society had situated them differently. Rather, I recall narratives which rationalized social stratification as divinely inspired. Those writers lived in a culture where there was a presumption that slavery and second class personages were part of a divinely inspired order, much as the capitalist system today is thought to be divinely inspired by those who reap its rewards.

Social realism in prose form was a transgressive act, and women were in the forefront of this revolution. Yet, even though women like Harding and Stowe were bestsellers, their work was not showcased as the transformative works they were by the literary canon. When I was growing up, I never heard about Rebecca Harding Davis, although *Life in the Iron Mills* was an instant sensation recognized as a literary landmark. "A wide and distinguished audience, shaken by its power and original vision, spoke of it as a work of genius" (Olsen 1978: 66). I certainly knew of Charles Dickens and his revelation of the shadow of Victorian culture. Unaware of Harding, how many of my readers know of Hawthorne, Emerson, and Whitman, her contemporaries? Harding's entry in *The Dictionary of American Biography* states unequivocally that her "stories were remarkable productions, distinct landmarks in the evolution of American fiction" (quoted in Olsen 1978: 113). If someone such as Rebecca Harding Davis could not make it into the canon, I am not surprised that Sue Grafton is not considered a major writer in contemporary times, despite her overwhelming success, or that Dana

Stabenow's revelations about the Aleut indigenous people and the native politics in Alaska do not garner more attention in the literary press.

The businesswoman novel

Standing alongside the social protest novel is the other strand in Anglo-American women's writing, which was concerned with women's employment outside the home. Louisa May Alcott's (1832–1888) *Little Women* (1868) belongs on the shelf beside the social protest novels because

> novels depicting women supporting themselves were shocking to some and headily new to many: the theme of the author-hero, which we see in Alcott's depiction of Jo March, remained a fascinating one to women readers throughout the period.
>
> (Pratt 1981: 114)

Annis Pratt in *Archetypal Patterns in Women's Fiction* (1981) finds the emergence of what might be called the businesswoman's novel, dealing with women who sought careers during the turn of the nineteenth century, a major evolution in women's writing. "This genre was to remain popular until the sexual counterrevolution overwhelmed it in the 1940's" (Pratt 1981: 115). Edna Ferber (1885–1968), Pulitzer prize winner and a bestselling author at the beginning of the twentieth century, wrote *The Business Adventures of Emma McChesney* (Ferber 1913) and *Emma McChesney and Company* (Ferber 1915), where the reader follows Emma as a traveling petticoat saleswoman for T.A. Buck's Featherloom Petticoats. It is this type of businesswoman novel of the post Civil War period that provides a bridge by giving the reader the image and narrative of a female character with the kind of independence and spirit of movement we find in the postmodern female Trickster.

The importance of being single and mysterious

Anna Katharine Green's (1846–1935) *The Leavenworth Case: A Lawyer's Story* (1878) is usually credited with being the first mystery written by an American woman but it would be more accurate to say that she was the first bestselling female mystery writer of a full-length novel published as a novel and for this she has been dubbed the mother of detective fiction. Green's (1878) work was so popular and well regarded that the Pennsylvania legislature debated whether the novel was a fraud. They reasoned that since a woman was not competent enough to write a novel which displayed the depth of knowledge found in the text, they concluded it had to be written by a man (Davidson and Wagner-Martin 1995: 597). While it may seem shocking to the postmodern sensibility that such a debate could and would be held in a state legislature, remember that Green's work was published at the same time (1876) that the Bradwell case was making its way before the United States Supreme Court. As the reader will recall, it was the Bradwell case which ultimately held that a woman was unfit to practice law. Green's (1878) novel introduced many elements that would come to be considered routine and conventional plot devices in mystery fiction:

> a rich old man about to sign a new will, a dignified butler, detailed medical evidence, a coroner's inquest with expert witnesses, a group of suspects . . . a diagram of the scene and a facsimile of a handwritten letter.
>
> (Davidson and Wagner-Martin 1995: 597)

Most significantly, Green's (1878) character, Miss Amelia Butterworth, became the prototype of the elderly busybody female sleuth. Humor is abundant as she bustles her way officiously through the two books that detail her cases, her indifference to hospital mutterings which call her a meddlesome, old maid presented a distinct contrast to the winsome delicacy of the same author's later girl detective, Violent Strange. Green's characters were not married, being either a spinster type or a young unmarried woman. An unmarried status was legally necessary to have freedom of movement and freedom to develop an independent identity. The reader will recall that when Green's detectives were born, only *unmarried* women were just beginning to have the legal capacity to own property in their own name. Both male and female writers used the fictive writing device of creating women characters as orphans or spinsters:

> An increasing number of unmarried women, near the end of the Century, broke away from the larger social community in which they were treated as marginal figures and, either by forming communities of like-minded woman or as we have seen, by living in solitary singleness, claimed the benefits off-centeredness; similarly, in late nineteenth-Century British fiction, the spinster who refuses to weave herself into the social fabric, the gesture which confounded such mid-Victorian novelists as Charlotte Bronte, Anthony Trollope and George Eliot (who ventures only a prospect-less widow at the end of *Daniel Deronda*), begins to open up new formal, thematic and characterological possibilities. The detective story, a fictional form that gained widespread leadership in England during the 1890's after Sherlock Holmes made his first appearance, provided a medium for the fictional spinster to emerge as a central character and seize upon self fulfilling opportunities.
>
> (Katz 1988: 298–299)

Katz in "Singleness of Heart: Spinsterhood in Victorian Culture" (1988) makes the argument that the female sleuth is not a derivative figure in literature but is unique (Katz 1988: 302). When we read closely we get a sense of the identity-making aspect of these early female sleuths. Instruments of identity prominently appear, including wills, lost letters, mistaken identities, dishonored reputation, and fraudulent documents. Katz (1988) terms this plot device

> dispossession . . . which frequently expresses a confusion about the origins of the self. The lost, forged, or invalid will; the in-authenticity or misappropriation of written documents; competing claims to family jewels; changed identities; and lost reputation all remind us that a person's identity, his or her origins, proclaims a person's right to property and conversely that a person's legal claim to certain property may affirm his or her identity.
>
> (Katz 1988: 311–312)

Katz identifies, as I do, the psychological connection between legal status, i.e., the right to own property and the forging of an identity. What type of identity can one hope for when one has no legal right to own property in a property-based world? If the law prohibits your having an identity which is legally recognized, how does one go about creating an identity psychologically? Katz's study is based primarily upon narratives about fictional women sleuths written by men, yet the stories display certain formal innovations which indicate that at least some of these authors created female detectives in order to free their narratives from the conventions of domestic containment thereby launching heroines who sought adventures outside of courtship and marriage:

> in the Glover-Greene catalogue only 3 out of 17 women detectives are married, while approximately 17 out of the 20 female sleuths on Michelle Slung's list are unwed. In other words, by the time the most renowned fictional spinster sleuth, Agatha Christie's Miss Jane Marple, started sniffing around St. Mary Mead in 1930, the spinster sleuth had already been fully formulated as a heroine by British authors. Sleuthing, one might say, was an occupation for which the stereotypical spinster, had in effect, been training in literature since the eighteenth Century, propelled by cunning rather than courtship, detective fiction was the genre in which spinsters and widows, instead of respectable married ladies, could inhabit the center of narrative and perform inspiring acts of heroism.
>
> (Katz 1988: 304–305)

Why a single woman detective?

The innovation of characters such as V.I., Kinsey, Kate, and Blanche, among others, is how "they challenge the world view that informs most classic detective fiction" (Katz 1988: 307). They can challenge this world view – first as a single woman – and this occurs in tandem with women being released, in a legal sense, from the absolute confinement of the enclosed nature of their reality. Fictional characters at the turn of the nineteenth century questioned the status quo in the same time frame that women, like Mott and Stanton, were questioning the legal and economic status quo. One example of how this operated in early female detective fiction can be seen in the *Experiences of Loveday Brooke, Lady Detective* (1894) who is portrayed as a spinster, because, after all, she is slightly over 30 years old. Author Catharine Louisa Pirkis' (1839–1910) choice of authoring fictional detective novels defied the conventions of her time and cut her off from society, yet it also offered her, according to Katz, "unprecedented mobility and resourcefulness" (Katz 1988: 342). Like Kinsey, Loveday has a standard uniform which immediately removes her from the dissipation of energy involved in focusing much of your waking conscious energy upon your clothing. The void of energy regarding clothing choices is also a reinscription regarding the cultural imperative to wear certain types of clothing to announce a persona, a role and status in society. For Loveday it is a black dress, for Kinsey it is the black turtleneck with jeans. Loveday's physical features, like Kinsey, are nondescript, thus in addition to her mobility she has the ability to adapt to context and does not stand out as a spectacle. Another example of the use of a single woman as sleuth can be found in Matthias McDonnell Bodkin's (1850–1933) *Dora Myrl, the Lady Detective* (1900). Using the device of parody on Poe's *The Purloined Letter* (1845), physical movement takes center stage as Dora rides a bicycle, plays golf and uses a gun, all wearing her ubiquitous skirt.

Whether written by men or women, these pioneering female Tricksters in the guise of sleuths had to be imagined outside of the enclosure of marriage in order to infuse them with the sense of autonomy and agency required for investigative work. In order for them to have the freedom of independent movement, which is a condition precedent to the embodiment and manifestation of Trickster energy, they had to have psychological freedom as well. This could be achieved only through the sense of self which comes from living an individual existence, and not the derivative one most Anglo-American women, who were married, were forced to live. These pioneering fictive women developed a popular cultural phenomenon all their own which could not then be enclosed within the canonical literary view of women detectives as derivative of the mystery genre of male writing.

The zenith of this masculinized canonical approach occurred in 1930 when the (mostly male) Detection Club of Britain promulgated (playground type) rules about what a detective novel was. One of them said that clues must be presented "fairly" to the reader and the detective must solve the crime exclusively through a process of "deduction" (Reddy 1988: 3). Not only is this the epitome of a hierarchical enclosure for imaginative manifestation but also this formulaic approach values solving an artificial puzzle at the expense of personal relationships, which are considered extraneous to plot development. These rules can be viewed as a rejection of the popularity of the spinster sleuth, businesswoman and Gothic novels which were crossing the boundaries artificially set up between detection and suspense. Howard Haycraft's *Murder for Pleasure: The Life and Times of the Detective Story* (1941) reports on a survey of detective story readers which criticized women writers for their "prime betes noires, nosy spinsters" calling them "women who gum up the plot." Apparently readers needed to be warned against "super feminine stories" that have "heroines who wander around attics alone" (Haycraft 1941: 239). I have to wonder which readers took part in this 1941 survey of readers. These heroines wandering about alone, which so upset the critics, somehow managed to give birth to the postmodern fictive female sleuth who exploded onto the popular culture scene at the end of the twentieth century as female Trickster.

The importance of being a (woman) mystery writer

If Austen, Alcott and the others I have already discussed were the spiritual mothers of the fictive female Trickster, what legacy and what blessings did the women mystery writers of the first three-quarters of the twentieth century give to Kinsey and her cohorts? Whether women like Agatha Christie (1890–1976) and Dorothy L. Sayers (1893–1957), who were major players in the golden age of British mystery fiction, brought gifts to the fictive female sleuths is a source of controversy among scholars. While most writers in this field would agree that these golden age women mystery writers were not feminists, these women, while still embedded within that patriarchal society did manifest, through their writing, energies of independence, wit, and intelligence. These earlier women mystery writers provide a psychological legacy in their identification of an individual's psychology as a critical determinant of criminal behavior. Women like the later Christie, Ngaio Marsh (1895–1982), and Dorothy L. Sayers began the tradition of revealing a character's true intentions through dialogue and not through gaps in alibi's or the careless word that had traditionally been used as a plot device in puzzle narratives to guide the sleuth as well as the reader. That said, it is important to keep in mind that these women did not create fictive female sleuths acting with autonomy and agency as we find in the female sleuths of today. When they did present fictive female sleuths, more often than not they worked in conjunction with men, such as we find in Dorothy L. Sayers' work, whose famous sleuth Lord Peter Wimsey worked with Harriet Vane.

P.D. James' work, especially her creation of Cordelia Gray in *An Unsuitable Job for a Woman* (1972), can be visioned though, as an "action-oriented" female detective who is a lead character (Woeller and Cassiday 1988: 154). However, Cordelia Gray is not a professional female sleuth and, like most fictive female sleuths before the late twentieth century, she gets into the business accidently. It is not until the 1980s that James breaks through with novels which have the kind of social sensitivity the postmodern fictive female sleuth possesses, but James has yet to write a strong female sleuth in the line of Kinsey, V.I. or Kate. Ruth Rendell, another major female player in the mystery fiction genre, does deal with emerging social concerns in "plots treating of sexual repression and its fatal consequences, transvestism, lesbianism, and all manner of modern psychological ills" yet she does not place a female sleuth at the helm (Woeller and Cassiday 1988: 154) and her characters are not especially humorous. This is where the controversy about these authors centers. On the one hand, they can be viewed as opening up the genre to concerns which were seen as within the special purview of women, yet they did not showcase the autonomous female sleuth as a female Trickster, as Paretsky, Grafton, Neely and Stabenow do. The same critique applies to Agatha Christie: although she might have radically departed as to form, her characters did not have the kind of reflective natures, about the contradictions and conflicts in their own life and how these concerns impact their lives and investigations or ironic stances, which the female sleuths I have introduced as female Tricksters employ.

I suggest revisioning these women mystery writers rather than classifying them as male critics have done according to the structural conventions of the mystery genre such as those which attach to the mystery in a country house. I view these women writers as the direct precursors of contemporary novels where explicit themes concern female victimization. In this sense they are radical novelists, yet, too often, they have been minimized in feminist analysis because of a singular focus that the detectives they wrote about were highly born, white and intellectually oriented. To ignore or minimize that they posed questions regarding the shared moral conditions people found themselves embedded in modern society is to read them myopically. Susan Rowland's *From Agatha Christie to Ruth Rendell* (2001) has done much to remedy this incorrect viewpoint. Other criticisms against the classic women mystery writers have identified the enclosed nature of the communities within which these women work, but in traditional Trickster fashion this can be seen as working to open up the genre as well as to keep it contained. Women's colleges were not even around when the first mystery writers, of whatever sex, started writing. Virginia Woolf reminds us that 1866 was the first year there were two women's colleges in Britain (Woolf 1929: 112). In the United States, coeducational land grant colleges developed after the Morrell Act of 1860. Although many women feel that Sayers' *Gaudy Night* (1935) ultimately lets them down because Harriet Vane marries Lord Peter

Wimsey, one can also view the novel as a vindication of the academic anti-domestic woman in a period when such women were generally regarded as peculiar and freakish (Coward and Semple 1989: 46). Women's hospitals and nursing homes were used by Christiana Brand (1946) and P.D. James (1971). Hilda Lawrence (1947) used a women's hostel and apartment complex inhabited solely by women. What is important about these locales is how relationships developed between women in these exclusively female locations were presented as deep, and often passionate, in a way few other novels of the period achieved. As Coward and Semple note, "the closed community of women has allowed a fiction which could reflect and explore the full complexities of relationships between women" (Coward and Semple 1989: 53). These women plotted their novels in locations which inclined towards radical areas of investigation. These radical locations were those that could support women as the subjective central focus rather than the object of the mystery novel. In these early mysteries issues of illegitimacy, abortion, the isolation of mothering, the powerlessness of women and the displacement of unmarried women can be seen long before the term *feminist mysteries* was coined (Coward and Semple 1989: 47). The Cassandra archetype was dealt with (although not named as such) in *The Spinster's Secret* (Brand 1946) where a lonely older woman witnesses a crime and nobody believes her. P.D. James wrote of the dependency of women in old age in *A Taste for Death* (1986). Thus these early women mystery writers showed a strong grasp of the social position of women and its relevance to crime writing through the use of themes such of powerlessness and isolation thereby bringing these works within the purview of postmodernity.

The role of the outsider, those marginalized by society and how they transgress and transform through a subversion of form will be dealt with in a later chapter. Here I want to briefly illuminate just the outside contours of why women, who have been the victims of the law throughout the hegemony of patriarchal consciousness, are so drawn to crime writing as their psychological exegisis. I would suggest that those whom the law does not protect in their autonomous nature have used the form of the crime novel to explore transgressions of the law itself. While, in the classic mystery, the law is restored, that does not negate what goes on, in the shadow of the law, during the novel's existence. Thus we can understand from the proliferation of women as amateur sleuths who, not permitted into the established legal order, bested the best at their own game, solving crimes while being legally manacled. This is an essential component of Trickster energy, not recognizing the boundaries which others have imposed.

The 1970s and women's literature

The golden age of British mystery writers which was dominated by the women discussed above followed closely on the heels of the first women's movement of the twentieth century. The popularity of the postmodern fictive female sleuth could be said to be a second golden age and this follows closely on the heels of the second women's movement of the twentieth century. This second wave is different in that there is a valuing of women as readers and writers of texts, and a respect for women's imaginative manifestations that was just emerging during the first golden age of women's mystery fiction. Kathleen Klein (1988), traces the seismic shift in detective fiction to the 1973 meeting of the Modern Language Association Convention. As Klein tells us:

> Nothing in my experience of twenty four years as a feminist critic equals the feminist sessions at the 1973 MLA Convention. Relegated to tiny rooms, women sat on top of furniture and each other, hung in the doorways, and ranged themselves down the halls. These were the places that now familiar names like Sarah Ome Jewett, Willa Cather, Kate Chopin, Doris Lessing, Dorothy Richardson, and others were first scribbled in dozens of notebooks to make their way onto syllabi back home.
>
> (Klein 1988: 6)

Klein's experience occurs in the early 1970s, Grafton has not yet given birth to Kinsey Millhone and Sara Paretsky has not thought of V.I. Warshawski. During this time frame, Klein pervasively concludes that while the female detectives of the 1960s and 1970s, who were created immediately preceding the fictive female sleuths I am discussing, might have been *female sleuths* (written by men as well as women), they were critically different from those created by women writers in the late 1970s and 1980s. Klein uses the examples of the bestsellers of Arthur Kaplan, Michael Hendricks, and Patrick Buchanan to illustrate that the female sleuth was a fictive device to titillate male readers sexually:

> the novels are male centered in presenting women as objectification of sexuality; they are conventionally patriarchal in their dismissive assumptions about women's limited values. The writers are male by sex and gender, the implied readers are gendered male although they may be biologically either male or female.
>
> (Klein 1988:12)

Klein argues that it is not until women learned how to resist the phallocentric instructions of contemporary and historical education and to read with resistance that the women's mystery, with its feminist female sleuth, could be born, and born she was in 1982 with the publications of Sara Paretsky's V.I. Warshawski and Sue Grafton's Kinsey Millhone.

Jungian approaches to popular cultural forms

> There is a fundamental difference of attitude between the psychologist's approach to a literary work and that of a literary critic. What is of decisive importance and value for the latter may be quite irrelevant for the former. Indeed, literary products of highly dubious merit are often of the greatest interest to the psychologist. The so-called "psychological novel" is by no means as rewarding for the psychologist as the literary-minded suppose. Considered as a self-contained whole, such a novel explains itself. It has done its own work of psychological interpretation, and the psychologist can at most criticize or enlarge upon this.
>
> In general it is this non-psychological novel that offers the richest opportunities for psychological elucidation. Here the author, having no intentions of this sort, does not show his character in a psychological light and thus leaves room for analysis and interpretation, or even invites it by his unprejudiced mode of presentation. Good examples of such novels are . . . that most popular of literary mass-production, the detective story, first exploited by Conan Doyle. . . . An exciting narrative that is apparently quite devoid of psychological intention is just what interests the psychologist most of all.
>
> (Jung *CW* 15: pars 136–137)

Jungian psychology relies in its grand theoretical incarnation upon the search for a dynamic transcultural universal structure. Jung's theory of archetypes and the collective unconscious as grand theory are examples of a structural approach in depth psychology.[3] While Jung's later work focuses more on his personal mythology and is sufficient as a support for a more balanced psychological approach to literature, traditional Jungian literary theory relies upon his grand theory of archetype.[4]

The psychological and the aesthetic attitudes

Some Jungian writers see an inherent split between literary interpretation done from a psychological rather than the aesthetic attitude more associated with traditional literary studies. This is the point I think Jung was trying to make in the passage with which I opened this section. A psychologist does see with different eyes, or perhaps it is a different set of lens through which the psychological attitude visions than what the aesthetic attitude dons but there is a distinction. Joseph Henderson distinguished the psychological attitude and the aesthetic attitude in *Cultural Attitudes in Psychological Perspective* (1984). Herrmann's "The Visionary Artist: A Problem for Jungian Literary Criticism" (1997) resolves the split by focusing on how one arrives at meaning in a text. Commenting on the issue of the psychological and the aesthetic difference using Miguel Serrano's

C.G. Jung and Hermann Hesse: A Record of Two Friendships (1966), Herrmann makes the argument for a bifurcation and subsuming of the aesthetic attitude:

> What Serrano didn't see is that Jung had arrived not at an artist's standpoint but at a psychological attitude – which Henderson calls the quintessential attitude, one that subsumes other cultural attitudes – the religious, the social, the philosophic, and the aesthetic by including an overarching perspective that sees the role of psyche in the creation of meaning.
>
> (Herrmann 1997: 39)

Focusing on meaning in making the determination as to which attitude is more applicable to a particular work of literature is what Morris Phillipson (1966) suggested as a way to heal the (apparent) split:

> If the interpretation is right, it does bring about an improvement in the service of wholeness. If it is not right, and the advance is not derived from it, then the symbol remains only an un-comprehended event. The valuable critic, like the effective analyst, is the one who helps the audience (like the cooperating patient) to interpret those manifestations that are symbolic in purport. By doing so, he exemplifies the expression of wisdom, relating what is known to proposals for how to live better.
>
> (Suggs 1992: 227)

What I find illuminating about the passage is that Phillipson moves beyond the either/or dichotomy in favor of asking whether the interpretation moves towards wholeness. Wholeness in the sense that I take it means towards awareness of difference and diversity as part and parcel of a postmodern multicultural psychological attitude, whether this is wielded by an analyst, a literary critic, popular writer, or performance artist. An aesthetic attitude identifies and describes symbols and images found in a literary work. The psychological attitude asks how these images make meaning; it is more process oriented than identification. I agree however with how Herrmann synthesizes the two attitudes through the image of binocular vision:

> I have suggested there are two ways of approaching works of art within the Jungian literary tradition, two ways of seeing or visioning a work of art. These viewpoints form two eyes that are needed to see with, if we are to arrive at an integrative standpoint. The fields of psychology and literature must be seen as two distinct complex-fields but they need not be viewed as antagonistic to each other.
>
> (Herrmann 1997: 39)

Herrmann's suggestion as to how to integrate these two visions is especially applicable to the contention that the image of the female Trickster can be approached through meaning as a psychological process:

> When *poesies* and *therapeutica* have been joined to their "source" what emerges is a realization that the split in the shamanistic archetype of the poet-healer is no longer valid. While on a higher professional plane, aesthetic and psychological criticism maintain their fundamental differences – as separate fields in their own right – both serve a similar function of healing for a person who submits to a work of art; and it is this variable of healing, I believe, that can lead us to a higher integration in the field of Jungian literary criticism.
>
> (Herrmann 1997: 40)

Bifurcation of the archetypal contents from the artist

Jung (1971) argued that there must be a bifurcation between the individual and the archetypal aspects of art which is a direct refutation to the poststructuralist and politics of location postmodern approach which finds these positions undividable. Yet, there is something in what he advises which I have synthesized in my own approach:

> It is obvious enough that psychology, being a study of psychic processes, can be brought to bear on the study of literature, for the human psyche is the womb of all arts and sciences. The investigation of the psyche should therefore be able on the one hand to explain the psychological structure of a work of art, and on the other hand to reveal the factors that make a person artistically creative. The psychologist is thus faced with two separate and distinct tasks, and must approach them in radically different ways.
>
> (Jung *CW* 6: par 131)

Jung (1971) is aware that these approaches can never be totally separate but rather even though they are "intimately related and even interdependent, neither of them can explain the other" (Jung *CW* 6: par 131). He cautions not to assume that they are the same entity because of this interconnectedness:

> The personal psychology of the artist may explain many aspects of the work, but not the work itself. And if ever it did explain his work successfully, the artist's creativity would be revealed as mere symptom. This would be detrimental both to the work of art and to its repute.
>
> (Jung *CW* 6: par 221)

Jung is not arguing for a melting together of the collective and individual consciousness in literary analysis, rather he seems to be advising a methodology which is workable in approaching a literary work by arguing for a conscious awareness of bifurcation in the interpretation of a text, with the text or the expression standing separate from the creator of the work. Jung is not asking the interpreter to ignore context or the dynamics of the hermeneutical circle, otherwise he would not go to such lengths to explicate the confluence of the influences. What Jung is arguing for is an artificial separation so that the archetypal aspects of a work of art can be identified. In doing this type of archetypal excavation, one must be aware of context but one must not allow the personal contexts of the artist to obliterate the focus of the dig. Adding complexity to the hermeneutical task is the awareness of what the researcher herself brings to the dig. The process therefore requires an exposition of the context while keeping one's focus on the text/artifact itself. This alleviates the fantasy that there can ever be a final explanation which is itself based upon a falsely objective stance.

Problems with traditional Jungian literary criticism

Traditional Jungian literary criticism is based upon Jung's work with archetypes, primarily focusing upon identifying the archetypal underpinning of the text under analysis. Freud and Jung both used literature as primary source material of the psyche and in many ways replicated a structuralist orientation towards understanding the dynamism of the psyche through its literary manifestations. Freud, through his interpretation of Sophocles' *Oedipus Rex* and Shakespeare's *Hamlet*, "revolutionized the reading of two canonical texts of Western culture and placed the imagination at the center of subjectivity" (Leitch 2001: 916). The only problem with the imagination at the center of subjectivity occurs when that imagination is exclusively one embodied in the male, when the female imagination is included, we have a step towards completion, the goal of the individuation process.

Jung's archetypal theories have proven to be problematic in the way they have been applied in the field of literary studies. The problem is that theorists from *all* schools of thought regularly conflate the irrepresentable archetypal energy with the culturally inflected archetypal image when engaged in Jungian-oriented literary analysis. Since the majority of theorists in the academe are men whose implied readers are men, the phallocentric archetypal images their imaginations produce have been presumed to be the universal norm for psyche's structure, but this problem occurs in traditional (non-literary) Jungian theory as well. It is critical to the way I interpret the fictive female sleuth to be aware of the dispositive contextual difference between a culturally inflected archetypal image and an "archetype." Rowland (1999) accurately locates the theoretical conundrum in the transcultural, transhistorical, transnational approach of traditional Jungian literary analysis using the conflation of the feminine and the great mother to arrive at an illusionary definition of the feminine (Suggs 1992: 4). I agree with Rowland that there has been a conflation of archetypal image with archetypal energy and also that there is a foundational impediment in continuing to see validity in Jung's concept of the feminine since it is so bound by Jung's time and place.

The images that are being produced by the female imagination is the starting point for deducing what the female imagination is saying. We can not know what will come from the imaginations of the future any more than we knew in the past about today. Any belief that there can be found a universalizing archetypal pattern replicated in every culture and over every time period is an act of colonization which imposes a particular culturally inflected archetypal image upon subsequent archetypal energies. There are too many cultural artifacts to come from the imagination of the previously marginalized for judgment to limit their reception into the collective culture.

Summary

In this chapter I have reviewed some of the major literary antecedents to the manifestation of the fictive female sleuth as postmodern female Trickster through the female imagination. I have also explicated the Jungian approach to literary interpretation, critiquing a structuralist approach which negates the female imagination in the production of universal archetypes. I have emphasized the importance of recognizing a psychological interpretation which is different from the aesthetic, finally arguing for an awareness of the distinction between a culturally inflected literary archetype and a universal archetype.

Notes

1 I think work such as that done by Susan Gilbert and Sharon Gubar (1979a, 1979b) and Elaine Showalter (1977) cannot be minimized once proper consideration is given to the time frame in which they were writing.

2 The first public library was founded in the fourth century BCE in Heraclea and soon Rome could boast of as many as 28. The biggest library of antiquity was in Alexandria with 500,000 scrolls, while that of Pergamon contained 200,000.

3 Traditional Jungian literary hermeneutics has been defined as the process of "discovering and explaining recurring, archetypal patterns (of symbols, character, theme, and genre) and myths – whether found in the traditional literary canon or in an area of more recent prominence, such as women's popular genre fiction" (Suggs 1992: x).

4 In Jung's first work published after his break from Freud (subtitled in the original as *The Psychology of Individuation*), *Psychological Types* (1923), he identified six universal templates of psychological energy which Jung argued could be found in

the personalities of cultures as well as people. Continuing in this line of inquiry are those forms of literary interpretation which have as its foundation the explication of universal types. This approach can be based upon Jung's work on the archetypes of the collective or on classical Greek mythology as symbolic of psychological processes. Northrop Frye, one of the most prominent literary critics of the twentieth century, initially established his reputation through applying Jung's archetypal theory to literature. Frye's work was considered a breakthrough in literary criticism and inspired others to incorporate Jung's psychological approach to literature. Julia Kristeva thought Frye's *Fearful Symmetry: A Study of William Blake* (1947) was a "revelation." Frye's work in *Anatomy of Criticism* (1957) has become a classic in literary theory, and for Kristeva the vehicle through which she began to grasp the "extraordinary polysemy of literary art and take up the challenge it permanently poses" (Leitch et al. 2001: 1443). Rather than using an essentialist or constraining universalist argument, Kristeva identified within the Jungian approach a process for eliciting diversity.

Part III

Honoring the traditions

Chapter 8

The traditional Trickster

> The symbol which Trickster embodies is not a static one. It contains within itself the promise of differentiation, the promise of god and man. For this reason every generation occupies itself with interpreting Trickster anew. No generation understands him fully but no generation can do without him. Each had to include him in all theologies, in all its cosmogonies, despite the fact that it realized that he did not fit properly into any of them, for he represents not only undifferentiated and distant past, but likewise the undifferentiated present within every individual. This constitutes his universal and persistent attraction. And so he became and remained everything to every man – god, animal, human being, hero, buffoon, he was before good and evil, denier, affirmer, destroyer and creator. If we laugh at him, he grins at us. What happens to him happens to us.
>
> (Radin 1956: 169)

Introduction

Trickster may be the most archaic of all mythologies because all other myths are contained within her. It is incontrovertible that the Trickster has hitherto, like most literature and the arts, been a manifestation of the male imagination and thus carries that imprint, yet Trickster represents universal energies which I found in the images and narratives of the fictive female sleuth in the last quarter of the twentieth century as well as a plethora of other imagery and narrative in popular culture originating in the imaginal realms of women's psyches. As in any area of scholarship there are divergent views on the Trickster. Culture hero, breaker of taboos, magician, shaman, buffoon, fool, jester. Sacred religious figure and profane clown who defies and deifies just about everything. The only thing scholars agree on is that once thought to be primarily of American Indian origin, specifically the tales of the Winnebago, and others of Raven, Coyote, Hare, it is now clear that the Trickster is of worldwide origin and is (with an ironic nod to postmodernity) one of the most universal of folk tales. There is Coyote of the North American Plains Indians, Great Hare of the

Woodland tribes of the North and East who became the inspiration for the
Br'er Rabbit stories of the American South, and Raven and Blue Jay from
the North West American Coast. From Africa come many tales of the
signifying monkey and Anansi the Spider. Recently discovered tales of
archaic origins have been found in Maui, Polynesia, Australia and New
Zealand. From Europe we have Reynard the Fox, Loki the Mischief Maker
and a variety of clowns and buffoons. Nietzsche (1844–1900) parodied the
eleventh century *festum asinorium*, where at the end of the mass the Priest
and congregation would bray three times.[1]

Traditional Trickster myths

Trickster figures have been with us for between 30,000 and 50,000 years
(Janik 1998). The first Trickster tales come from those North American
Indians who traveled from Asia over the Bering Straits when there was a
land bridge between the continents of Asia and North America. The Asian
émigrés brought with them a range of traditions of which Trickster is one.
The images and antics of Rabbit/Hare, Raven, Spider, Tortoise, Wolverine,
and Coyote are ubiquitous in oral and performative cultures (Janik 1998:
156). The Native American Trickster narratives analyzed by white ethnographers were fully developed between 1500 and 1300 BCE yet they integrated the values, content, and structure of later immigrants such as the
white European and thus appear to be even more chaotic and unstructured
than they actually are. This is because the only way to understand Trickster
is to understand how Native American epistemologies operate, especially
the role of comedy as a central communal dynamic. It is critical, according
to Gerald Vizenor, to know who the implied audience is if one is to make
any sense of Trickster stories (Vizenor 1990: 157). In "Trickster Discourse,"
Vizenor (1994) describes "Trickster hermeneutics" as a process where one
engages with

> the *holotropes* of imagination; the manifold turns of scenes, the brush
> of natural reason, characters that liberate the mind without the goal of
> reaching a closure in stories . . . Trickster hermeneutics is survivance,
> not closure, and the discernment of tragic wisdom in tribal experiences.
> (Leitch et al. 2001: 1984)

Vizenor is describing the process of wrestling comedy out of tragedy which
is applicable to any cultural group as long as one is aware of the perspective
of the group which produced the narrative. Much of the criticism regarding
traditional ethnographic work on Trickster is subject to the same criticisms
that other ethnographic work of indigenous cultures done by white men of
non-native cultures is; there was no awareness of how critical the frame of
perception is to what is perceived. Another problem with early work on

Trickster materials is that the observers came from cultures which relied upon written texts and did not fully appreciate the traditional cultures of orality. As soon as writing is introduced into a group, history, theology, and philosophy texts show up quite quickly. Writing changes the world one lives in the same way that literacy does. Those who could write and record, wrote and recorded what they perceived from their own frame of reference. This issue is important because of the postmodern critique that observers that are outsiders to a particular cultures, that is, the ethnographers who recorded the Trickster tales, brought with them their own unique perspective on the world and then – just perhaps – filtered the Trickster stories to fit a predetermined set of assumptions and expectations, thus making the cultures which had the Trickster tales the "other."

Occupying the liminal zone between the traditional and the postmodern Trickster is Paul Radin's evolutionary and analytical psychological interpretation in *The Trickster* (1956).

The Trickster of the Winnebago Tribe

In Paul Radin's (1956) recounting of the Winnebago Trickster cycle he interprets Trickster's solitary existence as symbolic of a break between man and society representing the undifferentiated and instinctual "primitive" self which corresponds psychologically to a young child before language acquisition. Language acquisition is the Lacanian precursor to integration into the symbolic order. In the initial moments of the myth when Trickster is submerged in water it signifies *mikvah*, the Jewish ritual cleansing upon which baptism and being *born again* into a new spiritual life are based. Following the submersion Trickster wants to be back on shore but gets no help – of course – because Trickster was already there, much as the grail castle was always there for Perceval. Unable to catch fish, he finds living waters, yet he remains incapacitated and unanchored, in isolation from humans and society as well as from nature and the universe. Trickster has just enough to survive on but nothing to be nurtured by. Trickster attempts to ease this frightful anxiety through mimicry, but what he mimics with his pointing turns out to be not a man but a tree. Miming is a stage in humor development that takes practice to get the performative masquerade correct.

When Trickster reflects upon the botch he has made of things Radin interprets it as the start of conscience awakening in the psyche for now Trickster knows his name – The Foolish One. Having a name signifies differentiation from the tribe and its participation mystique and movement to an individual identity. In the next section of the Winnebago tale, Trickster is outwitted by the fox, who ends up eating the ducks which Trickster spotted and planned on eating. Trickster decides to punish his anus, which demonstrates that he is disassociated from the anus/shadow as a body part of his own, yet the tale signifies that Trickster is coming into integration with the shadow aspects of his own body since he feels the pain of his punishment. The next part of the tale is a classic slapstick routine which has been repeated in many performative contexts, from The Three Stooges to Dr. Strangelove; Trickster's right hand beats up the left hand. At this stage in Trickster's psychological development all body parts undulate in frenetic motion as if they were trying to get united into some kind of bodily integrity. Trickster stands at a mid-point of awareness as he realizes that both the hands and the anus are him and is similar to what infants experience as they enjoy many weeks of amusement and awe waving their hands playfully in front of their eyes and discovering that they have an anal area which is part of them. This is the defining epiphany of bodily autonomy, yet awareness of the body does not mean Trickster is ready for responsibility in the world. For that to manifest, Trickster must get his sexuality, that variant of Eros energy with which he operates in the world, placed appropriately on his body.

In the next section of the tale, Trickster's appearance is altered as his intestines and anus are repositioned to reflect their actual positions in human anatomy. Trickster's next task is to integrate his penis appropriately into his body. Trickster's penis starts out having an independent existence and Trickster must carry it around in a box. At this stage of the tale the penis remains an enormous separate entity which causes Trickster to walk stooped over as he carries it around in a box on his back. In one scene he unrolls it and sends it to the chief's daughter. While the incident may be humorous there is no intimacy between the Chief's daughter and the Trickster's penis, just a disembodied sexual organ roaming around. What Trickster understands at this point is that his penis remains in a box on his back that he has to carry around. So Trickster shape-shifts into a woman and gets pregnant. She, the female part of the Trickster, does her own courting (a harbinger of future autonomous acts perhaps?) and the male/female Trickster gets pregnant again. Whose children are these? Next, the Trickster is chased around the fireplace by his mother-in-law but Trickster is revealed when his vulva drops out. In some versions of this story Trickster laughs at this but in the Winnebago saga he runs away; too many problems are developing, too many taboos have been broken and people are humiliated (Radin 1956: 139). Was it a taboo for Trickster to speak to his mother-in-law or was she in a position of authority over him and his masquerade is just a failure. It is only after Trickster runs away from the scene that he remembers he is a man with a wife and a child and returns to his home and becomes a socialized societal member, but then leaves again. Is he on another individuation journey so he can return once again? Is this a protest against domestication and society? Whatever the answer, Trickster starts acting out in an infantile manner by defecating on everything. Is this a male response to domestication? Is Trickster marking his territory? Or is this the psychological cleansing which occurs after hardship?

Trickster cleans himself but then he dives into his reflection in the water and regresses back into his carnivalesque masquerade. He runs into the Chipmunk while he is again carrying his penis and testicles on his back. Trickster's attack on the Chipmunk from a psychological standpoint can be viewed as the final protest of the Trickster before integration. It is at this point Trickster puts his penis into the hole of the tree trunk and it becomes a normal size through a series of shrinkings. Once it is the right size he is able to attach it to where it can be seen today on the modern male and he becomes a man and attains sexual consciousness.

Commentators on the story have suggested that since Trickster shape-shifts into a woman at one point in the story that it demonstrates a female Trickster. Hogwash. Perhaps this Trickster tale comes from a time when this tribe discovered that men had a role in procreation and the tale becomes a narrative regarding integration of that knowledge into a culture which was not previously aware of the male role in conception. Did they, like other pre-patriarchal tribes, attribute pregnancy to the moon visiting women?

Radin (1956) categorizes the humorous aspects of the Trickster as double paradox. An example of this occurs when the Chief refuses to engage in war, yet he invites the tribe to a war party and goes off with a woman. The Chief starts the war ritual but ends up destroying the key element needed for war, the war bundle. Radin interprets this aspect of the Winnebago cycle as a savage satire on war customs. War is made fun of by holding up to ridicule the rituals which serve to legitimize war.

Radin concludes that the main task of Trickster is to teach human beings to grow up. Trickster is perceived by Radin to be a mixed culture hero responsible for the creation of the world and the establishment of customs conflated with the myths of appetite, wandering and sexuality. Trickster's purpose is not to create anything new in culture but rather to rearrange the existing order so that excess behaviors will not be tolerated. Trickster's role is to place in high relief that which will be ridiculed by the culture and subject the individual to humiliation. Trickster in the Winnebago narratives as they have come to us through Radin's re/telling is a transitional figure, a remnant of an archaic past where there was "no clear-cut differentiation between the divine and the non-divine" (Radin 1956: 168). This is the realm of participation mystique.

Raven

The Raven narratives from the North West coast of the American con-tinent are quite different from the Winnebago Trickster cycle. Raven is an animal Trickster who creates the world and no matter the trick is always successful. Raven does not have the buffoon quality we find in the Winnebago Trickster. Perhaps the Raven myths more closely resemble the postmodern female Trickster as represented by the fictive female sleuth? After all, no matter what scrapes Raven gets into, or what tricks Raven plays or is subject to, Raven is successful in solving the case. Raven obtains satisfaction and creates whatever man/kind needs and thus fits more easily into a cultural hero mold notwithstanding Raven's animal embodiment. Raven and the Winnebago Trickster are two distinct types of Tricksters. Raven may be emblematic of Trickster in the role of transformer of the world while the Winnebago Trickster has more buffoonery, carnivalesque exaggerations and burlesques as humorous energy and portrays an earlier stage in psychological development, albeit still a stage in the individuation journey. Raven is focused on the physical transformation of the world, not the individual body. Perceived this way, Raven is more akin to the trans-formational Trickster energy of social work and refusal to be a victim which is manifesting through the postmodern female Tricksters.

Postmodern and traditional characteristics: food, movement and sex

Raven and other Tricksters have insatiable appetites. Food is the basic building block of life itself and is a focus of the traditional Trickster tales as well as those found in postmodernity. Kinsey is always eating, even though her diet consists of fast food, dining at her friend Rosie's dive of a café and the most simple of home-prepared foods, such as mashed egg sandwiches with gobs of mayo or peanut butter and pickle sandwiches. Expediency and ease is Kinsey's rule in her relationships to food. V.I. reflects upon food incessantly, but her palate is slightly, but only slightly more sophisticated, opting for delicatessens rather than fast food and occasionally even cooking a hot meal, but not too often. Like traditional Tricksters, the female Trickster finds her food outside of her home most often. Kate even hunts for hers and dresses them for storage, whether it's a bear or a moose. In fact, her being a subsistence hunter puts her in good company with the Trickster's characteristic of always on the hunt for food. Blanche is the only real cook among my quaternity of fictive female sleuth female Tricksters, cooking for herself and family as well as hiring out as a cook for other families. Blanche is also the most domesticated in the traditional sense of working as a housekeeper to earn money but she completely reinscribes the traditional perspectives regarding domestic work, especially cooking. While Tricksters have always been obsessed by hunger, the hunger is now more metaphorical and figurative in the postmodern female Trickster, more a symbolic hunger for integration and individuation. Yet, the getting of food does play a major role in all the postmodern Trickster narratives, from Kinsey's simple sandwiches to Shugak's subsistence hunting and fishing.

The urge for movement is an integral part of both traditional and postmodern Trickster. The sexuality of the Trickster is dominant in the

Winnebago myth but it is a male sexuality which is prominent in these traditional stories, not a female sexuality. I deal at length in the next section on the sexual activities of the female Trickster and discussion can be found there about this aspect of the Trickster.

Traditional Trickster as individuation myth

Karl Kerényi and Carl Jung both commented on Radin's interpretation of the Winnebago Trickster tales at his request, thus making Radin a bit of an outcast in anthropological circles, yet in doing so he became a Trickster himself, creating a liminal zone where others could interpret Trickster from new perspectives. Radin, Kerényi and Jung perceived the Trickster tales as an individuation journey, much as Edward Edinger did with his reading of the Old Testament in *The Bible and the Psyche* (1986). Karl Kerényi's interpretation focuses on Trickster as a narrative of creation origin where the duality of good and evil is the consistent theme rather than the characteristics of the Trickster. Kerényi focuses on the archaic (same root as archetype, arche-close to the beginning) aspect of the struggle between the dualities of good and evil. What I find troubling about Kerényi's view is that he does not place any emphasis on how significant Trickster's humor is in encouraging humans to integrate difficult aspects of existence such as good and evil. Kerényi also thinks that the penis is the essential core of the Trickster, thereby limiting it to its archaic phallic perspective. Kerényi disagrees with Radin's view that Trickster's role is to establish customs and boundaries within the symbolic order. For Kerényi, Trickster is outside of custom and law (Radin 1956: 185).

Jung's interpretation

Jung's commentary on Trickster does not focus on how humor is the transformative energy of the Trickster. Jung does agree that the Trickster is from a rudimentary time in our collective consciousness which "we may expect that with the progressive development of consciousnes the ruder aspects of the myth will gradually fall away" (Radin 1956: 205). This is what has happened with the manifestation of the postmodern female Trickster, the rudimentary aspects of the myth have indeed fallen away. Jung comments about the difficulty in attaining this level of consciousness because "outwardly people are more or less civilized but inwardly they are still primitives" (quoted in Radin 1956: 208).

Jung finds the doubling paradox concerning making war in the Winnebago tale as a representation of the carnival aspect of Trickster (Radin 1956: 152). The terrain of carnival as a subversive form of humor in popular culture is dealt with later in this chapter. Jung's primary interest is not in a causal relationship or a search for the myths origins, although he agrees that "Trickster haunts the mythology of all ages, sometimes in quite unmistakable form and sometimes in strangely modulated guise." Jung emphasizes the psychological function of the myth as the aspect which must take "undisputed precedence" in any analysis of the Trickster. Trickster, as found in archaic myths, thus functions as "the reflection of an earlier, rudimentary stage of consciousness." But is Trickster merely "an historical remnant" and if so why has it not "vanished into the great rubbish heap of the past?" Jung asks these questions because Trickster continues to "make its influence felt at the highest levels of civilization." Jung concludes that the archaic Trickster mythologies represent shadow energies that must be reflected upon:

> Only when his consciousness reached a higher state could he detach the earlier state from himself and objectify it, that is, say anything about it. So long as his consciousness was itself Trickster-like, such a confrontation could not take place. It was possible only when the attainment of a newer and higher level of consciousness enabled him to look back on a lower and inferior state.
>
> (Radin 1956: 200–206)

Jung's analysis posits two ways of looking back on the past, with contempt and derision over prior times of ignorance or as an idealized golden age, yet the postmodern female Trickster does not fit within either of these dichotomous perspectives. Trickster has not withered away but has shape-shifted into other forms, such as the fictive female sleuth, which as Jung prognosticated, is an evolution of traditional Trickster with its crude aspects. Yet the myth remains strong and vital because of the transformative possibilities Trickster offers to consciousness, which Jung calls it's "secret attraction and fascination." I would posit that the secret fascination and attraction is fueled through Trickster's humorous aspect which the consciousness of humankind will not and cannot give up. Humor is the thread which ties archaic mythologies about the Trickster, such as found in the Winnebago cycle with the postmodern female Trickster (Radin 1956: 200–206).

Other voices on the meaning of Trickster

One reason Trickster is so popular is that one can find whatever one wants within the image. Daniel Brinton (1896) thought the appearance of the Trickster image in a culture indicated a fall away from the sacred nature of a prior reality into temporal history, Eden, redux. Franz Boas (1898) considered the Trickster to be the original (albeit primitive form) of the culture hero. Joseph Campbell would agree with this view. According to Campbell, the Trickster "appears to be the chief mythological character of the paleolithic world of story" and is both the principle of disorder and the culture bringer (Campbell 1959: 272). Campbell is joined in this view by Joseph Henderson, who perceived Trickster as a primitive form of the hero. Both Brinton and Boas categorized Trickster as an example of an origin myth from an oral culture. Claude Lévi-Strauss (1963) thought Trickster was the image of complementary opposites. Victor Turner's (1967, 1969) work concerned the relational aspects of the Trickster which is especially significant considering how replicated research has established women's psyche as more relational and less hierarchal than the male psyche. It is how Turner (1967: 106) described liminality that takes us to the relational position; liminality as a psychic space where new energies could be brought into the community, which is the ideal space for sharing common values. Turner's concept is not dissimilar to Habermas' (1967, 1968) ideal speech situation and Bohm and Nichol's (1996) ideal dialogic. All three are describing a ritual space for transformative energy, as Woodman (1985) does in explaining the ritual spaces of rock concerts where Madonna and Cyndi Lauper appear. It is in these types of ritual spaces, which I maintain can be accessed through the reading process as well as attending performances, that the female Trickster has the radical potency to turn imagination into reality.

The most widely accepted collection of essays which appeared before Radin's work was Edward Evans-Pritchard's *The Zande Trickster* (1967). The significance of Pritchard's work was in moving what had been marginalized materials, the folk tale, into the mainstream of academic studies.[2] Hynes and Doty's *Mythical Trickster Figures: Contours, Contexts, and Criticisms* (1993) is the most important collection since Paul Radin's *The Trickster* (1956) and provides a useful cross-section of critiques and work done in the subject since Radin. For Hynes and Doty (1993), Trickster does outlandish ploys, uses irreverent language, displays extreme forms of individualism, uses deviant speech pattern to signal importance, poses a challenge to accepted ways of doing things, serves to highlight within a society creative reflection on the change of societal values, breaks down resistance to chaos disorder and is the gateway to insight and new knowledge. Robert Pelton (1993) tells us that Trickster is a metasocial commentary which is a display of hermeneutics in action and appears so that a culture can reflect upon their boundaries. To Mary Douglas (quoted in Hynes and Doty 1993: 21) the Trickster serves the social function of challenging the belief that any social order is absolute or objective. Trickster appears as a critique of the status quo and as a model for other possible arrangements in the culture. (Hynes and Doty 1993: 31–35). Doty (1993) lists many of the common characteristics found throughout world folklore but cautions that not all Tricksters will have them all since the essence of Trickster is the fundamentally ambiguous and anomalous personality, who deceives and plays tricks, shape-shifts and inverts situations. This word anomalous is significant because it means without normality, i.e., a-nomos. Abraham Maslow once said that we have a pathology of the average called normal, so Trickster challenges the norm immediately, whatever that norm may be.[3]

As a messenger of the gods, Trickster not only serves as a cultural transformer but also appears as the sacred/lewd bricoleur who exists in a bubble of immunity which protects Trickster from retribution. Perhaps that is because Trickster never has an ulterior motive or plan. The term bricoleur is one used by Lévi-Strauss (1966: 16–18) to describe Trickster as a tinkerer who fixes culture through ingenuity and creative solutions. The key to this Trickster is finding the lewd in the sacred and the sacred in lewd which seems to me to be another definition of humor. Because of the variety in the Trickster's bag of costumes we find a different Trickster narrative and imagery of the outlandish, outrageous and out of bounds always in correct juxtaposition to the specific culture Trickster appears in. What all the commentators agree upon is that Tricksters exhibit many contradictory traits. Having a paradoxical nature is the essential nature of any Trickster, and humor is based upon getting the paradox of the particular.

A paradox is a contradiction which turns out to be true; for example, the relationship of Eros and Logos is paradoxical in that they have been constructed in the patriarchal symbolic order as oppositional and disjunctive when they are actually related and conjunctive. Erotic does not mean obscene or exclusively sexual, it can mean relationship as in the myth of Psyche and Eros (Gilligan 2002). According to Doty, Hermes the Trickster embodies connectedness which occurs through "peaceful social intercourse, business, religion, travel, education, athletics, politics and even magic" (Doty 1978: 54). All of these activities have erotic energies and are not exclusively sexual, but, as I belabor the point, whose erotic consciousness have these traditional Trickster tales concerned? Yet, the best of these tales do leave the listener of whatever sex or race or ethnicity thoughtful as well as laughing. Whatever these Tricksters want us to know, it is done through humor.

Trickster is not shaman because shaman is not funny, although Campbell (1959) conflates Trickster with the shaman archetype (Campbell 1959: 267ff). He then conflates both as early prototypes for the hero's journey. While Freud saw sex everywhere, to Campbell every symbol represented a variant of the hero's journey. Campbell never differentiates the shaman's supernatural relationship and guiding energy, from the Trickster who goes it alone with only the energy of his wits to propel his behavior. If the Trickster is divine then why use tricks when he could use supernatural powers? Further, shamans have faith, an item specifically lacking in Trickster's tool chest. When Kinsey encounters faith, all she can muster is irony: "An early morning evangelist began to make his pitch and by the time I reached Ventura, I was nearly redeemed. As usual, I'd forgotten how often surges of goodwill merely presages bad news" (Grafton 1991: 3). Kinsey is using an ironic take on faith and belief which is Tricksterish, not Shamanic. Humor is the sine qua non of Trickster's existence, a factor which Campbell missed, but there is another distinction between Trickster and Shaman, perhaps just as critical. The shaman, wherever found, is an opening to another world. The Trickster, wherever she is found gives humanity insight and reflection into the existence of earth-bound creatures.

Doty argues that there is a western bias against allowing humor to represent serious and important cultural information (Hynes and Doty 1993: 18). This may be why the western mind limits Trickster to such outlandish images like the buffoon and the carnival clown, yet, I think that humor has been exactly the way that the most serious subjects have been brought to consciousness. Humor allows the speaker to claim misunderstanding. So, the use of costumes and masquerade is necessary to bring up the most important items which perhaps should be, but aren't on the public agenda. My argument is that the evolution of consciousness holds hands with, walks in tandem with humor and that is why the female Trickster in postmodernity can be humorous without being a buffoon or a clown.

Trickster as taboo transgressor

Is a Trickster who breaks taboos in a traditional culture really transgressive? Before answering this question the assumptions behind the question must be explicated; whose taboos are they, for what purpose were they developed and just who has to follow them? What about the social life of the people who created the taboo. Is magic an integral part of Trickster's violation of prohibition? Were the prohibitions against an idealized code of conduct or the actual status quo of the village? Who exactly is this Trickster transgressing against? These questions become very pertinent in my discussion of the transgressive nature of women's humor as compared with the non-transgressive nature of male humor in the next two chapters. Yet, what trick could be more cunning than a trick which breaks a societal taboo, be it intercourse with the Chief's daughter or working and supporting oneself as a single woman? I am thinking here of all the blood taboos in my own culture. Yet, I could find no Trickster tales which break this taboo. Trickster tales tell us nothing about blood, menstruation or childbirth. Trickster tales do almost always concern excrement. Why does Trickster not transgress those blood taboos which still remain at the heart of the majority of world cultures, those that identify women as impure and marginalized. Could this be mere ambivalence as Trickster picks and chooses what tales to tell? Perhaps Radin's critics are correct and the psychological theory of evolution and individuation is but another gloss on a reality which is, in Lily Tomlin's words, nothing but a collective hunch. But whose hunch is it then?

Enter Hermes

If Trickster is evolutionary, what does Hermes tell us about the Trickster, after all, Hermes, is closer on the evolutionary spiral to human than to Raven, Coyote, or the Winnebago Trickster, who is still trying to get his human body in some kind of order.[4] Hermes uses more satire and comedy to accomplish his tasks and is a more developed character from a psychological sense. As messenger Hermes carries knowledge but does not originate the materials. He is very much an agent, just as the fictive female sleuths do not originate their cases or investigations, someone else asks them to do so. But in completing his tasks Hermes is free to decide for himself how to go about the situation and that may of course include some tall tales. Hermes does not exactly tell lies, but he does not necessarily tell the entire truth. Think about the courtroom and how the oath asks you to tell not only the truth but also the whole truth, why is that? Although sins of omission are different from sins of commission they are both considered sinful, but are they really in the same league?

Hermes was Zeus' cleverest and wittiest son. His mother was Maia, daughter of Atlas and one of the Pleiades. All the Pleiades were retired maiden goddesses in the sense of the pre-patriarchal virgin. When Hermes' mother Maia was pregnant she stayed in a dark cave, a place of deep shadows where Zeus' wife Hera would not find her, for Hermes was one of Zeus' love children, a *spielkind* or play child. Humor was part of his gestation. On the day of his birth, Hermes sees a turtle and laughs. Here is the first hint of his wit and imagination as he was later to make music from the turtle's shell by adding nine strings to symbolize the nine muses. But I am getting ahead of the story here. Hermes, while barely a day old, figures out a way to get out of the cave and play with Apollo's cattle. He tries his hand at butchering two of them. Hermes then gets back into the cave through the keyhole. Apollo figures out who took his cows and comes to Hermes demanding that he give them back, but when Apollo picks Hermes up, Hermes empties his bowels on Apollo.[5] Hermes knew Apollo would not be able keep him in his grasp after he had excreted on his white toga. As expected, Apollo drops Hermes. Apollo is so frustrated by Hermes and his gift that he drags Hermes up to Mount Olympus, asking Zeus to pronounce judgment on him. Hermes tells Zeus that Apollo is making accusations without evidence and that Apollo threatened him in order to get a confession. Zeus bursts into laughter and tells Hermes to give Apollo the cattle back. It is at this point that Hermes fashions the lyre and plays it to soothe Apollo's anger. Apollo laughs out loud with joy when he hears the music. The song that Hermes sang praised Mnemosyne (memory) for as a son of Maia, Hermes was also a descendant of Mnemosyne. Apollo promises to make Hermes happy if he gives him the lyre. Apollo also makes Hermes messenger of the Gods and Zeus starts using Hermes for his most confidential matters. Apollo makes Hermes a herdsman, which is a humorous doubling since Hermes had already shown a talent for this job by converting the cattle to his own use. Conversion is different from theft in that conversion is a mistaken taking while theft is a specific intent crime so all the stories about Hermes stealing the cattle miss the point. Did Hermes have the requisite capacity as an infant to form an intent to steal the cattle or was he, like a young child, just playing?

The entire cattle incident is a gag, a skit, witty and irreverent, like a game of peek-a-boo but not ultimately changing the status quo. It is a humorous way for Hermes to enter the scene as Trickster and Hermes appears more than any other god in Greek mythology (Hamilton 1942), proving that the Greeks did have a sense of humor.

Jung differentiates the European Trickster, like Hermes, from indigenous Tricksters found for example in the Native American narratives such as the Winnebago or Raven narratives. In European Tricksters there is an assumption of evil intent and a greater need on the part of the populace for letting off steam in the form of jests and jokes. Therefore we find in Europe a proliferation of court jesters, of which Hermes is an example. In the Native American Trickster there is an assumption of intelligence that will make for an intelligent response. Nothing is forbidden in the culture in the same way as the legal systems and social mores one finds in the "civilized" society of Europe so the naive Trickster is more in evidence in "civilized" cultures than in cultures where Trickster is expected to be witty and wise. (Jung *CW* 17: par 230). Jung is saying that the Trickster is culturally inflected to mirror the culture it appears in and as such one would expect differences and that is why there is such a proliferation of characteristics associated with the Trickster figure. Yet, Hermes is European in origin and is witty and wise and in this sense the postmodern Female Trickster is more a cousin to Hermes than to Wakahunga of the Winnebago because of the hermetic tendency towards wit which is a psychological modality of evolution as compared to the lesser developed humor of jokes and jests. Another major point is that Hermes is not concerned with power (López-Pedrazsa 1989: 98). The power aspect or the lack of desire for absolute power in the female Trickster is dealt with in the conclusion materials at the end of the book.

Conclusion: Trickster is humor

Is the Trickster a humorous remnant from an earlier stage in human development or is it a mirror to the stage of conscious awareness that has developed in humanity? If, as researchers contend (McGhee 1979), the cognitive ability to understand humor occurs developmentally in the second year of life perhaps that is the stage reflected in Trickster myths of archaic origin. Humor becomes a shared experience when a child is between 2 and 3 years old. When humor is shared through play among boys the action becomes more boisterous than when humor is enjoyed alone or in the company of a female child. The traditional Trickster tales, whether European or Indigenous in origin, seem more like children's cartoons than stories. The traditional Trickster imagery is akin to Road Runner always getting flattened by a steamroller or The Three Stooges punching each other and poking themselves in the eyes without any harm suffered. This is considered humorous because they are caricatures and therefore are cognitively part of a fantasy structure; there *is* a fantasy *can't really happen element* about aggressive humor such as slapstick. Although slapstick appears to upset the apple cart, Road Runner gets up totally unscathed, so the apples are put back in the cart and the cart goes on its way. This is not transformational, although it may provide a steam vent for the psyche about the very real disparities in the world. These caricatures have to do with Trickster's conduit being the male imagination at an earlier time in the development of the collective consciousness. Cartoons are the province of children – in the main – and a child's psyche would be confused and frightened if Road Runner didn't get up or one of the Stooges got hurt. To resolve the incongruity Road Runner must get up and The Three Stooges must not be hurt. Traditional Trickster narratives, especially those of the Winnebago, used the Trickster as a facade so that defenses were down as the taboos of the culture were broken. All actions can be direct and open in cartoons. On the playground boys tease and taunt in a more physical manner than girls. Girls show cruelty in other ways, and they do resort to physical aggression more, now that it is a bit more permitted as behavior, but when children laugh at someone who is disabled it doesn't occur to them that they would be hurting someone's feelings. At that stage in development empathy has yet to develop and won't for several more years, and in some people empathy never develops. In later psychological development the joke facade can be used advantageously to distract from displaying underlying aggression or to camouflage a sexual theme. The move is more sophisticated with a shift from physical humor to the verbal witticism.

According to the Jungian view, the central purpose of Hermes or the more generic Trickster is inspiration through the imaginative balancing between the conscious and unconscious psychological worlds. This balancing is done through the use of humor as a primary psychological process of adaptation and integration. Hermes is an imaginative facilitator who brings cultural artifacts into temporal existence such as the gift of the lyre to Apollo. Music has always been a potentiality, but with the introduction of the lyre music became a reality in the temporal world and brought much pleasure. As many have noted, comedy is half music. It is from Hermes, the Trickster, that the music comes into the life of humanity. The Greek Tricksters, Hermes, Prometheus and Hephaestus, brought the possibility of pleasure to humanity through language, music, laughter, mathematics and agriculture. All these qualities can be used for positive or negative, language can be poetry or propaganda, math can be used to build bridges or weapons, metallurgy can be used to make jewelry or bullets. Trickster is the basic elemental nature of humor in life and humor can be used to heal or to hurt.

Trickster appears as most any thing the culture which imagines him to be. The universal characteristic of Trickster is his humorous take on a situation and the resolution of that situation through humor. Humor is the energy which upsets the apple cart. In the next chapters this unique Trickster quality of humor will be explored in further detail.

Notes

1 *Thus Spoke Zarathustra.*
2 Commenting upon Radin and Evans-Pritchard, Brian Street (1972) concluded that Trickster was the balancing medium between creativity and destructiveness:

> To question everything in society would lead to anarchy; to preserve everything would lead to stagnation; the conflict is presented, and the balance achieved, in Trickster tales which so many societies possess. And in all of them a universal feature of the Trickster is his role as both revolutionary and savior.
>
> (Street 1972: 72)

Street (1972) also emphasizes the boundary-crossing nature of Trickster which I term agency in the female Trickster. In order to cross boundaries, one must have agency, autonomy, and authority.
3 Unpublished lecture notes taken by the author in 1970 in Psychology 101, University of Florida, Gainesville.
4 All materials in this section are from the Fourth Homeric Hymn to Hermes.
5 According to Jung there is a "humorous significance that attaches to anal products in popular humor. It is like an animal marking territory." Jung offers what he considers to be a common joke to illustrate his point about the humor of excrement; there is a man who looks in a labyrinth for a hidden treasure and ends up depositing an "excrementum" as a "signpost" for the way out. The humor is the juxtaposition of hidden treasure with excrement. So the man looks for treasure and leaves garbage or what we think is garbage is the treasure. Now instead of leaving temporary markings humans make monuments. Excrement viewed this way is a marker/symbol/sign of our individuality (*CW* 5: par 279).

Chapter 9

Humor: Eros using Logos

All that humans have gained from the unseen powers beyond – fire, fish, game, fresh water, and so forth – have been obtained, by necessity, through trickery or theft. The reason we have these things today, according to the myths, is because the Trickster (that is, humans themselves) wrested from the owners "in the beginning." What the Trickster obtained from the supernaturals was their goods only; unlike the shaman he did not also obtain superhuman powers or spiritual friendship. The Trickster, apparently, sees no need to have powers other than those with which he is naturally endowed; his wit and wits.

(Ricketts 1993: 91–92)

Introduction

Trickster is a playful energy which has the capacity to produce humor that can trigger transformation. Trickster is Eros using Logos, producing pleasure through the cognitive apparatus of the psyche. Trickster humor mirrors the developmental state of the culture who imagines Trickster. Archaic consciousness gave us the buffoon trying to integrate his body parts. A more developed consciousness gave us the court jester and clown. Postmodernity has given us a female Trickster who manifests wit and irony. Wit is a highly developed variant of humor and is the essential energy that must be now be integrated if humanity is to transform itself and survive its childhood. The postmodern revolution in epistemology is based upon humor and the willingness to play with a humorous perspective. It is the move from a tragic world view to a comedic one. This chapter explores the developmental foundation provided by the transcendent nature of deep play and a Stage 4 sense of humor in the individuation process.

Deep play

Being in a state of deep play constellates a transcendental atmosphere conducive to producing erotic humor.[1] The human animal instinctually plays, just as there are animals who never play, like ants. Play develops as an adaptive survival tactic among certain complex animals. If animals survive solely on their instincts they do not have a sense of play. Play is critical to complex psychological aspects of human evolution because play and humor initiate a problem-solving process of making sense out of nonsense by encouraging humans to test their limits in developing survival – psychological and bodily – strategies. If you were fortunate as a child, you had the opportunity to go to playgrounds. A playground is like an alchemical vessel of transformation; it was sacred space, there was a time limit as to how long you could stay, and it had its own rules and ceremonies. Deep play, the kind which was constellated at the playground, in the depth psychological sense encourages an innate capacity for creativity.

The English word *play* comes from the Anglo-Saxon *pleg*, which means singing with gestures. Music and movement are considered playful activities around the globe. The Indo-European root word *plegan* means to risk, to take a chance, or to expose oneself to hazard, which seems to indicate that engaging in music and movement was erotic risky behavior which had to be controlled and contained by the evolving symbolic order. Perhaps that is why many languages join play with its twin, the sexually erotic; in Sanskrit copulation is the jewel of games, in German, *spielkind* means a play child or one born out of wedlock. In English to make a play for means to try to entice someone into an erotic arena. At the heart of both play and the sexually erotic is the desire for an elusive transcendent state of being, one where daring and risk join hands with ambiguity and uncertainty to produce ecstatic pleasure.

Johan Huizinga's classic *Homo Ludens: A Study of the Play Element in Culture* (1949) claims civilization itself grew out of play. Is this where we get our sense of *fair play*? However, when play and humor are used to uphold the status quo, marginalized populations might not get the same sense of fair play as elites in that culture. Were the Roman games considered playful and humorous? Not if you were the object of the game to see what happens when a man and a tiger were put in the same arena. Yet, research tells us that play is the brain's favorite way of learning something new. Is that why children must have play to develop into participating members of society? Is play rather than Lacanian theories of language acquisition the way of learning what the symbolic order expects of you? Girls and boys play very differently, so what is play as learning being used for? Yet despite their differences, both men and women continue to be magnetically attracted to playing.

The reason for this magnetic attraction to play and humor is because once constellated the individual, male or female, is offered an opportunity for engagement with the transcendent function. Jung said that the transcendent function "represents a function based on the real and 'imaginary,' or rational and irrational data, thus bridging the yawning gulf between conscious and unconscious" (Jung *CW* 7: par 121). Jung is describing movement between the poles of the real and imaginary as transcendence and Trickster is the embodiment of the archetypal energy which mediates between poles of opposites, in the liminal zone between the real and the imaginary where the transcendent resides. What "is capable of uniting these two" and "which itself transcends time and conflict, neither adhering to nor partaking of one side or the other but somehow common to both and offering the possibility of a new synthesis" is the metaphorical Trickster (Samuels et al. 1986: 150). In depth psychology the transcendental function is the most significant of the psychological functions; it is the function whose purpose is to allow an individual or a collective to move beyond the petty and pointless conflicts, towards conscience and beyond the personal point of view. Transcendence is what Maslow (1973) called a peak experience. Deep play is another way of describing this transcendent state which the psyche desires to constellate through humor and laughter.

How and when in the developmental sequence does humor develop?

Humor is based upon the release of the pleasurable erotic ability to perceive, enjoy, or express what is comical, but what is comical is dependent upon external as well as internal factors. Childish and underdeveloped jokes, puns, word plays and physical stunts were part of the evolution of Trickster humor but are no longer adequate markers for the appearance of Trickster archetypal energy in postmodernity. In postmodernity Trickster's toolbox is filled with parody, irony, wit and satire rather than simplistic jokes, buffoonery and cartoonish behaviors.

The ancients perceived that temperament was dependent upon what kind of humor was dominant in your body, sanguine, phlegmatic, melancholic, or choleric. In this sense, the word humor comes from the Latin moisture. Trickster humor – as moisture – is the fluid which greases the psyche. Without having a sense of humor life truly becomes what we fear most, meaningless and static. When does this psychic fluid called humor start flowing? Is it a response to frustration and fear or does it originate in an infant's first giggle after a tickle? Or is humor the playful movement between the poles of frustration and pleasure?

Humor is a cognitive experience which is dependent on the resolution of incongruity. While incongruity is necessary as a condition precedent to humor, incongruity is not sufficient in itself to produce humor. The social context of humor is also significant, but this element, like incongruity, is not determinative in the acquisition of a sense of humor. Sexual and aggressive elements play a significant role in much of everyday humor, yet sex and aggression are not funny in the absence of an incongruous context. Humor is an erotic method way of resolving or making sense out of what appears to be nonsense – the incongruity – through cognitive capacities: Eros using Logos.

All children laugh and play given the appropriate context, but at what point are they developmentally ready to perceive and resolve incongruity in a humorous way using their cognitive abilities? At what age does a child truly find something funny? Smiling makes its appearance in the first week after birth but research identifies this as a spontaneous activity of the central nervous system. The first wakeful smile follows within two weeks of birth and occurs when the infant is satiated and drowsy. The first fully awake, alert smile occurs when two prerequisites occur simultaneously; the mother's or other primary caregiver's voice and some form of tactile stimulation such as tickling. In the second month of life the smile develops into a broader grin and is stimulated by a wider variety of events in the infant's expanding universe. Sights and sounds replace an exclusive focus on physicality; moving objects which make a sound are the most likely to produce smiling (McGhee 1979: 48–50). It is during the third and fourth months of life that meaning making begins to play (pun intended) an important role in the infant's life. Piaget (1952) conceptualized this activity as resulting from the pleasure of recognition the infant feels as a face becomes familiar. Any familiar face will do until the sixth month, when the infant begins to differentiate and then, "if the child is so familiar with the object that it is immediately recognizable, little interest is aroused, and smiling does not occur" (McGhee 1979: 49). This finding supports the inference that humor is manifested only in that liminal terrain between knowing and the unknown. This pattern suggests that the child who is developing a sense of humor gains the greatest amount of pleasure, from the "exertion of moderate amounts of effort" and that this process is "built into children in a biological sense" (McGhee 1979: 50). Humor is like Hermes, interested in working just a bit to evoke laughter from Apollo and Zeus.

Infants do not have a sense of humor, their laughter and smiling signifies delight in mastery and recognition. If older infants are not displaying a sense of humor when they play peek-a-boo or laugh at Mom sticking out her tongue, could the laughter and smiling be an indication that there is a capability for the later development of a *sense of humor*. The condition precedent to experiencing incongruity as humorous and the subsequent development of a *sense of humor* depends upon having the capacity to engage in fantasy and make-believe play which Jerome Singer (1973) sees as a balancing act between too little and too much stimulation:

> The seemingly trivial make-believe play of the child grows essentially out of the very nature of the child's cognitive experience. It follows the assimilation and accommodation cycles and involves the seeking of

moderate levels of increasing stimulation or reducing such moderate levels of stimulation to produce an experience of joy.

(Singer 1973: 207)

But not all children engage in such fantasy play and there are widespread individual differences in fantasy and make-believe play as a child and witty interaction with the world as an adult. In childhood creative types tend to create fantasy incongruities as a way of maintaining a stimulating environment, but it may be an inherent capacity rather than a developmental stage all children go through. Children who do not have adequate caretaking or where critical environmental factors are lacking, such as adequate food, shelter and places to play in safety, do not develop along the lines I am postulating here because their energy is engaged in daily survival and thus there may be no extra psychic energy available to engage in fantasy play. There are five necessary environmental and social factors that encourage the evolution of pleasure in incongruity which leads to the development of a sense of humor; the first is privacy where the child is able to practice imaginative play in an environment where, second the external environment is routine and redundant and therefore greater attention can be paid to the internal environment. The third prerequisite is the availability of a variety of materials such as books, play things and stories which the child is encouraged to interact with, or at least not prohibited from interacting with. In this sense a pencil which can write or be imagined as a spaceship is better than a toy spaceship that can be imagined to be little else. The fourth prerequisite is the child's freedom from having to perform motor or perceptual skills on a preset schedule determined by adults and peers. The fifth condition precedent is the availability of adult models who encourage a sense of imaginative play and a cultural acceptance that privacy and make-believe are worthwhile forms of play critical to the development of a sense of humor as part of the individual's engagement with creativity.

Once children have a space and the encouragement to play in the world of fantasy and make-believe, mirroring becomes essential, for although children may be fascinated with what they dream up, unless they have an innate playful attitude which is nurtured in the environment, a sense of humor does not necessarily occur in the developmental cycle. "Humor in the young child, then, results from the playful contemplation of incongruity, exaggeration, absurdity, or nonsense only when the child realizes that the events exist in fantasy" (McGhee 1979: 61). Children must be aware that they are playing and what they are playing with is a fantasy that brings the pleasure of Eros energy and that kind of erotic pleasure must be encouraged in the environment. If these conditions are met, a young child has the opportunity to develop a Hermes-like fluidity which delights in movement between the inner and outer worlds as a way of seeking and enjoying the absurd. If all these conditions are met, a Trickster in training is the result.

The playful attitude that is a condition precedent to the development of humor occurs most often in social interactions, because children receive pleasure when they share their perceptions with others, regardless of whether it is their peers or adults who mirror them. That is why precocious children may use adults as mirrors more often than their age mates simply because adults have more highly developed cognitive abilities and thus can appreciate the child's attempts at humor. If the parent or caretaker views these playful experiments with positive attention the child learns how to use humor successfully in social situations. If a child is told that a playful attitude is foolish the value of imagination is diminished and either a sense of humor does not develop or it is repressed into the unconscious where it becomes shadow material not shared with others unless the child is fortunate enough to have an older sibling or other older playmates who can provide the positive feedback that the parents or primary caregivers cannot.

The stages of development in a sense of humor

Much of what is considered humorous has been limited to what is manifested during the earliest stages in the development of a sense of humor. Much of what is considered Trickster behavior mirrors these earliest stages of humor development in a collective cultural sense. The postmodern Trickster mirrors the more developed forms of humor: wit, parody and irony.

Stage 1 humor occurs in a child's second year when they are in a playful mood engaged in fantasy play with objects. For example, a child picks up a leaf and makes a telephone or portable media player out of it, causing her to explode in vigorous laughter. It is the incongruity of the act in conjunction with the playful mood that brings laughter which reflects the pleasure derived from creating in fantasy play a set of conditions known to be at odds with reality. Could this be the reason why Hermes laughs at the turtle on its back and turns it into the lyre? Or perhaps this is why Hermes has the cattle walk backward, simply for the incongruity? Can this be the reason we find Trickster's penis on his back as well?

In Stage 2 the child uses recently acquired language skills instead of objects to exploit incongruity as humorous. In Stage 1, a child might laugh when she uses a ruler to comb her hair, but in Stage 2 she will attempt to employ language to describe using the ruler to comb her hair. In Stage 1, physical action is critical while in Stage 2 the ability to abstract through language is the critical aspect even though both humorous situations concern the same action; it is the absence of action towards the object that marks it as Stage 2. Stage 1 is the slapstick humor of physicality while Stage 2 humor is an abstraction of the physical. Stage 2 humor development is when children find misnaming very funny, such as when they call a cat a dog or a tree a house, because they know that they are being absurd. Stage 2 humor predominates until the late preschool years of 3–4. In Stage 3, all the former stages are incorporated but now an attempt at making a joke is substituted for the nonsensical wrong name calling activity In this initial stage of joking nonsense words or distortion of familiar objects occur, so the cat which was called dog in Stage 2 is now drawn with two heads or a joke about a cat with two heads will be attempted. In Stage 3 humor, the child is shape-shifting the object through mental abstraction which indicates that she realizes that a name is not the same thing as the object yet objects remain the focus (Piaget 1952). Much of the humor then is directed at making incongruities out of familiar objects, like laughing at a picture of an elephant in a tree because the child knows elephants do not live in trees. This is also the time when nonsense words give great pleasure, so cutesey, bootsey, lootsey, mootsie, which play with the sound but not the meaning of words, can occupy a great deal of playtime as practice for punning. In Stage 4 humor a child steps beyond the appearances of objects and thinks about how they work. The elephant in the tree may become funny because the child knows a tree can't support the elephant's weight, not because it is the wrong place for an elephant to be. It is in Stage 4 that a child/person develops the possibility of a sophisticated sense of humor which incorporates wit. Wit is the cognitive ability to articulate the incongruities in a situation, to compare how the incongruities differ from what was expected and then being able to articulate a motivation for the character in the joke or cartoon, such as the elephant is in the tree because she wanted to smell the flowers on the top of the tree and got stuck there. It is when children recognize that there are fantasy motivations for actions and that the meaning of words themselves can shape-shift that they approach an adult style of humor. Stage 4 is when making puns demonstrates an emerging sense of humor because linguistic ambiguity and fluidity is incorporated into the adaptive responses of the child's psyche. For example, the following is a classic children's joke: "Hey, did you take a bath? No, is one missing?" A 7 year old understands this joke but the 3 year old does not because they cannot play with the meaning of *take*. To a 3 year old a bath is a bath and can be humorous if a monkey is in the bathtub because monkeys don't take a bath. One of the main markers of Stage 4 humor in a child is the delight they find in a riddle which has two answers, with the child recognizing that only one is funny, such as "Knock Knock, Who's there? Orange. Orange you glad I'm not an apple?" A child between the ages of 6 and 10 can also understand more abstract forms of humor, like the doubling of doing the opposite of what you intend to convey, which is a staple Trickster technique. No matter the stage of humor which is constellated by the child or in a culture through Trickster tales, it is the ability to move between different meanings and what they may imply that are the herm where a sense of humor develops.

Another aspect of humor development – empathetic response – is a reliable marker for mature humor. Older children have the possibility of adopting another's point of view; a young child may laugh at someone's disability, such as a limp, because they cannot put themselves in that person's shoes, but an older child can. This means that the older child will refrain from laughing at disabled people until they are at least out of sight. A child or person who has developed to Stage 3 in their sense of humor can laugh when someone gets hurt and slapstick is the prime example of this stage in a sense of humor. In Stage 4, the pain must be accidental or unintentional to constellate the possibility of laughter. In Stage 3, intent is irrelevant to how funny a joke is perceived to be and actually the more harm that is inflicted will make the action funnier to a child or adult whose sense of humor reflects the third stage of humor development. There is no way to place an upper age limit on either Stage 3 or Stage 4. Not all people develop empathy and many have a sense of humor which remains at Stage 3. Adolescents who evolve beyond Stage 3 are those who develop empathy and show a greater affinity for wit and anecdote than jokes. In the high school cafeteria, pulling out the chair from under someone may make some of the teenagers laugh and others look away in disgust at the childish nature of the prank, while others will rush to the aid of the object of the prank. It is during adolescence that an individual's humor gels into particular preferences which we retain throughout our life spans.

Psychoanalytic approaches to humor

Freud

Freud (1916, 1938) thought wit was used by those with unusual psychic abilities to derive pleasure out of pain and it is true that the witty have always been among the rarest of the species. Freud also realized that just as all cultures play, so do they dream, concluding that wit and dreams had much in common besides mutual residence in the psyche. Both involve the unconscious shape-shifting of one conscious perception into a different conscious perception. Both wit and the dream use a doubling technique of presenting imagery and narrative which is the opposite of what is intended to be meaningful. Absurdity abounds in wit, dream, and Trickster narratives. When the psyche uses humor, the absurdity is shape-shifted by a playful approach which releases a pleasurable sensation in the body. Humor is the psyche's way of acquiring pleasure while the dream guards against pain. Wit is to play as dream is to wish, in the Freudian sense.

Freud thought that wit was driven by two impulses – to evade reason and to become childish (Freud 1938: 722). He reasoned that as play becomes more restricted by reason during the socialization process inherent in "civilization," wit provides relief from reason's assumptive controlling position through the shape-shifting energy of playing with humor which confuses reason. Disguises such as masks, personas, and costumes fascinate because they also confuse reason by giving the wrong signal which then has to be properly decoded. With a playful attitude reason does not know what to expect, and if it can step aside and allow a playful attitude to occupy the consciousness, the pleasure of deep play can result.

Repartee in wit is like a paradox, it answers a foolish question with a condition that is equally impossible but absolutely accurate. Freud found the following examples particularly illuminating. For example, "Q: Can you color my white shirt blue? A: If you can stand the dying!" The following wit requires a greater degree of intellectual sophistication but employs the same process. "Q: Did you know that Rousseau wrote an Ode to Posterity? A: Voltaire said it would never reach its destination" (Freud 1938). For what reason does Voltaire use his wit against Rousseau? In a sense he is expressing the opposite of what he really thought but which he had to keep to himself. When a message is transmitted through using the opposite of what is meant we are in the land of irony, a place the postmodern female Trickster occupies with grace and pleasure, for she delights in the intuitive leap wit requires.

Psychological adaptation through the use of wit sets pleasure free by removing inhibitions. Wit begins in the innocence of play but in its adapted form it operates not only to assuage reason and critical judgment but to develop a totally new relationship with reason, critical judgment and aggression. Wit recombines in a new way that which is known but not connected and in that sense it is dialogic and relational not hierarchal. This kind of witty interaction happens only when the hearer and the teller have the same inhibitions and thus can enjoy the same humorous perspective, that is why *in-group* and *out-group* humor can be so different and explains why one group may find something witty while another just doesn't get it, like feminists listening to an obscene witticism. The obscene witticism overcomes societal inhibitions against the display of out of bounds sexual attitudes, images, or perspectives by offering pleasure as the inducement, but what is out of bounds and inhibited in one group may not be in another. Whether a joke is obscene, aggressive or cynical/skeptical, the natural instinct providing the psychic propulsion is the possibility of play or the received display of pleasure through words or a gesture. There is no universal norm regarding the content of jokes, the point is that humor and wit is an adaptive process aimed at resolving the absurdity of cultural restrictions whatever they might be.

As the individual grows up in a particular culture, more and more areas of play are roped off from ego consciousness by naming such behaviors and actions as "senseless." Maturation in civilization occurs as we accept that it is desirable to give up the absurd for the reasonable and so we lose the magical childlike transcendent perspective which is the natural psychological state during those years of innocent play. Freud posited that our natural instinct for play turns to the joke or witticism which can hold endless hours of pleasure as a source for liberation from ever increasing socialization into the normative symbolic order, but for the wit to be appreciated both the listener and the teller must have a similar set of inhibitions derived from growing up within the same culture, or have the openness to be willing to appreciate that other people may have a different sense of humor which can be integrated into our own limited consciousness, thereby enlarging that consciousness.

The three categories of wit posited by Freud – the obscene, the aggressive, and the cynical/skeptical wit – are derived from white European male culture. The obscene wit is the one most feminists have a bit of a problem with since the shared inhibitions required to get the joke don't exist in mixed company. The typical white male oriented obscene joke makes a confederate of a third party at the expense of the object, who usually turns out to be a woman or other marginalized group. Intimacy between the listener and teller about shared inhibitions is replaced with pleasure at the expense of another. The aggressive joke changes indifferent hearers into active haters and scorners. Racist jokes fall into this category. The skeptic or cynic shatters respect for institutions or truths the hearer believed. The usual technique here is to strengthen the argument for the object and then to attack it with a new perspective.

Wit removed from its moorings in the white male European imagination still has the capacity to be effective as psychological adaptation and is an invaluable aid in an intra-psychic individuation journey because wit has the capacity to resolve stressors which otherwise would require disassociation, denial, and a host of other defense mechanisms which the psyche has developed to grapple with the paradox of the everlasting mystery called life. Wit, that particular sense of humor which I am positing here as adaptation, operates by maintaining a fluid receptive terrain where the psyche finds pleasure in the integration of new perspectives; it is the grease of the psyche. In the sense of transformative play, wit (and Trickster) is a royal road to the transcendent function, "the function which mediates the opposites as it facilitates a transition from one psychological attitude towards another" (Samuels et al. 1986: 150).

Jung

From a Jungian/post-Jungian depth perspective humor's energy is held within the shadow until it is released as creative energy, which then has the possibility of manifesting through humor. Jung recognized humor, or play as the critical determinant in creativity when he said: "the creation of something new is not accomplished by the intellect, but by the play instinct acting from inner necessity. The creative mind plays with the objects it loves" (*CW* 6: par 198). Jung tells us that play is not something you want to do but is rather something you have to do thereby joining the two concepts of serious endeavor and playful creation to form the concept of serious play, which he claims lays at the base of all outward creativity, "If play expires in itself without creating anything durable and vital, it is only play, in the other case it is called creative work" (*CW* 6: par 197). To Jung, a humorous take on a situation then is creativity in the service of the self.

A brief gallop through humor's pasture

Clowns

Clowns wear costumes and are a caricature of an object which appears in reality. Costumes, disguises and masks confound and confuse reason. The perceiver is caught off guard and doesn't know what to expect. Vaudeville and burlesque are the province of clowns no less than the circus, but there are also other kinds of clowns who wear the clothing of mainstream culture and can be hard to spot. For example, there is the adult joker/clown who maintains control of a social interaction by creating the circumstances others are forced to react to. It's a win/win game, you control others and get rewarded by gaining pleasure from making humor all the while remaining in that liminal terrain where the dual possibility of constellating pleasure in others and being rewarded with positive mirroring can occur. Most children who develop into a class clown or have an aggressive social wit usually had aggressive patterns of behavior as a child along with the wit to channel these energies into the socially acceptable form of the joke or jest.

Of course, if you are a boy and smaller than your classmates a clever wit allows you to release aggressive energy while being able to claim misunderstanding if it is correctly perceived as the insult it was intended to be. Verbal dominance through wit is a tangible form of dominance in the normative symbolic order and is one of the reasons that women are supposed to be silent or demure in public, but I will leave that to the next chapter, which concerns how women and other marginalized groups have been silenced from using humor in public. Back to the class clown who may have difficulty if others in their age group do not appreciate their sophisticated parodies and satires. In that case, the child may find that adults are a better mirror and a young comedienne performing for the canasta and bridge crowd is born. Many comedians do report starting at an early age to entertain family and friends. Studies of comedians have shown that they self-report isolation, deprivations of many kinds and a generally traumatic childhood, but they are bright enough to consciously adopt another persona which channels their creativity into wit, such as we see in the female sleuths. They become Tricksters! Any child growing up in a marginalized group, such as Jews and African Americans in the United

States, may adopt this psychological strategy of finding humor everywhere in order to deal with the daily traumas they experience. This aspect of trauma and adaptation through humor is discussed in subsequent chapters of this book.

The soma of pleasure, desire, and jokes

Does it matter if the joke leads to a quick cheap laugh or does it have to make a deeper comment on the human condition for it to have value and integrity? Do jokes reflect reality and if so, whose? Is a joke merely an adaptation or does it have an aesthetic value as well as a physical value? Laughter and wit are differently processed in the body. When you laugh there is a moderate increase in your somatic arousal without any sudden drop immediately thereafter which is different from the body's reaction to something we find witty or humorous. The witty remark causes extreme divergences in psychic arousal; there is a sudden increase and then a sudden drop of energy. Although wit may produce laughter, it can also produce an intra-psychic reaction and just because someone is laughing it could be incorrect to draw the conclusion that something funny has occurred. Laughter can be a nervous response which discharges psychic energy that is not be related to humor at all. Laughing can be a coping mechanism in a social situation which produces anxiety. Sometimes we laugh so we don't kill.

Laughter, even without a joke which provokes it, and done for no other reason than the physical response, has a positive effect on the somatic body according to Dr. Madan Kataria, affectionately called the Laughing Yogi, who started a laughter club in Bombay in 1995. There are now 1800 laughing yoga clubs in India and another 700 worldwide. Laughter in the face of disaster has become a worldwide phenomenon. The first Sunday in May has been dubbed World Laughter Day where upwards of 10,000 gather each year in Copenhagen for a mass laugh. John Cleese, of *Monty Python* fame, and a recent attendee, called laughter a "force for democracy." Whether you agree with his politics or not, laugh anyway, since laughter can fool the body just as burlesque can fool the mind into laughing. As the Laughing Yogi says, "laughter can't solve your problems, but it can dissolve them."[2] Kurt Vonnegut in his memoir *A Man without A Country* (2005) commenting on *Slaughterhouse Five* (1969), his novel about the fire bombing of Dresden, recalls his humorous motivation for writing the famous novel: "all I really wanted to do was give people the relief of laughing" (p. 130). For Vonnegut, humor is a "way of holding off how awful life can be, to protect yourself" (p. 129). Even though Kant argues that humor can delude us only for a moment, but oh! what a moment it is![3] It is that transcendent moment which makes life worth living. It is the moments where Trickster lives.

Performance humor

Humor as performance is based in the desire for the pleasure of deeply transcendent play. Various words describe the process of attaining this state of reverie. Reverie provides the foundational support for tragedy and comedy, both of which can be traced to the rituals associated with the worship of Dionysius in Ancient Greece. Tragedy means goat song, from the Greek *tragos* and *ode*. The goat singers were intoxicated men dressed in goat skins celebrating wine as a homage to fertility during the Dionysian festivals. Cavorting like goats, townspeople would make fun of them and engage in witty criticisms of local politicians and other cultural elites. The word comedy comes from the Greek *konos* meaning to revel and make merry. The origin of all western conceptions of drama, whether performed or written, tragic or comedic, springs from the human desire to enter into the state of transcendent reverie one could experience as a participant of these Dionysian festivals. Parody, in its archaic past meant to mock by disguising in song, but it is essentially the art of disguise for humor's sake. The French *travestir* (to disguise) is used by the transvestite to humorously disguise their own sex. Other forms of comedic mockery are the burlesque, from the Italian *burla* meaning mockery. Burlesque is a comically exaggerated imitation which mocks but may not disguise. Trickster uses any and all of these forms with ease and always has.

Writing the Trickster

If the focus of Trickster humor is paradoxical absurdity, then Rabelais' (1494–1553) *Gargantua* (1532) and *Pantagruel* (1534 or 1535) written with the intent to make the reader laugh for joy while embracing the paradoxical reality of life must be considered as an exemplar of the form. Rabelais was a popular writer whose work was intended for the reader's private enjoyment subsequent to the widespread use of the new technology of the printing press. What ties Rabelais to the postmodern female Trickster in the guise of the fictive female sleuth is how he used written humorous narratives with subversive possibilities within the disguise of a simple tale. Mikhail Bakhtin (1968) the poststructural deconstructionist of the great carnivals of medieval Europe thought that Rabelais' work demonstrated a Trickster-like subversive element. Bakhtin, like Jung, linked the collective use of carnival with Trickster's appearance at critical junctures in the developmental cycles of culture. Focusing on the inversionary aspects of carnival where fools become kings, servants become aristocrats, priests become devils and scholars become dunces, Bakhtin concluded that these inversions opened a liminal space of transformation with these rituals and Trickster literary works actually creating the imaginal freedom of the Renaissance. Of course, others have criticized Rabelais as doing nothing but bringing buffoonery into the arts. Tainted or not by criticism, Rabelais' language oscillated between the serious and the salacious, the understandable to the obscure. While Bakhtin interprets the behavior of the Tricksters in Rabelais' work as opening the opportunity for new consciousness to integrate there is another aspect to carnival – the steam vent – that explains the vitality of Rabelaisian antics. The term Rabelaisian has come to mean a form of verbal comedy which concerns taboo areas in culture, using offensive language, exaggeration, and shape-shifting. To do this while maintaining your role and status in the collective required a cover and such was provided by the opportunity afforded in the liminal field the carnival constellated. Impropriety was tried out in a spirit of humor which could be easily disguised. Letting off steam is a variant of repression in the guise of fun and humor, but nothing is changed, rather the status quo is actually re-entrenched rather than destabilized. This kind of letting off steam may appear visually more intense, such as seen in exaggerated physical antics and grotesque costuming, but this variation of humor is not subversive because the individual participating in the humorous antics lacks the awareness that there is no ultimate resolution possible. The same antics, done with intentionality and consciousness, can be a subversive act of resistance and is one of the markers for Trickster energy in postmodernity.

Summary

Humor is a developmental adaptation which requires the mind and body to hold itself between the tension of the opposites in constant movement between the poles of reality and the imaginary as it makes sense of the nonsense and absurdity of life. Comedy, whether as performance or in written form, have both been used successfully by marginalized "others" within a culture to test the margins of safety and to let off psychic steam. All margins, like borderlands, are dangerous to a symbolic order based upon logos certainty. Where there is chaos there is no logos control and the fear that must be ameliorated is that Eros may rule in the borderlands without the legal or psychic restrictions found in communal culture.

Dionysius and Hermes add the emotional tone of melody and laughter to that dire Apollonian logos which has pre-empted the psychic field of humanity for too long. Apollo with the lyre is an image which evokes an awareness of the need for light of reason and the joy of music and humor to mediate both Apollo's and humanity's darkness because the compensation for the pain of life is joy. The orientation to joy – to have a sense of humor – is an affirmation of life in the face of pain and suffering. When Midas asked Silenus, Dionysius' companion, what is man's greatest happiness, Silenus laughs.

Trickster is an example of Eros using Logos – pleasure and thinking – as a way of being in the world that both appreciates the paradox and laughs in the face of that irresolvability. Humor and wit are also the most social forms of gaining pleasure outside of the dyad of sexual engagement. It is only through humor that we can face the horror of human life without turning to stone. Humor is essential to the transformative potentialities inherent in the Trickster and to the female sleuths I am investigating. Being humorous is a transgressive act because it encourages the critical eye to look the other way, thereby allowing the assumption to operate that these characters are "harmless and amusing teases, undeserving of serious, sustained attention," thereby missing the significance of the "unsettling impact of such a work" (Beebe 1981: 31). The most serious of themes can sometimes be presented only through humor which itself is Trickster energy; bridging seemingly contradictory and paradoxical elements. It is in this sense, of humor's ability to explicate a contradictory tone, to wrestle and harvest paradox, that humor can be used either to take control, to maintain power, or to overthrow authority. Trickster, the embodiment of humor itself, has constellated in postmodernity not to maintain power or take control but to overthrow. Humor can be a serious tool of transgression and transformation born of the imaginal realms as a psychological survival guide. It guides us to unite the paradoxical. It can teach us to unite all the while we are laughing.

Notes

1 The term "deep play" was first used by Clifford Gertz (1972).
2 Reported in *Time* Magazine, January 17, 2005: A26.
3 Citation found in Freud (1938: 636), citing *Zeitschrift für Psychologie*, XI, 1896.

Part IV

Re/storation

Chapter 10

Women *are* funny

Laughter as an antidote to dominance is perhaps indicated.
Virginia Woolf[1]

A revolution without humor is as hopeless as one without music.[2]

Introduction: is there a female sense of humor?

Is there a distinctly female sense of humor which differs from that which the mainstream culture considers humorous? Assuming arguendo that there is a difference when humor is imagined and shape-shifted through a female psyche do I label it *women's humor* or is there a distinct variant called *feminist* humor which can be imagined by either male or female if a female is at the center of the humor, as subject not object? Are the differences found between male and female humor the product of gender socialization which have merged into our collective conceptions of the feminine or are there distinct variants which identify a Feminine sense of humor which is archetypal in nature? Is there then an archetypal Masculine sense of humor, and does it manifest differently through the male and female body?

An example of a postmodern female Trickster

Mae West (1893–1980) was a postmodern Trickster. She spoke truth to power through humor and was not anybody's victim or adjunct. Mae West was different from other female comics because she offered her audience an image which signified a reinscription of sex as being both fun and an expression of love. Mae West's sexual honesty was similar to the self-conscious irony we find in the fictive female sleuths, especially Blanche White, whose humor infuses the next chapter. But Mae West did more than act, she was in charge of her own life, even choosing her own lead actors.[3] Six months after the release of *She Done Him Wrong* (1933) the National Legion of Decency pointed to Mae West and the film as one of the major reasons for the "necessity" of the organization.[4] In the film, Mae West plays Lady Lou, who offers up her subversive philosophical gems in the guise of comedy, "It was a toss up between whether I go in for diamonds or sing in the choir. The choir lost." She didn't just act and choose her lead actors, she retained final control over all aspects of her films, including writing the screenplays for *I'm No Angel* (1933) and *Belle of the Nineties* (1934), which broke the color barrier in American cinema by using an African American jazz band. West created the film persona of the bad girl with a heart of gold, mimicking and exaggerating vaudeville and burlesque personas found on the popular stage – but Mae West differed from other screen portrayals of heroines – she had agency, authority and autonomy. She does not get married, she doesn't die, she doesn't exile herself, she has no parents to contend with, no children and no husband, yet she triumphs in film after film. Her portrayals clearly linked sex and power in a woman, which standing alone is not anything new, woman have always exploited the power available to them through their sexual charms, but what Mae West did that was a postmodern female Trickster move is to use this Eros energy to attack social hypocrisy, the prevailing sexual double standards and all the pretensions of the rich and powerful she could lampoon with her wit. She was a social worker who refused to be a victim and like the fictive female sleuths and the postmodern virginal Tricksters, Mae West had no intention of changing who she was to fit anyone's perception of who she should be. Mae West got attention with her wisecracks, and that is exactly what they were, wisdom. She reinscribed the meaning of femininity and that's why she became the favorite of the drag crowd. She reveled in playing interesting women who took center stage without caring whether she was labeled as bad or good. She was much more interesting than stars like Lucy Ricardo whose existence and comic pranks always played off her role as housewife to Ricky Ricardo. In Lucy's world sex was never out in the open, but with Mae West you could count on hearing slightly salacious jokes all the time, which made her an outcast in polite society since all women who tell jokes, no matter where they live, are considered sexually promiscuous (Barreca 1991: 50). How Tricksterish!

Differences between male and female humor

That there is an observable distinction between male and female humor is now beyond serious discussion, the focus has moved onto cataloguing the characteristics which research has replicated and the research itself has found its way into popular culture. In the September–October 2005 issue of the popular magazine *Psychology Today*, the differences between male and female humor is broken down into the categories of attitude, modus operandi, focus, goal, and what the target is. According to *Psychology Today*'s review of the literature, men perceive joke telling as a competitive game, while women report feeling more cooperative when they tell jokes. No surprises there, this is the same finding from the playground and from same sex groupings throughout childhood development. The replicated research also found that men tend to focus their joking on a particular animate object while women tell jokes using ideas and concepts as objects. Women make general observations while men start jokes with, "Have you heard the one about?" Men tend to focus on what an individual does while women focus on what anyone might do in a particular situation. The male goal in telling jokes is to obtain a rhetorical one-upmanship while women tend to spotlight issues. Men target the weak while women target the powerful. Men tend to use sarcasm while women kid and men use a negative tone in jokes while women use a more positive tone. Is this popular cultural summary mirrored in the actual research done on women's humor? The answer is yes.

Regina Barreca, author of the classic text on women's subversive use of humor, *They Used To Call Me Snow White . . . but I Drifted* (1991) agrees with other feminist theoreticians that third wave women's humor, just like third stage women's writing, tends to place women at the center of their own narrative while earlier women's humor paralleled the "how to get a man" or "do I need a man" schools of women's writing discussed earlier in this work. Barreca found that women report experiencing particularly acute states of psychological dissonance when men are unaware of how their jokes cast a pejorative light on all women. This occurs because the context from which the male tends to make his jokes are within and from a position of being the implied norm of the collective culture, while women tend to question the normative structure itself. Women tend to question whether their perceptions are accurate, while men never ask whether their perceptions are accurate.

How do these differences in perceptions and subject matter play out (pun intended) in the sexual area of jokes? Research demonstrates that both sexes appreciate sexual jokes. Freud theorized that men like sexual jokes because it makes a confidant of the subject/hearer at the expense of the object/woman. This type of joking is based on a psychological conspiracy among members of the in-group (men) which makes fun of members of the out-group (women). This configuration operates both horizontally and vertically. Horizontally the positions are reversed in situations where the two groups have somewhat equal positions in culture, thus women as in-group members make fun of men as out-group members. Vertically, sub-ordinated peoples make fun of elites and elites make fun of subordinated peoples; this is the classic Trickster reversal discussed in Chapter 8. Replicated research has found however that there remain differences which are significant in how this in-group/out-group humor is manifested both horizontally and vertically. In the following example we have the classic in-group male-oriented joke. "Q: What's the difference between a wife and a job? A: After five years the job still sucks." Imagine being a woman in the room when that joke is told. If she doesn't laugh she (most probably) will be told or it will be implicitly assumed by the in-group that she doesn't have a sense of humor. The joke is about a woman refusing to perform a specific sexual act on a man which is then generalized as applicable to all women. Barreca (1991) reports that this joke is an advertisement for the explicit sense of contempt felt by the teller for the object of the joke. She illustrates with the following example as the difference in sexual joking between men and women that has a fundamentally different dynamic: "Q: Do you know why women have poor spatial perception? A: Because we've been told that 3 inches is 10." Barreca's example is sexual like the first joke and shares a mathematical orientation but it is not about a man refusing to perform a sexual act, it is a reversal on the male brag of penis size and makes fun of someone in a superior, not inferior, status position in culture. Another example would be Mae West's famous line, "Is that a pistol in your pocket or are you just happy to see me?" which also undercuts the male idealization as stealth aggressor. It brings out into open terrain that which is not supposed to be noticed, and if noticed, not said, and in doing so humorously shape-shifts the energy from aggression to erotic sexual energy. These reinscriptions examine relationships in a witty way, similar to the perennial joke I hear from middle-aged women: "I want a man in my life but not in my house." But I don't think I have ever heard that joke in mixed company, and this is another sexual difference which can be observed in the jokes told by men and women. Usually women will tell sexual jokes only when they are with other women, but men will tell any type of sexual joke in mixed company and then accuse a woman or anyone who doesn't laugh of not getting the joke. This explains why Mae West was considered a "bad girl" because she tested the margins by telling the pistol joke in mixed company, but the pistol joke is not a put down of men like the male joke about the blow job is a put down of women.

Women who laugh at jokes which put them down individually or put all women down are actually in a state of disassociation from their own feminine natures. This is an important point because the normative symbolic order could not have lasted as long as it has without some degree of disassociation of one half of its population; women. Using disassociation as a psychological defensive posture buttresses the argument that a diminished sense of individual identity is inevitable as a woman introjects the logical syllogisms of the normative symbolic order. An example would be this joke: "Teller to mixed group: All women are either bimbos or sluts, which are you?" The woman thinks (consciously or unconsciously) to herself, I am not a bimbo or a slut therefore I am not a woman you define. WHO AM I THEN? Or she laughs at the joke with the others, thereby colluding in the calumny but retaining her spot in the group. If this exchange takes place in the type of physical and psychological terrain which supports a joking response, a woman comfortable with her own autonomy, agency and authority and who is practiced in the verbal art of wit, returns the volley, thereby proving she is not a bimbo. This is what the female Trickster does. It is how V.I. responds when Bobby, her father's best friend, recommends that she go home and cook food and be a good little wife. She responds by joking and telling him she was already a lousy wife, thank you.

Is humor an alternative to fighting?

If humor encourages men to use words and not fists then it may be a cathartic experience and a developmental leap to reconfigure the hostility and aggression into a witty retort rather than physical force. But what about women, who are not supposed to have anger or hostility, especially towards the normative symbolic order, in comparison to men who are encouraged to engage in protective activities which include violence as an option to enforce rules or rights. Men are encouraged to confront from age 2, while women either because of their greater impulse control (see Chapter 3) or through gender socialization, avoid confrontation by walking away. If a woman defends herself through confrontation, whether physical or the intellectual jousting of joke and jest, the normative symbolic order names it as problematic. And if the subject matter is sexual, then the irrefutable presumption of promiscuity is triggered; that's why Mae West was labeled a "bad girl." For men, wit disguises feelings and provides an alternative socially acceptable way to demonstrate aggression and anger while for women, humor reveals rather than disguises feelings; that is why Trickster is the mask that reveals. Women do not make fun of what people cannot change such as social handicaps and physical appearance.

Women's humor tends to attack through subversion the deliberate choices of the powerful; their hypocrisies, affectations and the mindless following of the acquisitive and consumption oriented social status quo. The way that women's humor challenges authority – its subversive method – is by refusing to take it seriously. This is why the female Trickster is more dangerous than the traditional Trickster, who may serve a cathartic purpose in letting steam off from the symbolic order. The traditional Trickster, although testing boundaries, leaves the basic configuration, the existence of the social order, very much untouched. By not questioning its very existence traditional Tricksters may be boundary crossers, but they do not confront with the anger and truth that energize women's humor. The essence of the energy I call the postmodern female Trickster *must* question the very existence of the patriarchal symbolic order through humor. Where the traditional Trickster lets off steam by playing at the margins, the female Trickster in postmodernity deconstructs the margins and enters new terrain – the terrain of transformation of the order itself. And while this postmodern female Trickster energy may have begun as a culturally inflected archetype found only in the Anglo-American literary and popular culture scene, it now has international impact and part of my project is to name the new energy so that it can be a part of the ongoing discourse. This female Trickster transforms through the use of humor by channeling angry and rebellious energy into an adaptive phenomenon; a joke, a witty remark, or caricaturing something found offensive in the symbolic order. This female Trickster does not want to rebalance the old system, it wants to build a new system. This is certainly a different Trickster than Scheherazade, who had no chance of even dreaming of changing the system.

Whose culture is it anyway?

Let's assume for the moment that the psychological dynamic of humor in both women and men is propelled by the desire to satisfy aspects of the pleasure principle. Let's also agree arguendo that both men and women enjoy pleasure. If male and female humor is different, is pleasure different for men and women? If the pleasure principle is grounded for men in rising to the top of the hierarchy available to them within the symbolic order of the patriarchal epoch then perhaps for women, who have been caged within that symbolic order, it is the destruction of that order.

Women's jokes, just like men's, are based upon the culture from which the joker comes. Female culture is different from male culture, but male culture is the normative social order so as the dominant group men haven't historically gotten women's jokes, just as slave owners usually didn't get the jokes the slaves didn't want them to get. Dominant groups never have to know as much about the "other" as the "other" has to know about the dominant group's mores, customs, and humor. When the fictive female sleuths are witty they do not reaffirm women's traditional subordinate role in the normative symbolic order; when they do put women's weaknesses forward it is so the reader can re-evaluate them. The Trickster move is away from women using the humor of self-deprecation or deprecation of other women towards witticisms which showcase the play, delight, autonomy, authority, and agency involved. The Trickster energy here is not only humor reconfigured but also movement itself; the humor is not stuck in the same old place. Listen to how Kinsey Millhone reinscribes the traditional ideal of the wedding dress as desirable when someone questions her about her marriages and the reason they failed:

> Despite the fact that I had been married twice, I'd never had a formal wedding. The closest I'd ever come was a bride of Frankenstein outfit one Halloween when I was in the second grade. I had fangs and fake blood, and my aunt drew clumsy black stitches up and down my face.
>
> (Grafton 1993: 87)

In the selection Kinsey has successfully deflected the aggression of the inquiry which sought to establish her as a failure because she did not succeed in the designated way a woman finds fulfillment by reinscribing the image of marriage with the monster Frankenstein. When a female Trickster encounters aggression in humor which is hostile to women, it can be deflected or it can be directed by the woman. One way might be not to laugh but to show one's teeth, through a subversively intended smile, after all, teeth are weapons. When V.I. is questioned by her neighbor about why she let their dog go into a dirty lagoon she responds:

> Characteristic. In order to be forgiven I had to be scolded. I barred my teeth in the semblance of a smile. "I know, I know, I begged and pleaded with her, but you know how it is – lady wants to do something, she does it without taking advice from anyone."

To which her neighbor responds as a Trickster himself:

> He gave me a sharp look. "Seems to me I've known ladies like that, uh hah. And then you got to just ride it out until they're ready to listen to you again."

To which V.I. responds with her teeth again, but this time the meaning is quite different:

> I smiled significantly. "That's right. That's it exactly. Now, how about some coffee."
>
> (Paretsky 1990: 115)

What is a feminist comic sensibility?

The postmodern female Trickster I have been describing does have a feminist comic sensibility. What this means is that the details of women's lives are presented so women, the implied reader and audience, can mock traditional female roles. Revisions that encourage the mocking of the restricted roles historically permitted to women in traditional culture affirm rather than denigrate women's experience. This is not a competitive move, rather this is a mirroring dynamic which offers the opportunity for the type of psychic integration which occurs when you are not the "other" but are part of the group making and understanding the wit. Other marginalized groups, such as the slaves in the American South, used the technique brilliantly and this is discussed in the chapter on Re/storation The use of wit as a coping device indicates evidence of intelligence, personal strength, quick thinking and a sense of self as authority. These words are not usually used as descriptors of women in traditional cultures but do describe attributes of the female Trickster. Feminist humorists, such as Regina Barreca, correctly note that male humor acts as a safety valve which purges male desire and frustration while female humor is an incendiary device which transforms energy into action. Defined this way, female humor, like the fictive female sleuth, simply does not fit any "classic" definition of humor any more than the fictive female sleuth narratives fit within "classic" notions of the detective novel or Trickster narratives or Madonna and Cyndi Lauper fitting into traditional notions of women's performance art.

Prior to a feminist perspective being applied to humor, all theories, even those of postmodernity such as Bakhtin, who considered humor the "unofficial nature of the world explained" only brought into the foreground cultural energies which had been enclosed in the background, but the field, the normative order, was not challenged or changed. Thus, humor from a male point of view ultimately serves the purpose of upholding conservative conventions even while certain aspects are made fun of, thus providing the steam vent. Anything that has to do with renewal and regeneration by definition upholds the familiar symbolic order. Vulgar and debased presentations of the familiar provide a catharsis for desire and frustration which is the ritualistic purpose of an annual event such as carnival. When the spectacle and comedic reverie are over, it is time to go back to what was. Barreca correctly concludes that women's humor is like refusing to hand back the costume after the carnival is over.

Psychological considerations

Does putting on a comic persona fueled by wit provide the same impetus for psychic integration as having authority in the sense of internal psychic integration and sovereignty. Feeling comfortable enough to express your self by making your own jokes is a way of taking control of your own life away from the normative symbolic order. It is a refusal to introject their projections. Returning their volley with your own perceptions operates as a reinscription and resignification. The wit in any group has always been acknowledged as being among the most potent because when you make the jokes you become potent with authority. When you are someone who laughs along with the group, even when you do not think the joke or witticism is funny, you are complicit with the teller but are not the teller. When the fictive female sleuth narratives are read, the wit in the narrative produces an echo in the hearer, with the author as teller. The female Trickster may still be on the margins but her jokes and wit are shared through the permeable membrane that is the reading process. And this reading process as active imagination is transformative. Kinsey Millhone has the same experience with reading:

Afterward I did what any other trained professional would do: I walked the six steps into the living room, flipped off my shoes, and settled on the sofa, where I covered myself in a big puffy comforter and started reading a book. Within minutes, I'd been sucked through a wormhole into a fictional world, traveling faster than the speed of words into a realm without sound and without gravity.

(Grafton 2001: 85)

So does Kate Shugak:

Kate, let alone at the University of Alaska at Fairbanks [UAF], went into hibernation, emerging only at the invitation of an inspired English teacher, who taught her how to read recreationally. From that point on, she had never been lonely.

(Stabenow 2001: 49)

Humor has always dealt with the toughest matters; sex, death and all the other tragedies which are a regular part of life. For the female Trickster the use of sex and humor in situations which are filled with ambiguity and danger is a coping mechanism which brings pleasure. This type of humor can open the reader to explore hard subjects. The type of psychic exploration I am referring to is done through the process of sharing humorous stories rather than through jokes which shame or the one-upmanship (pun intended) of many traditional jokes. Using humor to share experience has the capacity to open a subject up, especially a taboo one, and thus humor can be a way of being in dialogic without frightening the listener with our deepest truths. Humor is the dialogic movement of energy is Trickster itself. As dialogic, humor gives a plasticity to the psyche which can hold the center between the paradoxical energies of strength and vulnerability. This is a divine method of finding meaning in the world and therefore I agree with Lewis Hyde that *Trickster Makes This World* (1998). Humor's energy affirms the self with a process and a methodology that meets challenges and channels fear into pleasure by translating pain into courage. Laughter, the natural constituency of humor, declares the person laughing an integrated individual because of the perspective and control they bring to the situation for the ability to laugh, to lose yourself in laughter is proof of an inner confidence. Of course I am not talking about nervous, anxiety produced laughter but the laughter of the belly laugh when you really get it.

A woman with a sense of humor is dangerous

The world tuned upside down can prove that the world has no rightful position at all. This kind of comedy terrifies those who hold order dear. It should.

(Barreca 1994: 33)

Women and humor are a dangerous combination because humor refuses to accept the givens and women are socialized to be a given. Even though women are now participating in the western normative symbolic order to a greater extent than ever before, there is still an implicit assumption that women are paradoxically entitled to a greater degree of protection from danger than other members of the culture except for children or the infirm. Yet, women are engaged in the most dangerous physical activities including childbirth and they still do most of the actual work in the world, dangerous or not. Even though western women have legal identity along with greater freedom of physical and psychological movement, life is still quite segregated, albeit in a more subtle fashion. Try to find a woman playing golf with men on a weekend morning without getting booed off the course or at least being made fun of for trying to keep up with the boys. In fact, weekend mornings on the golf course are still where major deals are made and women are simply not present. Women surgeons are suspiciously absent from operating theaters and women litigators are few and far between except in fields which focus on women and children. The dynamics discussed previously regarding jokes in mixed company are still in operation.

Since I am making the argument that Trickster as humor can be a subversive force which first challenges and then rearranges the symbolic order and women are in the public domain to a greater extent than before, why is a funny woman still considered dangerous? Let's recall that the traditional Trickster's appearance in a cultural milieu was twofold, not only; for the purpose of testing boundaries but also to provide a steam vent for frustrations in the hierarchal arrangement of a particular culture through the use of humor and nonsense. Women using humor become dangerous because they do not want nor intend to stop at the steam venting stage. I have discussed humor as an evolutionary process; how tickling gives way to body buffoonery which then morphs into word play and ends with the highly developed forms of humor in literary and performance satire and parody, but I have also discussed how girls develop differently in early childhood and that the symbolic order's normative humor is based on male subjectivity and female objectivity. Why would we as a culture expect that women would produce the same kinds of humor that men did once women are the subject rather than the object of the humor? And while women's humor uses similar forms such as irony, puns, repartee, irreverence, and sarcasm towards those in authority and those who act with arrogance, women have used not the carnival but literature and performance art. It is this act of encasing humor in normative forms of discourse such as literature and performance without the markers of mask and disguise, or excess and buffoonery, which is so dangerous to the symbolic order. Think of the laughter of Bertha as she burns down the house in *Jane Eyre*.

Another area of women's humor which is dangerous to the symbolic order can be seen in how women's comedy does not give the expected ending even though the context may be normative, so there is a sense of dislocation in juxtaposition with traditional cultural values and norms. In *Mansfield Park* (Austen 1814), Fanny's refusal to marry is seen as a refusal to supply closure. The symbolic order rests upon a foundational assumption that certainty can be brought out of chaos, that there is "proper" resolution even concerning humor, which has its basis in chaos. When there is conflict in the symbolic order, there are rules to apply for resolution and then there is the happy ending, all tied up. This is just an evolution on male child playground behavior where rules and regulations and a hierarchical structure is one of the first elements to emerge when boys play in groups. Humor as representative of the archetypal symbolic order follows the same pattern, there are rules and regulations on the timing and content of carnival and when all is over, not much has changed.

Women tend to look more for recognition rather than resolution – which they know is an illusion. Women ask questions about the structure of the symbolic order and whether it has any right to exist; they do not ask questions about whether the right rules were applied. This dynamic is similar to what occurs on the playground, where boys first set the rules for a game and then all conflict is handled within the rules structure, including at a later age, the rules for war. Girls change the game when there is a conflict; they do not resort to rules (Maccoby 1998). Carol Gilligan's *In a Different Voice* (1982) demonstrates the dynamic beyond the playground. When asked whether one should break into a drugstore to get drugs desperately needed for a dying spouse that were not affordable, women did not resort to rules but went beyond the posed question. Asked directly whether they would break into the building and steal the medicine, women sidestepped the question as they engaged in figuring out alternative ways to structure the situation, such as, perhaps I could go and talk to the pharmacist's wife about getting the medicine, or perhaps I could work at the drugstore to pay for the medicine. Women saw the question set up itself as too confining, and challenged the expectation that ethics or morality could be judged by how one applied the rules to the situation. Gilligan concluded that women did indeed speak in a different voice that was not less than but just different from how men viewed decision making (Gilligan 1982).

Women's different voice speaks in a variant of indirect subversive humor rather than humor which could be considered a direct confrontation to the symbolic order. This is the type of humor used by marginalized people when they are enclosed within a symbolic order which they did not design. Using humor with awareness does not engage in counter-productive strategy, therefore it is not in a woman's (or other marginalized others') best interest to anger those who are in absolute authority and control over their lives, even if they could imagine a witty and on point reply that would skewer those who were trivializing their role and status in a particular culture. One of the best examples of this can be seen in the work of Anita Loos (1889–1981), who wrote the brilliant play/movie *Gentlemen Prefer Blondes* (1926, 1953). Lorelei Lee, the main character, was witty, but she hid it, for if a man couldn't understand your wit he couldn't be mad at you. The entire play is double entendres and innuendo; the humor behind the witticisms can be characterized as "in-group" humor of women that most men do not get. However, men do like this film because the play/movie can be perceived as a simplistic exposé of big-busted women and therefore not to be taken seriously; that is, men do not have to suspend their disbelief in order to enjoy the narrative and performance aspects of the show. It is a spoof which allows multiple perspectives and illustrates why woman and other marginalized groups use irony so often, for the ironic witticism appeals to those in power who can misinterpret the joke and still think of themselves as correct and in control. Anyone can be taken in with false flattery, as in the story of the Emperor's New Clothes. Now that is an ironic tale, but did the Emperor get it?

It is well beyond discussion that women do speak in a different voice but at this point in the research we don't know whether it's nature or nurture, just that it is. I have also discussed the paradoxical nature of humor; motivation for it comes from the desire to satisfy the pleasure principle yet as a subversive technique for marginalized groups humor has both the energy and desire to destroy the symbolic order. Viewed from this perspective humor as a destructive force is also a reinscription which turns the aggressor's energy back on the aggressor. This is the essence of feminist humor, turning the aggressor's humorous energy back on the aggressor. Feminist humor is not about seeking resolution through some type of happy ending. For if humor has a happy ending I want to ask, whose happy ending? From a feminist point of view is marriage a tragedy or comedy? In Fay Weldon's *The Life and Loves of a She-Devil* (1983) the protagonist ruins her husband's career, she abandons her kids and kills her rival; there is no way to view the film as other than a direct confrontation to established values of home and family. As a book it was a bestseller, but when it was turned into a movie starring Meryl Streep and Roseanne Barr it did not do so well. Most of the reviewers of film are still men and they remain the dominant opinion makers in the mass media, but there is also another reason why the film did not do as well as the book. Women read the book, but men and women attend films and all the research shows that girls will watch what boys want to watch but boys refuse to watch what girls like. Girls will sit through *G.I. Joe* cartoons but boys will not watch *My Little Pony*. It starts as early as the cartoon age but continues unabated. Something written with woman as the implied audience is still used as stigmata; today bestsellers which center on women are dubbed *chick lit* as a marginalizing technique, just as when Nathaniel Hawthorne complained that those scribbling women were getting all the sales and notoriety.

Anger

> Comedy can effectively channel anger and rebellion by first making
> them appear to be acceptable and temporary phenomenon, no doubt to
> be purged by laughter, and then by harnessing the released energies,
> rather than dispersing them.
>
> (Barreca 1994: 33)

Those who are very angry with the culture they live in for the way they and
their kin are treated have successfully channeled their anger through
comedy. There has always been linkage between comedy and anger, but
there has always been a disjunction in that same culture; women are not
supposed to show or demonstrate anger, so what do we do when women
use anger in their comedy. Is any woman who uses anger in service of their
comedy a "bad girl?"

Humor can clear space within an unhappy situation by making what is
metaphorically dense more porous. As an alternative to complaining about
a situation, using humor can make it easier for the dominant culture to
integrate the dissension when anger is displayed through the adoption of a
playful and amusing stance towards the irritant. If a woman complains,
she is labeled an annoying neurotic, a bitch, a witch, or a hysteric or her
behavior may be blamed on hormones. Utilizing humor as subversive
creative energy therefore is a psychological trick of the female Trickster in
postmodernity. It is in the fluidity involved in psychologically inverting the
symbolic order that the Trickster develops the psychological authority that
is concomitant with mirroring, which is in essence positive attention. The
female Trickster laughs at herself before anyone else can. Instead of the fear
of looking like a fool the female Trickster decides herself to play the fool.

Women writing redux: women writing funny

In earlier sections of this book I made a point of differentiating a feminist
perspective, both in writing and analyzing the work of men and women and
writing by women. In this section I review what funny women have written.
In other sections of this work I focus on the characters produced through the
imaginations of women; here I focus on the work produced by those female
imaginations which utilized humor as primary process. As soon as women
began writing for money, they wrote humor. Anne Bradstreet (1612–1672)
was America's first published poet. She used her wit to challenge those who
thought she should not write. Her *The Tenth Muse Lately Sprung Up in
America* (1650 and 1675) (published before Jane Austen) perfected the
technique of staying within the domestic realm but hitting her target. The
early colonial period in America produced Mercy Otis Warren (1728–1814)
who wrote political satire which denounced the British before, during and

after the Revolutionary War. Ann Stephens (1813–1886) satirized the pretense and shallowness of urban high society in her novel *High Life in New York* (1843) but unfortunately she used a male protagonist. Frances (Fanny) Burney (1752–1840) was a Trickster figure who opened the doors of domestic comedy to later writers such as Jane Austen. Her novel *Evelina, or The History of a Young Lady's Entrance into the World* (1778) was praised for its comical qualities even as it was denigrated for not following the classical form. Burney challenged her critics by penning *The Witlings* (1779), a comedy which satirized the pretensions of those who criticized her work. Burney has enjoyed a Renaissance of her work, with her comedy *A Busy Day* (1800) being produced in London in 2000.[5] Burney did a stint as a lady's maid for Charlotte, queen consort of George III of Great Britain, a position she did not want nor enjoy but was forced upon her by her pretension-seeking father. In the following excerpt from a letter to her sister, Burney uses wit as her method for adapting to life's inevitable tragedies.

Directions for coughing, sneezing, or moving, before the King and Queen: In the first place you must not cough. If you find a cough tickling in your throat, you must arrest it from making any sound; if you find yourself choking with the forbearance, you must choke – but not cough. In the second place you must not sneeze. If you have a vehement cold, you must take no notice of it; if your nose membranes feel a great irritation, you must hold your breath; if a sneeze still insists upon making its way, you must oppress it, by keeping your teeth grinding together; if the violence of the repulse breaks some blood vessel, you must break the blood vessel – but not sneeze.

(quoted in Barreca 1996: 133)

Frances Miriam Berry (1814–1852) was writing at the same time as Mark Twain and although she died before the age of 40, her *The Widow Bedott Papers* (1856) sold over 100,000 copies and was a national bestseller. Emily Dickinson (1830–1886) doesn't usually come to mind as a comic writer but her poems are filled with satiric, playful and irreverent Trickster energy:

A little Madness in the Spring
Is wholesome even for the King,
But God be with the Clown –
Who ponders this tremendous scene –
This whole Experiment of Green –
As if it were his own!
    (quoted in Walker and Dresner 1988: 1333)

Josephine Dodge Daskam Bacon (1876–1961) wrote satires on child raising and even her titles are Tricksterish: *The Woman Who Used Her Theory, The*

Woman Who Took Things Literally, *The Woman Who Had Broad Views*
and *The Woman Who Caught the Idea* (Walker and Dresner 1988: 140).
Gertrude Stein (1874–1946) used the Trickster's doubling technique to
prominence in her work and Charlotte Perkins Gilman (1860–1935) had a
brilliant sense of irony; just take a look at her book *Herland* (1979) which
posits a culture made up by and for women where men are held in a corral
for breeding purposes. Alice Duer Miller (1874–1942) wrote the syndicated
newspaper column "Are Women People?" before World War I. Here's one
of her finest ditties:

> Father, what is a legislature?
> A representative body elected by the people of the state.
> Are women people?
> No, my son, criminals, lunatics and women are not people.
> Do legislators legislate for nothing?
> Oh, no; they are paid a salary.
> By whom?
> By the people.
> Are women people?
> Of course, my son, just as much as men are.
> (quoted in Walker and Dresner 1988: 203)

Anita Loos wrote *Gentlemen Prefer Blondes* (1926) which George Santayana
considered "the most philosophical book ever written by a woman" (quoted
in Walker and Dresner 1988: 228). The diary of Lorilei Lee, which is at the
heart of the play and film, was itself a take-off on H.L. Mencken's "boobus
americanus." Lorilei was an exemplar of the wise/innocent naive Trickster.
Zora Neale Hurston (1891–1960) was known as a wit in the Harlem
Renaissance as much as Dorothy Parker was known as the female wit of the
Algonquin Round Table. In Hurston's *Their Eyes Were Watching God*
(1937) Janie finds happiness with a man with whom she can laugh as an
equal.[6] William du Bois and Marcus Garvey were presented in coursework
about African Americans but not Jessie Redmon Fauset (1882–1961), who
was a contemporary of both and promoted the careers of Countee Cullen
and Langston Hughes. Her work had a sense of irony without outrage
because she knew that prejudice was self-evidently absurd. Alice Duer
Miller and Florence Guy were part of a group of early-twentieth-century
columnists and essayists who addressed the foibles of gender bias in popular
widely circulated magazines. A continuing series of any sort encourages a
relationship between the reader and the character's development, which is
why I use *Sex and the City*, a weekly cable television show which ran for
over six years as an example of female Trickster manifestation in the twenty-
first century.

If periodicals were the place Trickster could get a foothold in the late nineteenth and early twentieth centuries, then periodicals it would be. Helen Rowland used her column format along with others like Fanny Fern and Frances Whitaker in a similar way as Erma Bombeck and Ellen Goodman. Even Dorothy Parker, one of the few acknowledged female wits of the twentieth century, was conspicuous by her absence from Richler's *Best of Modern Humor* (1983). Parker used the form of light verse which has long been a favorite of women humorists:

> *General Review of the Sex Situation*
> Woman wants monogamy;
> Man delights in novelty.
> Love is woman's moon and sun;
> Man has other forms of fun.
> Woman lives but in her lord;
> Count to ten, and man is bored.
> With this the gist and sum of it,
> What earthly good can come of it?
> (quoted in Walker and Dresner 1988: 266)

At first reading, this verse seems to put Parker squarely in the biology is destiny camp, but her work can also be seen as a Trickster doubling on women's sentimental verse; is she commenting upon a universal truism about love or about how ridiculous that stereotypical view is? Margaret Halsey was one of a group of women humorists who didn't use a domestic situation as the basis for her humor. During World War II she saw first hand the discrimination African American and Jewish soldiers were subjected to at the Stage Door Canteen where she volunteered and where all service personnel were supposed to be welcomed. She wrote two books dealing with these issues – *Some of My Best Friends are Soldiers* (1944) and *Color Blind* (1946) – but the best example of her wry sense of humor can be found in her "Memo to Junior Hostesses" where she advised that "intelligence has nothing absolutely nothing to do with the amount of pigment in the skin, if it had, you would all be much stupider when sunburned" (quoted in Walker and Dresner 1988: 326).

Cornelia Otis Skinner, Shirley Jackson (who also wrote the classic short story, *The Lottery*), and Jean Kerr perfected the Trickster doubling style of comically playing up the domestic standards they couldn't master while simultaneously questioning those standards through the absurd situations they found themselves in. By sharing the absurdity, these humorists made the implied woman reader aware that everyone was falling short of standards that were impossible to attain. While none of these women created a serialized reoccurring character, the columns themselves and how often they appeared created the same opportunity for relationship as serial-izations and continuing characters; in many ways Erma Bombeck and many other women humorists used their own domestic situations as continuing and serialized character portrayals. In this group are Peg Bracken, Jean Kerr as well as Erma Bombeck, whose witty repartee about being a housewife ran in over 900 newspapers in the United States and Canada in 1985. Erma was always skewing experts who never changed a diaper or set foot in suburbia with the truth, as absurd as it was. She played both sides as Trickster when she used her humor to show both how absurd the experts view of what domestic life could be was as well as how absurd the actual reality was. She was a master at using wild exaggeration, parody and even burlesque to do away with the myth of the supermom. Women made Peg Bracken's *I Hate To Cook Book* (1960) a bestseller while men voiced the opinion that the title was inappropriate, giving women the wrong idea about the wonders of cooking for a family. Of course, that was precisely the point.

All the women writers I discuss in this section employed humor to undermine the propaganda machine after World War II which told Rosie the Riveter to go home and bake cookies and be happy while doing it. I am speaking about elite white women, of course, but these were the authors whose writing was popular in mainstream cultural contexts. There were women who satirized the righteous by making them look ridiculous through puns and word inventions like Felicia Lamport who transformed T.S. Eliot's "The Love Song of J. Alfred Prufrock" (1915) into "The Love Song of R. Milhous Nixon" (1973). The peach Prufrock wouldn't eat was transformed into Nixon's bout with impeachment, and Prufrock's meas-urement of his life through the metaphor of coffee spoons was transformed into Nixon's life measured in reels of tape. Although her work did not place women at center focus it demonstrated that women humorists could go head to head with any man. There was one female humor columnist who had a distinctly psychological tone to her work and eventually did go for analytical training, but before that period in her life, Judith Viorst articulated the ennui and anxieties felt by elite and mostly white middle-class women who were caught between the demands of being supermom and being a reluctant homemaker. Viorst's columns gave humorous voice to what it felt like being a social radical acting like a domestic conformist.

And then came Erica Jong's *Fear of Flying* (1972) and the reinscription of sexual mores through humor began in earnest. Here for the first time was outrageous humor and sexual fantasies in a woman with agency. When Isadora actually gets on the train she wryly scrutinizes herself and revealed comic acumen quite like the fictive female sleuths Tricksters. Isadora was certainly a Trickster and in her wake followed Rita Mae Brown (1973), who gave us uproariously funny gay women in *Rubyfruit Jungle*. Fran Leibowitz shifted from targeting the domestic world to looking the outside world squarely in the face and saying ugh to the ridiculousness of what passed for reality. But by this time things were really changing and women from all segments of society, not just the white elite were expressing their voices in humor. Chapter 11, which deals with Blanche White as Re/Storation Agent, explores the long history of female humor in the African American tradition.

Gloria Steinem deserves an entire book on how she has infused the feminist agenda with humor. Her work utilizes the classic reversal technique which she learned as a writer for the political television humor show *That Was The Week That Was* and as a writer for *Mad Magazine*. Her technique is the commonsense exposure of the absurdity of sexism. I loved reading her satires on men's superiority. "If Men Could Menstruate" and her piece for *Ms.* "On Womb Envy" were assertive takes on taboo subjects and are classics in the field. Below are just a few short excerpts from her work:

Reading Freud made me just as skeptical about penis envy. The power of giving birth makes "womb envy" more logical, and an organ as external and unprotected as the penis makes men very vulnerable indeed. . . . Whatever a "superior" group has will be used to justify its superiority, and whatever an "inferior" group has will be used to justify its plight. Black men were given poorly paid jobs because they were said to be "stronger" than white men, while all women were relegated to poorly paid jobs because they were said to be "weaker." As the little boy said when asked if he wanted to be a lawyer like his mother, "Oh, no, that's women's work." Logic has nothing to do with oppression.

So what would happen if suddenly, magically, men could menstruate and women could not?

Clearly menstruation would become an enviable, boast worthy, masculine event:

Men would brag about how long and how much. . . .

Statistical surveys would show that men did better in sports and won more Olympic medals during their periods. . . .

Street guys would invent slang ("He's a three pad man") and "give fives" on the corner with some exchange like, "Man, you lookin good!" "Yeah, man, I'm on the rag!" . . .

Medical schools would limit women's entry ("They might faint at the sight of blood").

Of course, intellectuals would offer the most moral and logical arguments. Without that biological gift for measuring the cycles of the moon and planets, how could a woman master any discipline that demanded a sense of time, space, mathematics – or the ability to measure anything at all? In philosophy and religion, how could women compensate for being disconnected from the rhythm of the universe? Or for their lack of symbolic death and resurrection every month?

. . .

In short, we would discover, as we should already guess, that logic is in the eye of the logician. . . . The truth is that, if men could menstruate, the power justifications would go on and on. If we let them.

(quoted in Walker and Dresner 1988: 431–432)

In this short piece above the shift is from complacency and complicity to action.

Conclusion

There was a plethora of women humorists writing after World War II, a selected few of which are showcased in this chapter. I have included some of my personal favorites in this chapter in order to dispel any notions that women were not writing plenty of humorous lines in the period before the fictive female sleuths and other female Tricksters occupied center stage in culture, but they were still dealing almost exclusively with domestic situations. Growing up I always felt slightly uncomfortable trying to fit my imagination around the stories which were offered to me, which were mainly about boys and men. I didn't realize why until I understood how being the implied reader changes the entire experience. What chagrin to discover these gems 40 years later and realize how differently I might have perceived my "strangeness" if I knew there were others who felt the same. The amazing thing is that the fictive female sleuths still had to reveal the same incongruities many years and even hundreds of years later. Women's strategic use of humor is like women's psychology, it is not about separation in the male sense. It is about being able to express anger or disappointment with a smile. Is it true or just an urban legend about the one where a woman after being dumped by her boyfriend called a recorded weather number in Cairo from her ex's phone in Detroit, and left it off the hook for ten days while he was out of town. Or how about the jilted ex-wife who lost her house to her husband in the divorce and sewed tiny shrimp into the bottoms of the curtains, forcing him to move out from the stench?

Women are now permitted increased freedom in terms of their sexuality. They are even allowed to try to get into the boardroom, where they haven't had much success, but are they allowed to be funny or mad? Regina Barreca contends that revenge humor is a way for powerless groups to use their creativity to regain their self-esteem. She sees humorous revenge as a way to displace anger with a joke which is the point of the two examples above. This is a technique which has been used by the African American culture as well as other marginalized groups throughout history like the Jews.

Helen Luke posits an archetypal Feminine as energy which manifests tangibly as humor. Referring to the statement attributed to Jesus that to enter the kingdom of heaven one must enter as a little child (Mark 10:15) Luke interprets this to mean that one must go beyond "all efforts of mankind to understand good and evil, matter and spirit" to find the gate through which we must pass:

> It is the gateway to the spontaneous play, not childish or childlike, of the feminine spirit. Without it there never could have been or cannot ever be any creation that knows eternity again after the long journey of the Return in the dimension of time. She is and always has been "playing in the world" in the sheer delight of the Fool and the Child hidden in every one of us. As we wait "at the posts of her doors" she may reveal herself to us: then indeed all work is transformed into play and play becomes the work that is contemplation and we know the delight of being with the sons and daughters of men.
>
> (Luke 1995: 80)

Notes

1 Woolf (1938: 182).
2 As I heard Gloria Steinem say, and which she attributed to fellow activist Flo Kennedy at the Reitz Union gathering in 1972 on the University of Florida campus.
3 Mae West is reported to have said, when she saw a picture of Cary Grant, that "if he could talk, he was in" her film, *She Done Him Wrong* (1933).
4 Founded in 1933 to combat objectionable content in motion pictures, the National Legion of Decency was sponsored by the Catholic Church and wielded great power in the film industry. Mae West probably had the Legion in mind as the model of the fictional Bainbridge Foundation in her satire on censorship, *The Heat's On* (1943).
5 Burney's play, *A Busy Day*, was produced at the Lyric Theatre, London, in Spring 2000 and was review by *Time Europe*, May 15, 2000, 155(19) www.time.com/time/europe/magazine/2000/0515/burney.html in an article titled, "Move Over Austen: The long-overlooked works of 18th century writer Fanny Burney are finally getting a wider audience," by Lauren Goldstein:

> Burney didn't chronicle her experiences for publication during her lifetime and she didn't make a penny from her life story. But she did write four novels and eight plays. Her seven-volume diary was published by her niece shortly after her death in 1840, almost certainly as Burney intended. It is those journals that Burney is best known for now. They inspired William Thackeray's *Vanity Fair* and Virginia Woolf's essay Dr. Burney's Evening Party. Her description of being chased around Kew Gardens was later a key scene in the film *The Madness of King George*. . . . It was her fiction, however, that made her famous in her own time – that led historian Thomas Macaulay to say she was a classic. Burney's books were more widely read than Jane Austen's and she counted Richard Sheridan and Samuel Johnson among her supporters. "She was the first female literary novelist," says Claire Harman, author of a biography of Burney. The women in Burney's books struggle in the midst of confining social mores. Her first book was *Evelina*, published anonymously, about a girl,

beautiful but lacking social connections or wealth, who falls in love with a lord. What made the novel a success was not the plot but the picture Burney drew of life in London. "Evelina was the first real heroine in contemporary circumstances," says Paula Stepankowsky, the president of the Burney Society, a group which promotes the study and appreciation of Burney and her family. "She was sort of like Bridget Jones: a contemporary woman dealing with the personal problems of her time."

History hasn't recognized Burney the way her peers and scholars have. She lacks the mass recognition of Austen, for example. "Austen may have done it better, more elegantly, have been more polished, but Fanny did it first," says Stepankowsky.

Now Burney is finally getting her due. In addition to Harman's extensively researched biography, the first major production of a Burney play, *A Busy Day*, is moving from the Old Vic Theatre in Bristol, where it has had rave reviews, to London's West End. "It was very moving," said Harman. "I had tears in my eyes because I thought how much she would have loved to see it." Burney only saw one of her plays produced – *Edwy and Elgiva* – and that ran for only one night. Appalled by cheap sets and poor acting, Burney had it pulled.

Kate Chisholm, author of a more narrative biography of Burney published in 1998, says she thinks it's likely that Burney would have preferred being known as a playwright – an occupation deemed unsuitable for women in her day. "Her writing is sharper and more controversial in her plays," Chisholm says. "But it is the diaries that give us the insight into the period." BBC Radio 4 will serialize her letters and journals for three weeks this summer. And a memorial to her will go into Westminster Abbey alongside the likes of the Brontë sisters and Austen in 2002, making Burney the only female writer who published in the 18th century to be so honored.

6 Zora Neale Hurston was born and grew up in the Southern United States (Alabama and Florida). She attended Howard University and then went to New York City, drawn by the circle of creative African American artists now known as the Harlem Renaissance. She continued her studies in anthropology at Barnard College under Franz Boas. It was during this period that Hurston won a grant that she used to collect African American folklore which gave her writing its distinctive style. While at Barnard, Hurston also worked as a secretary for Fannie Hurst, who later wrote *Imitation of Life* (1933), about an African American woman passing as white. Claudette Colbert starred in the 1934 film version of the story. "Passing" was a theme of many of the Harlem Renaissance women writers. *Their Eyes Were Watching God* (1937) was Hurston's most popular work, but it was criticized for being about African American themes which white readers would not understand. Zora Neale Hurston's popularity waned and her last book was published in 1948. She went back to Florida, dying in poverty, in 1960. Her work was almost forgotten until Alice Walker helped to revive interest in Hurston in the 1970s. Today Hurston's novels and poetry are studied in literature, women's and African American studies courses. *Their Eyes Were Watching God* was made into a motion picture in 2005, starring Halle Berry. Her books have also become popular with the general reading public. My personal favorite is *I Love Myself When I Am Laughing . . . and Then Again When I Am Looking Mean and Impressive* (Hurston 1979).

Chapter 11

The postmodern female Trickster

Best of all is Vic herself, spunky, fierce and funny.[1]

Kinsey is as candid, observant, funny, loyal and determined as ever.[2]

Stabenow handles her evergreen story with a wit and urgency that makes it fresh and exhilarating as the Alaskan wilderness.[3]

BarbaraNeely's latest mystery is as witty and wily as her beloved heroine [Blanche].[4]

Introduction

Humor and irony with movement results in a boundary-crossing process-oriented, postmodern Trickster. And what is the nature of the postmodern trick? It is this physical and psychological movement by a soul embodied as female crossing whatever boundaries they encounter with humor. Humor is the energy, movement is the process, and embodiment is in the female. These fictive female sleuths born in the last quarter of the twentieth century are funny, witty, and incisive women who no longer have to hide their wit and irony as their elite Anglo ancestors did.[5] The humor of the postmodern female Trickster is not the sarcastic biting humor meant to hurt, which is the shadow of humor. The humor I am speaking to here is revitalizing because it is playful, ironic, leaves one laughing at oneself and allows role playing and thus experimentation with alternative identities. This occurs because Trickster humor never has been and is not now motivated by power-seeking or arrogant motives. Trickster is humor focused upon the appetite for pleasure in life. Pleasure comes from engaging in activities which result in the successful attainment of the necessities of life. Unfortunately the patriarchal epoch has often substituted power over for the pleasure of humor, and Trickster has come to change this configuration through the process of resignification and reinscription of dominant value structures.

Reconsidering what Trickster signifies

Reconsidering "what Tricksters signify" is the first step in understanding how the postmodern female Trickster articulates and subverts dominant models of femininity through narrative laced liberally with humor and irony. To Henry Louis Gates the technique of signification is a "mode of formal revision . . . by creating ironic variations of these models" (Gates 1988: 52). Ironic variations on the theme of mystery fiction is the essence of the fictive female sleuth's ironic resignification; paying homage to and simultaneously reworking various aspects of the mystery tradition with a witty twist; thereby fulfilling the requisites to be called Trickster. Whereas Gates has used his concept of "signifying" as a way to revision the Trickster in an African American context, as a "set of rhetorical practices that evoke black differences by transforming mainstream literary and linguistic conventions" the same logic is applicable to all Trickster resignifications no matter where or what the subject matter. It is this process of ironic resignification which marks Trickster territory (Gates 1988: 52). After all, Gates, the Trickster, had no qualms about bridging the boundaries between African Tricksters, which appear predominantly as animal images, and African American Tricksters, who appear most often in a human form. Gates correctly identifies that it is the crossing of boundaries infused with ironic energy which is Trickster's modus operandi and it is precisely this process of re/creation by re/signification through irony and humor that makes the female Trickster at home in a postmodern context. Toni Morrison explains the resignification process she developed through ironic humor as transformative Trickster in *Beloved* (1987):

> The slave-holders have won if the experience of [slavery] is beyond my imagination and my power. It's like humor: You have to take the authority back; you realign where the power is so I wanted to have the power. They [the slave-holders] were very inventive and imaginative with cruelty, so I have to take it back – in a way I can tell it. And that is the satisfaction.[6]

To paraphrase Morrison, those who enclosed women's bodies and their imaginal realms have won if women cannot find a means to reestablish a connection to their own imaginal realms. But if you are a silenced minority or "other" – dominant modes of subversive power-oriented activity will not work – other ways of subversion are needed and Trickster's ironic manipulation of language through humor is an especially appropriate process for an alternative subversive transformative power that is not rooted in power over others' dynamics. In the excerpt above, Morrison challenges us to think about the very nature of power itself suggesting that one must take the power back but doing it through realignment with other forms of power. One of the most powerful forms of resignification or in Morrison's words, realigning where the power is, is through irony and humor utilized by an individual or collective in refusing to be a victim of the symbolic order any longer.[7]

When the female sleuth first appeared in the late nineteenth century, she was called a "freak." When she re-emerged during the late 1970s and early 1980s she was still considered an anomaly, as exemplified by characterizations of V.I. as "a quirky blend . . . full of wisecracking cussedness . . . a scrappy, entertaining, idiosyncratic fictional character who is a woman."[8] Notice that the descriptive words included the requisite reference to "woman," otherwise words like scrappy and wisecracking would have been assumed to describe a man. In the twenty-first century the fictive female sleuth is not considered a freak at all. Consider this more recent characterization of Blanche White as an example:

> Blanche White is a hoot. BarbaraNeely has crafted a wonderful character, a forty-year-old black domestic, with plenty going for her: wit, survival skills, and a wily intellect . . . an intriguing story about a feisty, funny black woman who keeps her dignity and self-worth alive while working for strange white people.[9]

In the following excerpt from the V.I. Warshawski's series we see that the way she uses humor's gift for wrestling with paradox makes it a serious tool of transgression and transformation:

> I pried her fingers from my arm. The smoke and noise and the sour cabbage smell were filling my brain. I put my head down to look at her in the eyes, started to say something rude, then thought better of it. I fought my way through the smog, tripping over babies, and found the men hovering around a table filled with sausages and sauerkraut in one corner. If their minds had been as full as their stomachs they could have saved America.
>
> (Paretsky 1993: 6)

This excerpt from Grafton's *"D" is for Deadbeat* (1987) is quintessential Kinsey – sharp, incisive, and ironic:

> Colgate is the bedroom community, attached to Santa Teresa like a double star. The two are just about the same size, but Santa Teresa has all the character and Colgate has the affordable housing, along with hardware stores, paint companies, bowling alleys, and drive-in theaters. Colgate is the Frostee-Freeze capital of the world.
>
> (Grafton 1987: 86)

Refusal to be a victim

Refusing to be a victim of the symbolic order is a resignification of traditional Trickster energy. To have a playful attitude is perennial Trickster, but to move psychologically beyond identification as a victim to identification as your own unique self utilizing your wit as the process which transforms pathos into pleasure is postmodern Trickster. To do this requires a playful attitude which can strategically deploy a comic sensibility; it is a refocusing from trauma towards doing or saying something witty about the incongruous absurdity of life which produces the trauma. For example, instead of actually planning on killing your mother for the harms and hurts you perceive she perpetrated upon you or someone else, you could play with the idea of wanting to kill your mother and plan a humorous demise in your imagination. In this example, humor is used to grease the psyche internally by resolving the "problem" hypothetically but humorously and in the process the psyche is transformed from victim to authority.

Refusing to be a victim as individuation: examples from literature, film, and life

Refusal to be a victim is at the heart of the postmodern Trickster as individuation motif. In the film *Catwoman* (2004), this refusal is through a show of physical strength.[10] But physical strength is only one aspect of refusing to be a victim. The post-Jungian Andrew Samuels (1993b) explicates a Trickster quality in the resistance movement of the Mothers of the Plaza de Mayo. To Samuels, the mothers' silent but unswerving attendance, standing witness to the horrors they had experienced in losing a loved one, transformed their suffering into political action and demonstrated that they would no longer be victims in the same way that they had been before their political behavior. Samuels thinks that the *trick* of the Mothers of the Plaza de Mayo was in how they expanded the role of mother through parody and thus triggered transformation: "Female masquerade, not as pathology or inevitable social fact, but as political strategy" (Samuels 1993b: 217). The actions of the Mothers of the Plaza de Mayo were symbolic speech, which is also a political strategy which is independent of their status as mothers. Symbolic speech is a form of direct confrontation and is not limited by biological status; the image that comes to mind is the 1968 Summer Olympics when African American black athletes stood silently with their fists held aloft during their medals ceremony. That act of silent resistance was as powerful as the Mothers of the Plaza de Mayo. But were either of these actions Trickster-like in the sense of being humorous? Both were silent and transformative, but they were not humorous. My sense of the Mothers of the Plaza de Mayo in postmodernity as female Trickster has more to do with their bodily presence *at* and *in* the terrain of the Plaza.

Capacity to inhabit a particular terrain is what connects the behavior of the Mothers of the Plaza de Mayo with an observation Samuels makes about the character in Margaret Atwood's *Surfacing* (1972). In *Surfacing*, it is the ability to inhabit the forest terrain which is critical to the character's transformation. One must be able to be present, in a bodily sense, in order for one's voice, whether shouted or symbolic, to be heard. If the "Mothers" were not permitted out of the house (as in the ancient Athenian *polis*), then they could not have stood silently in the Plaza. This is how I connect the mothers of the Plaza to the postmodern Trickster who refuses to be a victim, whether it means standing silently in a plaza, driving a car against legal rules imposed by a religious state,[11] standing silently with fists held aloft, or escaping from civilization and its discontents as the Trickster in *Surfacing* tells us:

> This above all to refuse to be a victim. Unless I can do that I can do nothing. I have to recant, give up the old belief that I am powerless and because of it nothing I can do will ever hurt someone. A lie was always more disastrous than the truth would have been.
>
> (quoted in Samuels 1993b: 218)

Refusing to be a victim parallels the progression of narrative and image found in elite Anglo-western women's literature; from writing within the assumed status of domesticity and dependency to being independent with psychological authority, bodily autonomy, and physical agency. When women first started writing they accepted their status as victims and wrote within the enclosed state of being. The next stage was feminist in the sense that women examined their perceived victimhood, playing with its inevitability, then women moved to the stage where they simply refused to be the victim. The progression in narrative and life moves away from a focus on how to find a man to how to avoid matrimony and have an identity towards the final stage where the individual identity is formed without the predominant consideration being your status in relation to the masculine, either father, husband, or collective culture. The refusal to be a victim parallels Jung's description of individuation:

> In general, it is the process by which individual beings are formed and differentiated; in particular it is the development of the psychological individual (q.v.) as being distinct from the general, collective psychology. Individuation, therefore, is a process of differentiation (q.v.), having for its goal the development of the individual personality.
>
> (Jung *CW* 6: par 757)

The individuation process requires the collective and those made a victim to move past this preliminary psychological stage of existence. Refusing to be a victim changes the questions that are asked, both of your external and internal world and by changing the questions that are asked, identity may be formatted in a new way. When one starts asking one's own questions, refusing to become the passive victim or conform to limiting roles imposed, one can use the foundation of difference for nomadic identity formation because one no longer is dependent upon mirroring from any single individual or culture to provide identity.

Identity then becomes integral and can be manifested no matter the culture or terrain one is inhabiting, whether actual, virtual, or imaginal. This ability to maintain identity no matter the terrain is a significant aspect of postmodern Trickster energy which encourages humor as adaptation to pathos. It is critical that women and other marginalized "others" – whatever their color, ethnicity, religion or socio-economic status – have the imaginal capacity and ability to communicate their desires if they are to refuse victim status because if one cannot portray or communicate who one truly is, then it makes even the desire to not be a victim, too dangerous to be spoken about in public and too dangerous to even imagine.

For women, speaking out – through performance and narrative – is a process of identity formation. Audre Lorde (1934–1992) describes how she has resolved this paradox between who you are and who they want you to be through her adaptation of a nomadic identity:

> I find I am constantly being encouraged to pluck out some part of myself and present this as a meaningful whole, eclipsing or denying the other parts of myself. But this is a destructive and frightening way to live. My full . . . energy is available to me only when I integrate all the parts of who I am, openly, allowing power from particular sources . . . to flow back and forth freely through all my different selves, without the restrictions of externally imposed definitions.
>
> (quoted in Eagleton 1996: 120–121)

Lorde is describing the liminal terrain where Trickster lives. Conceiving of liminality as identity in movement opens up the possibility of fluid/humorous movement across previous boundaries as part of the individuation process.

The postmodern female Trickster as social worker

The postmodern female Trickster manifests foolishness, play, wisdom and work. Work is critical to a full life, but so is humor and laughter. If you just have the play aspect dominating your persona then you may be disassociated from pernicious social causes. Humor and enlightenment go together like a horse and carriage. Samuels' (1993b) example heralding the appearance of female Trickster is Margaret Atwood's (1972) *Surfacing* which he reads to target "conventional political thinking about the environment – and conventional psychoanalytic thinking about the environment." Employing abundant Trickster qualities himself, Samuels connects the emergent female Trickster with social action and social work:

> my grim eco-targets are anything but fantasies, the possibility of global warming, deforestation and species depletion, damaging of the ozone layer, acid rain and other pollutions, the limits to growth, the feminization of poverty, the debate about population limitation, the general decay of urban civilization, the global injustice of Third World debt, the rights of the developing countries to those technological and industrial features that provide consumers of the developed world with all their goodies.
>
> (Samuels 1993b: 213)

Samuels' (1993b) sensitivity to environmental concerns which he finds reflected in Atwood's *Surfacing* (1972) is also presented to the readers of the fictive female sleuths. In Stabenow's *Midnight Comes Again* (2000), Kate is visiting with some members of the Yupik tribe, who we find out are the envy of other Alaskan Native tribes because they live along a river not wanted by western exploiters:

> The Yupik live along the Kushokwim River, whose water was too shallow for whales to swim up so the whalers left them alone and other rivers were more navigable along the route from the Klondike and Nome, so the gold rushers had left the area alone as well as those who were looking for timber, since the area lacked trees. The sparse and scattered nature of the villages along with the lack of resources valued by white Western standards had combined to allow the Yupik to retain their culture and even their language, which was presently taught half-days in the local school district, with English the other half of the day.
>
> (Stabenow 2000: 218)

Kate goes on to explain how the modern day Yupik exist through the Trickster behavior of making something out of nothing, sense out of nonsense. The reader finds out that what the Yupik subsist on is qiviut, which is the thick soft coat from the belly of a large, slow, not especially bright musk ox that once roamed Northern Alaska until hunters killed almost all of them, similar to what happened with the bison that were once so plentiful on the plains and prairies of the American West. They had been reintroduced in the 1930s by scientists at the University of Alaska and now numbered over 3,000 in a variety of herds:

qiviut, the softer hair that came from the belly, fell out naturally, was collected and spun into yarn and distributed among western Alaskan village women to be knit into hats, shawls, tunics and scarves, mostly for sale to tourists in Anchorage because nobody local could afford it.

(Stabenow 2000: 62–63)

The reader is offered a glimpse into the life of a Native Alaskan tribe whose people use what they have in order to get what they need without resorting to violence but the commentary is ironic.

Andrew Samuels (2001) posits that western culture is in dire need of what he calls the *Trickster leader* which is the social worker aspect of the female Trickster:

> We can see that the way the psyche is evolving in Western societies tends to foster the emergence of more female Trickster leaders. Sometimes the female Trickster enters the political arena by overdoing, in a transgressive manner, what is prescribed for women. For example, the Mothers of the Plaza de Mayo helped to topple the Argentine Junta by assembling, dressed in full maternal mourning dress, in the main square of Buenos Aires. Another area where we can see today's female Tricksters in leadership roles is in the environmental movement. The equation of women and nature or earth can be (but is not necessarily) one of the most oppressive equations for women when culture and power are then left for men. But when the equation of woman equals earth is exaggerated and parodied, as in some forms of eco-feminism, a new kind of energy becomes available for politics. The list of contemporary female Tricksters is almost endless. I think of the crop of female private investigators like V.I. Warshawski or sexually open film stars like Sharon Stone, with her one-liner that "having a vagina and a point of view is a deadly combination". Maybe some will say that the struggle for autonomy that characterizes the life of any and every woman in Western (or indeed, non-Western) societies makes her a female Trickster already. Perhaps. But the main point is that the blatant political flavor of the female Trickster highlights the argument with which we began: that political cultures need Tricksters as leaders and this is a far more complicated matter than the question of truth or falsehood, honesty or dishonesty, trustworthiness or untrustworthiness, in political conduct would suggest.

(Samuels 2001: 95–96)

Samuels juxtaposes Trickster and hero, concluding that the heroic ideal represents "the failure, in our time of the very idea of leadership" (Samuels 2000: 37). Yet, the heroic ideal still controls much of the psyche:

By now everybody knows that apparently strong and manifestly heroic leaders are deeply suspect. They are hyper-masculine or macho personages, and, intellectually speaking, we don't want them. They are "male" whatever their sex because, for heroes, the obstacles to be overcome are, in Western discourse, always "female." They are dangerous, whether in the role of the savior, explorer, king, philosopher, or warrior. And in the nuclear age in which we continue to live, it is quite clear why they are dangerous. Everyone knows this on an intellectual level. Women know it, for sure. All over the world women are deeply suspicious of male, and indeed female heroic leaders and leadership styles which are redolent of heroism. Yet, we don't let go of whatever hopes and desires are locked up in such leaders. This is the spilt and it would be hubris for anyone to claim to have gotten over it. The *idea* of the hero will not go away.

(Samuels 2000: 37)

The heroic standard of perfection is the problem, since according to Jung and the post-Jungians, the psyche longs for completion, not perfection. The collective is stuck in an adolescent psychology where perfection is the goal. And so as a collective we get, according to Samuels, "the pleasure of identification" with the perfection of the hero and that's why we can't give it up. When a culture or individual is striving for perfection, failure cannot be acknowledged as necessary to growth and so these failures are repressed into the shadow and ignored through a variety of disassociative techniques. The fictive female sleuths, as representative of the postmodern Trickster, know that failure is not only necessary but happens all the time, and so they do not repress or spilt themselves off, they deal with it through humor. As Samuels advocates, we need a politics of *play* that requires Tricksters as "in-house revolutionaries" (Samuels 2000: 40) simply because they are not rooted in reality. Now which reality is this? As Lily Tomlin said in her play, *The Search for Signs of Intelligent Life in the Universe* (Wagner 1986), "What is reality anyway but a collective hunch?" Perhaps it is time to move on to playing other hunches?

From characteristics to social practices

The emphasis placed upon social work practices found in the postmodern female Trickster have displaced the former focus on Trickster characteristics or characteristic behaviors. This social work aspect is brilliantly developed in the Kate Shugak series as a clash of values between Kate and her grandmother Ekaterina. In the following scene the reader confronts (along with Kate Shugak) the prejudice towards those categorized as "other," that occurs in many cultures. In doing so Kate's actions are

Tricksterish because she challenges the exclusively receptive role of dutiful daughter through an assertion of her own authority with humor:

> Your great-great-grandfather was a hundred percent Russian Cossack, your uncle was a Jewish cobbler who came north with the Gold Rush, and your sister married a Norwegian fisherman. We Aleuts are about as pure of ancestry as one of Abel's dogs.
>
> (Stabenow 1992a: 48)

The "blatant political flavor" (Samuels 2001: 96) of the postmodern female Trickster can be observed in *Burn Marks* (Paretsky 1990), where V.I. delves into the homeless situation in modern urban culture. The Indiana Arms, a vacant, once grand residential hotel, has burned down, and the homeless who lived there are now out on the streets. One of them is V.I.'s Aunt Elena and another is a young women named Cerise whom Elena is friendly with. Within a few days Cerise is dead from an overdose and V.I. is implicated because V.I.'s wallet was found on the body. In one scene V.I. talks to the owner of the burned building, and the reader finds out how a vacant building becomes a home for the homeless:

> It was an old building, no good to anybody, even me. You pay the taxes, you pay the insurance, you pay the utilities, and when the rent comes in you don't have enough to pay for the paint. I know the wiring was old, but I couldn't afford to put in new, you've got to believe me young lady.
>
> (Paretsky 1990: 127)

·The reader discovers that V.I. had let her aunt stay the night with her and then quickly arranged for another place, out of sight and presumably out of mind, repressing the shadow her aunt represents. Later V.I. discovers that her wallet was stolen the night her aunt stayed over and V.I.'s "anger faded, replaced by shame and a wave of hopelessness." But even amidst the shame V.I. feels about misjudging her aunt, she is in active movement between poles of awareness as she humorously notices that "out in front the couple had stopped arguing and were making up over a bottle of Ripple," but then pathos intrudes and she realizes that "sometimes life seems so painful it hurts even to move my arms" (Paretsky 1990: 120). While V.I.'s awareness of how little separates her from her aunt is presented as V.I.'s personal paradox, the commentary has wider implications for the implied reader's personal and political perspectives. V.I. shares her desire to "escape to a remote corner of the globe where human misery didn't take such human forms." But she realizes that she doesn't have the money to do that any more than people like Aunt Elena do. Even if V.I. doesn't leave but just goes to "bed for a month" she will have to face that her mortgage bill would come and go without payment and eventually the bank would kick me out and then I'd have some naked misery of my own, sitting in front of my building with a bottle of Ripple to keep it all out of my head.

(Paretsky 1990: 121)

So she moves back and forth between tragedy and comedy. She uses the bottle of ripple wine first for comedy and then to point up the tragedy of human existence, which is what makes humor so necessary.

In *Total Recall* (Paretsky 2001), V.I.'s case concerns the unjust enrichment of insurance companies that never paid out verifiable claims to Holocaust and slavery survivors or their families. The insurance company defends the theft because others do the same:

Our position is in line with the industry, that however legitimate the grief and the grievances – of both the Jewish and the African-American communities – the expense of a policy search shall be most costly for all policyholders.

The book continues to place before the reader discourse about insurance reparations for slavery and Holocaust claims. Later in the book, V.I. reads a letter to the editor which asks the reader to "imagine that you go into Berlin, the capital of Germany, and find a large museum dedicated to the horrors of three centuries of African slavery in the United States" and to further imagine that "Germany passed a law saying that any American company which benefitted from slavery couldn't do business in Europe. That's what Illinois wants to do with German companies." The insurance executive finally concludes that, "No one's hands are clean, but if we have to stop every ten minutes to wash them before we can sell cars, or chemicals, or even insurance, commerce will grind to a halt" (Paretsky 2001: 120). What exactly would grind to a halt here is the economic model that values only the bottom line. Justice is portrayed as an ideal that may be nice as a concept but really doesn't work too well in tough situations when there are competing interests. The ability to balance between the tension of the opposites is an integral element in both the postmodern and traditional Trickster energies. The difference, according to Samuels' reconfiguration of the Trickster in the political process, is how the postmodern Trickster employs without apology, a "blatant political flavor" (Samuels 2001: 96). Refocusing the reader's attention beyond the simplistic either/or dichotomies which are woven throughout the normative symbolic order and assumed to be natural as opposed to emphasizing that they are actually interpretations of social reality brings the reader to a new set of questions which are triggered when economics is no longer assumed to be the most important factor to be evaluated when making collective decisions about the future of any particular culture. The question becomes how do we transform the world so that the world itself, our environment, can flourish?[12]

Status within a culture

Women's status and role within a particular culture is an important consideration attendant to female Trickster manifestation. Franchot Ballinger (1988), who studied hundreds of North American Trickster stories for her paper, "Coyote, She Was Going There: Prowling for Hypotheses about the Female Native American Trickster," concluded that where the female Trickster appears, "it is a consequence of the ways in which power and gender are connected" in a particular tribe's life:

> The most obvious fact that we should note about stories with female Tricksters is that they are all from tribes that were or are yet matrilineal or matrilocal. In most, and maybe all of the tribes I've named, women have traditionally had significant de facto or official authority and power. For example, among the western Tewa and Hopi, women traditionally control the economic system and the home which is the core of that system. Women own the houses, the fields, and the fruits of cultivation through their clans, with the clan mothers having final say in matters of distribution. Furthermore, strong ties among mothers-daughters-sisters create a solidarity of opinion which in turn carries much authority.
>
> (quoted in Hyde 1998: 340)

A psyche embodied as a female living in a culture which recognizes the female as having (legal) identity through the capacity to own – houses, fields and decisions – is what Ballinger (1988) describes as a condition precedent to Trickster energies being manifested through the female. The indigenous cultures she describes are quite dissimilar from "civilized" Greek society where "the law expressly forbids children and women from being able to make a contract about anything worth more than a bushel of barley" (Stibbs 1992: 6).[13] Lewis Hyde in *Trickster Makes This World* (1998) agrees that "we find this female Trickster in the context of female power, a fact that, in the end, supports the idea that the canonical Tricksters are male because they are part of a patriarchal mythology" (Hyde 1998: 340). Thus when the female Trickster appears in postmodern culture, she would not be expected to be simply a double of the traditional male Trickster but would signify a change in the psychological terrain of the culture she manifests within, and this is precisely the point; late-twentieth-century Anglo-American culture became the kind of terrain where the female body could legally manifest agency, authority, and autonomy. This change in terrain signifies increased transformed feminine power in the collective as well as the collective consciousness. This is the central theme developed about the significance of, for example, these fictive female sleuths as postmodern Trickster, they are embodied as female but do not represent the traditional feminine imagery projected from the male imagination.

Sex and pro/creativity

The postmodern female Trickster demonstrates a different attitude than traditional Trickster relative to pro-creativeness. According to Hyde's analysis, "Trickster's fabled sex drive rarely leads to any offspring. Tricksters do not make new life; they rearrange what is already at hand" (Hyde 1998: 341). The simple fact is that men do not give birth and the Trickster has been embodied in men, thus giving birth was out of the question if Trickster was to have any credibility. But is this a distinction without a difference? No. A superficial comparison reveals that Kinsey, Kate, V.I., and Blanche do not have children of their own. In the case of Blanche and Kate, they may end up raising other women's children, but it is quite significant that they do not have pre-emptive childcare responsibilities during the pendency of their cases. The important point is that these women can manifest agency which rearranges culture *and* procreates human beings. This is a conjunctive, rather than disjunctive, psychological consciousness, and we see it in Blanche raising her deceased sister's children and Kate's willingness to consider taking her deceased lover Jack's son, Jimmy, into her home and heart.

When women starting writing novels, using the fictive device of making women single and outside the enclosure of marriage and childbirth was necessary to write a narrative where women could demonstrate independence and still be within acceptable traditional cultural norms. This outside the enclosure tradition was found when the fictive female sleuths were imagined by women in the last quarter of the twentieth century. However, in the later sleuths, like Blanche and Kate, we do see them wrestling with the conflicts inherent in working in the world and raising children.

There is a second aspect to this evolution which relates to technology and procreativeness. As reproductive technology continues to advance and women in western political democracies are no longer tied to the exclusive role of procreation with its attendant diminished life span, postmodernity has given two women the option to have children or two men the same option. It is mission impossible to fit these emergent postmodern female Tricksters into the same imagery and narratives of the Tricksters from cultures dominated by traditional patriarchal cultural norms. To attempt to do so is to ignore the distinction between the culturally inflected archetypal image and the archetypal energy.

Creativity

Another point which must be raised deals directly with creativity itself. Creativity can be manifested in many forms, and this diversity of creative form has been possible for highly born men throughout patriarchal cultures. However, one of the hallmarks of traditional cultural norms is the binding of women to pro-creativity – if women give birth, then their creative needs have been met. Any other creative needs can be met in the role of muse, but neither of these creative outlets available to women in patriarchal cultures includes the capacity to protect the environment and engage in the political process which seems so much a part of the post-modern Trickster, especially in her social work/leadership capacity.

Sex and marriage

The sexual antics and proclivities of the perennial Trickster were an inherent part of the imagery and narrative produced in traditional cultures but there is evidential support for the conclusion that Trickster's characteristics change when women have agency and authority within a culture (Ballinger 1988). In late twentieth century North American culture, women *did* begin to have legal capacity and rights which led to the imagining and then the actual development of power and authority in their public and psychological lives.[14] And although this has been especially evident in those women who did not marry, things have changed for all (western) women. Previously, women who wanted to manifest authority, autonomy, and agency did not marry or have children within that marriage in order that they could lay claim to a separate identity that was not (sub)merged with their husband upon marriage. Today, women are marrying but even if married, the American census information from June of 2002 indicates that among women age 15 to 44, 26.7 percent are childless. Women with the highest education rates are also the most childless. No longer can a woman's identity rest upon the production of children if the world is to survive over-population and the attendant diminishment of natural resources. Amy Caizza, who directs the Institute for Women's Policy Research in Washington DC, says the reason is because "you don't have to be a mother to be a complete woman." Another revealing statistic regarding identity formation in postmodern women is how the number of never-married woman who are in professional and managerial positions and who are having children has doubled. The reason, women earning enough money and the lack of stigma associated with raising a child alone.[15] Madelyn Cain's *The Childless Revolution* (2001) concludes that the very definition of woman is changing:

> It was considered "unwomanly" to admit to feeling happy and whole without children. Yet, the childless woman I interviewed spoke of many

benefits: the latitude to develop their careers fully; the intimacy they share with their mates; their lack of financial, emotional and time pressures; the freedom from fear of being a bad mother, or having a difficult child; the spiritual growth that takes place thanks to the availability of unfettered time; the relief of not having to raise a loved one in a world some view as too violent or selfish.[16]

The woman Cain describes is Carrie Bradshaw, the lead character in the cable television hit, *Sex and the City*, which is the focus of Chapter 13. Childlessness does not lead to unhappiness, according to the *Journal of Gerontology* in 1998, which found no "significant differences in loneliness and depression between parents and childless adults."[17] In the United States along with the majority of the western world and China, population growth is on the decline as the current birth rates will not replace the population. Other commentators note that the structure of the family has changed, or shape-shifted many times. The idea of the nuclear family as somehow naturally ordained is incorrect, since the idea and ideal of a one house family is of relatively recent origin. While the usual doomsayers portend the end of the traditional family, "more women than ever are choosing a life that does not conform to the old standard." Dr. Pearce advises that we "absorb into our consciousness a new version of femaleness, one that is predicated on the measure of a women's character, not on the issue of her body."[18]

It was not so long ago that the issue was not resignifying or reinscribing identity based on sex but race. California, in 1947, was the first state to permit mixed racial marriages; in the majority of states those laws were on the books until 1967 when the Supreme Court overruled the practice with the plastic language, the "freedom to marry or not marry a person of another race resides in that individual." The Supreme Court's own language is the best argument for same-sex marriages. In biblical culture, polygamy was the norm, not the idealized nuclear family of today.

The postmodern female Trickster might not marry, but that does not stop her from crossing the boundary of sex for women within marriage exclusively. Both Kinsey and V.I. did marry and divorce. Blanche and Kate have never married, although Kate and Blanche both thought a lot about what impact that would have on their lives. Blanche decides against it in *Blanche Passes Go* (Neely 2000), and her longtime beau, Leo, marries another. Kate decides for it and then her fiancée is murdered in *Hunter's Moon* (Stabenow 1999). The following passage from the Kinsey Millhone series fairly represents the perspective that the fictive female sleuths share with their readers:

Is that what marriages finally come down to? I've seen old couples toddle down the street together holding hands and I've always looked on faintly misty-eyed, but maybe it is all the same clash of wills behind closed doors. I've been married twice myself and both ended in divorce. I berate myself for that sometimes but now I'm not sure. Maybe I haven't made such a bad trade-off. Personally, I'd rather grow old alone than in the company of anyone I've met so far. I don't experience myself as lonely, incomplete, or unfulfilled, but I don't talk about that much. It seems to piss people off, especially men.

(Grafton 1985: 60)

Why is it that men are continually "pissed off" because Kinsey, V.I., Kate, and Blanche are not married? Could it be because women without agency, authority, or autonomy were necessary to support traditional patriarchal cultural norms?

One of the transgressive acts of these postmodern Tricksters is their authentic engagement with the mystery of erotic sexuality. This is a crossing of the boundaries previously assigned to women. In one memorable scene, Blanche goes to a bar with a new friend, and speculates about male sexuality:

A man in handcuffs and a T-shirt that said I'M YOURS threw himself on the floor in front of a woman carrying a whip. She lifted her foot, and he began passionately licking the bottom of her shoe. Blanche turned to find Lacey watching her with amused eyes.

"What can I bring you, ladies?"

Blanche couldn't stop herself from staring at the waiter's see-through plastic shorts and his pink penis with its cock ring clearly visible. Lacey could hardly order for laughing. Blanche didn't mind.

(Neely 1998: 174)

Most of the sex scenes are not a masquerade or parody of male sexuality, as this scene in the bar is. More usual is the type of sexual sensitivity Kinsey demonstrates as she reflects on the male fantasy:

Men are funny, you know? Big male fantasy about hookers? I see this in all these books written by men. Some guy meets a hooker and she's gorgeous: big knockers, refined, and she's got the hots for him. Him and her end up bonking, and when he's done, she won't take his money. He's so wonderful, she doesn't want to charge him money like she does everyone else. Now that's bullshit for sure. I never knew a hooker who'd do a guy for free. Anyway, hooker sex is for shit. If he thinks that's a gift, then the joke's on him.

(Grafton 1994: 93)

Dialogic about and openly erotic energy in a woman continues to shock those who are still embedded in traditional cultural norms. Thus the depictions we find of women enjoying, thinking about, and openly engaging in strategies to have sexual relations cross boundaries and reinscribe the cultural norms. This kind of sexual energy has been used in an especially subversive and successful fashion in the portrayals of lesbian relations within this genre. Although that specific consideration of sexual relations is beyond the scope of this work, the reader who is interested in this aspect of the genre will find the shelves bulging with possibilities.[19]

Kinsey as quintessential Trickster or how to deal with the tough stuff through humor

In *"P" is for Peril* (Grafton 2001) Kinsey offers the reader a fine example of the psychological, physical, and sexual fluidity which is characteristic of the Trickster archetype. Kinsey's travels are fueled by her being able to plug into a variety of energy sources, starting out in the following excerpt with the warmth of parental protection, similar to what Zeus offered Hermes. Kinsey then plans and participates in a theft – just as Hermes stole Apollo's cattle – and gets caught in what could have been a compromising position, but she manages to extricate herself through humor and irony, just as Hermes did with his invention of the lyre to soothe Apollo's wrath.

In this first scene Kinsey is reflecting on her reaction when she finds out that Tommy, a man she was attracted to, may have participated in the murder of his own parents. Initially Tommy had told Kinsey that his parents were murdered by burglars for their jewels, but as the narrative progresses, Kinsey learns that the "burglars" may have been Tommy and his brother, and that it looks as if they may actually get away with the crime of murdering their parents. Understandably, given Kinsey's own parental loss[20], she has a desire to do justice by taking the law into her own hands. What is postmodern Trickster is the ethical psychological attitude she brings to bear on the situation, reflecting upon the irony of law and justice within a humorous context even though her own feelings are in play:

> I could feel the Masked Avenger aspect of my personality girding her loins, prepared to seek justice and to right old wrongs. At the same time, Henry's [Kinsey's surrogate parent figure] accusations had hit perilously close to home. I'll admit I'm (occasionally) foolhardy and impetuous, impatient with the system, vexed by the necessity for playing by the rules. It's not that I don't applaud law and order, because I do. I'm simply indignant that the bad guys are accorded so many rights when their victims have so few. Pursuing scoundrels through the courts not only costs a fortune, but it offers no guarantee of legal remedy. Even assuming success, a hard-won conviction doesn't bring the dead back to life. In this matter, though I hated to be

practical, I'd come around to Henry's point view. I intended to mind my own business for once.

(Grafton 2001: 232)

Kinsey shares with her reader the psychological processes in which she reinterprets Tommy's behavior and her own complicity:

The mild Texas accent I'd found so attractive a day or two before, now seemed to be an affectation. He was wearing a cashmere sweater, a soft downy gray that played up his florid hair color and the greed of his eyes. I wanted to shiver not from arousal but from dread. What had once seemed seductive was only cheap display. In a quick recap, I realized that from the moment we'd met he'd worked to dominate, beginning with my declining to drink a beer with him. He'd proposed a Diet Pepsi instead, popping it before I could refuse. I'd taken the path of least resistance once he'd established his control. After that the transitions were smooth and well rehearsed. He'd enlist my sympathies by rolling out the reference to his parents' death and then he'd offered up his comment about California women being so stuck up. Immediately I'd work to prove him wrong. His final move was adroit. "Which do you prefer? Guys way too young for you or guys way too old?" I couldn't believe I'd been so easily taken in.

(Grafton 2001: 235)

Refusing to be Tommy's victim, Kinsey decides to have no further contact with Tommy, so she is surprised when she gets to her neighborhood bar, Rosie's, and he is there. She escapes momentarily to the bathroom, and when she returns she finds that Henry Pitts, her surrogate father/landlord/neighbor, is sitting at the table with Tommy:

Henry glanced over to me and we exchanged a brief look. I knew what he was up to. He was feeling protective. He had no intention of letting me consort with the enemy without a chaperone . . . here he was laying out the bait. Henry had launched himself on his maiden lie, which he'd offered in my behalf. I knew why he was doing it. If the jeweler's name came from him, how could I be blamed for it later when the deal went sour? Henry and Tommy had spent the previous evening together. Tommy would trust him. Everybody trusted Henry because he told the truth and he was straight as an arrow. . . . Meanwhile, Henry went on as smoothly as a con artist with an easy mark.

(Grafton 2001: 238–239)

After Kinsey manages to get out of the bar alone she shares with the reader her psychological take on the situation:

I went back to my apartment and locked myself in. Tommy gave me the creeps. I went from window to window, closing the latches, pulling the shutters across the panes so that no one could look in. I didn't relax until every possible bolt and bar had been secured. In his mind, whatever I was up to must have something to do with him. Narcissism and paranoia are flip sides of the same distorted sense of self-importance. In the eerie way of all psychopaths, he'd pick up on my newly minted fear of him. He must be wondering who or what had caused my attitude to shift.

(Grafton 2001: 245–246)

Too early to don her detective persona, she fills her "time with various household chores," reinscribing for the reader domestic cleaning using humor and irony:

Cleaning out a toilet bowl can be wonderfully soothing when anxiety levels climb. I scrubbed the sink and the tub, and then crawled around on my bathroom floor, using the same damp sponge to wipe down the tiles. I vacuumed, dusted and started a load of laundry. From time to time, I looked at my watch, calculating the hour at which the residents of Pacific Meadows would be bedded down for the night.

(Grafton 2001: 247)

Before leaving on her detective job, Kinsey gets in touch with Ruby, her sister in crime at the nursing home. A Trickster herself, Ruby extracts a promise from Kinsey to bring her that quintessential Trickster substance, food:

I hope your heart doesn't seize up, I said, taking a sip of my Coke. "Who cares? I've got a no-code on my chart and I'd rest in peace." She held up her Big Mac, delighted at the sight of juices dripping out the bottom. She licked a dab of Special Sauce from the corner of her mouth. "Not as big as the ones on TV, but it's good."

(Grafton 2001: 250)

Even when Kinsey switches back to the "serious" work of breaking and entering her ironic stance continues:

When I reached the administrative offices, I took a deep breath and tried the knob. Locked. I considered using my key picks, but I was uneasy at the prospect of loitering for fifteen minutes while I manipulated the tumblers with assorted snap picks, torqueing tools, and bent wires.

In the bottom drawer I saw a metal file box that opened at a touch. Inside was a small compartmentalized tray with various keys, all neatly tagged and labeled. Yea for my team. This was really more exciting than a scavenger hunt.

(Grafton 2001: 252)

Kinsey gets the files she wants but is stopped from leaving the area and gets caught in a confining physical predicament from which there seems no escape, a place much inhabited by all Tricksters:

11:34. Time to scram. I pushed through the hinged gate in the counter and I'd just reached the hall door when I heard approaching footsteps. I froze, trying not to panic. The tapping sound of hard-sole shoes was soft but distinct. I scanned the area for the easiest hiding place. I crossed to Merry's workstation, pulled out her rolling chair and crawled into the kneehole space under her desk. I found myself sitting on a tangle of fat power cords, my head angled unnaturally to keep it from banging into the underside of Merry's pencil drawer. The corners of Klotilde's chart cut into my stomach and chest and made a strange crackling sound and I drew my feet up and hugged my knees. The office door opened. I expected the light to be turned on, but the room remained dark. Who were these two? Maybe we were on the verge of a burglar's jamboree, all three of us stealing files for differing but nefarious purposes. They had to be up to no good or why not turn the lights on?

(Grafton 2001: 256–257)

Kinsey is stuck, but in a totally unexpected way. While the situation echoes traditional Trickster sexual imagery, it is totally reinscribed:

I heard a flurry of indistinct susurrations, a guttural moan, protest on his part, and intimate urgings on hers. I picked up the quiet but unmistakable rip of a zipper being lowered on its track. I nearly shrieked in alarm. They were about to play doctor and I was going to be stuck in the examining room! He leaned back against the desk – I could see his fingers grip the edge for support. Meanwhile she dropped to her knees and started to work on him. His protests began to die down as his breathing increased. He clearly had a letch for nursie types and she was probably turned on by the possibility of getting caught. I did my best to distract myself. I tried to think worthy thoughts, elevating myself to a Zen-like plane. After all I had only myself to blame for the predicament I was in. I decided to stop breaking and entering. I made up my mind that I'd repent my sins.

(Grafton 2001: 257–258)

Again we are drawn into laughter when we realize the reason for her repentance:

> Not that I wasn't already paying a stiff price, in a manner of speaking for someone who gets as little sex as I do, this surely constituted punishment of a most cruel and unusual kind. Pepper was only three feet away from me, happily occupied with the guy's throbbing manhood, as it is euphemistically referred to in novels that abound in such scenes. I have to tell you, other people's sex lives are not that fascinating.
>
> (Grafton 2001: 258)

And then she tricks us again with a bit of ribald humor:

> She began to make little encouraging noises in her throat. I was tempted to chime in. From under the desk even the surge protector made a small enthusiastic peep which seemed to spur him on. His vocalizing was muffled but the sound accelerated and began to rise in pitch. Finally, he turned as though his finger had been slammed in a door and he trying not to scream.

> All three of us fell back exhausted and I prayed we would have to pause for a post-coital smoke. Ten more minutes passed before they pulled themselves together. After a whispered discussion, it was decided that she would leave first and he would follow at a suitable interval. By the time I crawled out of my hiding place I was cranky and sore and had a crimp in my neck. This was the last time I'd ask Ruby to man the lookout post.
>
> (Grafton 2001: 258)

In the space of a few pages, we have a running psychological commentary on the attraction of bad types of men, a protective parental energy coming to her aid, the use of domestic chores to ease anxiety not cause it, and the use of fast food as bribe to make her way into the nursing home's medical records. Each scene is psychologically attuned, assisting the reader in reinscribing and revisioning women as autonomous, with agency and authority and perhaps, most significantly, someone who helps us survive the world through laughter.

Ethics and the postmodern female Trickster

What are ethics? I was taught that an ethical dilemma is one where two courses of action are both equally desirable. A dictionary defines ethics as moral philosophy; the study of the general nature of morals and the specific choices made by an individual in relationship to others.[21] The Greek word *ethos* means personal disposition, therefore it is not a collective judgment which ethics concerns but how a person interacts with the collective through their own personal disposition. Of course, this disposition can be influenced and molded – that's what religions do at an early age – but is there a type of ethical behavior which is determined upon a personally generated rather than collectively imposed morality? Nietzsche in *A Genealogy of Morals* (1899) asked the psychological question, what determines our morals, when he inquires under what conditions did culture construct these value judgments of good and evil and do they have any intrinsic worth? Nietzsche asks the postmodern question, how did we humans arrive at these moral principles? But when Nietzsche talks of humans, who is he really talking about? The problem I find with the questions he asks is that they assume a *power over* dynamic as the natural way that humans must live. Trickster is not interested in power and so this leads to the question of what kind of ethics am I speaking about when I discuss ethics and the postmodern female Trickster? Or put another way, how does a symbolic order based upon *power over* dynamics deal with paradox, which is both the ethical and Trickster's realm.

While an argument can be made that differentiating good and evil through moral philosophy is a step towards individuation, more compelling is the argument that the construct of good and evil as we now have it is a direct development based upon the need to consolidate and hold onto power within a designated group. As clans transited from nomadism to sedentary life an enclosure was placed around the group itself, identifying evil as that which occurred outside or in the shadows of the recognized power of the constituted group. Shunning or exile from a group has always been among the most direct forms of coercion into a group dynamic based upon the illusion of certainty and the possibility of control. Trickster, who is the paradoxical signification that there is no certainty or control, just movement and chaos, is a threat to such a group. Trickster in these "developing" groups is identified as evil, outside the group. Trickster's eroticism, irrational behavior, and magical qualities become equated with the worship of false gods. This exclusionary and repressive situation was exacerbated by the Christian Church necessitating the outrageous spectacles and carnivals as a psychological balancing mechanism. Christianity gave the Eros of the Trickster poison to drink but it did not die, although her reputation became associated with vice or shunned as abnormal.

Do women have different ethical consideration than men?

Our western conceptions of morality and ethics were spilt along an Eros and Logos division, but when the voice of girls and women are factored into the ethical equation the questions themselves are challenged. This is what Carol Gilligan (1982) concluded when she attempted to replicate Lawrence Kohlberg's scale of moral development by asking the same question of girls and women that Kohlberg asked of boys and men. Asked to decide whether a man named Heinz should steal a drug he cannot afford which the druggist refuses to lower the price of, in order to save the life of his wife, Jake, an 11-year-old boy, who preferred English to math, had no problem resolving the given hypothetical; Heinz was to steal the drug even if he didn't love his wife. In reviewing Jake's response, Gilligan points out that Jake's

> judgment that Heinz should steal the drug, like his view of the law as having mistakes, rests on the assumption of agreement, a societal consensus around moral values that allows one to know and expect others to recognize what is "the right thing to do."
>
> (Gilligan 1982: 26)

Jake is certain that "there can only be right and wrong in judgment," a statement which places him at the upper end on Kohlberg's scale of moral development:

> his ability to bring deductive logic to bear on the solution of moral dilemmas, to differentiate morality from law, and to see how laws can be considered to have mistakes points towards the principled conception of justice that Kohlberg equates with moral maturity.
>
> (Gilligan 1982: 27)

When Gilligan asked Amy, a bright 11 year old who planned on becoming a scientist the identical hypothetical her answer placed her on the Kohlberg scale as "an image of development stunted by a failure of logic, an inability to think for herself." The disparate results stem from Amy's deviation from Kohlberg's expectations. Amy questioned the options given to her by the hypothetical:

> Well, I don't think so. I think there might be other ways besides stealing it, like, if he could borrow the money or make a loan or something, but he really shouldn't steal the drug – but his wife shouldn't die either.
>
> (Gilligan 1982: 28)

Amy failed Kohlberg's test of morality because she did not consider mainstream property or legal factors in her analysis, rather she focused on the effect that theft could have on the relationship between Heinz and his wife:

If he stole the drug, he might save his wife then, but if he did, he might have to go to jail, and then his wife might get sicker again, and he couldn't get more of the drug, and it might not be good. So, they should really just talk it out and find some other way to make the money.

(Gilligan 1982: 28)

Gilligan concludes that Amy saw the hypothetical dilemma,

not as a math problem with humans but a narrative of relationships that extends over time. Amy envisions the wife's continuing need for her husband and the husband's continuing concern for his wife and seeks to respond to the druggist's need in a way that would sustain rather than sever connection.

(Gilligan 1982: 28)

Amy fails the justice test since the hypothetical requires her to deal with the facts as a self-contained problem to be resolved only using the internal information of the hypothetical. Amy's failure in moral development is based upon a moral standard of analysis which is exclusively drawn from the male psyche. But what happens when we seek to find out what Amy's reasoning is for dealing with the hypothetical dilemma the way she does rather than simply judging her to be a moral failure? Gilligan posits that the world which Amy inhabits is different from that refracted by Kohlberg's construction of Heinz's dilemma:

Seen in this light, her understanding of morality as arising from the recognition of relationship, her belief in communication as the mode of conflict resolution, and her conviction that the solution to the dilemma will follow from its compelling representation seem far from naive or cognitively immature. Instead Amy's judgments contain the insights central to an ethic of care, just as Jake's judgments reflect the logic of the justice approach. Her incipient awareness of the "method of truth," the central tenet of nonviolent conflict resolution, and her belief in the restorative activity of care, lead her to see the actors in the dilemma arrayed not as opponents in a contest of rights but as members of a network of relationships on whose continuation they all depend. Consequently her solution to the dilemma lies in activating the network by communication, securing the inclusion of the wife by strengthening rather than severing connections.

(Gilligan 1982: 30–31)

Amy does not answer the question posed, which is *should* Heinz steal the drug; rather she asks *how* Heinz should act. Gilligan concludes that the problem lies in the interviewer's failure (not Amy's) to understand a logic which searches for a more adequate solution, just as girls do on the playground when they change games rather than impose rules. Jake has fully introjected the rules and regulations approach, so he decides that theft is okay in order to avoid confrontation, and he feels comfortable in relying on the law, "the judge would probably think it was the right thing to do" to mediate the dispute, should one arise. Jake has transposed a hierarchy of power into a hierarchy of values, which is the mainstream method of defusing potentially explosive conflict by rendering people into impersonal representatives of conflicting claims. This is an abstraction of the moral dilemma which obfuscates the fundamentally personal situation which is presented. Hierarchical ordering is based upon competition, who wins and who loses, and what rules are applied to the game in order to lessen the very real possibility of violence when one does not ascend the hierarchy. Amy perceives the dilemma as part of a network of connections which can be solved through increased communication. For Amy, the moral problem "changes from one of unfair domination, the imposition of property over life, to one of unnecessary exclusion, the failure of the druggist to respond to the wife" (Gilligan 1982: 32).

Gilligan concludes that "men and women may speak different languages, [which] they assume are the same, using similar words to encode disparate experiences of self and social relationships" (Gilligan 1982: 73). She explains that "while an ethic of justice proceeds from the premise of equality – that everyone should be treated the same – an ethic of care rests on the premise of non-violence – that no one should be hurt" (Gilligan 1982: 174). The basis upon which the mainstream formulates its ethical considerations have, by definitions of equality, excluded most of the world until very recently. The ethics of the postmodern female Trickster more closely resemble an ethics of care rather than an ethics of justice.

Summary

The female Trickster in postmodernity has reinscribed sexuality, social work, ethics, and the generally accepted characteristics of traditional Tricksters into a culturally inflected archetypal energy which refuses to be anyone's victim while constellating an ethics of care rather than an ethics of justice. Accomplishing these tasks with a comedic context which assumes that chaos and paradox are perennial while relationships are the constant if treated with care and awareness is emblematic of the postmodern female Trickster. The most serious of themes can sometimes only be presented through humor which itself is Trickster energy, bridging seemingly contradictory and paradoxical elements. It is in this sense, of humor's ability to explicate a contradictory tone, to wrestle and harvest paradox, that humor can be used either to take control, to maintain power, or to overthrow authority in postmodernity. The female Trickster, the embodiment of humor itself, has constellated in postmodernity not to maintain power or take control but to reinscribe and revalue the hierarchy of values which has brought the modern world to the brink of extinction. Humor is a serious tool of transgression and transformation born of the imaginal realms as a psychological survival guide. It guides us to unite the paradoxical. It can teach us to prosper while we are laughing.

Notes

1 *St. Louis Dispatch* on Paretsky (1982): book jacket.
2 *Los Angeles Times* on Grafton (1992): book jacket.
3 *Kirkus Reviews* on Stabenow (2000): book jacket.
4 *Essence Magazine* on Neely (2000): book jacket.
5 For further discussion of this topic the reader is referred to *The Penguin Book of Women's Humor* (Barreca 1996), especially the excerpts from the Brontë sisters, Jane Austen, and Charlotte Gilman Perkins.
6 "Author Toni Morrison Discusses her Latest Novel *Beloved*," interview with G. Caldwell (1987).
7 The humor of irony has been noted by other scholars working on the manifestation of the female Trickster in postmodernity. Lori Landay (1998) in *Madcaps, Screwballs and Con Women: The Female Trickster in American Culture* found that "female Tricksters use linguistic trickery and ironic layering, of resistance and dominant meanings" to transform culture (Landay 1998: xx). Unfortunately, Landay's research into the female Trickster does not consider the Jungian or post-Jungian work on the Trickster archetype, such as López-Pedraza (1989), Beebe (1981) or Samuels (1993b, 2000) which would have been particularly illuminating. Landay's (1998) analysis is sociological and linguistic (not psychological) in the same way that Lewis Hyde's (1998) and Henry Louis Gates's (1988) work on the Trickster are. However, the question posed by these theorists is certainly psychological; what does the Trickster's appearance in postmodernity signify?
8 Excerpts from quotes at the beginning of *Indemnity Only* (Paretsky 1982) where V.I. made her first appearance (Dell Paperback edition).
9 *Washington Times* and the *Christian Science Monitor*, Neely (1994): back cover.
10 Lori Landay (1998) concludes that the appearance of Trickster energy is a precursor marker to revolution in a particular culture's mores, thus the appearance of the female Trickster in American culture is the precursor of a major revolution in American cultural mores. She identifies female Tricksters who appeared immediately before World War II and precursed the "different from" second wave of the women's movement. She identifies *Catwoman*, the film, as demonstrating how the Trickster refuses to be a victim through a show of physical strength.
11 I am thinking here of those brave Saudi women who drove cars in protest against the law which said they could not drive.
12 This concern with and action which preserves the environment is occurring in temporal space as well as the fictional world. In 1960, a group of women from the San Francisco Bay area decided to restore the polluted cesspool called the San Francisco estuary. How they did and their story was made into the book, *San Francisco Bay: Portrait of an Estuary*. In the fictional world, Nancy Drew in

her latest incarnation is driving a hybrid car instead of her roadster, and she's now volunteering at a animal shelter.

13 The quote is attributed to Isaeus (c.420–c.350 BCE), a Greek speech writer.

14 This is what Samuels (1993a: 95; 1993b; 2000: 45) has been referring to since he began writing about this subject in relation to the feminine in the mid-1990s and for which I have attempted to find evidential support in the literary arena, as he does in the political one.

15 All figures from the National Center for Health Statistics, Washington, DC and the National Marriage Project, a research group at Rutgers University based upon Census Bureau Data from a June 2002 survey, reported in the *Marin Independent*, October 25, 2003: A13.

16 Madelyn Cain, *The Childless Revolution* (2001) was excerpted in *Utne* magazine, July–August 2002: 72.

17 Age did have something to do with feeling comfortable with or awful about the decision to not have children. Women in their fifties felt inadequate, women in their forties reported mixed reactions and women under 35 felt no sense of obligation to have children and accept the notion fully that they were entitled to having many options and choices other than marriage and child-rearing.

18 All statistics and quotes are taken from *Utne* magazine, July–August 2002: 72–74.

19 *Detecting Women* (Heising 2000) lists 52 lesbian female sleuths. The reader is referred to this publication for guidance in tracking down some of these sleuths. I have especially enjoyed Nikki Baker's series with Virginia Kelly, a black lesbian stockbroker from Chicago; Rose Beecham's Amanda Valentine series set in exotic Wellington, New Zealand; and Irene Lin-Chandler's Holly-Jean Ho, a bisexual living in London. Claire McNab has written ten Carol Aston adventures set in Sydney, Australia. It is interesting to note that the majority of the 52 authors writing in excess of 229 novels featuring fictive lesbian female sleuths were created in the 1990s. Those created in the late 1970s and early 1980s were lesbians but they were white: Vicki McConnell's Nyla Wade (1982 – three novels), Eve Zaremba's Helen Keremos (1978 – six novels), and Sarah Dreher's Stoner McTavish (1985 – seven novels) are examples. As the genre opened to diversity, so did the range of lesbian sleuths imaged. Now there are black lesbian sleuths (Virginia Kelly), Anglo-Chinese bisexuals (Holly-Jean Ho), Hispanic-Black sleuths (Elizabeth Mendoza), and Chicana lesbian sleuths (Lucia Ramos) (Heising 2000: 309–310).

20 Kinsey's parents were killed in a car accident when she was 6. She was in the back seat of their car and had to wait several hours to be rescued while she heard her parents dying in the front seats.

21 *American Heritage Dictionary* (1981).

Chapter 12

Blanche White, re/storation agent

The revolution is simply not going to be made by literary journals.
Lillian Robinson[1]

Introduction

Discourse about the subaltern "other" was not located exclusively in academia. The fictive female sleuth narratives are examples of how the discourses of postmodernity were offered to the reader of popular fiction through a narrative which is carefully woven around the awareness of one's location and the location of others. This excerpt from the Blanche White series, written by BarbaraNeely,[2] is evidence and example of how the postmodern Trickster makes an appearance within a situated location and remains fluid while exploring her truth humorously:

> Blanche was unimpressed by the tears, and Grace's Mammy-save-me eyes. Mammy-savers regularly peeped out at her from the faces of some white women for whom she worked, and lately, in this age of the touchy-feely model of manhood, an occasional white man. It happened when an employer was struck by family disaster or grew too compulsive about owning everything, too overwrought, or downright frightened by who and what they were. She never ceased to be amazed at how many white people longed for Aunt Jemima. They'd ease into the kitchen and hem and haw their way through some sordid personal tale. She'd listen and make sympathetic noises. She rarely asked questions, except to clarify the life lessons their stories conveyed, or to elicit some detail that would make their story more amusing to her friends. She told employers who asked what she would do in their place, or, what she thought they ought to do, "I sure wish I knew, I truly do," accompanied by a slow, sad smile, a matching shake of her head, and arms folded tightly across her chest.
>
> (Neely 1992: 39–40)

Blanche is an example of the postmodern Trickster who crosses inter-sections with a knowledge of where she has been and where she is going. In postmodernity, however, simply *crossing boundaries* between the dichoto-mies of either/or is not enough. The trick comes when there is bridge-building activity between previously uncrossable boundaries and borders – this is the re/storation work the postmodern female Trickster is involved in. Building bridges across dichotomies, between boundaries with an awareness of one's own self-interest and the interest of the collective, beyond the earlier stage of tribal affinity and even beyond nationalism, to an awareness of being on planet Earth together and the need to survive together – this is the energy of the postmodern female Trickster of which Blanche is a prime example of. Surviving the world is what African American women have had to do since they were stolen from their lands and sold into the system of slavery which extinguished their inherent human rights. Much of Blanche's life has been spent in reacting to racism and sexism. How does one who is politically powerless rectify her situation? One way is through

> Contrived laughter as a means of appeasing, conciliating, and protesting against her masters and mistresses. Much early humor was based upon shirking work, escaping a whipping, causing the master or mistress some physical harm or humiliating them. Similar tales of aggressiveness against white racism continue to serve the same purposes for African American women today.
>
> (Dance 1998: 458)

The element which brings psychological rewards is the revenge aspect, which Freud said was based upon the pleasure that one gets from belittling and humbling an enemy, but in marginalized groups this belittling has to occur ironically and be easily misinterpreted by the symbolic order, in other words, it has to be obtuse. It is the doctrine of

> fight, and if you can't fight, kick; if you can't kick, then bite – and if you can't do that, make them and their foolish behavior the butt of your humor and hold them up to the ridicule of the world.
>
> (Dance 1998: 459)

Introducing Blanche White: re/storation agent

Blanche White is a re/storation agent par excellence. She reinscribes prosti-tution as sex work. Motherhood is reinscribed with the imagery of a mule. Refusing to be a victim becomes a refusal to introject the meaning of the "other." Literature and the writing of it are reinscribed to include the imaginal manifestations of all classes of persons. Naming African American children with names that are difficult for white tongues to articulate is reinscribed as value laden in their creativity and lack of tie to European origins (Neely 1998: 78). An older woman living alone is honored for her independence, and being a maid is reinscribed into a "profession" offering independent agency, autonomy, and authority. Blanche reinscribes the traditional middle-class white view of those who clean houses for a living because she refuses to introject and reproject a hierarchal political structure of master/servant. She offers another perspective all together to the reader, for Blanche, relationship is not only the primary constituent of whether she takes a position or not but also an integral part of her relationship to her profession as well since "understanding houses was part of how she made her living" (Neely 1998: 1). She continues the reinscription by analogizing cleaning homes to a "good surgeon [who] didn't open up a patient without an examination, [likewise] she didn't clean or cook in a house until she'd done the same." In the next sentence Blanche recalls that "she couldn't remember when she'd first understood how much houses had to say about themselves, but it was information she had come to depend on" (Neely 1998: 1–2). Blanche establishes a tone of integrity about her work, which takes cooking and cleaning out of the "other" category, including the ethical considerations which are a part of the fiduciary duty a professional has to their community:

> This was not the sort of job Blanche liked. Being housekeeper-cook was the kind of position she woke up worrying about in the middle of the night. She wasn't scared of it. There was no type of domestic work that she hadn't aced in the twenty-six years since she'd taken up the profession. It was her ability to cook, sew, clean, launder, wait table, and all the rest that made it possible for her to make her way in the work and feed and clothe her dead sister's two children. Part of the problem with this job was that she never liked supervising folks – too much like being an overseer. She hoped that Carrie, the housemaid she'd met yesterday and Wanda the cleaning woman didn't need somebody looking over their shoulder, because she already had two kids at home.
> (Neely 1998: 2)

In the next scene, Blanche reinscribes the hierarchical structures of employer and employee, humorously establishing that she decided whom to work for and not the other way around:

> She'd made a note of which ones complained [her clients] so she could replace them. Any employer who couldn't understand an emergency would likely be a problem before long. One of the major reasons she chose to do day work was being able to pick up and drop off clients as

she saw fit. This meant she didn't have to take no mess from nobody, her preferred way of living.

(Neely 1998: 3)

For Blanche, the work of cleaning houses allows one to be your own boss. This insistence on having an independent source of money makes Blanche like Kate or V.I. and Kinsey, who all insist on the same independence in their choice of work, the dispositive feature being that they are not dependent upon anyone else's direction or decision making. And while they all work alone, this is not to say that they don't have many relationships, but it is this act of living alone, having an independent source of income and liking it which is the reinscription for women. At the same time that Blanche is reinscribing the value of working she is also deconstructing race politics and love from a postmodern postcolonial perspective. She punctures the idealized projection of love when she realizes that "the more a person believed love was a part of what they got from an employer, the more likely it was that the person was being asked to do things that only love could justify" (Neely 1998: 5).

The disassociative state which occurs when there is fusion abuse and love is shown in her dealings with a family who has servants which must be hidden from public view because "it wasn't right for somebody running for governor to have personal servants like that in these times" (Neely: 1998: 6). Blanche cannot help herself from becoming involved in those shenanigans that this kind of house inevitably produces. From a structural perspective, not much has changed about big houses having an upstairs and downstairs culture from *Mansfield Park* to *Wuthering Heights* and *The Age of Innocence*. The postmodern trick is that now the ones who live "upstairs" are the "other" and Blanche, the housekeeper, is the storyteller:

> Sweet ancestors! If she'd known she was going to have to arm-wrestle the housemaids, she'd have gotten more rest. And what a hypocrite this Brindle character was, sending off their personal servants! As if anybody would mistake someone who lived in this kind of house for just your average Joe.

(Neely 1998: 7)

Blanche doesn't limit her targets, as she punctures every grandiose illusion with an ironic deconstructive equanimity. Racial prejudices are not so subtly deconstructed when Blanche eavesdrops on a conversation regarding the handling of the African American community:

> 'We'll give 'em a bang-up lunch, make them feel included. They all need that you know, all of them. They are like children!" Allister Brindle spoke like an authority.

"Oh, it'll be fine sir. You've got them in your pocket. They are behind us a hundred percent."
Brindle reached over and slapped Sadowski on the back. "That's why I hired you, Ted. Even I believe you when you mouth that bullshit."
Brindle's smile faded. "Let's not be overconfident, Ted. You can never quite trust them. You must never forget that."
He gave Sadowski's shoulder a little shake for emphasis. "They got different values. In the end, they're in the pocket of whoever pays them."
Blanche left for the kitchen. She wondered which *they* Brindle and Sadowski meant – Blacks, women, gays, Puerto Ricans, people in wheelchairs? It didn't matter which.
What mattered was that Brindle and Sadowski believed in *They*; talked about *they* as though *they* lived on the underside of the public toilet seat. Is that what Inez listened to every day. Poor Inez. Poor Inez, hell! Poor Blanche [emphasis in original].

(Neely 1998: 8)

Before Blanche can decide whether to remain in this house, the doorbell rings, triggering her sexuality and a deconstruction of racial characteristics:

the man on the other side was the color of old, old gold. He could have been a mulatto or a Latino, but the ease with which he stood at rich white folks door in his shorts and T-shirt convinced her he was Caucasian.

(Neely 1998: 9)

Then Blanche reinscribes the erotic:

He gave her one of those Mr. Mona Lisa smiles as he passed her. I bet his dick curves up when it's hard, she thought. Every man she'd known with an upturned dick had sex seeping out of his pores, just like this boy. . . . Pity the poor cow who thought it had anything to do with her. Alright, Blanche, get your mind out of your drawers, she told herself. Still, how long had it been? She got to two years and stopped counting.

(Neely 1998: 9)

This preoccupation with graphic sexual imagery is reminiscent of Trickster from the Winnebago tribe, but the postmodern twist is in how Blanche reflects the energy back upon herself, reflectively.
Blanche employs a Tricksterish doubling technique when we see how she can get caught by prejudice. Blanche is waiting for Wanda Jackson, the cleaning woman, when a strange white woman walks into the kitchen. Blanche knew "this white woman surely wasn't Wanda Jackson" (Neely

1998: 10). But of course, this white woman is Wanda, and it is Blanche who has to reevaluate her presumptions. But we are not done with Wanda in this story, for Wanda turns out to be quite a Trickster of her own. She begins by challenging Blanche on her assumptions, asking her if she was "that taken with your own good sense, darlin?" Blanche answers affirmatively and then reflects to herself, "maybe the Ancestors put Wanda in her path to remind her not to fall into a *They* trap of her own" (Neely 1998: 11).

This is cross-cultural bridge building at its best and demonstrates why popular culture serves as an important locale where these racial, social, and religious boundaries can be crossed, whether by whites, off-whites, or blacks. Blanche fully embraces the paradox when she states, "what a dull place the world would be if people only did what was expected, eh?" (Neely 1998: 13). Which is why she is such a restorative postmodern Trickster. In the next scenes, *They* turn out to be Black leaders and while Blanche "was generally delighted to come across a group of black people" this group makes her "jaw drop" for another reason, for *They* were the "Blacks with positions and titles to support the latest cut in programs for the poor, or to amen some closet racist like Brindle (Neely 1998: 14). *They* are the black leaders of the community.

At the luncheon Blanche realizes that there was "nobody from what she considered the helpful groups in the community . . . everyone of these suckers expected something in return for their sellout" (Neely 1998: 15). But her real vengeance is reserved for the black minister:

> whose Temple was a new kind of African-American religion where Christian, Jewish and Muslim holy books and beliefs were mixed together . . . she was suspicious of anyone who was pushing not one, not two, but three boy-led religions rolled into one.
>
> (Neely 1998: 15)

In less than 15 pages, the reader has received a trenchant racial, political, and class commentary, delivered with Blanche's prodigious sense of humor. And we have just started the book! As the luncheon proceeds and Brindle courts the black minister the reader finds out which boundaries Blanche is willing to subvert:

> "Now about this election . . . . I really need your help in Roxbury, Maurice."
> "Not to worry, not to worry," Samuelson asserted him. "Aunt Jemima and Uncle Ben know which side their bread is buttered on. And if they don't it's my job to tell them."
> Both men laughed.

Flames engulfed Blanche's brain. She'd never before heard a Black person promise to keep the Darkies in line for Masa . . . before she could stop herself, she turned abruptly and jabbed a sharp elbow into Samuelson's lower spine, knocking him off balance and splashing whatever he was drinking onto his shirt.

"Uncle Ben and Aunt Jemima that, you butt-sucking maggot!"

(Neely 1998: 16)

Psycholinguistic reinscription or just plain rage in the service of good? Shadow energy eruption or shadow energy brought up to consciousness for integration? After the incident Blanche goes to the kitchen and reflects with wit and irony about these issues:

So why she had acted like it was? Had she passed her sell-by date? Had she lost the looseness needed to roll with the kind of blows that came with this work? Or maybe she was just sick to death of nigger-minded dickbrains like Samuelson making pacts with the devil in the name of Black Folks.

"Spiritual leader my foot." She fiddled and fumed, moving pots from the sink to the dishwasher, emptying the kettle, wiping the counter, anything to keep moving, to help her fidget away the last of her outrage. At the same time, she was depressed by the knowledge that there was really nothing surprising about what Samuelson had done. She knew that all these years of being hated for no reason beyond color had convinced some Black people that the racists must be right. Did Samuelson hate himself as much as he did the people he called Aunt Jemima and Uncle Ben? Or did being a man of the cloth make him an honorary white in his own eyes?

(Neely 1998: 17)

The most difficult issues are brought to the foreground for the reader's reflection through the clear dialogue. Carrie is prejudiced against lesbians and Blanche confronts her reliance on religion to diss them. Carrie defends herself:

"Cause God doesn't mean for women to do what she do."

A lesbian, huh?

Had Carrie been a few shades light Blanche was sure she'd have seen blood rush to the woman's face.

"It's against God. It say so in the Bible."

"But what's it got to do with you?"

"Ain't none of my business but my pastor say it ain't natural. It's ungodly," Carrie hissed.

"I don't get it," Blanche said. "You Christians say God made every-thing and everybody which has gotta include lesbians. But then you say lesbians are ungodly. Seems to me that you, your pastor, or your God is very confused, honey."

(Neely 1998: 18)

Adrienne Rich (1980) would be happy with the confrontation Blanche has with Carrie's notion of compulsory heterosexuality. The next transgressive linguistic subversion we see in this narrative occurs in the context of Blanche's style of mothering. Blanche takes on the raising of her sister's children after her sister dies. Taifa and Malik are both teens in the book, *Blanche Cleans Up* (Neely 1998), and it is through her relationship with them that Blanche has an opportunity to turn her gaze towards the insti-tution of mothering. Blanche and her niece Taifa disagree about hairstyles, which prompts another deconstructive dialogue, specifically concerning identity as represented by African American hair:

Blanche washed her hands then squished meat loaf ingredients together and tried not to pretend it was Taifa's tender throat between her hands. She took a deep breath.
"I ain't even sure what a geek is, and I don't want nobody to make fun of you baby, including yourself which is what you'll be doing if you grow up to be a Black woman who thinks your hair's gotta be pro-cessed or have some Dacron extensions on it to be beautiful." Blanche mentally patted herself on the back for sounding so reasonable and even-tempered. She turned the meat loaf into the pan, covered the potatoes with a bit more water and went on.
"Look, if I had my way, every Black person in the world would wear their hair in some kind of natural style instead of making themselves look foolish imitating white folks hair."

(Neely 1998: 32)

Blanche demonstrates how wit operates as psychological adaptation when she imagines wringing Taifa's neck while challenging her adopting a white viewpoint on the beauty of hair:

[Taifa] Oh Moms! That race stuff is so old. I keep tellin you it ain't even about white people.
Blanche held up her hand. "Yeah, yeah. So you say. I think it is about white folks. I think it's about being ashamed of having nappy hair."
"Yeah, but my girlfriends' mothers don't."
Blanche felt her left nerve beginning to fray. She couldn't seem to stop herself from reacting to this holdover from years of having Mama tell her she needed to be more like Miz Mary's or Miz Caroline's

daughters, who'd be happy to lick the kitchen floor clean, let alone mop it, if their dear old mother even looked like she wanted the floor cleaned.

"and Rasheeda's mother said she'd never let Rasheeda go out with naps all over her head like some kinda . . ."

That did it! Blanche spun around and leaned across the table so that her face was close to Taifa's. "Now I've let you get your hair straightened. Even let you get a permanent. If that ain't good enough for you, put a paper bag over your head and stop bugging me about it!"

(Neely 1998: 33)

The physical outburst is unusual for Blanche but it does happen, as it does in the scene above and when she shoves the Pastor at the Brindles. Blanche is not perfect and perfection is in the realm of the hero, not the Trickster. Even so, this kind of behavior is unusual for the wise-cracking Blanche, who usually seems to take everything in stride but the significance of Taifa's desire to change her hair to more closely resemble the blonde, flowing tresses of the Northern European female which the North American culture idealizes is just too much for Blanche. The action quickly shifts and the reader goes back with Blanche to the Brindles the next day. The next person Blanche meets is Mick Harper, Mrs. Brindle's masseuse. Before saying hello, Blanche reflects upon the transgressive potential inherent in Mrs. Brindle's choice of a masseuse:

If Mick Harper's mannish haircut, bone-crushing handshake and butch walk didn't deliver her message, her purple T-shirt did. I CAN'T EVEN THINK STRAIGHT was plastered across her chest in hot pick letters. She was one of those mid-size women who managed to make themselves seem taller and bigger by the way they moved their bodies. Blanche was tickled. She knew instinctively that Felicia's having a very out lesbian masseuse was meant to be a slap at the righteous-assed Allister.

"Love that shirt," she said.

(Neely 1998: 44)

Blanche's boss employs a black lesbian masseuse as an act of resistance against her husband and traditional cultural norms. Blanche, as Trickster social worker, invites Mick to lunch with her and Carrie as an act of resistance. "Mick gave Blanche a skeptical look. You don't really think Carrie's gonna sit down with me, do you?" Blanche's reply turns the challenge into a win situation by building bridges through sharing food, "Bet you a nickel food will win out over foolishness." To which Mick replies, "You're on" (Neely 1998: 44). After Mick has enjoyed Blanche's cooking, Blanche *shape-shifts* into a differing sort of Trickster, prodding Mick for information about the Brindles. It's in this passage that we get a sense of how Blanche constructs her own identity and then offers to share her process as bridge-building material with Mick: "Mick fiddled with the coffee cup and didn't speak. I'm just not sure I oughta be talking about my client's business." And it is at this point that Blanche reinscribes that what they are doing is not gossiping but "a little talk between two professionals about our mutual client":

> Well, I don't know how it is in your business, Blanche told her, but in my business, information is just like a pot or a broom, just another something. I need to do my job in a way that works for all concerned, just like you need to know if your client's got a bad back or a tricky kidney so you can give them the best service. And anyway, I'm working for Felicia, too. So, this is just a little talk between two professionals about our mutual client.
>
> (Neely 1998: 46)

This is a deconstruction and reinscription of the traditional boundaries set up between an employee/employer or master/slave. It challenges the presumption supporting the illusion in the symbolic order that economics trumps all other activities. This reinscription continues as Mick tells all about the history of the Brindles, including how Mr. Brindle was "related to people who own this state." Then Mick reinscribes the comment, "Or should I say, people who killed the Indians and stole their land" (Neely 1998: 47). This excerpt is an example of how popular cultural fiction can provide an educatory function to the reader in how to resist traditional cultural norms while contributing imagery which reinscribes North American history and by implication, colonial world history. The reader is then offered a potent example of how Braidiotti's (1994) theoretical concept of *nomadic identity* works phenomenologically:

> Like everyone else, Felicia was put together with pieces from different jigsaw puzzles so you got a bit of a tree, half of a horse's leg, and a bit of lake that taken together meant something different from anything the individual pieces showed.
>
> (Neely 1998: 48)

Now the night-time and her children take over, which is what happens for most people who work outside their homes – if they happen to have children. The reader is drawn into Blanche's musing on the tension of the opposites, which many parents face regardless of how their egos are encapsulated in a body – male, female, of color, white, or mixed heritage:

Once again she was faced with the major contradiction of her parent-hood: wanting both to be shed of these kids and to be as much of a mother as they needed for as long as they needed her – within reason, of course. It was like wanting to be a rock and an eagle at the same time.

(Neely 1998: 52)

As soon as Blanche walks in the door the pragmatics of daily life take over:

Blanche was almost grateful when Malik reminded her of the environ-mental meeting he wanted to get to that evening. Almost. She'd much rather take a hot bath and go to bed early, but she knew this meeting was important to Malik, and she had no intention of letting him go alone. She wasn't one of those parents silly enough to think the child wasn't the type to get into trouble.

They almost missed the place. They'd been looking for an office type building or storefront, but the office of the Community Reawakening Project was up a narrow stairway to the third floor apartment across the street from the check cashing place. A hand lettered sign invited them to walk right in.

There were fourteen people already there. Six of them were white, the largest group of white people Blanche had ever seen in Roxbury, except cops. They were all sitting together with tight little smiles on their faces, their hands folded in their laps like schoolchildren under a mean teacher. If they were so uncomfortable, why had they come? She took the flyer from Malik and read the answers down at the bottom in very small letters: "Also sponsored by the Multi-Cultural Environmental Coalition."

(Neely 1998: 52–53)

The reader gets to scan the crowd along with Blanche. Hair makes another appearance as a central image of identity:

She watched a young dred sister gather her hair in one hand and dig in her shoulder bag with the others. She pulled out a pair of chopsticks and used them to pin her hair on top of her head. When a couple of stray dreds fell in her face, she flipped them back with a toss of her head that made Blanche smile.

She used to think the Hair Ballet that white girls did was all theirs until she'd noticed dred sisters flipping their hair over their shoulders, lifting it from their necks to catch a breeze, flinging it back from their faces in ways that women with false or processed hair rarely seemed to do. And wasn't it funny that after all these years of horsehair, other people's hair, Dacron weaves, wigs and extensions, it was our own naturally nappy hair that was making black women's blow hair dream come true? Like Lady Day sang: God bless the child that's got her own.

(Neely 1998: 54)

Encouraging being and loving oneself is reinforced to the reader when Blanche meets someone who identifies herself as "Lacey Monroe, sex worker." Blanche immediately gets into the transcendent joy of jest, replying, "Blanche White, temporary celibate" (Neely 1998: 55). Here we see linguistic subversion openly acknowledged between Tricksters when they meet. This humorous energy exchange may be between people dissimiarly situated according to traditional cultural norms yet these women are postmodern Trickster souls and though they travel psychologically in different embodiments they make a connection across difference. Then the reader is drawn into the social worker aspect of the narrative when the purpose of the meeting is revealed by Aminata Dawson of the Community Reawakening Project:

Tonight is one in our series of events to make sure the community knows how our lives, and our children's lives, are being affected by pollution, toxic waste, and other environmental hazards, especially lead poisoning.

(Neely 1998: 55)

This is an example of a community refusing to be a victim. Several speakers follow, mostly in inflammatory language intended to incite anger and hatred towards others. Then Mr. Othello Flood begins talking with an authentic reassuring joke: "Most of y'all know me. I grew up around here. Probably stole something from half the people in this room" (Neely 1998: 57). After the audience laughs with him, Othello shares his transformational story:

But I looked up one day and understood I'd been doing wrong and what I needed to do to make things right. So me and a couple other brothers started Ex-Cons for Community Safety. Our group tries to get brothers coming home from prison to take responsibility for making our neighborhoods safe and to help turn our young brothers around so they don't go the prison route. As far as lead poisoning and the environment is concerned, we have an environmental patrol that deals with illegal dumping and trashing. We make sure abandoned buildings are secured and not being used by junkies or drug dealers. We also provide security for meetings like this and escorts for our elders and other people who need it. We're working with some of the youth to start a breakfast program for the little ones next year. Thank you.

(Neely 1998: 58)

Sexuality and social work converge comfortably when Blanche finds Lacey at the meeting, and asks her, "So what kind of sex work are you in exactly?" Lacey replies:

"The rent-my-body-for-pleasure line." Lacey took a leather case from her handbag and handed Blanche her card. "We're a cooperative. We work with the big hotels and private parties for men with lots of money."

Blanche looked down at that card:

Family Values, Inc.

555-767-7979

She covered her mouth with her hand, but not quite soon enough to stifle the wop of laughter that turned the heads of people standing nearby.

"Girl! Are you serious?"

"As any other incorporate identity out there," Lacey didn't even smile when she said it.

"Yeah, I nearly split my sides the first time I saw that card," Joanie said. "They even got an investment club."

(Neely 1998: 60)

In this bit of expert reinscription sex workers turn a new trick by making the exploitive capitalistic system work for them through the adaptation of irony. Yet, Blanche also seriously questions the economic basis upon which prostitution is built:

She thought about the times in her life when her money was so low, her prospects so dim that if the right stranger had asked her to have sex for the right price, she didn't know how she would have answered. She thought about the more than handful of women she knew and worked for who talked about sex with their husbands and lovers as though it were a price they had to pay for help with the cost of foods or school clothes for their children.

(Neely 1998: 64)

The trick is not about explicitly using the economic system to one's own benefit, the trick is to be aware of what you are doing and for what end. Blanche's perception is similar to how she perceives *Darkie's Disease*, which is discussed in the opening pages of this chapter. The narrative then moves seamlessly into a consideration of teenage pregnancy. Shaquita, Blanche's cousin Charlotte's 16-year-old daughter, has been staying with Blanche while Charlotte was on vacation. Blanche discovers that Shaquita is pregnant. When Shaquita refuses to consider an abortion, Blanche "heard jail doors clanging shut" as she reminisces about her own abortion at the age of 19:

> Blanche shut her bedroom door and sat on the side of the bed rocking and hugging herself as the memory of her own teenage pregnancy and decision to have an abortion played in her mind. She'd been older than Shaquita, almost nineteen, and determined to do what Mama would not have her do: get out of Farleigh, take her life in her own hands and try to live it her own way. Had she had already decided at nineteen that she didn't ever want to have children?
>
> (Neely 1998: 67)

The paradox shown here is of a woman who knows she does not want to have children yet could not turn her deceased sister's children away. A woman who knew what she wanted from life yet must balance the tensions of being deeply connected to her living and lineal kin. For Blanche, as for many women regardless of ethnicity or culture, the ethics of care which focuses on relationships and how to keep them intact trumps the ethics of justice with its focus on rules and regulations. Blanche comforts herself by resorting to sacred technology, her "altar" where she "lit a candle and a stick of incense," as prelude to speaking "to the Ancestors about what was on her mind" (Neely 1998: 67). Blanche is the embodiment of independence and connection. Do autonomy and community really represent the fundamental contradiction that critical theorists say it does?[3] Through reading these narratives and embracing the images the reader is made aware that what has been presented by the patriarchal symbolic order as an irreconcilable opposing unresolvable tension can be brought into relationship by connecting the dichotomous ends of the continuum. Blanche shows how through her connection to the Ancestors; through the rituals she enacts she is restored. That process done, she can go to sleep.

When Blanche goes back to work the next morning, she finds out that Mrs. Brindle's trainer, Saxe, her "joy boy," has been murdered. Blanche goes to get herself a drink of water and runs into Mr. Brindle's political advisor, who informs her, "I don't think that glass was meant for you." It made Blanche feel as though he'd caught her stealing the silverware (Neely 1998: 71). Blanche turns it around by recognizing explicitly that they are both similarly situated as both were employed by the Brindles: "Thanks for telling me, I'll ask the Brindles which glasses were bought for the help's use and make sure to serve your drinks in them next time you eat here" (Neely 1998: 72). Blanche refuses to introject Sadowski's projection on her as the "other," and this is how she manifests her refusal to be a victim. In addition to this image, Blanche fulfills an educatory function for the reader, instructing on how to trick by tossing back the nonsense as a strategic move fueled by an ironic wit. In the next scene Blanche has to deal with Mr. Brindle and strategically decides not to tell him the whole truth when she is asked about someone visiting the house yesterday:

"If somebody was in here, I'd say he must have had a key."
"What the hell does that mean? Either he was here or he wasn't."
She'd never seen someone's eyes get bloodshot while she watched. Could she make him froth at the mouth next?
"If someone with a key came quietly in the door, I wouldn't know a thing about it." They say if you're gonna lie, stay as close to the truth as you can.

(Neely 1998: 74)

Is what Blanche does an ethical move here, after she has told a lie? Since I have made the argument that an integral part of the Trickster energy in postmodernity is its ethical cast and also that females demonstrate an ethics of care as opposed to the ethics of justice recognized by the symbolic order, does Blanche's strategic lie demonstrate integrity? According to Gates (1988), linguistic subversion is the most potent part of reinscription. Toni Morrison (1987) tells us that linguistic subversion through reinscription must be done to take back the authority. Lying isn't wrong when it's done in the service of a greater good (like hiding Jews during the Holocaust or helping slaves escape through the Underground Railroad before the Civil War). All of these issues and more are raised by Blanche as the murders involving the Brindles start to pile up, literally at their doorstep. It seems that Mr. Brindle had a visitor who came in and took a videotape that revealed something about Brindle which could cost him the election. This is not the transgressive part of the narrative, though; what is transgressive is how Blanche uses these events to place before the reader imagistic narrative which moves beyond the binaries of race, class, or sex to an awareness that what really marks you as the "other" is character and the integrity you reveal in your everyday behaviors. By the time Blanche leaves the Brindles that day, she has morphed into the gleeful traditional Trickster who walks away after starting the pyrotechnics, "giggling with relief that this was her half day so she didn't have to hang around the fire raging in the Brindle house" (Neely 1998: 75).

As Blanche rides home she shares how Boston was still segregated, using clothing, hair, and parenting as metaphor:

She was ignored by salesclerks and followed by store security people downtown which was just one more sign that this city wasn't putting out the welcome mat for her. Boston didn't seem to allow much room for differences either. If you were white and lived on Beacon Hill, you had to wear a lot of navy blue and worship old money. If you were an Irish Catholic from South Boston, you had to have big hair and a bad racial attitude. As for Roxbury, when she'd first moved in, three women in Rudigere Home had without being asked given her the names of their hairdressers, as if there was something wrong with her un-straightened hair. And practically every mother in the housing development had found time to tell how wrong she was when she'd said it was just as bad to scream at, curse and dis your kids as it was to beat them.

(Neely 1998: 77)

Blanche has established herself as an outsider to traditional static Anglo-American and African American culture, yet she demonstrates a dynamism in terms of psychological awareness, humor, and irony. In the next few pages of the narrative the reader is treated to a reinscription of an unmarried woman automatically assumed to be lonely to the awareness that the unmarried state for a woman can offer opportunity for lifelong independence (Neely 1998: 83). Blanche then reinscribes the writing of literature from an exclusive purview of the upper classes to a gift of imagination fully available to those in the working classes. This reinscription not only gives the imprimatur of credibility to those who have not imagined themselves as writers because they must work with their hands but also provides the reader with an image of how it actually could be accomplished:

She leaned over and picked up her copy of *Working Writer* from the floor beside her chair. It had become one of her favorite books. Joanie, who worked as dietician at Boston Medical Center, had given it to her. The poems and stories by hospital laundry workers who had recently gotten their GED and improved their English skills through Worker Education Project were about people like her – people who worked with their hands at jobs that could murder your back and didn't provide a liveable pension. They wrote about things she understood too well – like hardly ever having enough but deciding to love life anyway. Reading the book she wondered what would happen if she and everybody like her decided to take the same week off and let their employer scrub the floors and empty the garbage while the worker got massages and sailed around the harbor on the old yacht.

(Neely 1998: 84)

Throughout the remainder of the book, Blanche continues to reinscribe her life and the lives of those around her. At the end of the book, we find Blanche connecting to her ancestors again in order to resolve a paradoxical justice situation which she is confronted with:

The next morning, Blanche spent nearly an hour in front of her Ancestor's altar, trying to find a way to make peace with the knowledge that Donnie's family didn't and would likely never know what happened to him. She knew she couldn't tell his wife, could never do anything that would endanger Othello and the Ex-Cons for Safety. She also knew this wasn't justice, and she apologized to her forebears for it. When she had first gotten Othello's group to help her, she'd been glad to know there were black men in the community prepared to protect people, make the bad actors pay for what they did, and keep the neighborhood safe. She still thought this was a good idea – just as soon as folks figured out how to solve the same problem they had with the downtown system: Who polices the police? Who decides who should be punished and how?

(Neely 1998: 255)

No sooner has Blanche left the house to go meet her friend's train than she is confronted with the justice question again when she sees the man who impregnated Shaquita and finds herself "tempted to slip back around the corner until he got further away":

Why? Because he was one of those young men some people called an endangered species. Was that a reason to turn up her nose at him? After all, people didn't stop speaking to FDR's granddad when he was dealing drugs. His little enterprise got him into the president's family. Maybe Pookie would get lucky. He tried in his own way to get Shaquita to change her mind about the baby, and it still might work. Anyway, treating him like he was dog poop on the pavement wasn't likely to help him come to a good end. If nobody even wanted to speak to these kids, how could anyone then turn and criticize them for their choices?
    "Hey, Pookie! Wait up," she called.

(Neely 1998: 257)

This is an ultimate moment not only for Blanche but also for the reader. Everything has been reinscribed, even drug dealing. Truth has been told and the questions that are asked by Blanche are some of the most important ones that need to be asked if humanity is to survive in a postmodern world of diversity and limited resources with a sense of humor.

Blanche's ancestry

Blanche comes from a unique background which buttresses the perspective that she is emblematic of the transformation possible through using humor as an adaptive psychological dynamic. Nikki Giovanni says we can all be this kind of black woman:

> One of the reason I personally like the word "Black" not as a description but as a sociological term is that we can all be Black women. In any given room everyone from blonde to red-haired to silver-haired to bald can be a Black woman. Even a room full of men would benefit from saying once or twice a day to themselves, "I'm a Black woman; I can do anything." Oh sure, you laugh, who would want to be a Black woman if they didn't have to be? And that is my point exactly. If you could be anything at all without penalty or punishment, why wouldn't you want to be a Black woman?
> We are the folks who took rotten peaches and made cobbler; we took pieces of leftover cloth and made quilts . . . every time something was taken away we took something else and made it work. . . . We understand the trials and tribulations of being women, let alone Black women; we find a way to laugh because we know that the only way to win this battle of life and liberty is with the pursuit of happiness. . . . Cause we start with that belly laugh and tears roll down our cheeks; we throw up our hands and all is right with the world. . . . Who wouldn't want to be a Black woman knowing nothing can defeat the indomitable spirit that is determined to love and laugh. Who can help but be a fan of the greatest, most wonderful creature on the planet. And when things are not going well with you, why not gather a few friends, fry a chicken or two and sit around the table saying: "I am a Black woman. I am the best thing on Earth." Then laughing your foolish head off. "Yeah. We're wonderful. Honey, Hush!"
>
> (quoted in Dance 1988: xix–xx)

Who are these Black women with a playful attitude that have the golden sense of proportion which makes having a sense of humor the divine delight it can be? To survive the horrors of slavery, Jim Crow, the broken promises, the betrayals and dehumanization of their time on American soil Black women found the relieving balm of humor because they had to, as the old blues song goes, "I laugh to keep from crying." Out of their tragedy, a most delicious, life affirming humor has developed. African American women use humor to hide pain, mask attacks, put sensitive subjects on the table, walk gently around that which is too hard to look at straight, to warn of lines not to cross, as a tease or compliment, and to bring about change. African American women know that laughter is more serious and complicated than tears. Like all marginalized groups, including white women, humor for the African American women has been an in-house affair. The reasons are the same for all trivialized groups, it was a way to conceal inappropriate behavior around the dominant classes. There is a story that Negroes were not allowed to laugh out loud on the street in a particular Southern town. If they felt a laugh coming on they had to stick their heads in a laughing barrel marked "For colored" in order to protect whites from the infectious and corrupting nature of their humor (Dance 1988: xxii). The act of putting their heads in water was also symbolic of repression into the unconscious, the place where all women's humor, including African American women's humor, because humor in a woman was stamped as undignified buffoonery.

Despite a rich tradition of female humorists, including Ethel Waters and Zora Neale Hurston among many others, African American women are ignored in most any study of American humor: "all the Americans are WASPs, all the women are white, and all the African-Americans are men" (Dance 1998: xxxii). And when the African American humor of men or women is analyzed, it is of course done by whites. For example Arthur Hudson's two-volumes on *Humor of the Old Deep South* (1936) has a chapter "Darkies" but all the selections are from white male authors. Even the more recent *Encyclopedia of American Humorists* (Gale 1988) does not have a single entry on an African American women (Dance 1998: xxix). Even in studies of women's humor, African American women are suspiciously absent or relegated to a few paragraphs at most even though the humor is unique in its irony and satire:

> In addition to a propensity of subject matter and themes that most often speak to our experience in this nation, African American women's humor is often characterized by a certain style that includes a predilection for satire and irony, a delight in the irreverent, a vigorous style of *force vitale*, an insistence on reality ("be real"), a love of contest/challenge/debate, and a delight in drama and kinesics: the black woman worldwide is noted for that most atavistic of all African American gestures – cut-eye, suck teeth, an insulting gesture of disdain, eliciting one of the vehement reprimands from black mothers: "Girl, don't you roll/cut your eyes at me"! The black women is also noted for that arching of the eyebrow and "the stare" as well as some unique head bobbing, neck swiveling, hip swinging, finger pointing, hands on hips stances, and other gesticulations that form a dynamic vocabulary of their own. But the most distinctive aspect of the style of black women's humor is her language.
>
> (Dance 1998: xxxii–xxxiii)

This excerpt describes a Tricksterish energy which "delight[s] in experimentation with sound, imagistic phrases, musical expressions, and with the catchy rhythms of the old-fashioned church service" (Dance 1998: xxxiii). Blanche demonstrates these linguistic experimentations when she deals with the hard subjects of race, gender, sexual identification, social class, economic status, occupation, politics, domestic life, neighborhood dynamics, and families through her sassiness. Sassy means impudent while sassitude is the combination of sass and attitude, such as "I don't care much for your sassitude today." If you look at most mainstream dictionaries in the United States you will find that the origin of the word sass is attributed to its being a derivation of sauce or saucy, but the *Oxford English Dictionary* attributes the origin of the word to the West African poisonous sassy tree whose sap was used to test witches. If a purported witch could survive nearly two gallons of sass, they won their case. To sass an elder, a master, or a spouse was the worst thing to do in public but behind closed doors it was the way of resignification. Verbal repartee, sharp signifiers, rhyming rappers all come from the sass tradition which women shared with men in Africa. We see it in female responses in raps and in blues songs like Ida Cox's "Wild Women Don't Have the Blues," "wild women are the only ones who get by/ Wild women don't worry/Wild women don't have the blues."

African American women's humor is unique because an African American woman was more likely than an elite white woman to have grown up in a house run by working women. There was no cult of domesticity for the working African American woman to embrace, she worked inside her own home and inside the home of others, which is what generates the Mammy or Aunt Jemima stereotype. Blanche's reinscription is brilliant because she takes the stereotypical Mammy and completely reinscribes the big, bossy and ever-loyal woman to her master and flips it.

But what about that other stereotype for African American women, the oversexed and always willing partner based on her youth and beauty. If no Mammy, then she was the Jezebel modeled on the so-called Hottentot Venus, the captured African who was shown throughout Europe naked and caged in circuses to reveal her genitalia.[4] Identity formation for the young African American girl and woman was as narrow and predetermined as it was for white elite women:

> There is hardly a novel by a black woman that does not touch upon the issues of complexion, hair, and general physical appearance, i.e. beauty; as, as Gloria Wade-Gayles tells us in *Rooted Against the Wind* (1996), pretty for black women means "not overweight, nor too dark, attractively coiffured, well-dressed, and young looking.
>
> (Dance 1998: 92)

The insidious effect of these cultural stereotypes are portrayed in Alice Walker's *The Color Purple* (1982) where Celie is repeatedly told she is ugly, to Toni Morrison's *The Bluest Eye* (1970) whose Pecola wished for only the thing she could never have, blue eyes. Whoopi Goldberg, the African American comic and actress, made a joke out her own inability to meet the idealized image: "If you were like me, you knew you stood a better chance of winning the Nobel Prize than waking up beautiful" (Dance 1998: 94).

Conclusion

We have seen in this chapter how Blanche White utilizes with wit and grace the process of the postmodern female Trickster, reinscribing everything which has oppressed her; psychologically, metaphorically and literally. I think that Blanche may be the incarnation of Marion Woodman's Dark Goddess, the one who guides and advises and acts with absolute clarity, often with a startling sense of humor that delights in play. Or perhaps she is a reincarnation of Baubo, who inhabited the alchemical kitchens in Asia Minor before the fifth century BCE making all laugh at her baudy and bodacious ways. Yet, Blanche White is an absolute original, who represents the confluence of all the aspects of the postmodern female Trickster which are discussed throughout this book; she is witty, wise, and funny, and also happens to solve crimes and misdemeanors of every sort and variety.

Notes

1 Robinson (1972), cited in McDowell (1980).
2 From the internet site http://www.blanchewhite.com:

> BarbaraNeely is a novelist, short story writer, and author of the popular Blanche White mystery novels. The first book in this series, *Blanche on the Lam*, won the Agatha, the Macavity, and the Anthony – three of the four major mystery awards for best first novel – as well as the Go On Girl! Book Club award for a debut novel. The subsequent books in the series, *Blanche among the Talented Tenth*, *Blanche Cleans Up* and *Blanche Passes Go* have also received critical acclaim from both fans and literary critics. Books in the Blanche White series have been taught in courses at universities as varied as Howard University, Northwestern, Bryn Mawr, Old Dominion, Boston College, Appalachian State University, Washington State University and Guttenberg University in Mainz, Germany. Books in the series have been translated into French, German and Japanese.
>
> Neely's short stories have appeared in anthologies, magazines, university texts, and journals including: *Things that Divide Us*, *Speaking for Ourselves*, *Constellations*, *Literature: Reading and Writing the Human Experience*, *Breaking Ice*, *Essence*, and *Obsidian II*.
>
> Ms. Neely has also had an extensive public sector career. She designed and directed the first community-based corrections facility for women in Pennsylvania, directed a branch of the YWCA, and headed a consultant firm for non-profits. She was part of an evaluative research team at the Institute for Social Research, the Executive Director of Women for Economic Justice, and a radio producer for Africa News Service. For her activism Neely has received the Community Works Social Action Award for Leadership and Activism for Women's Rights and Economic Justice, and the Fighting for Women's Voices Award from the Coalition for Basic Human Needs.
>
> In addition to writing, BarbaraNeely is also host of *Commonwealth Journal*, a radio interview program in Massachusetts. *Commonwealth Journal* airs at 7:00 PM on Sundays, and can be heard online at http://www.wumb.org/commonwealthjournal/.

3 Duncan Kennedy and the Critical Legal Studies Group who taught at Harvard Law School in 1990–1991 structured much of their inquiry around what they saw as the fundamental contradiction between autonomy and community.
4 Saartjie Baartman's genitals were on display in the Musée de l'Homme in Paris until 1974. See Sander Gilman, "Difference and Pathology," 85–90, in Dance (1998: 91).

Chapter 13

New sightings, *Sex and the City*

Carrie: Maybe our mistakes are what make our fate. Without them, what would shape our lives? Perhaps if we never veered off course, we wouldn't fall in love, or have babies, or be who we are. After all, seasons change. So do cities. People come into your life and people go. But it's comforting to know the ones you love are always in your heart. And if you're very lucky, a plane ride away.

Carrie: Later that day I got to thinking about relationships. There are those that open you up to something new and exotic, those that are old and familiar, those that bring up lots of questions and those that bring you back. But the most exciting, challenging and significant relationship of all is the one you have yourself. And if you find someone to love, well, that's just fabulous.

Introduction

The postmodern female Trickster energy is a contemporary manifestation of an inchoate dormant archetypal capacity repressed by the normative symbolic order of patriarchal consciousness millennia ago. While this female Trickster came in through women's written literature, she can now be found in the cyberspace of cable television as Carrie Bradshaw, the lead character in the series *Sex and the City*.

A television series can infuse the psyche with new imagery and narrative in the same way that novels do. Both fulfill the desire of the reader to have a continuing relationship with fictional characters. This desire for relationship to fictional characters is not limited to women, it can be seen in the mainstream media, where the desire for continuing relationship is manifested through a proliferation of sequels, prequels and postquels to successful films, books and television series.

Sex and the City

Sex and the City ran for six years with 94 episodes,[1] won every award it could and is a pop cultural phenomenon around the globe. There are clubs, multiple web sites and articles available to a fan. Special edition sets of all the series episodes sold out before Christmas 2005.[2] Seminars and panels on the cultural significance of the show have been held throughout the United States, similar to what happened after the fictive female sleuth made her appearance in the early 1980s.[3]

There are four women who make up the entourage on *Sex and the City*. Samantha is a publicist and the most blatant sexual predator on the show, her character is a parody of all those bachelor shows, of the 1960s and 1970s, where the guy's working life was played second fiddle to getting the girl. The reinscription here is that it is Samantha getting a man and many times any man will do. Miranda is the women who has the outside trappings of the successful male; a partnership in a prestigious law firm, owning her own apartment and living alone quite happily. She starts out in the series symbolizing the hard edged, logos based, skeptical bordering on cynical female lawyer stereotype. Charlotte represents the prim and proper Upper East Side silver spoon in her mouth "belle" who runs an art gallery and is heavily invested in her idealization of the perfect marriage and family. Based on Candace Bushnell's provocative bestselling memoir, the fictional Carrie writes the column "Sex and the City," which chronicles the state of sexual affairs of fin-de-siècle Manhattanites. The series is a weekly carnival of boundary-crossing behavior, using the stage props of Carrie's omniscient voice-overs about relationships as internal dialogue shared with the viewer along with a weekly session at a coffee shop in Manhattan where the friends work their shape-shifting magic on every possible permutation of sexual adventure previously off-limits for women to "voice" in mainstream culture:

> Samantha: Is he that bad in bed?
> Miranda: No. He's just . . . a guy. He can rebuild a jet engine but when it comes to a woman . . . what's the big mystery? It's my clitoris, not the Sphinx.
> Carrie: I think you just found the title of your autobiography!

including but not limited to lesbian lovers:

> Samantha: You know when I was a lesbian . . .
> Carrie: I saw that one coming
> Samantha: I could get in and out with nothing but a fine lip gloss.

> Maria [Samantha's current sexual partner]: You call this a relationship?
> Samantha: Well, it's tedious and the sex is dwindling, so from what I've heard, YES!

penis size:

> Samantha: You dated Mr. Big. I'm dating Mr. Too-Big!
> Carrie: You broke up with your last boyfriend because he was too small, now this one's too big. Who are you, Goldie-Cocks?

dating:

> Carrie: Men who have had a lot of sexual partners are not called sluts. They're called very good kissers, a few are even called romantics.

extramarital affairs, impotence, models, oral sex:

> Miranda (to Charlotte): Are you telling me you would never perform this act?
> Carrie: She'll juggle, she'll spin plates, but she won't give head. The reality is the only thing that went down with any regularity on Charlotte's dates was a Gold American Express card.

even anal sex:

> Carrie: How did this happen? How did they get the message that the ass is now on the menu?
> Miranda: I bet there's one loud-mouthed guy who found some woman who loved it and told everyone "women LOVE this!"
> Carrie: Who is this guy?
> Miranda: Who's the woman who loved it?
> Samantha: Don't knock it till you've tried it!
> Carrie: Bingo!

adultery:

> Carrie: Well, I think maybe there's a cheating curve. That someone's definition of what constitutes cheating is in direct proportion to how much they themselves want to cheat.
> Miranda: That's moral relativism!
> Carrie: I prefer to think of it as quantum cheating.

> Samantha: All married couples stop having sex eventually.
> Miranda: That's not true, you've had sex with plenty of married people.
> Samantha: That's how I know!

dildo's:

> Carrie: I'm not going to replace a man with some battery-operated device.
> Miranda: You haven't met "The Rabbit."
> Samantha: Oh come on, if you're going to get a vibrator, at least get one called "The Horse."

erotica:

> Charlotte (looking at a catalog): Oh my god! Vagina weights!
> Samantha: Honey, my vagina waits for no man.

and fellatio:

> Samantha: Maybe there's something he can eat to make it sweeter.
> Carrie: Maybe you should write to Martha Stewart.
> Miranda: "Dear Martha: Funk Spunk. Help."

> Adam [Samantha's current sexual partner]: Come on, give me a little BJ, up and down a couple times, you're done, it's easy!
> Samantha: Easy? You men have no idea what we're dealing with down there. Teeth placement, and jaw stress, and suction, and gag reflex, and all the while bobbing up and down, moaning and trying to breathe through our noses. Easy? Honey, they don't call it a job for nothin'!

Carrie is the head Trickster in this series and her credentials include the traditional Trickster markers of wit, constant dynamism in her relationships, sexuality in the foreground and outrageous costuming. Carrie has no money but she has a closet full of high-heeled stilettos which are a parody of oversized clown feet:

> Carrie: If I spent forty-thousand dollars on shoes and I have no place to live, I will literally be the old woman who lived in her shoes!

When she is mugged, the only thing Carrie cares about is her strappy sandals which she got on sale and cannot be replaced! It is Carrie's role to continually pointing out the paradoxical reality of relationships between men and women always in a witty manner:

> Carrie: When men attempt bold gestures, generally it's considered romantic. When women do it, it's often considered desperate psychotic.

Even when discussing the most serious of issues, her philosophical commentary on relationships and sex is wrapped up in humor:

> Carrie: I'd like to think that people have more than one soul mate.
> Samantha: I agree! I've had hundreds.
> Carrie: Yeah! And you know what, if you miss one, along comes another one. Like cabs.

Samantha is the show's foil for the doubling technique used to call attention to the sexualized male psyche. The implicit mainstream perspective is placed before the viewer in the guise of a beautiful woman:

> Samantha: Money is power and sex is power. Therefore getting money for sex is just an exchange of power.

> Samantha: Carrie, you can't date your fuck buddy.
> Carrie: Say it a little louder, I don't think the old lady in the last row heard you.
> Samantha: You're going to take the only person in your life that's there purely for sex, no strings attached, and turn him into a human being? Why?

The show, over the six seasons it was on, totally reinscribed and resignified sex and the single woman as Carrie, Samantha, Charlotte, and Miranda dealt humorously with the sexual and relational questions facing the single urban dwelling woman as she tried to live out a life filled with her own agency, authority and autonomy.

In the first season the four women discuss the risks and benefits of adopting the male perspective on sexual relations. Samantha, the parody on male sexuality, suggests that the group should begin by objectifying men the way that men have always objectified women. Charlotte, in a satire on Gracie Allen, takes the literal meaning of object and replies, "does that mean having sex with a dildo," to which Samantha replies, "no – just have sex without feelings." Samantha philosophizes about the end of the twentieth century being the first time in history that women have had as much power and money as men and thus, have the luxury of treating men as sex objects, which she demonstrates throughout the series. Miranda, ever the analyst, tells Samantha that her plan is a Catch-22; yes, Samantha is right that men don't want to have a relationship but when women just want to have sex, men can't perform, so they leave anyway.

Samantha's philosophy is based upon the premise that women are no longer enclosed within a male economic system which results in women having access to sexual freedom because they are no longer dependent upon the male. Of course, Samantha is living an illusion, but an imaginative one which has the potency and capacity to expand consciousness for the viewer. The world Samantha and the other very elite and affluent New Yorkers which the show portrays live in has economic equality and this may be true for the age group of the women in *Sex and the City*, (30–40), but baby boomer women (aged 50+) will make 55 cents to the male $1.00 over their lifetime and younger women, like Carrie, Samantha, Charlotte and Miranda, still make less than 80 cents on the dollar to men. However, the point Samantha is making is one I support; this is a unique period of time for many women on the planet one that opens them to the possibility of psychological authority, physical agency and bodily autonomy.

Carrie cuts through the sexual paradox of adopting the male perspective when she ponders, "are women giving up love and throttling power?" Her voice-over asks the viewer to consider whether being "equal to" men, here in the sexual arena, is what women really want. Samantha seems to be stuck in the first wave of women's liberation with her "equal to" philosophy, while Carrie is more interested in figuring out the third wave question of, if women can have it all, what do they really want and is acting like a man what they really want? To answer her own question we find Carrie, the sexual anthropologist, in a bar where she sees her old boyfriend, "the creep." Her voice over tells the audience that while she has no feelings for him she did have the best sex of her life with him. This is a complete reinscription of the old canard that women don't like to have sex at all and do it so they can have babies, except of course those "other" kind of women who do like sex and make jokes, but alas, do not have babies. Carrie decides she can have "sex for sex sakes, right?" She goes over and says hi to "the creep," telling him he looks great and asks him what he is doing later. He replies, "I thought you weren't talking to me for the rest of your life?" to which Carrie retorts: "Who said anything about talking?" After this bit of witty repartee the two of them leave and have sex; Carrie has an orgasm and when it's his turn Carrie turns the tables and tells him that she isn't concerned with meeting his needs, only her own. The guy is nonplussed and says he likes her better this way than the last time they hooked up. So he is okay with her walking out, but Carrie, who just had great sex, wonders why, if she is having sex like a man, she doesn't feel more in control. After all, she did the "equal to" men activity and doesn't feel what she projected she would feel. As many women in the first wave of women's liberation found out, being equal to a man only places you in the world they have designed and promoted as desirable, but what is actually desirable for a woman is something yet to be worked through in this series and in independent women's lives.

This first episode sets up the narrative arc which is played out over the next six years as guys come and go. The reinscription of sexual relationships occurs, but the bonds of female friendship always trumps the girls' sexual and emotional relationships with men. As Samantha says, "women are for friendship, men are for fucking." These women, although they interact with men, remain at the center of their own lives and each others. This plays out (pun intended) when the girls decide that if you make plans with someone, you keep them, no matter what. No longer can plans with a girlfriend be jettisoned without accountability for plans with a man. In *Sex and the City*, this kind of behavior is challenged as tacky and insulting to those who are most important in your life – other women. The women of *Sex and the City* play a doubling game. They enjoy the energy that comes from having a man in their lives, but they demonstrate to the postmodern viewer how to integrate the "how to find a man" and "how to live without a man" stages with the "who am I and what do I want" to do with my life through wit and irony.

Each episode is a witty play on words as well as a humorous burlesque on the traditional types of activities that are supposed to occupy a woman's imagination. Do women really want to have babies or have they been brainwashed to believe they do is the topic when Carrie, Samantha, Charlotte, and Miranda go to a baby shower for a former party girl friend turned Soccer Mom. Carrie is late with her period and can't decide whether she wants the test to turn out positive or negative, Charlotte fears she will never have the baby girl she has been preparing for her entire life while Laney, the about to be Mom, yearns for the freedom and independence she sacrificed to have a family. Then the question becomes, if there aren't going to be babies, why marry? This question cuts away at over 4,000 years of women's enclosure within marriage and rips the assumptions to shreds.

In "The Caste System" episode from the second season, the girls explore the impact that social class, earning capacity, and sexual compatibility can have on relationships. Miranda admits to herself that she has fallen in love with Steve, the bartender, and so she invites him to her firm's annual dinner. Steve is initially excited to go with her until he hears that his corduroy suit isn't suitable for the occasion. Miranda and Steve go shopping, but Steve can't afford the clothes in the shop Miranda takes him to. The scene switches to the coffee shop where Miranda shares her yuppie guilt over being the wealthier of the two. Samantha offers a reinscription by asking, how he is in bed? Carrie admits that she feels poor compared to Mr. Big but Miranda (correctly) notes that money is an issue only when it is the woman who is earning more. The episode ends with Carrie wondering if "New York is really any different than New Delhi."

Carrie demonstrates her authentic self at a cocktail party she attends with Mr. Big, where the hostess prohibits "brown food." Carrie concludes that the "no brown food" lady is cultivating this eccentricity so no one will notice she is devoid of personality. Mr. Big replies, "You're being a bitch." Carrie uses this opportunity to differentiate who she is, "No, I'm being myself." Big attempts to tell Carrie how a date *should* act in this situation to which Carrie replies, "No, not having any, I'll just *be* rather than *perform*, thank you."

In the third season episode "Boy, Girl, Boy, Girl," sexual flipping and ambiguity as the new norm is explicated. Charlotte puts on men's clothing for an exhibition at her gallery, finding that she likes her masculinized portrait persona and Carrie stops dating a younger man when she is introduced to his ex-loves, a guy and a girl. In "Are We Sluts" the topic under discussion is how many men are too many and whether there is any boundary between being respectable and being a slut. In the fourth season Samantha tries monogamy for the first time, but with a gender bender; she falls in love with an exotic lesbian artist who teaches her what an intimate relationship between two people of whatever sex can offer. In the fifth season Carrie and Miranda wrestle with being manless. Miranda is a single mother with her son Brady in tow while Carrie finds herself deep in the publishing world promoting her book of columns. Charlotte divorces her perfect-on-paper husband because he decides he doesn't want children, a dream she will not give up. Prim, proper and Protestant Charlotte falls in love with her bald, hairy Jewish divorce lawyer, Harry.

The fifth season's climactic episode, "I Love a Charade," dissects the elements that truly make a relationship worthwhile and satisfying. The set up is the marriage announcement of one of Carrie's friends, gay Bobby Fine, a Broadway piano bar legend. At the coffee shop, the girls discuss how Mitzi and Bobby had to be just "acting" like they were madly and passionately in love with each other since it is obvious that they are getting married because of their advancing ages and desire for steady companionship. The discussion moves to the question of whether sex is even necessary in a marriage; Samantha says sex doesn't matter because all marriages stop having sex. Miranda quips that Samantha has had plenty of sex with married men and Carrie wants to know how you sustain a companionship relationship if there was never the *za za zoo*. In an earlier show, the question was, why marry if there are not going to be kids; the question has morphed into why marry if there was no sexual attraction. On the issue of sexual attraction we find out that Charlotte is attracted to someone who is definitely not her type; short, bald, and hairy, and as a joke, of course, his name is Harry. Samantha just wants to know about the sex between them and Charlotte says it's the best in her life and she really likes him. Then the climax scene where Charlotte and Harry are dancing and they admit to each other that they are falling in love but then Harry tells her he's Jewish and the relationship can't go anywhere because he has to marry a Jew, Charlotte is astounded and wants to know why if Mitzi can marry a gay guy, why Harry can't marry a Episcopalian. The final word is Carrie's in a voice over where she says that, when it comes to relationships, "Maybe we are all in glass houses; some are settling down, some are settling and some refuse to settle for less."

In this last season of the series, Charlotte converts to Judaism and gets married to Harry; however, she remains infertile and her desire to have a child dominates their relationship. Miranda has an affair with her neighbor, who happens to be a hunk of man, an African-American man who is team doctor to the New York Knicks Basketball Team. But she breaks up with him to marry her baby's father and move to Brooklyn. Carrie decides to give up her column for a chance at love with a Russian artist and Samantha meets a waiter and actor named Smith and stays with him practically the whole season. He is younger, but much wiser in the ways of love than her. When Samantha discovers she has breast cancer he doesn't flinch, even shaving off his hair when Samantha loses hers from chemotherapy. When she loses her sex drive as well, he tells her he will wait for spring. Samantha finds out that love can wait for sex.

Each character's initial presumptions are shape-shifted and redefined in the series. Charlotte starts out as the stereotypical Park Avenue WASP, looking for the man of her dreams. He doesn't turn out to be the perfect-on-paper Protestant rich doctor with an illustrious lineage, he is the bald, hairy, divorce lawyer Harry. For this true love, Charlotte becomes a Jew. Miranda moves from power-suited lawyer to earth mother, finding love with her bartender Steve in a Brooklyn house filled with kids and in-laws. Samantha, the promiscuous – even in this group – hedonist extraordinaire, finds love after a season of personal trauma with a younger man who is wise beyond his years. The coffee table discussions range from the unpleasant taste of punky semen after a blow job and the problems of anal intercourse to what is the perfect mate and how to make a life that isn't dependent upon men. *Sex and the City* is the Jane Austen of the twenty-first century.

The serious nature of being: *Sex and the City*

Throughout the series Carrie moves as Trickster between the serious and the funny, using the funny to make the serious palatable. The series is truly subversive in the way it reinscribes sex from a woman's point of view, thus the need for comedy to introduce it into the collective. One of the most significant issues the series confronts is how to identify the critical emotional supports in a woman's life. The series concludes that friendship is what holds life together and what is a man worth compared to having great friends? Trickster energy is present as these women move between what seems to be the paradoxical poles of Eros and Logos through humor, reinscribing what appears as a dichotomy into a circle by seductively attacking our prejudices with snide remarks about a make-believe happy life. For example, asking the rhetorical question of should a women go with the head or the heart and then humorously working in a discussion of giving men head (oral sex) and what happens if it doesn't taste good. Alchemically mixing base elements along with transformational imagery is Trickster territory. When Carrie is selected to walk the runway as a model,

she doesn't get the dress they promised, rather they make her wear rhine-
stone panties and a bra. She falls on the runway. Trickster Carrie picks
herself up and totally reinscribes this serious faux pas, thereby transforming
the tension through humor, making the audience question the values given
to walking perfectly down a runway.

Sex and the City is a worldwide phenomenon, and cyberspace demonstrates the radical potency of popular culture to turn imagination into
reality as viewers share how influential the show has been in their own lives
proving that the best method of bringing up subversive and transgressive
issues is through humor. The comments excerpted are representative of
those I found regarding the show:[4]

> As a straight male viewer of this show, I think that it gave me a lot of
> insight into the female aspect of a relationship and the world as a
> whole. This show also changed the way the public views women. Carrie
> and company are strong, self-sufficient women who even dislike serious
> relationships and the prospect of marriage. This is far from the house-
> wife days of "Leave it to Beaver" and "Father Knows Best".

> Sex And The City is one of the comedies for the '90's, a slick, classy
> affair that's not afraid to push the boundaries to the limit. It's graphic
> (sort of) depiction of sex is ground-breaking, yet it doesn't forget it's
> main reason for being out there, to be funny. Thankfully, it succeeds.

> I appreciate the fact that the show touches on some major issues of
> singles in the dating world while, at the same time, not having an overly
> dramatic or depressing tone. It's fun and light hearted – it celebrates
> the shallowness in each one of us while also recognizing the basic faults
> that make us human.

> I love these ladies! They're devastatingly witty, they go after what they
> want, and even when they don't get it they stay upbeat. The support
> they give each other is wonderful to watch. My favorite, though, has to
> be Miranda – I can totally identify with her ambivalence about a guy
> that anyone can see is perfect for her.

> And to address the sex issue . . . I am so tired of the Madonna/Whore
> complex everyone in the country seems to be up to their eyeballs in. Get
> over it! Women like sex, they have sex, and they have sex with men they
> don't like. So what? And so what if they continue to look for Mr. Right
> even when they're with Mr. Right Now. What person man or woman
> hasn't consistently done something, seemingly at cross-purposes with
> their intended goal in the name of love, lust, or companionship? Stop
> with the tired double standards.

From Carrie's first date with Big, to Miranda's unexpected pregnancy, to Charlotte's divorce, to Samantha's outrageous statements, Sex and the City has touched all of us in one way or another, whether you're a woman or a man, I am brave enough to admit. The common misconception surrounding this show is that it is pornography, that these women are sluts, that they are "male-bashing, unmoral, unfocused, drunken losers" to quote a certain user. At the beginning, we were introduced with the theme of Sex and the City: If men can go around having sex with as many women as they want, why can't women benefit from the same right. Thus began an era of cosmopolitans, manolos, men, breakups, makeups, shakeups, tears, and many surprises. The show expressed a series of views, social standards and taboo statements opinionated by the women, which before were considered to be unladylike, associated with men's sleazy minds.

The following are a highly selective group of comments from the worldwide viewing audience of Sex and the City.

From Asia: Coming from a non-liberal Asian culture, this show is a breath of fresh air and I relished the sexual escapades these 4 women shared. I'm also glad that in the end the show finally proved the bottom-line of the whole saga – it was more about the friendship these 4 women shared more than anything else.

(IMDb.com)

From the United Kingdom: "Sex" is truly a rare programme because it manages to be incredibly stylish (in terms of everything from the fashion, to the way it is shot, to how the characters are presented by the four very talented stars) yet it still had a great deal of substance to it. The writing was simply a joy – the dialogue between the characters always sparkled and yet there was a real truth and honesty to all of it. A lot of the best humor from the programme was born out of this honesty between the characters – the way their different opinions bounced off each other and how they interacted was always honest, always entertaining and sometimes totally hilarious.

(Author: Trey Mercartne from United Kingdom, 5 May 2005)

United Arab Emigrates: I started watching this movie 2 yrs ago from a friend of mine, but haven't completed the whole episodes. And as everybody knows DVD's and CD's are not available in the market here in UAE. Until I found out that I could make a reservation in one of the exclusive shops here, I didn't took a chance and grab the DVD's. So these time I got all the episodes from Season 1–6 I will treasure it for the rest of my life. Well FYI there are too much single ladies here in

UAE mostly expatriates, me and my girlfriends really adore the movie and as we watched it, it really applies with our lifestyle. It's really applicable in all aspects, and the movie is not a typical movie it's a realistic, the way the cast portray their role, they act so naturally and it really suits they're personality. The movie is really useful especially with singles. The topics are wide, sex, relationship, friendship, career, feelings the individual choices. And it really affects the watcher. . . . All I can say is I really enjoyed the movie. I will never get fed up in watching it over and over again. Keep it up!!! Wishing you all the best. (8 October 2005, Author: donna_dxb_77 from United Arab Emirates)

Romania: Hello peoples, I am a girl from Romania. . . . Yesterday was the last episode from "Sex and the City" here in Romania, I watched with no breath, like I watched the whole story. It was just great, and I associate the entire story with my life and my friends girls life. The thing is that we are four, just like in the movie, and one of us has a child. It is incredible how the things work and progress in life, and after a certain age everything it seems to lay down in our life, not calculated, but from inside of our personality. I saw the movie from the beginning, I loved this movie and the characters. I used to associate some time the peoples and situations from reality, with the ones in the movie, this for fun only of course, even that some times the real life was impressive exactly like in the movie. I want to see this movie again . . . or maybe a brand new series? . . . With deeply respect Teodora.

From Brazil: The fourth season of the saga . . . the discussions among them about many themes are very funny and delightful. . . . I conclude stating that I am a 'Sex and the City' addicted. Now I will start seeing the Fifth Season, which has just been released on DVD in Brazil.

Are Carrie, Samantha, Miranda, and Charlotte social workers?

While the characters from *Sex and the City* demonstrate agency, authority and autonomy throughout the show and refuse to be a victim, is there a social work aspect to Carrie as Trickster, which is an important post-modern characteristic of the Trickster? The women of *Sex and the City* are social workers in questioning the stereotypes assigned to women, thus making the answers available to the viewer for integration. The courage to ask the right question triggers the initiation process. When the term "social worker" is removed from its moorings in therapia and reperceived as energy which gets other energies moving into a dynamic state of trans-formation through the initiatory process, then Carrie, Samantha, Miranda, and Charlotte fulfill all expectations of social workers in the sense of asking questions which break and reinscribe former taboos. There can be no doubt that this show is a taboo breaker extraordinaire which demonstrates to the viewer's imaginal realms that taboos can be broken without society falling apart. Women who are sexual and funny is nothing new, we had Mae West for that, but women who talk openly about anal intercourse, farts, and blow jobs is new. We have moved from a pistol in the pocket to a dick in the mouth and on the bed. Women's use of sexual innuendo, language, and graphic sexual imagery, is one of the taboos broken consistently through humor by Carrie and her friends. The show does not belittle men, as men's humor does to women, rather it places before the viewer the image and narrative of a group of women who have agency, authority, and autonomy and are not willing to give it up for a man.

Does watching this series enlarge the imaginative capacities of the viewers as it did with the readers of the fictive female sleuths? Well, according to the comments of those men and women who have watched the show around the world this show accurately reflects and enlarges the possibilities for both the feminine and masculine imagination. And now the show may be coming back, according to a *TV Guide* article, "Life After Sex," which asks what if Carrie, Samantha, Charlotte and Miranda popped out a few kids?[5] It would be a hit. Sources say the cable network has quietly begun production on an as-yet-untitled half-hour comedy pilot that is being billed as *Sex and the City* for the Mommy and Me set. "It's about being a new mother in New York City," confides our mole. Working title: "Sexless and Bound for the Suburbs."

Other Trickster sightings

Sex and the City is joined by a plethora of other manifestations of Trickster energy in the female body. The British *Calendar Girls* used the genre of the pin-up calendar but reinscribed the meaning and intent when they artfully covered up their natural endowments and had a worldwide hit, including having their story made into a film. A book titled *Female Chauvinist Pigs: Women and the Rise of Raunch Culture* (Levy 2005) celebrates "feminism gone wild."[6] While the reviewer didn't get it that women were reinscribing the idea of the male chauvinist pig through irony, the book has been a bestseller with women. In the May–June 2004 issue of *Utne* magazine, there was an article by Bradford Keeney titled "Tricksters of the World Unite: How Going Crazy Will Help Save America" which emphasizes the transformative value of Trickster's energy, which can turn "fantasy into something really powerful." The article credits Tricksters with "tripping ourselves into seeing, hearing, and feeling the world with a different awareness (pp. 56–57) The California Institute for Integral Studies ran a workshop titled "The Trickster in Tibetan Buddhist Practice: Working with Paradox, Provocation and Humor" in May, 2005 and a professor from the University of Alabama published a book on *Hermes and Aphrodite Encounters*

(Zupancic 2004) with 27 essays examining how these mythological figures and the human characteristics they embody are portrayed or reportrayed in modern culture."[7] There is a new comic book on the scene, according to the *New York Times*, which breaks with the male drawn big-tits femme fatale of the super hero comics. The new series taps the girl market with strong women and while "the girls are cute, they're never insulting and they never have big breasts . . . referring to the overly endowed women drawn in superhero comics."[8]

Bridget Jones? No, It's Jane Bond, according to Helen Fielding, who admits that she is now using James Bond instead of *Pride and Prejudice* as her template for her new series because it promotes a more developed sense of identity: "Olivia is what Bridget would be if she stopped worrying about her weight and what people expected of her, but just made the decision to just get on with things." Critics may have been put off by her "hodgepodge of genres" but Fielding feels "now that there are more books with women looking outward . . . women are not worrying about the size of [their] thighs but are looking out at the world."[9]

Conclusion

Sex and the City, while ostensibly about sex, operates between and betwixt, traversing the levels of the comic and the cosmic, between earth and heaven, the gods and humanity. *Sex and the City* operates on two levels as all good Trickster tales do, the sexually humorous top level and the deeper level of the real thing, which is the real subversive transformative essence of the Trickster archetype. Like traditional Trickster tales, *Sex and the City* presents us with all the absurd and obscene gestures and ridiculousness of anal sex, bed farts, bad tasting spunk, and blow jobs but the real deal is always about connections and relationships among and between people. And this is where Carrie and her friends share lineage with Austen's Tricksterism. Even though Jane had to work with the raw data of her time, which mandated that her characters operate within a domestic realm, on the deeper level her work endures because it is quintessentially profound about the central aspects of everyone's life, our relationships with other people. In *Sex and the City*, the set up is sexually starved single women living in a fin-de-siècle urban environment. The show also parodies male buddy shows of the 1950s and 1960s, like *Route 66* and *Sunset Strip*, where the search for women and cars were only stand-ins for getting sex; the doubling maneuver in *Sex and the City* is in how the search for sex is actually a search for relationship.

Is *Sex and the City* truly transformative or is it just another funny show about women breaking taboos? Comments from the United States and from around the world indicates that *Sex and the City* has opened the imaginative capacities of men and women, whether in Manhattan or Saudi

Arabia, thus *Sex and the City* is not just another steam vent using non-traditional forms of humor which encourage the patriarchal symbolic order to continue. I have found that no matter the setting, groups of younger women and men discuss the plots and images of *Sex and the City*, dissecting the characters and situations found as much as an earlier generation did with V.I. Warshawski, Kinsey, Kate, and Blanche.

Notes

1 1998–2004, Home Box Office Subscription Service.
2 I know this because I tried to purchase it from several stores, both brick and mortar and on-line, who were back ordering the set for January 2006 delivery.
3 The influence of the fictive female sleuth has continued through the proliferation of the *Sisters in Crime* clubs, special audio and printed materials, web sites for all the major authors dealt with in this book and a plethora of both popular and academic articles.
4 All comments were found on IMDb.com user comments for *Sex and the City*.
5 *TV Guide*, October 28, 2005.
6 *Miami Herald*, September 17, 2005: 3E.
7 http://uanews.ua.edu/feb05
8 *New York Times*, December 28, 2004: B1, "Girl Power Fuels Manga Boom in U.S."
9 *New York Times*, June 6, 2004: 6ST

Chapter 14

Conclusion

The divine comedy of being

A sense of humor is the only divine quality of man.[1]

It is impossible to define that which we call a "sense of humor." Yet perhaps by playing around it in the imagination we may bring to light a little of the wonder, the mystery of that divine and human gift.[2]

Humor is what you wish in your secret heart were not funny, but it is, and you must laugh. Humor is your own unconscious therapy.[3]

History Repeats Itself First in Tragedy and then as Farce.[4]

Introduction

Humor is a divine quality of humanity which requires a playful imagination to constellate the wonder and mystery of this transformative human gift. And when we are able to bring a sense of humor to a situation, we become our own therapists since "laughter and good will are a gracious and contagious catalyst to continued transformation" (Zweig 1990: 252). If one substitutes Trickster for humor it becomes clear why Trickster offers the individual and collective psyche the opportunity to transform itself. My thesis throughout this book has been that what has been manifested in the female body in the last half of the twentieth century, while certainly standing on the shoulders of all those witty women and men who have come before them, is a new variant of Feminine energy manifesting through humor which can be embodied in many forms: a heterosexual woman or man, a cross-dresser, a transvestite, a homosexual, and other gender forms not yet known or named. This Feminine sense of humor I am describing requires a psychological orientation of maturity, one that can appreciate and understand difference and diversity (Luke 1995: 72). Only with this mature understanding of diversity can those with a post-tribal perception penetrate to the "laughter at the heart of things" as T.S. Eliot said.[5] Helen Luke concludes correctly that a healing sense of humor is dependent upon a sense of proportion between the inner and outer worlds, where it can "strengthen the compassion in which all our pains and joys become whole" (Luke 1995: 74). This type of humor must have a particular context in order to constellate:

> Unless a man or woman has experienced the darkness of the soul, he or she can know nothing of that transforming laughter without which no hint of the ultimate unity of opposites can be faintly intuited.
>
> (Luke 1995: 74)

What Luke is referring to is how a mature sense of humor embodies pleasure by having a playful attitude which can manifest only when the psyche faces the savagery of truth. In this way, the pleasure of play takes the edge off the *too* real. I am not referring to intellectual wit that is caustic or the superficial joking of buffoonery, both of which are evidence of a protective armoring surrounding a frightened ego and do not represent the sense of humor which develops from the ability to laugh at how your own ego painfully operates in the conscious world. When you can laugh at yourself you have a sense of proportion about life, that you are but an infinitesimal part of the unknowable whole. A sense of humor gives us delight in the ordinary, but it is not the humor of laughing at a person and it is not a condemnation of another's way of perceiving, it is the laughter which, as Eliot said, "is at the heart of things."

Individuation

Individuation is the core concept at the heart of Jungian psychology. It is a process of becoming aware of, familiar with, and in dialogue with the unconscious. It is a doubling Trickster process; the first step requires differentiation of the individual from the collective. The second step requires that the individual psyche comes into greater relationship both intra-psychically with the self and with the collective. I am not talking about individualism since individuation is a different concept: individualism is based upon a rejection of the collective in favor of the individual; individuation respects the collective while being aware of the need for differentiation from it. As Jung put it:

> Individuation has two principal aspects: in the first place it is an internal and subjective process of integration, and in the second it is an equally indispensable process of objective relationship. Neither can exist without the other, although sometimes the one and sometimes the other predominates.
>
> (Jung *CW* 16: par 448)

From a Jungian perspective no one ever succeeds in becoming individuated, it is a goal, a process and a journey, the true value being in what happens along the way, "the goal is important only as an idea; the essential thing is the opus which leads to the goal: that is the goal of a lifetime" (Jung *CW* 16, para 400).

If individuation is the process of becoming who you already are, and I have argued that there is a difference between the psyche of the male and female, does the process described as individuation hold the same hope for the female as it does for the male psyche? Research is just at the stages where enough data is being collected and what we are finding out is that our previous ideas about the absolute nature of identity based upon sexuality was wrong, identity is more fluid and indeterminate and based upon a different configuration of nurture and nature than what humanity could perceive in its psychological childhood. My question then, is the Jungian model of individuation as applicable to the female psyche as to the male? Previously, the Jungian perspective was quite attractive to women since it was based upon the presumption that each individual was unique, thus the search to realize one's own real inner dimension seemed applicable to either sex. Jung's perspective differed from Freud's reductive psychology which had an irrefutable presumption that adaptation to the existing society was necessary for a healthy psyche. Freud did not ask whether the existing society was healthy for women, he assumed that women had a subservient psychological context to men. Jung offered a concept which encouraged an initial separation from existing society and then a reintegration based on the relational dynamics of an interior dia-logic. Yet, Jungian psychology does not generally recognize the inequities between the weights on each side of the balancing scale and thus follows the follies of systems which are based on overvaluing the male and devaluing the female. Jung was a product of his own context and may have assumed that balance could be wrought from a fundamentally out of balance world, after all power and access to developmental processes were much greater for the class which Jung belonged to, the white European elite male. However, to throw out his entire theory because contrasexuality is not proportionally in balance in patriarchal societies is similar to throwing out the baby with the bath water. Concepts which initially sound wonderful but are applied in limited contexts because of time and place are capable of becoming more inclusive, if the originating idea is well founded. An example of this can be found in the ideal of classical liberalism born of the Enlightenment and which is the foundation of the United States' system of government. When the United States was founded, equality meant that a white man, who was over 21 and owned property, got to vote. The concept of equality has proved more inclusionary than exclu-sionary over time and now all those over 18 may vote in the United States. Other traditional psychological theories are similarly based upon a male norm, but my question is, are they similarly capable of being inclusive, as the concepts of liberalism have been?

Aspects of the postmodern female Trickster supportive of individuation

I have discussed the unique energy of the virgin as a "woman unto herself" who is potentially conscious in the same way that the trickster has the potentiality of consciousness. The promise of potency can be intimidating and this is the reason why women's potency has been held inchoate by the symbolic patriarchal order. The virgin accepts life as it is in all its permutations and diversity which also threatens the illusion of certainty upon which the symbolic order rests. The virgin energy encourages movement from potentiality to an individual truth. The postmodern female trickster brings the potential of consciousness through humor. I think that Blanche White fits Marion Woodman's description of the appearance in our time of the Dark Goddess in the dreams of people around the world. Woodman contends that:

> Although she takes many different forms, this goddess – sometimes a Black Madonna or an Asian or Indian Madonna – always carries authority. She guides and advises and acts with absolute clarity, often with a startling sense of humor that delights in play.
>
> (Woodman and Dickson 1996: 2)

This energy of the Dark Goddess is evident in the worldwide hit series, *Sex and the City*, and in the evolution of Madonna as pop icon. In the beginning of this work I discussed the influence that certain fictive female sleuths had upon my psychological development in opening new avenues for my imagination to travel upon. As I was finishing writing this book the *New York Times* published Stephanie Rosenbloom's "Defining Me, Myself and Madonna,"[6] an article about how Madonna had similarly influenced someone who grew up in the 1980s which demonstrates both the importance of popular culture on emerging identity development and how dominant patriarchal imagery remains. The memoir article starts the recollection at the age of 8, when Rosenbloom wanted to wear a cross because it was "the essential accouterment of those determined to dress like Madonna." The problem for this girl was that she was Jewish and wearing a cross had to be done surreptitiously, so that is what she did. What was it that awed this 8 year old along with millions of other girls about Madonna:

> Like countless girls of my generation I was captivated by her style (the fingerless gloves, the navel-baring shirts, the armloads of bracelets, the forbidden cross) and awed by her cocky defiance of gender

conventions. Never had we seen someone so powerful, so sexually agressive who was not a man. At times she was crass. At times she was mean. But she made us consider the kind of women we wanted to be.

When Madonna's burning crosses and interracial love scenes caused her work to be banned, Rosenbloom found that it "helped me to crystallize my views on freedom of expression." Even though she didn't like it when Madonna moved to the English countryside and started writing children's books, she emphasized that the essential nature of Madonna was humor and her Trickster-like qualities: "Still, Madonna continued to be a sharp businesswoman with a biting sense of humor. And she stayed true to the one thing she has always been – a chameleon." It is this Trickster-like chameleon nature which encourages each fan to identify with Madonna, whether she was celebrating interracial relationships, gay life in clubs or S and M, the point was she was a mirror to the many who saw no place for themselves in mainstream culture:

> To see even a part of yourself embraced by her, especially a part that you feel is marginalized, can be heady validation . . . my preoccupation with Madonna has always been less about her life choices than mine. Whether I liked what she was doing or not, she pushed me to consider the choices I made for myself.

And this is exactly the point of this book and my argument about the female Trickster, whatever package we find her in, whether embodied in a female body or some other body, it is the enlargement of the individual conscious through humor which is at the heart of postmodernity and the individuation process, which if we are lucky, will save us all.

Does literature have the radical potential to change imagination into reality?

Time Magazine reports that "one of the most interesting things about the present moment in U.S. literary history is that the tough, fibrous membrane that used to separate literary fiction from popular fiction is rupturing." Mystery fiction is now a cultural psych-pomp according to the *New York Times* article, "Solution to a Stalled Revolution: Write a Mystery Novel," noting that "the book follows the conventions of detective fiction, yet it is also laced with references to Mexican politics, past and present, opening up a wide range of possible story lines for Marcos [the author] to develop." The authors of the fictive female sleuths were writing about social injustice and power politics a quarter of a century ago, but in the hands of a revolutionary (male leader) it becomes a political tool. So, when the "elusive and charismatic leader of the Zapatista movement in Southern Mexico" wanted to write a crime novel he acknowledged mystery novels as "the best genre for describing social injustice, the abuse of power, the inequality that exists in a society."[7] That is an example of the radical potency of literature to turn imagination into reality as well as how the postmodern female Trickster energy can be embodied in a man, that is, of course, if the mystery is ironic and witty.

Another example of the radical potency of Trickster literature to turn imagination into reality can be found in Nancy Drew, that first fictive female sleuth, who turned 75 in April 2005. When she was born she was utterly her own young woman and she is still there influencing an entire generation of feminists. In 1976 the president of the National Organization for Women (NOW), Karen Decrow, told the *Boston Globe* that, "I was such a Nancy Drew fan." Ayaan Hirsi Ali, an outspoken member of the Dutch Parliament and writer of the film *Submission* (2004) concerning Islam's mistreatment of women, thought Nancy Drew was her inspiration for the courage to break with her religion and alienate her parents, "From the time I started reading novels of Nancy Drew and Hardy Boys, I wanted to be like Nancy Drew," she told Morley Safer in an interview. Nancy has shape-shifted out of the literary realms and is a three-dimensional computer game produced by a company which promises that its games are free of "gender stereotypes."[8] Are they funny too?

Is mainstream culture capable of adopting the humor sassitude found in out-group humor?

Out groups behave differently when they are with their own kind as compared to when they are in the dominant *in*-group. This difference in behavior occurs whether the *out*-group is sexually or racially categorized. The white elite world has trekked into the African American world to find the energy of humor many times. In Countee Cullen's *One Way to Heaven* (1932), Constantia Brandon declares "I could go white if I wanted to, but I am too much of a hedonist; I enjoy life too much, and enjoyment isn't across the line." Nikki Giovanni's poem "Nikki-Rosa" is often misinterpreted by white Americans because they can perceive only her hard childhood and do not understand that being rich in "Black love" made her always "quite happy" (quoted in Dance 1998: 136).

This lack of understanding on the part of the well off that those who seem poor and downtrodden in the economic sense can be happy and uplifted in their relational sense is an example of Gerald Vizenor's (1990) admonition that Trickster discourse must take place in its own context and outsiders simply don't get it. African American life is still segregated to a significant extent. This is evident in the service-oriented sector of the economy as African Americans still frequent their own beauty salons, churches, residential areas for the most part, funeral parlors, and doctors' offices and it is in these places that the unique forms of humor of the African American are born and then transmitted to the rest of the culture. Out of the overwhelming hardships which African Americans have faced, like another group known for its humor amidst suffering, the Jews, both groups have made laughter out of anything; their homes, their poverty, their religion, their relatives and neighbors, their illnesses, even death and starvation:

> When Bertrice Berry and her siblings asked their mother what was for dinner, if there was no food she would reply, "Poke, rolls and grits. Poke your mouth out, roll your eyes, and grit your teeth, 'cause that's all you're getting."
>
> (Dance 1998: 139)

Can you even imagine a mother having to make a joke out of the fact that her children have nothing to eat, but what better way to handle it than with humor?

Other areas which have been masterfully handled in marginalized cultures with humor is the art of romantic banter. Based upon what is called "dozens" which is the popular term for a verbal duel common throughout Africa and the African diaspora. Zora Neale Hurston has dramatized these bouts of teasing banter which are part of the courtship rituals in works such as *Jonah's Gourd Vine* (1934) and *Mule Bone* (1931), which she co-authored with Langston Hughes. This form of banter found its way into the Plantation Minstrel Shows and later Minstrel Shows based upon them and vaudeville acts. Humor was used for that most serious of tasks – determining whether people were well suited to each other.

Ethics and the postmodern female Trickster

The emerging postmodern female Trickster demonstrates an ethics of care rather than the traditional ethics of justice as perceived by the symbolic patriarchal order. The traditional definition of ethics encompasses both the moral choices to be made by an individual in relationship with others as well as the study of the morals and moral choices imposed upon an individual by the culture they are brought up in. Again, western culture has overemphasized one end of the ethical continuum while ignoring the other. And women have somehow come up short when it comes to ethics. How did this occur? Carol Gilligan (1982) summarizes the history thus:

> The criticism that Freud makes of women's sense of justice, seeing it as compromised in its refusal of blind impartiality, reappears not only in the work of Piaget but also in that of Kohlberg. While in Piaget's account (1932) of the moral judgment of the child, girls are an aside, a curiosity to whom he devotes four entries in an index that omits "boys" altogether because "the child" is assumed to be male, in the research

from which Kohlberg derives his theory, females simply do not exist. Kohlberg's (1958, 1981) six stages that describe the development of moral judgment from childhood to adulthood are based empirically on a study of eighty-four boys whose development Kohlberg has followed for a period of over twenty years. Although Kohlberg claims universality for his stage sequence, those groups not included in his original sample rarely reach his higher stages. (Edwards 1975; Holstein 1976; Simpson 1974) Prominent among those who thus appear to be deficient in moral development when measured by Kohlberg's scale are women, whose judgments seem to exemplify the third stage of his six-stage sequence. At this stage morality is conceived in interpersonal terms and goodness is equated with helping and pleasing others. This conception of goodness is considered by Kohlberg and Kramer (1969) to be functional in the lives of mature women insofar as their lives take place in the home. Kohlberg and Kramer imply that only if women enter the traditional area of male activity will they recognize the inadequacy of this moral perspective and progress like men toward higher stages where relationships are subordinated to rules (stage four) and rules to universal principles of justice (stages five and six).

(Gilligan 1982: 19)

Gilligan concludes that the problems inherent in Freud, Piaget and Kohlberg come from their exclusive focus on the male which "informs a different description of development" (Gilligan 1982: 19). In Nietzsche's *Genealogy of Morals* he asks under what conditions did culture construct these value judgments of good and evil and what is the intrinsic worth of these value judgments? While it is the correct question, Nietzsche makes the same fundamental mispresumption that cultural development is synonymous with the male perspective. Yet, he does ask the postmodern question: how did we humans arrive at these moral principles? Gilligan understands that "men and women may speak different languages, [which] they assume are the same, using similar words to encode disparate experiences of self and social relationships" (Gilligan 1982: 173). She explains that "while an ethic of justice proceeds from the premise of equality – that everyone should be treated the same – an ethic of care rests upon the premises of non-violence – that no one should be hurt" (Gilligan 1982: 174). The collective western collective conception of morality and ethics, our conceptions of moral development have been based upon an ethic of equality, which is a legal fiction since women along with most of the world's population have been perceived as not equal to the norm of the elite white male. Women and other marginalized groups have not been even been conceptualized as coming within any conception of equality until the late twentieth century. The basis upon which the collective formulates its ethical considerations have, by definition of equality, excluded most of the world.

Gilligan (1982: 19) concludes that this ethic of care is based upon "conflicting responsibilities rather than competing rights and requires for its resolution a mode of thinking that is contextual and narrative rather than formal and abstract." While Gilligan did not label this energy as Trickster, she is describing an energy which is centered in an ability to remain fluid between the differing poles of context and relationship and I would argue that this requires Trickster's dynamism; that ability to move between differing poles without losing sight of either.

John Beebe in *Integrity in Depth* (1992) analyzes Gilligan's work in relationship to Jung finding that her ethics of care describes Jung's individuation journey as coming from within rather than from an imposed set or morals from the collective:

> We can see in Gilligan's formulation, which has been so helpful in teaching us to read women's lives for what they say about their style of integrity, a vision of two styles of moral consciousness that ultimately derives from Jung. Jung gives the styles that Gilligan calls "care" and "justice" the names *eros* and *logos*.
>
> (Beebe 1992: 81)

Although Beebe goes on to comment about the unfortunate use of the words *eros* and *logos* by Jung, Beebe does clarify their meaning in a way that I have adopted implicitly throughout this work:

> It would help to follow Gilligan in realizing that eros is a moral attitude. By eros, Jung means neither sex nor relatedness in any casual sense, but rather the need to cultivate caring for the wholeness of others as well as oneself. Jung's eros is not unlike Austen's amiability, and is part of a conception of integrity which he does not explicitly define. To borrow the language of Taoist philosophy, eros would be the *te* that senses the feminine Tao. Logos in contrast, means the capacity to differentiate and discriminate, implying a conception of justice by which such discrimination can be made.
>
> (Beebe 1992: 81)

Beebe has reinscribed *eros* with morality which I argue can be integrated with humor to arrive at the postmodern female Trickster's energy – humorous and ethical. Are these two conceptions capable of being integrated? Yes, and the representation is Woodman's lusty Dark Goddess who signifies a new conception of morality inclusive of the cognitive adaptation of humor through the manifestation of Trickster energy as psychopomp. This is why Trickster has manifested, not only to rebalance the symbolic order, but also to transform it into a dynamic and humorous energy which is then manifested in the world.

Recent sightings or just another first wave?

In Chapter 13 I reviewed recent sightings of the female Trickster, concluding that when women imagine the feminine, they imagine it differently
than when the male imagines the feminine, but has this information been
integrated into the collective awareness? One positive outcome is that as
more women enter the ranks of mainstream media they expose the unfortunate but still evident exclusion of women in the arts. One study regarding
playwrights and other forms of written literature published by the New
York State Council on the Arts found after three years of research that
"only 17 percent of plays produced in America were by women and, the
January 2002 report revealed, the smaller theaters were the more inclusive
ones."[9] In written literature the research indicates that:

> books written by men were significantly less intimate than those written
> by women. Men's texts referred typically to sex, exteriors, violence, work
> and tools. Women's texts referred typically to relationships, interiors,
> clothing, children, women inside. Men outside.[10]

The study also found that while "women are the ones buying and reading
books" it is "men, male publishers, reviewers and award givers [who] continue to define public taste."[11]

This is quite a conundrum and brings up the issue of whether separate
prizes and awards are necessary since the male-dominated mainstream
apparently still refuses to recognize women artists as more than token
representatives of the collective culture. Sara Paretsky, the author of the
V.I. Warshawski detective series, started the organization *Sisters in Crime*
for that very reason. When asked to speak about the creation of *Sisters in
Crime*, Paretsky had this to say:

> *Sisters in Crime* was started back in 1986 with a group of other women.
> We were trying to help women get in print, stay in print, and come to
> the attention of booksellers and libraries. At that time, books by men
> mystery writers were reviewed seven times as often as books by women,
> so libraries and booksellers didn't know we existed. Thanks to heroic
> work by women like Linda Grant, Sharyn McCrumb, and Carolyn
> Hart, we got a Books in Print project off the ground that made a big
> difference in readers learning what women were writing. *Sisters in
> Crime* now has more than four thousand members worldwide.
>
> (Paretsky 2001: 3)

Ms. magazine asked where the women were as directors and producers in
the film and television field and found that the 2002–2003 television season

matched what they had found the previous three years: "white men directed 82 percent of the 860 episodes tallied. Ten of the top 40 shows hired no female directors, 13 hired neither female nor minority directors" (*Ms.*, Fall 2003: 12). Television and movie demographics are still based on teen boys with producers being stunned (over and over again!) when a movie like *My Big Fat Greek Wedding* (2002) is successful. Why is it that so many middle-aged men are producing movies where 50–60-year-old men successfully woo and win women half their age? Are those involved with the movies and televison stuck in a puer complex repeating their visions of never having to grow up through the medium of the visual imagery of films and television?

When women do produce and direct do they produce a different entity even when they are using the imaginal realm material of the male, such as a play which was written by William Shakespeare? When the all-female Queen's Company tackled Shakespeare's famous war-of-the sexes comedy, *The Taming of the Shrew*, the reviewer found that "the use of women to play men turns the usual Shakespearean gender-bending . . . on its head . . . in this version there's no question that women rule." But the point of it all, is that the troupe "just wants to have fun." From the beginning of the prologue where there is a lip-synch version of Cyndi Lauper's *Girls Just Wanna Have Fun* to "the eight women (many of whom play multiple roles) are entirely convincing as men," then the coup de grace, "the inflatable doll who plays Bianca" reducing her to a "very funny sex toy" and a hilarious dream sequence leading to the "madcap wedding [which] has become a multi-cultural affair, with Indian music and garb."[12] While the show remains a comedy, it is subversive in how it visions the action itself, and no longer do we have a woman tamed by a mean man, we have a fun romp through a gender-bending world filled with ironic twists, such as the blow-up doll in place of the one-dimensional Bianca.

The film *The Aristocrats* (2005) purportedly a "brilliant" essay on humor done through the technique of interviewing some of the world's funniest comics about the world's "dirtiest" joke provides additional insight into how a female humorously reinscribes the male world view. The joke is about excrement and represents an early stage in humor development. None of the male comics, such as George Carlin, Bill Maher, Martin Mull, Don Rickles, Chris Rock, Dick and Tommy Smothers, Jon Stewart, and Robin Williams, did anything but a straightforward interpretation of why the joke was funny. It fell to the female comic Sarah Silverman to provide "one of the few genuinely unsettling and provocative moments" in the film:

> Stripping away the frame ("a guy walks into a talent agent's office . . ."), she tells the joke from the inside perspective of someone for whom it is not funny at all. Which makes it funnier than ever, as well as decidedly squirm-inducing.[13]

Sarah Silverman shifted the perspective from the power dynamic to the view of the victim and in so doing totally reinscribed the joke, kept it funny, showcased her wit, and obliterated the old way of looking at the joke. Sarah Silverman is an example of how the postmodern female Trickster is manifesting in the collective consciousness. Women are in the culture to a greater extent than ever before, recognized as world leaders, and many of them are reinscribing female Tricksters, much like Gates' signifying monkey. As this energy is integrated will women be marginalized again? This is an important consideration because the female Trickster was able to manifest only through women's humor and literature. How do we, as a culture, continue to encourage the development of women's imaginal realms so that the entire collective can benefit? In an article about girl chess players it was reported that, "When girls play against girls they still play as girls," that is strategically rather than aggressively and they can thank an opponent for beating them with a "beautiful finish, something few could imagine in mixed play." It seems that for boys it is still about a "take no prisoners mentality", which girls are punished for having. The article asks the question of whether to continue the all girls chess tournaments.[14] Isn't separate inherently unequal? Does the problem stem from the early segregation of the sexes during play? Most women leaders in the United States report that they came from all-girls schools, and that would include Hillary Clinton and Pat Schroeder. To redress the imbalance in literary awards the Orange Prize in Great Britain and the Prix Femina in France were developed, but there is no all women's literary prize yet in the United States. In other areas women are making inroads (pun intended). Volvo asked women to design a car they would like to drive, and what did they come up with? They wanted everything the men wanted in terms of style and performance "plus a lot more that male buyers have never thought to ask," said Hans-Olov Olsson, Volvo's president and chief executive. He added that "we learned that if you meet women's expectations, you exceed those for men." So what did the women design? A car that's nearly maintenance free, an oil change every 30,000 miles and the car sends a wireless message to a local service center which notifies the driver when to schedule a servicing. The car designed by women has a less messy way to fill up the tank and there's no hood, the whole front lifts up for easy access.[15] Including women's imagination at the design stage changed the car into one that better met the needs of the consumer. Now, can you imagine what might have been designed in law, religion, and politics if women had been invited to attend the design sessions all those millennia ago?

Conclusion

The desire for the state of transcendence fixed to an undeveloped and immature psyche has resulted in a false security in certainty. This imbalanced masculine symbolic order has attempted to control through power the natural cycles of chaos, cycles which cannot be controlled. This has resulted in an economic and social order which has repressed for thousands of years its role in deforesting and deflowering the world. This phallic ideal that it can rise from the land towards the sky without regard to natural cycles requires that man lie on his back like a dog with its belly exposed; it is a vulnerable position which requires much armoring. The postmodern female Trickster is here to get the penis off our collective backs so that we may walk upright into the future.

George Bernard Shaw is reputed to have said that if you wanted to tell people the truth you had better make them laugh or they'll kill you. The fictive female sleuths, Madonna and other female performers, and the women of *Sex and the City* are representative examples of the radical deployment of this Trickster energy in postmodernity as embodied in the female. Their mission is no less than to remake the world through laughter.

Notes

1 Attributed to Jung referring to Schopenhauer, cited in Luke (1995: 72).
2 Helen Luke (1995: 72).
3 Langston Hughes, in Dance (1988: 97).
4 Anonymous.
5 In Eliot's introduction to Charles Williams' novel, *All Hallows' Eve* (1945), cited in Luke (1995: 72).
6 *New York Times*, November 13, 2005: ST2.
7 *New York Times*, December 13, 2004: A4.
8 All materials from *New York Times Sunday Magazine*, April 24, 2005: 30.
9 *New York Times*, Sunday, December 21, 2003: 4AR.
10 *New York Times*, Sunday, December 21, 2003: 4AR.
11 The actual study results can be found at www.Mslexia.co.uk cited in *New York Times,* June 23, 2005: B7.
12 *New York Times*, November 14, 2005: B4.
13 *New York Times*, November 11, 2005.
14 *New York Times*, May 16, 2005: A12.
15 *Marin Independent Journal*, March 3, 2004: C9.

Bibliography

Abram, D. (1996). *The Spell of the Sensuous: Perception and Language in a More-than-human World.* New York: Pantheon.

Ackerman, D. (2004). *An Alchemy of Mind: The Marvel and Mystery of the Brain.* New York: Scribner.

Alcott, L.M. (1994 [1868]). *Little Women.* London: Little, Brown.

Allen, P.G. (1986). *The Sacred Hoop: Recovering the Feminine in American Indian Traditions.* Boston, MA: Beacon.

Anzaldúa, G. (1987). *Borderlands/La Frontera: The New Mestiza.* San Francisco, CA: Spinsters/Aunt Lute.

Armstrong, K. (1993). *A History of God: The 4000-year Quest of Judaism, Christianity, and Islam.* New York: Knopf.

Atwood, M. (1972). *Surfacing.* London: Virago.

Auden, W.H. (1948). "The Guilty Vicarage". In R. Winks (ed.) (1981) *Detective Fiction: A Collection of Critical Essays.* Englewood Cliffs, NJ: Prentice-Hall.

Austen, J. (1811). *Sense and Sensibility.* London: T. Egerton.

Austen, J. (1813). *Pride and Prejudice: A Novel.* London: T. Egerton.

Austen, J. (1814). *Mansfield Park.* London: T. Egerton.

Ayto, J. (1991). *Dictionary of Word Origins.* New York: Arcade.

Bachelard, G. (1987). *On Poetic Imagination and Reverie: Selections from Gaston Bachelard.* Dallas, TX: Spring.

Bakhtin, M. (1968). *Rabelais and his World.* Cambridge, MA: MIT Press.

Ballinger, F. (1988). "Coyote, She Was Going There: Prowling for Hypotheses about the Female Native American Trickster." Unpublished talk given at the Modern Language Association meeting, December 1988.

Barreca, R. (1991). *They Used To Call Me Snow White . . . But I Drifted: Women's Strategic Use of Humor.* New York: Penguin.

Barreca, R. (1994). *Untamed and Unabashed: Essays on Women and Humor in British Literature.* Detroit, MI: Wayne State University Press.

Barreca, R. (ed.) (1996). *The Penguin Book of Women's Humor.* New York: Penguin.

Bartky, S. (1988). *Foucault, Femininity, and the Modernization of Patriarchal Power.* Boston, MA: North Eastern University Press.

Becker, C., Bowman, C.G. and Torrey, M., et al. (1994). *Cases and Materials on Feminist Jurisprudence: Taking Women Seriously.* St. Paul, MN: West.

Beebe, J. (1981). "The Trickster in the Arts." *San Francisco Jung Institute Library Journal* 2(2): 21–54.

Beebe, J. (1992). *Integrity in Depth*. College Station, TX: Texas A&M University Press.

Behar, R. (1996). *The Vulnerable Observer: Anthropology that Breaks your Heart*. Boston, MA: Beacon.

Berry, F.M. (1856). *The Widow Bedott Papers*. New York: J.C. Derby.

Besant, W. (1896). *The Revolt of Man*. London: Chatto and Windus.

Bhabha, H.K. (1994). *The Location of Culture*. London: Routledge.

Blackstone, W. (1979 [1765]). *Commentaries on the Laws of England: A Facsimile of the First Edition of 1765–1769*. Chicago, IL: University of Chicago Press.

Boas, F. (1898). "Introduction." In J.A. Teit, *Traditions of the Thompson River Indians of British Columbia*. Boston, MA: Houghton Mifflin.

Bodkin, M.M. (1900). *Dora Myrl, the Lady Detective*. London: Chatto and Windus.

Bohm, D. and Nichol, L. (1996). *On Dialogue*. London: Routledge.

Bollas, C. (1992). *Being a Character: Psychoanalysis and Self-Experience*. New York: Hill and Wang.

Bracken, P. (1960). *I Hate To Cook Book*. New York: Harcourt, Brace.

Bradstreet, A. (1650). *The Tenth Muse Lately Sprung Up in America*. London: Stephen Bowtell.

Braidotti, R. (1994). *Nomadic Subjects: Embodiment and Sexual Difference in Contemporary Feminist Theory*. New York: Columbia University Press.

Brand, C. (1987 [1946]). *The Spinster's Secret*. London: Pandora.

Brann, E.T.H. (1991). *The World of the Imagination: Sum and Substance*. Savage, MD: Rowman and Littlefield.

Brinton, D.G. (1896). *Myths of the New World*, 3rd edn. Philadelphia, PA: David McKay.

Brodkin, K. (1998). *How Jews Became White Folks and What that Says about Race in America*. New Brunswick, NJ: Rutgers University Press.

Brontë, C. (1847). *Jane Eyre*. London: Smith, Elder.

Brontë, E. (1847). *Wuthering Heights: A Novel*. London: Thomas Cautley Newby.

Brown, L.M. and Gilligan, C. (1992). *Meeting at the Crossroads: Women's Psychology and Girls' Development*. Cambridge, MA: Harvard University Press.

Brown, R.M. (1973). *Rubyfruit Jungle*. Plainfield, VT: Daughters.

Buck, C. (ed.) (1992). *The Bloomsbury Guide to Women's Literature*. New York: Prentice-Hall.

Burlinson, K. (1992). "Nineteenth-century Britain." In C. Buck (ed.) *The Bloomsbury Guide to Women's Literature*. New York: Bloomsbury.

Burney, F. (1778). *Evelina, or The History of a Young Lady's Entrance into the World*. London: T. and W. Lowndes.

Burney, F. (1984 [1800]). *A Busy Day*. New Brunswick, NJ: Rutgers University Press.

Burney, F. (1995 [1779]). *The Witlings*. East Lansing, MI: Colleagues Press.

Butler, J. (1990). *Gender Trouble: Feminism and the Subversion of Identity*. London: Routledge.

Butler, J. (1997). *Excitable Speech: A Politics of the Performative*. London: Routledge.

Cain, M. (2001). *The Childless Revolution*. Reading, MA: Perseus.

Campbell, J. (1959). *The Masks of the Gods: Primitive Mythology*. New York: Viking.

Césaire, A. (1972 [1950]). *Discourse on Colonialism: An Interview with Aimé Césaire*. Trans. J. Pinkham. New York: Mr Books.

Chodorow, N. (1978). *The Reproduction of Mothering: Psychoanalysis and the Sociology of Gender*. Berkeley, CA: University of California Press.

Cixous, H. (1976)."The Laugh of the Medusa." Trans. K. Cohen and P. Cohen. *Signs* 1: 875–893.

Cixous, H. and Clément, C. (1976). *The Newly Born Woman*. Trans. B. Wing. Manchester: Manchester University Press.

Claremont de Castillejo, I. (1973). *Knowing Woman: A Feminine Psychology*. New York: Putnam.

Cottle, T.J. (1974). *Black Children, White Dreams*. New York: Delta.

Coward, R. and Semple, L. (1989). "Tracking Down the Past: Women and Detective Fiction." In H. Carr (ed.) *From My Guy to Sci-fi: Genre and Women's Writing in the Postmodern World*. London: Pandora.

Craig, P. and Cadogan, M. (1981). *The Lady Investigates: Women Detectives and Spies in Fiction*. New York: St. Martin's Press.

Cullen, C. (1932). *One Way to Heaven*. New York: Harper and Bros.

Dance, D.C. (ed.) (1998). *Honey, Hush! An Anthology of African American Women's Humor*. New York: W.W. Norton.

Darwin, C. (1981 [1871]). *The Descent of Man*. Princeton, NJ: Princeton University Press.

Davidson, C.N. and Wagner-Martin, L. (eds.) (1995). *The Oxford Companion to Women's Writing in the United States*. New York: Oxford University Press.

Davis, R.H. (1998 [1861]). *Life in the Iron Mills or The Korl Woman*. Boston, MA: Bedford.

de Beauvoir, S. (1953). *The Second Sex*. New York: Knopf.

de Lauretis, T. (1993). "Feminist Genealogies: A Personal Itinerary." *Women's Studies International Forum* 16(4): 393–403.

Derrida, J. (1967). "Writing and Difference." In V.B. Leitch, W.E. Cain, L. Finke, B. Johnson, J. McGowan and J.J. Williams (eds.) (2001) *The Norton Anthology of Theory and Criticism*. New York: W.W. Norton.

DeWall, C.N., Altermatt, T.W. and Thompson, H. (2005). "Understanding the Structure of Stereotypes of Women: Virtue and Agency as Dimensions Distinguishing Female Subgroups." *Psychology of Women Quarterly* 29(4): 396–405.

Dilley, K.J. (1998). *Busybodies, Meddlers, and Snoops: The Female Hero in Contemporary Women's Mysteries*. Westport, CT: Greenwood Press.

Donovan, J. (1990). "The Silence is Broken." In D. Cameron (ed.) *The Feminist Critique of Language: A Reader*. London: Routledge.

Doty, W. (1978). "Hermes, Heteronymous Appellation." In J. Hillman (ed.) *Facing the Gods*. Irving, TX: Spring.

Doty, W. (1993). "A Lifetime of Trouble-making: Hermes as Trickster." In W.J. Hynes and W. Doty (eds.) *Mythical Trickster Figures: Contours, Contexts, and Criticisms*. Tuscaloosa, AL: University of Alabama Press.

Douglas, C. (1990). *The Woman in the Mirror: Analytical Psychology and the Feminine*. Boston, MA: Sigo Press.

Downing, C. (1984). *The Goddess: Mythological Images of the Feminine*. New York: Crossroad.

du Bois, P. (1998). "Introduction to The Love Songs of Sappho". In P. Roche (ed.) *The Love Songs of Sappho*. Amherst, NY: Prometheus.

Dyer, L. (2001). "The Guys, the Gals – Who's on First?" *Publishers Weekly* (Internet edition) September 4: 1–9.

Eagleton, M. (1996). *Working with Feminist Criticism*. Cambridge, MA: Blackwell.

Edinger, E.F. (1986). *The Bible and the Psyche: Individuation Symbolism in the Old Testament*. Toronto: Inner City.

Edwards, L.R. (1984). *Psyche as Hero: Female Heroism and Fictional Form*. Middletown, CT: Scranton, PA: Wesleyan University Press.

Eliade, M. (1987). "Images and Imagination." *The Encyclopedia of Religion, Vol. 7*. New York: Macmillan.

Eliot, T.S. (1948). *Selected Poems*. Harmondsworth, UK: Penguin.

Ellenberger, H.F. (1970). *The Discovery of the Unconscious: The History and Evolution of Dynamic Psychiatry*. New York: Basic Books.

Evans-Pritchard, E.E. (1967). *The Zande Trickster*. Oxford: Clarendon.

Fanon, F. (1967 [1952]). *Black Skin, White Masks*. Trans. C.L. Markmann. New York: Grove.

Felstiner, W.L.F., Abel, R.L. and Sarat, A. (1980–1981). "The Emergence and Transformation of Disputes: Naming, Blaming, Claiming." *Law and Society Review* 15: 631–654.

Ferber, E. (1913). *Roast Beef, Medium: The Business Adventures of Emma McChesney*. New York: Frederick A. Stokes.

Ferber, E. (1915). *Emma McChesney and Company*. New York: Frederick A. Stokes.

Fierz-David, L. (1988). *Women's Dionysian Initiation: The Villa of Mysteries in Pompeii*. Dallas, TX: Spring.

Foster, H.W. (1986 [1797]). *The Coquette*. New York: Oxford University Press.

Foucault, M. (1979). *Discipline and Punish: The Birth of the Prison*. New York: Random House.

Foucault, M. (1984). "What is an Author?" In P. Rabinow (ed.) *Foucault Reader*. New York: Pantheon.

Frederick, H.V. (2000). "Mystery: Revisiting the Scene of the Crime." *Publishers Weekly* (Internet edition) April 24: 1–14.

Freire, P. (1972). *Pedagogy of the Oppressed*. New York: Herder and Herder.

Freud, S. (1938). "Wit and its Relation to the Unconscious." In A.A. Brill (ed.) *The Basic Writings of Sigmund Freud*. New York: Random House.

Freud, S. and Brill, A.A. (1916). *Leonardo da Vinci: A Psychosexual Study of an Infantile Reminiscence*. New York: Moffat Yard.

Friedan, B. (1963). *The Feminine Mystique*. New York: W.W. Norton.

Frye, N. (1947). *Fearful Symmetry: A Study of William Blake*. Princeton, NJ: Princeton University Press.

Frye, N. (1957). *Anatomy of Criticism: Four Essays*. Princeton, NJ: Princeton University Press.

Gale, S.H. (ed.) (1988). *Encyclopedia of American Humorists*. New York: Garland.

Gates, H.L. (ed.) (1986). *"Race," Writing, and Difference*. Chicago, IL: University of Chicago Press.

Gates, H.L. (1988). *The Signifying Monkey: A Theory of Afro-American Literary Criticism*. New York: Oxford University Press.

Geertz, C. (1972). "Deep Play: Notes on a Balinese Cockfight." *Daedalus* 101: 1–37.

Giegerich, W. (1984). "World as Mirror." *Spring* 1984: 61–75.

Gilbert, S.M. and Gubar, S. (eds.) (1979a). *Shakespeare's Sisters: Feminist Essays on Women's Poets*. Bloomington, IN: Indiana University Press.

Gilbert, S.M. and Gubar, S. (1979b). *The Madwoman in the Attic: The Woman Writer and the Nineteenth-Century Literary Imagination*. New Haven, CT: Yale University Press.

Gilbert, S.M. and Gubar, S. (1988). *No Man's Land: The Place of the Woman Writer in the Twentieth Century*. New Haven, CT: Yale University Press.

Gilligan, C. (1982). *In a Different Voice: Psychological Theory and Women's Development*. Cambridge, MA: Harvard University Press.

Gilligan, C. (1988). *Mapping the Moral Domain: A Contribution of Women's Thinking to Psychological Theory and Education*. Center for the Study of Gender Education and Human Development Harvard University Graduate School of Education. Cambridge, MA: Harvard University Press.

Gilligan, C. (2002). *The Birth of Pleasure*. New York: Knopf.

Gilligan, C., Lyons, N.P. and Hanmer, T.J. (1989). *Making Connections: The Relational Worlds of Adolescent Girls at Emma Willard School*. Troy, NY: Emma Willard School.

Gilligan, C., Rogers, A.G. and Tolman, D.L. (eds.) (1991).*Woman, Girls and Psychotherapy: Reframing Resistance*. New York: Haworth Press.

Gilman, C.P. (1979). *Herland*. New York: Pantheon.

Gimbutas, M. (1989). *The Language of the Goddess*. New York: Harper and Row.

Goswami, A. with Reed, R.E. and Goswami, M. (1993). *The Self-Aware Universe: How Consciousness Creates the Material World*. New York: Putnam.

Gottman, J. (1994). *Why Marriages Succeed or Fail: And How To Make Yours Last*. New York: Fireside.

Grafton, S. (1982). *"A" is for Alibi: A Kinsey Millhone Mystery*. New York: Holt, Rinehart and Winston.

Grafton, S. (1985). *"B" is for Burglar: A Kinsey Millhone Mystery*. New York: Holt, Rinehart and Winston.

Grafton, S. (1986). *"C" is for Corpse: A Kinsey Millhone Mystery*. New York: Holt, Rinehart and Winston.

Grafton, S. (1987). *"D" is for Deadbeat: A Kinsey Millhone Mystery*. New York: Henry Holt.

Grafton, S. (1988). *"E" is for Evidence: A Kinsey Millhone Mystery*. New York: Henry Holt.

Grafton, S. (1989). *"F" is for Fugitive: A Kinsey Millhone Mystery*. New York: Henry Holt.

Grafton, S. (1990). *"G" is for Gumshoe*. New York: Henry Holt.

Grafton, S. (1991). *"H" is for Homicide*. New York: Henry Holt.

Grafton, S. (1992). *"I" is for Innocent*. New York: Henry Holt.

Grafton, S. (1993). *"J" is for Judgment*. New York: Henry Holt.

Grafton, S. (1994). *"K" is for Killer*. Hingham, MA: Wheeler.

Grafton, S. (1995). *"L" is for Lawless*. New York: Henry Holt.

Grafton, S. (1996). *"M" is for Malice*. New York: Henry Holt.

Grafton, S. (1998). *"N" is for Noose*. New York: Henry Holt.

Grafton, S. (1999). *"O" is for Outlaw*. New York: Henry Holt.

Grafton, S. (2001). *"P" is for Peril*. New York: G.P. Putnam's Sons.

Grafton, S. (2002). *"Q" is for Quarry*. New York: Putnam.

Grafton, S. (2004). *"R" is for Ricochet*. New York: Putnam.

Grafton, S. (2005). *"S" is for Silence*. New York: Putnam.

Graves, R. (1966). *The White Goddess: A Historical Grammar of Poetic Myth*. New York: Farrar, Straus and Giroux.

Green, A.K. (1878). *The Leavenworth Case: A Lawyer's Story*. New York: Putnam.

Habermas, J. (1967). "The Structural Transformation of the Public Sphere: An Inquiry into a Category of Bourgeois Society." In V.B. Leitch, W.E. Cain, L. Finke, B. Johnson, J. McGowan and J.J. Williams (eds.) (2001) *The Norton Anthology of Theory and Criticism*. New York: W.W. Norton.

Habermas, J. (1968). "Knowledge and Human Interest." In V.B. Leitch, W.E. Cain, L. Finke, B. Johnson, J. McGowan and J.J. Williams (eds.) (2001) *The Norton Anthology of Theory and Criticism*. New York: W.W. Norton.

Haddon, G.P. (1990). "The Personal and Cultural Emergence of Yang-Femininity." In C. Zweig (ed.) *To Be a Woman*. Los Angeles, CA: Jeremy P. Tarcher.

Halsey, M. (1944). *Some of My Best Friends are Soldiers: A Kind of Novel*. New York: Simon and Schuster.

Halsey, M. (1946). *Color Blind: A White Woman Looks at the Negro*. New York: Simon and Schuster.

Hamilton, E. (1942). *Mythology: Timeless Tales of Gods and Heroes*. Boston, MA: Little, Brown.

Haraway, D. (1985). "A Manifesto for Cyborgs: Science, Technology and Socialist Feminism in the 1980's." In E. Weed (ed.) *Coming to Terms: Feminism, Theory, Politics*. London: Routledge.

Haraway, D. (1991). *Simians, Cyborgs, and Women: The Reinvention of Nature*. New York: Routledge.

Harding, M.E. (1955). *Woman's Mysteries: Ancient and Modern – A Psychological Interpretation of the Feminine Principle as Portrayed in Myth, Story, and Dreams*. New York: Pantheon.

Harding, M.E. (1961). *The Way of All Women: A Psychological Interpretation*. New York: D. McKay.

Hawley, R. (1992). "Women's Literature in Greek and Roman Antiquity." In C. Buck (ed.) *The Bloomsbury Guide to Women's Literature*. New York: Prentice Hall.

Haycraft, H. (1941). *Murder for Pleasure: The Life and Times of the Detective Story*. New York: Appleton-Century.

Heilbrun, C.G. (1988). *Writing a Woman's Life*. New York: Norton.

Heising, W. (ed.) (2000). *Detecting Women*. Dearborn, MI: Purple Moon Press.

Henderson, J. (1984). *Cultural Attitudes in Psychological Perspective*. Toronto: Inner City.

Hennessy, R. and Ingraham, C. (eds.) (1997). *Materialist Feminism: A Reader in Class, Difference, and Women's Lives*. New York: Routledge.

Herrmann, S.B. (1997). "The Visionary Artist: A Problem for Jungian Literary Criticism." *San Francisco Jung Institute Library Journal* 16(1): 35–68.

Hillman, J. (1977)."An Inquiry into Image." *Spring* 1977: 62–88. First presented at the annual conference on Jung, University of Notre Dame, IN, April.

Hillman, J. and McLean, M. (1997). *Dream Animals*. San Francisco, CA: Chronicle.

Hohmann, M. (1997). *Gone is the Shame: A Compendium of Lesbian Erotica*. New York: Masquerade.

hooks, b. (1984). *Feminist Theory: From Margin to Center*. Boston, MA: South End Press.

hooks, b. (1989). *Talking Back: Thinking Feminist, Thinking Black*. Boston, MA: South End Press.

hooks, b. (1990). "Postmodern blackness." In V.B. Leitch, W.E. Cain, L. Finke, B. Johnson, J. McGowan and J.J. Williams (eds.) (2001) *The Norton Anthology of Theory and Criticism*. New York: W.W. Norton.

hooks, b. (2002). "C-Span Interview." May 5, 2002.

Hudson, A.P. (ed.) (1936). *Humor of the Old Deep South*. New York: Macmillan.

Hughes, L. and Hurston, Z.N. (1991 [1931]). *Mule Bone: A Comedy of Negro Life*. New York: HarperPerennial.

Huizinga, J. (1949). *Homo Ludens: A Study of the Play Element in Culture*. London: Routledge and Kegan Paul.

Hurst, F. (1990 [1934]). *Imitation of Life*. New York: Perennial Library.

Hurston, Z.N. (1934). *Jonah's Gourd Vine*. Philadelphia, PA: J.B. Lippincott.

Hurston, Z.N. (1937). *Their Eyes Were Watching God*. Philadelphia, PA: J.B. Lippincott.

Hurston, Z.N. (1979). *I Love Myself When I Am Laughing . . . and Then Again When I Am Looking Mean and Impressive: A Zora Neale Hurston Reader*. Edited by A. Walker. Old Westbury, NY: Feminist Press.

Hyde, L. (1998). *Trickster Makes This World: Mischief, Myth and Art*. New York: Farrar, Straus and Giroux.

Hynes, W.J. and Doty, W. (eds.) (1993). *Mythical Trickster Figures: Contours, Contexts, and Criticisms*. Tuscaloosa, AL: University of Alabama Press.

Iser, W. (1974). *The Implied Reader: Patterns of Communication in Prose Fiction from Bunyan to Beckett*. Baltimore, MD: Johns Hopkins University Press.

Jackson, S. (2000). *The Lottery and Other Stories*. New York: Modern Library.

Jacoby, M. (1992). "The Analytical Psychology of C.G. Jung and the Problem of Literary Evaluation." In R.P. Sugg (ed.) *Jungian Literary Criticism*. Evanston, IL: Northwestern University Press.

James, P.D. (1971). *Shroud for a Nightingale*. London: Faber and Faber.

James, P.D. (1972). *An Unsuitable Job for a Woman*. London: Faber and Faber.

James, P.D. (1986). *A Taste for Death*. London: Faber and Faber.

Jameson, F. (1988). "Postmodernism and Consumer Society." In V.B. Leitch, W.E. Cain, L. Finke, B. Johnson, J. McGowan and J.J. Williams (eds.) (2001) *The Norton Anthology of Theory and Criticism*. New York: W.W. Norton.

Janik, V. K. (1998). *Fools and Jesters in Literature, Art and History*. Westport, CT: Greenwood Press.

Johnson, R.A. and Ruhl, J.M. (1998). *Balancing Heaven and Earth: A Memoir*. San Francisco, CA: HarperSanFrancisco.

Jong, E. (1972). *Fear of Flying*. New York: Holt, Rinehart and Winston.

Jung, C.G. (1923). *Psychological Types: or, The Psychology of Individuation*. Trans. H.G. Baynes. London: Kegan Paul.

Jung, C.G. (1933). *Modern Man in Search of a Soul*. New York: Harcourt, Brace.

Jung, C.G. (1959, 1969). *The Collected Works of C.G. Jung*. Princeton, NJ: Princeton University Press.

Jung, C.G. (1971). *The Problem of Types in Classical and Medieval thought Psychological Types*. Princeton, NJ: Princeton University Press.

Jung, C.G. and Franz, M.L. von (1964). *Man and his Symbols*. Garden City, NY: Doubleday.

Jung, E. (1981 [1957]). *Analytical Club of New York*. Dallas, TX: Spring.

Jurich, M. (1998). *Scheherazade's Sisters: Trickster Heroines and their Stories in World Literature*. Westport, CT: Greenwood.

Katz, S.L. (1988). "Singleness of Heart: Spinsterhood in Victorian Culture." Arts and Sciences, Ph.D. Dissertation. New York: Columbia University.

Kittelson, M.L. (1998). *The Soul of Popular Culture: Looking at Contemporary Heroes, Myths, and Monsters*. Chicago, IL: Open Court.

Klein, K.G. (1988). *The Woman Detective: Gender and Genre*. Urbana, IL: University of Illinois Press.

Klein, K.G. (1994). *Great Women Mystery Writers: Classic to Contemporary*. Westport, CT: Greenwood.

Klein, K.G. (1995). *Women Times Three: Writers, Detectives, Readers*. Bowling Green, OH: Bowling Green State University Popular Press.

Kohlberg, L. (1958). *The Development of Modes of Moral Thinking and Choice in the Years 10 to 16*. New York: Longman.

Kohut, H. (1971). *The Analysis of the Self: A Systematic Approach to the Psychoanalytic Treatment of Narcissistic Personality Disorders*. New York: International Universities Press.

Kristeva, J. (1974). "Woman Can Never Be Defined." In E. Marks and I. de Courtivron (eds.) *New French Feminisms: An Anthology*. Brighton, UK: Harvester.

Kugler, P. (1997). "Psychic Imaging: A Bridge between Subjects and Objects." In P. Young-Eisendrath and T. Dawson (eds.) *The Cambridge Companion to Jung*. Cambridge: Cambridge University Press.

Lacan, J. (1955). "Seminar on 'The Purloined Letter'." In V.B. Leitch, W.E. Cain, L. Finke, B. Johnson, J. McGowan and J.J. Williams (eds.) (2001) *The Norton Anthology of Theory and Criticism*. New York: W.W. Norton.

Lamport, F. (1973). "The Love Song of R. Milhous Nixon." Schlesinger Library, Radcliffe Institute for Advanced Study, Harvard University, Cambridge, MA.

Landay, L. (1998). *Madcaps, Screwballs, and Con Women: The Female Trickster in American Culture*. Philadelphia, PA: University of Pennsylvania Press.

Landry, D. and Maclean, G. (eds.) (1996). *The Spivak Reader: Selected Works of Gayatri Chakravorty Spivak*. New York: Routledge.

Lauter, E. and Rupprecht, C.S. (1985). *Feminist Archetypal Theory: Interdisciplinary Re-Visions of Jungian Thought*. Knoxville, TN: University of Tennessee Press.

Lawrence, H. (1985 [1947]). *Masoko Togawa: The Master Key*. London: Penguin.

Leitch, V.B., Cain, W.E., Finke, L., Johnson, B., McGowan, J. and Williams, J.J. (eds.) (2001) *The Norton Anthology of Theory and Criticism*. New York: W.W. Norton.

Leonard, L.S. (1982). *The Wounded Woman: Healing the Father–Daughter Relationship*. Boulder, CO: Shambhala.

Leonard, L.S. (1990). *Witness to the Fire: Creativity and the Veil of Addiction.* Boston, MA: Shambhala.

Leonard, L.S. (1993). *Meeting the Madwoman: An Inner Challenge for Feminine Spirit – Breaking through Fear and Destructive Patterns to a Balanced and Creative Life.* New York: Bantam.

Lévi-Strauss, C. (1963). *Structural Anthropology.* New York: Basic Books.

Lévi-Strauss, C. (1966). *The Savage Mind.* Chicago, IL: University of Chicago Press.

Levy, A. (2005). *Female Chauvinist Pigs: Women and the Rise of Raunch Culture.* New York: Free Press.

Lindgren, J.R. and Taub, N. (1993). *The Law of Sex Discrimination.* St. Paul, MN: West.

Loos, A. (1926). *Gentlemen Prefer Blondes: The Illuminating Diary of a Professional Lady.* New York: Boni and Liveright.

López-Pedraza, R. (1989). *Hermes and his Children.* Einsiedeln, Switzerland: Daimon.

Lorde, A. (1996). "Sister Outsider." In M. Eagleton (ed.) *Working with Feminist Criticism.* Cambridge, MA: Blackwell.

Lugones, M.C. and Spelman, E.V. (1983). "Have We Got a Theory for You! Feminist Theory, Cultural Imperialism, and the Demand for the Women's Voice." *Women's Studies International Forum* 6(6): 573–581.

Luke, H. (1986). *Women: Earth and Spirit – The Feminine in Symbol and Myth.* New York: Crossroad.

Luke, H. (1995). *The Way of Women: Awakening the Perennial Feminine.* New York: Doubleday.

Maccoby, E.E. (1998). *The Two Sexes: Growing up Apart, Coming Together.* Cambridge, MA: Belknap Press of Harvard University Press.

McDowell, D.E. (1980). "New Directions for Black Feminist Criticism." *Black American Literature Forum* 14(4): 153–159.

McGhee, P.E. (1979). *Humor: Its Origin and Development.* San Francisco, CA: W.H. Freeman.

McNeely, D.A. (1996). *Mercury Rising: Women, Evil and the Trickster Gods.* Woodstock, CT: Spring.

Maslow, A.H. (1973). *Dominance, Self-esteem, Self-actualization: Germinal Papers of A.H. Maslow.* Monterey, CA: Brooks/Cole.

Mather, L. and Yngvesson, B. (1980–1981). "Language, Audience, and the Transformation of Disputes." *Law and Society Review* 15: 775–822.

Meador, B.D. (1990). "Thesmophoria: A Woman's Fertility Ritual." In C. Zweig (ed.) *To Be a Woman: The Birth of the Conscious Feminine.* Los Angeles: Jeremy P. Tarcher.

Meador, B.D. (2000). "The Feminine and Politics." In T. Singer (ed.) *The Vision Thing: Myth, Politics and Psyche in the World.* London: Routledge.

Meyers, C. (1978). "The Roots of Restriction: Women in Early Israel." In R.M. Golden (ed.) *Social History of Western Civilization.* New York: St. Martin's Press.

Minh-ha, T.T. (1989). *Woman, Native, Other: Writing Postcoloniality and Feminism.* Bloomington, IN: Indiana University Press.

Moore, B. and Moore, M. (1997). *Dictionary of Latin and Greek Origins: A*

Comprehensive Guide to the Classical Origins of English Words. New York: Barnes and Noble.

Morrison, T. (1970). *The Bluest Eye*. New York: Holt, Rinehart and Winston.

Morrison, T. (1973). *Sula*. New York: Knopf.

Morrison, T. (1987). *Beloved*. New York: Penguin.

Morrison, T. (1993). *Jazz*. New York: Plum.

Neely, B. (1993). *Blanche on the Lam*. New York: Penguin.

Neely, B. (1994). *Blanche among the Talented Tenth*. New York: St. Martin's Press.

Neely, B. (1998). *Blanche Cleans Up*. New York: Viking.

Neely, B. (2000). *Blanche Passes Go*. New York: Penguin.

Neumann, E. (1963). *The Great Mother: An Analysis of the Archetype*. New York: Pantheon.

Neumann, E. (1994). *The Fear of the Feminine and Other Essays on Feminine Psychology*. Princeton, NJ: Princeton University Press.

Ngugi wa Thiong'o (1972). *Homecoming: Essays on African and Caribbean Literature, Culture and Politics*. Studies in African Literature. London: Heinemann.

Nicholson, L.J. (ed.) (1990). *Feminism/Postmodernism: Thinking Gender*. New York: Routledge.

Nietzsche, F.W. (1899). *A Genealogy of Morals*. Trans. W.A. Hausmann and A. Gray. London: Unwin.

Nussbaum, M.C. (1986). *The Fragility of Goodness: Luck and Ethics in Greek Tragedy and Philosophy*. Cambridge: Cambridge University Press.

Olsen, T. (1978). *Silences*. New York: Delacorte.

Ott, B. (1999). "Review." *American Libraries* 30(2): 61.

Palmer, R.R. and Colton, J. (1971). *A History of the Modern World to 1815*. New York: Knopf.

Paretsky, S. (1982). *Indemnity Only: A Novel*. Garden City, NY: Dial Press.

Paretsky, S. (1984). *Deadlock: A V.I. Warshawski Mystery*. Garden City, NY: Dial Press.

Paretsky, S. (1985). *Killing Orders: A V.I. Warshawski Mystery*. South Yarmouth, MA: J. Curley.

Paretsky, S. (1987). *Bitter Medicine*. New York: W. Morrow.

Paretsky, S. (1989). *Bloodshot*. Boston, MA: G.K. Hall.

Paretsky, S. (1990). *Burn Marks*. Boston, MA: G.K. Hall.

Paretsky, S. (1991). *A Woman's Eye*. New York: Delacorte.

Paretsky, S. (1992). *Guardian Angel*. New York: Delacorte.

Paretsky, S. (1993). *Deadlock: A V.I. Warshawski Mystery*. Boston, MA: G.K. Hall.

Paretsky, S. (1994). *Tunnel Vision*. New York: Delacorte.

Paretsky, S. (1995). *Three Complete Novels*. New York: Wings.

Paretsky, S. (1996a). *Windy City Blues: V.I. Warshawski Stories*. Thorndike, ME: G.K. Hall.

Paretsky, S. (1996b). *Women on the Case*. New York: Delacorte.

Paretsky, S. (1998). *Ghost Country*. Rockland, MA: Wheeler.

Paretsky, S. (1999). *Hard Time: A V.I. Warshawski Novel*. New York: Delacorte.

Paretsky, S. (2001). *Total Recall*. New York: Delacorte.

Paretsky, S. (2002). Interview with Sara Paretsky. www.VIWarshawski.com/sarainterview.html

Paretsky, S. (2004). *Blacklist*. New York: Delacorte.

Paretsky, S. (2006). *Fire Sale*. New York: G.P. Putnam's Sons.

Paretsky, S. and Mystery Writers of America (1989). *Beastly Tales*. New York: Wynwood.

Paris, G. (1992). *The Sacrament of Abortion*. Trans. J. Mott. Dallas, TX: Spring.

Pearsall, M. (ed.) (1999). *Women and Values: Readings in Recent Feminist Philosophy*. Belmont, CA: Wadsworth.

Pelton, R. (1980). *The Trickster in West Africa: A Study of Mythic Irony and Sacred Delight*. Berkeley, CA: University of California Press.

Pelton, R. (1993). "West African Tricksters: Web of Purpose, Dance of Delight." In W.J. Hynes and W. Doty (eds.) *Mythical Trickster Figures: Contours, Contexts, and Criticisms*. Tuscaloosa, AL: University of Alabama Press.

Perera, S.B. (1981). *Descent to the Goddess: A Way of Initiation for Women*. Toronto: Inner City.

Phillipson, M. (1966). *Leonardo da Vinci: Aspects of a Renaissance Genius*. New York: George Braziller.

Piaget, J. (1932). *The Moral Judgement of the Child*. London: Kegan Paul Trench Trubner.

Piaget, J. (1952). *The Origins of Intelligence in Children*. New York: International Universities Press.

Pirkis, C.L. (1894). *Experiences of Loveday Brooke, Lady Detective*. London: Hutchinson.

Plaut, A. (1973). "Reflections on Not Being Able to Imagine." In M. Fordham and the Society of Analytical Psychology (eds.) *Analytical Psychology: A Modern Science*. London: Heinemann Medical.

Poe, E.A. (1992). *The Best of Edgar Allan Poe*. Old Greenwich, CT: Listening Library.

Pratt, A. (1981). *Archetypal Patterns in Women's Fiction*. Bloomington, IN: Indiana University Press.

Puigvert, L. (2001). "Dialogic Feminism: 'Other Women's' Contributions to the Social Transformation of Gender Relations". In J. Butler, E. Beck-Gernsheim and L. Puigvert, *Women and Social Transformation*. New York: Peter Lang.

Qualls-Corbett, N. (1988). *The Sacred Prostitute: Eternal Aspects of the Feminine*. Toronto: Inner City.

Radin, P. (1956). *The Trickster: A Study in American Indian Mythology*. London: Routledge and Kegan Paul.

Radway, J. (1984). *Reading the Romance: Women, Patriarchy, and Popular Literature*. Chapel Hill, NC: University of North Carolina Press.

Reddy, M.T. (1988). *Sisters in Crime: Feminism and the Crime Novel*. New York: Continuum.

Rich, A. (1976). *Of Woman Born: Motherhood as Experience and Institution*. New York: Norton.

Rich, A. (1980). "Compulsory Heterosexuality and Lesbian Existence." In V.B. Leitch, W.E. Cain, L. Finke, B. Johnson, J. McGowan and J.J. Williams (eds.) (2001) *The Norton Anthology of Theory and Criticism*. New York: W.W. Norton.

Richler, M. (1983). *Best of Modern Humor*. New York: Knopf.

Ricketts, M.L. (1993). "The Shaman and the Trickster." In W.J. Hynes and W. Doty (eds.) *Mythical Trickster Figures: Contours, Contexts, and Criticisms*. Tuscaloosa, AL: University of Alabama Press.

Ricoeur, P. (1977). *The Rule of Metaphor: Multi-disciplinary Studies of the Creation of Meaning in Language.* Toronto: University of Toronto Press.

Riviere, J. (1986 [1929]). "Womanliness as a Masquerade." *International Journal of Psychoanalysis* 10: 35–44.

Robinson, L.S. (1972). "Cultural Criticism and the Horror Vacui: Response to Sonja Weita." *College English* 33(6): 731–735.

Robinson, O.F. (1988). "The Historical Background." In S. McLean and N. Burrows (eds.) *The Legal Relevance of Gender.* Atlantic Highlands, NJ: Humanities Press.

Rohrlich, R. (1980). "State Formation in Sumer and the Subjection of Women." *Feminist Studies* 6(1): 76–102.

Rossi, A.S. (ed.) (1973). *The Feminist Papers: From Adams to de Beauvoir.* New York: Columbia University Press.

Rowland, S. (1999). *C.G. Jung and Literary Theory: The Challenge from Fiction.* New York: Macmillan.

Rowland, S. (2001). *From Agatha Christie to Ruth Rendell: British Women Writers in Detective and Crime Fiction.* Basingstoke: Palgrave.

Rowland, S. (2002). *Jung: A Feminist Revision.* Cambridge: Polity.

Rowson, S.H. (1986 [1794]). *Charlotte Temple.* New York: Oxford University Press.

Said, E.W. (1978). *Orientalism.* New York: Pantheon.

Samuels, A. (1985). *Jung and the Post-Jungians.* London: Routledge and Kegan Paul.

Samuels, A. (1993a). *The Political Psyche.* London: Routledge.

Samuels, A. (1993b). "I am a Place: Depth Psychology and Environmentalism." *British Journal of Psychotherapy* 10(2): 211–219.

Samuels, A. (2000). "The Good Enough Leader." In T. Singer (ed.) *The Vision Thing: Myth, Politics and Psyche in the World.* London: Routledge.

Samuels, A. (2001). *Politics on the Couch: Citizenship and the Internal Life.* London: Profile.

Samuels, A., Shorter, B. and Plaut, F. (1986). *A Critical Dictionary of Jungian Analysis.* London: Routledge and Kegan Paul.

Sanday, P.R. (1981). *Female Power and Male Dominance: On the Origins of Sexual Inequality.* Cambridge: Cambridge University Press.

Sanday, P.R. (1990). *Fraternity Gang Rape: Sex, Brotherhood, and Privilege on Campus.* New York: New York University Press.

San Juan, E. (1997). *Beyond Postcolonial Theory.* New York: St. Martin's Press.

Sayers, D.L. (1935). *Gaudy Night.* London: Victor Gollancz.

Schafran, L.H. (1990). "Gender and Justice: Florida and the Nation." *Florida Law Review* 42(1): 181–208.

Schroeder, P. (2002). "Book and Author Breakfast." New York: BookExpo America. Broadcast on C-Span, Book TV, May 5.

Sealey, R. (1990). *Women and Law in Classical Greece.* Chapel Hill, NC: University of North Carolina Press.

Serrano, M. (1966). *C.G. Jung and Hermann Hesse: A Record of Two Friendships.* New York: Schocken.

Shinn, T.J. (1996). *Women Shape-shifters: Transforming the Contemporary Novel.* Westport, CT: Greenwood.

Showalter, E. (1977). *A Literature of their Own: British Women Novelists from Brontë to Lessing*. London: Virago.

Showalter, E. (1985). *The Female Malady: Women, Madness, and English Culture, 1839–1980*. New York: Pantheon.

Singer, J. (1973). *Boundaries of the Soul: The Practice of Jung's Psychology*. Garden City, NY: Anchor.

Singer, J. (1976). *Androgyny: Toward a New Theory of Sexuality*. Garden City, NY: Anchor.

Singer, T. (ed.) (2000). *The Vision Thing: Myth, Politics and Psyche in the World*. London: Routledge.

Slung, M.B. (1975). *Crime on her Mind: Fifteen Stories of Female Sleuths from the Victorian Era to the Forties*. New York: Pantheon.

Smart, C. (1990). "Law's Power, the Sexed Body, and Feminist Discourse." *Journal of Law and Society* 17: 194–210.

Smith, B. (1977). "Toward a Black Feminist Criticism". In G.T. Hull, P.B. Scott and B. Smith (eds.) (1982) *All the Women are White, All the Blacks are Men, But Some of Us Are Brave*. Old Westbury, NY: Feminist Press.

Spivak, G.C. (1987). *In Other Worlds: Essays in Cultural Politics*. New York: Methuen.

Sprinkler, M. (ed.) (1992). *Edward Said: A Critical Reader*. Oxford: Blackwell.

Stabenow, D. (1992a). *A Cold Day for Murder*. New York: Berkley Prime Crime.

Stabenow, D. (1992b). *A Fatal Thaw*. New York: Berkley Prime Crime.

Stabenow, D. (1993). *Dead in the Water: A Kate Shugak Mystery*. New York: Berkley Prime Crime.

Stabenow, D. (1994). *A Cold-Blooded Business: A Kate Shugak Mystery*. New York: Berkley Prime Crime.

Stabenow, D. (1995). *Play with Fire: A Kate Shugak Mystery*. New York: Berkley Prime Crime.

Stabenow, D. (1996). *Blood will Tell: A Kate Shugak Mystery*. New York: G.P. Putnam's Sons.

Stabenow, D. (1997). *Breakup: A Kate Shugak Mystery*. New York: G.P. Putnam's Sons.

Stabenow, D. (1998). *Killing Grounds: A Kate Shugak Mystery*. New York: G.P. Putnam's Sons.

Stabenow, D. (1999). *Hunter's Moon: A Kate Shugak Mystery*. New York: G.P. Putnam's Sons.

Stabenow, D. (2000). *Midnight Comes Again*. New York: St. Martin's Paperback.

Stabenow, D. (2001). *The Singing of the Dead*. New York: St. Martin's Minotaur.

Stein, M. (1980). "Review of Paul Friedrich, 'The Meaning of Aphrodite'." *San Francisco Jung Institute Library Journal* 2(1): 18–22.

Stein, M. (1993). *Solar Conscience, Lunar Conscience: An Essay on the Psychological Foundations of Morality, Lawfulness, and the Sense of Justice*. Wilmette, IL: Chiron.

Stephens, A.S.W. (1843). *High Life in New York*. New York: E. Stephens.

Stibbs, A. (ed.) (1992). *A Woman's Place: Quotations about Women*. New York: Avon.

Stowe, H.B. (1983 [1852]). *Uncle Tom's Cabin*. New York: Bantam.

Street, B.V. (1972). "The Trickster Theme: Winnebago and Azande." In A. Singer and B.V. Street (eds.) *Zande Themes: Essays Presented to Sir Edward Evans-Pritchard*. Totowa, NJ: Rowman and Littlefield.

Suggs, R.P. (1992). *Jungian Literary Criticism*. Evanston, IL: Northwestern University Press.

Tannen, R. (1990a). "The Historical Foundations of Gender Bias in the Law: A Context for Reconstruction." *Florida Law Review* 42(1): 163–180.

Tannen, R. (1990b). "Report of the Florida Supreme Court Gender Bias Study Commission." *Florida Law Review* 42(5): 803–997.

Taub, N. and Schneider, E. (1990). "Women's Subordination and the Role of Law." In D. Kairys (ed.) *The Politics of Law: A Progressive Critique*. New York: Pantheon.

Todd, J.M. (ed.) (1987). *A Dictionary of British and American Women Writers, 1660–1800*. Totowa, NJ: Rowman and Allanheld.

Tuchman, B. (1978). *A Distant Mirror: The Calamitous Fourteenth Century*. New York: Knopf.

Turner, V.W. (1967). *The Forest of Symbols: Aspects of Ndembu Ritual*. Ithaca, NY: Cornell University Press.

Turner, V.W. (1969). *The Ritual Process: Structure and Anti-structure*. Chicago, IL: Aldine.

Vickery, J. (ed.) (1966). *Myth and Literature*. Lincoln, NE: University of Nebraska Press.

Vizenor, G. (1990). "Trickster Discourse." *American Indian Quarterly* 14(3): 277–287.

Vizenor, G. (1994). "Manifest Manners: PostIndian Warriors of Survivance." In V.B. Leitch, W.E. Cain, L. Finke, B. Johnson, J. McGowan and J.J. Williams (eds.) (2001) *The Norton Anthology of Theory and Criticism*. New York: W.W. Norton.

Vonnegut, K. (1969). *Slaughterhouse Five*. New York: Dial Press.

Vonnegut, K. (2005). *A Man without a Country*. New York: Seven Stories Press.

Wagner, J. (1986). *The Search for Signs of Intelligent Life in the Universe*. New York: Harper and Row.

Walker, A. (1982). *The Color Purple*. Boston, MA: G.K. Hall.

Walker, A. (1983). *In Search of our Mothers' Gardens: Womanist Prose*. San Diego, CA: Harcourt Brace Jovanovich.

Walker, N. and Dresner, Z. (eds.) (1998). *Redressing the Balance: American Women's Literary Humor from Colonial Times to the 1980's*. Jackson, MS: University Press of Mississippi.

Walton, P.L. and Jones, M. (1999). *Detective Agency: Women Rewriting the Hard-Boiled Tradition*. Berkeley, CA: University of California Press.

Weldon, F. (1983). *The Life and Loves of a She-Devil*. London: Hodder and Stoughton.

Whitmont, E.C. and Perera, S.B. (1989). *Dreams: A Portal to the Source*. London: Routledge.

Williamson, M. (1986). "The Greek Romance." In J. Radford (ed.) *The Progress of Romance*. New York: Routledge and Kegan Paul.

Winks, R.W. and Corrigan, M. (1998). *Mystery and Suspense Writers: The Literature of Crime, Detection, and Espionage*. New York: Scribner's Sons.

Wiseman, S. (1992). "Britain 1500–1800." In C. Buck (ed.) *The Bloomsbury Guide to Women's Literature*. New York: Prentice Hall.

Wittig, M. (1981). "One is Not Born a Woman." In V.B. Leitch, W.E. Cain, L. Finke, B. Johnson, J. McGowan and J.J. Williams (eds.) (2001) *The Norton Anthology of Theory and Criticism*. New York: W.W. Norton.

Woeller, W. and Cassiday, B. (1988). *The Literature of Crime and Detection: An Illustrated History from Antiquity to the Present*. New York: Ungar.

Wolff, T. (1934). "A Few Thoughts on the Process of Individuation in Women." *Spring* 1941 (1): 81–103.

Woodman, M. (1982). *Addiction to Perfection: The Still Unravished Bride. A Psychological Study*. Toronto: Inner City.

Woodman, M. (1985). *The Pregnant Virgin*. Toronto: Inner City.

Woodman, M. (1990). "Conscious Femininity: Mother, Virgin, Crone." In C. Zweig (ed.) *To Be a Woman: The Birth of the Conscious Feminine*. Los Angeles: Jeremy P. Tarcher.

Woodman, M. and Dickson, E. (1996). *Dancing in the Flames: The Dark Goddess in the Transformation of Consciousness*. Boston, MA: Shambhala.

Woolf, V. (1929). *A Room of One's Own*. London: Hogarth Press.

Woolf, V. (1938). *Three Guineas*. London: Hogarth Press.

Woolf, V. (1976 [1939]). "A Sketch of the Past". In *Moments of Being: Unpublished Autobiographical Writings*. Edited by J. Schulkind. New York: Harcourt, Brace.

Young, S. (ed.) (1994). *An Anthology of Sacred Texts by and about Women*. New York: Crossroad.

Young, S. (ed.) (1999). *Shape-shifting: Encyclopedia of Women and World Religion*. New York: Macmillan.

Young-Eisendrath, P. (1984). *Hags and Heroes: A Feminist Approach to Jungian Psychotherapy with Couples*. Toronto: Inner City.

Young-Eisendrath, P. (1987). *Gender and Desire: Uncursing Pandora*. College Station, TX: Texas A&M University Press.

Young-Eisendrath, P. (1999). *Women and Desire: Beyond Wanting to be Wanted*. New York: Random House.

Zimmerman, B. (1981). "What Has Never Been: An Overview of Lesbian Feminist Literary Criticism." In R. Warhol and D. Herndl (eds.) *Feminisms: An Anthology of Literary Theory and Criticism*. New Brunswick, NJ: Rutgers University Press.

Zoja, L. (2001). *The Father: Historical, Psychological and Cultural Perspectives*. London: Brunner-Routledge.

Zupancic, M. (ed.) (2004). *Hermes and Aphrodite Encounters*. Birmingham, AL: Summa.

Zweig, C. (ed.) (1990). *To Be a Woman: The Birth of the Conscious Feminine*. Los Angeles, CA: Jeremy P. Tarcher.

Index

abortion 113, 216
absurdity 142, 143, 145, 171, 172;
    adaptive process aimed at resolving
    146; incongruous 179; paradoxical 150;
    sharing 170
abuse 14, 16; fusion 206
accommodation cycle 141
Ackerman, D. 73
acting out 42
active imagination 63; reading as 5, 60,
    162
Adams, Abigail 84, 90
adaptation 38, 39, 43, 136, 149; girls and
    women using natural gifted ability for
    47; necessary for healthy psyche 242;
    nomadic identity 181; nuances of 47;
    psychological 210; psychological 49,
    146, 147
adolescents 145
adultery 90, 227
adversity 10
advertising 9, 38
Aeschylus 80
aesthetic criticism 117
aesthetic value 149
affirmation 44
affirmative action 23
Africa 124, 246
African Americans 14, 20, 21, 22, 32–3,
    206–7, 233; art 68; athletes 179;
    bridging the boundaries between
    Tricksters 177; coursework about 169;
    female stereotypes 222; grievances of
    communities 186; humor 148–9, 172,
    173, 221, 222, 246; identification as 50;
    identity as represented by hair 210; jazz
    156; naming children 204–5; protesting
    students 26; segregated 245–6;

situation for women worse than under
    slavery 86; soldiers subjected to
    discrimination 170; women surviving
    the world 204
Agamemnon 81
age expectancy 48
agency 7, 15, 103, 110, 111, 156, 160, 189,
    229, 236; autonomous, authoritative
    women with 41, 70; constructing a life
    replete with 33; divine 62; independent
    205; legal 82, 85, 187; non-profit 45;
    outrageous humor and sexual fantasies
    in a woman with 171; woman
    comfortable with her own 158; women
    without 191; see also physical agency
aggression 46, 146, 158; alternative
    socially acceptable way to demonstrate
    159; child behavior patterns 148; in
    humor hostile to women 161; male 39;
    physical 136; sex and 140; successfully
    deflected 160, 161; underlying 136
Alaska 19, 107
Alcott, Louisa May 107, 111
Aleut people 106–7
Algonquin Round Table 169
alienation 34
Allen, Gracie 229
Allen, Kate 24
Amazon concept 67, 70, 105
ambiguity 9, 131–2, 139, 144, 163
ambivalence 51
American dream 106
American South 124, 161, 221
Amphimedon 81–2
amphitheaters 80
amygdala 73
anal area 126
analogy 64, 70

Anansi the Spider 124
ancestors 57–120
Ancient Greece 72, 84, 150; *see also*
    Athens
Andrews, Sarah 25
androgens 39
anecdotes 145
anger 159; ability to harness 103;
    inflammatory language intended to
    incite 214; linkage between comedy
    and 167; way to displace with a joke
    173
anima 35, 38, 43, 44, 75
animals 138–9
animus 38, 43, 67, 68–9, 75; phallic 46
Anti-Slavery Convention (London 1840)
    85
anxiety 51, 125, 149, 171, 193; avoiding
    42
Apollo 134–5, 136, 141, 192
apperception 64
appetite 127, 176; insatiable 128
Aquarius 42
archaic tales 124, 130
archetypal energy 3, 4, 7, 8, 9, 73, 188;
    available for integration into woman's
    psyche 72; conflation of archetypal
    image with 118, 119; embodiment of
    140; emergent 63, 64; feminine 73;
    irrepresentable 118; not restricted to
    any sex 41; universal 80; virginal
    energy re-emerging through 72; *see also*
    agency; authority; autonomy
archetypal images/imagery 66, 67, 93,
    119; culturally inflected 62, 64, 118,
    188; phallocentric 118
archetypes 4, 5, 192; Cassandra 113;
    concretized versions of 74; culturally
    inflected 159; emerging, virgin 74;
    equality 94; grand theory of 115;
    mother 67, 68, 69; new, law and 93–4;
    psychological 35; shamanistic 117, 132;
    unconscious 51
Argentine Junta 183
aristocracy 52
Aristotle 106
Armstrong, Karen 42
arousal 149
arrest 86
art 9, 65; archetypal aspects of 117;
    bifurcation between the individual and
    archetypal aspects of 117–18;

neurobiology and 73; performance 164;
    Trickster energy transforms culture
    through 9; visual 66, 68; women's, men
    appearing in 69; *see also* works of art
Artemis cult 80
Asia 124
Asians/Indians 50
Askelpios cult 80
assimilation 104, 141
Athena cult 80
Athens 79–82, 106, 180
attention 167
attitudes 14, 143; aesthetic 115–18;
    ethical 192; parental 16; playful 146;
    playful 179; psychological 17, 74,
    115–18, 147, 192; quintessential 116;
    racial 218; sexual, out of bounds 146
Atwood, Margaret 180, 181–2
Aunt Jemima stereotype 222
Austen, Jane 25, 83, 102, 111, 165, 167,
    168, 174, 175, 233, 238, 248
Australia 124
authenticity 10; compassionate demand
    for 46
authority 6, 10–11, 103, 156, 160, 162,
    189, 229, 236; assertion of own, with
    humor 185; constructing a life replete
    with 33; independent 205; legal 82, 187;
    psyche transformed from victim to 179;
    sense of self as 161; solidarity of
    opinion which carries 187; taking back
    177; woman comfortable with her own
    158; women without 191; *see also*
    psychological authority
auto-eroticism 74
autonomy 6–7, 70, 85, 102, 103, 110, 111,
    156, 160, 189, 229, 236; comfort with
    own 158; community and 216;
    constructing a life replete with 33;
    diminished status 79; economic 84;
    independent 205; leadership
    obligations and 20; physical 78; same-
    sex boy groups achieve more 36;
    struggle for 183; terrain where female
    body could legally manifest 187;
    women without 191; *see also* bodily
    autonomy
awareness 13, 33, 43, 61, 118, 218, 237;
    cognitive 65; conscious 42; difference
    and diversity 116; environmental 36;
    incipient 199; mid-point of 126;
    psychological 16; using humor with 165

Axial Age (800–200 BCE) 42
Ayto, J. 6

baby boomer women 230
Bachelard, G. 59
Bacon, Josephine Dodge Daskam 168–9
"bad girl" persona 156, 158, 159, 167
Bakhtin, Mikhail 150, 151, 162
Ballinger, Franchot 187, 189
Bantam 23
baptism 125
Barnes, Linda 24
Barr, Nevada 25
Barr, Roseanne 166
Barreca, Regina 100, 101, 102, 156, 157, 158,
    161–2, 163, 167, 168, 173
beauty 39, 50; youth and 222
Beauvoir, Simone de 32, 51, 90
Becker, C. 88
Beebe, John 5, 102, 152, 248
being: divine comedy of 4, 240–52;
    importance of 79–82; radical openness
    to new forms of 34; serious nature of
    233–6; woman's natural state of 45
Bering Straits 124
Berkeley Press 24
Berle, Milton 38
Berry, Frances Miriam 168
bestsellers 105, 106, 114, 166, 237
biblical culture 190
big-box type stores 14
Billops, Camille 68
binary opposition 34; redeployment of 62
binocular vision 116
biological predispositions 39
biology 49; reproductive 35
birth rates 190
birthing process 43; creative, pushy
    attitude necessary for 44
black arts 41
Black Codes 86
Black Death (1347–61) 61, 62
Black Madonna 243
black men 172
Black Student Unions 26
Black women 220
Blackstone, William 83
blaming 91
"Blanche White" 10, 12, 20–2, 23, 24, 33,
    41, 74, 110, 155, 172, 176, 178, 188,
    190, 191, 203–24, 239, 243

blood taboos 133
Blue Jay stories 124
blues songs 222
Boas, Franz 130, 131, 175
bodily autonomy 20; being
    independent with 180; defining
    epiphany of 126; how to construct
    an ethical life with 14; lack of 90;
    possibility of 230
Bodkin, Matthias McDonnell 110
body 8–9; awareness of 126; elite male 8;
    energies which reside in 44; laughter
    can fool 149; no dialogic relationship
    permitted between psyche and 62;
    relational perspective between mind
    and 62
Bohm, D. 131
Bollas, Christopher 12
Bombay 149
Bombeck, Erma 170, 171
Books in Print project 249
Boston Globe 245
boundary-crossing behavior 25, 204,
    226
Bracken, Peg 171
Bradley, J. P. 87
Bradstreet, Anne 167
Bradwell, Myra 87, 88, 108
Braidiotti, R. 212
brain stem 73
Brand, Christiana 113
Brann, Eva 59–60, 72
Br'er Rabbit stories 124
bricoleur term 132
bridge-building 10
Brinton, Daniel 130, 131
Brontë, Charlotte 100, 102, 108
Brontë, Emily 101
Bronze Age 78
Brown v. Board of Education (1955) 94
Buchanan, Patrick 114
Buck, C. 79
Buddhism 42
Buenos Aires 183
buffoonery 124, 133, 140, 151; body 164;
    undignified 221
burlesque 39, 128, 148, 149, 150, 171;
    humorous 231
Burlinson, K. 101
Burney, Frances (Fanny) 168
Bushnell, Candace 226
Butler, Judith 35, 51

C. G. Jung Conference (1976) 70
Cain, Madelyn 189–90
Caizza, Amy 189
Cali 45
California 190
California Institute for Integral Studies 237
California Supreme Court 91
Campbell, Joseph 130–1, 132, 133
capitalism 42
caricatures 136, 148, 160
Carlin, George 250
carnivals 127, 128, 129, 133, 151, 162; collective use of 150; outrageous 197
cartoons 136, 140, 144, 166
Cassandra archetype 113
Cassiday, B. 80, 112
castration 44
catharsis 159, 162
Cather, Willa 114
Catholic Church 42, 83
Caucasians 50
certainty 165; false security in 251; illusion of 43, 59, 197, 243
Cervantes, M. de 62
chaos 131, 165, 200; movement and 197
chaperones 79
characters 104, 110; being able to articulate motivation for 144; idiosyncratic 178; more developed 134; not especially humorous 112; relationships with 225; revealing true intentions through dialogue 111; serialized, continuing 171
Charlotte, queen consort of George III of Great Britain 168
cheating 227
Chicago Legal News 87
chick lit 16
child abuse 14
child rearing 47
childbirth 133, 164; making women single and outside the enclosure of 188
childcare responsibilities 188
childless women 189–90
China 42, 190
Chipmunk 127
Chopin, Kate 114
Christianity 82, 83, 197
Christie, Agatha 25, 109, 111, 112
circuses 148, 222
citizenship 80

civil law 87
Civil Rights Act (US 1964) 89
civil rights movement 94
class clowns 148
cleansing: psychological 126–7; ritual 125
Cleese, John 149
clerical law 83
Clinton, Hillary 251
clothing: appropriate 38; focusing conscious energy upon 110; restrictive 47
clowns 124, 138, 148–9
Clytemnestra 81
Code of Urakagina of Summer 78
coeducational institutions 40, 112
coercion 197
cognition: imaginative 72; psychological 59
cognitive abilities 40, 135, 141, 144
collective consciousness 3, 9, 23, 26, 42, 51; captured imagination of 59, 70; development of 136; female image who refuses to be a victim of 10; imaginative manifestations recognized as cultural artifacts 80; increased transformed feminine power in 188; "prototypes" of 64; re-emergence of female Trickster energy 12; transforming 10; Trickster is from a rudimentary time in 129; valid prototypes of 63
collective unconscious 7, 51, 62, 115
colonization of the mind 34
color barrier 156
columnists 169, 171
comedians 148
comedic effect 38, 43
comedy 72, 103, 134, 136, 164–5, 250; anger successfully channeled through 167; divine 4, 240–52; domestic 168; foundational support for 150; subversive philosophical gems in the guise of 156; terrifying 163; tragedy to 124, 138, 186; verbal 151; women use anger in 167; *see also* humor, sense of humor, irony, satire, wit
comic books 238
comic pranks 156
comic sensibility 161–2, 179
commercials 38
commonalities 20, 22; self-censorship regarding 34; shared 32

communal matrilineal systems 78
compassion 46
complacency 102, 173
complaints 167
complexion 222
complicity 173
compulsory heterosexuality 210
con artists 74
Conan Doyle, A. 63, 114
conflict 20, 112; gender 25; mainstream
    method of defusing 200; symbolic
    order 165; within-group 36
conflict resolution 199
confrontation 210; avoidance of 159, 200;
    direct 85, 102, 165, 166, 179
Confucianism 42
connectedness 132
conscience 140
consciousness 8, 41, 42, 151, 190;
    allowing a playful attitude to occupy
    146; attainment of newer and higher
    level of 130; capacity to 5; cultural 64;
    cyborg 25, 39; dialectical relationship
    between art and 62; disjunctive,
    psychological 188; earlier, rudimentary
    stage of 130; ego 146; enlargement of
    63; enlarging 147; erotic 132; evolution
    of 133; illusion which has the potency
    and capacity to expand 229–30; images
    take possession of 60; limited 147;
    moral 248; more developed 138; new,
    opening the opportunity to integrate
    151; opportunity and encouragement
    to move beyond present boundaries 61;
    patriarchal 4, 43, 45, 66, 78, 113, 225;
    postmodern time-traveling cyborg-type
    25; potentiality of 243; progressive
    development of 129; quantum 85;
    sexual 127; shadow energy brought up
    to 209; shape-shifting metaphor
    expands 60; transformed 10, 48;
    triggering an enlarged image in 82;
    work towards 6; yang-masculine 46;
    see also collective consciousness
conspiracy 14
Constantine the Great, emperor of Rome
    42
contempt 158
contexts 35, 118; comedic 200;
    incongruous 140–1; performative 126;
    social 36
contrasexuality 242

control 46; possibility of 197; see also
    impulse control
cooking 171
cooperation 39, 49; cross-sex 40; same-
    sex 40
Copenhagen 149
coping mechanism 149, 161, 163
copulation 139
Cornhill Magazine 104
corruption 13, 14
cosmic renewal 103
costumes 133, 148; grotesque 151;
    outrageous 228
court jesters 135, 138
courtesans 79
coverture 83, 89
Coward, R. 113
Cox, Ida 222
Coyote tales 123–4, 134
creation 43; opening the way for seeds of
    44
creativity 14, 103, 142, 189, 205;
    channeled into wit 148; critical
    determinant in 147; innate capacity for
    139; outward, base of all 148; revealed
    as mere symptom 117
crime writing 113
criminal activity 89–90; critical
    determinant of behavior 111
criminal justice system 14
critical judgment 146
crones 7
cross-pollination 26
Crown 24
cruelty 136, 177
Cullen, Countee 169, 245
cults 42, 80
cultural artifacts 5, 30, 60, 66, 98;
    imaginative 41, 79
cultural norms 8, 35, 165, 211, 214; how
    to resist 212; one of the hallmarks of
    189; patriarchal 188, 191; reinscribing
    192
cultural restrictions 146
culture shock 104
culture(s) 34, 160–1; ability and capacity
    to change 46–7; ability to move
    between 20; archaic, goddess imagery
    of 70; collective 5, 9, 41, 59, 157;
    dominant 167; gender distinctions 36;
    indigenous, ethnographic work of 124;
    inhibitions derived from growing up

within same 147; men and women made in 51; mirrored 8; oral 124, 125; performative 124; political 183; postmodern 14; prosperous 49; restricting women 78; ridicule by 127; scarcity 49; status within 40, 187–8; subsistence 35; Trickster energy transforms 9; Trickster's appearance at critical junctures in developmental cycles of 150; Victorian 106; white European male 147; world 133; see also patriarchal culture; pop(ular) culture
custody of children 83, 89
cyborgs 25–6, 29, 39; consciousness and time traveling 25, 39
cynics 147

Dance, D. C. 86, 204, 220, 221, 222, 245, 246
danger 163–6
Dante Alighieri 62
darkness 6
Darwin, C. 85
Davidson, C. N. 104, 105, 107, 108
Davis, Rebecca Harding 106
Declaration of Rights and Sentiments 84, 85
deconstruction 150; implicit and explicit phallocentric power structures 31; traditional boundaries 212
Decrow, Karen 245
deduction 111
deep models 48
defecation 126
defense mechanisms 147
deforestation 182
delusion 43
Demeter-Persephone story 67–8
Dengler, Sandy 25
denial 147
dependency 113
deprecation 160
depression 190
Depression (1930s) 88
deprivations 148
depth psychology 10, 139, 140; crossroads of humor 3; structural approach in 115
Descartes, R. 62
desire 68, 139, 149, 150; catharsis for 162; male 162; to enter a woman 67; unconscious 39

Detecting Women (compendium) 24
Detection Club of Britain 110–11
detective fiction 108, 109, 115, 162; early 110; mother of 107; seismic shift in 114; spinsters and widows in 109; see also fictive female sleuths
developing world 32
development stages 125, 140–5
deviant speech pattern 131
DeWall, C. N. 49, 50
dialectic 62
dichotomous model 47
Dickens, Charles 106
Dickinson, Emily 168
Dickson, E. 4, 6, 41, 243
differentiation 125, 127, 180, 241
Dilley, K. J. 25
Diogenes 82
Dionysius 150, 151
Diotima 81
disabilities 136, 145; pregnancy-related 89
disassociation 41–2, 43, 72, 147, 158, 181, 206; repression of 73
discrimination 170; serious 88; sexual 89, 91
disenfranchisement 33
disguises 145–6, 148, 150
dislocation 165
dispossession 109
diversity 24; commonalities across 20
divination tools 75
divine inspiration 106
divine prophecy 103
divorce 90, 190, 235
domestic realm 67–8
domestication 126
domesticity 84, 88, 222
dominance 43, 49, 49; tangible form of 148
Donovan, J. 98
Doty, W. 8, 131, 132, 133
double entendres 166
doubling 67, 129, 144, 145, 170, 229, 231, 241
Douglas, Mary 131
drag 39, 156
drama 79, 221; origin of all western conceptions of 150
dreams 145
Dresner, Z. 168, 169, 170, 173
Drood Review 23
duality 129; integration of 64

Du Bois, William 169
Dutch Parliament 245
Dyer, L. 23, 24

Eagleton, M. 31, 181
eco-feminism 183
Edinger, Edward 129
education: access to 85, 98; highest rates
    189; phallocentric instructions of 114;
    sex-segregated 89; upper-class girls 99
Edwards, Grace 24
Edwards, Lee 84, 101
ego 5, 46; frightened 241; weak 4
ejaculation 43
elderly abuse 14
Eliade, M. 60, 62, 63, 64
Eliot, George 101, 108
Eliot, T. S. 171, 240–1
elite males 8, 32, 157, 242
elite women 38, 84, 222; affluent 230;
    ennui and anxieties felt by 171; identity
    formation narrow and predetermined
    222; mothers 37; privileged 33; writers
    98, 101–4
Elizabethan period 25
Ellenberger, H. F. 61
Ellison v. Brady (1991) 93
Elysian Fields 72–3
Emancipation 86
embeddedness 21
emergencies 45
Emerson, Ralph Waldo 106
empathy 136, 145
employment opportunities 89
empowerment 40; symbolized 103
enclosure 46, 78–9, 188; collective,
    madwoman role as a way out of 102;
    crumbling of 82–93; hierarchical 111;
    placed around the group 197
Encyclopedia of American Humorists
    (Gale) 221
energy 20, 21, 26, 32, 33, 68, 103, 181;
    aggressive 148; angry and rebellious
    160; autonomous and authoritative 81;
    chaotic 103; contradictory 102; creative
    38, 41, 103, 147, 167; dark 103; dialogic
    movement of 163; different 6;
    dissipation of 110; dynamic 59;
    embodiment and manifestation of 110;
    Eros 126, 142, 156; erotic 132, 158,
    191; essential, must be integrated 138;
    exertive 43, 44; frenetic, demanding,

yielding to 47–8; guiding 132;
    humorous 128, 166, 214; integrated
    251; ironic 177; manic 74; Masculine
    43; negative 103; new kind of 183;
    numinous 5, 106; psychic 142, 149;
    psychological 38; reciprocal 48, 64; re-
    emergence of 12; repressed 43; sexual
    158, 192; shadow 130, 209; shape-
    shifting 145; shared 25; split-off 103;
    sudden increase and sudden drop of
    149; superhuman surges of 4; thrusting
    43; transformed/transformative 34,
    103, 128, 129; transgressive 102;
    universal 123; virginal 72, 75; yang 45,
    46; see also archetypal energy;
    Trickster energy
enfranchisement 33
England 83; novel form and early
    women's literature 97–105
Enlightenment 242
ennui 171
Environment and Wilderness
    Background Types (Heising) 24
environmental issues 182, 183, 189;
    critical factors 142
Epidarus 80
epistemological revolution 65, 138
equal opportunity 92
equality 32, 40, 200, 242; archetype of 94;
    economic 230; gender 93; innate 84
Ereshkigal 103
Eros 75, 126, 132, 156; Logos and
    138–52, 197, 233, 248
eroticism 132, 140, 141, 191, 197; risky
    behavior 139
essayists 169
essentialism 34
ethics 16, 197, 200, 205, 216, 217; and
    postmodern female Trickster 196–200,
    246–8
ethnic minorities 91
ethnicity 24
ethnography 124, 125
Euripides 80
Europe 124
European Americans 50
Evans-Pritchard, Edward 131
evolution 133–4; complex psychological
    aspects of 139; psychic 63;
    psychological modality of 135; see also
    psychological evolution
evolutionary model 38–40

evolutionary psychology 39
exaggeration 39, 180, 151, 183; wild
    171
exclusion 84; unnecessary 200

fairy tales 4
faith 132
familiarity 141
family structure 190
fantasy 65, 71, 118, 136, 142, 143, 237;
    capacity to engage in 141; male 191;
    motivations for actions 144; sexual 171
fatherhood 39
Fauset, Jessie Redmon 169
fellatio 228
female behavior 37
Female Chauvinist Pigs (Levy) 237
femaleness 190
feminine 101; archetypal 173; collective
    conceptions of 155; conceptualization
    of 67; conflation of great mother and
    119; context dependent term 35;
    illusionary definition of 119;
    intrinsically 37; Jung's highly reputed
    reverence for 70; Jungian and post-
    Jungian perspectives on 41–50;
    metaphysical principle 75; pre-
    patriarchal virgin and today's virginal
    presence 73–5; research on 34–40
femininity 35, 39; behaviors strongly
    associated with 37; culturally
    appropriate ideal of 45; dominant
    models of 177; dramatic assertion of
    45; ideas about 43; Maccoby's second
    category of 36; only biological marker
    for 50; patriarchal 50; phallic side of
    43; reinscribed meaning of 156;
    resumption of more traditional notions
    of 38; taking a shower not a marker for
    38; yin and yang 43–4
feminism 10; approach to text 30–4;
    comic sensibility 161–2; critical
    discourses in 24; crossroads of 3;
    dialogic 34; first wave 25, 32, 33, 88;
    goddess 75; Jungian 75; obscene wit a
    problem for 147; postmodernism and
    33–4; question of how to avoid
    matrimony 101; second wave 25, 32,
    90; sessions at MLA Convention 114;
    third wave 25, 33
feminist humor 155, 161–2; essence of
    166

Ferber, Edna 107
Fern, Fanny 170
fertility 150
festum asinorium 124
feudal system 83, 89
fictive female sleuths 9–11, 12, 25, 51,
    65, 101, 118, 128, 130, 148, 176, 182,
    188, 243; antecedents of internal
    dialogues found in 104; energy found
    in 73; essence of ironic resignification
    177; female detectives created
    immediately preceding 114; first
    appeared in late 19th century 178;
    images and narratives of 123; most
    renowned 109; overwhelming
    proliferation of texts 23; postmodern
    111, 112, 114; self-conscious irony
    155; uniqueness of 109; witty 160;
    writer in the guise of 150; see also
    "Blanche White"; "Kate Shugak";
    "Kinsey Millhone"; "V. I.
    Warshawski"
Fielding, Helen 238
fighting 159–60
film reviewers 166
Finch, Anne, Countess of Winchelsea 100
flappers 88
flattery 166
flirting behavior 39
Florida Supreme Court Gender Bias
    Commission 90
folk tales 131
food 128
fools 150
Foster, Hannah Webster 105
Franz, M. L. von 4
fraud 13
freaks 178
Frederick, H. V. 23
freedom 32, 90; imaginal 150; increased
    in terms of sexuality 173; psychological
    110; sexual 229
freedom of movement 108, 110;
    psychological 164
Freud, Sigmund 118, 132, 145–7, 157,
    172, 204, 242, 246, 247
Friedan, Betty 90
Fritchley, Alma 24
frustration 140; catharsis for 162; male
    162
fun 40, 151, 155–75
fundamentalists 14

games 139
gangbangers 14
gangs 40
Garvey, Marcus 169
Gates, Henry Louis 7, 8, 177, 217, 251
gay women 171
Gemini 42
gender 23; critical discourses in 24;
  importance of 36; incorrectly used as
  synonym for sex 37; male writers by
  114; power and 187; societal rules 40
gender bias 91–2; columnists and
  essayists who addressed the foibles of
  169
genetic predispositions 39
genitalia 222
gentrification 14
gestures 221; obscene 238
Giegerich, Wolfgang 12–13
gifts 80
Gilbert, S. M. 86, 87, 102–3, 119
Gilligan, Carol 37, 132, 165, 198–200,
  246–8
Gilman, Charlotte Perkins 169
Ginsburg, Ruth Bader 91
Giovanni, Nikki 220, 245
global warming 182
Glover-Greene catalogue 109
goat singers 150
God 42, 123, 209–10; mysterious
  purposes 61
goddesses 70, 74, 75; dark 45, 103, 223,
  243; retired maiden 134
gods 134–5; false, worship of 197
Goethe, J. W. von 13
Goldberg, Whoopi 222
golf 164
good and evil 129; differentiating through
  moral philosophy 197
Goodman, Ellen 170
Goswami, A. 85
Gothic literature 104, 111
Gottman, J. 48
Grafton, Sue 10, 17, 18, 19, 23, 105, 106,
  112, 114, 133, 160, 162–3, 178, 191–5
Grant, Linda 249
Great Hare tales 123–4
great mother 69; conflation of feminine
  and 119
Great Mother, The (Neumann) 35, 67
Greek mythology 135
Green, Anna Katharine 107–8

grotesque costuming 151
group cohesion 36
groups: boy and girl 36; boys play in 165;
  cultural 40; dominant 160;
  marginalized 48, 148; primate 39;
  same-sex 39, 40, 157; sexually
  segregated 36; shunning or exile from
  197
guardianship of children 87
Gubar, S. 86, 87, 102–3, 119
guilt: avoiding 42; yuppie 231
Guy, Florence 169

Habermas, Jürgen 94, 131
Haddon, Genia Pauli 43–4, 45, 46
Hager, Jean 24
Halsey, Margaret 170
Hamilton, E. 135
Hammurabi's Code 79
hands 126
Haraway, Donna 25–6, 39
Harding, Esther 66, 70, 73–4
hardship 126
Hardy Boys 245
Harlem Renaissance 169
harm 145
Hart, Carolyn 249
hatred 214
Hawley, R. 82
Hawthorne, Nathaniel 25, 105, 106, 166
Haycraft, Howard 111
healing 117
Hebrew prophets 42
Hecate 45, 103
hegemony 113; patriarchal 59, 66, 113;
  worldwide 47
Heilbrun, Carolyn 41
Heising, W. 24
Helen of Troy 81
Henderson, Joseph 115
Hendricks, Michael 114
Henry VIII, king of England 99
Hephaestus 136
hermeneutics 118, 124, 131
Hermes 10, 41, 132, 134–5, 136, 141, 142,
  143, 192
Hermes and Aphrodite Encounters
  (Zupancic) 237–8
heroism/heroines/heroes 41, 109, 111,
  176; cultural 128, 130; female leaders
  and leadership styles redolent of 184;
  screen portrayals of 156

Herrmann, S. B. 115–17
heterogeneity 34
hierarchical structure 165, 205
hierarchies 40, 200; in-group dominance
    39; interracial 84; rules and regulations
    61
Hill, Benny 38
Hillman, James 64–5
Hinduism 42
Hipparchia 82
hippocampus 73
Hirsi Ali, Ayaan 245
holding 50
homelessness 14
homemaking 50, 171
Homer 81–2
hookers 191
hooks, bell 34
hopelessness 185
Hopi women 187
Horace 98
hormones 167
hostility 10, 159
Hottentot Venus 222
Huang, Jim 23
Hudson, Arthur 221
Hughes, Langston 169, 246
Huizinga, Johan 139
human rights 204
humiliation 127
humor 8, 10, 15, 38, 43, 102, 134;
    abundant 108; aggressive 136, 140;
    assertion of authority with 185;
    bodily functions 17; channeling
    shadow energy into 103; childish 48;
    cognitive ability to understand 135;
    consciousness through 243;
    corrupting nature of 221; critical
    determinant in creativity 147;
    crossroads of 3; dealing with tough
    stuff through 192–6; definition of
    132; deploying as psychological
    adaptation 49; development of 48,
    125, 140–5; early 204; enlightenment
    and 181; erotic 138; evolution of
    consciousness walks in tandem with
    133; female, male reflection of 40;
    feminist 155; foreground 74; gaining
    pleasure from making 148; girls and
    37, 40; in-group 146, 157–8, 166;
    irony and 9, 33, 176, 177, 192, 193,
    221; male and female differences 133.

156–61; marginalized groups silenced
    from using in public 148; out-group
    146, 245–6; outrageous 171;
    performance 150; phallic talent found
    to operate with 46; psychoanalytic
    approaches to 145–8; relatively
    undeveloped variant of 48; revenge
    173; sex wrapped up in 229; sexual
    elements in 140; shadow of 176;
    shared 135–6; significant 129;
    subversive 123, 157, 164, 167; trauma
    and adaptation through 149;
    Trickster quality of 102, 135–6,
    150–1; unique 221, 222, 246; used to
    make invective 100; variation of 151;
    see also cartoons; clowns; comedy;
    feminist humor; irony, fun; jokes;
    laughter; satire, sense of humor; wit
hunger 128
Hurston, Zora Neale 169, 221, 246
Hyde, Lewis 163, 187, 188
Hynes, W. J. 8, 131, 133

idealization 106, 226; housewife 49;
    male 158; role of mother and child
    67
ideals 31, 33, 39; heroic 183; patriarchal
    46; politically articulated 94
ideas: archetypal 63; from male embodied
    psyche 65
identification 50; pleasure of 184; self-
    object 13; victim to 179; virginal energy
    repressed and disassociated from 72
identity 125; construction of 8, 9, 26, 212;
    diminished sense of 158; feminine 51;
    fixed 8; forging of 109; imagination's
    role implicated in creation of 65;
    importance of popular culture on
    emerging development 243;
    independent, freedom to develop 108;
    instruments of 109; intra-psychic 37,
    38; legal 90, 164, 187; legally
    extinguished 78; nomadic 20, 181, 212;
    psychological 10; psychological model
    underlying 37; represented by African
    American hair 210; separate, claim to
    189; sexual 51; stable 6, 8
identity formation 6, 8, 34, 65, 180;
    narrow and predetermined 222;
    nomadic 181; revealing statistic
    regarding 189; young African
    American girl and woman 222

ideologies: dominant 21; legal and philosophical 85; mother 68; regional, distinctive 42; separate spheres 85; traditional home and motherhood 88
illegitimacy 113
Illinois Supreme Court 87–8
illusion 43, 59, 165, 197, 212, 243; imaginative 229
images/imagery 4, 9, 31, 117, 123, 212; animal 177; animus 69; cyborg 25–6; dominant 43, 243; doubling technique of presenting 145; emergent 65; evocative 60; feminine 38, 42, 43; genuine creator of 6; God 42; goddess 41, 70; graphic sexual 237; idealized 222; male 42, 62; metaphoric 10, 60, 61, 62, 63, 64; mother 68; motherhood 204; need to work 64–5; out of bounds 146; outlandish 132, 133; popular cultural 65; previously separated, slamming together 64; psychic 75; traditional feminine 188; traditional Trickster 48; transformative 60; unconscious archetypes 51; visual 66, 250; women as imagined by women 59; women with authority, agency and autonomy 8; see also archetypal images
imaginal zone 60; freedom of imaginal zone 150
imagination 8, 44, 74, 134; encouragement to use to heal 75; gift of 218; law and 78–96; metaphor and 59–71; placed at the center of subjectivity 118; planning a humorous demise in 179; potency to turn into reality 9, 10, 234, 244–5; process where one engages with holotropes of 124; reader encouraged to enlarge 16; recovered memory and 59–60; value is diminished 143; see also active imagination; male imagination
imitation 150
immigrants 104, 124
impropriety 151
impulse control 47, 48; women, greater 159
impulses 145; threatening 42
in-breeding 39
in-groups 39, 146, 157–8, 166
in-house revolutionaries 184
inadequacy 45

incongruity 140, 141, 143; cognitive ability to articulate 144; factors that encourage the evolution of pleasure in 142
independence 205, 206; embodiment of 216; lifelong, opportunity for 218
independent women 67, 69–70
India 42, 149
individualism 131
individuation 7, 126, 128, 133, 241–4; archetypal energy of 3; goal of the process 118; intra-psychic 147; Jung's description of 180; male images of 62; refusing to be a victim as 179–81; step towards 197; symbolic hunger for 128; traditional Trickster as myth 129–30
Industrial Revolution 85
inference 141
inhibitions 146, 147; shared 147
initiative 102
innate possibilities 62, 64
inner confidence 163
innuendo 166; sexual 237
instincts 139; play 147
insult 148
integration 42, 64, 72, 74, 126, 136, 209; final protest 127; psychic 162; psychological 73; symbolic hunger for 128
integrity 149, 205
intelligence 111, 170; assumption of 135; evidence of 161
intensity 46
intentionality 151
interaction: distinctive 39; divergence in styles 40; equal status 46; social 143, 148; witty 146
interconnectedness 117
intimacy 147, 190
introjection 36, 47, 49, 158, 162, 200, 204, 205, 216; patriarchal 103
intuition 65, 85
intuitive knowledge 103
Iran 42
Iron Age 78
irony 8, 48, 132, 133, 138, 140, 143, 146, 164, 209; adaptation of 215; brilliant sense of 169; funny, witty, incisive women who no longer have to hide 176; humor and 9, 33, 176, 177, 192, 193, 221; marginalized groups use 166; realigning power through 178;

reinscribing the male chauvinist pig through 237; self-conscious 155
irrational behavior 197
irreverence 131, 164, 221
Islam 245
isolation 113; self-reported 148
Israel 42

Jackson, Shirley 170
Jacoby, M. 63
James, P. D. 112, 113
Jane Eyre (C. Brontë) 101, 103, 164
Janik, V. K. 124
jest 148
Jesus 173–4
Jewett, Sarah Ome 114
Jews 14, 33, 148, 173, 232, 243; grievances of communities 186; humor amidst suffering 246; ritual cleansing 125; soldiers subjected to discrimination 170
Jim Crow 220
Johnson, Samuel 105
jokes 136, 145, 148, 149, 162; aggressive 146, 147; attempt at making 144; childish and underdeveloped 140; cynical/skeptical 146; in-group male-oriented 157; jests and 135; misinterpreted 166; mixed company 147, 158, 164; obscene 146, 147; one-upmanship of many 163; racist 147; reinscribed 251; salacious 156; sexual 157–8; shared inhibitions required to get 147; typical white male 147; way to displace anger with 173
Jones, M. 12
Jong, Erica 171
Journal of Gerontology 190
joy 142
Jung, Carl Gustav 12–13, 35, 67, 85, 129, 184, 248; dynamic approach to psychological materials 66; highly reputed reverence for the feminine 70; imagination work 62; works: *Collected Works* 5, 7, 42, 62, 63–4, 65, 115, 117, 135, 139–40, 147–8, 180, 241, 242; *Man and his Symbols* 4
Jungian psychology 50, 242; archaic goddess myth tradition 75; core concept at the heart of 241; problem in 43; reliance upon search for dynamic transcultural universal structure 115

justice 86, 192, 198, 199; equal 92; ethics of 200, 216

Kahlo, Frida 67–8
Kali 103
Kant, Immanuel 149
Kaplan, Arthur 114
Kataria, Madan 149
"Kate Shugak" 10, 12, 19–20, 23, 33, 74, 110, 112, 128, 163, 182–3, 184–5, 188, 190, 191, 206
Katz, S. L. 108–9, 110
Keeney, Bradford 237
Kerényi, Karl 129
Kerr, Jean 170, 171
kinesics 221
"Kinsey Millhone" 10, 12, 17–19, 22–3, 74, 91, 93, 110, 111, 112, 114, 128, 132–3, 160–1, 162–3, 176, 178, 188, 190–6, 206, 239
Kittelson, Mary Lynn 66
Klein, Kathleen 114
Kohlberg, Lawrence 198, 199, 246–7
Kohut, H. 12
Kugler, P. 61, 65

labels 155, 156, 159, 167
Lacan, J. 125, 139
lactation 68
Lamport, Felicia 171
landowners 86
language 137, 139; inflammatory 214; ironic manipulations of 177; irreverent 131; offensive 151; serious and salacious 151; sexual 237
language acquisition 40; Lacanian theories of 125, 139; recent skills 143
Latinos/Latinas 50
laughter 140, 141, 143, 181; anger and rebellion purged by 167; belly 163; contrived 204; mass 149; possibility of 145; quick cheap 149
Lauper, Cyndi 73, 74, 76, 131, 162, 250
Lauter, Estella 66, 67–70
law 113, 192; and imagination 78–96
Lawrence, Hilda 113
leadership 36
Lee, Lorilei 169
legal issues: independent domicile 90; lack of recognition 86–8; private rights 83; restrictions 79
Leibowitz, Fran 171–2

Leitch, V. B. 25–9, 34, 118, 124
lending libraries 103, 104
Leonard, Linda 103
lesbians 192, 209–10, 211, 226, 232
Lessing, Doris 114
Lethe, River 72–3
Lévi-Strauss, Claude 131, 132
liberalism 94, 242, 243
liberation movements 32
life givers 59
light verse 170
liminality 5, 6, 21, 34, 60, 125, 129, 140,
    141, 148, 150, 151; as psychic space 131
Lin-Chandler, Irene 24
Lindgren, J. R. 84
linear model 47
literacy 99, 125; increased 103
literary criticism 63, 115, 117; problems
    with 118–19
literary theory 97–120; critical 30
literature 65, 79, 164; detective 10, 63–4;
    popular 9; psychological approach to
    115; radical potential to change
    imagination into reality 244–5; relating
    to Tricksters 97–120; see also women's
    literature
location 30–55, 117; radical 113
logic 172, 173, 177; deductive 198
logical syllogisms 158
Logos 132; Eros and 138–52, 197, 233,
    248
Loki the Mischief Maker 124
London 168
loneliness 190
Loos, Anita 166, 169
López-Pedrazsa, R. 135, 201
Lorde, Audre 181
loss of consortium 90
love 206; reinscription of sex as being fun
    and an expression of 155
love children 134
lower classes 85
Lowndes, Tom 104
Luke, Helen 75, 173–4, 240–1
lying 217

Maccoby, Eleanor 35, 36, 37, 38, 40, 46,
    47, 48, 165
macho behavior 40, 184
Mad Magazine 172
Madonna 51, 73, 74, 131, 162, 234,
    243–4, 252

madwomen writers 102–4
magazines 103, 104; widely circulated,
    popular 169
magic 133, 197
Maher, Bill 250
Maia 134
make-believe play 141, 142
male editors 23
male imagination 103, 123; delusion
    which has captured 43; gestating womb
    idealized 45; projective 37, 188; texts
    produced by 31; women finished being
    held within enclosure of 46
male peer model 48, 49
male readers 114
Mammy stereotype 222
Manhattan 226
marginalization 30, 34, 48, 113, 133,
    148–9; belittling 204; relating to
    slavery 91, 161
market economy 42
marriage 22, 78, 89, 189; boundary of
    class and 101; chief legal effects of 83;
    happy, one of the prime markers of 48;
    legal identity merged into husband's
    90; making women single and outside
    the enclosure of 188; minimum ages for
    89; mixed racial 190; most women
    enclosed by 88; property in 86, 90;
    restricting women to exclusively
    procreative role 78; same-sex 190; sex
    and 189–92; ultimate patriarchal prize
    102; women's place within the
    enclosure of 84
married women 110
Married Women's Property Acts 86, 87,
    90
Marsh, Ngaio 25, 111
Martin, Allana 25
masculine 41; reinscription of 45; women
    do not often present images of self as
    69
masculinity 35, 36, 39, 43; distorted 42;
    ideas about 43; inner 45; marker of 38;
    patriarchal 50; phallic 43, 45, 46;
    testicular 44; yin and yang 43–4
masks 72, 145, 148; gynophobic 97
Maslow, Abraham 132, 140
masquerades 45, 50, 51, 125, 133;
    carnivalesque 127; costuming 25; failed
    126; female 179
mastery 141

matrilineal/matrilocal tribes 187
maturation 146
Maui 124
McCarthy era Blacklists 14
McCrumb, Sharyn 249
McGhee, P. E. 135, 140–1, 142
Meador, Betty D. 42
meaning(s) 44, 117, 144; divine method of finding 163; how one arrives at 115; multiple 3, 39; reinscribed 156, 237; role of psyche in creation of 116
memory 134; archetypal, archaic 72; conscious 73; implanting 72; recovered 59–60; repressed 73; unconscious 73; willingness to value and interact with 73
Mencken, H. L. 169
menstruation 68, 133, 172
Mercartne, Trey 235
Mercurius 7
metaphor 9, 171; imagination and 59–71
metaphysics 62
Meyers, C. 78
Miciak, Kate 23
Midas 151
middle-aged women 158
middle classes 84, 205; ennui and anxieties felt by elite women 171
Middle East 42
mikvah 125
military service exemption 89
Miller, Alice Duer 169
mimicry 125
Minor v. Happersett (1885) 88
Minstrel Shows 246
mirroring 181; positive 148; psychological authority concomitant with 167
misnaming 143, 144
Mississippi 86
mixed company 147
Mnemosyne 72–3, 134
mockery 161; comedic 150
Modern Language Association Convention (1973) 114
Monfredo, Miriam 24
monkeys 39, 124, 251
monotheism 42
mood swings 48
Moore, B. & M. 7
moral development 198, 199, 247
morals 196–7
Morell, Mary 24

Morrell Act (US 1860) 112
Morrison, Toni 177–8, 217, 222
mothering 31, 210; isolation of 113
mothers 7; bad, fear of being 190; black 221; desire to return to 67; elite 37; employer who refused to hire 89; expanded role of 179; good 67; harms and hurts you perpetrated by 179; phallic 42; spiritual 111; teenage 14; terrible 67, 68; see also great mother
Mothers of the Plaza de Mayo 179, 180, 183
Mott, Lucretia 84, 85, 110
Ms. Magazine 249–50
Mull, Martin 250
muses 69, 72, 104, 134, 189
music 136, 137; and movement 139
mysterious women 107–9
mystery fiction 12, 23, 31, 63, 108; British, golden age of 111, 113; first golden age of 114; major female player in the genre 112; series 13, 24; variations on the theme of 177
myths 4, 67–8, 72–3, 123, 138; archaic 75, 130, 135; customs conflated with 127; individuation 129–30; traditional 124–9

naming 91, 94, 204–5
Nancy Drew Mystery Series 13, 245
narcissism 193
narrative dialogues 104–5
narratives 8, 20, 32, 60, 70, 82, 106, 109, 123, 127, 132; authoritative, autonomous women 41; cultural expectations confronted 101; doubling technique of presenting 145; easily accessible 104; exciting 64, 115; humorous 150; Native American 124, 135; non-patriarchal 75; sacred 71; wit in 162
National Judicial Education to Promote Equality for Women and Men in the Courts 92
National Legion of Decency 155
natural law 49, 89, 105
necessity 155, 176, 192; complicity out of 78; inner 147
Neely, Barbara 20–1, 22, 112, 176, 178, 190, 191, 203, 205–19, 223
negotiation 49
Neumann, E. 35, 67

neurology 48
never-married women 189
New Jersey State Supreme Court 91
New York 91
New York State Council on the Arts 249
New York Times 238, 243, 244
New Zealand 124
newspapers 103, 104
Nichol, L. 131
Nicholson, L. J. 33
Nietzsche, F. 124, 197, 247
noise nuisance 49
nonsense 144, 164
normality 51, 132
normative symbolic order 147, 148, 158,
    159, 160, 164; inchoate dormant
    archetypal capacity repressed by 225;
    taking control of your own life away
    from 162
norms 190; challenged 132; collective 91;
    male 242; masculine and feminine 46;
    universal 118, 146; *see also* cultural
    norms
North American Indians 123–4
novels 97–105, 225; businesswoman 107,
    111; crime 245; detective 64, 110, 111,
    162; domestic 67; Gothic 111; male
    centered 114; mystery 12, 113;
    psychological 63, 115; serialized 104;
    social protest 106–7
NOW (National Organization for
    Women) 245
nuclear family 190
nurturance 35–6, 37, 68; resumption of
    more traditional notions of 38

object naming 144
objectification 114, 130, 229
objectivity 65; false 59; female 164
O'Connor, Sandra Day 91
O'Connor, Susan 24
Odysseus 81–2
old age 113
Old Testament 129
Olsen, T. 106
Olsson, Hans-Olov 251
Olympic games 80
oppression 172
opus alchymicum 7
oral sex 227, 228, 233
orality 125
Orange Prize 251

order 163; illusion of 43; social 131, 159;
    see also symbolic order
orphans 108
Otherness 34
out-groups 146, 157
outsiders 113, 125, 218
oversexed women 222
Ovid 106
Oya 103

paid labor 84
pain 61, 73, 126; accidental or
    unintentional 145; dream guards
    against 145; pleasure out of 145;
    translating into courage 163
Pan-Hellenic Council 26
paradox 25, 68, 146, 152, 178, 181;
    doubling 129; for all its worth 74; of
    the particular 132; perennial 200;
    sexual 230
paranoia 193
parenting 217; male 39
Paretsky, Sara 10, 13, 14, 15, 16, 17, 105,
    112, 114, 161, 178, 185–6, 249
Parker, Dorothy 169, 170
parody 140, 143, 150, 164, 171, 179, 183,
    226; on male sexuality 229;
    sophisticated 148
parturition 68
passive gestation 46
passivity 67
patience 44
patriarchal competitiveness 48
patriarchal culture 42, 94, 188, 189, 191;
    conscious 45; creativity and highly born
    men in 189; fight for dominance 49
patriarchal mythology 187
patriarchal symbolic order 33, 42, 71, 73,
    132, 216; female role in 37; questioning
    the existence of through humor 159;
    relationship to 41; repressed energy of
    Feminine 43; shadow of 46; stalled 47;
    worldwide enslavement of women 46
patriarchy 48, 73; creation of system 78;
    institutionalized 72
Patriot Act (US 2001) 14, 17
Pauli, W. 85
Pearce, Dr. (*Utne* magazine) 190
Pearl Harbor 88
peasant classes 82
peer groups 39, 40
Pelton, Robert 131

Penelope 81–2
penis 143; archaic phallic perspective 129;
    disembodied 126; pink, with cock ring
    191; shrinkings 127; size 158, 172, 226;
    see also phallus
penis envy 172
Pennsylvania legislature 107
perception(s) 85, 124, 162; accurate 157;
    conscious 145; differences in 157;
    psychological 62; shared 143
Perceval 125
perfection 184
performance 164
periodicals 170
personality 131–2
phallus/phallic states 31, 42, 43–4, 45, 46,
    114, 129
Phillipson, Morris 116
philosophical rationalism 42
philosophy 65, 79, 82; moral 196, 197
physical agency 3, 8, 10, 12; being
    independent with 180; how to
    construct an ethical life with 14; lack of
    90; possibility of 230
physical appearance 159, 222
physicality 141; slapstick humor of 143
physiology 37
Piaget, Jean 141, 144, 246, 247
pin-up calendar genre 237
Pirkis, Catharine Louisa 110
Pisces 42
Plains Indians 123–4
Plato 81, 106
play 160; boys, boisterous 136; critical
    determinant in creativity 147; deep
    138–40, 146; deeply transcendent 150;
    different styles 40; fantasy 142, 143;
    girls on the playground 37; imaginative
    142; innocent 146; make-believe 141,
    142; politics of 184; possibility of 146;
    restricted by reason during
    socialization process 145; rough and
    tumble 36–7, 39, 40, 48; segregated
    same-sex groups 39; serious 148; toys
    which really do maim and kill 48; wit
    begins in the innocence of 146
plays 80–2
pleasure 136, 137, 140, 149; belittling and
    humbling an enemy 204; children
    receive 143; coping mechanism which
    brings 163; deep play 146; desire for
    150; ecstatic 139; endless hours of 147;

erotic 142; gaining from making humor
    148; humor is the psyche's way of
    acquiring 145; in incongruity 142;
    laughter reflects 143; methodology that
    channels fear into 163; nonsense words
    give 144; possibility of constellating in
    others 148; received display, through
    words or gesture 146; recognition 141;
    unusual psychic abilities to derive out
    of pain 145
pleasure principle 160, 166
Pleiades 134
plot devices 108, 109, 111
Poe, Edgar Allan 110
political strategy 179
polygamy 190
Polynesia 124
pop(ular) culture 9, 65, 73, 99, 208, 225;
    culturally inflected archetype found
    only in 159; differences between male
    and female humor 156; female
    imaginings emanating from 104; forms
    most readily available to mass
    population 104; icons 51, 64; imagery
    and narrative in 123; importance on
    emerging identity development 243;
    important locale where boundaries can
    be crossed 208; Jungian approaches to
    115; novels received appreciatively in
    101; outlets in 103; postmodern fictive
    female sleuth 111; radical potency to
    turn imagination into reality 234;
    subversive form of humor in 123
population growth 190
postcolonialism 24, 32, 33
postmodern female Trickster 23–6, 41,
    60, 64, 130, 176–202; aspects
    supportive of individuation 243–4;
    characteristics 128–9; crossing
    boundaries 204; deconstructs margins
    and enters new terrain 159; different
    from traditional Trickster 8–9;
    emerging images of 62; energy 225;
    ethics and 196–200, 246–8; example of
    155–6; fictive female sleuth as 9–11;
    humor 143, 146; liminal zone between
    traditional and 125; Rabelais and 150;
    Raven myths closely resemble 127–8;
    restorative 208; social worker aspect
    36, 181–7; spirit of movement 107;
    virginal energy re-emerging through
    archetypal energy of 72

postmodernity/postmodernism 8, 10, 74, 104, 113, 123, 128–9; crossroads of 3; female Trickster can be humorous without being buffoon or clown 133; feminism and 33–4; humor 138, 140; politics of location 117; psychological trick of female Trickster in 167
postquels 225
poststructuralism 33, 117, 150
power: absolute, lack of desire for 135; balance of 40; defined 50; dichotomous 47; dominant characteristic in groups 36; gender and 187; hierarchy of 200; naming 91, 94; patriarchal 41; phallocentric 31; realignment with other forms of 177–8; shifting to the marketplace 42
powerlessness 113, 173; political 204
Pratt, Annis 97, 107
pre-Christian mythologies 75
pregnancy 126, 127, 134; patriarchal 46; teenage 215–16; unexpected 235
prejudice 169, 184; racial 206
prequels 225
presumptive laws 90
Priestesses 103
privacy 142
privileged women 32–3
Prix Femina 251
problem-solving process 139
procreation 37–40, 78, 188–92
projections 162
Prometheus 136
promiscuity 156, 233; presumption of 159
propaganda 9, 171
property: in marriage 86, 90; right to own 108, 109
prosperity 49
prostitution 89, 204, 215
Proust, M. 59
psyche 5, 8, 9, 10, 60, 82, 93, 145; archetypal energies available for integration into 72; autonomous 15, 65; child's, adaptive responses of 144; collective 64; confused and frightened 136; defense mechanisms developed by 147; embodied as female 187; energies in 44, 61; female, emergence of the masculinity found in 45; healthy 242; heroic ideal still controls much of 183; humor and 145, 163, 179; imaginal realms of 123; infused with new imagery and narrative 225; inner attitude of 73; investigation of 117; Jung's grand theory 62; literature as primary source material of 118; male 73, 131; neurobiology and art meet in 73; psychological appreciation of literature can influence 13; role in creation of meaning 116; sexualized male 229; splitting of 41–2; start of conscience awakening in 125; understanding the dynamism of 118; undeveloped and immature 251; way it is evolving in Western societies 183; world 42
Psyche and Eros myth 132
psychiatry 61
psychic life 51
psychoanalysis 182; approaches to humor 145–8; notions about the nature of woman 88
psychological authority 3, 8, 10, 12, 167; being independent with 180; how to construct an ethical life with 14; lack of 90; possibility of 230
psychological considerations 34–40, 162–3
psychological conspiracy 157
psychological criticism 117
psychological development 126, 243; earlier stage in 128; later 136; male peer model that specifically discourages 48
psychological dissonance 157
psychological evolution 62, 63; collective 71
psychological growth 64
psychological misidentification 90
psychological model 37–8
psychological movement 7, 11, 176; fluidity of 15; freedom of 164
psychological opposites 65
psychological shunning 47
psychological strength 70
psychological transformation 103
psychology 37, 104, 111, 116; adolescent 184; archetypal 70; crime 23; evolutionary 39; male 43; personal, of the artist 117; reductive 241; women's 66; see also depth psychology; Jungian psychology
Psychology Today 156
psychopaths 193
publishing houses 103

pulp fiction 104
punishment 47, 126
puns 140, 141, 144, 163, 164; making the
   righteous look ridiculous through 171
pushy behavior 44
Putnam 23

Quinn, Elizabeth 25

Rabbit/Hare images and antics 124
Rabelais, F. 150–1
race 190, 210
racial minorities 91
racism 147, 204; aggressiveness against
   204; closet 208
Radin, P. 8, 123, 125, 126, 127, 129, 130,
   131, 133
rage 103, 209
rape 93
raps 222
Raven tales 123, 124, 127–8, 134, 135
reaction: intra-psychic 149; psycho-
   neurotic 42
reading 72, 99, 162–3; as active
   imagination 5, 60
realignment 177–8
reality 66, 130, 148, 171, 184; gloss on
   133; insistence on 221; jokes and 149;
   paradoxical 150; psyche creates 65;
   psychological 13; re-visioning of 71;
   ridiculousness of 172; turning
   imagination into 9, 10, 131, 234,
   244–5; women's sense of 66
reason 145–6, 148
receptivity 50
recognition 141
recovered memory 59–60
Reddy, M. T. 111
re-enslavement 86
Reformation 99
regression 127
reinscription 43, 45, 46, 110, 156, 158,
   166, 205, 226; brilliant 222; dominant
   value structures 176; expert 215;
   linguistic subversion through 217;
   psycholinguistic 209; resignification
   and 162; sex as being fun and
   expression of love 155; sexual mores
   171; traditional boundaries 212;
   unmarried woman 218
relationships 22, 158; constant dynamism
   in 228; deep and passionate 113;

dialogic 60; family 82; female's
   independence threatens 70; fictional
   characters 225; intact 216; intimate
   232; lifelong 48; master-slave 62;
   network of 199; paradoxical 132;
   patterns of 20; status 79; supernatural
   132; women find creativity primarily
   through 66
religion 82; courage to break with 245;
   functions and rituals 80; insights 42;
   reliance on 209
remarkable women 12–29
remembering 86; numinous process of
   59–60
Renaissance 61, 62, 150; reification of 68
Rendell, Ruth 112
repartee 146, 164; witty 171
repressed shadow 103
repression 43, 72, 73, 143, 221; sexual
   112; variant in the guise of fun and
   humor 151
reproductive technologies 35, 188
resignification 176, 179; ironic 177; one of
   the most powerful forms of 178
resistance 104, 114, 131; silent 179;
   subversive act of 151
resolution 165
revelation 62, 102, 106–7
revenge 173, 204
reverence 59
reverie: comedic 162; transcendent 150
reversal technique 172
revolutionary times 104–5
Reynard the Fox 124
Ricardo, Lucy 156
Rich, Adrienne 31, 210
Richardson, Dorothy 114
Richler, M. 170
Ricketts, M. L. 138
Rickles, Don 250
Ricoeur, P. 60, 62, 63
rights 83, 86; equal, struggle for 34
risk 139
ritual spaces 131
rituals 72, 162; cleansing 125; courtship
   246; liminal space of transformation
   with 150; religious 80; war 127
Riviere, Joan 50
Road Runner 136
Robb, J. D. 24
Robinson, Lillian 203
Robinson, O. F. 83

rock concerts 131
Rock, Chris 250
role expectations 101
roles: confusion of 88; cultural 40; gender 35, 40; housewife 156; maintaining 151; maternal 89, 179; mother and child, idealization of 67; outsider 113; public 80; sexual 80; socialized 37; subordinate 160; traditional female 161
Roman Empire 82–3, 106
romances 103–4
Rosenbloom, Stephanie 243–4
Rosenstein, Natalee 24
Rosie the Riveter 38, 89, 171
Rossi, A. S. 84
Rowland, Helen 170
Rowland, Susan 75, 112, 118–19
Rowson, Susanna Haswell 105
rules and regulations 200; focus on 216; hierarchical 61; playground 165
Rupprecht, C. S. 66, 67–70
Rutter, Peter 93

sacred technology 216
Safer, Morley 245
Saint Phalle, Niki de 67
same-sex partners 36
Samuels, Andrew 35–6, 64, 82, 140, 147, 179–80, 181–2, 183–4, 185, 186
Sand, George 38, 101
Sanday, Peggy 49
Sanskrit 139
Santa Barbara 17
Santayana, George 169
Sappho 81
sarcasm 157, 164, 176
sassiness/sassitude 222
satire 7, 69, 134, 140, 164, 171, 229; humor unique in 221; political 167–8; savage 127; sophisticated 148; see also comedy, humor, irony, sense of humor
Sayers, Dorothy L. 25, 111, 112–13
scarcity 49, 69
scarification 39
Schafran, Lynn Hecht 92
Scheherazade 160
Schneider, E. 85
Schroeder, P. 23, 251
scientific theories 85
scribbling women 105
sculpture 67
Sealey, R. 80, 81–2

seductress image 67
segregation 36, 39, 164; childhood 40; gender 36; sex 40, 49, 88, 89
seigniors 79
self 7, 163; authentic 97; confusion about the origins of 109; creativity in the service of 148; "primitive", undifferentiated and instinctual 125
self-censorship 34
self-deprecation 160
self-determination 50
self-esteem 173
self-importance 193
self-object 12; evocative, identification with 13
self-regulation 62
self-worth 6
Semple, L. 113
Seneca Falls 85–6
sense of humor 14, 145, 147, 158, 240; acquisition of 140; ancient Greek 135; archetypal Feminine/Masculine 155; con artists 74; danger of woman with 163–6; development of 141, 142, 143–5; different 147; emerging 144; female 155; not having 140; prodigious 208; sophisticated 144
sensitivity 33, 34; environmental 182; gentle 74; sexual 191; social 112
sentencing provisions 89
sentimental literature 104
sequels 225
serialization 104, 171
Serrano, Miguel 115–16
sex: differential treatment because of 90; food, movement and 128–9; Freud and 132; gender word incorrectly used as synonym for 37; marriage and 189–92; pro/creativity and 78, 188–92; psychological considerations attendant to 35; reinscription of 155; world 156; wrapped up in humor 229
Sex and the City (television series) 36, 39, 169, 237–9, 243; characters: Big 227, 231, 235; Bobby 232; Carrie 51, 73, 190, 225, 226, 227, 228–9, 230, 231, 232, 233–4, 235, 236; Charlotte 226, 227, 228, 229, 231, 232–3, 235; Harry 232; Miranda 226, 227–8, 229, 231, 232, 233, 235; Mitzi 232; Samantha 226, 227, 228, 229, 230–1, 232, 233,235; Smith 233; Steve 231, 233

sex differences 36, 37, 47, 49
sex scenes 191
sex workers 204, 215
sexism: absurdity of 172; reacting to 204
sexual attributes/behavior 51, 93, 139;
    adventurous women 39; antics and
    proclivities 189; film stars 183;
    groupings 32; harassment 93, 94;
    honesty 155; mores 171; promiscuity
    156; titillation 114; unusual habits 82;
    women openly engaging in strategies to
    have relations 192
sexuality 74, 126, 127; dominant 128–9;
    erotic 191; foreground 228; increased
    freedom in terms of 173; male 129, 191,
    229; restricting 78; vulnerable without
    false bravado 14; women as
    objectification of 114
shadow material 143
Shakespeare, W. 62, 98–9, 118, 250
shamans 132, 133
shame 163, 185
shape-shifting 6, 7, 8, 32, 126, 127, 129,
    130, 131, 144, 151, 155, 211–12, 233,
    245; family structure 190; humorous
    158; in the imaginal realm 60–1;
    transformative 3; unconscious 3, 145
Shaw, George Bernard 252
Sherlock Holmes 108
Shinn, Thelma 71
Showalter, Elaine 101
sights and sounds 141
signification 177
Silenus 151
Silverman, Sarah 250–1
simians 39
Singer, Jerome 141–2
Singer, T. 42, 93
single women 107–11
Sisters in Crime 249
skeptics 147
Skinner, Cornelia Otis 170
slapstick 48, 126, 136, 143, 145
slavery 48, 73, 79, 85, 86, 94, 102, 177,
    204; culture of 106; insurance
    reparations for 186; not viewed as a
    "problem" 91; reparations for 17;
    surviving the horrors of 220
Slung, Michelle 109
smiling 141
Smothers, Dick and Tommy 250
social changes 46–7, 104

social class see lower classes; middle
    classes; peasant classes; upper classes;
    working classes
social construction 91; sex role 37, 40
social handicaps 159
social hypocrisy 156
social realism 106
social stratification 106
social work(er) aspect 13, 14, 15, 17, 36,
    128, 156, 211, 236; cultural and
    psychological revolution through 8;
    integral role of 9; postmodern female
    Trickster 181–7
socialization 36–7, 41, 43, 79, 126; gender
    155, 159; liberation from 147; play
    restricted by reason during 145
sociological/anthropological model 35–6
sociology 49
somatic arousal 149
Sophocles 80, 118
spectacles 197
Spider images and antics 124
spinsters 108; popularity of 111;
    stereotypical 109
splitting 41–2, 43
Stabenow, Dana 10, 19, 20, 106–7, 112,
    163, 176, 182–3, 185, 190
stability 44
standards 170
Stanton, Elizabeth Cady 84, 85, 86, 110
state of mind 20
status 40, 84, 101, 187–8; derivative 79,
    81; diminished 79; domesticity and
    dependency 180; equal 46; legal 83, 85,
    86, 109; maintaining 151; political
    strategy independent of 179; superior
    158; unmarried 108; victim 180; victim
    181
status quo 133, 135, 151; acquisitive and
    consumption oriented 159; critique of
    131; legal and economic, questioning
    110; play and humor used to uphold
    139
steadfastness 44
steam venting 151, 159, 164
Stein, Gertrude 169
Stein, M. 5, 60
Steinem, Gloria 172
Stephens, Ann 168
stereotypes 33, 46, 49, 109, 170, 233;
    cultural 222; cynical female lawyer 226;
    deviant 103; gender 49

Stewart, Jon 250
Stewart, Martha 228
Stibbs, A. 9, 187
stigma 189
stigmata 166
stigmatization 49
stimulation 141, 142
Stone, Sharon 183
Stowe, Harriet Beecher 105, 106
Streep, Meryl 166
subjectivity 51, 65; changed perception about 64; constructed in postmodernity 26; imagination placed at the center of 118; male 164; masculine and feminine 50
subjugation 21, 31
submissiveness 41
subordination 33, 79, 82
subsistence hunting and fishing 128
subversion 49, 123, 150, 151, 156, 157, 161, 167, 233; linguistic 214, 217; other ways needed 177; transgressive linguistic 210; women's humor tends to attack through 159
sue sponte thought 9
suffering 18, 41, 151, 179; humor amidst 246
suffrage 88, 94
Suggs, R. P. 116, 119
Summer Olympics (1968) 179
superiority 172
supermom myth 171
supernatural powers 132
surgeons 164
survival 49; adaptative 139; daily 142
survival of the fittest 39
suspense 111
Switzerland 12
symbolic order 160, 163, 204; humor and 164–5, 166; illusion in 212; patriarchal 243; refusing to be a victim of 178, 179; see also normative symbolic order; patriarchal symbolic order
symbolic speech 179
symbols 132

taboos 47, 151, 163, 172, 235; assertive takes on 172; broken 123, 126, 133, 136, 236–7, 238
Tannen, R. S. 79, 90
Taoism 42, 248
Taub, N. 84, 85

teasing banter 246
teenage mothers 14
television 104, 169, 190, 225; political humor 172; women directors and producers 249–50
temporal existence 60
tension 23; irreconcilable opposing unresolvable 216; transgressive 101
testicles 44, 127
Tewa women 187
text(s): boundary crossing 25; conscious awareness of bifurcation in interpretation of 118; female sleuth 23; feminist approach to 30–4; how one arrives at meaning in 115; written, cultures which relied upon 125
Thalia 72
That Was The Week That Was (TV satire) 172
theory-into-myth paradigm 75
Three Stooges, The 48, 126, 136
Thurlo, Aimee 24
tickling 164
Time Magazine 244
Todd, J. M. 104, 105
Tomlin, Lily 66, 133, 184
Tortoise images and antics 124
toughness 40
traditional Trickster 123–37; imagery of 48; lets off steam by playing at the margins 159; postmodern female Trickster is different from 8–9
tragedy 103, 124, 138; foundational support for 150; move back and forth between comedy and 186
traits: feminine, positive 43; masculine versus feminine 36
transcendence 138, 139, 140, 149; desire for 251; magical childlike 146
transformation 60, 178, 179–80
transgressive behavior 101, 102, 133
transvestites 150
trauma 148, 149; refocusing from 179
Trickster energy 10, 12, 20, 23, 34, 41, 93, 152, 160; accessed 72; archetypal 3, 7, 8; embodiment of 110; essential component not recognizing boundaries 113; ethical 21; humor and irony in 9, 33; integral part in postmodernity 217; manifested 8, 11, 25, 32, 33, 101, 110; one of the markers for, in postmodernity 151; shape-shifting 32;

significant aspect of 102; transformational, of social work 128; transformative value of 237

Tricksters: con artist 74; definitions 4–7; detective of marital politics 83; ethical 20; fictional, first 85; humor 135–7, 138, 150–1; linguistic subversion openly acknowledged between 214; literature and literary theory as it relates to 97–120; meaning of 130–3; nature of 74; quintessential 192–6; sightings 225–39, 249–51; social worker aspect 17, 211; traditional myths 124–9; wise/innocent naïve 169; *see also* postmodern Trickster; traditional Trickster

triggering event 39

Trollope, Anthony 108

Tuchman, B. 61–2

Turner, Victor 5, 34, 131

Twain, Mark 168

Twiggy 39

uncertainty 139

unconscious 60; bridging the gulf between conscious and 139–40; dialogue with 241; divine beings in human imagination in 75; images from 4; metaphoric image and its integration into 64; repression into 221; sense of humor repressed into 143; *see also* collective unconscious

unionization 94

United States: Abolitionist Movement 85, 86; books published in 23; census figures (1860/2002) 84, 189; coeducational land grant colleges 112; Declaration of Independence (1776) 84, 85; elite college students 49–50; female literacy (17th century) 99; foundation of system of government 242; Fourteenth and Fifteenth Amendments 86; gender bias problem 91–2; marginalized groups 148; middle-class women (World War II) 38; novel form and early women's literature 97–105; population growth 190; slave culture 106; "standard practice" throughout parts of 91; women leaders 251

United States Supreme Court 87–8, 89, 90, 91, 108, 190

unity 62

University of Alabama 237

University of Chicago 50

University of Florida 26

University of Notre Dame 70

unmarried women 78, 83, 88; displacement of 113; legal capacity to own property 108; reinscription of 218; young 108

upper classes 14, 84, 85, 104, 218; literature of white women 101; reading and writing 99

Utne magazine 237

"V. I. Warshawski" 10, 12, 13–17, 23, 36, 74, 91, 93, 110, 112, 114, 128, 159, 178, 183, 188, 190, 191, 206, 239, 249

vagina 183, 228

vagrancy and idleness statutes 86

values 31, 33; common 131; cultural 37, 165; hierarchy of 200; home and family 166; infringed 21; limited 114; societal, change of 131

vaudeville 148, 246

vengeance 208

verbal witticism 136

victims 93, 112, 113; refusal to be 9, 10, 33, 128, 156, 178, 179–81, 204, 214, 236

violence 99, 103, 159; crimes of 90; domestic/family 14, 79; possibility of 200; sexual 93; underlying threat of 93

Viorst, Judith 171

Virgil 98, 106

virgins 7, 70, 72, 90, 243; mature 15; pre-patriarchal 73–5, 86, 134

Vizenor, Gerald 124, 245

Volvo 251

Vonnegut, Kurt 149

vulnerability 14; conscious 15; strength and 163

Wade-Gayles, Gloria 222

Wagner, Jane 66, 184

Wagner-Martin, L. 104, 105, 107, 108

Wakahunga 135

Walker, Alice 222

Walker, N. 168, 169, 170, 173

Walton, P. L. 12

Warren, Mercy Otis 167

wars 84–6, 88–91, 127, 129

"Warshawski" *see* "V. I. Warshawski"

Washington DC 189
WASPs (White Anglo-Saxon Protestants) 221, 233
Waters, Ethel 221
Weldon, Fay 166
West, Mae 155–6, 158, 159
Whitaker, Frances 170
Whitman, Walt 106
wholeness 62, 116
widows 83, 109
Williams, Robin 250
Williamson, M. 104
Winnebago cycle 8, 123, 125–7, 129, 134, 135, 136
wisdom 156
wise women 62
wisecracks 156
Wiseman, S. 99, 100
wit 43, 48, 63, 111, 134, 138, 140, 143, 156, 158, 167, 169, 209, 228; absurdity abounds in 145; adoption of persona which channels creativity into 148; affinity for 145; aggressive 147, 148; appreciated 147; clever 148; comic persona fueled by 162; cynical/skeptical 147; funny, witty, incisive women who no longer have to hide 176; ironic 217; laughter and 149; obscene 147; operating as psychological adaptation 210; repartee in 146; showcased 251; sophisticated sense of humor which incorporates 144; use as a coping device 161; verbal dominance through 148; see also comedy, humor, irony, satire, sense of humor, witticisms
witches 62
witticisms 136, 160, 162; humor behind 166; ironic 166; obscene 146
witty remarks 149
Woeller, W. 80, 112
Wolff, Toni 68, 69, 70
Wollstonecraft, Mary 84
Wolverine images/antics 124

womanist perspective 33
womanliness 50
womb 43, 172; exertive 44, 45, 46; gestating 44, 45
women of color 32, 84; confined to marginal jobs 88
women's colleges 112
women's literature: early 97–105; 1970s and 113–14; wit and irony in 48
women's movement 90, 94; second wave 114
Women's Policy Research 189
Women's Rights Convention (1848) 85–6
Wood, Marian 23
Woodland tribes 124
Woodman, Marion 4, 6–7, 15, 41, 42, 43, 72, 74, 131, 223, 243
Woolf, Virginia 59, 98–9, 112, 155
word play 164; see also puns
working classes 23; enjoyment of popular narratives 104; gift of imagination fully available to 218
working women 85
works of art 70; archetypal aspects 118; psychological structure of 117; transformative 62; two ways of seeing or visioning 116
World War II 38, 88, 170
writing 125
Wuthering Heights (E. Brontë) 101, 103, 206

yang-femininity 43–4, 45; emergence of 46
yang-masculinity 43–4, 47; shadow 46
yoga clubs 149
Young, S. 61, 81
Young-Eisendrath, Polly 6, 41

Zapatista movement 244–5
Zeus 72, 134, 141, 192
Zoja, Luigi 39
Zoroaster 42
Zweig, Connie 41, 240

THE
WORKING
PARENTS
HELP
BOOK

THE WORKING PARENTS HELP BOOK

by Susan Crites Price and Tom Price

Peterson's

Princeton, New Jersey

Library of Congress Cataloging-in-Publication Data
Price, Susan Crites
    The working parents help book / Susan Crites Price and Tom Price.
    p. cm.
    Includes index.
    ISBN 1-56079-333-3
    1. Parents—United States—Life skills guides. 2. Working mothers—
United States—Life skills guides. 3. Work and family—United States. I.
Price, Tom.   II. Title.
    HQ755.8.P746 1994
    649'.1—dc20   94-19035
                                                           CIP

Cover and interior design: Greg Wozney Design Inc.

Printed in the United States of America

10   9   8   7   6   5   4   3   2   1

To our daughter, Julie, and to our parents.

CONTENTS

Acknowledgments xi

Introduction xiii

YOUR PARENTAL LEAVE 17

Planning your leave...19
Negotiating with your boss 21
Your legal rights 22
Making time for childbirth classes 26
Paternity leaves 30
Getting help after birth...33
When to begin the child-care search 36
Returning to work...37
Breastfeeding while working 38

CHILD CARE IN YOUR HOME 43

The upside/downside of in-home care 45
The hiring process...46
Placement agencies..54
Getting along with your caregiver..............................58
Au pairs 61
Special considerations for live-ins 64
Sharing care...65
Taxes and immigration issues.....................................68

CHILD CARE OUTSIDE YOUR HOME 73

Family daycare...74
The upside/downside of family daycare 75

Daycare centers 83
The upside/downside of daycare centers 84
The separation blues...87
Maintaining a good relationship with the daycare center...........90
Sick-child care 92
Drop-in daycare centers..93
Caregiving by relatives 95
Preschools 99
The school of the 21st century 101

YOUR SCHOOL-AGE CHILD............................103

Your options for school-age programs 104
Choosing the right program for your child 107
Getting kids from here to there 107
Setting up a new program.....................................109
Summer care 112
Year-round school 116
Home alone after school.......................................118

THE TEENAGE YEARS 127

A tough age to parent 128
Supervising from a distance 129
Have car, will travel 134
Part-time jobs for teens......................................137
Teen volunteering..140
Parent peer groups..141

Reducing risky behavior..................................144
About sex..144
Underage drinking and illegal drugs.......................145
Teen parties...151
Teenage depression 152

TIME WELL SPENT 155

Shortcuts on the home front................................156
Reducing your time on the road 166
Spending your "free" time well 167
Time with the children.....................................168
Volunteering...171
Staying involved in your children's school 173
Family vacations...174
Couple time, personal time.................................179

SHARING THE LOAD................................183

Divvying up the labor......................................184
Sharing sick-child care 189
Resolving conflicts..189
Involving the kids in chores 191
Help from friends 192
Car pools..196
Sharing the babysitting....................................197
Support groups 198

WORKPLACE DILEMMAS 205

Resolving conflicts with your supervisor 206
The Neanderthal boss 208
Special problems for fathers 208
The overtime trap 209
Have job, must travel 210
Relocating for work 213
Overcoming the guilts 215
A report card for parents 218
When your kids make you late 220
Helping your children understand your work 220

CAREERS WITH FLEXIBILITY 223

Making the case for a flexible schedule 224
Working from home 229
Going part time 233
Job sharing 236
Finding a flexible new job 238
Slowing down on the fast track 238
Combining more family time with rewarding work 239

Evaluating a firm's "family-friendliness" 240
Making the break to your own business 242

PREPARING FOR THE FUTURE 249

Saving dollars by pinching pennies 250
You don't have to be rich to save 250
Taking advantage of noncash benefits 252
Financing your child's education 253
Preparing for your retirement 257
Insuring your future—and your kids' 259
Wills and guardians 263
What if you're incapacitated? 267
Getting professional financial advice 267
Managing your own money 269
Raising money-savvy children 271

Appendix: Further Reading 273

Index 277

About the Authors 285

ACKNOWLEDGMENTS

In the course of writing this, our first book, we needed a lot of help. Fortunately, we got it. We owe thanks to many people. At the top of that list is our editor, Carol Hupping, who conceived the idea, supported our efforts to bring it to fruition, and made this a better book through her careful attention to every detail, from the content to the graphics. Carol and all the other members of the Peterson's staff have been a pleasure to work with.

We are also indebted to our friend Susan Dynerman, who convinced us we should write this book and then gave us much encouragement and help throughout the process.

Many parents and experts shared their time and thoughts about coping with careers and children. Two people, Jannet Carpien and Barbara Warner, should be singled out for their considerable help on the financial planning section. Thanks go also to those parents we quoted and to many others we interviewed, especially Lisa Brown, David Chu, Daniel Thorner, Kevin Greer, Bob and Joy Kraft, Margaret Bradley, Sarah Toth, Randy Wynn, and Marcia Vines. Kathryn Ray helped us with library research.

We also want to thank friends who cheered us on

and helped out in myriad ways while we were writing this book. They include Ann Hoenigswald, Mary Broderick, Karen Tcheyan, Laura Tosi, Avery Dizard, J. E. McNeil, Mary Alice Levine, Ginny Curtin, Mary Beth Greene, Kathleen Partridge, and the members of the Washington Independent Writers Mothers Group.

We are grateful to our parents, Sam and Anna Mae Price, Margaret Crites, and the late Franklin D. Crites, for their belief in us.

Finally, and most important, we thank our daughter, Julie, for her patience and good humor while we spent many evenings and weekends completing this book.

INTRODUCTION

In the back of our daughter's baby book is a piece of graph paper with a crude bar chart. We saved it because it became a symbol of our naive attempt to apply problem-solving skills from our orderly work worlds to the most overwhelmingly chaotic—and fulfilling—experience couples can have: parenthood.

Our newborn cried a lot. We didn't know this was normal for some babies. We figured we must be doing something wrong, failing to meet some obvious need. And we began to wonder how we'd ever function at work if we couldn't get a decent night's sleep. Hence the chart, where, in half-hour intervals, we used colored markers to track the times when Julie was either eating, sleeping, fussy, or quiet. We thought that a flow chart of her moods could help us identify the problem and arrive at a solution.

The project lasted two weeks—until we tired of remembering to fill in the chart and fell to arguing about whether she deserved a red mark (fussy) or a green mark (quiet) for that half hour. The evidence was inconclusive to say the least.

Relief came from experienced friends who assured us that fussy babies are normal, that this stage would pass (only to be replaced by some other challenge), and that it *is* possible for couples to have careers and still be good parents.

Julie is an elementary school student now, but our questions never stop. We still seek advice. But we've had enough experience to give some, too, and there's a growing number of dual-earner families who need it.

More Working Parents Than Ever

In 1970, 39 percent of mothers with children younger than age 18 were in the work force. By 1990, that had risen to 62 percent. The 1990 census showed that approximately half the mothers of babies younger than age 1 worked at least part time outside the home.

The trend even reached the White House when the Clintons became our first presidential couple to combine dual careers with child rearing.

And who'd have thought that, after sixty years of staying at home, Blondie Bumstead would start her own catering business—thus turning the "Dagwood" comic strip into a home for working parents?

If there are so many of us in the same boat, why is it so tough to sail a clear course? One reason we're floundering is that we didn't have many role models, since most of our mothers managed the home while our fathers brought home the single paycheck.

Another problem is the workplace itself, which has been slow to adjust to families' needs. Too many bosses still act as if every father has a wife at home all day and every working mother should be able to juggle work and family without any special favors. The highly touted Family and Medical Leave Act of 1993—by which the federal government supposedly rode to the employed parent's rescue—covers less than half of America's workers and requires only unpaid leave, a luxury many parents can't afford.

An Increasingly Family-Friendly Workplace

The good news is that a small but growing number of companies are trying to meet the needs of modern families. They've figured out that if they want to attract and retain qualified employees in the future, they can't ignore the dual roles that employed parents are juggling. Workers distracted by child-care difficulties, for example, are less productive and have higher absenteeism and turnover.

Companies are learning that if they accommodate pregnant workers with reasonable maternity leaves, the women are more likely to come back to work. Studies conducted for the U.S. Small Business Administration and the Families and Work Institute calculated that it's much cheaper to provide the leave than to replace a good worker.

For too long, parents have felt it was their fault if they couldn't keep all the balls in the air. Slowly we're recognizing that we've set impossible standards for ourselves: We can't be in two places at once if the boss calls a 5:30 P.M. meeting and the daycare center closes at 6 P.M. We can't arrive home from work and simultaneously play with our children, cook a gourmet meal, and make the house sparkle with cleanliness.

We have to stop comparing ourselves with unrealistic ideals. We have to set priorities. We have to learn to ask for help when we need it. And we have to think creatively, taking ideas from others and adapting them to our own situation.

An Exchange of Good Information and Wise Advice

The information in this book comes primarily from our interviews with mothers and fathers across the country, in small towns and big cities. We participated in group meetings and talked individually with secretaries, teachers, lawyers, nurses, writers, computer programmers, a veterinarian's assistant, and people in many other lines of work. They told us about the frustrations of combining work and family, as well as the joys. And they shared their methods of coping—ideas that we incorporated into this book.

We also interviewed people who often are described as experts—pediatricians, child-care professionals, psychologists, corporate benefits managers, career counselors, and business consultants, for example. Many of them answered our questions not only from their perspective as experts but also as parents themselves.

We discovered no magic formula for success—no perfect model for child care, no ideal length of a parental leave, no single method for coping with an inflexible boss. What we did find were countless good ideas that can be copied or adapted to your particular needs.

Many parenting books focus primarily on mothers. We think raising kids is a team sport, and many of the fathers we talked with agree. More dads want to be equal participants, sharing in the responsibilities and rewards of shaping the lives of their children, and we've treated them as such in this book.

As working parents, we've brought our own views and ideas to the chapters that follow. As journalists, we've gathered and sifted the ideas of others. The questions we tackled are the ones parents tell us they grapple with every day. If we help each other meet the challenges of the balancing act, we can focus on the fulfillment that can be ours from successfully combining kids and careers.

YOUR PARENTAL LEAVE

HERE'S HELP ON:

Planning your leave, page 19
Negotiating with your boss, page 21
Your legal rights, page 22
Making time for childbirth classes, page 26
Paternity leaves, page 30
Getting help after birth, page 33
When to begin the child-care search, page 36
Returning to work, page 37
Breastfeeding while working, page 38

Nothing will change your life more profoundly than becoming a parent. From the moment you learn you're expecting, you see everything in a new light. Now you're making decisions that affect not just your own life or that of your partner but also the child you are going to rear. Parenthood changes your work life, too. Suddenly you think about how your child will be affected by the hours you put in, the flexibility you have, and how much money you make.

And the first manifestation of this workplace impact is when you go to your boss to ask for parental leave.

If you're expecting, your first inclination may be to shout the good news from the rooftops. Before you tell your boss, co-workers, or subordinates, however, you should gather some information and make some decisions about the leave you want.

LEAVES FOR MOMS—AND DADS, TOO

Spending those first few days or weeks with your newborn is one important way to begin forming strong attachments as a family. The dads we spoke with told us that they really valued the time they spent at home getting to know their baby. A father's presence also can be a big help for the mother, who is recovering from the physical stresses of childbirth.

The first days after the baby arrives can be a very special time for a new family—a time to just rest and be together, a time to spread the good news and begin to get used to the new roles and responsibilities of Mom and Dad. For some couples, however, taking parental leave together isn't possible. And some choose to take their leaves back to back to stretch out the time their infant can be home with a parent before a hired caregiver takes over.

WORKPLACE ACCOMMODATIONS FOR NEW PARENTS

Unlike some so-called "family-friendly" benefits that are given only at the discretion of an employer, there are certain accommodations for new parents that are guaranteed by law. For instance, federal and state laws grant many parents the right to unpaid leave.

Many new mothers also are eligible for paid disability leave. And a boss can't fire a woman just because she's pregnant.

A union contract or an employer's policies may provide other benefits. And in some organizations, additional benefits can be negotiated, often on a department-by-department basis.

PLAN FOR FLEXIBILITY

Making a plan, approaching your boss, and negotiating a leave are things over which you have some control. You can't pinpoint exactly when the baby will be born, however, or how you'll feel once you become a parent. Some babies are early and others are late—giving you a quick introduction to how uncontrollable your life as a parent will be.

You also may be quite surprised at what you want to do with your life after your baby is born. You may plan to go back to work in the shortest possible time but then discover you can't pull yourself away from your infant. Or you may think you want to stay home as long as your boss will let you but find yourself anxious to trade the exhaustion of full-time child care for the familiar routine of your office.

As with just about every other aspect of parenthood, a successful parental leave requires planning for as many contingencies as possible so you're prepared for whatever comes next!

Planning Your Leave

The first step in your planning should be to answer some questions about your own wishes, needs, and capabilities. Before you can talk to your boss, you need to discuss the following with your spouse:

- ❏ how much time Mom would like to be home with the baby
- ❏ whether she'd like to phase back into her job, returning part time at first
- ❏ whether Dad should request a leave, too, and whether it should be at the same time or after Mom goes back to work
- ❏ how much unpaid leave your family budget can handle
- ❏ what child-care options you have
- ❏ whether flexible work arrangements would enable you to coordinate your schedules so you could reduce the number of hours you need paid child care

YOU DON'T KNOW UNTIL YOU'VE BEEN THERE

During my career, I've had management responsibilities and subordinates. I'd taken a time management course and understood the principles of setting priorities, concentrating on the important tasks, and delegating or eliminating the less important ones. So when friends told me that, after giving birth, they'd had days when they didn't have time to change out of their pajamas, I'd smile knowingly. I assumed they just weren't organized. That wouldn't happen to me. Then, a couple of weeks after Julie was born, when I'd been up half the night and didn't even know what time it was, I discovered it was noon and I still hadn't gotten dressed.

Suddenly, I understood. Babies are not like subordinates who can be managed dispassionately. In fact, they turn the superior-subordinate relationship on its head; the parents become the ones jumping through hoops. Time-management training goes out the window when you finally get the baby to sleep and then can't decide which is the more important priority—eating a meal or napping yourself.

Susan

MATERNITY AND PATERNITY BENEFITS

Once you've got those answers, you need to find out from your personnel office, your union representative, or your supervisor exactly what maternity and paternity benefits your company offers.

Be sure to ask not only about the availability of paid and unpaid leave but also about whether benefits such as health insurance are continued during the leave. You may have to pay some or all of the cost of continuing your insurance benefits, for example. If you are paid commission, ask how it would be affected by your leave.

If you're adopting a child, be aware that some companies will pay some of the costs of adoption, just as their insurance plans cover the medical costs of childbirth.

Disability Coverage

Many companies provide disability coverage that pays all or part of a new mother's salary. The length of the disability leave is dictated by doctors, who usually recommend six to eight weeks for uncomplicated pregnancies, sometimes more for cesarean deliveries. You may be allowed to tack vacation time on to your paid leave. But that may not seem like such a great idea later, when you have no paid days off for a break from work or to stay home with your baby when she's sick.

Job Protection

Inquire about your employer's job protection policy. It could promise you an equivalent position if you return within a certain period of time, but not necessarily the same job you had before your leave. During times of employer retrenchment, some new mothers have complained that they got their maternity leave but were laid off shortly after they returned to work.

Prenatal Benefits

Both husband and wife should ask their employers about any other benefits offered to expectant parents. Some employers sponsor prenatal classes during lunch hours and provide paid time off for prenatal doctor visits. This is not just altruism. Ensuring that mothers get good prenatal care means fewer babies born with medical complications that can skyrocket a company's health insurance costs.

Help with Child Care

Growing numbers of firms will help their employees find child care, and some will help pay for it. These firms believe employees will be absent less frequently and will be more productive on the job if they aren't worrying about the quality of their children's care or trying to cope when child-care arrangements fall through. Such family-friendly benefits also are tools for employee recruitment and retention (*see* Employer Assistance *on page 77*).

Checking with Co-Workers

Dana Friedman, co-president of the Families and Work Institute, a New York–based research group, advises prospective parents to ask their co-workers what arrangements other new parents have been able to make in the company. Managers often have discretion to let new mothers return to work part time or on flexible schedules even if there are no written policies covering such arrangements. Managers also may be able to accommodate new fathers who want time off. It helps if you can show your boss other cases in the company where the arrangement you are proposing has been successful.

Don't be surprised, though, if other parents are unwilling to reveal the specifics of deals they cut with their bosses.

Negotiating Your Maternity Leave with Your Boss

It's probably best to wait to discuss your leave with your supervisor until at least the end of your first trimester, when you are past the highest risk of miscarriage. It might not be possible to wait, however, if you suffer from morning sickness and frequently have to excuse yourself from staff meetings, for example. Just make sure your boss gets the news from you. Don't tell others who might tell her before you do.

You should open your negotiations by emphasizing your commitment and value to the company and your plan to continue working after the baby is born. Then suggest how your job responsibilities could be handled in your absence.

"Broach the topic with the manager as honestly as you can," says Dana Friedman of the Families and Work Institute. "Let him know you've thought

YOUR LEGAL RIGHTS

For all the controversy surrounding passage of the Family and Medical Leave Act of 1993, the law does not do as much as most people think nor as much as most parents need. Less than half of all workers are covered. The law requires employers to offer those workers twelve weeks of unpaid leave with continuation of health benefits. For parents who can't afford to take off without pay, that is slim comfort.

The Pregnancy Discrimination Act of 1978 requires companies to cover time off for childbirth in the same way that they cover other temporary disabilities such as a heart attack. Beyond that, few employers offer paid maternity leave.

Paternity leave has been slow to catch on in any form, even in companies that have adopted specific policies permitting it. A major reason for this is that men fear their careers will suffer if they appear to be less dedicated to their work.

The Family and Medical Leave Act

You're covered by the Family and Medical Leave Act—with some exceptions—if your employer has at least fifty employees, you've been there at least a year, and you worked at least 1,250 hours in the past twelve months. You aren't covered if your employer doesn't have at least fifty employees working within 75 miles of your work site.

Under the law, your employer must allow you to take up to twelve weeks of leave during any twelve-month period for childbirth, adoption, or acquisition of a foster child; care of a seriously ill child, spouse, or parent; or your own serious illness. The employer does not have to pay you, but he must continue your medical benefits. You have the right to return to your old job or an equivalent job with the same pay and benefits.

An employer can deny job restoration to salaried employees who are among the highest paid 10 percent of employees within 75 miles of their work site. The employer has to show that the leave would cause "substantial and grievous economic injury" to the organization.

Your employer can require you to use paid leave for any part of the twelve-week period. If you and your spouse work for the same employer, the two of you together have a right to just twelve weeks of leave to care for a new child or sick parent. You must give your employer thirty days' notice if your need for the leave is foreseeable.

The Federal Pregnancy Discrimination Act

Under this law, an employer with fifteen employees or more cannot fire you, reassign you, force you to take a leave, or refuse to hire you simply because you are pregnant.

If you become temporarily unable to work because of pregnancy, your employer must treat you the same way he treats any other temporarily disabled employee. You are eligible for any disability leave that your employer regularly provides to others. Your job must be held open for as long as jobs normally are held open for other disabled employees. Your benefits must be continued as they are for other employees who take leaves.

State Leave Laws

According to a 1993 U.S. Labor Department report, thirty-four states, Puerto Rico, and the District of Columbia have leave laws; twenty-three cover private and government employees, and thirteen protect government employees only. Some are more generous than federal law in certain aspects.

Negotiated Contracts

Some labor-management contracts provide child-related benefits that exceed legal requirements. Your employer's policies may be more generous than the law requires. And you can always try to negotiate a better deal on your own if a union contract doesn't preclude you from doing so.

For More Information

To get more information on your state's laws, contact the state's labor department or commission on civil or human rights. For more about the federal leave law, call the nearest office of the Wage and Hour Division of the U.S. Department of Labor (listed in the government section of your phone book). Information about the Pregnancy Discrimination Act can be obtained from the U.S. Equal Employment Opportunity Commission. Call 800-669-4000 to be connected to the nearest EEOC office.

about the implications. Look at your job and dissect it. What skills are needed? Then figure out who else can do it." Include plans to train that person or those persons early.

THINK IT THROUGH AHEAD OF TIME

There are several elements to this negotiation—expected departure and return dates, for instance, as well as benefits and paid and unpaid leave—which is why careful planning is required. For example, you need fall-back positions in case your initial requests get turned down.

If you ask for a five-month leave but the boss wants you back in three, be prepared to propose another alternative—such as returning sooner on a part-time basis or working from home. Once you've completed the negotiation, put the plan in writing. You can do this in a routine memo to your boss, summarizing your understanding of the plan.

Jean Marzollo offers these tips in her book, *Your Maternity Leave: How to Leave Work, Have a Baby, and Go Back to Work Without Getting Lost, Trapped, or Sandbagged Along the Way* (Poseidon Press, 1989):

❑ Don't wrap up the deal too quickly because your boss may offer other ideas designed to lure you back to work.

❑ Don't sign on for more at-home work than you can reasonably handle during your leave. You always can volunteer for more work later.

❑ Don't suggest doing an important managerial job part time at a reduced salary because you could end up working nearly full time for less money.

❑ Ask for more than you expect to get, so you can compromise.*

DECIDING HOW LONG YOUR LEAVE WILL BE

"My boss wants to know how long I expect my maternity leave to be, and I don't have an answer. I'm torn because I'll be giving up income if I take more than eight weeks but I want to get my baby off to a good start."

This is the key question in your parental leave plan, and it's the hardest to answer. You don't know how you're going to feel—physically or emotionally—until you're actually in the situation.

---

* Marzollo, p. 47.

THE WORKING PARENTS HELP BOOK

If you have a cesarean delivery, for example, you may need more time to recover physically. If you have a colicky baby, you may want to stay home with her longer, especially if you are nursing and she finds comfort in frequent feedings. On the other hand, you may miss your job and find it preferable to long days of infant care.

In fact, at the outset of your negotiations, you don't even know when your leave is going to start. Some babies arrive early, others late. Pregnancy complications could force you to quit work weeks before your due date.

Some experts advise mothers to take a minimum of three to four months after the birth so they can form attachments with their babies. The health of babies who will be in group care also benefits from extra weeks at home. Exposure to the germs of other children is delayed while their immune systems mature.

Try to Keep It Flexible

You should try to persuade your boss to leave your return date somewhat open-ended, with the promise that you'll keep her regularly updated about your plans. If you're pushed to give a date in advance, and

SOME PITFALLS OF GOING BACK TOO SOON

Cathy Crouch knows what can happen when you return to work too soon.

"When I had my second child, I felt better physically, so I cut my leave short and went to a four-day business conference in Florida," she recalls. "But I had no business being there." Her baby, whom she had just weaned, was only a month old, and Crouch soon discovered she was neither physically nor emotionally ready to be away that long.

Crouch also echoes the new parent's common lament that you won't really understand parenthood until you're there. "My company gives six weeks paid medical leave and eight if you have a cesarean," she says. "With my first pregnancy, I thought: 'My gosh! What will I do with all that time off?' I thought I'd get work projects done at home—things like budgets and performance appraisals."

Instead, she found that caring for her baby exhausted her. "I thought I was busy before," she recalls. "But then you become a mother, and it's entirely different."

MAKING TIME FOR CHILDBIRTH CLASSES

Will you find it difficult to attend evening childbirth classes because of unpredictable work schedules? There are alternatives to the standard six-week course.

Some hospitals now offer the option of a course that meets for two days on one weekend. If you can afford it, another option is to hire a childbirth educator to give you the course in your home.

Weekend Getaway Classes

Even more expensive, but also more fun, is to combine a getaway weekend with childbirth classes. Couples buy a hotel package that includes room, meals, and a childbirth course, usually offered in conjunction with a nearby hospital.

Mercy Hospital in Miami, for example, runs a weekend getaway at the Sonesta Beach Hotel in the summer and fall. Parents-to-be can stroll the beach in between meals and classes on Saturday and Sunday. There's even a free children's camp program so couples who already have kids can bring them.

Making Up Missed Classes

A crash course, however, is not necessarily the preferred way; the regular courses are designed to build on what you learn each week and to leave time for practicing the breathing techniques in between classes. If you sign up for the conventional weekly program and you miss a class, you may be able to make it up if the instructor is teaching other sessions. Instructors also tell wives to attend even if their husbands can't make it, with a friend in his place, if possible.

Childbirth Videotapes

These can supplement your class instruction if you miss a session, but instructors advise against using them as a substitute for attending any classes at all. Videos also are an option if you've taken a course for a previous birth and just want a refresher.

Videotapes are available in some stores and libraries and also through the Lamaze Information Line at 800-368-4404. Lamaze can also give you a list of certified instructors in your area.

you decide during your leave that you want to extend it, alert your boss as soon as possible. You may find she's willing to grant your request if she's convinced that returning later will make you more productive.

Your departure date should be flexible, too. Some women work right up to delivery, but others need time off early, especially if their jobs require physical exertion or constant standing. You might benefit from being able to shorten your working day as your due date nears.

Kathy Strawn, a mid-level manager in a large Midwestern corporation, wishes she had reduced her workload as her delivery date approached. Toward the end of the pregnancy, "I was only performing about 50 percent," she says. "The quality of my work suffered. I should have worked half days and given the company 100 percent during the time I was there."

Strawn's experience also illustrates another reason for negotiating a flexible departure date. Her baby arrived seventeen days ahead of schedule!

Keeping in Touch

Feeling isolated from the office drives some women back to work early or leads them to perform some office duties while they are officially on leave. Occasional contact with colleagues can be good for you emotionally. And your boss may appreciate being able to contact you as the need arises.

Your maternity leave agreement should include a plan for accepting business calls. You may want to limit the number right after delivery and increase them later. Using an answering machine lets you return calls when the baby is napping instead of taking them when she's nursing or crying. Of course, that doesn't preclude calling friends at the office who can keep you posted on what's happening.

THE RECOVERY PERIOD

"My six-week disability leave is almost up, and I don't feel I've fully recovered. I'm worried about how I'll get through the day when I return to work."

There's company policy, and then there's real life. Many doctors use six weeks as the rule of thumb for recovery from a vaginal delivery (eight for a cesarean). But new research suggests that many women need more time to recover fully.

A study by Dr. Dwenda K. Gjerdingen, a family

practitioner who also teaches at the University of Minnesota, found that a variety of symptoms—such as breast soreness, hemorrhoids, hot flashes, constipation, fatigue, and vaginal discomfort—can persist for several months.

Her personal experience after the birth of her own child spurred Dr. Gjerdingen's interest in the birthing recovery period. Her conversations with other mothers confirmed her view that recovery takes longer than the medical community says it does. "We need more flexibility in this area," she says. "Some women need more time. Six weeks isn't the end of the story."

Dr. Gjerdingen says the reproductive organs usually return to their nonpregnant state in about six weeks. That benchmark does not take into account the rest of the body, however. Effects of the delivery itself—or hormonal changes that occur afterward—can cause discomfort for a longer period of time. Some of these problems then may be aggravated by the stress of caring for an infant.

One surprising finding in her study was that new mothers experience respiratory infections more frequently in the third month after delivery than in the first month. Women who returned to work had a higher rate of such infections than mothers who were at home. Possible explanations include exposure to colleagues' germs at work, increased susceptibility due to work stress, or infections their babies brought home from group daycare.

Not Ready to Go Back to Work?

If you don't feel you have fully recovered by the end of your scheduled leave, you may be able to have it extended by getting your doctor to certify your continued disability. Or your boss might be willing to negotiate a longer maternity leave. If you must go back before you feel physically ready, try to get more help at home and avoid overloading yourself with too many tasks at work. You also can take some comfort in knowing you're not alone in feeling less than fully recovered six weeks after childbirth.

GOING BACK PART TIME

When her first son was born, Kim Boltenhouse used her six weeks of disability leave and two weeks of vacation and then returned to her job.

"I have to work," says Boltenhouse, a veterinarian's assistant in a small Ohio town. "We need the money. But it was terrible to go back so soon. For a while I cried every morning and every night." She wasn't worried about her son, who was being cared for by her mother-in-law. She simply had trouble adjusting to being away from him all day—she missed her baby.

After the birth of her second child, she again took a six-week disability leave. But then she returned to her job for 20 hours a week, gradually working up to a full-time schedule. And she coped much better. "If you can take the extra time to ease yourself back into the work situation, it makes so much difference," Boltenhouse says.

Her view is supported by the extensive research on parental leave done by Catalyst, a national organization based in New York that works with corporations to foster women's career development. "A sense of resentment builds if a mother doesn't get enough leave," says Marcia Kropf, Catalyst's research director. "We hear over and over about how tired women are physically and emotionally" when they return to work after childbirth.

She advocates that companies adopt flexible policies to allow women to return to their full-time jobs gradually. For example, a woman could return for two days a week, then increase to three, then four, and finally five days a week.

Going back on a transition basis, first to part time and then to full time, eases the stress on the mother and her family, Kropf says. "And full time in many companies means long hours coupled with a long commute."

Many mothers who return part time prefer to work a few days each week rather than a few hours each day. Of course, what schedule you adopt will depend on what you can convince your employer is to your mutual advantage.

Some bosses will be happy to have you back part time if it means they get you back sooner. Proposing that you take a shorter leave in return for starting back part time might work to your advantage in your negotiations.

A part-time schedule not only gives you time to rebuild your stamina but also can allow you to ease your child into daycare and give you more opportunities to observe your child-care provider in action.

WORK-AT-HOME ARRANGEMENTS

"I'm thinking of suggesting to my boss that I work at home for a few weeks to extend my leave and still keep some paychecks coming. What's the best way to structure such an arrangement?"

"Working at home is a great way to transition back into the job, but be clear that working at home is not a substitute for child care," says Dr. Kropf of Catalyst. If you expect to get any work done, you'll have to hire a caregiver. "But being at home satisfies many needs," she says. "You can juggle household tasks and be close to your infant."

How much work you'll get done also depends on your child, as Jan Hodson, a university administrator in Ohio, found out.

"I made a deal with my boss that I'd do some work from home and I'd be off for four months," she remembers. "I'd never had a baby before, so I thought I could show him I could do everything. I had assumed I'd have a baby who'd sit in her little seat while I used the Dictaphone. When my secretary would arrive with piles of files, I'd try to work but the baby would be screaming." Hodson stuck out her work-at-home struggle because she was the only woman on her department's professional staff and she

"felt I had to prove something to my office. I sensed they were worried that I wasn't going to be serious about my career anymore," she says.

Home Sweet Office

If you want to work at home, you should talk to your boss about what specific tasks could be handled away from the office. If it's appropriate, ask to borrow a computer, modem, and fax machine. Find a space in your house that you can devote to office work, and try to set some regular hours for working while your baby is with his caregiver.

If you find you've taken on more work than you can handle, renegotiate the workload with your supervisor.

Paternity Leaves

Except for the physical aspects of pregnancy, childbirth, and recovery, we offer the same advice for expectant fathers that we do for expectant mothers. When negotiating for paternity leave, you need to:

❑ learn your legal rights and your company's policies

- ❏ find out what your co-workers have done
- ❏ present your boss with a plan for covering your work in your absence

NEW ROLE MODELS NEEDED FOR DADS

That being said, we know that it's often difficult to find bosses and co-workers who are as accepting of paternity leaves as they are of maternity leaves. Women, not men, are considered the nurturers in our society, and there aren't a lot of role models for fathers who want to take more than a week or so to be home with their new babies.

Even in companies that have a policy expressly permitting paternity leave, few men take advantage of it for fear their careers will suffer. And most paternity leave is unpaid.

The First in Your Office

"I think I'd like to take a leave. But no other man in my office has ever done it, and I'm afraid the boss will think I'm not serious about my career. Is it really all that worthwhile?"

Many of our fathers weren't in the room for our births. Today, however, it's rare for a husband not to be holding his wife's hand during labor. Just as we have discovered that a father can play a valuable role in childbirth, we now know that he can be quite important at home afterward as well. It's helpful to Mom, good for Baby, and rewarding for Dad.

The new family-leave law gives many fathers the opportunity to take up to twelve weeks of unpaid leave. A small but growing number of employers offer paid paternity leave. And many fathers arrange to take vacation when their children are born.

The bosses who are most receptive probably are those who have children themselves. Paternity leave is used most often where senior managers are most supportive. The practice will grow as more men take leaves and become role models for others.

"I think it's going to snowball," says Steven Shorkey, vice president of a bank subsidiary in North Carolina. Shorkey took advantage of his company's new paid paternity-leave benefit when his wife, a partner in a large accounting firm, went back to work. "We've tried to be very supportive of each other's careers and divide things up," he explains. "It was only fair that I would take a paternity leave."

Shorkey was the first—and, for a year, the only—man to take advantage of the paid leave at his workplace. He could have taken up to six weeks but chose to take only two—an illustration of how even open-minded men are reluctant to push very far. Shorkey says he couldn't take more time off because his job requires him to stay current with a lot of fast-breaking information.

Among the benefits of having been at home with his new baby, Shorkey says, is the knowledge that "it was me he smelled and felt. I'm sure he could tell it was my hands holding on to him. Our relationship is different than it would be without that time to bond."

Shorkey feels there is general acceptance of paternity leave throughout his company because there is support from the top. In the future, when one of his subordinates wants to take time off with a new baby, "I won't give it a second thought," he adds.

If you sense that your supervisor is not sympathetic, you may have to be the pioneer who starts the trend. If you're a valued employee, a brief absence shouldn't jeopardize your career, but several months off might. If you have made yourself especially valuable to your company—by working long hours without complaint, for instance, or by doing things no one else does—now is the time to collect your reward.

PLANNING HELPS . . . SO DOES LUCK

Because I am my newspaper's lone Washington correspondent, my work life is replete with long days, long weeks, odd hours, and late-night phone calls from editors who have just discovered a breaking story that needs reporting from the nation's capital. The upside to my chaotic work schedule is that it earns me some flexibility in taking time off.

I prearranged a three-week leave for immediately after our child's birth, and it worked out better than my bosses or I could have imagined.

I worked late one Friday night, finishing up a major project. At bedtime, Susan said she was beginning to feel contractions but suggested that I go to sleep anyway. She woke me about 6 A.M. Saturday, saying it was time to head for the hospital. Julie was born that evening, ten days past her due date, and I started my paternity leave with a clean desk at work (to the extent that my desk ever can be said to be clean).

Unfortunately, I have no advice about how you can arrange such exemplary timing!

Tom

CONSECUTIVE OR SIMULTANEOUS LEAVES?

If a father takes his leave when the mother's ends, the family maximizes the time the child receives full-time care from a parent and delays the expense of child care. On the other hand, taking leave simultaneously can bring the family closer together while reducing the parental workload during that time.

Having help from relatives also can influence your decision. Grandparents may relish the opportunity to spend a few weeks assisting with the care of a new grandchild. If Grandma is going to be home with Mom for the first two weeks, Dad may want to delay his time off until after her visit so he can support his wife when she's alone and stressed out from full-time child care.

Getting Help After Birth

"Neither of our mothers is well enough to come and help out when our baby is born, and my husband can take very little time off. I think I'm going to need some extra help, especially from someone who knows more about baby care than we do!"

Ever heard of a "doula"? A Greek term meaning "to mother the mother," the word describes a woman who assists new mothers during and after the birth. Doulas are common in Europe and have been introduced in the United States in the past decade. Few Americans are familiar with the term, however.

DOULAS

The first doula service in the United States started in New York, and the National Association of Postpartum Care Services was created in 1988, according to Gerri Levrini, owner of Mother's Matters in Alexandria, Virginia, one of approximately one hundred association members. Levrini, a registered nurse, is in charge of the association's accreditation program, which certifies doulas after they have received training and passed an examination.

A family might hire a doula to assist with the labor and delivery if, for example, the father is traveling abroad on business or is just too nervous to participate in the birth. Most hire doulas after the birth to help the family during the first few trying days or weeks of parenthood. The women from Levrini's agency are experienced mothers who are trained to assist in the new mom's recovery from the physical stress of childbirth while helping her learn the basics of infant care—such as bathing, breastfeeding, and calming a fussy baby.

Hours and Costs

Typically, the doula will visit the home for two to four hours a day for two to three weeks. Costs vary widely around the country, but the average is $25 per hour. A few hospitals are including doula services as part of their maternity care package for early-discharge patients. In rare cases, insurance companies will cover the cost.

Services Doulas Provide

In addition to teaching the new mother and helping her gain confidence, the doula will prepare meals or do light housekeeping so Mom can rest. Sometimes the doula will stay with the baby so the mother can go out or spend time with her other children. Other times the doula will care for the older children while the mother devotes herself to her infant.

Levrini's service also includes a lending library of tapes and articles for new mothers and an on-call nurse who can be reached by pager if a new mother has medical questions.

A quarter of Levrini's customers are second- or third-time moms. "Maybe they didn't have a good breastfeeding experience the first time around," she explains. Or they may need help caring for other children in the family.

> **TIP:** You'll want to contact a service early so you have a chance to interview prospective doulas before your baby is born. To find out about doulas in your area, contact the National Association of Postpartum Care Services, 326 Shields Street, San Francisco, CA 94132-2734, 206-672-8011.

BABY NURSES

Although the number of doula services is growing, not many communities have them yet. Baby nurses are more commonly available. They will take care of your infant while you recover from childbirth, and they can teach you baby-care basics. But they won't take care of your house.

HOUSEKEEPERS AND MOTHER'S HELPERS

Some new mothers hire housekeepers to cook and clean for a few weeks after birth so Mom can concen-

A DOULA FOR HELP AND MORAL SUPPORT

Amy Mann is one of Gerri Levrini's satisfied customers. Her daughter was a cesarean delivery and her husband could take off work only during the first week she was home from the hospital. Nursing wasn't going well, and her recovery from the surgery was slow.

Mann's mother is deceased, and her mother-in-law couldn't travel from Wyoming, so she found herself consulting her 87-year-old grandmother, who hadn't nursed her children and couldn't remember much about baby care.

When her daughter, Sydney, was three weeks old, Mann called Levrini in desperation and was matched with her doula, Susan, who visited two or three hours a day until the baby was almost two months old. Susan is a nurse who has children of her own and who became a doula so she could work around her children's school schedules.

"What she did more than anything was talk to me and help me relax," Mann remembers. "Before Susan came, nursing hurt. She helped with that and also taught me to pump and store milk." She taught both Mann and her husband how to bathe Sydney. And she'd vacuum, tidy the house, and take care of the baby so the new mother could run an occasional errand.

"I would so look forward to that time of day when she would come," Mann says. "And if I had a question, I knew I could get it answered when she got there."

Mann thinks that even when a father can stay home with his wife, a doula can help. "With your hormones raging, it helps to have a mom who's been through it. I love my husband, and he helped a lot, but husbands expect new mothers to know more than they do."

trate on getting the rest she needs and on getting to know the new baby.

A teenager can be hired as a mother's helper after school to watch the baby or your other children. A few hours here and there will give you some welcome time to do laundry, write thank-you notes for your baby gifts, or just sleep.

HELP FROM EXPERTS AND FRIENDS

If you just need some professional advice, consider hiring an expert for one home visit. Lactation consultants, for example, will help you get started with breastfeeding and teach you to pump and store milk. Or maybe you can get a friend who's an experienced mother to teach you the basics. You also can check out infant-care classes offered by local hospitals or community groups; some are geared for expectant parents, and others are for parents whose children already have been born.

Don't be shy about asking for assistance. Unlike other animals, humans aren't born with innate knowledge about caring for their young. In the past, some aspects of new-baby care—bathing, nursing, etc.—were taught before new mothers left the hospital. Now, with insurance companies demanding that mothers go home 24 to 48 hours after birth, there's hardly time for a shower, let alone infant-care instruction.

When to Begin the Child-Care Search

"Our baby isn't due for six months, but I feel anxious about how long it will take us to find child care. I have only six weeks of leave, and I hear horror stories about waiting lists. When should I start looking?"

Timing depends on the kind of care you want. If you're going to hire an in-home caregiver, you'll probably have to wait until a few weeks before you return to work because most nannies aren't job hunting months in advance (*see* The Hiring Process *on page* 46). The exception is the foreign au pair. Agencies need three months or more to process your application and match you with a person who then travels to the United States (*see* Au Pairs *on page 61*). If you plan to use a nanny placement service, you can spend time now researching and choosing a qualified agency (*see* Placement Agencies *on page 54*).

A LITTLE HELP FROM YOUR FRIENDS

If you can't afford to hire assistance, now is the time to be straightforward with all your friends who ask what they can do to help you. Most of them really mean it, but you have to be honest and specific about your needs.

Maybe you'd be uncomfortable asking a friend to do your laundry or housecleaning (or maybe not!); but you could ask her to organize your friends or co-workers to bring you dinner for the first couple of weeks. Experienced mothers can be good teachers.

And if someone offers to give you a baby shower, you can suggest that it be a "voucher shower." Getting all those cute little outfits at a typical shower is fun, but they are soon outgrown. It can be better to get presents in the form of vouchers, in which the givers pledge to do babysitting, meal preparation, grocery shopping, or errand running when you need it most.

If you're interested in group care—such as a daycare center or a family daycare home—signing up early is a good idea; there often are waiting lists for infant slots. After your first trimester, when you're feeling more energetic, you can visit centers or homes, talk with providers, and make your final selection (*see* Family Daycare *on page 74 and* Daycare Centers *on page 83*).

Returning to Work

When your leave is almost over, it's time to reconnect with your colleagues. Even if you've been checking in by phone or receiving your business mail while at home, some mothers recommend visiting the office a week or two before to catch up on memos or current projects. You might want to take the baby with you so your co-workers can see you in your new role as a parent as well as an employee. After that, refrain from talking about your child too much at work. You need to keep things on a professional basis.

Try to start back on a Wednesday or Thursday so you have the weekend to regroup and ease into the separation from your baby, especially if you are continuing to breastfeed. Expect to have feelings of anxiety about leaving your baby at first—it's natural.

To ease your way through the transition, you need to focus on the satisfaction you get from being in the work world again. Some parents find it comforting to display baby pictures at work. Others say pictures cause stress by making them long for their child. You'll have to figure out what's best for you.

BREASTFEEDING WHILE WORKING

"I'd like to continue to breastfeed when I return to work. How do other mothers manage this?"

Combining breastfeeding with a full-time job takes commitment on the mother's part and support from her spouse, caregiver, pediatrician, and workplace. There are several options for nursing mothers when they go back to work:

❑ Wean the baby when the maternity leave ends.
❑ Work at home.
❑ Continue to breastfeed by expressing milk at work so your caregiver can feed the baby breast milk during your absence.

❑ Reduce breastfeedings to the hours when you're at home and have the caregiver use formula when you're at work.
❑ Continue nursing even while at work. This is possible if the baby is near the mother's workplace—at an on-site daycare center or with a caregiver who lives nearby, for example—and the mother can nurse during her breaks and lunch hour.

If you want to breastfeed for several months, you might extend your leave that long and then wean the baby. If you have a job requiring travel, weaning is probably the easiest option.

Expressing Milk at Work

Some mothers are able to express milk at work—if they can take breaks and if they have privacy. Those are two big ifs. Usually these mothers use pumps—manual, battery-operated, or electric. The last are faster, pumping both sides at once in 10 to 15 minutes. Electric pumps cost several hundred dollars, so most women rent them for $2 to $3 a day or less from hospitals or a group like La Leche League. A few mothers learn techniques to express milk manually so they don't have to deal with pumps, but that takes a lot longer.

You'll need an insulated cooler or refrigerator for milk storage. You should practice the pumping process so you get the hang of it well before you return to work.

A nurse in a doctor's office told us she pumped three times a day, in an unused office, during morning and afternoon breaks, and on her lunch hour. She had good support from co-workers and somewhere to call when she had questions—the lactation center at the hospital where she gave birth.

Expert advice is important when you first start pumping at work. Your pediatrician may be helpful, but not all are supportive of working mothers. Some pediatric practices have lactation consultants. Experienced mothers who have pumped at work also are a source of help.

For Some, It's Not Worth It

One mother told us she tried pumping but soon gave it up. It wasn't because her workplace was unsupportive. She's the top person in a health-care agency, and she makes the rules. "I'd close my door, take off my blouse, and use an electric pump. But the whole process was awkward and messy. And the pump was noisy, so even with my door closed I was self-conscious, thinking that my staff was hearing it." She also had to schedule meetings around her pumping sessions. And travel meant lugging the heavy pump along.

With her second child, she stayed home three months, even though she was ready to go back to work sooner. She did it because she wanted to breastfeed her baby until he was three months old without having to struggle to pump milk at work.

Company Support for Nursing Moms

A few companies are setting up nursing suites equipped with electric pumps so mothers have a comfortable place to express milk. This makes good business sense, since nursing mothers might return from maternity leave sooner if they can pump at work. There's also considerable evidence that breastfed babies are healthier. So encouraging mothers to combine nursing and working may reduce the days they have to be absent to care for sick babies.

Breast and Bottle

Many mothers told us they don't pump at work but

continue breastfeeding before and after work hours. Here's how they do it:

Before their leaves ended, they started gradually substituting bottles of formula for the breast during the hours when they'd eventually be at work. Breasts adjust to the decrease in demand by producing less milk. They also asked other people—Father and caregiver, for example—to do some of the bottle-feeding during this transition so the baby got used to a change from Mother. Usually, the sooner a baby starts with a bottle, the easier it is to get her to accept it in place of the breast.

If you opt to continue breastfeeding when you go back to work, be sure to get plenty of rest, drink *lots* of fluids, and eat nutritious meals to keep up your milk supply.

> **TIP:** La Leche League has pamphlets on breastfeeding while working and on expressing milk. It also has a hotline with counselors who will answer questions and send you a catalog of books and tapes. Call 800-LA LECHE.

MINIMIZING CHILD-CARE ANXIETY

The biggest cause of anxiety for parents at work is their child-care arrangements. That's a good reason to ease into child care before you return to work.

Have the caregiver start a week or two early—or place your child in the daycare center then—beginning with a couple of hours the first day and gradually working up to full time. This lets you observe how your baby is adjusting and makes you feel more confident when you return to work. Don't hesitate to call the caregiver several times during the first few days so she can keep you posted on how things are going. You will need this reassurance in the beginning (*see* Easing Your Anxiety *on page 87*).

Establishing Your Morning Routine

Before you return to work, practice a morning routine. Time how long it will take to nurse, shower, dress, eat breakfast, pack the diaper bag, load the car, drive to the sitter, and get to work. Then add some extra time to allow for the unexpected, such as the baby spitting up on your suit just as you're walking out the door!

If your baby will be cared for at home, this practice time is when you can check your house for safety hazards and show your caregiver where you keep the fire extinguisher, first-aid kit, and emergency phone numbers.

BE EASY ON YOURSELF AND YOUR FAMILY

And finally, don't expect this time to be easy. If your baby is still getting up at night, you may be dragging through the day at work. Don't demand too much of yourself. You may have to let the housecleaning go or eat take-out food a lot until you learn how to juggle all the balls and still get enough rest.

Spouses can be a source of emotional support. So can other working parents who offer sympathy and understanding. Go ahead and talk about your feelings. Expressing your guilt or anxiety is a healthy way to make the transition from home to work smoother.

CHILD CARE IN YOUR HOME

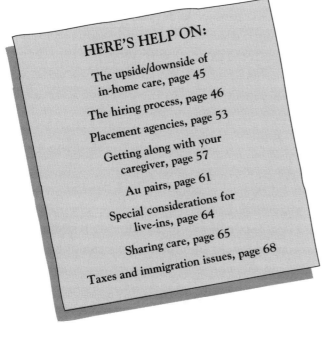

HERE'S HELP ON:

The upside/downside of
in-home care, page 45

The hiring process, page 46

Placement agencies, page 53

Getting along with your
caregiver, page 57

Au pairs, page 61

Special considerations for
live-ins, page 64

Sharing care, page 65

Taxes and immigration issues, page 68

Ever notice how many articles on finding the ideal nanny mention Mary Poppins? Mary was, of course, a real find—efficient, wonderful with children, and able to perform magic (literally). Yet, in Disney's version of the story, she also manipulated her employers and left abruptly without giving notice or even saying good-bye to her two young charges. Alas, Mary wasn't perfect either.

Having a caregiver in your home is just one of several child-care options available to working parents. Others, including family daycare (providers who care for children in their homes) and daycare centers, are discussed in *Child Care Outside Your Home*, starting on page 73. Before- and after-school care are covered in *Your School-Age Child*, starting on page 103. Many families use a variety of in-home and out-of-home arrangements during their children's preschool years.

Whatever you decide, nothing is forever. Of the

1,733 readers who responded to a *Working Mother* magazine survey, a whopping 97 percent said they had changed their caregiver at least once within the past year.* Forty-eight percent had changed two or more times. In some cases, the caregiver was a daycare center and, in others, an individual.

Changes are necessary in part because of the natural progression of children's development. You may want a nanny for your infant but decide on a pre-school or daycare center when your child is older so she can be with other children and have more varied experiences. Other changes are beyond your control. Given the low pay and long hours, caregivers often leave for greener pastures with another family or move to another line of work.

Cost is a key reason why only an estimated 3 percent of working parents have in-home caregivers.† Costs range from $175 to $350 a week, depending on which part of the country you live in and the level of the caregiver's training. Parents who can afford this option often prefer it because of the greater flexibility it offers them and because their children can remain in familiar surroundings, having their individual needs met more fully than in group care.

After weighing the pros and cons and deciding to hire an in-home caregiver, the challenge is to find—and keep—the right one. As the Mary Poppins story illustrates, there is no perfect nanny nor one magic solution for locating the caregiver who would be best for your family. What we think we want is someone just like us . . . except never impatient or bored or less than enthusiastic at the end of a long day of child care. Some perfectionists wouldn't hire themselves for this job if they could stand back and observe how they relate to their kids on a particularly trying day!

WHAT QUALITIES MATTER MOST IN A CAREGIVER?

The key is for both parents to identify those qualities most important for their family. For example, do you want someone who is:

❏ mature and experienced or young and energetic?
❏ able to drive?
❏ looking for a live-in or a live-out position?

---

* Jan. 1993, p. 48.
† *"National Child Care Survey, 1990,"* Hofferth et al, Urban Institute, 1991.

THE UPSIDE/DOWNSIDE OF IN-HOME CARE

The Upside

- There is more flexibility for parents than in family daycare or daycare centers, which are only open certain hours.
- You save time by avoiding the drive to and from daycare.
- Your work schedule isn't disrupted if your child is ill.
- Children, and especially infants, don't get pushed into schedules for eating, napping, or play time as they might in group care. Sleeping kids don't have to be awakened and dressed to leave with you in the morning.
- Infants aren't exposed to as many germs as in group care.
- The caregiver can accommodate the needs and schedules of children of different ages. She can care for your toddler at home and also pick up your older child at school.
- Your caregiver also may perform other household duties. Some do light housekeeping, wash the children's laundry, and prepare meals. You also have someone to let service people into your home.
- If you have more than one child, it may be cheaper than out-of-home care, where you pay per child (although you may get a discount for every child after the first).

The Downside

- When the nanny is sick, you're without child care.
- It's more expensive than group daycare, unless you have more than one child.
- You become an employer and have to deal with taxes and other government regulations.
- The caregiver is on her own, and you don't know what goes on when you're not there, especially when your child's too young to talk.
- Turnover can be frequent, leaving you without child care while you find someone else.
- If the person lives in, you relinquish some privacy and assume some added responsibilities for the caregiver.

□ willing to let you share her services with another family?

□ similar to you in religious views or family values?

□ a take-charge type who doesn't want or need much supervision or one who prefers specific direction from the parents?

You also must decide whether to find a caregiver on your own or to use a placement service (*see* Placement Agencies *on page 54*).

NANNIES, AU PAIRS, AND BABYSITTERS

Throughout this chapter, we use the term caregiver to apply to nannies, au pairs, and babysitters. Some people use these terms interchangeably, but there are differences between them:

Nannies are best defined as people who have had some formal child-care training, often at one of the nanny training schools that have mushroomed around the country. They command larger salaries than caregivers without formal training.

Au pairs usually are young women from other parts of the country or from Europe (through the international exchange program) who live in and are almost like family.

Babysitters generally are all others who care for children. Most of their knowledge comes from personal experience with their own children or siblings. Some young sitters have taken babysitting classes through their school or a community organization.

We refer to caregivers as women because the number of male caregivers, although growing, is still a tiny fraction of the total.

The Hiring Process

Assuming you've decided not to use a placement agency, your first step is finding candidates.

Advertising

Be as specific as possible in your ad. If you're in a big city, you may want to pick smaller neighborhood papers instead of a major daily to reduce the cost of the ads and to avoid massive numbers of responses. If you want a young woman from another state (several Western states have become popular hunting grounds for nannies), advertise in a newspaper there.

> **TIP:** Use an answering machine to record calls in response to your ad so that you can speak to applicants at your convenience.

Informal Networks

Ask friends, neighbors, pediatricians, ministers, and colleagues. Put up signs in neighborhood churches, libraries, and grocery stores. Talk to caregivers at playgrounds and ask if they have friends looking for new positions. (But beware the appearance of trying to steal someone else's nanny!)

Schools

You can call local community colleges, which may have recent graduates who studied child development. Another option is to contact one of the country's approximately fifteen nanny schools.

> **TIP:** You can get a list of nanny schools from the American Council of Nanny Schools, Delta College, University Center, MI 48710, or by calling 517-686-9417.

EVALUATING CANDIDATES

"I've been swamped with calls about my ad, and I've eliminated some people on the phone. But now that I've got several to interview, I'm worried that I won't know which one is right for us. Is previous experience the most important thing? References? Gut feeling?"

In the first sentence of *Baby and Child Care*, Dr. Spock tells parents: "You know more than you think you know." Judging the qualifications of applicants can be approached methodically, with different weights given to various factors. But in the end, you also must rely on your instincts and common sense.

As the box on the following page illustrates, by getting clear in her own mind what traits were most important to her and to her husband, Rosann Wisman was able to be more confident in her decision. The relative importance of such traits will be different for each family. Previous experience, references, the person's child-rearing philosophy, and how the candidate interacts with the child are factors to consider. Couples who establish beforehand which qualities are their top priorities will improve their chances of finding a caregiver with whom they'll be comfortable.

THE INTERVIEW

Interview a candidate in your home so she can see where she'll be working and you can see how she interacts with your children. It's best if both parents are present, because one of you may pick up on

LISTEN TO YOUR INSTINCTS

Rosann Wisman learned this lesson when she hired a nanny for her 3-month-old son, Sam. As the executive director of a health-care agency, she has plenty of experience interviewing and hiring employees. So does her husband, Michael Lilek, a service manager for a communications firm.

But with this hiring decision, "the element of risk was a lot different," Lilek says. The vision in his mind wasn't the movie *Mary Poppins* but rather *The Hand That Rocks the Cradle*.

Wisman was more confident. She had heard from friends that finding the right caregiver is mostly a matter of luck. And sure enough, about the time she was placing a carefully crafted ad in the paper, she heard about an experienced woman who would be available soon.

"I thought I'd already gotten lucky," Wisman recalls.

At first the candidate seemed perfect for the job, and she took to Sam immediately. But as the interview wore on, the woman complained a lot about her previous employer and then tearfully shared some personal problems she was having with her adult daughter. Clearly the woman carried a lot of emotional baggage.

"When she left, I told Michael I thought the most important quality for our nanny should be that she is a happy person," Wisman says.

Eventually, a woman named Alma answered their ad. "I asked her on the phone to describe herself," Wisman explains, "and she said, 'Well, I'm basically a happy person.' Right away I felt she was the one."

A lengthy personal interview and reference check confirmed Wisman's first impression. Alma turned out to be a real find.

things that the other doesn't. You both should be comfortable with the person you hire.

Interview Questions to Ask

Ask the candidate about her education, child-care training, employment history (including references with phone numbers), and health. Try to assess her knowledge of child development by asking open-ended questions about how she would play with your child and how she'd handle certain situations. Ask her views on such issues as discipline, toilet training, sleep schedules, TV watching, and outdoor play. Also ask her to describe the other families she worked for, their children's ages, and how she handled these issues in their homes.

Make a list of questions you want to ask and information you want to give during the interview. Photocopy the list—with spaces for filling in the answers—to help you remember the details of the interview when you compare the candidates later. We've provided a sample one on the following page; you can copy and use it, or customize it as you see fit.

Job Description

Give applicants a detailed job description, including starting date, salary (regular pay and overtime pay or compensatory time), and hours (include whether she will occasionally be asked to stay late, spend the night, or work a weekend or holiday). You should also include a list of employer-provided benefits, such as:*

- ❑ Social Security
- ❑ Workers' compensation
- ❑ Unemployment compensation
- ❑ Disability insurance
- ❑ Health insurance
- ❑ Vacation (How many days? Restrictions on when?)
- ❑ Holidays (Which ones?)
- ❑ Sick days or personal days (How many?)
- ❑ Training (a first-aid course, for example)

The job description should also include a list of responsibilities, such as:

- ❑ Child care, including age-appropriate activities, outdoor play, protection of their health and safety, etc.

---

*Some of these are required by law; see Taxes and Immigration Issues, page 68, for your general obligations as an employer.

QUESTIONS FOR AN INTERVIEW

Basic Information:

Why are you looking for a new job? _____
_____
_____
_____

What is your employment history (employers, addresses, dates, ages of children cared for)?
_____
_____
_____
_____
_____
_____
_____
_____
_____
_____

What education have you had? _____
_____
_____
_____

Do you have a driver's license (if one is needed)?
_____

Do you smoke? _____

Can you provide evidence of a recent physical or are you willing to have one (at our expense)? _____

Can you show proof of American citizenship or eligibility to work in this country? (*See* Taxes and Immigration Issues, *page 68*.) _____

Whom may we contact for references? (Get at least two names.) _____
_____
_____
_____

Open-ended questions:

What do you enjoy about working with children?

_____

_____

_____

What kinds of activities will you engage in with our child? _____

_____

_____

_____

Do you think it's important to be out-of-doors for some part of most days? _____

Do you think babies should be picked up whenever they cry (for parents with infants)? _____

_____

How do you handle discipline? _____

_____

_____

How did your parents discipline you as a child?

_____

_____

How would you handle...? (Fill in situations a nanny in your home might encounter, such as a specific medical emergency, a tantrum, potty-training, sibling conflict, etc.) _____

_____

_____

_____

_____

The Applicant's Turn (make note of her questions; they could give you insight into her expectations):

What questions do you have for us? _____

_____

_____

_____

Are the job requirements satisfactory? _____

_____

What would you like to know about our children?

_____

_____

_____

_____

- Transporting children to school or activities
- Supervising other children who play with yours
- Taking children to dentist or doctor appointments
- Miscellaneous (include any that apply): meal preparation (just for the children or also for the family?); shopping, chores, errands; laundry; light housekeeping (be specific); pet care

Reference Checks

Checking references is an inexact science at best. Some parents are uncomfortable being totally honest about their former caregiver's performance. Talk to several references, even if not all of the jobs involved child care. Ask about the candidate's reliability, strengths and weaknesses, and why she left her former jobs. Also ask about the ages and number of children she cared for and how she handled problems that arose. Check the answers with the candidate's own answers to the same questions to see that they match.

Getting to Know Each Other

Prior to hiring a candidate, have her spend a couple of days with your child while you are there to observe, paying her for the time, of course. A weekend might be best, when both parents can be involved.

A Clean Bill of Health

Before coming to your final decision, make sure the applicant you want to hire has had a recent physical exam, or require one and offer to pay for it. With her permission, you can get a health report from the doctor so you are assured the candidate doesn't have a communicable disease or other medical condition that would impair her ability to care for children. One woman told us of a friend whose infant caught tuberculosis from her caregiver.

Legal and Criminal Checks

If the candidate is not a U.S. citizen, ask to see evidence that she is legally permitted to work (*see* Work Permits *on page 70*). You also should check whether the person has a criminal background. States vary on the procedures and charges for this, so call your state police office for more information. Ideally, you want to know about felony and misdemeanor arrests as well as traffic violations such as speeding and drunk driving.

REFERENCE CHECKS

Here are some sample questions to ask when you call a potential caregiver's references. You may find it useful to make copies of this page and take notes right on it.

When was the caregiver in your employ? _____
_____

How many children did she care for and what were their ages? _____
_____

Why did she leave? _____
_____
_____

What did the job responsibilities entail and how well did she meet them? _____
_____
_____
_____
_____
_____
_____

What activities did she plan for the children? _____
_____
_____
_____
_____
_____

How did she handle discipline? _____
_____
_____

Was she reliable and prompt? _____

Was she in good health? _____

How was your relationship with her and were you able to communicate about any issues that arose?
_____
_____
_____

What are her biggest strengths? _____
_____

What are her weaknesses?_____
_____
_____

Some parents choose to hire an investigative service instead of attempting the background check themselves. Michael Adamson, vice president of American Background Information Service in Middleburg, Virginia, provides checks for both placement agencies and parents around the country. He estimates that 10 percent of his firm's investigations of child-care candidates reveal criminal records. Using the addresses where the candidate has resided, his firm also checks credit reports and traffic arrests.

> **TIP:** To find such an investigation service, look under "Investigators" in the *Yellow Pages*. Typical charges are $65 to $75.

MAKING YOUR DECISION

After you've been through all these steps and gathered adequate information, you must listen to your gut instincts.

Don't hire a person you have reservations about, even if no one else is waiting in the wings. Usually those doubts are there for good solid reasons, even if you can't articulate them.

If You've Made a Mistake

If you discover you've hired the wrong person, terminate the arrangement as soon as possible. Nothing is worth the agony of worrying that your child is not being well cared for.

Placement Agencies

"We'd like to save ourselves the hassle of finding nanny candidates and just go through an agency. But friends of ours had a bad experience with an agency. How do we pick a good one?"

CHOOSING THE RIGHT AGENCY FOR YOU

Agencies differ a lot in terms of size and the types of caregivers they place. Some specialize in young girls from Western states, others—primarily on the East and West Coasts—may have mostly foreign-born women. Because the agencies usually aren't licensed or regulated, you're on your own to judge quality. Agencies also don't do all the work for you. They find candidates, but you still have to do the interviewing and often your own reference checks.

Getting recommendations from friends is a good way to find an agency. The wrong way is to call those listed in the phone book, ask their prices, and pick the cheapest.

NANNY STORIES THEY CAN TELL

One Washington, D.C., couple we know became firm believers in the gut-instinct approach after bumbling through five live-in caregivers in as many years. They know several of their hiring failures happened because they didn't follow their instincts. The reason they didn't is familar to many working couples.

"You get desperate," says the mother, who was too embarrassed to let us use her name. "And here is this live body who looks honest and industrious, and you think you might not find anybody else, let alone someone better. We were so naive."

The couple's first caregiver was a recent high school graduate from Utah. Rural Western states such as Utah and Montana are popular recruiting grounds for caregivers; many young women there want to experience big-city life and see new parts of the country. The couple had acquaintances who had a caregiver from a small Utah town and who had heard of a young woman from another family who wanted to come to Washington.

The mother interviewed her on the phone, checked references, and then paid to fly her in for an interview. The couple hired her despite some uneasiness, partly due to the young woman's lack of experience as a full-time caregiver.

"When I was hesitant, my husband kept saying, 'You won't think anybody is good enough,'" the mother says, and she suspected he was right. "But it was a big mistake. She lasted two months. She told us on a Monday she was leaving for home on Wednesday. She really had no interest in children or in the other things she had agreed to do, like starting dinner."

Deciding they wanted someone with more experience, the couple turned to a placement agency. Their next caregiver had worked for another family in Washington. "They gave her a decent reference, but not a glowing one," the mother remembers.

Overall, the couple's experience with her was positive, but there were a few negatives—like when she started a fire in the kitchen!

"She had put a bottle and nipple into boiling water on the stove and then forget about them and took my son for a walk," the mother says. The flame burned itself out in the pan, but not before black soot had covered the walls. They had to repaint their kitchen.

When that nanny decided to quit to enter nursing

(continued on next page)

school, the couple tried a new agency. Unlike the first one, this agency interviewed the couple in their home and seemed intent on finding the perfect match for their family.

This time, the candidate they chose seemed almost too perfect—energetic, industrious, great with the kids. She had a glowing reference from her previous employer. Only later did the couple discover that their nanny was bouncing checks all over town.

At first, they believed her story that she was inexperienced with a checking account and had gotten in over her head with bounced check charges. After they tried to help her straighten it out, they discovered she was pocketing the cash they were giving her to buy the family's groceries and was paying for them with more bad checks. Needless to say, she was quickly let go.

Their next caregiver also came through an agency. "My gut told me this wouldn't work," the mother recalls, because the nanny's previous position was with a family that needed her services only when their only child came home from school.

"At their house, she had access to a pool and a car with a car phone. She quit us within five months because she wanted to find another family that would let her work less than 40 hours a week."

The parents, who now have two children, finally lucked out with their current caregiver, a young woman from Wisconsin who loves children and had previous experience at a daycare center.

Looking back on her family's revolving nanny door, the mother concludes that, although she considers herself a very protective mother, she's like many other harried working parents. Rather than follow her gut instincts, she made compromises because she needed child care and it's a scarce commodity.

"As in all things, you get what you pay for," says Judi Merlin, owner of a placement agency called Friends of the Family. It's an easy business to get into, she cautions. One person with a phone can buy a few ads and start making placements. Agency fees can range from $500 to $2,500. What you are paying for are prescreened candidates.

If you don't know someone who has used the agency, ask the staff for the names of a few families who have. While you're at it, find out about any other services the agency provides that you may need at some point. Merlin's firm, for example, has a roster of caregivers for emergency care (if your caregiver calls in sick), sick-child care, weekend and overnight care if you travel, and help for mothers and newborns in those first few days or weeks after the birth.

Agencies usually have access to group health-care plans, which may save you money if you buy insurance for the caregiver you hire.

BACKGROUND CHECKS OF CANDIDATES

Ask if the agency's caregivers are bonded, although that only protects you against theft and then only if the caregiver is convicted. Ask how extensive a background check is performed. Some agencies only check criminal records of the current state where the caregiver lives and not other states. A thorough background check should include driving violations and credit history.

Doing Your Own Reference Checks

Even if the agency says it checks references, you should, too. You'll want to know specific information about how much another family is like yours in discipline style, for example, whereas the agency will have asked about such matters as promptness and reliability (see Reference Checks on page 52).

REFUND AND REPLACEMENT POLICIES

Merlin suggests asking a prospective agency how long the firm has been in business and how many placements it does a year. Also ask about the replacement or refund policy if the initial caregiver doesn't work out. Many agencies will offer replacement candidates. Depending on the firm, replacement offers are good for periods ranging from thirty days to a year.

To avoid the need for replacements, many agencies do follow-up evaluations of the caregiver and will mediate disputes. Also ask if the firm's candidates have received training.

Getting Along with Your Caregiver

"I've had friends who got along fine with their nannies at the beginning, but over time the relationship deteriorated. How can we avoid this?"

This is where a written agreement—and some common sense—come in. False expectations mixed with poor communication is a recipe for high turnover.

Caregiver turnover is especially high among young women because many decide that they want to pursue their education or move on to higher-paying jobs with more chance of advancement. Sometimes they quit to get married and have children of their own. And—young, old, or in-between—caregivers sometimes quit because their employers have unreasonable expectations or don't give them the respect they feel they deserve.

YOUR WRITTEN AGREEMENT

Drawing up a written agreement when the caregiver is hired is the best way to avoid expectation problems on both sides. Placement agencies often provide fill-in-the-blank agreements and help with the negotiations, but you can easily draw up your own in simple, everyday language. An agreement should include:

❑ Salary. Check your state's minimum wage requirement, which may be higher than the federal minimum. Talk with friends about the going rate in your area.

❑ Usual working hours. Include whether you will ask for evening or weekend babysitting and how that will be compensated.

❑ Holidays, vacations, and sick days. Specify how

NANNIES' PET PEEVES

Costello Williams has been a nanny for the same family for nine years, since the oldest of the two children was a few days old. She's been happy in her job because she and the parents have regular—and candid—communication and because she feels she's a valued member of the team. But she's become something of a mother confessor for other caregivers in the neighborhood who complain that their employers treat them unfairly. Here's a sampling of the complaints she hears:

❑ Parents start taking their nanny for granted, coming home late a lot and expecting her to work more hours than the original agreement.

❑ Especially with live-ins, parents want the nanny to be available for evening and weekend babysitting, too. "Nannies have a life of their own" and need time for their families or other obligations, Williams points out.

❑ Some families take their nannies along on their vacations and expect some child care. This is not a substitute for the nanny receiving her own vacation time.

❑ Extra duties get added to the job that weren't originally mentioned, such as pet care, housecleaning, or cooking. If you want her to do the housecleaning as well as child care, pay her more, Williams stresses.

❑ Parents don't tell the nanny how she's doing. She needs to hear praise if things are going right and, if the parents are unhappy about something, they must explain what they want done differently.

❑ Parents aren't in agreement and therefore give the nanny conflicting instructions.

❑ Some parents allow another family to share their nanny occasionally without asking the nanny's permission first or offering to pay her for the additional children.

❑ Kids are allowed to have authority over the nanny or are not reprimanded by the parents when they refuse to mind her. "Parents on a guilt trip because they are working will sometimes let their kids do whatever they want," Williams explains.

Most of all, Williams says, parents should respect their caregivers and foster an atmosphere of mutual respect and trust.

(*Also see* Keeping Communication Lines Open *on page 60.*)

many she gets and which will be paid.

- ❏ Any other benefits you plan to offer. You might want to offer health insurance, although most families don't.
- ❏ Added responsibilities. Be specific about what that means: laundry, meal preparation, light housekeeping, grocery shopping, transportation to preschool, play-group participation, pet care, etc.
- ❏ Additional considerations for live-in caregivers. You'll need house rules regarding such matters as her use of the telephone and whether she may entertain guests in your home (*see* Special Considerations for Live-Ins *on page* 64).

TIP: If your caregiver needs health insurance, she can qualify for lower group rates by joining an organization like the National Association for the Education of Young Children, 1509 16th Street NW, Washington, DC 20036, 800-424-2460. Regular membership is $25; insurance costs vary.

Working Hours

Placement agency owner Judi Merlin says the hours a caregiver is expected to work often become a major issue, and she won't accept clients who want a person to work an unreasonable amount of time.

"Parents say they want a caregiver to be flexible, and what that means is they feel the caregiver should be willing to work infinitely expanding hours," Merlin says. She recalls one client who complained when her caregiver made a doctor's appointment in her off-hours without getting permission. The client, a doctor herself, wanted the caregiver at her disposal around the clock.

"After 50 hours a week of child care, she may not feel like babysitting on the weekend," even with extra pay, Merlin points out. "And so many people are still paying their caregivers the same salary after three years. Businesspeople would never put up with that."

Keeping Communication Lines Open

Merlin also thinks it's important to offer caregivers positive reinforcement. "They work long and hard for not a lot of pay, but they'll feel better about it if they know they're appreciated." And she recommends regular performance reviews. "Otherwise, little things will fester."

Paula Schwed, a working mother who's hired nannies to care for her children, thinks parents avoid telling caregivers what's wrong because "it's hard for our generation to do. We're uncomfortable with the master-servant relationship. But you have to do it. My friends who don't [speak up] have disasters."

One mother we know handles the performance review by hiring another babysitter for an evening so she and her husband can take their caregiver out to dinner at a nice restaurant occasionally.

"We use a positive approach," she explains. "We tell her she's doing a good job, but here's what we want her to work on." They also ask if she has any concerns or complaints about her job.

Au Pairs

The controversy over hiring undocumented workers as nannies has led parents who want live-in help to queue up at the handful of government-designated agencies that recruit legal au pairs from Europe. For a cost less than the typical live-in, parents get a young, energetic caregiver and don't have to deal with any government paperwork. If they're lucky, a bit of culture and foreign language rubs off on their kids in the bargain.

From the French for "on par"—a helper equal to others in the family—au pairs are English-speaking men and women ages 18 to 25 who are recruited from European countries. Special one-year visas, authorized by a 1986 law, permit au pairs to trade 45 hours of child care and light housekeeping for a private room, board, a $100-a-week stipend, and the opportunity to learn about America.

Qualifications

Most have driver's licenses, and all must show evidence of prior child-care experience, including references. They must have a doctor's certificate as evidence of good health and up-to-date immunizations.

Costs

Families work with one of several government-authorized agencies to find a good match. The agency's fee covers orientation for families and their au pairs, medical insurance, and all paperwork. The family also pays the au pair's plane fare. The total tab, not counting the room and board, averages between $170 and $180 a week—less than the cost of a typical live-in. Families with more than one child often find hiring an au pair is less expensive than using a daycare center, which charges per child.

Big cities are popular with au pairs, but some are willing to go to smaller communities; one agency we know of has arranged placements with families in upstate Alaska and on cattle ranches in Colorado.

IS AN AU PAIR RIGHT FOR YOU?

It takes a certain personality to adjust to a caregiver who is not supposed to be treated as an employee but more like a member of the family. You have to be more flexible, less concerned about privacy, and comfortable having an extra person at the breakfast table or on a family outing. You also have to adhere to the 45-hours-a-week limit.

Although you hire an au pair because you want child care, the government views this as a cultural exchange. The au pair is supposed to spend part of her time taking a class or engaging in some other educational activity.

> **TIP:** Find au pair agencies in the *Yellow Pages*, but make sure the one you call is on the government-approved list. Some families have been defrauded by unapproved groups that illegally arrange for foreign au pairs to enter the

country on tourist visas. To get the official list, call the U.S. Information Agency, 202-475-2389.

DEALING WITH AN AU PAIR'S HOMESICKNESS

"Our au pair is terribly homesick. She's a 19-year-old from rural Austria, and it's her first time away from home. How can we help her?"

Being confined for long hours with a baby is hard enough. Couple that with adjusting to a different culture—unfamiliar food, customs, kitchen appliances—and you've got the potential for an au pair who wishes she were home.

Au pair agencies typically have counselors in the communities in which they do placements. To lessen the degree of culture shock and homesickness, the counselors hold regular meetings with groups of au pairs so they develop their own circle of friends. Some agencies also have a buddy system, linking two au pairs in the same neighborhood.

For their part, families are expected to include au pairs in family meals, activities, and outings. Offering access to the family car lets the au pair enjoy a social life outside the family as well. Local coordinators work with families and au pairs on an individual basis if they have adjustment problems.

HOW ABOUT A MALE AU PAIR?

"The agency offered us a male au pair. We were taken aback at first, but then thought this might be fun for our two boys."

Scott Shepard recommends families consider a male au pair. His first two were young men from Spain. "Since fewer families want men, the competition for positions is keener, so you get a more mature and experienced au pair who is here to perfect his English and improve his career opportunities in his own country," Shepard explains.

Does he worry about sexual abuse when using a male sitter with his daughter, Aliana? "I get asked that all the time and had to do some explaining to my in-laws," Shepard says. He pointed out that any sitter, male or female, might physically or sexually abuse a child. "But we spent time with our au pairs when they first came, to see how they related to Ali. You have the right to reject an au pair you're not comfortable with. We trusted our instincts, and they turned out to be two of the finest young men I've ever known."

YEARLY TURNOVER

"It seems as if she just got here, but our au pair's year is up. How can we help our kids cope with saying good-bye and also make our new one feel welcome?"

It's not just a problem for the kids. Parents get attached, too. Scott Shepard says the annual good-byes are the hard part for his family. When he took their last one to the airport, he had to pull over and let his wife, Deborah, drive because his eyes had clouded with tears. The Virginia family is on its third au pair for three-year-old Aliana.

"She was too young to understand they were leaving" when the first two departed, Shepard says. "But the next time may be tough."

The Shepards keep in touch with their former au pairs through letters, Christmas presents, and occasional phone calls. They hope to take Ali to Europe to visit them someday.

Helping Children Say Good-bye

For young children, the frequent turnover of au

pairs—or other caregivers for that matter—can become a serious issue. The children may feel it's their fault that their au pair is leaving.

Janice Abarbanel, Ph.D., a child and family psychotherapist in Portland, Maine, says kids sometimes feel abandoned when a favorite sitter leaves, and "those negative feelings can get transferred to the next sitter."

She recommends letting children go through a grieving process. "Parents need to acknowledge the loss with their child," she says. "That part is rarely done. Children should be helped to talk about the loss, remembering a variety of occasions shared with the au pair. Parents can involve the children in good-bye rituals, such as a farewell party. Kids can participate in the party and can accompany the au pair to the airport as part of the closure."

She also suggests that one or both parents take a few days off from work during the transition. "That way they can be supportive when the children say good-bye to one and welcome the next."

Abarbanel, who had personal experience with European au pairs for her two sons, says regular turnover is not harmful if the transitions are handled carefully and with thought for the child's feelings.

With children who are old enough, it's best to address the issue up front. Explain that the au pair will be with your family for just a year, but that this will be an opportunity to learn about another country and to develop a relationship that can last a lifetime.

Special Considerations for Live-Ins

"We'd like the convenience of a live-in, but we're nervous about the loss of privacy and are uncertain about what ground rules we should set."

Success depends on the physical layout of the caregiver's quarters and respect for each other's needs.

Living Arrangements

The quality of the living quarters you offer may affect your ability to attract and retain child-care help. The caregiver's living area should be clean and comfortable, a place you'd feel okay having your own daughter live in if she'd gone away from home to be a nanny. If you are converting a basement or attic into living quarters, find out about your community's zoning and building codes. They often dictate minimum requirements for size, ventilation, and egress. Sleeping rooms should have an operable window or exterior door for emergency escape.

For maximum privacy, it's best if you can offer a separate bathroom. Or it might be one the caregiver shares only with the children. Consider providing a television and a clock radio for her room. A separate phone line keeps your phone from being tied up and keeps her long-distance bill separate. Access to your car for personal use, rather than just for chauffeuring your children, lets the caregiver have a better social life. Check your car insurance to see if additional coverage is required.

Meals Together or Separately?

Mealtimes require advance discussion, too. Some caregivers prefer to feed the children early, fix their own food later, and eat in private. In other homes, the family and the caregiver dine together. Try to accommodate her food preferences.

Entertaining

Other issues include whether the caregiver may entertain friends in your home, including overnight guests. You might be happy to have her parents visit from out of town but not be pleased if her boyfriend spends the night. If she wants to have a couple of friends over in the evening, would you rather she entertained them in her room or in the family room? Spell these things out in advance.

Show Respect

Inevitably, sharing your house with someone else means sharing your private lives with each other, too. If she becomes too much like part of the family, it may harm the employer-employee relationship. If you set some boundaries, and show her respect and appreciation as a valued participant in your child's care, some of these problems can be avoided.

Sharing Care

"We can't afford to hire a full-time caregiver, so we're thinking about sharing with another family. Is this a good idea?"

With costs of in-home care so high, this arrangement makes good sense for some families. The key issue is compatibility. You not only have to find a

SAMPLE HOUSE RULES FOR LIVE-INS

1. The employer will provide a private room with television. The bathroom is shared with the children.
2. The caregiver may entertain guests in her room or may entertain in other rooms of the house that are not then in use by family members. When not in use, the VCR in the family room is available to the caregiver.
3. The caregiver may have occasional overnight guests (not of the opposite sex) if she has prior approval from employer on each occasion. The caregiver should refrain from entertaining guests after 11 P.M. on weeknights.
4. The caregiver has full use of the kitchen, and employer will provide whatever foods the caregiver chooses. She may join the family for meals if she desires.
5. The employer will provide a telephone on a separate line in the caregiver's room. The caregiver is responsible for her own long-distance charges.
6. The caregiver will have the use of one of the employer's two cars. The employer will provide insurance coverage. The car will be used to transport the children and also is available for the caregiver's personal use.
7. If the caregiver is involved in an accident, it should be reported to the employer immediately. If an insurance deductible must be paid as a result, the caregiver will pay half the amount. The caregiver is responsible for any traffic or parking tickets she receives.
8. There will be no smoking in the house or car or around family members. This applies to both the caregiver and her guests.

caregiver you can work with but another family as well. With shared care, parents and children are going to be closely linked in many ways. You may even coordinate vacations (probably when the nanny takes hers).

Randy Rieland and Carol Ryder adopted their son, Ben, about the same time some good friends were welcoming the birth of their first child, Matthew. By pooling their money, the families could pay more than the going rate to get a quality caregiver and still pay less than they would have individually. Rieland and Ryder believe an additional advantage is that their son is developing social skills by being with a playmate.

"We think Ben's less likely to be spoiled" than if he were alone with his caregiver, Rieland says. Another advantage is that when the caregiver gets sick, four parents can share the burden instead of only two. And the caregiver likes supervising two children instead of one because the kids entertain each other.

Ryder says it helps that the couples were good friends before they had kids. That made it easier to work out the many issues that inevitably arise in such arrangements. The parents jointly decided on instructions for the caregiver on such matters as discipline, schedules, and food to be served to the children. Rieland and Ryder accepted the other couple's offer to handle the paperwork and have the care done at their house.

"They have a bigger house with a yard and live on a cul-de-sac," Rieland says, and the house is only five minutes from his wife's office. The other family doesn't have to haul their child somewhere in the morning, and they get a little extra service from the caregiver, who tidies the house when the kids are napping. But they also have the wear and tear from two little boys. The couples share food buying. Rieland and Ryder contributed a few toys so Matthew wouldn't always have to share his.

FINDING A FAMILY TO SHARE WITH

If you're not fortunate enough to know someone who wants to share, you may find help through local referral networks or parent support programs in your community. The Parent Connection in Bethesda, Maryland, for example, operates Share, a data base that matches families with similar child-care needs and compatible locations. The service costs less than

$20 and is usually used by parents of children from birth to age 3.

Ann Byrne, who directs the project, advises parents not to limit consideration to people whose address is near theirs. It may be just as easy if the home is near one of the parent's workplaces, especially for a mother who wants to nurse her baby during lunch hour. Byrne also suggests being open to families whose children are not exactly the same age as your own or who have more children than you do.

Making Decisions Together

She thinks both sets of parents and the children should get together for an initial meeting. If they decide they are compatible, a host of other decisions must be made, including:

- ❏ Whose house will be used?—or should they alternate every month?
- ❏ Who will handle paperwork?—or should they hire an accountant?
- ❏ Who will take calls and screen applicants? (Both families should participate in the candidate interviews.)
- ❏ What are their attitudes about nutrition, toilet training, TV watching, naps, and discipline?

Licensing and Insurance

You should also check your community's requirements for licensing family daycare homes. Although there is little or no enforcement in shared-care arrangements, many state and local governments require licensing of homes in which just one unrelated child is cared for. This means the home must meet certain health and safety standards. Byrne says the process of complying is not as difficult as you might think (*see* Typical Licensing Standards *on page* 76).

She also suggests contacting your insurance agent to find out if you will need additional liability coverage in your homeowner's policy.

Taxes and Immigration Issues

"Some of the candidates we've interviewed insist they be paid under the table. Many of our friends do this. As long as we're not planning to run for public office, what's the harm in hiring the best person and ignoring the government's rules?"

The government doesn't devote a lot of energy to snooping for parents who don't deduct Social Security taxes from their payments to the neighborhood babysitter. And the Immigration and Naturalization Service (INS) probably won't stake out your home to find out if you've hired an undocumented worker for regular child care. But obeying the law is a good idea.

If you do get caught, the back taxes, interest, and penalties can be steep. Also, by not paying your help on the books, you forfeit your access to child-care tax benefits. If you hire an undocumented worker—or anyone else under the table, for that matter—you're not the only person who avoids scrutiny by the authorities; so does the person to whom you are entrusting the care of your most precious asset, your child.

You're not necessarily doing your caregiver a favor by helping her avoid taxes. She's also forfeiting Social Security payments in her old age and unemployment benefits should she lose her job. And isn't it worth something to show your children by example that they should play by the rules? •

YOU AS EMPLOYER

If you hire the girl next door to babysit, she becomes your employee. If you pay her $50 in a three-month period, you both have to pay Social Security taxes. But if you hire her twin brother to mow the lawn,

COMPLYING WITH THE RULES*

Taxes

If you pay your caregiver at least $50 in a calendar quarter, you and she must pay Social Security and Medicare taxes. If you pay at least $1,000 in a quarter to all of your household employees combined, you are subject to the tax for federal unemployment compensation. You should contact your state unemployment office for information about your state obligation.

You do not have to withhold federal income tax for your caregiver, but you may do so if she asks you to. She also may ask you for help in obtaining advance payment of the federal earned income tax credit.

Labor regulations

You also should contact your state labor department if your caregiver works more than 20 hours a week. That makes you subject to labor regulations, such as the minimum wage, and some states' requirements are tougher than the federal government's.

*As of June 1994.

and he brings his own lawn mower, he's an independent contractor, and the Social Security system is his problem, not yours. That may not make sense to you, but that was the Internal Revenue Service rule as this book went to press.

The box *Complying with the Rules* on page 69 explains your general obligations as an employer as best as they could be determined as we were writing this book. But Congress was considering significant revisions to the Social Security law in the summer of 1994. And remember: If your tax situation is complicated or you don't understand our explanations, you need to consult a professional tax adviser.

There are lots of twists and turns and exceptions in the tax code. Congress regularly tinkers with the law. And some states and localities impose stricter employment regulations than the federal government. If you employ certain relatives, for instance, your federal tax obligations are different than if your caregiver is not related to you. Read the tax forms and instructions carefully. Some parents avoid the paperwork hassle by hiring an accountant.

TIP: You can obtain free federal forms and instructions by calling 800-TAX-FORM (800-829-3676). Particularly useful is IRS Publication 926, *Employment Taxes for Household Employers*.

TAX BREAKS

The good news is that, by doing things legally, you can cut your taxes. Depending on the size of your income and whether you have one or more children, the child-care tax credit can reduce your federal income tax by $480 to $4,800. Some states also offer a credit.

The tax code also allows employers to set up dependent-care flexible spending accounts through which employees can exempt up to $5,000 of their income from federal—and most state—taxes. Check with your personnel department to see if your company has such a plan.

WORK PERMITS

"We've heard you can sponsor a foreign-born nanny until she gets her work permit. How complicated is it?"

Since the process can take years, many immigration lawyers don't recommend that parents do it anymore.

If a caregiver you want to hire is not a U.S. citizen, you are obligated to ascertain that she is legally eligible to be employed. There are several documents that candidates can offer to prove this besides a so-called green card (which no longer is green!). The INS can tell you what documentation you need to see.

> **TIP:** For more information on determining employment eligibility, call the Immigration and Naturalization Service, 800-755-0777, and request the employer handbook or contact one of the 30 INS district offices around the country.

CHILD CARE OUTSIDE YOUR HOME

HERE'S HELP ON:

Family daycare, page 74

The upside/downside of family daycare, page 75

Daycare centers, page 83

The upside/downside of daycare centers, page 84

The separation blues, page 87

A good relationship with the center, page 90

Sick-child care, page 92

Drop-in centers, page 93

Caregiving by relatives, page 95

Preschools, page 99

The school of the 21st century, page 101

If only 3 percent of working families have an in-home caregiver, who cares for the rest of the children? Some are cared for by their parents, who work different shifts or have part-time schedules. Some stay with other relatives, although this is becoming less common. The rest are in daycare centers or in family daycare homes.

Nationally, among children under age 3 in out-of-home care, slightly more are cared for in family daycare homes than in daycare centers. But when it comes to children between ages 3 and 5, far more attend daycare centers or nursery schools than go to family daycare homes.*

Although the trend is toward center-based care, the majority of parents of infants and toddlers still prefer some kind of home-based care, according to Barbara Reisman, executive director of the Child Care Action Campaign, a New York–based advocacy

---

* *"National Child Care Survey, 1990."*

group. The rising costs of an in-home caregiver, plus the inability to monitor what goes on when parents aren't around, are two reasons why more parents don't hire one, Reisman says. Thus, many families turn to family daycare.

Center-based care is not an option for many parents with babies because it is either too expensive or not available at all. Many centers don't take infants. If they do, the centers charge more because infant care is more labor intensive than care for older children. Centers that do take infants usually have few slots, so there are long waiting lists.

It's common for a family to start an infant with a family daycare provider, then switch to a daycare center when the child is older to take advantage of the broader range of experiences centers usually offer.

Family Daycare

Parents have always used what today is called family daycare. Children were left with other mothers in the neighborhood or a nice grandmother up the street. Today's family daycare providers often are mothers who quit their jobs because they couldn't find satisfactory child care for their own children and still want to earn an income. Others have children who have left the nest, and child care is the profession for which they have the most experience.

Where such homes are regulated, they typically are limited to six children (including the caregiver's own preschoolers), with generally no more than two children under 2 years old. Sometimes the provider will hire assistants so she can care for more children, usually seven to fourteen. Such homes are called large family daycare homes or group homes.

LICENSED OR NOT?

"Our friends have a wonderful family daycare provider in our neighborhood, but we don't think she's licensed. Should we consider using her anyway?"

This is a dilemma for many parents. First, not all providers have to be licensed. And even in states where a license is required, the vast majority of family daycare providers operate without one. Some estimates run as high as 90 percent. Finding a licensed or

THE UPSIDE/DOWNSIDE OF FAMILY DAYCARE

The Upside

❑ Usually it's the least expensive, although sometimes the cost is comparable to daycare centers.
❑ Your child may be happier in a homelike atmosphere than in a daycare center.
❑ Many providers have flexible hours that might better fit your schedule. Some will even keep children overnight when parents travel on business.
❑ Some family providers will take children when they are slightly ill.

The Downside

❑ Usually the caregiver has little or no formal training in child development and may not provide the kind of stimulation your child needs as she gets older.
❑ Turnover can be high. Providers sometimes go out of business after their own children start school, or move away if their husbands are transferred.
❑ Some family daycare homes close for the summer.
❑ With several children in the home, your child may not get as much attention as you'd like.

registered provider may be difficult in your community.

A study on family daycare licensing published by the Children's Foundation, a Washington, D.C.–based education, research, and advocacy organization, found that eighteen states require licensing.* The rest use various forms of voluntary registration or self-certification, or they don't regulate at all. With licensing, states typically set minimum standards and inspect the homes. States that require only registration usually let the caregiver do a self-study to determine if she is meeting the standards. Often inspections are not made unless complaints are lodged.

State standards vary dramatically and do not insure a quality program. For example, the Children's Foundation reports thirty-two states have a 1-to-2 or 1-to-3 ratio of providers to children younger than 2. But several allow six infants per caregiver and one, Idaho, allows twelve!†

Regardless of the regulations, you should thoroughly investigate the family daycare home you are

---

* "1993 Family Day Care Licensing Study," May 1993.
† Ibid

considering and continue monitoring it if you send your child there.

Typical Licensing Standards

Although licensing requirements for family daycare providers vary radically from state to state, these are the typical areas of regulation:

- ❑ staff-to-child ratio
- ❑ provider training in such areas as child development and first aid
- ❑ provider qualifications, such as passing a health exam, tuberculosis screening, and background check
- ❑ immunizations for the children
- ❑ fire safety
- ❑ liability insurance
- ❑ parental rights to pay unannounced visits
- ❑ whether or when smoking is allowed in the home
- ❑ discipline procedures, such as whether corporal punishment is permitted
- ❑ washing hands after diapering and before food handling
- ❑ safety of playground equipment and surfaces

If you are considering a provider who's new to the business, she might not know whether the state requires licensing. You might offer to help her with the licensing procedures. The benefits to her, aside from staying within the law, are that she can be listed with local resource and referral agencies and can take advantage of special training programs they offer.

But don't be surprised if a provider who cares for one or two children prefers to ignore the law rather than get involved with government red tape. She knows she'll have customers whether she's licensed or not.

RESOURCES AND REFERRAL AGENCIES

"We've just moved to this town. How do we find out about the family daycare providers in our area?"

Many people hear of providers through friends, colleagues, and neighbors. A more systematic approach is to contact one of the more than 500 resource and referral agencies across the country that can supply the names of licensed family daycare providers and daycare centers in their communities. Funded by a combination of government funds, grants, and employer contributions, the agencies also have listings of preschools, summer camps, and after-school-care programs.

Nearly half the states have statewide agencies as well. The typical agency charges a small fee (some are free) and will provide computer printouts of providers by zip code. Agencies have counselors who can answer questions and provide printed materials such as checklists to be used when you evaluate a provider.

Agency data bases contain listings only for providers who meet their state's regulatory requirements, but the staffs don't evaluate or endorse individual providers. It's up to you to judge the quality of the program.

> **TIP:** To get the number of your local agency, call Child Care Aware at 800-424-2246. They'll answer questions and send you a checklist.

EMPLOYER ASSISTANCE

Don't overlook your employer as a possible source of help. Some hire firms to provide child-care consulting, helpful booklets, and other resources to their employees. Others contract with an agency that will help you in your child-care search by, for instance, making initial contact with a few providers for you.

A few employers have on-site child care, and others have slots reserved for their employees' children with nearby providers. Although rare, some companies even have provisions for emergency and sick-child care and offer child-care subsidies. Check with your personnel office to see what, if anything, is available through your company (*see also* Employer-Subsidized Sick-Child Care *on page 95*).

FINDING A PROVIDER YOU LIKE

"I've got a printout with a dozen names of providers in my area. How do I pick the right one?"

First screen them by phone, preferably in the evening, when the provider is not busy caring for children. At that point, you're checking basics, such as whether she has an opening for your child, how many children she cares for, hours, costs, and how long she's been a provider. You may be able to get the names of other parents to talk to, or she may want to have you visit first. Either way, be sure to check references at some point.

WHY TWO FAMILIES CHOSE FAMILY DAYCARE

Judy David

Coauthor with Ellen Galinsky of *The Preschool Years*, Judy David chose family daycare when her son was born. "I did not want group care for Andrew when he was very young," she told us. "I wanted a home environment. I wanted him not to have to have a schedule."

She eliminated the idea of hiring a nanny because she had studied early peer relationships and thought Andrew, an only child, would benefit from being with other children. With a doctorate in education from Harvard, she is more qualified than most parents to judge the quality of a family daycare home.

A real estate agent in her church led David to a highly recommended family daycare provider. When David took her son to visit the woman's home, Andrew was fussy. "She calmed him by laying him on the couch and showing him the colors in a quilt draped over the back," says David, whose instincts told her this was a warm and loving caregiver. But David checked many other aspects of the home before deciding.

The adult-to-child ratio was good. The woman cared for only one other infant and two older children. Her own kids were in school. Because her husband worked a night shift, he sometimes helped out during part of the day. There was a crib for each baby, high chairs, plenty of toys, and a backyard with play equipment.

"I also watched her with the older children, because I thought Andrew might still be there when he was a toddler," David explains. "Some people are loving with infants but might not be as sensitive with toddlers when they get into battles of autonomy.

"I spent time with her and transitioned Andrew in slowly. I left him for only a couple of hours initially."

When David finally dropped Andrew off for his first full day and drove from her New Jersey neighborhood to her job in New York City, she recalls that, even though she was comfortable with her provider, "I cried and cried." When she got to the office, David called her caregiver, who was very reassuring. Good ones not only help kids adjust to daycare, but also help the parents.

The Marcanos

Frances and Ray Marcano picked family daycare because the provider's flexibility accommodated Ray's changing work schedule as an editor at a Midwestern newspaper.

When she learned she was having twins, Frances started looking at daycare centers but found the cost for two infants was prohibitive. A neighbor recommended a woman with grown children who "is very motherly," Frances says. "We've been really lucky." The provider cares for several children, but not on the same day; some of her clients are nurses who work only one or two days a week. On days when Ray worked 2 to 11 P.M., he cared for the twins part of the day, and Frances picked them up when she left her secretarial job at 5 P.M.

Eventually the Marcanos decided their daughters needed more structured activity. The twins, now 4, go to a morning preschool that transports them to the family daycare provider's house at midday. The Marcanos now have a 2-year-old son at the daycare home, too.

Initial Visit

After you narrow the list of possibilities, visit the homes. But don't take your child to visit until you find one you like. On the initial visit, just observe. If you think this is the place, schedule time later when the children are napping or in the evening so you can interview the caregiver at length.

You should observe how she relates to the children (and whether they are enjoying themselves), her activity plans, meals, snacks, safety, cleanliness of the house, and the adequacy of equipment, toys, and books. Check the outdoor play space or, if there isn't one, find out if she takes the children to a park.

Ask if the caregiver is licensed. She might even be accredited through a program run by the National Association for Family Child Care, an organization of early-childhood professionals. To earn this accreditation, the caregiver must have completed a self-study, been inspected by the association, and been found to meet its standards of quality (see Licensed or Not? on page 74).

Pay attention to your instincts in making your decision. Do not choose a caregiver who sets restrictions on when you can come and see your child, and don't settle for a provider about whom you are even slightly uneasy. Hard as it is, it's better to keep searching.

When you do decide, get a written agreement so obligations on both sides are spelled out. Continue to monitor the program's quality once your child is enrolled by making periodic visits and having occasional talks with the caregiver about your child's development.

> **TIP:** An excellent, in-depth guide for evaluating this and other forms of child care is *The Complete Guide to Choosing Child Care*, by Judith Berezin for the National Association of Child Care Resource and Referral Agencies (Random House, 1990). To order, send $14.95 to NACCRRA at 1319 F Street NW, Washington, DC 20004.

Before leaving your child, give the caregiver the phone numbers of friends or relatives to call in case you can't be reached in an emergency. Make sure she has medical information, such as any allergies your child has, and a signed consent-to-treat form to ensure an emergency room will treat your child if you can't be contacted immediately. If the caregiver doesn't have the form for you to sign, you can request one from your doctor or send a postcard to McNeil

FAMILY DAYCARE CHECKLIST

If you plan to visit several family daycare providers, it may be helpful to bring along a checklist of important information such as the following:

Basic Information

☐ Program licensed
☐ Hours acceptable
☐ Fees affordable

General Atmosphere

☐ Home safe and well maintained
☐ Setting cheerful
☐ Toys safe and appropriate
☐ Good light and ventilation
☐ Smoke detectors, fire extinguishers
☐ Medicines/household products locked away

The Program

☐ Provides varied and age-appropriate activities
☐ Allows time each day for children to play outdoors

Caregivers

☐ Seem to enjoy children
☐ Respond quickly to children's needs
☐ Play with children
☐ Gentle in handling children

Parent Involvement

☐ Are welcome to spend time in the home
☐ Meet with caregiver on a regular basis

Reprinted with permission from The Complete Guide to Choosing Child Care, *by Judith Berezin for the National Association of Child Care Resource and Referral Agencies.*

EMERGENCY CONTACTS

Use this form to provide emergency contacts to your family daycare provider. (This should be used in addition to the consent-to-treat form mentioned on page 80.)

Child's name: _____

Address: _____

Home phone: _____

Father's name: _____

Daytime phone: _____

Mother's name: _____

Daytime phone: _____

Relative or friend to contact in case parents can't be reached (you may want to list more than one):

Name: _____

Relationship: _____

Phone: Day _____ Night _____

Name: _____

Relationship: _____

Phone: Day _____ Night _____

Child's pediatrician: _____

Phone: _____

Child's specialists (if child sees an allergist, for example, or you use a particular plastic surgeon in the event of facial cuts):

Doctor's name and specialty: _____

Phone: _____

Doctor's name and specialty: _____

Phone: _____

Preferred hospital: _____

Address: _____

Medical history of child (list any conditions or allergies the caregiver and treating physicians should be aware of):

_____

_____

_____

Special notes (offer caregiver any information you think is appropriate, such as child's fears, disabilities, etc.): ___

_____

_____

Consumer Products Co., 7050 Camp Hill Road, Fort Washington, PA 19034.

Daycare Centers

Between 1976 and 1990, the number of child-care centers in the United States tripled and the number of children cared for in these programs quadrupled.* Centers that serve 3- to 5-year-old children are the most common, although a growing number are adding infant and toddler slots. Good centers not only provide basic care and opportunities for children to socialize but also have age-appropriate educational activities.

CHOOSING A CENTER THAT SUITS YOU

A check of the *Yellow Pages* or a call to your local child-care resource and referral agency (*see* Resources and Referral Agencies *on page 76*) should give you the names of centers near your home or work. Also check with your employer to see if it has special

---

* *Barbara Willer,* The Demand and Supply of Child Care in 1990, *National Association for the Education of Young Children, 1991.*

arrangements with a center, such as reserved spots for employees.

Factors to Consider

Some parents prefer a center close to work so they can drop in during the day to see their children. Others like one close to home so their children don't have to make a long commute, especially if the parents use public transportation.

Call the centers to eliminate those that have hours incompatible with your schedule or that don't have an opening for a child the age of yours. Other factors that might eliminate a center are the cost, the staff-to-child ratio, or the lack of an open-door policy. If a center won't let you drop in to see your child at any time, cross it off the list.

Evaluating Centers

"We have to budget our time because we're missing work to check out centers. What's a reasonable amount of time to spend in a center in order to get a good picture of its operation?"

Barbara Reisman of the Child Care Action Campaign tells of an old saw in the child-care business that the three questions parents ask are: "What are

THE UPSIDE/DOWNSIDE OF DAYCARE CENTERS

The Upside

❑ The teaching staff usually is trained in child development.

❑ There's a wider range of activities and toys than in home care. Usually there is a playground, too.

❑ Centers tend to stay in business longer than in-home or family providers, so you don't have to search for new caregivers so often.

❑ Centers don't call in sick. If caregivers are off, the centers find substitutes.

❑ Children get to be with a variety of children and adults.

❑ Most centers are regulated by state or local governments so they meet at least minimum standards.

The Downside

❑ The hours may not fit with your work schedule.

❑ Infant and toddler care is expensive. Some centers charge $800 a month for infants.

❑ Most are strict about not taking children who are sick. (A rare few have set up separate areas to care for mildly ill children.)

❑ There's a set time for naps, meals, and outdoor play; your child may have trouble conforming to the schedule.

❑ There is less individual attention than in a setting where the caregiver has only one or two children to care for.

❑ In some communities, especially in rural areas, lack of transportation can be a barrier.

your hours? What do you charge? Can I bring my child on Monday?"

Some parents spend more time choosing a car than choosing a daycare center, adds Suja Ali of the Child Care Connection, a resource and referral agency in Montgomery County, Maryland. Her organization conducted a survey of child-care providers—both family daycare and daycare centers—that reported 75 percent of parents spent less than an hour observing a program before enrolling their children. More than 11 percent of parents signed up their kids without visiting the program first.

The survey results led the Child Care Connection to develop a course to teach parents how to evaluate child-care programs.

"You have to look at what's going on in a center," Reisman says. "You've got to stick around a while, and you've got to go back after your child is enrolled—all of which is not easy because you're doing this so you can work."

Two Trips Recommended

Experts suggest making at least two trips to a center and observing for several hours before deciding to send your child there. Schedule the first visit and go unannounced after that. Spend time discussing the program with the director and visit more than one class, not just the one your child will be in, so you can see what the program will be like when your child is older.

Kim Boltenhouse was familiar with her small town's leading daycare center because a friend had been the director and she had filled in for two weeks when the staff was shorthanded. She thought it would be a good place for her son when he was old enough to go, at age 2. But by that time, the center had a new director.

"I went to check the place out, and it was totally changed," Boltenhouse says. She visited three different times. In the morning, things were very chaotic, with children wandering between the first and second floor without the caregivers knowing exactly where they were. She went back at lunchtime, which seemed fine. But when she went back at 3 P.M., the lunch plates were still on the table and kids were occasionally returning to eat the leftovers. Boltenhouse doesn't think she'd have had as clear a picture of the operation if she'd visited during only one part of the day.

What to Look for When You Visit

"I'm no child-care expert, so I'm not sure of all the things I should be looking for. The center may look good on the surface, but how do I really know if it's good for my child?"

Some of the most important things you should look for are:

- ❑ **Accreditation.** All states require daycare centers to meet minimum licensing standards. But one mark of quality is whether the center is one of the approximately 2,500 accredited by the National Association for the Education of Young Children (NAEYC). As the nation's largest organization of early childhood professionals, it has set the standards many people look to for judging quality child care (*see* Tip *on page 87*).

  Another indicator of quality is whether any of the staff has earned Child Development Associate (CDA) credentials from the Council for Early Childhood Professional Recognition.

- ❑ **A stable, caring staff.** How do the center's workers relate to the children? What is their education level? What is the turnover rate? Does the staff communicate well with parents? What is the child-to-adult ratio and the group size? NAEYC recommends that all groups have at least two caregivers and that group enrollment be no more than six to eight infants, ten to fourteen 2- and 3-year-olds, and sixteen to twenty 4- and 5-year-olds.

- ❑ **Adequate stimulation.** Are activities appropriate for the children's ages? Does the center have a variety of materials and toys? Are infants moved around to experience different parts of their environment, not just kept in their cribs? Is language development encouraged in older children? Is there a mixture of active play, quiet play, and rest time?

- ❑ **A healthy and safe environment.** Is the facility clean and cheerful, and are there separate areas for rest and play? Are there hazards, such as uncovered electrical outlets or stairs without gates? Does the center have fire extinguishers and smoke detectors? Is the playground fenced and the equipment well maintained? Is the playground covered with a soft composite material instead of a hard surface such as asphalt? Do staff members wash their hands after changing diapers and before handling food?

TIP: It helps to take a daycare evaluation checklist with you. To get one, call your local resource and referral agency (*see* Resources and Referral Agencies *on page 76*), phone Child Care Aware (800-424-2246), or send a self-addressed, stamped envelope to NAEYC, 1509 16th Street NW, Washington, DC, 20036, and ask for the booklet on choosing an early-childhood program.

The Separation Blues

"My infant just started daycare, and I'm feeling miserable. I know it's a good facility, but I just hate to leave him there in the morning. How can I cope with this?"

First, understand that your feelings are normal. As you get into the routine and your confidence in the caregiver builds, you will become less anxious. Also, don't be shy about expressing your feelings to the caregiver or calling the center from work during those first few days to reassure yourself that your baby is adapting. Having a caregiver tell you that your child is getting along fine, as you worry needlessly but understandably in the middle of the morning, will make you feel a lot better.

Easing Your Anxiety

It takes a couple of weeks for mothers, especially the mothers of infants, to get over the worst of their anxiety, says Nancy Hey, who has directed daycare centers in Massachusetts and in Washington, D.C. "We're used to mothers in tears and frequent phone calls the first few days. I understand that. I did it myself," says Hay, who left her own daughter with caregivers to go back to work.

Hey advises parents who choose a daycare center to stay with their children in the center for the first couple of mornings—or even the first two days—to get comfortable with the program. She also suggests asking the staff to pair you with a parent whose child has been in the center for a while so you have another parent to turn to with questions.

WHY TWO FAMILIES CHOSE DAYCARE CENTERS

The Strawns

Kathy Strawn never seriously considered a daycare center when her son, Christopher, was born. Her image of daycare was institutional, and the vision she had for her son was of a homey atmosphere and a single person to substitute when Mom and Dad were at work. But after going through three caregivers in the first year, she and her husband decided a quality daycare center had to be better than what they'd had up to that point.

They were lucky. The Strawns found a church-affiliated center with the highly regarded accreditation from the National Association for the Education of Young Children (NAEYC). Although the center had a waiting list, a slot for a 1-year-old opened soon after they applied.

"One of the things I like about it is that it is church-related, and I think that's preferable to for-profit centers; the church gives a greater priority to community service," Strawn says. The church also has a preschool program in the mornings for older children that Christopher, now 3, attends.

The Hodsons

Jan Hodson, a university administrator, placed her 6-month-old daughter in the college's child-development center after being on the waiting list for more than a year. It is the only center in her county that will take infants.

Hodson returned to work two months before her daughter entered the center. During the interim, Hodson used two family daycare providers. One was a friend who kept the infant three days a week, and the other lived nearby and took her the other two days.

In hindsight, Hodson thinks this plan was a mistake. "What you should try to create for a very young child is stability," she says. "That can't happen with a different caregiver every day." She also warns that family daycare may not offer your child as much attention as you would like if the caregiver is occupied with her responsibilities to her own family.

Getting into the center was a relief for Jan and her husband, Tom. "I didn't realize how hard it is to find good care," Hodson says. "Now I know how truly blessed we were to get in there." Her daughter, Lauren, was a fussy baby who suffered from colic. "I learned quickly I wasn't a good mother for an infant like that. These people were professionals and they knew what to do with a colicky baby. I learned a lot from them."

Because the center is part of the university's education department, the caregivers have degrees in child development and are assisted by students-in-training. The ratio of children to staff is very good, but that means the costs are higher than at other centers in the area.

Hodson thinks Lauren has benefited from daycare in ways she wouldn't have if she'd been with a single caregiver. "I always thought it was good for Lauren to have other adults she felt comfortable with." Because of her daycare experiences, "she's now the kind of child who's not the least bit shy to try new things." And yes, even though Lauren mostly liked it, "everyone has different moods. There were days she didn't want to go or she didn't want me to leave. I'd get to work and call and they'd say, 'As soon as you left, we got her playing at the water table.' That reassured me so that I could focus on work."

Both the Strawns and the Hodsons found daycare centers preferable to family daycare because of the staffs' expertise and the variety of activities their children were exposed to. They were lucky in finding centers with well-trained, stable staffs and openings for their children. Unfortunately, the demand for such care is often greater than its availability.

Maintaining a Good Relationship with the Daycare Center

"Now that my child's in daycare, I want to feel connected to the staff. But I don't want to interfere or seem too pushy."

Try dropping in for visits or lunch with your children so you can get to know the staff. Volunteering time is another option. Depending on your center's policies, you might be able to:

- work in the center a couple of hours a month, maybe during a long lunch break; jobs can be as simple as reading to children or watching them at nap time so the staff can have meetings
- shop for snacks or check out picture books from the library
- go on field trips
- start a parents' newsletter
- organize an event, such as a barbecue or potluck supper, so staff and families can get to know each other better
- serve on the parent advisory board or board of directors (in some non-profit centers, parents are responsible for hiring the director and setting policy)

Kathy Strawn says she developed a good relationship with the staff at her child's center by helping with parties and decorating for holidays. "Part of my vacation time is allocated for volunteering," Strawn explains.

She also thinks it's important to show the staff you appreciate them. She gives gifts to her child's caregiver at Christmas and when her son leaves one caregiver to move to the next age group each year. She is surprised that more parents don't do this.

Co-op Centers

A few centers are run on a co-op basis, requiring parents to commit some time to the operation. If your work schedule permits, you might choose this kind of center so you are assured of regular opportunities to interact with the staff.

ENSURING GOOD COMMUNICATION

"We'd like more staff feedback on how our daughter is adapting to daycare, but we're usually too

rushed at drop-off and pick-up times to have any meaningful conversation. And the caregiver who's there at 7:30 A.M. isn't the same one we see in the late afternoon. Are there other ways to share information?"

Staff and parents should be partners in ensuring the child will have a positive daycare experience. The key is communication. It takes effort, but it helps build trust. And parents then find it easier to relax, knowing the center is meeting their child's needs.

Finding the Time to Communicate

Try to leave time for at least a brief word with the caregiver morning and evening. The caregiver should be told, for example, that your baby has started teething, or that last night's storm kept your toddler awake. If you really don't have time to chat, at least write a note.

Hiring Staff as Sitters

You might hire staff members for evening and weekend babysitting in your home. We found that some aides in our daughter's nursery school were glad to earn extra money, and they enjoyed the chance to spend one-on-one time with Julie on her home turf. You and the staff member get to know each other better, too.

Improving the Way the Staff Communicates

If you think the caregivers need to improve their part in communication, suggest they try the following:

❏ Give parents daily, written reports—on simple, fill-in-the-blank forms—that tell how much the child ate, how long she napped, and any other bits of information about the child's day. That way, parents are forewarned that their child might not be as hungry as usual at dinner or that a long nap during the day may keep him up later that night.

❏ Hold at least two staff-parent conferences each year to jointly assess the child's development and strategies they ought to be implementing together.

❏ Keep notebooks with morning messages from parents so, if shift changes occur, the information is passed to the afternoon caregiver.

WHAT GOES ON WHEN WE'RE NOT THERE?

"Things seem okay when we visit the center. But I can't help wondering what goes on when we're not there, and our child isn't verbal enough to tell us."

Barbara Reisman suggests "dramatic play," a technique she used when her two children were in daycare. The idea is to get the kids to act out their daycare experiences by suggesting a pretend game in which they play the parts of caregiver or child while you watch for clues about how things are going.

"They'd play 'school,' and I'd watch them, and they'd model what went on at the child-care center," she recalls. Reisman says she realized how accurately the center was portrayed when one of her children mimicked a caregiver who had a characteristic way of walking with her hands in her pockets.

Parent Talk

Sharing experiences with other parents is another way to learn what's going on. You also should watch for any changes in your child's behavior that may signal a problem. If you are worried about any aspect of the center's care, talk to the staff. The issue you raise may be one they were unaware of and could easily solve. If after such a discussion you remain concerned, it might be time to look for a new place for your child.

Sick-Child Care

"I come to work even when I'm sick because I have to save sick leave for when my child is ill. Since our company only allows sick leave for the employee, I have to lie to my boss, which I hate doing, and which I'm sure she suspects. But what alternative do I have?"

Nothing strikes fear in the hearts of working parents like the sound of a hacking cough coming from their child's room early in the morning.

In one survey, 35 percent of employed mothers said one of their children had been sick on a workday in the last month.* More than half the mothers stayed home. Others left the child with the father, a regular caregiver, or a relative.

It's a vicious cycle. Kids in daycare are exposed to illness more often than those kept at home. Yet family daycare providers and daycare centers usually

---

* *"National Child Care Survey 1990."*

DROP-IN DAYCARE CENTERS

Rare is the town that has a daycare center that will take drop-ins. But some are starting to appear, especially in shopping centers, and more are expected to open in the future.

Rick Shaye of Birmingham, Michigan, saw this as a niche market ten years ago and started My Place for Kids, where all the little customers are drop-ins.

"This is total flexibility," Shaye explains. "We want to replace Grandma and the girl next door," who may not be available at short notice. "Or if your babysitter calls and says she's got a date with Dreamy Jimmy, you can bring the kids here instead." Shaye's first center was so successful that he started a second one in nearby Bloomfield Hills.

Open until 10 P.M. weeknights, 8 P.M. Sundays, and 1 A.M. Saturdays, the center serves parents who need to work late or who just want an evening out. Reservations are required only for infants, because Shaye must plan extra staffing for the crib room. If parents will not be reachable by phone, Shaye gives them beepers. Some of his regular clients are the children of Detroit Tigers, who go to My Place instead of accompanying their moms to the baseball team's games.

The center offers activities for different age levels in separate areas: elaborate climbing equipment, blocks, arts and crafts, computer games, and movies. "The kids also enjoy the constantly changing group dynamics" as one child gets picked up and another arrives, Shaye says.

Drop-in daycare typically costs $4 an hour, slightly more for babies. Discounts sometimes are offered for siblings. To find out if there are drop-in centers near you, check the *Yellow Pages* listing for "child-care centers" or call your local resource and referral network (*see* Resources and Referral Agencies *on page 76*).

won't take kids when they are obviously sick.

A few centers have created sick rooms where they can care for mildly ill children. Some doctors think this makes sense because the children remain in familiar surroundings and because, by the time symptoms appear, other kids already have been exposed to the illness. But this setup requires extra space and staff that many centers can't afford. Most simply give you a list of ailments—sometimes dictated by state regulation—and if your child gets one, she can't come.

Working parents say this is one of their biggest headaches. If a child wakes up with a runny nose, you scramble to find alternative care or decide which parent will stay home. Especially frustrating are times when the child feels fine but is considered contagious. After the actual outbreak of chicken pox, for example, kids usually feel okay. But they can't go back to daycare or school until all the blisters have crusted over.

In an ideal world, employers would grant parents paid sick leave to care for their ill children. Since most don't, parents must fend for themselves. Some couples split the day in half so the child gets parental care and both parents spend some time at work. More often, it's the mother who stays home the full day.

If you can't stay home, you need to have back-up plans so you don't have to scramble for last-minute care and so your child knows what to expect. If you're anxious about the temporary care, the child will detect that and get anxious, too. Some parents arrange to call on relatives or neighborhood friends in an emergency (*see* A Neighborhood Emergency Network *on page 106*).

SHORT-NOTICE CARE FOR HIRE

A more impersonal—and costly—approach is to call a local home nursing service that can provide short-notice care for a sick child in your home. Some services are available to the general public; others are only for employees of companies that have contracted for the service. This plan may be the least appealing for your child because the caregiver is likely to be a stranger.

SICK-CHILD CENTERS

An alternative for mildly ill children is provided by sick-child centers, which are becoming more common, especially in hospitals (*see* An In-Hospital Sick-Child Center *on page 96*).

Using a sick-child center typically costs $4 to $6

an hour. Home nursing runs $10 an hour and up, depending on where you live. To find care near you, try calling local hospitals or the nearest child-care resource and referral agency.

EMPLOYER-SUBSIDIZED SICK-CHILD CARE

A few large employers subsidize sick-child care—either in sick-child centers or by home nursing services. Not only is it a nice employee benefit but it also saves companies money in the long run in reduced absenteeism and productivity loss.

Honeywell in Minneapolis, for example, subsidizes 80 percent of the cost of sick-child care—either in one of two sick-child centers or from a home health service—and also offers paid leave for a parent to care for a sick child.

In 1989, several large New York City companies—including Colgate-Palmolive, Time Warner, Home Box Office, and Consolidated Edison—joined together to give their employees access to home-based child care on short notice for illnesses, snow days, and so forth. Some of the firms pay the full cost, others a portion. The city's child-care resource and referral agency coordinates the service.

Parents with access to subsidized sick-child care have mixed reactions to it. Some appreciate and use it. Others feel it coerces them into working when they'd rather be able to use sick leave to stay home and care for their children themselves.

Caregiving by Relatives

"My mother-in-law has offered to take care of our baby when I go back to work. I know she'll love him and take good care of him, but I'm afraid she'll want to do things her way instead of our way, which could cause conflicts."

Having grandparents or other family members living close enough to help with child care is an option for fewer and fewer people in our increasingly mobile society. Couples who delay childbearing may also find their babies' grandparents are no longer physically capable of taking care of an infant or toddler. Or they may have just retired and have plans of their own that don't include full-time child care.

If you're lucky enough to find that your parents or other relatives are willing to help out, you can go to work knowing your child is in the hands of someone

AN IN-HOSPITAL SICK-CHILD CENTER

Mend 'n Tend at Miami Valley Hospital in Dayton, Ohio, takes children 6 weeks to 12 years old with temporary illnesses. Parents pre-register their children and can tour the center with them in advance. Then, when the child gets sick, the parents call to see if space is available. If it's not, the staff will refer them to a nursing service that will care for the sick child at home.

The supervisor is a nurse who can decide if a child needs to be isolated. A doctor is available to check on a child's condition if the staff requests it.

Stephanie Hamilton, a staff member, says a lot of kids actually enjoy the change from their normal daycare routine. "The more often they come, the more comfortable they feel," Hamilton says. "Instead of being home and bored out of their minds, we give them Popsicles and Disney videos. There are toys and other kids to play with, too."

Mend 'n Tend has its own entrance, so children aren't frightened about going to a hospital. The staffers wear street clothes, not medical uniforms. They don't give shots, but they can administer prescribed medications and take temperatures.

Hamilton says parents usually know if a child is too sick to be cared for outside the home. Minor illnesses—such as a low-grade fever or one bout of diarrhea—can keep a child out of daycare but not necessitate staying at home. Those are the times parents feel comfortable using Mend 'n Tend. The staff encourages parents to call to check on their children's condition. Parents can chat with their children on the phone or drop in at lunch or any other time during the day. "Kids like it here," Hamilton says, "and that makes parents feel better."

who loves him and who most likely shares your values. But as with any other caregiver, open and honest communication is needed to keep inevitable conflicts to a minimum.

TWO GRANDMOTHERS TO SHARE THE CAREGIVING

Brenda and Dick Coyne of Munhall, Pennsylvania, feel blessed that both of their mothers wanted to care for their son, Billy, although the Coynes had never thought to suggest it initially. A friend of theirs ran a daycare center, and that had been the couple's original child-care plan. But a few days after Billy was born, Dick's father died. Another family member suggested that to ease her loneliness, Dick's mother might want to babysit her new grandson.

"She'd had ten kids of her own, and I thought this would be the last thing she'd want to do," Brenda recalls. On the contrary, her mother-in-law was thrilled to do it, and Brenda's widowed mother offered, too. At the end of her eight-week maternity leave, Brenda went back to work as a transcriptionist at a local hospital. She works four days a week and every other Saturday. The grandmothers each take Billy two days a week. Dick has charge of Billy on the alternate Saturdays.

"I wouldn't want either of them to do it full time," Brenda says, because caring for an infant or toddler is so exhausting. Both women are in their 60s and have personal interests they want to pursue. Brenda thinks Billy is the winner because "they teach him more than I could. They have more experience."

The grown-ups all get along well, too, although Dick is amused that the grandmothers let Billy get away with things they never allowed their own children to do. Now, at age 5, Billy goes to preschool two mornings a week, so the amount of time the grandmothers babysit gradually has declined.

POTENTIAL PROBLEMS WITH RELATIVES

Spoiling became a big issue for Kim Boltenhouse, whose 4-year-old son has been cared for by her mother-in-law since he was 8 weeks old. Although she has a good relationship with her husband's parents, she wishes "they'd be more open to my suggestions. They think they should be able to spoil him. When he comes home from their house, it's an hour and a half before he learns to go by my rules. Lots of times I've had to sit down and talk about these things, and sometimes they still won't listen."

Jealousy

Boltenhouse also thinks that she was jealous of her mother-in-law at first, which may have strained their relationship. "She got to see all the things the baby was doing, and I didn't."

She admits she'd rather be home with her children, but the family can't make it on her husband's salary as a city maintenance worker. If she must leave her children with someone else, she'd rather it be family members. Her infant daughter is being cared for by her sister-in-law. Her son now goes to a YMCA preschool from 8:30 A.M. to 4:30 P.M. and spends late afternoons at his grandparents' home.

Family Differences

The distance between your home and the grandparents' doesn't necessarily preclude their babysitting. Angela Mickalide's in-laws moved in with her to care for her daughter, Anna. The tricky part is that the grandparents are from Iran and speak only Farsi. The language barrier is not as big a challenge for the family as the cultural differences and lack of privacy caused by living with relatives. But

the pros far outweigh any cons in Mickalide's mind.

"It's difficult to express how confident I feel with relatives raising my child," says Mickalide. "Anna is being exposed to her cultural heritage, one that is very child-centered."

She recalls one difficult three-week period when her in-laws had to attend to family business in Iran and her own parents were unavailable. She and her husband took Anna to a family daycare provider who came highly recommended and who seemed to be very good with their baby. But they couldn't get over the insecurity of having a stranger caring for Anna. They also hated getting the baby up early, commuting to the sitter's house, and hauling an assortment of baby equipment each day.

Mickalide says the key to living with relatives is compromise. (That, and having a roomy house: Theirs in suburban Maryland has four bedrooms and three baths.)

"You have to decide what you can let go of," says Mickalide, an admitted control freak. One thing she let go of was her kitchen, which she finally let her mother-in-law organize in her own way. She's laid down only a few rules regarding child care. For example, she requires that Anna always be kept in her car seat on trips, even though her mother-in-law is tempted to take the child out to comfort her when she's fussy.

"Mostly it's a matter of artful negotiation," Mickalide explains. "If you're not willing to negotiate, this arrangement won't work."

SHOULD YOU PAY RELATIVES?

Should you pay a family member for babysitting? Kim Boltenhouse does, because her mother-in-law gave up a paying job to babysit her grandson. Paying your relative may make you more comfortable because you don't feel you're imposing.

If money isn't changing hands, you can offer services instead—not as a quid pro quo, but to show your gratitude. A grandparent might appreciate having help with yard work or home repairs, for instance. If the relative, such as a sister, has children, too, you can offer to babysit for her some nights and weekends.

Preschools

Most daycare centers serve the function of a preschool. But parents with other child-care

TIPS FOR RELATIVES AS CAREGIVERS

❑ Set clear ground rules for the child-care issues that are the most important to you, then give the relative freedom to use her own judgment and experience beyond that.

❑ Communicate regularly about how you both feel the arrangement is going. Don't be reluctant to express your opinions, even if it's to your parent.

❑ Be prepared to compromise and negotiate.

❑ Take into account the physical strain child care may place on older relatives; limit their hours accordingly.

❑ Show your appreciation for the valuable service the relative is providing.

arrangements sometimes want to use a half-day preschool when their children get older. By the time a child is 3 or 4, his imagination and curiosity demand a broad range of activities that usually aren't provided by an in-home caregiver or a family daycare home. He also can benefit from socializing with more children his age. Using a half-day preschool appeals to parents who don't want their child in a formally structured preschool program all day long.

Transportation can be a barrier to this option. You have to find a way to get your child between the preschool and your home or the daycare home. Some nannies, au pairs, or family daycare providers will be able to take your child; sometimes preschools will provide transportation. If these are not available for you, you can try to arrange a car pool with parents who are home during the day.

Evaluating Preschools

Many of the criteria we talked about in choosing a daycare center—such as staff qualifications, a safe and cheerful physical environment, and staff-child ratios—apply to preschool selection, too.

You'll want to look carefully at the activities offered, the classroom layout, and the teaching style. Classrooms should have separate areas devoted to such activities as science and math games, art supplies, blocks, books, music tapes, and puzzles.

Kids should be allowed to choose activities. They should be able to work alone or in groups to experiment and solve problems, with teachers facilitating the children's opportunities to find their own ways of doing things.

Early childhood experts caution parents about preschool programs that emphasize "academics" by using work sheets and rote memorization, or that introduce reading and math concepts too early or in ways that are inappropriate for the age group. The experts worry that elementary school curricula will be applied to children who are too young. When children are forced to read before they are ready, for example, they can come to think of it as drudgery rather than something they really want to do.

Public School–Sponsored Preschools

Public schools are becoming key players in preschool programs. A growing number offer programs that operate half a day or match the regular school hours, often with after-school care available. In some communities, the classes are intended for low-income children, but more are cropping up in middle-class neighborhoods. Some charge fees, and some are free.

Competition for the available slots can be fierce, especially in free, full-day programs. In our neighborhood, where each elementary school has only one preschool class for 4-year-olds, parents commonly camp out overnight at their local school to be at the front of the line on registration day.

The School of the 21st Century

Child-care expert Edward Zigler, director of the Bush Center in Child Development and Social Policy at Yale University, has developed what he calls "the School of the 21st Century." Zigler believes that the neighborhood school is the ideal facility for various kinds of child-care programs as well as for education of parents and training of family daycare providers. Zigler's idea is catching on fast, with variations of his model being tried in more than 200 schools in fifteen states.

One of the first communities to open a school based on the concept is Leadville, Colorado, one hundred miles south of Denver in the center of rural Lake County (population 5,700). The Center, as it is called, opened in 1988 in a remodeled school building that had been closed because of declining enrollment. Start-up funding came from various state and local government sources, a small amount of private money, and sliding-scale tuition.

Under the auspices of the local school district, the Center originally served children who were at least 2 1/2 years old. In 1991, it expanded to include infants and toddlers.

The daycare program dovetails with the half-day preschool program and is open from 5:30 A.M. to 6:30 P.M., 365 days a year. Many of the parents who use the center leave the county each day, traveling over mountain passes to work in ski resorts in other towns. The schedule accommodates these parents, who have long commutes and sometimes work on holidays when the resorts have peak business.

The Center's services have grown to encompass many other child-related programs, such as parent education, teen pregnancy intervention, family counseling, services for children with disabilities, Scouts, and ski lessons. It has served as a model for other communities, especially because it has managed to operate without subsidy from property taxes. In Zigler's model, the schools are designed to be self-supporting.

Other communities are opening such schools with fewer components of Zigler's model—preschool but not daycare for younger children, for example. Each school district's approach must fit its own community's needs and resources, and the model allows for that. These programs often get started through parental pressure on—and cooperation with—school and community officials. The Bush Center offers technical assistance.

> **TIP:** To find out more about how to initiate a School of the 21st Century in your community, write to the Bush Center in Child Development and Social Policy, Yale University, 310 Prospect Street, New Haven, CT 06511-2188.

YOUR SCHOOL-AGE CHILD

The day your child starts school, your daycare needs take a turn for the better—and for the worse. Schools keep kids approximately six hours a day (less for half-day kindergarten). If you use a public school, you eliminate the need for costly child care for a substantial block of time each week. But you now have a need for a few hours of supplemental care that may be hard to find.

The typical school day may be 9 A.M. to 3 P.M. But that's not a typical workday, which is more likely to be 8:30 A.M. to 5 P.M., with commuting time tacked on to each end. So you have to arrange child care before and after school and possibly transportation as well. Add the days when schools are closed for teachers' meetings, holidays, snow storms, and summer vacation—and the inevitable times when your child gets sick—and you'll discover a whole new meaning for the word "patchwork."

Most child-care experts rank school-age care right

HERE'S HELP ON:

Your options for school-age programs, page 104

Getting kids from here to there, page 107

Setting up a new program, page 109

Summer care, page 112

Year-round school, page 116

Home alone after school, page 118

up there with infant care as the hardest kinds to find.

Some parents rely on an in-home caregiver, particularly if they also have a younger child who has not started school yet. But if there are no preschoolers at home, it can be difficult to find someone to work the few hours you need care before and after school. And many parents are reluctant to employ full-time help to fill what is a part-time need. This is when some families decide to have a live-in au pair or a college student, who will trade a few hours of morning and afternoon child care for room and board.

If you have jobs that allow flexible schedules, you may be able to arrange for one of you to start work after the children leave for school while the other works an early shift and gets home before the kids do.

Some families work out deals with neighborhood parents who are home and willing to keep extra kids before and after school—perhaps in exchange for reciprocal care at other times. Others use nearby family daycare providers or one of the few daycare centers that take school-age children. Older kids often care for themselves at home when they aren't in school.

Family daycare may lose its appeal for older children if the provider also cares for very young children and if there aren't enough activities for the school-age group. A growing number of parents are choosing before- and after-school (sometimes called extended-day) programs at their school or in a local YMCA, YWCA, recreation center, church, or synagogue. Some in-school programs are set up by parents. Others are run in the schools by outside groups, such as a youth service organization or a for-profit daycare center.

Your Options for School-Age Programs

"We are fortunate to have a choice of after-school programs in our community. How do we judge which is best for our daughter?"

From the standpoint of convenience for you and your child, a program right in her school, if it's available, could be your best option.

IN-SCHOOL PROGRAMS

"The whole country is moving more toward programs in the schools," says Rhea Starr, director of association and network services for the YWCA. "Everybody is realizing that it's a waste of resources to close a school at 3:15."

Having care at school means children have an easier time participating in extracurricular activities such as soccer practice or Scout meetings. And parents don't have to worry about transportation. Sometimes, however, kids aren't kept at their home school if one building houses extended-day programs for several schools in the area.

One drawback of programs in school buildings, as opposed to those run by outside entities, is that the building may be closed during school holidays, teacher training days, or snow days. This compounds the number of times you have to scramble for emergency care. Then you're left to find a relative, neighbor, a friend's nanny, or an emergency child-care service to cover while you're at work. (*See* A Neighborhood Emergency Network *on page 106; also see* Sick-Child Care *on page 92.*) Some parents even take their kids to work with them, but not many have this option, even in an emergency; they're more likely to take a personal or vacation day and stay home with their children if they've got no backup.

The best advice we can offer is to plan ahead. It's easier to do this when there is advance notice, such as with a school holiday. But don't wait until the radio reports school is closed for snow or a water main break or a power failure to identify your options. The same holds true for days when your child is sick.

The best programs offer not only supervised child care but also enrichment opportunities. But experts advise against programs that require children to follow rigid schedules of activities. If kids have already spent several hours at school, they need time to unwind and have some choice in how they will amuse themselves.

YWCA AND YMCA PROGRAMS

Rhea Starr says YWCA school-age programs typically offer a quiet place for homework as well as activities for children to select. "We try to provide opportunities for children to do the things parents would like to them to do if the parents were home, such as attend swimming lessons or dance classes," she says. But formal activities aren't imposed on the children. "Sometimes they just need time to sit and talk," Starr explains.

Another group with many years of experience in

A NEIGHBORHOOD EMERGENCY NETWORK

In close communities with many stay-at-home parents, getting neighbors to help out in an emergency may be as simple as making a phone call. But, when all the neighborhood parents are working, you need to prepare in advance.

In a working parents' child-care network, each participating family chooses one day to be responsible for emergency care. Part-time workers might find this more doable than those who work every day. But full-timers may be willing to pay for help or to call upon relatives to fill in for them when they're on duty.

Be sure that every parent has each other's at-home and at-work phone numbers and that all schools and after-school programs have each participant in the network listed as an approved pick-up person.

school-age care is the YMCA. Ken Vogt, associate director of program services, says 65 to 75 percent of the association's 2,200 sites have child-care programs, mostly for school-age children.

"We were doing school-age care years before we knew it," Vogt says. "We had game rooms where parents dropped kids off. Or kids would come two or three times a week for gym class or swimming lessons and stay around afterward. But they weren't creatively involved. They were just hanging out, and that caused behavior problems." Once the need for organized after-school care became apparent, the Y took elements of what it already offered and packaged them into a comprehensive program.

Each YMCA has the freedom to tailor its program to the local community. The typical YMCA program is organized much like a school, with homerooms and specialized classes. Like-aged children are assigned to a home group with a staff person they can relate to. Students can choose from several activities, such as sports or crafts. There is time for homework, and sometimes there is tutoring by volunteers. There is "circle time" when the children sit and talk with their home group. "Sometimes they talk about values issues, such as drugs or peer influence," Vogt says.

CHOOSING THE RIGHT PROGRAM FOR YOUR CHILD

Your child probably would prefer an after-school program attended by some of her friends. You'll need to find out costs and hours of operation. Some programs offer both before- and after-school care, but others operate only in the afternoon. Some have part-time options, so you don't have to enroll five days a week if your child has one afternoon occupied with music lessons or a sport.

> **TIP:** Most child-care resource and referral agencies have listings for school-age programs and summer camps. You can get the phone number for your local agency by calling Child Care Aware at 800-424-2246. You also should check with your employer. A few businesses subsidize child care for their employees, and some reserve slots with school-age care providers (*see* Employer Assistance *on page 77*).

When choosing among school-age programs, you'll use many of the same criteria you used if you selected a daycare center or preschool when your child was younger (*see* Evaluating Centers *on page 83, and* Evaluating Preschools *on page 100*). This time you should involve your child in the decision-making so he'll be happier with the final choice.

> **TIP:** For a booklet on how to evaluate school-age programs, write the National Association of Elementary School Principals, 1615 Duke Street, Alexandria, VA 22314. Enclose a check for $3 and ask for *The Right Place at the Right Time*.

Getting Kids from Here to There

"Finding an after-school program wasn't as hard as finding transportation to get my child there. How have other parents solved this?"

Transportation will be a key factor in your selection of school-age care. A family daycare provider may be willing to pick your child up at school. You might be able to pay an older student to walk your child to a family daycare home. Or you could carpool with another parent—you taking her kids to school in the morning in exchange for her taking yours to daycare in the afternoon, for example (*see* Car Pools *on page 196*).

School Buses

If your child rides a school bus, ask if he could be

WHAT TO LOOK FOR IN A SCHOOL-AGE CHILD-CARE PROGRAM

- ❏ Is the facility clean, pleasant, and safe?
- ❏ Are the equipment and materials in good condition? Note especially whether there are books, toys, and sports equipment suitable for your child's age.
- ❏ Is there an outdoor play area and is it well maintained? If there isn't, are children taken to a well-maintained site elsewhere for outdoor activities?
- ❏ Is there a quiet place for children who want to do homework or who want to chat with a few friends?
- ❏ Is this just a babysitting service or are there enrichment activities that your child would enjoy?
- ❏ Do children have the freedom to pick activities, and does the staff ask for their input when planning activities?
- ❏ Are nutritious snacks offered?
- ❏ What are the staff's qualifications? Are they caring people who relate well to school-age children's needs? Do they listen to the children? Do they offer assistance but refrain from dominating the children's activities?
- ❏ What is the staff turnover rate? Consistency of care is important, especially for younger children.

- ❏ What is the age span and how are children grouped? If all ages are mixed together, an older child may become bored. On the other hand, a program that uses both mixed-age and single-age groups for different activities gives older students a chance to serve as role models and develop leadership skills.
- ❏ What is the adult-to-child ratio? The National Association of Elementary School Principals recommends at least one adult per twelve children. You don't want a program with so many children that your child won't receive the individual attention she needs.
- ❏ Has the program obtained all required licenses?
- ❏ Is the program accredited by a state agency or outside group such as the National Association for the Education of Young Children?
- ❏ What do parents who have used the program say about it? They can be the best source of first-hand observations about the program you're considering.

dropped off at his after-school program. A few communities allow this, especially if a number of children are going to the same location.

But many school districts require that buses take children directly to their homes. "Some are easing up on this," the YMCA's Ken Vogt says. "But schools have been slow to realize that families have changed." Getting a school district to change its policies may require another kind of parental pooling—to lobby school board members and administrators.

Program-Provided Transport

Many programs run their own vans to pick kids up after school. You should find out the drivers' qualifications, how well the vehicles are maintained, and whether there is a working seat belt for each child.

Setting Up a New Program

"There is no after-school care in our neighborhood aside from a few family daycare providers. We've been talking to other parents about setting up a program, but we don't know where to start."

There are two ways to go. Parents can establish and run it themselves, or they can get someone else to provide the service.

PARENT-RUN PROGRAMS

With the typical do-it-yourself approach, parents conduct a survey to see how great the need is, then form a board, find a space and hire a director who in turn hires staff. During the planning phase, it's a good idea to visit other parent-run programs to learn what's involved.

Finding Space

This can be the toughest part. Schools that are overcrowded may have trouble accommodating an after-school program if the only available space is in classrooms. Teachers are reluctant to let others take over their rooms after school, for fear they'll cause wear and tear, rearrange things, and fill storage space with their own toys and equipment.

When our daughter's school no longer could accommodate its growing extended-day program, the parents moved it to two churches within a block of the school, putting older kids in one and younger kids in the other. The students still use some school

TRANSPORTATION FOR HIRE

The transportation woes of working parents have spawned a new mini-industry—van services for children. One of the first was started by Pam Henderson of Birmingham, Michigan.

As a single mother with three elementary school children, Henderson found herself constantly driving her children to athletic events and other activities. "I wanted to work, but I also wanted to be there for my kids," she recalls, "and the toughest part to juggle was transportation."

One night, she had to pick up her twins at separate places three miles apart. Rushing between stops, it occurred to her that there ought to be a taxi for children.

The idea led her to create Kids Kab, a company that is spreading franchises to other cities around the country. For an average fare of about $6.50 per ride in a seven- to ten-mile radius, a Kids Kab van will transport a child to after-school care, soccer games, Scouts, home, or anywhere he needs to go. Henderson says it's cheaper and safer than taxis.

Parents charter the service on a monthly or annual basis. Kids are issued photo ID cards. They don't have to carry cash because trips are charged to credit cards.

Though the twelve-passenger, radio-equipped vans can transport children of any age, the kids usually are between ages 4 and 15, Henderson says.

Some parents use the service to get their kids to and from child care every day. Others use it occasionally, such as when they get stuck in the office later than usual.

In Birmingham, Henderson has an arrangement to take children to a drop-in center if the parents can't make it home in time.

facilities, such as the gym and playground.

Our school's extended-day program includes enrichment classes that are offered as after-school activities to the rest of the student body for a fee. That provides a service to the whole school and helps to finance the extended-day program. The two dozen class topics range from karate and ballet to cooking and chess.

Insurance, Licenses, Costs

If you help to establish an after-school program, you'll need to get insurance and fulfill your community's licensing requirements. You'll also need to provide toys, books, and sports equipment. Fees have to be adequate to cover known as well as unanticipated costs. You will want to find out if yours is among the states that offer start-up grants for school-age child-care programs. Some states also help to pay the fees of low-income children.

> **TIP:** To find out about start-up grants, call your state's department of education or human services. The welfare department would be the likely source of aid for low-income children.

Parent Volunteers

Some parent-run programs require a volunteer commitment of a few hours a year from participating families. Tasks might include painting, cleanup, clerical work, driving for field trips, or serving on the parent board.

> **TIP:** For a manual on how to set up a program, write the School-Age Child Care Project, Center for Research on Women, Wellesley College, Wellesley, MA 02181. The 400-page manual, *School-Age Child Care: An Action Manual for the 90's and Beyond*, by Michelle Seligson and Michael Allenson, costs $19.95, plus $3 shipping. Write the center for ordering information and a publications list.

OUTSIDE PROVIDERS

If all of this seems like too much to take on, then look for an outside group that would set up a program for you. Organizations that have put programs in schools include the YMCA, Camp Fire, 4-H, Boys and Girls Clubs, and private daycare providers.

You also can investigate whether a program could be established by another institution in your neighborhood, such as a recreation center, church, or synagogue. Institutions with existing child-care programs are prime spots for establishing school-age care because they already have licenses, child-care staff, and facilities, often including outdoor play space.

Chevy Chase Presbyterian Church's after-school program in Washington, D.C., was created after a popular family daycare provider went out of business. Some church members who were left without child care distributed flyers around the neighborhood to ascertain how many other families might use the service.

The church already had a half-day nursery school, and opening up an after-school program gave it extra rental income and a greater opportunity to reach out to the community, director Tempe Thomas says. "We have a sense of mission. We're providing a place where the children of our community can come and spend a safe afternoon." Because the kids aren't all from the same school, they get to make new friends.

YWCA Assistance

Another source of help is the YWCA. Not all of the country's 4,000 YWCA sites offer care for school-age children. But part of the organization's mission is advocacy. So, even if your YWCA can't set up a program, the staff may be able to help you and other parents form a coalition to get a program going elsewhere.

KINDERCARE

This national child-care chain offers a year-round school-age program called Klubmates in its daycare centers and also runs programs in schools.

And it is establishing programs for school-age children in shopping centers. Older children prefer programs in schools and malls because they think it's "babyish" to be with younger children in daycare centers.

Summer Care

"Our elementary school has an extended-day program during the school year but closes down when classes end in the summer. All of a sudden, we'll have no child care. What will we do then?"

The kind of summer a lot of us remember—three whole months of unstructured time when we played in the yard, rode bikes, and hung out with our friends—is not the norm any more. Nowadays, even children at home with parents or caregivers will beg to go to camp just because all their friends with working parents are gone during the day and there are few neighborhood children to play with.

Your options depend on what's available in your community. Some child-care resource and referral agencies have listings for summer programs. Some YWCAs and YMCAs run summer day camps. So do private schools, community recreation centers, and the large daycare-center chains. If your child is old enough (typically 8 or older), you might choose sleep-away camp for a portion of the summer.

Informal Arrangements

A high school student in our neighborhood runs a small "camp" for a few children in her family's backyard with her mother's help. You may be able to find someone in your area who has a similar setup, or you might want to help someone get started by helping her find other parents looking for summer child care.

Some family daycare providers have openings in the summer because their enrollment drops during vacations. You may be able to fill up part of your children's summer with a family vacation and visits with grandparents and other relatives.

SUMMER CAMPS

"My community has several summer camps. I hate to pick one sight unseen. But I need child care this summer, and the applications are due this spring when the camps aren't operating."

Although some experts advise visiting a camp with your child the summer before she enrolls, none of the parents we talked to had done this. Making the rounds of camps during a few weeks in summer—and a whole year ahead—is just not practical for many working parents. And program quality can vary from one year to the next.

Choosing the Right One

We found that parents' typical selection method is to start with recommendations from friends whose children have attended camp. Your kids probably would prefer one where some of their buddies will be, and knowing other families who send their children to the same camp may make car pooling easier for you. Your children probably will want a say in the type of camp they attend. Some camps have a variety of activities to choose from and others are devoted to one area such as sports, nature study, fine arts, or computers.

As with any child-care arrangements, you'll be concerned about cost, transportation, and hours of operation when you pick a camp.

Hours and Sessions

Some camps have hours similar to a school day and provide before- and after-camp care at extra cost. Camps often divide the summer into sessions (typically two or three weeks long), so kids can sign up for one and have time free for a family vacation or a switch to a different camp for variety. Even if you have your child at one camp most of the summer, the last session may end in early to mid-August, which may mean that you'll have to find a "gap camp" to provide care until school starts.

Costs

The cost of camp can be steep, and some camps may be beyond your family budget, especially if you have more than one child. For-profit camps typically charge more than nonprofit camps. If finances are a problem for you, ask if the camps offer scholarships, sliding scales for fees, or discounts for siblings. If your child attends a summer day camp so that you can work, you can qualify for the Federal Child Care Income Tax Credit. The credit does not apply for overnight camp costs or any camp after your child turns 13.

Visiting Camps

Once you've identified camps that meet your time, money, and transportation needs, you should dig deeper than the camp brochures to determine quality. A number of camps have open houses on spring weekends so that parents and children can visit, look around, and ask questions.

Check to see that the equipment is well maintained, the outdoor space is safe, and the swimming pools or ponds have shallow ends divided from deeper parts for children who can't swim.

Questions to Ask

If you can't see the camp in operation or attend an

open house, call the director. Ask about the qualifications of the staff and the training they receive. If high school and college students serve as counselors, how closely are they supervised?

Check the daily schedule for your child's age group to get a sense of the number and types of activities they'll be involved in. If campers are driven on field trips, ask about the drivers' credentials and whether the vehicles have seat belts.

Also ask if the camp is accredited by the American Camping Association (ACA). ACA-accredited camps are visited every three years and judged against a set of 300 standards ranging from the qualifications of the lifeguards to the temperature of the hot water in the dishwasher. It is a voluntary program, and lack of accreditation does not mean camps aren't good. But, if they aren't accredited, it's worth asking why.

Ask the ratio of children to adults. The ACA suggests one staffer for every eight campers age 6 to 8 and one for every ten campers age 9 to 14. For risky activities, such as swimming or horseback riding, more adults are needed. ACA also recommends that at least 80 percent of the staff be 18 or older.

TIP: If you don't know any parents whose children have attended the camp, ask the director for parent references and check their impressions of the staff and programs.

Camp Fairs

One easy way to get lots of information at once is to attend a camp fair, sometimes held by local organizations or schools. If your area doesn't have one, talk to your PTA about setting one up as a fund-raiser by renting table space to participating camps. You can also invite other groups that provide activities for children such as music lessons, tutoring, or birthday party entertainment.

The ACA has thirty-two offices around the country. If one is listed in your phone book, ask for camp fair schedules and a directory of accredited camps in your area (see Tip on page 116 for ACA's address).

Registering

Many camps fill up fast and some send out applications as early as February. Don't wait until May to start your search or you might end up with few, if any, options.

SLEEP-AWAY CAMPS

Sleep-away camps provide kids opportunities to develop independence and gain confidence by learning new skills, such as canoeing or horseback riding. But camp can be miserable if a child is too homesick to enjoy it.

Is Your Child Ready?

You should be sure that your child is ready to be away from home before you send him off to overnight camp. Think about how he's handled other periods away from home, such as a visit to his grandparents or a vacation trip with a friend's family. His first camp experience could be more pleasant if one of his friends will be there, too. You might start with a week at a close-to-home camp sponsored by a familiar organization, such as the Boy Scouts, Girl Scouts, YMCA, or your church.

Choosing the Right Camp

Investigate sleep-away camps the same way you'd check out day camps—through conversations with experienced parents, a call to the camp director, and a visit, if possible (*see* Summer Camps *on page 113*). Some of the fancier camps go beyond glossy bro-

chures and now send videotapes to prospective campers.

> **TIP:** For more information about sleep-away camps, day camps, religious camps, and camps for kids with disabilities, contact the American Camping Association (ACA). The staff will answer questions, make referrals, and send you a free brochure on how to choose a camp. For $12.95, you can order ACA's *Guide to Accredited Camps*, which has 2,000 listings by geographic region. Call 800-428-CAMP to order the book, or call 317-342-8456 to speak to the staff. The ACA address is 5000 State Road 67 North, Martinsville, IN 46151-7902.

Year-Round School

"Just when we thought we'd licked our summer child-care problem, our school district has started talking about year-round school! Do they know how hard it's going to be to find child care for several small vacations scattered throughout the year?"

The possibility of year-round school is popping up across the country, and it's important for parents to get involved in the early planning and to keep an open mind. Parents in year-round schools don't necessarily have a harder time finding child care; they just have different needs.

Some parents prefer the year-round schedule because their heaviest child-care expenses are spread out over the whole year rather than concentrated in three months of summer.

Flexibility in scheduling family vacations is another advantage. You could visit Disney World in October, enjoying the warm southern weather and avoiding the summer crowds, for example. Or, if you live in the cold North, you could save your pennies for a trip to the Caribbean in February, when other families with school children are stuck home shoveling snow.

Approximately 2,000 schools in thirty-one states have converted to a year-round schedule, according to Don Jeffries, program specialist for the National Association for Year-Round Education, in San Diego, California.

Seventy percent of those schools are in California, where overcrowding and lack of funds for new buildings have forced school districts to find ways to get more use from existing facilities. A fifth of Califor-

nia's schools go year-round. Florida, Texas, and North Carolina are the states with the fastest growth in year-round schools.

HOW YEAR-ROUND SCHOOL WORKS
A typical year-round plan divides students into four clusters, with three groups going to school while one is on vacation. Schedules adopted by school districts vary. Some kids go to school for nine weeks, then are off for three weeks. Or it could be six weeks in school and two off, or one of several other combinations. The students still get nine months of schooling. But, instead of having the summer off, their vacations are shorter and scattered throughout the year.

If your school is considering this kind of plan, make sure siblings can be put into the same cluster so your kids are on vacation at the same time, if that's your preference.

Jeffries says overcrowding motivates just half of the schools that adopt the year-round schedule. The rest, he says, do so because they believe it's better for learning than the old system of summers off, a legacy of our 19th-century agricultural economy. Formerly a teacher and principal for thirty-five years, Jeffries spent twenty of those years on a year-round schedule and is a strong proponent of the concept.

He says teachers don't have to spend so much time reviewing material as they do when students have three months to forget what they learned in the previous nine. Shorter but more frequent breaks reduce stress and burnout for students and make it easier for teachers to adjust their lesson plans to fit their students' individual needs.

Keys for Success

School systems that are most successful in implementing year-round operations consult with parents, child-care providers, and other groups serving children, such as recreation centers and YMCAs. Some districts set up child care in their schools for students who are on breaks.

Businesses that traditionally hire teenagers for part-time or summer work should be involved in planning, also. Some parents worry that year-round school will shut their kids out of summer jobs. But Jeffries says businesses can adjust to the schedule—by hiring three students to rotate in one job as each goes on and off vacation, for example.

> **TIP:** For more information on issues for parents and the role they can play in planning, contact the National Association for Year-Round Education, P.O. Box 711386, San Diego, CA 92171-1386, 619-276-5296.

Home Alone After School

"Our child came home from school one day and declared: 'I don't need a babysitter anymore! All my friends are staying home by themselves after school; I'm old enough, too.' Is he?"

Any parent who's read Dr. Seuss' *The Cat in the Hat* (and what parent of a school-age child hasn't?) has an all-too-clear vision of the mischief kids can get into when their parents are away. As if that weren't enough, remember the movie *Home Alone?* An eight-year-old, accidentally left by himself, spends his hours eating junk food, watching videos, and fending off burglars.

Both are only fiction. But, unfortunately, reality can be as bad or worse. Children left to care for themselves may spend their afternoons lolling mindlessly in front of the television. Even if being alone was their idea, they may end up feeling lonely and unwanted. They can become victims of violent crimes or serious accidents. And adolescents can take advantage of empty houses to drink alcohol, use drugs, or have sex.

Despite the potential problems, thousands of children are home alone every day. Some parents can't afford child care. Many communities offer no—or inadequate—after-school programs for older children. And some parents decide that their children are capable of caring for themselves.

HOW OLD IS OLD ENOUGH?

When is a child a reasonable candidate for self-care? Experts are reluctant to set a specific age because kids mature at different rates. However, many say children under 11 or 12 are too young. Some 15-year-olds aren't ready, either. And, no matter how mature the child, if the neighborhood is unsafe or no neighbors are home during the day, self-care is not a good idea.

"It really isn't an issue of age because school-agers develop differently," says Margaret Plantz, an expert on self-care who directed Project Home Safe, a program sponsored by the American Home Economics Association and the Whirlpool Foundation. "They need to have enough life experience and level-headedness so that if an emergency arises, they can make a life-saving choice," Plantz explains.

If there's a fire, for example, your child must instantly sort out and choose the right course of action. Is he first going to call 911, save the cat, or immediately leave the house, choosing the safest exit?

Like many child-care experts, Plantz is concerned about the psychological effect on children who are "on their own for long periods of time, day after day and year after year. Children may never be mature enough to handle that kind of isolation," she says. "They're at a stage in their lives when they learn a lot from interaction with other people."

Why Teenage Programs Fail

She believes that supervised care can be valuable even for older teenagers but that current programs aren't meeting the needs and interests of this age group. "The child-care community needs to address older children," she says. "I think they require a different model." (*For more on the teenage years, see pages 127-154.*)

Kids often suggest self-care because they are unhappy with their after-school care. Programs that fail to challenge and interest fifth and sixth graders lose those children fast. If you don't want your older child to go home alone, you could try to find another after-school program that he would find more challenging.

When Not to Start Self-Care

Self-care definitely is a bad idea if a child is going through a period of heightened emotion or stress. Being home alone can create enough anxiety by itself. Self-care should not be started when the family is coping with divorce, death, a new baby, or a move to a new home, for instance.

PREPARING A CHILD TO BE HOME ALONE

If your child is going to be home by himself, you need to prepare him well. Then you must never stop evaluating how the arrangement is working out.

Outside Help

Your child could prepare for being home alone by taking a self-care class at a local organization such as the YMCA, Scouts, or Camp Fire. There are also books and other publications that can help you learn about self-care (*see* Tips *on pages 122 and 125*).

Practice Sessions

Before you implement this new arrangement, you

IS YOUR CHILD READY TO STAY ALONE?

If you are considering self-care for your child, Project Home Safe recommends you answer such questions as:

❑ How mature is my child—not just in years, but emotionally, intellectually, and in his ability to make sound judgments?

❑ How has he handled brief periods of being left at home alone up until now?

❑ Will he be lonely or frightened to be by himself?

❑ How long will he have to be alone?

❑ Will he use the time safely and productively or will the hours be spent eating junk food and watching television or worse?

❑ Does he solve small problems himself but also know when and how to seek help?

❑ Does he have enough confidence to contact an adult when he needs assistance?

❑ Is he physically able to lock and unlock the doors and windows in the house?

❑ Can he manage simple tasks like fixing a snack and taking phone messages?

should help your child practice making emergency telephone calls (without actually dialing) so he learns to give his name, address and the nearest cross street, and a simple description of the emergency. Teach him that, in cases of fire, he should leave immediately and go to a neighbor's home before calling the fire department. You also should practice fire drills and identify backup exits in case one is blocked.

Finally, role play various situations until you and your child are comfortable that he'll know what to do if the unexpected happens.

Emergency Supplies

Teach your child basic first aid, such as how to apply pressure to stop bleeding. Make sure your house has a well-stocked first-aid kit and that your child knows where it's kept. Have a flashlight handy in case the electricity goes off, a battery-powered radio to monitor severe weather warnings, and a supply of fresh replacement batteries.

Dealing with Strangers

Your child should not reveal to outsiders that he is alone. If a stranger telephones or comes to the door, your child should say that his parents can't come to the phone (or door) right then but that he'll take a message. Doors should be kept locked and should have windows or peepholes so children can see who's on the doorstep while keeping the doors closed.

Handling Keys

Your child must keep his keys in a safe place— attached to a chain around his neck and tucked inside his shirt, perhaps, or chained to a belt loop and carried in a secure pocket. There should be no identification attached to the keys so that, if they are lost, they can't be traced to your house. Leave extra keys with trusted neighbors in case your child gets locked out.

Important Phone Numbers

Next to each telephone in your house, you should display important numbers—parents at work, neighbors or relatives who can be called for help, police, fire, ambulance, poison control center, family doctor, and so forth.

Some families have gotten their home-alone children a dog for protection and companionship.

TIP: Several books have been written for home-alone kids. Check out *Alone at Home* by Ann Banks (Puffin Books, 1989), a workbook with advice and ideas for kids and a special section for parents.

Easing into Self-Care

There are ways to ease into self-care. For example, you could start with one afternoon a week and build up gradually while continually evaluating how well your child is managing on his own.

CHECKING IN

Another smart way to start self-care is with a plan for checking in. A check-in system can ease a parent's mind. For a child, it offers a way to be independent without the loneliness or fear of being totally on his own.

The idea is to find an adult who is available to your child when you're not at home. The child is allowed to go to pre-approved places—your home, certain friends' homes, after-school activities, and so forth—as long as he keeps the adult informed of his whereabouts. He might also be required to phone the adult at particular times or even to stop by the adult's home.

You might set up your check-in system with a neighbor who—perhaps for compensation—would be available to your child between school dismissal and your return from work.

ESTABLISHING HOUSE RULES

It is essential that you and your child agree on a clear and comprehensive set of house rules. You might want to put them in the form of a contract that everyone signs. Post the rules on the refrigerator, so your child sees them when he gets his snack.

You need to decide if he is allowed to have visitors and, if so, whom. May he go to a friend's house, the park, or the library? What time is he to arrive at home from school? When must he check in by phone? Which appliances is he allowed to operate? How is he expected to use his time? Must he do chores? When must he complete his homework? Are there limits to what he can watch on television and for how much time?

MAINTAINING PHONE CONTACT

"Sometimes I'm not available when my child calls from home or I'm not able to talk for very long.

A MODEL CHECK-IN PROGRAM

Named one of the ten best daycare centers in the country in 1992 by *Child* magazine, the Reston Children's Center in Virginia cares for children from 6 weeks through 14 years. It is a nonprofit cooperative owned and governed by parents.

Although there is an after-school program on site, the staff also coordinates a check-in program for children up to age 15 with carefully selected and trained family daycare providers.

Often the provider is a neighborhood mother with school-age children, who is paid to let others come to her home after school for a snack and conversation. The children then go to their own homes but check in with the provider by phone at regularly scheduled intervals until the parents return from work. If a child fails to call, the provider will check on him.

The parents and provider agree in advance on what the child is allowed to do, such as visit friends in the neighborhood or go to a scheduled activity such as soccer practice.

How can I deal with this without hurting her feelings?"

It is not always easy to take personal phone calls at work. But that afternoon chat can be an essential link for children in self-care. "An afternoon check-in means the parent knows the child is home, and the child has the incentive to get home in a timely manner," says self-care expert Margaret Plantz. "Requiring a call also says that I care about you and what's going on."

Have a Backup When You Can't Take the Call

Plantz suggests arranging for someone who can talk with your child if you're not available. This could be a colleague at work who could pick up the phone if you're not there. It could be a neighbor or relative whom your child knows to call if she can't reach you. Or it could be both.

Some communities have telephone services staffed by volunteers who will take calls from children who get lonely at home. You might find one in your phone book under such listings as "PhoneFriend," "Kidsline," or "Careline." The Girl Scouts match home-alone Scouts with elderly or homebound adults so they can keep each other company over the phone. The adults also will alert parents if a girl fails to make her scheduled call.

If you want to be able to call your child, you may need to restrict how long he can chat on the phone with friends. Or you can buy the call-waiting service from your phone company so you can get through even when the line is busy.

PARENTING BY PHONE

"Normal is…solving complex emotional problems of sibling rivalry and adolescent moral dilemmas of right and wrong in 3-minute telephone segments in mid-afternoon under the disapproving eye of a supervisor who lives with a parakeet for which he has health insurance."

Ellen Goodman, The *Boston Globe*, August 22, 1993

EVALUATING YOUR SELF-CARE ARRANGEMENT

"Lately, my child has been more clingy and seems to be having trouble sleeping. I'm wondering if it could be that she's not happy being home alone after school even though she's the one who suggested it."

Experts stress that parents continually need to monitor how well self-care is working. And that means more than just being certain that the house rules are being obeyed. Any change in behavior—becoming argumentative or passive, sleeping more or less, becoming withdrawn, or having trouble at school, for example—could signal that your child is not entirely happy with self-care even if he doesn't admit it or perhaps doesn't even realize it.

If you think the problem can be traced to self-care, repeat the transition measures we suggested above or consider alternative after-school arrangements.

PUTTING A SIBLING IN CHARGE

"My older child goes home alone after school, and now my younger one wants to join her. Should we let him?"

You need to be very careful about placing one of your children in another's charge, day after day, when you're not at home.

Being responsible for a sibling is a burden that a child may not be ready for. It also limits her after-school activities because she has to stay at home to watch her little brother or sister. Even if your older child is a teenager who babysits occasionally, she may resent the burden of tending to her sibling every day.

According to Margaret Plantz, unless the older child is of "substantial maturity"—say 15 or 16—she should not be expected to care for a younger sibling.

You may want to hire a college student to care for your younger child and provide gentle supervision of the older one (*see* A College Student to Help *on page 131*).

(*For more about after-school care for teenagers, see also* Supervising from a Distance *on page 129.*)

> **TIP:** For free booklets produced by Project Home Safe on preparing your child for self-care, write to AIS-Whirlpool, P.O. Box 405, St. Joseph, MI 49085. The National SAFE KIDS Campaign has booklets on safety for kids. Write them at 111 Michigan Avenue NW, Washington, DC 20010-2970 or call 202-884-4993.

THE TEENAGE YEARS

HERE'S HELP ON:

Supervising from a distance, page 129

Have car, will travel, page 134

Part-time jobs for teens, page 137

Teen volunteering, page 140

Parent peer groups, page 141

Reducing risky behavior, page 144

Teen sex, page 144

Underage drinking and illegal drugs, page 145

Teen parties, page 151

Teenage depression, 152

One mother we know told us she worked full time when her children were young but cut back to part time when they hit the teen years because "I worried about what might happen during those hours they were unsupervised at home."

She's not alone in worrying. There's no question that teens today face more grown-up challenges at earlier ages than we did in our youth. The magazines we read as teenagers coached us on the latest beach-party fashions and how to talk to the opposite sex. Today's teens read about sexually transmitted diseases and date rape.

Peer pressures—coupled with exposure to television, movies, and music that glamorize drinking and sex—are threats to teenagers of all ages. Drugs, violence, depression, and even teen suicides also are serious concerns for teens and their parents.

Adolescents who go home to empty houses may be responsible when they are alone. But will they be vulnerable to the influence of their friends who drop by and want to take advantage of the absence of adults in the house? Many parents want to be home in the after-school hours, not so much because of worry about what their kids will get into, but because their young teenagers are at an emotionally volatile stage when they may need an adult to confide in—even if they won't admit it.

A TOUGH AGE TO PARENT

Raising teenagers is an especially difficult challenge for you as a working parent. Much like the challenge you faced when your child first went off to school, your job as a parent becomes easier and more difficult at the same time. No longer are you preoccupied with maintaining a corps of babysitters, but you can't leave your child to rear himself. And the problems he faces now are more complex and consequential than those you solved when he was ages 3, 6, and 10. You've got to strike the best balance you can between supervising and letting go.

Build a Good Relationship Early

If we want our teenagers to accept our help and adopt our values, we have to begin building strong relationships with them when they are young. And

then we have to keep communication lines open and set good examples during the teen years. What you say, how you listen, and what you do will go a long way toward determining whether your child can resist peer pressure, get out of dangerous situations, and ask for your help when he needs it.

Life Gets More Hectic, Not Less

Many parents of younger children think (and hope) that when their children get older and become more independent their frantic pace will ease up a bit. They look forward to the day when they can go out for an evening without having to scrape up a babysitter. What you find, however, is that your time still is not your own. Instead, it's monopolized by your teen's many activities.

More sports events, more class plays, more recitals, and more social life—scattered all over town and often beyond—make the teen years as hectic for parents as they are for the kids. If you feel you're just barely keeping your head above water, you need to get serious about managing your time as efficiently as possible (see Time Well Spent, *starting on page 155*). You can enlist the help of other parents to carpool. And you can limit the number or kinds of organized activities in which your child participates. While you may want to keep your teen busy after school with sports, clubs, or music lessons, for example, you can avoid signing up for too many that require big commitments of your time on nights and weekends.

Supervising from a Distance

"It's those after-school hours I worry about the most. Even though I trust my kids, I know the temptation to experiment is always there. How can we make those hours safe and productive?"

In the chapter *Care for Your School-Age Child* we discussed self-care, when kids around middle-school age often begin staying by themselves after school (*see* Home Alone After School *on page 118*). Initially, parents set rules about staying in the house, locking doors, using electrical appliances, and handling emergencies. As the kids get older, the rules relax because the parents gain more confidence in their children's abilities to keep safe and act responsibly. How well the arrangement works depends on how responsible the child is and how many hours she is left unsupervised.

DON'T LOSE TOUCH WITH SCHOOL

When you're deciding which commitments to cut back on, put your teenager's school high on your "keep list." Educators find that parent participation falls off in junior high and gets even worse in high school.

Public opinion surveys have shown that people who are closest to a school feel best about it. The Gallup Organization has repeatedly found that individuals rate their local schools higher than the nation's schools in general, that parents rate the local schools better than non-parents, and that parents rate their own child's school better than they rate the local schools in general.

Gallup says these findings suggest that "the better people know the public schools, the higher their opinion of school quality."*

*"25th Annual Phi Delta Kappa/Gallup Poll of the Public's Attitude Toward the Public Schools," *Phi Delta Kappan*, October 1993.

More Time Equals Greater Risk

Peter Scales, director of the Center for Early Adolescence at the University of North Carolina's School of Medicine, says research shows the chances of adolescents engaging in risky behavior goes up with the number of hours they are unguided.

"The cut-off point seems to be 10 to 11 hours a week" with no adult guidance, Scales says. Left to their own devices for longer than that, children are more likely to experiment with alcohol, drugs, or sex. This is true no matter what the economic level of the family, he adds. "When kids are guided by adults in activities that are wholesome—to use an old-fashioned word—their risk of engaging in these behaviors goes down dramatically."

As children grow older, they need "successively fewer layers of supervision," says Scales, author of *A Portrait of Young Adolescents in the 1990s: Implications for Promoting Healthy Growth and Development* (The Center for Early Adolescence, 1991). "But they do need adults to be around without hanging over them."

FLEXIBLE WORKING HOURS CAN HELP

This is one of the times in your child's life when flexible work schedules can be a special blessing. One parent might work 7 A.M. to 4 P.M. and the other 9 A.M. to 6 P.M., so there is someone at home before and after school. A few parents are opting for telecommuting, when their employers allow it, so they can spend all or some of their working hours at home.

Claudia Winkler, a single mother of two, carved out more time for her children by living close to her job and working a very early shift. She could get to work in 6 minutes and would be at her desk at a Cincinnati newspaper by 5:30 A.M. "I didn't think the kids needed me as much in the morning," Winkler says.

Starting to work early meant she could be home early. She hired a college student to fix dinner and tutor her children on the one day a week she worked into the evening to write a column.

Winkler's daughter visited the office occasionally to help with the filing because of her "natural ability to organize." Other parents might find it attractive to use their children as part-time assistants if their workplace rules allow. It can give an adolescent valuable work experience and parental supervision at the same time. Be sure to pay your child for the work, and don't forget to praise her efforts.

A COLLEGE STUDENT TO HELP
Some parents of teenagers hire college students to be in their homes weekdays after school, either to care for the teens' younger siblings or to do housecleaning. The students also are available to help with homework, to provide companionship, and to subtly supervise the teens. Many teenagers are comfortable with this arrangement; they don't perceive the college students as their babysitters, but they also aren't home alone.

AFTER-SCHOOL ACTIVITIES
Other parents take the keep-'em-busy approach, using lots of extracurricular activities and sports to reduce or eliminate the time their children are home alone. Unfortunately, school budget shortages and lack of adult volunteers have forced cutbacks of these programs in some communities, especially at the

middle school level. Transportation also may be a problem.

Peter Scales urges communities to provide a wide range of after-school activities. "It's not enough to stick up a basketball net and say we've taken care of early adolescents," he says. "We have to have a lot more formal programs through religious organizations, schools—and especially businesses, which can kick in money to pay adults to run the programs."

Businesses are becoming more involved in providing child care for younger children but still do little for older ones. Seeking help from employers "is an avenue that has been untapped," Scales says.

CHECK IN BY PHONE
Many parents require their home-alone teens to keep one parent informed of their whereabouts at all times. If they don't have a scheduled activity and are expected to be home, they have to call to say that they're going to the library or to a friend's house. As adolescents grow older and demonstrate sound judgment, they deserve more freedom—but that doesn't mean parents should give up all supervision.

"We had one rule throughout high school," says Carolyn Leatherman, working mother of two chil-

A WEEKLY CALENDAR FOR BUSY FAMILIES

Day	Monday	Tuesday	Wednesday	Thursday	Friday	Saturday	Sunday
Menu	vegetable soup, cheese, bread	Spaghetti, salad, celery + carrot sticks	leftovers	Sauteed chicken breast, rice	hamburgers French fries, salad	lasagna, vegetables	chuck roast, potatoes, coleslaw
Paul		village council 7:00		in Columbus 6:30 am- midnight	BB game 6:30	concert 8:00	church 9:15-12:00 Grandma's birthday dinner 12:00
Carolyn	book club 7:30		choir 6:30- 9:00			haircut 10:00	
Jenny	piano lesson 4:30	work 4:00-7:00	choir 6:30- 7:45	work 4:00-7:00	movie 6:30	work 6:00 am- 2:00, April's 8:00-11:00	youth group 7:00- 8:00
Jay	BB practice 4:00-6:00	BB practice 5:00-8:00	BB practice 4:00-6:00 choir 6:30-7:45	BB practice 4:00-6:00 dr. appt. 6:30	BB game 6:30	BB practice 9:00-12:00 movie 7:30	Jim's 5:00- 8:00

dren who now are grown. "They could not bring friends home unless we were there." She also kept track of where her kids were when she wasn't home.

"Every Sunday night we sat down with a master calendar and went through the next seven days," she recalls. Each family member had a column to record where he would be, whether he needed a ride, and when he expected to be home. Anyone who was going to be an hour late, including the parents, had to call in.

"If we had told them we would be home at a certain time and then found we were going to be late, we'd call the kids because they would worry about us," Leatherman says. "It's only common courtesy. Things we demanded of them, we also did ourselves." Meals were on the calendar, too. Leatherman planned the week's menus, and whoever got home first was responsible for starting dinner.

SETTING RULES

Teenagers need rules about their after-school hours, some of which are negotiable and a few that aren't. Kids who have no rules or structure may feel their parents don't care about them. Parental rules also can help teens get out of difficulties with their peers. For example, they can tell friends that "I'm not allowed to invite people over after school" or "I have to be home before dinner."

"I always told the kids that, if they needed to use me to get out of tough situations, they could just say that 'my mom won't let me,' and they could let me know later what I was supposed to have said," Carolyn Leatherman recalls. "They could use their dad this way, too."

Kids react better to rules if they understand what's behind them, so you should explain why each particular rule is important. Some families hold periodic meetings to review rules and see if changes are in order. Adolescents should understand the consequences of breaking the rules, and parents should be consistent in enforcing them.

TIP: The Center for Early Adolescence has publications for parents about understanding and communicating with 10- to 15-year-olds, as well as information about preventing risky behavior. It also offers a curriculum for parent discussion/support groups. Write the center at the School of Medicine, University of North Carolina at

Chapel Hill, D-2 Carr Mill Town Center, Carrboro, NC 27510, or call 919-966-1148 and ask for a publications list.

Have Car, Will Travel

"My son will be old enough to get his driver's license next year, and already I'm worrying about how to make sure he'll be a safe driver."

That license produces one of the great approach-avoidance conflicts in a working parent's life. You enjoy relief from your chauffeuring duties but dread the visions of car crashes that may dance in your head. Although the anxiety diminishes over time (if your teen proves to be a responsible driver), you're never totally free of it.

Set Limits

Ruth Crone, mother of two, remembers her own mixed feelings when her teenagers got their licenses. When they were younger, she laughs, "I was afraid of them driving bumper cars at the beach!" When they started to drive automobiles, she set very conservative rules until she felt comfortable about their driving abilities and sense of responsibility. She limited the hours in which they could drive, how far they could go from home, and what routes they could take—no superhighways at first.

Some parents permit only daytime driving initially or won't let their teens drive with other kids as passengers. Some establish responsibilities for car maintenance and for keeping the gas tank filled. Many families set penalties if their teenager gets a ticket or dents the fender.

Because different children achieve different levels of the skills and attitudes essential for safe driving at different ages, you may have to set different rules as each of your teenagers becomes a new driver.

Be a Good Role Model

The key to rearing good teenage drivers is starting them on the right route when they're young, says Charles Butler, director of driver safety for the American Automobile Association. "Parents need to be aware that, whether they like it or not, they are role models for their children. If you wear your seat belt, you're teaching them. If you speed or are very

AAA'S TEEN DRIVER'S CONTRACT

The American Automobile Association advises all families to have a written driver's contract spelling out the rules, signed by both the teenager and the parents. AAA's sample contract includes the following items, which can be adapted by each family:

❏ what the teen driver is required to pay for (gas, tags, insurance, fines, for example)

❏ what upkeep she is responsible for (such as washing, taking the car for maintenance)

❏ whether user privilege is to be linked to grades in school or performance at home (such as prompt completion of chores)

❏ limits (if any) on the number of miles and the number of times the teenager may drive per week

❏ penalties (e.g., withdrawal of driving privileges for a specific time) for traffic offenses or at-fault crashes

❏ other rules (such as requiring the driver and passengers to wear seat belts, banning drugs and alcohol from the car, requiring the teen to tell her parents her destination and time of return and call if she will be late)

emotional behind the wheel, you're modeling how your child will operate a car."

Ride with and Supervise Your Teen Driver

Butler also cautions parents not to rely solely on a driver's education course to prepare teens to be safe drivers. The standard course in high school is 30 hours in the classroom and 6 hours in the car, he points out. Not all 6 hours are necessarily behind the wheel—some may be spent observing while another student drives. And some schools devote even less time to the course.

"Going through a training course doesn't make you a safe driver," Butler says. "It just gives you enough information to pass the licensing exam." He advises parents to provide a year to eighteen months of "supervised, supplemental training." He recommends spending about 200 hours riding with your teenager in various driving situations, especially those not encountered in a course—such as driving at night, in the rain, or on a busy highway.

It may sound like a big investment of time, but it can be accomplished in three to four hours a week over that twelve- to eighteen-month period. He suggests that you have your teenager drive when you go to the grocery store or run errands and that you set aside some time on the weekend for driving practice.

Choose a Driver Ed Course Carefully

He also tells parents to check out the quality of driver education programs before their children enroll. In many communities, the course no longer is offered through the high school, so parents have to turn to commercial driving schools. "Make sure it's a quality program," Butler says, adding that there are bad programs both in high schools and in the private sector.

> **TIP:** AAA offers a free booklet on how to evaluate a driver training course and sells a parent involvement package. The package tells parents how to provide supplemental driving experiences and includes a videotape, parent-student guides and a sample written contract. Check your phone book for the AAA office in your area.

HAVING THEIR OWN CARS

"My daughter wants to get her own car. She's been responsible with ours, but we wonder if having her own will give her too much freedom."

A growing number of two-earner families with teens are parking three and four cars in the driveway. It's a way to provide the teenagers transportation to school, jobs, and far-flung activities while both parents commute by car to work.

Before you allow a teenager have her own car, you need to evaluate how she has handled the responsibility of driving and caring for a family car and if she has complied with the rules you've established. Your car-use contract then needs to be updated to fit the new situation.

Check Your Teen's Car Regularly

When a teenager drives the same car you do, you should be able to notice whether it's being well cared for and is in good running order. That won't happen with the teenager's own car unless you make a point to check it periodically. The AAA suggests keeping

THE THREE-CAR FAMILY

Like many parents, Herb and Jo Ann Amey had looked forward to the time when their daughter Emily would be old enough to drive herself to her numerous activities. The Ameys assumed that Emily would share the family's two cars—especially since Jo Ann teaches at Emily's high school and mother and daughter could ride to school together.

Unfortunately, Jo Ann and Emily found that their after-school schedules seldom meshed. Summers were even worse, with Emily heading to tennis team practice and her mother attending graduate school classes in the opposite direction. Finally the family decided to buy Emily a used car.

"It's scary when you think of her having the responsibility of driving, but we felt confident she was a good driver," Jo Ann says. "Emily took driver's education, and we rode with her a lot so we could observe her driving skills."

Satisfaction with a teen's driving ability is one thing; worry about where she goes when she has her own car is something else again.

"There's a definite lack of control," Jo Ann says. "When she was driving our cars, she would ask permission and say where she was going. Once it's her car, it's a little more freedom. If she wants to go to a friend's house after school, she can just go."

an eye on mileage, tires (for adequate air pressure and abusive use), maintenance, vehicle damage, and clues to drinking or drug abuse.

Who Pays for It?

Because a car carries a substantial purchase price and operating expense, many families expect—and need—teenagers to help pay the cost, usually with part-time jobs. That's okay as long as the teenager doesn't work so many hours that she neglects her school work or misses out on the social aspects of high school.

Part-Time Jobs for Teens

Some teenagers work so they can buy stylish clothes, expensive athletic shoes, or other material things their parents can't afford or won't buy. Some work to buy gas and pay car insurance. Still others work to save money for college or even to help with the family's living expenses. Some are lucky enough to work because they enjoy the job.

Many of us parents had part-time jobs in high school that helped us learn valuable work skills, develop independence, and earn money for higher education. Teenagers' jobs are particularly helpful to working parents because they leave the children with fewer hours of unsupervised time on their hands.

PUT A LIMIT ON WORKING HOURS

But teachers say some kids are working so many hours that their school work suffers. If a teenager puts in late hours at a fast-food restaurant, it's hard for him to complete his homework, get a good night's sleep, and enjoy a normal social life. Teens who have too much disposable income may be tempted to spend it on alcohol or drugs. And too much focus on making and spending money can warp their values.

Marguerite Kelly, co-author of *The Mother's Almanac* (Doubleday, 1975; revised edition, 1992) and author of *The Mother's Almanac II* (Doubleday, 1989), thinks all teens from age 14 on should have some kind of job. "If they work, they feel good about themselves," she explains. The job can be as simple as babysitting or lawn mowing for neighbors. Kelly says parents need to limit the number of hours worked, so jobs don't interfere with school. She also believes children should save a major portion of their earnings.

Kelly—the mother of four and grandmother of three—doesn't think kids should be paid for chores they do at home. "For family things, I don't believe in paying until they start paying me to make dinner!" she says. "Kids deserve to be needed. They should go to bed at night knowing the world was improved because they were in it and that they give as much as they get."

Also author of the syndicated newspaper column "The Family Almanac," Kelly employs a couple of young teenagers to help in her home office after school. They open mail, file, and do simple chores on the computer. "It's fun for me to have them around, and they like the sense of doing something important," she says.

Peter Scales of the Center for Early Adolescence says that holding a part-time job "seems to be good because it gives (young teens) some extra money and a feeling of being on their own and being responsible for themselves."

Children younger than 15 should not work more than 10 to 15 hours a week, however, he says. "The more time they spend at work, the less time they are spending on school work. Also, the more they work, the more they are associating with older kids who work longer hours. They're more exposed to various behaviors of older kids, such as sex or drinking and driving."

Other experts say juniors and seniors in high school should be limited to no more than 20 hours of employment a week. And they will benefit most if the jobs offer real opportunities to learn.

(LOW-KEY) JOB GUIDANCE FROM PARENTS

Service jobs, such as working in fast-food restaurants, are the most readily available for young teenagers. And "there's nothing wrong with that for a while," Scales says. "But the learning curve at McDonald's flattens out fast." He suggests that parents encourage their children to think about moving into more challenging jobs. "A culinary talent won't be expanded at McDonald's," he says, but it might in a restaurant kitchen where the teenager can move from salads to pastries to main dishes.

Scales doesn't suggest that parents pressure kids into certain jobs but that they serve as a resource. "Parents can clip things from the paper about the world of work and say, 'I just thought you might be interested,'" he explains.

Parents also can help by looking for job opportunities at their own workplaces, as long as the teenager is agreeable to the idea. Working in the same place can help parent and child feel closer. And children often cherish the opportunity to see what their parents do at work.

Talk About Work Hours and Money Earned

Before your adolescent takes a job, discuss the hours you will allow him to work. Some parents don't permit younger teens to work on school nights, for example, and they may limit how late at night a child can work on weekends.

You should agree in advance about what portion of the teenager's wages will be put into savings. Once your child locates a job, find out who the boss is. Try to meet with that person, so you and he can agree on the hours and tasks your child will be assigned.

TIP: Some high schools have work-study programs that offer better vocational preparation than jobs kids find on their own. Contact your school to see if it offers any work programs.

Teen Volunteering

Volunteering is another productive use of an adolescent's time. In the chapter *Time Well Spent* we discuss community service projects that parents can do with their younger children (*see* Volunteering *on page 171*). When kids are old enough to volunteer on their own, one afternoon a week spent helping others offers big payoffs to young teens. In the best volunteer jobs, adolescents get to interact with adults, are exposed to career ideas, see concrete results from their efforts, and reap the reward of feeling competent and needed.

Peter Scales of the Center for Early Adolescence says parents ought to encourage their children to perform community service from an early age because those who are involved in helping others are less likely to get into risky activities. He says research shows that when kids are 10 or 11 they have the greatest interest in community service, because that's when they begin to recognize the needs of others instead of focusing only on their own needs.

If you encourage them at that age, they'll be more likely to continue to be active volunteers as they grow older. If you wait until they are 14, they usually are less interested in taking on volunteer roles, Scales says.

SCHOOL-SUPPORTED VOLUNTEERISM

Some schools have started offering opportunities for children to volunteer, and there is a growing trend for high schools—both public and private—to require their students to perform community service.

Elementary schools can get into the act by organizing students to plant flowers in the school yard, clean up litter, or collect canned goods for needy families at Thanksgiving. Children and parents at our daughter's elementary school prepare and serve dinner at a shelter for homeless women once a month.

Schools can incorporate their students' public service work into the curriculum. Volunteer experiences that include cleaning the environment or reading to the blind can be linked to science or English classes, for example. This helps students to "see the relationship between the classroom and the real world," says Joan Schine of the National Center for Service Learning in Early Adolescence. School-sponsored service also enhances a school's reputation in the surrounding community.

COMMUNITY OPPORTUNITIES

Community service opportunities also can be found in such organizations as the Girl Scouts, Boy Scouts, Camp Fire, Boys and Girls Clubs, and churches. Children who have outgrown their after-school programs might be able to return as teacher's helpers. Daycare centers and senior citizen centers often need volunteers.

Your children don't have to be involved with a formal organization to be a volunteer. A teenager can run errands for an elderly neighbor, for example. Or your family can take on a project on its own.

Such activities can instill positive habits in children and let busy parents spend some rewarding time with their teens.

Every Sunday, for example, Claudia Winkler, her teenage daughter, and two adult friends used to go to the home of an elderly blind woman where they took turns reading books to her. "We had the pleasure of friendship and of sharing books," Winkler remembers. Today, Winkler's now-grown daughter still reads for the blind and volunteers in a hospital. Scales reminds parents that younger adolescents have short attention spans. A 12-year-old may not like taking judo class once a week for a year, even though she did when she was a first-grader. The same applies to volunteer activities. "It's normal for them to get tired of an activity in a month or two," Scales explains. "Don't apply an adult framework, saying they should stick with it." At this age, kids like to sample a variety of activities, so Scales suggests that children rotate among several volunteer projects.

Parent Peer Groups

"We seem to be battling a lot with our teenagers over things like curfews and where they can go with friends. We don't want to be unreasonably strict compared to other parents, but it's hard to know how we stack up with what others allow."

Every parent hears the lament: "All my friends are allowed to _____(fill in the blank). It can make you wonder if you really are the overly restrictive old fogy that your kids would have you believe.

The only way to find out what rules their friends' parents are setting is to ask those parents, not your kids. This not only helps you gauge common practice but also can alert you to parents who are too permissive for your taste. If, for example, another family does something you find unacceptable—such as let-

MAKING VOLUNTEERING MEANINGFUL FOR KIDS

Historically, children had real responsibilities in their homes and communities, says Joan Schine of the National Center for Service Learning in Early Adolescence, based at the City University of New York. Children have fewer duties today, but volunteers are needed for many community services.

Schine says early adolescents think it "a great privilege to enter the adult world." Community service allows them to play adult roles "when they are yearning for them and have no entry point of their own."

The National Center is helping to establish what are called "service learning projects" in schools, after-school programs, and community organizations. "Service learning" describes community service projects with an added component of "preparation and reflection." Before and during a project, volunteers meet in a group with a qualified adult to prepare for the work they'll be doing, discuss the problems they run into, and reflect on how their community service is going. Adults at the volunteer site also receive special training.

"Ideally, young people should have a voice in selecting the kinds of places they want to work," Schine says. And they shouldn't be exploited by being assigned to do nothing but clean up the paint pots in a daycare center, for example. If they volunteer in a convalescent home, adults making assignments must gauge students' readiness to deal with the possibility that those they work with—and become attached to—may be impaired or might die.

If your school has a program, ask what kind of adult supervision your child will get and how the service program connects with the curriculum. If it has no program, talk to the principal or school board about starting one.

For help in bringing service learning to your school, contact the National Center for Service Learning in Early Adolescence, 25 W. 43rd Street, Room 620, New York, NY 10036-8099, 212-642-2947.

ting teenagers drink alcohol in their home—you could forbid your child to visit there but allow him to invite that family's children to your house instead.

GETTING TO KNOW OTHER PARENTS

You already know the parents of some of your child's friends from the neighborhood, the PTA, sports, or other places parents congregate. As your child's circle of friends expands, you'll have to reach out to become acquainted with new parents.

When children are still of the age that they must be driven everywhere, take a minute to go to the door and introduce yourself when you drive your child's new friend to her home, for example. Or go out to the car and greet a parent you haven't met when she drops off her child for a visit to your house. You could host a small gathering of parents in your home. At the very least, you should introduce yourself by phone to parents you haven't met.

Parent Group Meetings

Parent peer groups offer a more formal way to meet other parents and learn how they set limits on their children's behavior. Sometimes the groups are off-shoots of the PTA. Others are sponsored by schools, and there might be a group for parents of children in each grade level. Usually a school representative attends, and the meeting is run by a parent facilitator.

Diane Brewer has been in peer groups in two different schools as her daughters have progressed through the grades. She says a group works best with certain ground rules. Children and parents aren't identified by name when problems are discussed. All discussion is confidential. "You aren't allowed to repeat anything outside the room, so the children's privacy isn't violated by the things discussed," Brewer says. "The point is to make parents into colleagues who are working together to make a better social and academic climate for their children."

While Brewer thinks it's important for the school staff to attend the meetings because many issues involve the school, the sessions should not be used to "complain about teachers or academics. There are other forums for that."

Naturally, the issues covered at meetings change over the years. "In fourth grade, it might be talk about too much homework or how many after-school activities are appropriate or what's a proper bedtime," Brewer says. "In sixth grade, it's how long kids can talk on the telephone and if they can call the opposite sex."

Now in the high school grades, her peer group talks about curfews and under-age drinking. No one votes, but parents get a sense of the community view on an issue or learn if there is no consensus. "You find there is a real range of parental attitudes," Brewer says. "You also build relationships with other families" so you know who has a parenting style similar to yours.

Reducing Risky Behavior

Parents have learned the hard way that it's not enough to "just say no" to alcohol, drugs, sex, or other risks.

Long before our children become teenagers, we have to start giving them practical education about the dangers they will face and teaching them our moral values. In that way, we arm them with the ability to make good decisions for their own protection.

We always must remember that our good—or bad—examples are our children's most effective teachers.

ABOUT SEX

"How can we minimize the likelihood that our teenagers will be harmed by early experiments with sex?"

Debra Haffner, executive director of the Sex Information and Education Council of the United States, speaks regularly to parent groups about how to talk to children about sex. She says there is "no such thing as 'The Big Talk.' " Teaching kids about human sexuality, she says, "is developmental and it has to start early.

"Unfortunately, the media have become the sexuality educators for our teenagers," Haffner says. The television series *Beverly Hills 90210* sets the standard for "what is cool," she says, and most of the main characters are having sex.

Haffner recommends using the media creatively to educate children. Basketball star Magic Johnson's announcement that he had tested HIV-positive, for example, provided an opportunity for unusually effective discussions about the risks of unprotected sex. TV shows and movies watched with your children can be catalysts for discussions of your values and what you think about teenage sexual behavior.

Some parents fear that sex education promotes

sexual activity, but research indicates the opposite. "In homes where there is open communication, sexual activity starts later," Haffner says. "If sex is a big mystery and a big taboo, you can create an area of rebellion" for your teenagers.

Young people who are involved in churches and extracurricular activities and who do well in school are less likely to engage in sex early and are more likely to use birth control when they do, Haffner explains.

COMMUNICATION REDUCES RISKY BEHAVIOR

Parents who are involved in their children's lives reduce the likelihood of all kinds of risky behavior, not just unsafe sex. Education and communication are key weapons for combating under-age drinking, drug abuse, drunk driving, and other dangerous activities as well.

"There's an assumption that, at a certain age, they don't need us," Haffner says. But that's not true. When teens go out, she explains, it's important for parents to ask where they're going and who they're going to meet. When they return, the questions are about what they did and who they were with.

TIP: The Planned Parenthood Federation of America has a free booklet called *How to Talk to Your Child About Sexuality*. Request it from the organization's marketing department, 810 Seventh Avenue, New York, NY 10019.

The Sex Information and Education Council of the United States has a pamphlet on talking with children and a bibliography, both available for small fees. Write the council's publications department at 130 W. 42nd Street, Suite 2500, New York, NY 10036, or call 212-819-9770.

UNDERAGE DRINKING AND ILLEGAL DRUGS

"I feel I'm a pretty involved parent, and I've tried to teach my kids about the risks of alcohol and other drugs. But I know there's a lot of drinking going on among my kids' peers, and I worry about harder drugs."

"If you want to reduce the chance your child will use cocaine," says drug and alcohol therapist Lee Dogoloff, "focus on marijuana, tobacco, and alcohol." All are drugs, and their use can be interrelated.

Kids make decisions about trying tobacco as early as age 11 and illegal drugs before they become teenagers, according to Dogoloff, former director of the

KEEPING COMMUNICATION OPEN
WITH A BOOK CLUB

Finding opportunities to discuss issues with early adolescents is tough, not just because of the time involved but also because your children's growing sense of independence may make them less than enthusiastic about having heart-to-heart talks with Mom or Dad.

Myra Paul, a middle-school librarian, started a mother-daughter book club as a vehicle for talking about issues and preparing her child for the tricky transition from elementary to middle school.

Paul and three other mothers started the club with their fifth-grade daughters. The books lead to lively discussions about such issues as dating, peer pressure, and cliques. The biography of young AIDS victim Ryan White stimulated a conversation about the risks of contracting the disease.

Another story about a girl who had a very young mother got the girls talking about how old women should be before they start families. The girls are more comfortable talking about characters in books than about themselves.

Now that her daughter is an eighth grader, Paul finds the book club offers a rare opportunity for such discussions because, like most kids her age, Sara is less communicative at home these days. "When the club talks about something like sex, we get the perspective of four daughters and mothers, which is more interesting than me just giving Sara a lecture on AIDS," Paul points out.

Meetings often end with the girls wandering off for some time together while the moms compare notes on the phases their kids are going through. "It's almost like a support group," Paul says.

Paul thinks a book club could work with boys, too, as long as they are independent readers. Dads could have a book club with either their sons or their daughters to get an interesting perspective on their young adolescents' viewpoints. While boys' tastes might run to sports books or science fiction, these genres include many titles that address the issues of growing up.

Paul offers these tips to parents who want to start a book club:

- Don't form one before the kids are enthusiastic and independent readers, probably not before fifth grade. The motive shouldn't be to get adolescents to become readers. Otherwise, it will seem like just another parent-imposed chore.
- Limit the size to no more than about six children so everyone has a chance to talk.
- Let the kids take turns picking the book to be discussed. They can get suggestions from school and public librarians. "It shouldn't be the parents' agenda," Paul cautions.
- Allow at least six to eight weeks between meetings, so kids and parents both have enough time to read the books.
- Be creative about meeting places. Paul's group usually meets in homes or restaurants. When they read *Of Mice and Men* by John Steinbeck, they discussed it and then watched the video in the hostess' family room. A book about a girl who lived in an American internment camp for Japanese-Americans during World War II was discussed at a Japanese restaurant. The group also attended a bookstore appearance by one of the authors they had read.

American Council for Drug Education. You must use education and discipline to assure that your children's decision is "no."

Convey to your teen both the value of not using drugs and the consequences of using them, Dogoloff suggests. If you and your children see a drunk-driving accident reported in the news, use that "teachable moment" to talk about the danger of alcohol. Dogoloff advises parents to forbid the use of alcohol, tobacco, and illegal drugs and to "come down hard" with sanctions if a child disobeys. "Your job as a parent is to get in the way of behavior that is unhealthy and destructive," he says.

Working parents sometimes are reluctant to impose discipline because they feel guilty about the time they spend away from home. But "if you are a working parent who has some guilt already," Dogoloff says, "you aren't going to make it up in overdosing on permissiveness." He also advises keeping your liquor supply locked if your child spends unsupervised time at home.

If your family has a history of drug or alcohol abuse, your child is especially at risk, Dogoloff says, and so are children with learning disabilities and attention deficit disorder.

Signs of Drug Abuse

Spotting drug abuse can be tricky because some of the signs are similar to common adolescent behavior. Things to watch for are declining school performance, slovenly appearance, interest in drug symbols and paraphernalia, secrecy, and withdrawal from the family.

"Part of adolescence is healthy withdrawal," Dogoloff says, as teens strive to become independent. "But (drug-users) pull away because they know they are doing something wrong and feel guilty."

If you suspect your child is using drugs, you should contact an experienced professional for help, Dogoloff says. Your pediatrician or family physician probably could refer you.

Abusing Legal Substances

Teens also can hurt themselves through the misuse of some fairly common household products. Searching for highs that don't require the purchase or possession of illegal substances, kids inhale fumes from glue, propane, butane, aerosols, paint thinner, and gasoline.

They don't associate danger with items regularly available at grocery and hardware stores. Yet inhaling these legal substances can do serious damage to the heart, lungs, brain, liver, kidneys, nerves, or bones, and even cause sudden death to otherwise healthy youngsters.*

TIP: The federal government operates a hot line with information on substance abuse, including free materials for parents. Call the National Clearinghouse for Alcohol and Drug Information at 800-729-6686.

PREVENTING OPPORTUNITIES TO DRINK

"Teen drinking seems to be so common. Is there any way to keep my child from joining in?"

A key is to try to keep your child away from places where teenagers drink—a tough task in this day and age. Ruth Crone, executive director of the Metropolitan Council of Governments in the Washington, D.C., area, tells of a survey done by her agency in which 20 percent of parents said they suspected their teenagers had come home drunk from a party at least once, while 72 percent of teenagers said they actually had.

---

* The Washington Post, 30 January 1994, p. 1.

DRUG USE RISING AMONG TEENAGERS

A Department of Health and Human Services study, released in January 1994, showed teenage drug abuse rising again after having declined for a decade. And it found a reduction in the number of students who disapproved of illicit drug use or thought it poses a risk.

The survey of 50,000 junior and senior high school students also revealed that:

❑ The biggest increase was in marijuana use; 26 percent of twelfth graders reported smoking it within the last 12 months, up 4 percentage points from the previous year.

❑ 9.2 percent of eighth graders reported smoking marijuana.

❑ 8.4 percent of tenth graders abused inhalants.

❑ 8.4 percent of seniors abused prescription amphetamines.

❑ Cocaine use remained at low levels and alcohol use declined, but cigarette use was up.

Crone describes a common scenario: A teenager, whose parents are away for the weekend, invites a friend over for Cokes and a video. Then a couple of acquaintances drop by with a six-pack of beer. Other kids at school have heard of the house where the parents aren't home and come bearing a keg. More kids walk in, not even bothering to ring the bell. The party expands to the backyard, attracts other neighborhood kids, and gets completely out of control.

Even if your child doesn't drink anything (although the peer pressure is great to go along with the crowd), it's probable that other party-goers will get drunk, leading to violence or vandalism. Kids who drink too much are more likely to engage in sex or become dangerous behind the wheel of a car.

Teen Supervision While You're Away

Crone thinks parents shouldn't put their kids in such a vulnerable position. She and her husband avoided leaving town together unless they took their kids along. If parents must leave town without the kids, she says, they should ask a trusted friend or relative to stay at their home or they should arrange for their children to stay in the home of responsible adults.

Crone and her husband left their high-school-age son home once while they attended parents' weekend at their daughter's college. Before they left, Crone wrote what she calls a "Domicile Protection Plan." It said their son could be at home briefly during the day but would sleep at the home of a buddy whose parents Crone trusted. A couple of Crone's friends agreed to drop in to check on the house, and a neighbor across the street also was enlisted to keep watch.

All of the adults involved had copies of Crone's plan, which contained all of their phone numbers, descriptions of their cars, and the numbers where the Crones could be reached. Any unauthorized people or cars at the house were to be reported to the police. Despite all of the preparations, Crone recalls, "we still worried the whole time."

Rules for Evenings Out

Crone thinks parents have to be vigilant when they are home, too. When your teenagers go out, you should know where they are going and when they will return. If Crone's kids wanted to stay out later than planned, they had to call to obtain permission before doing so. She required her children to give her a good-night kiss when they returned—even if they had to wake her—so she'd know they were home safely with no smell of alcohol on their breath.

Parent Networks

Crone and Dogoloff both stress the importance of parent networks. Parents should be active in the PTA, Crone says. "That's where you hear who had a party, what's going on, or who the troublemakers are."

By forming a peer group of the parents of your child's closest friends, Dogoloff explains, "you can talk about curfews and supervision at parties so you can share standards."

TEEN PARTIES

Though the kids might not like it, teen parties need adult supervision. It's your responsibility to supervise when the gathering's at your house. You also want to make sure adults oversee the parties that your child attends elsewhere.

Some parents advise keeping your refrigerator stocked with snacks and soft drinks and making your children's friends feel welcome to congregate in your

PARENT AS DIPLOMAT

Diane Brewer says that when her daughter is invited to a party, she calls the host's parents to make sure the parents know about it and will be home.

The call doesn't always generate a warm reception. "Some parents don't see it as a big problem for kids to collect unsupervised," she says. Others think the question implies that you don't trust their judgment or their child's.

To avoid this, Brewer starts the call with, "I understand you're having a party Friday night." Then she asks what her daughter can bring, such as chips or soft drinks.

During the conversation, she can then learn if the party will be chaperoned, and she doesn't let her daughter go if it won't be.

home. That way, you can keep an eye on the activities and get to know your kids' friends.

You don't want to be obtrusive when your child hosts a party at your house. But you also don't want to disappear into your own bedroom for the evening and leave the teens on their own. Your adult presence is needed.

One trick Marguerite Kelly used when her children were teens was to serve tacos for a snack. Going in and out of the party from the kitchen, bearing the many ingredients, gave her an excuse to keep an eye on things. "Kids won't object to food being brought in!" Kelly stresses.

Prom nights are notorious for after-dance drinking parties. An alternative is for the school's PTA to host an all-night after-prom party with food, nonalcoholic beverages, casino-type games, movies, and places for kids to sit and talk. Diane Brewer helped with an all-night party at her daughter's school. No one left to get drunk, she says, because the teens who attended had to agree to stay for the whole party.

To succeed, such parties have to be truly entertaining for the teenagers, says Sharon Murphy, a consultant to the Virginia Department of Education. As a PTA president, she organized all-night celebrations for students on prom and graduation nights, and now teaches parents how to do it.

> **TIP:** Sharon Murphy has compiled a 178-page book of tips for party-planners that can be obtained at no charge by writing to the Virginia Department of Education, Richmond, VA 23216. Murphy also is willing to answer questions over the phone at 703-620-9743.

TEENAGE DEPRESSION

"My teenager has bouts when he's moody and withdrawn. How can I tell if this is just normal adolescent behavior or if it could be real depression?"

Since suicide is one of the leading causes of death among teenagers, parents are understandably concerned if their child seems unhappy or depressed. Of course, we all remember those turbulent years when our hormones kicked in, magnifying life's inevitable ups and downs into major emotional upheavals. All teenagers go through periods of sadness, irritability, or disappointment. But usually they bounce back quickly. Depression is longer-lasting and interferes with the teenager's ability to function in day-to-day activities.

Dr. David Mrazek, chairman of psychiatry at Children's National Medical Center in Washington, D.C., says parents have a hard time recognizing depression because teenagers are good at masking it. In their efforts to become more independent, they're more emotionally distant from their parents, spending more time with friends. And often they are going through some rebellion.

Another reason some parents fail to pick up on the early signs is that they don't want to believe their child is unhappy, something they would feel responsible for, says Mrazek, co-author of *The A to Z Guide to Your Child's Behavior* (Perigee, 1993).

"Depression is the result of multiple factors coming together," Mrazek says. There are people who have a genetic vulnerability to it. It's also related to stress caused by events such as loss of someone important through death or divorce or the end of a romantic relationship. Another influence is loss of self-esteem from such disappointments as not making the sports team or not getting into the college of the teenager's choice. "Some kids are very vulnerable to such losses," Mrazek adds.

Dr. Mrazek offers several signs to watch for:

- ❑ sudden lack of interest in clothes, personal appearance, friends, school, or getting into college
- ❑ lethargy, lack of interest in sports or other physical activities
- ❑ inability to sleep or oversleeping
- ❑ changes in appetite; sudden weight loss or weight gain
- ❑ sudden increase in risk-taking behavior; a serious car collision, for example, might be suicidal or mental health–related
- ❑ statements from the teenager about how miserable she is or about how she doesn't want to live anymore

There can be explanations other than depression for some of these symptoms. Fatigue or weight loss, for example, could be due to a physical illness. And certainly it's not abnormal for a teenager to be mopey for a week or two if he's just broken up with his girlfriend, Mzarek explains. But three or four weeks is not normal.

If your child's depressed mood is mild, and he's willing to talk to you about it, the best thing to do is remain available, be supportive, and avoid putting him under additional stresses. If he doesn't open up to you, Mzarek says, you might consult first with a minister or rabbi who knows your child well and could be more objective than you are about whether there really is a problem. If you suspect there is, seek professional help.

> **TIP:** For more information, call the National Mental Health Association at 800-969-6642 and ask for the free brochures called *Teens and Self-Esteem* and *A Teenager's Guide to Surviving Stress*. The association also can answer questions, refer you to other materials, and give you the phone number of the nearest local chapter. There are about 350 around the country.

TIME WELL SPENT

HERE'S HELP ON:

Shortcuts on the home front, page 156

Reducing your time on the road, page 166

Spending your "free" time well, page 167

Time with the children, page 168

Volunteering, page 171

Staying involved with school, page 173

Family vacations, page 174

Couple time, personal time, page 179

More time is at the top of every working parent's wish list. Yet we know we can't add to the 24 hours we're given each day. What we really want is fewer hours eaten up by work, domestic chores, and sleep, so we have more time for our kids, our spouses, and ourselves.

To free up that time, we have to remove some of the things already on our plates. And, because it takes thought and discipline to use time more efficiently and to concentrate on our real priorities, we have to do some planning.

When we asked Tom's sister Ellen Pinker, a mother of three young children, what she'd do if she had an afternoon to herself, her instant response was: "Shave both my legs on the same day." She wasn't kidding. Anyone who's had even one baby knows that life passes in a blur during the early stages of parenthood.

It gets better when the kids get older and at least you're able to sleep through most nights. But by then you're juggling not only your own calendars but those of your kids, who now have dance classes, birthday parties, soccer, and a zillion other things to squeeze into their schedules.

It's no wonder parents look ahead with mixed feelings to the day their child gets her driver's license. They're scared of the added risk this brings to their child's life—but relieved not to have to do all the chauffeuring anymore!

Shortcuts on the Home Front

"Our house is a mess. We spend our nights and weekends doing chores and errands. We're overcommitted. How can we find some time to have fun?"

Working parents have to be very inventive to become more efficient. The only way they're going to gain more family time is to cut out the time-wasters. Here are some of the strategies we've heard from parents or tried in our own family.

SET PRIORITIES

With all of the competing demands on your time, you have to learn to say no to the things that aren't that important to you.

Try this little exercise: With pencil and paper, record all the optional activities in your life and estimate how much time you spend on them. Re-list those activities in order of importance and consider whether some should be eliminated.

Then, before you say yes to a new commitment, consider whether it is a high priority for you and what on your list you're willing to give up in its place. Help your children do this, too. It's common for even young children to have days that are too full of scheduled activities.

HIRE HELP

In her first prime-time interview a few months after becoming first lady, Hillary Clinton revealed that she still did some laundry occasionally. Working parents probably wondered why—when she has the whole White House staff at her beck and call, and she had a major health care reform package to produce—she would be doing housework. For her it seemed to be an attempt to maintain some normalcy in her life, even while married to the leader of the free world. Most of the rest of us, however, would be quite happy to turn the laundry over to someone else and never look back.

While it's true that not everyone can afford housekeepers, those who can't might be able to pay for smaller services—sending shirts to the laundry, hiring a housecleaning service on an occasional basis, getting a neighborhood kid to mow the lawn, paying someone to get the car inspected or to wash the windows. Some parents hire a neighborhood preteen to entertain their children while they make dinner. (Incidentally, this is a good way to groom a future babysitter!)

"I hired someone to do the grocery shopping," says Jan Hodson, who dreaded this chore, which took two hours by the time she drove, shopped, and stowed the food away in her kitchen. Because she lives near a college campus, she was able to hire the wife of a graduate student to handle this each week for her family.

SIMPLIFY MEALTIME

You can cut a lot of activities out of your daily schedule, but eating isn't one of them. Add cooking and cleanup time, and you've used up a substantial chunk of your day.

One way to tackle this is to simplify the meals. Give up homemade dinners as much as your taste buds—and parental guilt level—can tolerate. There's a wide array of convenience foods out there for you to explore.

Spaghetti sauce in a jar can seem almost as good as homemade if you're a harried parent, and stir-fry dishes are easy now that you can buy frozen vegetables and meat already cut up. When you do your grocery shopping, stop at the salad bar and pick up tomorrow's cold lunch or supper. And think takeout; there's more than just pizza and Chinese to choose from today—and many places deliver.

Using shortcuts doesn't mean giving up good nutrition. In fact, it's quicker and more nutritious to serve raw fruits and veggies with a low-fat dip than to cook them.

Picnic Suppers

Our family enjoys picnic suppers in summer. In winter, we sometimes put a plastic tablecloth on the floor in front of the fireplace and have an indoor picnic. No one has to cook—we get the food from a neighborhood deli or the supermarket—but the meal seems festive because it's served in an out-of-the-ordinary setting.

Make Simple Special

Something as simple as candles on the table can make a soup-and-sandwich meal seem special. When they are old enough, kids enjoy lighting the candles before the meal and snuffing them out afterward.

But Don't Overdo It!

We ignore those magazine articles that show you how to turn food into "works of art your children will love." A couple of times, we tried using cookie cutters on bread. (It's not as easy as it sounds!) But Julie still didn't like tuna salad, even if it was in sandwiches shaped like stars or animals. Luckily, as she got older, she grew to like it, even on plain bread.

Guests In? Take Out

You don't have to slave in the kitchen all day to produce a dinner good enough for guests. You can get lasagna at the Italian deli, buy prepared dishes and salads from your supermarket, or wait until the guests arrive and order takeout from a restaurant and have it delivered. The company matters more than the meal.

Neighborhood Cooking

There's a neighborhood near us where five families do cooperative cooking. Each family is responsible for preparing and delivering dinner to the other four on one weeknight. There's some planning involved, of course, especially to find dishes that can be made in quantity and that accommodate the tastes of the others in the group. And there's more work in making a large batch of something instead of just a single-family-size one—but think of the reward of not having to cook the other four nights!

Involve the Whole Family

If you want to combine cooking and spending time with your kids, find simple tasks they can do, such as washing vegetables or setting the table. Motivate them with their own kid-size aprons or children's cookbooks. The cooking probably will take longer when they "help," but at least you're doing something together.

Very young children enjoy having a play area adjacent to or in the kitchen so they can be with you while you cook, even if they aren't actually involved in the process.

SIMPLIFY SHOPPING
This can be a big time-waster, especially if you have to drag the kids along. Here are some shortcuts.

Shop by Catalog
Our family has become big catalog shoppers. Sometimes we make mistakes and have to send something back. But if we stick to catalogs we've already used or friends have recommended, it doesn't happen too often. And we figure we can afford to return something once in a while for all the time we save not having to drive to the stores in the car.

Ordering flowers or gift baskets by phone for distant friends or relatives is a double time-saver: It not only saves shopping time but also eliminates a trip to the post office.

EATING OUT—WITH KIDS

If you like to dine out, start taking your children to restaurants at a young age so they will become comfortable and learn what kind of behavior is expected. Here are a few tips on eating out with the very young:

❏ Check ahead to make sure the restaurant is a place families go with children. It's probably okay if it has a children's menu and high chairs.

❏ Go early or make reservations so the kids don't have to wait to be seated.

❏ Place your order quickly so your meal arrives before the troops get restless.

❏ Ask for crackers, bread, or something else for your child to munch on to take the edge off hunger until the meal arrives.

❏ Take along small toys or other amusements so the kids can entertain themselves.

❏ Don't ignore restaurants with international cuisine just because your kids tend to order burgers and fries. Many ethnic restaurants are family-run and welcome children. Less-spicy appetizers in Chinese, Greek, or Mexican restaurants make great finger-food meals for children.

Keep a List

For things you need to pick up in stores, keep a running list so you can consolidate trips. Then, if you go to the dry cleaners and see on your list that you need something from the hardware store next door, you can cut down on repeat trips.

Buy in Quantity

We keep a stash of children's birthday presents in a closet so we don't have to shop every time Julie gets a party invitation. We never buy just one greeting card, but check our list of upcoming birthdays and holidays and stock up. The food warehouse stores offer another way to buy in bulk—and save money—as long as you have a place to store large sizes and quantities of grocery items.

Shop the Off-Hours

Finally, shop when other people don't. If you can hit the grocery store on a weeknight instead of the weekend, you'll find it less crowded. Shopping then is less stressful, and you'll spend less time standing in line at the checkout.

USE TECHNOLOGY TO YOUR ADVANTAGE

Some modern gizmos, chosen and used wisely, can be godsends for busy families. Here are the most popular products of modern technology that working parents told us they'd rather not live without.

Microwave Oven

It's worth the price, even if all you do is thaw out food you forgot to take from the freezer before you went to work. It's also great for heating leftovers and making a single-serving meal for a finicky eater or a parent working odd hours.

Answering Machine

You get all your messages, can return calls at your leisure, ignore calls you don't want, and spend uninterrupted time with your child or spouse without missing an important call.

Cordless Phone

It lets you talk on the phone while you're putting in laundry or doing other chores around the house.

Call Waiting

This phone feature saves you from having to keep redialing to reach your older kids if they're home alone and on the phone a lot.

Beeper

On-the-move parents and children can be reached no matter where they are. From a touch-tone phone, you can call the most convenient beeper models and key in the phone number you want the beeper carrier to contact. Your home-alone child can call you at any time. You can give your beeper number to teachers, babysitters, other caregivers, and the parents whose homes your children frequent.

Cellular Phone

More versatile than a beeper and no longer confined to automobiles, cellular phones now can be purchased in portable models small enough to fit into your pocket. The carrier can answer calls instantly and make outgoing calls as well.

Recorded Books on Cassette

You can keep up with your reading—or, rather, listening—while you commute, cook dinner, or wait for soccer practice to be over. The selection is now quite large, with fiction and nonfiction tapes available for sale or rental through stores and mail order. Many libraries stock them, too.

Finance by Wire

Find a bank that lets you use the telephone to pay bills and move money between accounts. Ask your employer's payroll or accounting department if your paycheck can be deposited directly into your bank account.

VCR

You can watch the movies you don't have time to see in the theater anymore, and you can tape your favorite TV shows to view at your convenience. A VCR can help you control your child's entertainment, too. And—talk about saving time—you can watch a football game in an hour by fast-forwarding through the time-outs and halftime!

Tape Recorder

Some parents take one along to dictate notes or

ideas when they are away from their desks—in the car, pushing the stroller, or standing in line, for instance. It's a handy device, so long as you don't overdo it to the point of annoying the people around you.

Computer

The home computer has many uses, from keeping track of your finances to printing your holiday newsletter. Kids can use it for learning as well as entertainment. You don't have to haul kids to the library, for example, if they can tap into a computerized encyclopedia. You can buy programs that teach anything from chess to typing.

HOUSEKEEPING SHORTCUTS

Some of the following ideas might be obvious to you, but there may be others here you haven't thought of.

No-Fuss Clothes

Don't be tempted to buy clothes that must be hand-washed or line-dried, or that require more than touch-up ironing. Remember, you not only have to pay for those silk shirts, but you also have to cart them off to the dry cleaners or wash and iron them

TECHNOLOGY ON THE GO

We spotted the ultimate working parents' use of technology on a weekday afternoon visit to the Santa Fe, New Mexico, children's museum. A father, clearly torn between wanting to be with his kids and having to finish some office work, had come toting a cellular phone and a laptop computer.

While we don't encourage bringing your office with you on all your outings with your children, technology can help out in a pinch when the press of work makes compromise necessary.

Take, for example, our neighbor, Barry Morewitz, whose job involves monitoring the stock market from his home office. He often takes his daughter Risa to a nearby park and carries a portable receiver that feeds him up-to-the-minute stock quotations. He turns a few heads as he gazes at his hand-held screen, but he puts in a lot more park time than most dads do.

by hand! Sensible working parents look for items that go from washer to dryer to drawer with minimal fuss in between.

No-Fuss Interiors

Look for "dishwasher-proof" labels when you buy items for the kitchen, and make sure they also can go into the microwave oven. You'll save cooking and serving time by heating leftovers on the dinner plates, and you'll face an easier cleanup when the meal is over.

You don't have to wash drapes if there are none on your windows. A no-wax floor with no rugs is easier to maintain than a wood floor with small carpets scattered about.

We're not suggesting that you turn your home into something stark and cold that can be cleaned with a hose once a month. But the very design of your house and what you put into it will influence how hard it is to keep presentable.

When you paint the walls, buy carpet, or shop for new furniture, you should always be asking: How much maintenance does this require? If the carpet is white, the furniture isn't stain-resistant, and the paint can't be washed, the answer is: too much.

Folks we know have only perennials in their garden so they don't have to plant their flower beds every year.

Get Rid of Clutter

We know, you're thinking that getting rid of clutter is easier said than done. But keeping it picked up, stored, or pitched simplifies housecleaning and means you don't waste time trying to find lost items. Giving kids storage bins or large baskets to stow toys helps them keep their own messes under control. And for every purchase you consider, first think about whether you want to store it, dust it, or clean around it.

Dispose of things that make you feel guilty. If unread magazines or drooping houseplants are playing on your conscience, don't suffer any longer: Get rid of them.

Practice Preventive Housekeeping

At our house, Julie's friends know that food is to be eaten at the kitchen table, not dribbled through other rooms. (We started confining snacks to the kitchen when she was a toddler.) Hands coated with paint or mud are taken immediately to the sink. Having good floor mats, both inside and outside the exterior doors, cuts down on tracking dirt through the house.

We don't restrict kids from engaging in messy activities, but we've learned to use cookie sheets on the kitchen table for projects involving paint, glitter, or clay. In good weather, we send messy projects outdoors to the picnic table covered with old newspapers.

It's also a good idea to make sure that the materials used in inherently messy play are easy to clean up. In a toy store, we overheard an exasperated mother say to a clerk about a children's paint set: "I don't care that it's nontoxic. I want to know if it's washable."

A Stitch in Time

If you stack pans and dishes in the sink until the food dries, you've got twice as big a job. If wash-and-wear clothes sit in the dryer, they'll wrinkle and need touch-up ironing. If your car doesn't get its regular maintenance, you could end up stuck on the highway or with a car in the shop for days. If you ignore the filling that fell out of your tooth...well, you get the idea. Before procrastinating, think about all the time you'll save by getting a job done when it's easier to do.

Delegate Chores

Assigning chores to children teaches them responsibility and eventually can make your household run more efficiently. They learn that they are contributing members of a family where individuals pitch in for the good of all. Even very young children can be given simple assignments that provide a sense of accomplishment.

Don't expect perfection. And don't redo a slightly imperfect job or you'll undermine your child's feeling of achievement. Be explicit with a child when assigning a big chore, such as cleaning her room, and help her break it down into several small tasks— make the bed, put the dirty clothes in the hamper, stow the toys on the shelf, and so forth. Completing each task then becomes an accomplishment. Rotate the assigned chores so your kids don't get bored.

Involving children doesn't necessarily save you time at first because you might be able to do the chores faster by yourself. But, while you're imparting the message that every family member is part of a

LOWER YOUR STANDARDS, PROTECT YOUR SANITY

Most parents are forced to lower their housekeeping standards out of sheer necessity, and it can be downright upsetting if you're a neatness freak or if you constantly compare yourself to other parents and their standards. You can drive your kids or your spouse crazy, too, if you're constantly chiding them for making messes.

Will it make you feel better to know you're not alone? Housekeeping standards have been going down for several years, especially in dual-earner homes with young children. The evidence for this includes surveys of moving companies, maid services, and exterminators who regularly visit private homes, and from research showing a decline in the hours families spend each week on housework.

The *New York Times* reported, on April 11, 1993, that home economics experts are accepting—some, endorsing—this change, describing it as parents "reprioritizing" or having better things to do with their time. As mothers work more outside the home, they have less time to devote to traditional housekeeping chores. While fathers are taking on more housekeeping responsibilities, they are not filling all of the gap, these experts have found.

Working parents who can afford it—and are so inclined—are hiring others to do their housekeeping for them. Many of the rest are buying cleaning products that promise to do several jobs at once. They also are more content to let the hidden dirt lie while trying to keep visible surfaces clean.

Instead of getting frustrated about your less-than-pristine home, remind yourself that you'll have time to focus on your nest once the kids have left it. Most of us would rather our children remember that we had time for them than that we had the cleanest house on the block.

team, you're also paving the way for your child to be a big help to you when he's older.

Reducing Your Time on the Road

You can make a sizable reduction in your commuting time by changing your job or moving closer to work. A bit radical, perhaps, but some parents actually do this when the grind gets to be too much. Telecommuting—working at home for all or part of the week, often with a computer and a modem—is gaining popularity as another way to stop wasting time on the highway, enjoy a more flexible work schedule, and spend more time near the kids. (*See* Working from Home *on page 229.*)

Many people, however, don't have the option of telecommuting or of easily switching jobs or neighborhoods; they're committed to homes and workplaces that are miles apart. Some of these parents opt for mass transit because they can read, knit, or make other productive use of commuting time. Others choose child care near their workplace so that commuting time becomes an opportunity to spend time with their children.

Choose Services Where Most Convenient

If you can't cut your commute to work, small reductions in other car trips may be possible. Find a hairdresser, dry cleaner, physician, and dentist close to work but a pediatrician close to home.

It's certainly important to find a pediatrician with a good reputation, a comforting manner, and a child-rearing philosophy compatible with yours. But, if he or she has an office miles from your home, keep looking. The numerous trips you'll make to the pediatrician will add up to a lot of time in the best of circumstances. No need to pile on extra hours in the car. While you're at it, try to find a practice with evening or weekend hours. Some doctors have schedules that accommodate families with two working parents.

Organize Your Errands

A lot of driving time can be wasted on errands. Use your phone before you jump into your car. Call around to determine which hardware store has the item you need; check the pharmacy's hours to make sure it will be open when you get there to pick up your child's prescription.

Try to cluster errands. If your supermarket sells stamps and has a bank machine, you can can cut three stops down to one. (At ours, we even can get flu shots in the fall!) Go to places where parking is easy or where there's a drive-up window.

Take Little Chores with You

Don't leave home empty-handed if you suspect you'll have time to kill. Carry chores with you for times when you're standing in line or waiting in the car. Balance your checkbook, catch up on your reading, or make lists.

Car Pools for the Kids

You'll spend fewer hours on the road if you take the time to organize car pools to take your kids to school, ballet, soccer, and birthday parties.

Spending Your "Free" Time Well

The point of using time more efficiently is so you have more of it to give to your children, your spouse, and yourself. But that takes some careful planning, too. It's easy to fall into the trap of spending all your free time with the kids, partly because you feel guilty about being away from them.

But healthy marriages need nurturing, too, the kind of nurturing that comes from spending time as a couple. And you need personal time to relax in your own way and to recharge your battery.

Make Room for Fun—and Chores

When you schedule family recreation time, agreeing on how you spend it can be tricky. The mere act of having fun as a family unit is fraught with peril if everyone has his or her own definition of fun. Yes, there are families in which every member adores camping, for example. But we think this is the exception rather than the rule. And, as children grow from toddlers to teenagers, their ideas of a fun weekend change dramatically.

While you're blocking out time for leisure, you may want to put chore time on your calendar, too. Setting aside Saturday mornings for housecleaning, when everybody pitches in, can have a positive effect on the preceding six days. Family members will clean up their messes as they go through the week, so they can finish the housework faster on Saturday and get an earlier start on weekend fun.

Time with the Children

"We're always hearing about quality time, but too often the time I spend with my kids is when I'm doing something else, like grocery shopping or cooking dinner. If I plan some special activity with them, they don't always want to do it or we feel rushed to finish."

REDEFINING "QUALITY TIME"

Sometimes parents get caught up in the idea that quality time has to involve some special "Kodak moment" kind of experience. But, for a child, it's probably those times when we just interact with them on their level, listening to their concerns or joys, comforting them, or laughing with them. Quality time doesn't need an agenda or a special setting. It just needs you and your child.

If it's so simple, why is quality time so hard to come by? Because unstructured, uncommitted hours aren't found in our day unless we make a conscious effort to block them in. Your child knows you're only

SCHEDULING LEISURE TIME

Free time has a way of evaporating. That's why Pam Ripley, an Arizona schoolteacher, schedules leisure activities on her calendar. This way, she avoids letting other things encroach on family time.

Her calendar might include a weekend camping trip with the family or a personal treat such as getting a massage. She writes down time for exercise, sometimes a brisk walk with her husband or a neighbor.

She's usually too tired at the end of the day to enjoy reading, "so sometimes I block out two hours of reading on a Saturday as a reward to myself," Ripley says. If someone asks her to do something during those hours, she simply checks her calendar and says she has another commitment.

half listening if you're also plowing through rush hour traffic or cooking dinner. To give kids undivided attention, especially if you have more than one child or if you are a single parent, takes real effort.

One-on-One Time

Whether you use Stanley Greenspan's concept of "floor time" (*see box on page 170*) or some version of your own, the important thing is to deliberately plan for frequent one-on-one time with each of your children. If you can't work in 30 minutes per child each day, try 15. It could be part of your bedtime ritual, just as long as each child has a chance, free of distractions (including siblings), to share with one of his parents his feelings about what's going on in his life. Establishing the habit early will make it easier to keep communication lines open when your child hits the teen years.

Night Walks

For regular quality time with the whole family, some parents like night walks. Even when the weather's cold, you can bundle up, take the dog, and go out after dinner to enjoy the night air, the smells, the stars, and all the things that look different by night.

It's good exercise and can stimulate your child to be more candid since you don't have to make eye contact in the dark.

Family Fun Can Be Simple, Spontaneous

Having fun as a family doesn't have to be complicated. The fact that you've allotted a particular time for it doesn't mean it has to be a major event. It's easy to throw together a picnic, head for a park, set up the badminton set, or pull out the Monopoly board.

The Art of Compromise

It's more fun if you try to find some common interests that everyone in the family can enjoy. But that doesn't mean every activity has to be equally enjoyable to each family member. Children learn valuable lessons about compromising and sharing when you take turns planning family outings. It means trying to make sure that nobody has a miserable time and everybody has a fair share of turns to have a great one.

Reading Together

Reading is another important family activity. Too often, parents who read religiously to their pre-

"FLOOR TIME"

In his book, *Playground Politics: Understanding the Emotional Life of Your School-Age Child* (Addison-Wesley, 1993), psychiatrist Stanley Greenspan advocates what he calls "floor time." It's a concept he teaches parents to use as a way to better understand what is going on in their children's lives and to help them work through the challenges they are confronting, especially during the school-age years.

Simply described, floor time means spending about half an hour a day with your child during which the child sets the agenda. With preschool children, you'd typically get down on the floor and engage in make-believe play that the child directs. For school-age children, you could sprawl on the bed or take a walk, while chatting about whatever is on their minds.

"The idea behind floor time is to build up a warm, trusting relationship in which shared attention, interaction, and communication is occurring on your child's terms," Greenspan writes.

The concept sounds simple, but in practice many parents find it difficult to do, Greenspan says. A key problem, of course, is finding the 30 minutes each day to devote total attention to each other. Busy schedules conspire to keep us from interacting. But that's why Greenspan is so determined that we find that 30 minutes when we turn off the TV, postpone the dinner dishes, and give undivided attention to our children.

A pitfall to avoid in floor time is orchestrating it yourself instead of leaving it to your child. It's tempting to suggest a plot line if your child has engaged you in a fantasy with dolls and a castle of blocks. Or if your older child says, "I have a really lousy teacher," Greenspan warns, don't say "Don't talk about your teacher that way!" Instead, you might say: "Yes, teachers can be difficult sometimes. What did yours do today?"

If your child doesn't feel like talking at first, don't give up. Instead, ask why he doesn't want to talk about it, or tell him about times in your childhood when you didn't feel like talking either.

schoolers get out of the habit when the children learn to read to themselves. But teachers tell us that parents should continue to read regularly at least through the elementary years.

Even children who read well benefit from hearing a story because it helps develop their listening skills and allows them to enjoy books with a wider vocabulary. They can concentrate without having to stop every time they come to a word they don't recognize. They can ask you what words mean. You can discuss the meaning of the story together. You are demonstrating that you believe in the importance of reading. And it can lead to the kind of discussions that Greenspan encourages through floor time.

(Role reversals are fine, too. Julie likes to read to us from time to time.)

Volunteering

"I'm so overcommitted with volunteer work that I'm thinking about withdrawing from everything! How can I keep it under control?"

Although volunteering is an area where you can easily fall prey to creeping commitment, it can be personally rewarding for parents and good for your family, especially if the volunteer activity involves more than one family member. Being a volunteer for school, church, Scouts, or your child's sports team, for example, shows her you care about the things that are important in her life and in the lives of others.

ACCOMMODATIONS FOR WORKING PARENTS

Some organizations are better than others at involving working parents as volunteers. Meetings held at night or on weekends and with child care provided will attract more parent volunteers than those that don't. If your church, school, or volunteer group doesn't do this, speak up. Also, don't assume a group's volunteer activities won't fit your schedule. Some, like the Girl Scouts, have changed out of necessity.

CHOOSING FAMILY-ORIENTED ACTIVITIES

If your volunteer time is limited, try finding activities that involve the whole family, so you have the bonus of spending time together while contributing to the greater good and teaching children the value of community service. Picking up trash in the park, planting

GIRL SCOUTS—CHANGING WITH THE TIMES

The biggest impact on the Girl Scouts of mothers leaving the kitchen and going into the work force hasn't been a jump in cookie sales. It's the challenge of finding volunteer troop leaders. But the organization must be doing something right, because the number of adult volunteers—male and female—is at an all-time high.

"We certainly had to change," says Mary Rose Main, national executive director of Girl Scouts of the USA. Leaders used to have to attend many hours of training during the day. Now training is more compressed, is scheduled at night or on weekends, and is augmented by videotapes and phone conferences.

Troop and patrol meetings can be held on evenings or weekends, and several parents can band together to share leadership responsibilities. "Many couples now serve as leaders together," Main adds. The only restriction on a father's involvement is that he must work with a woman leader, "because we think a female role model is so important for the girls," Main says.

flowers at your school, organizing a clothing drive, or visiting shut-ins on holidays are just a few ideas (*see also* Community Opportunities *on page 141*).

Time Commitments

When choosing a project, consider the level of commitment you're willing to make. It can be a one-time activity or something you do every week or every month. Many organizations have adjusted their volunteer jobs to fit the tight schedules of working parents.

Consider Your Children

Tailor the activity to your family's interests and the ages of your children. For example, if you're concerned about the hungry but think serving meals in a soup kitchen may be too intense an experience for your younger children, you could help your local food bank sort, shelve, and repackage food.

Or try gleaning. Some cities have gleaning programs in which volunteers go to nearby farms to harvest leftover fruits and vegetables that are edible but don't meet the appearance standards required by supermarkets. The harvested crops are used by local soup kitchens or distributed to needy families (*see also* Making Volunteering Meaningful for Kids *on page 142*).

> **TIP:** If you need ideas for family volunteer opportunities, one place to contact is your local United Way office, which is listed in your phone book. It has information on many local nonprofit organizations with a variety of volunteer needs.

Staying Involved in Your Children's School

"Our work schedule means we can't get to our son's school very often. And if we forget to check his book bag regularly for newsletters or fliers, we don't know what's going on until it's too late. How can we stay up-to-date and feel better connected to his school?"

Involvement in their children's school should be on all parents' agendas. Research shows a direct relationship between parental involvement and a child's academic success. Getting to know the staff, keeping up on what's happening, and providing much-needed parental support go a long way toward ensuring your child's success. Yet much goes on at school while you're at work. And parents with children in more than one school have an even harder time.

PARENT-TEACHER ORGANIZATIONS

Events sponsored by parent-teacher organizations are good vehicles for school involvement. But you can't pay attention if your kindergartner is squirming in the chair beside you.

Our Parent-Teacher Association (PTA) provides child care for all of our meetings, and parents chip in a couple of dollars per child to cover the cost. One year, the school's Girl Scout troop took this on for their child-care badge. Other years, we've hired junior high students or the teacher aides who work in our after-school program.

School budgets are tight everywhere. Many of the parent volunteer jobs are in either fund-raising or providing help that the school can't pay for—anything from assistance in the classroom to clerical work, yard work, painting, and repair.

Don't wait for the parent association to call you. Call the officers to find out what jobs need doing so you can have first pick of one that suits your skills, interests, and schedule. If your work load at the office is heavier in spring, pick a volunteer project that is done in the fall. If your work schedule is erratic, choose something you can do on your own time, such as phone-calling, rather than serving on a committee that holds meetings at the same time every week.

> **TIP:** The National PTA is a good source of ideas for getting involved in your children's school. The organization has pamphlets on such topics as making parent-teacher conferences work and evaluating your school.
>
> You can get the publications list for $1. The publications are available to anyone, whether you belong to the PTA, some other parent-teacher organization, or no parent-teacher group at all. Write the National PTA, P.O. Box 88873, Chicago, IL 60680.

KEEPING IN TOUCH WITH TEACHERS

"How can we schedule teacher conferences when we're both working?"

Some schools will arrange conferences early in the morning or at night to accommodate working parents. Unless your child is having problems in school, a conference's primary purpose is to give you a progress report and an opportunity to ask the teacher questions. While it's best for both parents to participate, one couple told us they take turns. The one who goes takes written questions from the other and tape-records the conference. That way, nothing is lost in the translation.

Communicating by Phone

Phone calls provide another vehicle for keeping in touch with teachers in between or in lieu of face-to-face conferences. Ask your child's teacher if he or she prefers calls at certain times during the school day, after dismissal, or at home in the evening. Or send in a note and request a written reply.

Some schools have established voice-mail systems that allow you to call the teacher to hear a recorded explanation of that day's homework assignment and any news that parents need to know. That way, you're not dependent on your child remembering what's going on.

Family Vacations

"Before we had kids, our vacations were relaxing. Now we have to come home and rest up after a trip with our children! Do family vacations have

to be this stressful? How can we make them more fun for us all?"

For two-earner families who crave more time together, vacations are a much-needed respite from hectic, everyday life.

Some spouses agree on what makes a perfect vacation, but many don't. Throw children into the equation, along with the family budget and limited vacation time, and planning the perfect trip can be a real challenge. Here are some ideas for meeting everybody's needs and desires.

Give Them a Break

When children are very young, shorter trips closer to home may be easier on the parents. Long car rides with infants and toddlers can put a real strain on family fun. Look for parks or other kid-oriented places to take breaks from long drives and seek out hotels with playgrounds and swimming pools.

Bring Along Amusements

Be sure to pack toys and games to entertain the kids while you're getting to where you're going and also for those inevitable rainy days. Soccer balls or jump ropes are good for releasing pent-up energy at roadside rest stops. Take a blanket for babies who are crawling so they can move around when you stop for a break.

If you're flying, ask if the airport has a kids' space. Several now provide areas with climbing equipment and toys where children can play while awaiting flights.

Take Along Tapes

Music tapes and recorded books also make travel time go faster. If your library's selection of recorded children's books is limited and you don't want to buy them, you can record your own. Let your children choose the stories they want. Or you can surprise them with your own choices. Older children can record books for younger siblings, and families can trade with each other to get different tapes.

Consider Everyone's Interests

As kids grow older, give them a say in where the family will go on vacation, and involve them in the planning. Let them follow maps of your route and let them choose some spots to visit along the way.

If family members' interests vary, incorporate more than one destination in the vacation. Or choose one location with a wide range of attractions. A major metropolitan area, for instance, will offer something for almost everybody: museums, sports, shopping, zoos, and outdoor recreation, for example.

Remember that children have short attention spans. Pace yourself, allowing time for regular rest breaks, cold drinks, and snacks. Use strollers for the younger set, and don't try to cram too much activity into one day.

If we want to see a museum we know Julie won't enjoy, we take turns so one of us can tour while the other finds a nearby park or child-friendly activity to keep her occupied.

> **TIP:** Many cities have magazines or newspapers for parents and children that publish information about local attractions and schedules of events for kids. Before your trip, write to the publication in your destination city to request a recent copy. To get the name and address of the publication, write to Parenting Publications of America, 12715 Path Finder Lane, San Antonio, TX 78230, or call 210-492-3886.

Take Along a Sitter

If you take the kids on vacation but want time

COMPROMISE CAMPING

I'm an avid outdoorsman, and Susan's idea of roughing it is a hotel without room service. Because we've found ways to meld our disparate interests, Julie is growing up with a taste for mountain climbing in the wilderness as well as hotels with heated pools and fancy restaurants.

For a long-weekend getaway, we rent a cabin in the Shenandoah Mountains for what we call "Compromise Camping." Julie and I take hikes, photograph wildlife, and cook the meals over a campfire. Susan appreciates the bed and indoor plumbing. She'll read in the shade outside the cabin or attend historical or cultural programs at the nearby national park lodges.

On longer trips, we try to spend part of the time in a national park for me and part in a city with museums and shopping for Susan. Julie enjoys the junior ranger programs offered at many national parks, and we always try to pick cities with some special kid-oriented attraction.

If Julie and I want to do real camping in a tent, we leave Susan at home.

Tom

together as a couple, you could take along a babysitter. Some teenagers are happy to exchange babysitting for room and board at the beach.

A grandparent also might make a great addition to your traveling party. Grandma gets to travel, and you get some evenings off while she enjoys spoiling her grandchild.

We've done this on two vacations to Hawaii when Julie was 3 and 5 years old. All of the adults had time to pursue their own interests as we took turns entertaining Julie. The benefits extended far beyond babysitting.

Tom and his mother cherished the times the two of them went sight-seeing together, taking long drives that Susan and Julie prefer to avoid. Susan and her mother-in-law enjoyed time together in museums and quilt shops while Tom and Julie played on the beach. Tom and Susan had quiet dinners and walks along deserted beaches while Julie and Grandma had their own adventures.

FAMILY PACKAGES

Hotels and resorts are trying harder than ever to attract families. They're offering supervised programs for children and teens so the kids can have fun while their parents go off on their own. For the younger set, there are toys, crafts, games, movies, cooking with the hotel chef, tours, and the like. Teenagers can choose day trips with other teens and dances or movies in the evening.

Hotels without full-fledged programs frequently offer babysitting services, and some have supervised meals for children in separate dining areas.

If you are considering a resort's children's program, call ahead to find out age limits, the qualifications of the child-care supervisors, whether special reservations are needed, costs, hours of operation, and program content.

Family Cruises

Cruises with separate children's programs are popular with parents who enjoy visiting different locales with minimal hassle. They don't have to move from one hotel to another or deal with transportation. There's plenty to do, even if they don't leave the ship. And the children's programs allow the parents to go on historical tours or shopping trips in port cities without having bored children in tow.

FAMILY CAMPS

Some parents are going to camp with their children instead of sending them off alone. The American Camping Association reports that a number of children's sleep-away camps are being converted into camps for the whole family for all or part of the season.

At these new family camps, everyone can enjoy canoeing, swimming, campfires, horseback riding, crafts, and group meals free from the distractions of television and telephones. A range of supervised activities allows family members to do some things together and some apart. The cabins may be Spartan, but you won't worry about your kids making a mess or creating too much noise, as you might on a vacation spent in hotels.

> **TIP:** The current camping association guide lists more than 200 family camps that have sought and earned ACA accreditation. To order the directory for $12.95, call 800-428-CAMP (800-428-2267). (*For further information on ACA, see* Summer Camps *on page 113.*)

SHARE VACATIONS

Some parents like to join others on vacation. Relatives or good friends chip in on a beach house, for example. If you're going to try a shared vacation, do it with relatives or long-standing friends whom you know very well. Don't focus only on whether the adults are compatible; the kids should be, too.

If you want to share vacations without living together as a big group, go with friends but stay in separate hotel rooms or cottages. That way, your families can be together or apart as the mood strikes you, letting you retain some level of privacy.

SHARE KIDS

An older child may enjoy a vacation more if you let her invite a friend along. And the friend's family can reciprocate another time.

Jo Ann and Herb Amey have done this since their 16-year-old daughter Emily was in fifth grade. Their vacations went smoother when Emily's best friend joined them. And then they'd get a week to themselves when the friend's family took Emily on a trip. One summer the families had their vacations coincide so the girls spent one week with the Ameys at a beach and the next week on an island with the friend's family.

Shared vacation or shared kids can be particularly good for only children. No matter how well you and your child get along, there will be times she'll have more fun with a companion her own age.

Couple Time, Personal Time

Too often time with your spouse gets put at the bottom of the priority list once children come along. But marriages need nurturing if they are to remain strong. And kids need to know that they aren't the center of the universe—that you are a couple and you need time alone.

PLAN FOR SPONTANEITY

If you think planning couple time seems to lack spontaneity, you're right. You lost most of your ability to be spontaneous when you became parents. The closest we get to spontaneous couple time is when Julie gets a last-minute invitation for a sleep-over. If you wait for spontaneity, you'll never spend time together. So go ahead and plan for it.

Some couples put a babysitter on retainer for one or two Saturday nights a month so they'll get regular time alone for dinner or a movie. Others take vacations, or just long weekends, without the kids. Sometimes when we visit the grandparents, we leave Julie with them, go out on the town, and spend the night in a nearby hotel. We know a grandmother who has taken her grandchildren on a vacation so the parents could have a break.

Monthly Dates

If you think a bit of mystery is romantic, try taking turns planning a monthly date. The person whose turn it is arranges child care, picks the activity, makes the reservations, and keeps the plans a surprise for the spouse.

PERSONAL TIME

You've got to block out time to do your own thing or you'll never do it. Relieving the stress of careers and parenthood includes taking care of your personal need for relaxation. Too often, if given a free afternoon, we feel guilty if we relax rather than tackle neglected chores. But enjoying ourselves and indulging in our own personal interests isn't wasting time; it's a necessity for keeping ourselves on an even keel.

Reserve Time for Yourself

Think about something you'd really like to do and reserve a time for it on your calendar. You'll be refreshed and better able to cope with your kids, your spouse, even your boss. Take a class, enjoy a hobby, play a sport, read a book, go out to lunch with a friend, visit a museum, meditate—do anything that gives you pleasure. And, once you've done it, schedule a time when you can do it again soon.

Take Time for Exercise

While it may not be on your list of fun things to do, regular exercise belongs on your agenda, too. Maybe you don't exercise because you don't have time to go to a gym, a pool, a jogging track, or an exercise class. But that isn't a good excuse; you don't have to engage in a lot of strenuous activity or use fancy equipment to make a difference in your physical condition. Health experts say moderate activity—such as a brisk half-hour walk four or five times a week—produces significant health benefits.

Take a walk on your lunch hour, in the evening with the baby in a stroller, or while you're waiting for your daughter's dance class to end. Use the stairs instead of the elevator at work. Get off the bus a couple of stops early. Just do something to get your heart pumping and your limbs moving.

SHARING THE LOAD

HERE'S HELP ON:

Divvying up the labor, page 184
Sharing sick-child care, page 189
Resolving conflicts, page 189
Involving the kids in chores, page 191
Help from friends, page 192
Car pools, page 196
Sharing the babysitting, page 197
Support groups, page 198

That West African saying "It takes a village to rear a child" may seem like an admirable but impractical goal for working parents in the United States today. Extended families are almost extinct, and communities aren't as close-knit as they used to be. Many neighborhoods are virtually deserted for large chunks of the day, with parents at work and children in school or daycare. In fact, instead of a village, just one person often is left with the primary responsibility for child care and housekeeping: Mom, even if she also works outside the home. And single parents have it tougher still.

Going it alone is never as easy as getting help from others. Nowhere is this more true than in child rearing, especially when both parents work full time. Our challenge is to forge partnerships, both within our families and within our communities. It takes some effort on the front end but reaps rewards later.

Divvying Up the Labor

There's a Whirlpool appliance ad that has a member of a modern American family proclaim: "Around here, the homemaker is anybody who happens to be home." Unfortunately, in most families, reality hasn't quite caught up to that ideal.

Many couples are mired in the traditional roles they were raised with—Mom taking care of the kids and home, Dad earning the paycheck—even though today's Mom is working part time or full time outside the home, too. This puts many working mothers into two jobs instead of one: the first shift at work, the second at home.

WOMEN STILL BEAR THE BURDEN

Arlie Hochschild describes that phenomenon in her book *The Second Shift* (Viking, 1989). In the families that Hochschild studied, the women felt more strain than the men (even when husbands shared the work) because:

❑ The women did two-thirds of the daily jobs, such as fixing dinner, while the men did the jobs that don't have to be done regularly at a specific time, such as changing the oil in the car or repairing an appliance. The women, thus, had the pressure of a task facing them every night at 6 P.M., whether they were in the mood or not.

❑ The women were more likely to do two or more things at once, such as ironing and supervising a toddler. The men tended to focus on one thing at a time, folding the laundry *or* playing with the children.

❑ Of the time each devoted to domestic duties, the men's was weighted more than the women's toward child care and the women's more than the men's toward housework. The women tended to do more of the undesirable chores, such as cleaning bathrooms. Of the time devoted to child care itself, the women's was more focused on maintenance (feeding and bathing, for instance) and the men's on play (taking the children to the park). Even while sharing the load, the men got to do more of what they preferred.

❑ The women typically were the ones who kept the family on schedule—always hurrying the children to get ready to go somewhere, for instance, and feeling like the villain.

FATHERS CONFRONT BARRIERS

In our society, men's identity still stems in large part from their success in the workplace. And most employers don't make it easy for men to accept more domestic responsibilities. Employers are more likely to make accommodations for working moms than for working dads, because they assume men will put work before family when there are school closings or sick children at home. Even where benefits such as paternity leave are available, sometimes there's an unspoken message that using the benefit may jeopardize a man's career advancement (*see* Paternity Leaves *on page 30*).

GETTING DADS MORE INVOLVED

"In the early weeks with our baby, I breast-fed her. Now that she's on a bottle and my husband could take over more of the child care, he seems reluctant. How can I get him more involved?"

Mothers have a leg up on fathers when it comes to baby care. Even if they don't know any more about it

CHANGING FOR THE BETTER

Obstacles to fathers fulfilling their roles as complete parents can be found everywhere. We once were in the children's clothing section of a major department store when a man spread a cloth on an out-of-service cash register counter and started changing his baby. A young clerk rushed over to protest. Ignoring her request that he stop, the father complained loudly that there was no changing table in the men's room so he had no choice.

Of course, lots of women's rest rooms don't have changing tables either, so some hassles stem from lack of consideration for parents in general. But things are getting better.

We discovered a shopping mall with a "family room" beside the men's and women's rest rooms. Inside are a private nursing area, baby-changing facilities, and enclosed stalls where parents can take older children. A park we frequent has several unisex rest rooms, so a father spending an afternoon with his small daughter doesn't have to choose between sending her into a women's room alone or taking her into the men's room.

than their husbands, they've formed a close connection to the baby through the unique experience of pregnancy, childbirth, and often nursing. Men know this, of course, and society still tells them infant care is primarily the woman's bailiwick.

Sometimes mothers say they want help but are reluctant to give up their role as the parent in charge. Some men complain that when they take charge of the children, their wives second-guess their decisions or criticize their techniques for changing diapers or preparing baby food, for example. It's no wonder they see their role as secondary.

Let Dad Be a Real Partner

If you want your husband to be an equal partner, you have to treat him like one. Leave him alone with the baby sometimes, so he gains confidence in his ability to care for her. Don't criticize his technique if he doesn't do the diapering exactly the way you do. Your method may be different but not necessarily better. Let him feel his way as a new parent, just as you are. The more you view child rearing as a collaboration, the more likely it actually will become one.

Ask for Help When You Need It

Also, don't wait for him to read your mind. Open a dialogue in which you calmly lay out your case in a nonaccusatory way and ask for his cooperation in finding a solution to your problem of being overburdened. And tell him he's as much needed at home as he thinks he is at work. Many men don't realize how essential their role as father is (*see also* Paternity Leaves *on page 30*).

TRADING RESPONSIBILITIES

"I do more of the child care and housework than my husband does, and I resent it. I always have to ask him to pitch in. How can I get him to do his share without prompting from me?"

Many a working couple's arguments stem from a feeling that one partner isn't pulling a fair share of the domestic load. Especially when it comes to infant care, men may be less involved because they believe their wives are more expert. Caring for children is such an intense, energy-sapping experience that a parent who bears a disproportionate share can come to crave time for herself.

Debra Haffner set up a system to address that problem in her family. One parent has total charge of the children in the evenings on Monday and Wednesday, the other on Tuesday and Thursday. They can trade nights, but the even sharing of labor must be preserved.

Having two nights completely free every week gives each spouse the luxury of taking a class, going out with a friend, staying late at work, or just relaxing in bed with a good book.

"Structure helped us," Haffner recalls. "I felt I had no time for myself when I went back to work, and constantly having to negotiate was crazy."

TO EACH A FAIR SHARE

Debra Haffner and her husband also have their own system for splitting up weekend chores—one her mother used when Haffner and her sister were kids. It's known as "divide and pick," she says. One person divides the chores into two groups and the other gets to pick which group to do. For example, the divider might break down the housecleaning into the upstairs and downstairs or offer the alternative of doing laundry or grocery shopping.

The one who does the dividing is motivated to make the groups equal because she knows she's going

WEEKEND RESPITES

Although Tom always has been a very involved father and handled baby care from day one, our weekends were a big bone of contention. When you're suffering from lack of sleep and see your weekends evaporate in chores and infant care, it's easy to fall into arguments about who got up the most times in the night or who changed the last diaper.

Our solution during Julie's infancy was to give each other one weekend day off. On my day, I could sleep late or go off for an afternoon without the slightest guilt because Tom would get his time off the next day. In practice, neither of us chose to while away the day in idle pleasures very often. Usually, we'd tackle a big household chore or pick a family activity that involved all three of us. But we still had the freedom to choose.

One rule was that the partner who had the day off would step in at dinnertime to feed and bathe Julie and put her to bed. That way, no one got exhausted from rising early and devoting all day and evening to baby care.

Susan

to get stuck with one of them. They also have the commonly used rule that whichever spouse cooks, the other cleans up. The first parent home starts dinner.

Most of the couples we spoke with split the labor according to each spouse's abilities and interests, and that often follows traditional gender lines. The men are more likely to handle car repairs or plumbing. Cooking falls more to the women. Seldom is a chore such as bill paying shared. Instead, it's usually handled by the spouse who's better at math and finance.

Even with Haffner's divide-and-pick system, some jobs are permanently assigned. "Ralph is in charge of yard work because I couldn't care less about that," she says. "I buy the kids' clothes and take them to the doctor."

Exchange Roles Sometimes

Some parents feel each spouse should share every chore in the interest of fair play and so that partners develop expertise in all areas. Even though such perfect sharing is not a common arrangement, it is good if children at least sometimes see Dad cooking and

Mom taking care of the car so they'll be less likely to grow up with a stereotyped view of women's and men's roles.

What is very important is sharing the daily child-care jobs, because your child may develop a strong preference for one parent if you don't. If Mom always is in charge of bedtime rituals, for example, your toddler may be upset when Dad takes over during Mom's business trip. If possible, take turns picking up your child at daycare or taking him to the doctor. Even when you share, children usually go through phases of preferring one parent for a particular activity, but it won't be so pronounced.

Lists and Charts Can Help

Pencil and paper can help you to avoid chore-sharing arguments. List all of the jobs that need to be done and divide them so each parent gets at least some of the ones that he or she prefers. A calendar might help, or use a chart on which you list each week's assignments. When listing chores, set priorities. You might decide to dust furniture every two weeks instead of weekly, if this is not as important to you as another household task. Trade jobs occasionally, or renegotiate, so the work doesn't become so monotonous.

If you hire someone to clean your house or take care of your lawn, your list will be shorter. But every family has chores that should be shared.

A SAMPLE CHORE CHART

MOM

Gas car. Dust and vacuum. Take out trash. Take kids for haircuts. Make dinners. Clean kitchen. Do Saturday morning errands. Take bedtime duty.

DAD

Mow lawn. Wash dishes. Laundry. Car pool to Scouts. Pack lunches this week. Clean bathrooms. Grocery shop. Take morning duty.

Sharing Sick-Child Care

"A big issue at our house is who stays home with the kids when they're sick. It often leads to an argument about whose job is more important."

One couple we know got tired of negotiating this issue and established a rotation. "The person who has to take the day off is the one who didn't do it the last time," the father told us. "It's automatic. No discussion." The other spouse can volunteer to stay home, "but you're not allowed to ask. I can't tell you how many fights we've avoided."

Another way to share this responsibility is for each parent to stay home half the day and work the other. For some couples, however, sick-child duty may always fall to one spouse—because of the nature of their jobs, the amount of latitude each of their employers allows, or there being a loss of income if one spouse is home but not the other.

To avoid recurring arguments about who will stay home, agree to a plan in advance so you don't waste time negotiating every time your child wakes up with a fever. (*See Sick-Child Care on page 92 for how to cope if neither of you can stay home.*)

Resolving Conflicts

Sharing responsibility also means sharing authority, which can lead to parental conflicts that are more profound than whose turn it is to load the dishwasher. We tend to consult our own childhoods when we think about how we should conduct ourselves as parents and what rules we should set for our kids. Because Mom and Dad come from different families, they can bring very different childhood memories to this process. So the potential for disagreement is high.

You shouldn't try to shield your children from your disagreements. Differences of opinion are a natural part of life. And it's healthy for children to learn how people can disagree, argue—even be angry with each other—and then settle a difference, make up, and go on with a healthy, loving relationship.

Julie has observed us working on this book, sparks flying between our computers as we disputed some family-management principle or writing technique. She's seen that, eventually, we'd come to an agreement and move on. The lessons were that conflicts are natural and can be resolved and that an argument about a business matter doesn't have to have any impact on a personal relationship.

You should find a private place to resolve disputes about child rearing, however. Your child could become confused by witnessing you disagree in this circumstance. And he could be disturbed by feeling that he is the cause of your conflict.

This is another place in parenting where communication, compromise, and priorities are keys to success. By calmly talking out a dispute, you may find strengths in both of your positions and be able to meld them into a family policy you both can support enthusiastically. When that doesn't seem possible, each parent must consider how truly important this particular issue is. A good rule of thumb in this circumstance is to let the parent with stronger feelings prevail—as long as it isn't always the same parent.

It's time to consult a professional if you profoundly disagree about a matter that you believe can have an important effect on your child's health, safety, or development. Depending on the topic, you might turn to your pediatrician, your clergy, your child's teacher, or a family therapist.

Parents shouldn't pretend to agree when they don't. "It's subterfuge that drives kids mad," says Marguerite Kelly, co-author of *The Mother's Almanac* and author of *The Mother's Almanac II*. But once you come to an agreement, you both must enforce it. If Dad accepts Mom's desire to limit the time the children can watch television, for instance, Dad can't go slack on enforcement when Mom's not around.

Involving the Kids in Chores

"We think our elementary school children are old enough to help with chores, but it seems more hassle than it's worth when we have to nag them constantly about remembering to do their jobs. How can we get them to help out more?"

In the chapter *Time Well Spent* we discuss the importance of starting kids on chores when they're very young, to set a pattern for when they'll be old enough to provide real help. Unfortunately, over-worked parents know it's often quicker to do a chore themselves than to involve the kids in it. When children dawdle or complain about picking up toys or cleaning the gerbil cage, you might be tempted to stop asking them to. Yet it's important that every family member make a contribution to maintaining the household. Children who master chores have a feeling of accomplishment and self-reliance, and it

trains them for the time when they'll really be a help to you.

HELP YOUR KIDS HELP

The mistake some parents make is to expect too much too soon. Experts say that, until children are around age 8, they need supervision when performing chores. And most kids under 10 still need to be reminded to do a chore.

You need to start small and to expand the child's responsibilities with age. Toddlers can help to put away their toys. In early elementary grades, kids can make their beds, tidy their closets, feed their pets. As they get older, they can get into real housekeeping—cleaning their bedrooms and bathrooms, for example. Building on this through the teenage years will equip your children with the housekeeping skills and attitudes they'll need to maintain homes of their own.

To help young children remember their duties, some parents make charts with words or pictures, and then just remind the kids to check the chart. Children may be more willing workers if they get to pick their chores and can change occasionally. We've tried a job jar with moderate success in our family. Along with a few regular chores, such as making her

A CHORE CHART FOR KIDS

Every day: Make your bed. Feed the cat. Put your dirty dishes in the sink.

Every Tuesday: Clean your bathroom.

Every Thursday: Clean your bedroom.

Every Saturday: Help Daddy with a chore.

Every Sunday: Help Mommy with a chore.

bed and feeding the cat, Julie can pick a task at random from several written on pieces of paper in a jar.

Try anything that will make a chore seem like fun. Even toddlers will pick up their blocks if they think it's a game. Remember, too, that a child usually will have more fun doing a chore with a parent than doing it alone. And children want to copy their elders and to feel grown up. Imitating Tom Sawyer, Susan will merrily announce how much fun she's about to have cleaning the bathroom, and Julie will beg for the chance to do it herself. Julie also volunteers for tasks that she sees us doing but doesn't get asked to do—helping to wash the car, for example, or straining to push our human-powered lawn mower.

Kids are different. You may have to experiment to find what works with yours. Remember that what works when your child is 4 years old may not when she's 6—but something else will.

Most experts say children shouldn't be paid for routine household chores and that an allowance should not be tied to household duties. Performing chores is a child's contribution to making a home and family run well. An allowance is money he is given to manage, no strings attached. But it's all right to offer a special payment for an out-of-the-ordinary task, such as cleaning the garage.

Help from Friends

For harried working parents, friends provide important emotional support and practical help. Yet among the first things to go when couples become parents are some of the friendships they had before the baby arrived—especially friendships with nonparents.

Holding down a paying job and caring for a baby

TIPS FOR GETTING KIDS TO HELP

❏ Start when they're ages 2 to 4 and eager to help.
❏ Make chores fun.
❏ Buy child-size tools: toy rakes and brooms, for instance.
❏ Work together.
❏ Don't expect perfection.
❏ Be generous with thanks and praise.
❏ Point out the importance of their contribution to the family.
❏ Keep the chores and your supervision appropriate to the child's age.
❏ Put chores on lists or calendars.
❏ Let your child chose her chores.
❏ Try a job jar (*see page 191*).

leave little time for leisurely evenings and weekends out. Becoming a parent also can make you less compatible with some of your childless friends, who have no interest in talking about the child-related matters that have taken center stage in your life.

MAKING NEW FRIENDS
WITH OTHER PARENTS

As workers, you may have tended to find your friends on the job and to have had your friendships grow around shared career interests. Now you need to build friendships around the shared interests of parenting as well.

Some of your co-workers may fill that bill. But you'll also want to look elsewhere, especially in the neighborhood where your children will grow up. Obvious places to start are your childbirth class, the pediatrician's office, the playground, the daycare center, your place of worship, and neighborhood homes with strollers parked on the porch.

It's a good idea to include at-home parents in your circle of friends. They can be important allies, especially if they live nearby and are willing to help you out in a pinch, such as when your car pool or child-care arrangement falls through. But be careful not to take advantage of them (*see* "Mommy Wars" Prevention Measures *on page 195*).

Socialize Simply and Often

Socializing doesn't have to be elaborate. Invite another family for an outing in the park or just to stroll around the neighborhood with the kids. Have potluck dinners or invite other families to your house and order pizza. Include friends and their children in the activities you would be doing with your kids anyway.

Couples with very young children can enjoy dinners at each other's house while the kids sleep. When the children are older, they can play together as their parents socialize. Rented videos can provide some of the kid entertainment.

This can help your children cultivate friendships at the same time you do. You can avoid the expense and bother of procuring a sitter. Or you can use a younger sitter than usual because you're right there in the home, too. We have friends who hire our 9-year-old to entertain their 4-year-old from time to time, for instance. Julie makes a little money and enjoys having a friend she can treat like the little brother she thinks she wishes she had.

STAYING CLOSE TO CHILDLESS FRIENDS

This is not to say you should abandon acquaintances who don't have kids. You may find few opportunities to see old friends who aren't fond of children. But those who enjoy being with kids may become more important to you than ever before. A single friend or childless couple may relish the chance to be with your children as well as with you, becoming almost like surrogate family.

If you live far away from your relatives, having an "Aunt" Bridget or "Uncle" George—who enjoys taking your kids on outings or who is happy to babysit occasionally—can be a big help to you and can give your children an opportunity to form relationships with other adults.

These types of friendships are best nurtured in all of their facets. You should continue your old relationship—going out with them, without your children, to dinner, movies, concerts, and so forth. You also should include them in events that involve your children, inviting them to your home for an evening when your children join you for dinner and then are put to bed or go off to entertain themselves, for instance. Your friends may want to reciprocate, inviting you and your children to their house for dinner.

And if your friends want to, you should give them opportunities to spend some time with your children when you aren't around. An occasional trip to the movies or the pizza parlor could be a treat for your friends and your kids.

Depending on the nature of the relationship, you may want to invite these friends to your children's birthday parties, exchange presents at holiday time, and so forth. You should encourage your kids to send these friends birthday and holiday cards and to write thank-you notes when they're appropriate.

"MOMMY WARS" PREVENTION MEASURES

Much has been made of the "Mommy Wars," the supposed conflict between mothers who are employed and those who choose to stay at home with their kids. The topic has been a subject for women's magazines and talk shows in the last few years. But the differences between these two groups of mothers don't have to materialize into conflicts if parents respect each other's choices and are sensitive to each other's feelings.

Mothers who work and those who stay home are both capable of raising happy, healthy children. And they also are capable of having close, mutually beneficial relationships with each other, if they recognize that every mother has to make decisions that are right for her and her family.

Conflict or unease might arise when one parent feels she is being imposed upon too often. At-home parents get hit up to help out during the day by their working friends as well as by their child's school. Most won't mind, as long as they can count on you to help them in return when you can.

Return the Favor

Don't wait to be asked to do a favor for a stay-at-home parent. Show your appreciation by offering to babysit on weekends, for example. If you have a nanny or an au pair, ask if she'd be willing to watch your friend's kids as well as your own from time to time—with extra pay, of course.

One woman told us how she and another employed mother led a Brownie troop on Saturday mornings and didn't ask the Scouts' at-home mothers to do any of the work. "This was our way of showing our appreciation for all the times they bailed us out during the week," the career mother explains.

Be careful, too, of imposing on parents who have home offices. While they may have more flexibility than you do, it's easy to forget that they are employed, too, and may resent interruptions or requests to drive after-school car pools. Find out what is really convenient for them, and respect the limits they set while making sure you reciprocate for their help to you.

Car Pools

"I got soured on car pools when our son was in nursery school. I tried it for a month and gave up because the other parent was always late. Now that my child is entering elementary school, it would help me a lot. How can I head off problems before they happen this time?"

Car pooling is the great salvation of working parents whose children have places to go...and go and go. For the little effort that it takes to make the

arrangements, you save yourself time, wear and tear on your car, and the stress that comes from being your children's chauffeur all the time. As kids get older, car pooling becomes ever more necessary, especially if your children need transportation when you are at work.

Anne Goff of Tampa, Florida, mother of 14-year-old Rachel, told us she always offers to do more than her share of driving. "Once I'm in the car," she says, "I'll take any number of kids." That way, she doesn't feel she's imposing if an emergency at work forces her to call other parents to drive Rachel somewhere. Another benefit of driving is that "our quality talking gets done" when she and Rachel are in the car together with nothing to distract them. "At home, she's on the phone or doing homework, and I'm always busy."

Finding Potential Poolers

Some schools and summer camps provide lists of student addresses so parents can locate neighbors who might be interested in sharing rides. If you don't have access to such lists or directories, try putting a note on the bulletin board asking interested parents to contact you.

Sharing the Babysitting

"We'd like to go out more, but we aren't comfortable leaving our infant with a teenage sitter. The expense is a problem for us, too."

As we mentioned earlier in this chapter, family and friends can make great babysitters. And often they enjoy spending time with your children.

Some of your friends may have nannies or au pairs who'd be interested in earning some extra money at night; but be sure to ask your friends' permission before recruiting their employees to work for you. Nursery school teachers and teachers' aides are mature caregivers who could be interested in moonlighting.

BABYSITTING CO-OPS

Another place to find experienced caregivers—in this case, other parents—is a babysitting cooperative. These sitters don't cost you a cent. And you get as many hours of babysitting as you provide in trade.

If there isn't a co-op with an opening in your neighborhood, you can organize one by publicizing your intentions through bulletin-board notices in nearby grocery stores, churches, schools, or pediatricians' offices. Or you can take fliers house to house.

A co-op membership of about two dozen families seems to be the ideal. With too few families, it's hard to meet everyone's sitting needs. Too many can complicate administration, and you have less chance of getting a sitter you know. If you need help with structure, contact an existing co-op and use their bylaws as a model. You probably can find one through the PTA officers of local schools, who often know of such groups.

Some co-ops publish a newsletter in which parents can advertise other services they would like to trade, such as computer instruction in exchange for help with wallpapering. Co-ops can be used for clothing and toy exchanges, too.

Co-ops usually are restricted to operating in the evenings or on weekends, if they are composed of couples who work full time. Finding some members who work odd shifts or who stay at home can be a lifesaver for working parents who need emergency child care during the day. In such situations, the daytime sitter often hosts the other children at her house while she also watches her own.

Support Groups

"Ever since we brought our baby home from the hospital, I've worried about everything. Is she getting enough to eat? Does she cry more than other babies? I feel there's a limit to the number of times I can phone my pediatrician, but I don't know where else to turn."

Many new parents describe similar feelings of isolation and insecurity. You weren't born knowing how to be a parent. Without other people around who have been through it, you can feel you're on pretty shaky ground. Certainly, having experienced parents for friends can be a source of comfort. But if you're juggling work and child rearing, you may not have contact with them on a regular basis. What you need is a support group.

PLAY GROUPS

The most common support group, and the simplest to set up, is a play group. These tend to be organized by and for mothers and their babies, although some include fathers regularly or for an occasional event such as a group picnic. Parents who work weekdays

NURTURING A BABYSITTING CO-OP

Doug Wolf, a college professor in Syracuse, New York, was president of his co-op when his two children were young.

"The thing that drew us to it was that the problem of searching for a responsible babysitter was automatically solved by joining a group of thirty couples who all had kids about the same age as our own," Wolf says.

In Wolf's co-op, the president's job rotated every six months. That person was responsible for interviewing new couples if vacancies occurred. "You had to visit them and form an impression of whether they were responsible people," he says. The president also totaled the balance of credits or debits periodically. Parents who accumulated too large a negative balance or who seldom used the co-op were asked to resign.

Every two weeks the co-op rotated the secretary's job, which involved receiving requests for sitting and matching them with sitters. Every couple had to take a turn as secretary.

In his family, Wolf did most of the sitting while his wife stayed home with their own kids. He liked to do it because, after his charges went to sleep, he often got work done. "Babies might already be asleep when I got there," he recalls.

"About half the sits in our group were done by men. One guy brought his computer to our house." Some couples who planned to do computer work after the children were asleep kept track of which families had IBM-compatible or Macintosh computers.

FAMILY ACTION: POWER IN NUMBERS

Babysitting co-ops and car pools are just two examples of the creative ways parents are getting together to make life better for themselves and for their children. In communities across America, parents have organized to improve neighborhood playgrounds, to set up after-school programs, and even to establish daycare centers and cooperative nursery schools. They've also joined forces to lobby their employers for family-friendly benefits.

Famed anthropologist Margaret Mead once said: "Never doubt that a small group of thoughtful, committed citizens can change the world." And sometimes even better is a large group. That's why nationally known pediatrician and author T. Berry Brazelton co-founded Parent Action, an advocacy group for parents and their families, in 1989.

One of the group's purposes is to bring parents together at leadership training conferences, to help them prepare to tackle family issues in their own communities and workplaces. It also sponsors what it calls "The Big Listen," periodic forums for parents to talk while government officials listen.

Direct services for members include a quarterly newsletter as well as access to a resource service that can answer questions about everything from the Family and Medical Leave Act to college financing. Members also can request "Short Cuts," a series of information packets on a variety of parenting topics. Local parent groups can get technical assistance from Parent Action. And members pool their buying power to get discounts on travel, food, books, videos, toys, a national mortgage plan, long distance phone service, income tax services, and more.

Annual dues for Parent Action are $10. To join, call 410-PARENTS (410-727-3687), or write Parent Action, 2 North Charles Street, Suite 960, Baltimore, MD 21201.

typically get together on Saturdays, often rotating the meetings in each other's homes. Some groups have topics and occasional speakers, while others just use the time to share their joys or concerns while the children play.

It's a great comfort to find you aren't alone. You discover other parents are coping with many of the same problems you are—everything from stress at work to a child who isn't sleeping through the night. Because several heads are better than one, you'll also get ideas for coping.

Prospective play-group members can be found in the same places we suggested finding new friends (*see* Making New Friends with Other Parents *on page 193*). You might try announcing your interest in starting a new group by putting a notice on the bulletin board at your pediatrician's office or community center.

It's best if the children in the group are close in age so you're going through the same stages at roughly the same time. Keep the group small—six to ten parents—so everyone gets ample time to participate in the conversation.

PLAY-GROUP MEMORIES

Our play group was formed by half a dozen mothers whose babies were born within three months of each other. We became acquainted at a baby-care class run by our pediatric practice, and we just kept meeting once a week after the course concluded.

We got together, kids in tow, for four years. And we still have 'mothers' night out,' when we leave the kids with their dads and go to a nice restaurant. I don't think I could have gotten through those first few months of worry and uncertainty if I hadn't had the other mothers to talk to.

One of my fondest memories was the day Julie first walked. She did it at the play-group meeting, timing it, I suspected, just to have a big audience to rejoice with her mother at this important milestone. Since Julie also was the last child in our group to walk, her feat was a milestone for the play-group moms as well. We had survived infants and now were embarking together on toddlerhood. And we'd need each other more than ever.

Susan

MOTHERS' CENTERS

A more formal support group is the National Association of Mothers' Centers, the hub of more than one hundred centers across the country. The association can refer you to a center in your area or can help you start one yourself.

Most centers have a meeting site, but some rotate meetings in members' homes or among various public facilities. Most have fifty to one hundred members. Because they are locally operated, their programs differ.

Typically, the centers serve as places for mothers to meet and for children to play. Initially, the centers tended to be organized by at-home mothers or mothers on extended maternity leaves. But working mothers participate in some centers on evenings or weekends. Mothers with nontraditional working hours can participate during weekdays. And some centers have developed programs for fathers as well.

Brown-bag dinners are convenient for working parents. "Daddy and Me" events are specially designed for groups of children and their fathers.

The centers provide the support and education that come from parents sharing their own experiences. Some also sponsor programs led by professionals and collect and distribute information useful to parents.

The association's national headquarters publishes a newsletter, offers information over a toll-free phone line, provides training for the centers, and sponsors an annual conference.

> **TIP:** To locate a center near you, learn how to organize one yourself, or just obtain additional information about the association, you can write to the National Association of Mothers' Centers, 336 Fulton Avenue, Hempstead, NY 11550, or call 800-645-3828.

SUPPORT AT WORK

As more mothers enter the labor force and fathers increase their share of parenting responsibilities, family matters are becoming more important to employers. Child-care centers are being opened at or near work sites. Some employers now sponsor parent-support groups and parent-education classes. Some discussion groups and classes are organized by employees who are parents, in meeting space provided by employers. Others are offered through the employers' personnel departments.

Ask what programs your employer offers. If there's nothing to meet your needs, ask the personnel department if the company might sponsor a program or allow you to organize one. The start could be as simple as a brown-bag lunch for parents in a company conference room.

PARENT EDUCATION CLASSES
Parent-education classes also are sponsored by hospitals, mental health associations, local governments, and profit and nonprofit organizations. The courses can cover everything from toilet training to first aid, sibling conflicts, how to communicate better with your children, and how to educate your kids about sex.

Many nursery and elementary schools sponsor such programs, inviting guest speakers, then dividing the assembly into small discussion groups. School programs usually are free and are attended by parents from the neighborhood. In addition to enriching your parenting skills, the programs may deepen your relationship with other participating parents and

expand your informal support group of friends.

Your pediatrician probably can put you in touch with parent education groups in your area.

SUPPORT THROUGH LEADERSHIP
Parents also can build relationships that resemble support groups by coaching a soccer team, being a Scout leader, or participating in parent-child programs sponsored by the PTA, YMCA, YWCA, church, or synagogue. Taking a leadership role—such as coaching—in a children's activity lets you bond with your fellow leaders differently than if you simply are the parent of a participant.

This can be especially valuable to fathers, who aren't as likely to participate in a play group. In learning together how to motivate, organize, and teach the children on their soccer team, the fathers who coach also teach each other how to be better parents.

Working parents may find it difficult to keep a commitment to get to every Wednesday evening practice and every Saturday morning game. But they can solve the problem by banding together and accommodating each other's schedule. Four fathers (including Tom) coach Julie's sixteen-player soccer team, for instance, and a couple of others attend the games regularly enough to be counted on to help out in a pinch. That's a high and helpful coach-to-player ratio. We're confident that at least two coaches will be at every practice and every game.

If you're new to a community, leading a children's group can be a quick way to build a circle of friends. And you will receive emotional rewards from this time with your child and from knowing you're making a contribution to the community.

COMMITMENT HAS ITS REWARDS

Carol Hupping, our editor, was reluctant about coaching her 7-year-old daughter's Little League team. "It was a real trial to rush home from work two days a week all season, pick up my children from after-school care, get some supper into them (often in the car on the way), drop my son off at his baseball practice or at the car pooler's house, and then drive over to my daughter's practice.

"But once we got on that field, I got caught up in the excitement of the sport and I loved it. And it was good for my daughter, the youngest on the team, who appreciated my support during her first softball season.

"What's more, as a newcomer in town, I found that I quickly became a known quantity to the girls and to many of their parents—people I might never have met. Now, when I see one of them at the local shops, at school, or at other sporting events, we nod and say hello. I feel much more a part of the community."

WORKPLACE DILEMMAS

HERE'S HELP ON:

Resolving conflicts with your supervisor, page 206

The Neanderthal boss, page 208

Special problems for fathers, page 208

The overtime trap, page 209

Have job, must travel, page 210

Relocating for work, page 213

Overcoming the guilts, page 215

A report card for parents, page 218

When your kids make you late, page 220

Helping your children understand your work, page 220

We recently saw a car with a bumper sticker that read: "I can handle any crisis. I have children." How true it seems. Being a parent (and therefore being prepared for almost anything) sounds like the kind of credential that would look good on any resume. Yet it's not one that many employees want to advertise. On the contrary, most play down their parenthood at work.

Employers aren't exactly opposed to the existence of children—after all, that's how all their customers and workers started out. But by and large, the boss's life is easier if employees' family responsibilities don't spill over into the workplace. This attitude drives many parents underground. They view the conflicting demands of jobs and kids as a personal problem, not a responsibility employers should share.

Until recently, few employers felt otherwise. But change is coming, as more bosses see the value of offering family-friendly benefits. The reason is highlighted in a study of American workers, called *The Changing Work Force*, published in 1993 by the Families and Work Institute. Workers with greater access to work/family assistance are more committed to doing their jobs well, are more loyal to their employers, and take more initiative on the job, the study says.

The importance of such assistance grows as the number of mothers in the work force increases. And it's not just employers with mothers working for them who are affected. Because fewer men have wives taking care of the home front, fathers bring family issues to the job, too. Someone has to pick up Baby at the daycare center at the end of the day, and sometimes that's got to be Dad. That means Dad can't always be counted on to work overtime. These changing demands on parents can cause frustration even in workplaces with family-friendly policies. Theory and practice aren't always identical.

Some employers proclaim their family-friendliness but refuse to put policies in writing, leaving real work/family issues to be dealt with inconsistently on a case-by-case basis, for instance. Formal policies can vary from division to division within the same company. Parents can be blocked from taking advantage of benefits because implementation is left to the discretion of middle managers, who may be resistant.

Men may forgo available paternity leave for fear of subtle reprisals (*see* Paternity Leaves *on page 30*). There may be restrictions on which employees are allowed to take advantage of flexible work schedules (*see* Presence Is Performance to Some Bosses *on page 228*). And no matter how enlightened your employer, on-the-job dilemmas are bound to crop up.

Resolving Conflicts with Your Supervisor

"My relationship with my boss has been strained every since I became a parent, and it's getting worse as time goes on. I missed a few days of work this winter when the daycare center closed because of snow. And I can't work late as often as I used to. But I don't think that should ruin what used to be a good relationship."

Lynne Waymon, a consultant whose services include resolving conflicts between supervisors and employees, suggests that you ask a trusted friend to help you think through your situation.

"It should be someone outside the place where you work or maybe someone in a distant department" whom you could trust to maintain confidentiality, says Waymon, co-author of *Great Connections: Small Talk and Networking for Businesspeople* (Impact Publications, 1992). "Have that person help you think out loud what the possible solutions are that you might propose. What is the boss's side of the story? Am I expecting more (accommodation) than I ought to?"

If you can't express clearly to your friend what you want from your boss, then you have to rethink how to communicate it better. Rehearse what you'll say and have your friend help you anticipate the points your boss might raise.

When you meet with the boss, Waymon suggests, start out by expressing appreciation for the support you've received in the past. After that, say: "The situation I want to talk about today has to do with…" or "I've been concerned about your perception of me lately." Then cite the problem—the snow days, for example. Suggest two or three alternative solutions,

such as how you might make up the lost work time or how you could stay in touch by phone when future snow days occur.

"Propose solutions, but don't issue ultimatums," Waymon says. "Then sit back and listen. Try to find some commonality."

If you sense resistance, don't ignore it. "Most people want to stuff resistance down and get rid of it," Waymon notes, "but a serious negotiator will try to bring it out in the open." Say: "Tell me the difficulties you see with us doing this." If the boss says he can't think of any objections but you sense he has some, rephrase the question and ask it again.

If you don't come to agreement right away, or the boss needs time to mull things over, say: "Why don't I check back with you on (a specific date)?" You can suggest this also if the boss proposes something you hadn't considered. Say: "That's a good point; I'd like some time to think about it." When you've reached agreement, it's a good idea to turn it into a written understanding, unless that runs counter to your organization's culture.

THE NEANDERTHAL BOSS

"My supervisor frequently insists that I work overtime, even though I've tried to explain how hard this is when I have kids to pick up at daycare. In many ways, he's made it clear that he doesn't care that I have a life that extends beyond my job. Am I crazy to think that I need to find another boss?"

You might have rights—under the law, company policy, or a union contract—to protest this kind of treatment. If you don't—or if you just would rather avoid the conflict that enforcing those rights might entail—changing bosses could be your best option.

Brenda Cooper says that, in her experience, bosses who don't accept her dual role as employee and mother are difficult to work with in other ways as well. "I've found that a boss who doesn't understand why you have to be at your child's spring recital or at home when a child has strep throat is someone who is unrealistic about expectations in general," she says. "He doesn't have his priorities in the same place I do, so we have a hard time reaching consensus."

Finding another position can be hard to do. But inertia or fear of the unknown often keeps people in intolerable work situations when they could move to better ones.

You may be reluctant to quit your job if you've built up seniority and benefits during a long tenure with your company. But, in a big organization, you might not have to quit—you might be able to transfer to another department. Try looking for someone to trade jobs with. If you're a secretary, for example, you might be able to find another secretary in the company who would welcome the chance to earn the overtime pay that you want to turn down.

Before you decide to leave your company, make sure you aren't jumping from the frying pan into the fire (*see* Evaluating a Firm's "Family-Friendliness" *on page 240 for tips on assessing whether potential employers are family-friendly*).

Special Problems for Fathers in the Workplace

"My company is willing to give some slack to mothers who have conflicts between work and home, but the corporate culture isn't as understanding of fathers. Almost no man has taken paternity leave or asked for time off to care for a sick child. I want to spend more time with

my family, but I'm afraid that could ruin my career."

Psychologist Brad Sachs, director of The Father Center in Columbia, Maryland, says that's not an unreasonable fear. He consults with companies that are instituting paternity leave and other benefits for fathers, but says change has been "much slower than we'd like to imagine. I've read articles that say the change is revolutionary, but it's really more evolutionary. There's still much resistance to men making family life a priority over, or equal to, their work."

Lacking role models, "men are entering a territory they don't have a road map for," says Sachs, author of *Things Just Haven't Been the Same: Making the Transition from Marriage to Parenthood* (William Morrow, 1992). He says a father first must convince himself that making more time for his children is a legitimate goal. "Men may feel ambivalent themselves, so they come across as tentative" when they ask their supervisors for family-friendly work arrangements, Sachs says. "The boss picks up on that and may be negative [in responding to the request]. You must believe your request is legitimate, and you must be clear" in how you make it.

Sachs warns that many bosses don't care whether you're able to spend much time with your children. Your boss "may not have made that commitment to his own family," Sachs says. That's why it's most effective to explain how the change would make you a better employee. (*See also* Paternity Leaves *on page 30. For more on negotiating tips, see* Making the Case for a Flexible Schedule *on page 224.*)

The Overtime Trap

"My wife and I share the responsibility of picking up our son at the daycare center. If my boss suddenly puts a crash project on my desk or calls a meeting at 5 P.M. on a night when Kathy already is committed to working late, I have to tell him I can't stay, and I'm worried that that is hurting my career."

The overtime dilemma is at the top of many parents' lists of workplace problems. One father told us he helps his boss by offering to work extra hours on evenings or weekends during busy periods at the office when that doesn't conflict with his parental responsibilities. That way, he's less uncomfortable when he has to beg off an overtime assignment since he's built up some credits with the boss.

Try showing the boss you're flexible. When a conflict arises, stress that you want to do that last-minute project and offer an alternative, such as coming in early the next morning.

"Your willingness to suggest such alternatives will stand you in better stead than simply refusing," says Dana Friedman, co-president of the Families and Work Institute.

If you anticipate being asked to stay late occasionally, arrange for the availability of short-notice child care when you need it. Talk with other parents who use your daycare center and offer to pick up their children in an emergency if they'll do the same for you. It's good to have this pact with several families in case one can't help on the night you need it.

Have Job, Must Travel

"My job requires me to make frequent out-of-town trips. How can I make this easier on my kids?"

There is a surprising range of views on this subject. Some parents phone home regularly; others don't, because they think their young children would be upset by the calls reminding them of the parent's absence. Some bring home presents from each trip; others don't, because they say their kids focus more on the booty than on their returning mom or dad.

You may question the wisdom of gift giving if the first words of greeting from your child are: "What did you bring me?" But many parents think occasional or regular presents are okay, as long as they aren't lavish and don't send kids the message that you feel guilty about being away (even if you do). A small token can convey the idea that you were thinking about your kids while you were gone.

Debra Haffner brings her daughter a T-shirt from each city she visits. If she doesn't have time to shop, she can always get one at the airport gift store. A friend of hers has eliminated the need to shop on trips by keeping a stash of small gifts in her closet at home. When she returns from a trip, she just sneaks one out and presents it.

Matt Quinn points out that you don't have to buy a present to impress very young children. On a business trip to New Hampshire, he saved a couple of peppermint candies from a restaurant and brought them to his toddler. Now, whenever Quinn's daughter hears New Hampshire mentioned, she says that's where peppermints come from.

Phone Home?

When Quinn's wife, Paula Schwed, travels, she doesn't call home to talk to their two preschoolers. "They cry when I leave but then it's over," she says. "They deal in the present. If I call, it makes them sad all over again and it makes me sad."

Other parents find that their young children may not feel like talking when they call home, which can be a real let-down for the traveler who's missing her kids.

If your children are very young, take a cue from them about whether phone calls make your absence easier to tolerate. Older children usually appreciate regular phone contact.

We try to phone home every day when we travel, and we usually bring Julie some kind of present. The point is to let her know that she's always in our thoughts, even when one of us is away.

Counting the Days You're Away

Young children have trouble understanding time.

So, even if you say you'll only be gone three days or you'll be back on Thursday, your child may not have much concept of how long that is.

Some parents use terms like how many "sleeps" they'll be gone, meaning how many bedtimes the child will have before the parent returns. Others give their kids small candies equal to the number of days their trip will last. The child is to eat one a day so she can visualize the parent's return getting closer as the candy supply dwindles.

Preparing Kids for Your Trip

Don't give toddlers much advance notice. Wait until the night before your departure to tell them you are going away so they don't have as much time to fret. But older kids usually appreciate knowing ahead of time so they can talk about your trip and help you get ready for it.

Doug Leavens, an international financial consultant, frequently travels overseas, usually to Africa, for as long as three weeks at a time. Because of the expense and difference in time zones, he can call home to his wife and 6-year-old son Andrew only about twice a week. If no one is home, he leaves messages for Andrew on the answering machine.

Leavens also helps his child handle the heavy travel schedule by discussing the countries he visits, both before and after the trip. With the help of a globe and maps, "we start talking about my next trip well ahead," Leavens explains. He and his wife have found children's books of African folk tales, and Leavens uses the stories and pictures to help Andrew visualize where his dad will be.

While abroad, Leavens buys postcards with local scenes that include children. Upon his return, he and his son talk about the trip, relating it to things Andrew understands, such as what the schools are like or what kinds of games the children play.

Taking Children Along

One way to give your child positive feelings about your business travel is to take him along sometimes. If you're attending a conference, for example, you could ask the organizers to help you arrange child care; some hotels have special programs for kids. A few parents occasionally take along child and nanny, although that can get to be an expensive excursion. And grandparents have been known to go along on

---

TIPS FOR EASING YOUR ABSENCE

❏ Give your child a calendar with the days you're away marked clearly on it. Put a big star on the date you're scheduled to return.

❏ Read children's books on to an audiotape so your child can listen to a story in your voice when she goes to bed.

❏ Give your child pictures of yourself, maybe even one of you reading to her.

❏ Send postcards addressed to your children. You could mail the first one the day before your trip, or drop it into the mailbox at the airport just before you leave town. Kids love to get mail.

❏ Try to avoid business trips that coincide with your spouse's. Children, especially very young ones, can get quite upset if both parents are gone at the same time.

❏ If both of you do travel at the same time, leave your kids in the care of a family member or someone else your children know well.

❏ Don't forget how travel affects the parent who stays at home. When you're gone, the entire child-care burden falls on your spouse.

trips to look after the kids. A particular advantage of traveling with a baby is that it can allow a mother to continue nursing.

Brenda Cooper, a communications vice president for a health-care agency, has taken each of her three children on business trips since the youngest was 6. By taking only one at a time, Cooper assured that the traveling child got one-on-one time with Mom and learned to adapt to an adult world.

Some of the trips were to conferences for which Cooper was arranging programs. As the kids got older, they were able to help with simple tasks, such as delivering messages. On one trip, Cooper's daughter got to meet actress Cicely Tyson, who was a conference speaker.

"The meetings were in the summer, so the kids didn't miss school," Cooper recalls. "My room was already paid for, so that cut down on the expense." She says her children knew they had to be quiet when sessions were going on, and they thought it was worth it to have Mom to themselves while traveling and during meals.

Relocating for Work

"My company wants to transfer me to another city. They've agreed to help my husband find a new job, and we're both excited about the prospect of new opportunities. But we're also worried about how the move will affect our kids. How can we help them adjust?"

Moving is stressful for everyone in a family. How much it affects your children depends in part on their age. Babies and toddlers can adjust easily, as long as they can take some of their favorite objects with them. Elementary school children will miss their bedrooms, their park, other special places, close playmates, and maybe their teachers. Teenagers will feel the biggest impact because of the disruption of their social and academic lives.

But moving doesn't have long-term negative effects on well-adjusted kids. And it can be positive in giving them experience in handling change and forming new relationships.

The fact that you are happy about the move will help your children cope. Keep stressing the positive aspects, such as the sense of adventure in going to a new place. Involve the children as much as possible in planning the move and selecting your new home. Take photos or a videotape of the new home, if your children won't be able to see it before the move, so they will be less fearful of the unknown.

Also arrange special send-off events, so your kids can say good-bye to friends and collect addresses and photos. One father we know gave his adolescent daughter a long-distance phone allowance to help her keep in touch with friends she left behind.

It's good to maintain former friendships, but not to the exclusion of making new ones. You have to help your children find those new acquaintances, too.

The Best Time to Move Kids

Many parents try to move in the summer, thinking that's less disruptive for kids than moving during the school year. But, particularly for younger children, that's not necessarily true. It can be harder for kids to make new friends in summer, when other children are scattered in summer programs or away on vacation. The new kid in town also can get lost in the shuffle of those first confusing days and weeks of the new school year. In the middle of the school year, teachers have more time to help ease your child's adjustment.

> **TIP:** Parent Action offers its members a useful information packet on preparing children for a move. For more information, call 410-PARENTS (410-727-3687) or write Parent Action, 2 North Charles Street, Suite 960, Baltimore, MD 21201.

Find Activities to Smooth the Transition

One way to ease the transition is to help your children continue some of their favorite activities. If they play baseball or soccer, for instance, find the leagues in your new town.

Pam and Jim Ripley did this when they moved from Ohio to Arizona. Their son quickly found a group of ready-made friends in a Boy Scout troop. They picked their new house in part because it was in a neighborhood with a school that had a good debate team; that was something their teenage daughter had excelled in at her old school. The Ripleys chose their new church in part because of its youth programs, which their children had enjoyed in their old community.

Choosing New Schools

School selection can be the biggest issue in your

move. Don't rely on information from a single real estate agent. He may not have direct knowledge of the school system. And his comments might be designed to sell you a particular house rather than to give you an objective analysis of school quality. Ask your new employers and co-workers for help. (*For more advice on selecting schools, see* Evaluating Schools *on page 255.*)

> **TIP:** Some of the major moving companies have booklets on helping your children adjust to the move. Ask what yours offers.

Overcoming the Guilts

"I feel so guilty about leaving my child to go to work every day that I have trouble concentrating. I know this is affecting my work, but I can't seem to overcome it."

If you're a parent, guilt just goes with the territory. Women tend to feel it more than men. But all parents—working or not—have those occasional pangs about whether they're doing enough for their kids, or doing too much, or doing the wrong thing.

One mother told us she felt guilty about not feel-ing guilty! She loves her career and was glad when her maternity leave ended, so she could flee the stress of mothering a very fussy baby full time and get back to her office. Yet she couldn't completely shake the feeling that she must be a bad mother to want to leave her baby for a chunk of the day.

Parents have to change what they can change and learn to live with what they can't. Otherwise, guilt will consume a lot of psychic energy that could be expended much more productively and creatively at work and at home.

You also must avoid the overcompensation trap. If guilt leads you to lavish gifts on your children or to go easy on discipline, you're not doing them any favors. Do things for your kids because you love them, not because you feel guilty.

To see what can be changed, dig through the guilt to unearth the specific cause. For example, guilt about leaving a child may be due to your dissatisfaction with the quality of your child care. A change in caregivers might make you feel much better. (*For advice on searching for a better caregiver, see* Child Care in Your Home, *starting on page 43, and* Child Care Outside Your Home, *starting on page 73.*)

Maybe your guilt stems from the amount of time

you're away from your children. If so, you need to try to reduce your overtime, cut the amount of paperwork you bring home, and see if you've got a flextime option that would let you spend more time with your kids. (*For advice on pursuing flexible job arrangements, see* Careers With Flexibility, *starting on page 223.*)

> **TIP:** Some of your guilt may have little to do with how well your children are faring and more to do with your reaction to society's expectations of parents. Read Melinda Marshall's book *Good Enough Mothers* (Peterson's, 1993) for help in working through your parental guilt.

THINK ABOUT THE POSITIVE

Katherine Wyse Goldman, author of *My Mother Worked and I Turned Out Okay* (Villard, 1993), says working parents should frequently remind themselves of the positive things they do for their children. Her own mother, advertising executive and author Lois Wyse, was a rarity—a woman with a career in the 1950s, when Goldman was growing up and all of her friends' moms were at home. "She gave me a sense of the world," Goldman recalls. "She was happy with what she was doing. She transmitted that feeling to my brother and me."

"THE FIRST AND LAST DAY OF SUMMER"

Even little things can make a difference. It was during the summer that single mother Betsy Crane felt the most guilt about not spending enough time with her son, Jesse. She remembered childhood vacations filled with free time and seven siblings to play with. And she "had angst that Jesse wasn't having the experiences I had."

When Jesse started elementary school, Crane hit on an idea she calls "the First and Last Day of Summer." Every year, she takes off work the day his summer vacation begins and the day before he goes back to school in the fall. She devotes those days to Jesse, letting him decide how they spend the time. When he was younger, they'd go for ice cream, play at a playground, and have his favorite foods at mealtime. When he got older, he picked a day at a water park one time and a long hike another, and he invited his best friend along.

"It was special," says Crane, "because it was different from the rest of his summer vacation. It was all his day."

When Goldman started her own career in advertising, her mother was her role model as well as a font of advice for negotiating job offers and making career decisions. Goldman also benefited from her mother's large network of contacts in the business world. Goldman believes the workplace will change for the better as the children of working couples grow up, enter the work force, and become managers.

Even Goldman—working mother of a 6- and a 7-year-old—has moments of guilt. An especially bad one was when she forgot Parents' Day at her son's school. "Max came out of school and cried," she recalls. "I finally realized he didn't feel as bad about it as I did, and he got over it. But I'll never forget another Parents' Day!"

HOW KIDS FEEL ABOUT WORKING PARENTS

In *Speaking of Kids: A National Survey of Children and Parents* (1991), the National Commission on Children reported that kids with employed mothers were almost as satisfied with the amount of time they spent with their moms as kids whose mothers were home full time. Kids with working moms also were not significantly more likely to feel that their mothers frequently missed important events in their lives.

Men Feel Guilt, Too

The survey also found that children want more time with fathers who work long hours. And, even though society hasn't laid the same guilt on dads as it lays on moms, men are saying they would like to spend more time with their kids.

Some of this desire for father-child closeness can be attributed to the fact that 90 percent of fathers now attend the births of their children, says psychologist Brad Sachs. "Once the fathers started becoming intimately involved in the birth, that bonding had a profound carryover" into child rearing, he says. Men are feeling torn when job demands leave them little time for their children.

Sachs set up The Father Center to help new and expectant fathers. The center isn't an actual location but a series of classes offered at various sites throughout the community. It has evolved into helping fathers beyond just the initial stages of parenthood.

Sachs advises fathers to discuss feelings of guilt with other men. "Women do this more naturally," he says. "They explore these issues, so they feel less

A REPORT CARD FOR PARENTS

While writing this book, we had less time to spend with Julie than we usually do. One day when guilt was really getting to me, I came across a parent report card in Working Mother magazine (January 1993).

Designed for third to ninth graders by Linda Berg-Cross, Ph.D., director of the clinical psychology program at Howard University in Washington, D.C., the report card gives kids a chance to rate their parents. The idea is to use the card to stimulate parent-child communication, and it does that. But, more important, it gave me a sense of relief. I was expecting some tough marks from a daughter who felt deprived. Instead, I got pretty high grades. She wasn't feeling as deprived as I thought!

Like a mind reader (or an experienced clinical psychologist), Dr. Berg-Cross predicted the two areas where we would score low because it happens to many parents: "Lets me act my age" and "Watches TV with me." The first wasn't a surprise to us, but the second was. Like most parents, we use the time Julie watches television to do other things. But, Dr. Berg-Cross says, kids want parents to watch with them, not use the TV as a babysitter.

I passed the report card on to a doctor friend whose two children were really starting to complain about her long hours. She, too, got higher marks than she expected, and some insights into the things she was doing well. I can't promise this will happen to every parent who uses the report card. But I suspect most of us are a lot harder on ourselves than we should be.

Instead of wallowing in guilt, you can try the report card, too. Discussing the grades gives your children a chance to raise concerns that you didn't even know they had and it can help you find ways to address them.

Susan

Dr. Berg-Cross offers these instructions for using the report card:

- ❑ Have each child fill out the card privately rather than compare notes with siblings, to prevent them from giving a parent higher marks to gain favor.
- ❑ Add questions related to your specific concerns. For example, add "Helps me get to school on time" if your family seems to cut this too close too often. This might elicit ideas about what kind of help your child needs in the morning.
- ❑ After your child completes the card, have him explain each grade. Don't argue, explain, or defend yourself. Just listen or ask: "Can you tell me more about this grade?" Then ask: "How can I improve?"

Try to get a couple of specific suggestions.

After the discussion, thank your child for his honesty and give him a big hug. Then wait 72 hours before mentioning the report again. This gives you a cooling-off period to get over any hurt feelings and to acquire some perspective. Later, you can talk to your child about the grades again and even say you were hurt by some of them. This starts a dialogue about areas you don't see eye-to-eye on, which is a key point of the exercise.

Don't even start the exercise if you don't handle criticism well. This is supposed to be a tool to help you, not something that will make you feel worse.

The Report Card

For each item, circle the grade your parent has earned this month.

1. Helps me with my homework when I ask.	A B C D F
2. Understands my moods.	A B C D F
3. Gives me hugs.	A B C D F
4. Tells me he or she loves me.	A B C D F
5. Lets me act my age.	A B C D F
6. Is nice to my friends.	A B C D F
7. Keeps my secrets.	A B C D F
8. Helps me look my best.	A B C D F
9. Cooks good meals.	A B C D F
10. Keeps the house nice.	A B C D F
11. Watches TV with me.	A B C D F
12. Listens to my problems.	A B C D F
13. Tries to explain things to me.	A B C D F
14. Doesn't scream at me when angry.	A B C D F
15. Thinks about me enough.	A B C D F
16. Spends time with me alone.	A B C D F
17. Makes me laugh.	A B C D F
18. Makes the holidays special.	A B C D F
19. Lets me make my own decisions.	A B C D F
20. Helps me make my room special.	A B C D F
21. Helps me get up when I oversleep.	A B C D F
22. Treats all kids in the family fairly.	A B C D F
23. Answers my questions about sex.	A B C D F
24. Helps me buy the things I want.	A B C D F
25. Is understanding about poor grades.	A B C D F
26. _____	A B C D F

(Add your own questions if you wish.)

Copyright © 1990 by Linda Berg-Cross. Used with permission.

alienated and disconnected. Men feel more alone. They need to help each other."

Like mothers, fathers can get together in places like parenting classes, Sachs says. Widespread participation in childbirth preparation classes has paved the way for that by introducing men to the experience of group sessions focused on parenthood, he says.

SEEKING AN OUTSIDE OPINION

If you're overwhelmed by guilt, professional help might be in order. A family therapist or psychologist, for example, can help parents sort out their priorities and examine which parts of their lives could be changed to ease the guilt. An alternative is a class or group sessions run by a professional, such as those offered by parent education programs (*see Parent Education Classes on page 203 for more on finding classes*).

When Your Kids Make You Late

"My 4-year-old dawdles so much in the morning that I'm sometimes late for work, and my boss is losing patience. How can I avoid the mad rush in the morning?"

If your child is hard to wake in the morning, try putting him to bed a half hour earlier at night. Do as many things as you can the night before, such as laying out his clothes, packing his lunch, and organizing his belongings for daycare. You may have to get up earlier yourself, too, to help him to get ready.

One mother told us she used games with her 5-year-old to jump-start the morning. She and her son would race to see who could get dressed first and—surprise!—he always won. A father told us he used a timer to help his son judge how much time he had left to finish getting dressed before breakfast.

Helping Your Children Understand Your Work

"My children resent the time I'm away from them, and they complain about it a lot. Is there a way to explain how important my job is to me and to our family finances?"

Don't tell them; show them. It is important for

kids to understand that work is an important part of who you are.

TAKE YOUR KIDS TO WORK
Even if you sit behind a desk all day, there probably are things your kids would enjoy seeing and doing with you at your office, such as trying out the copy machine, using the electric pencil sharpener, meeting your co-workers, or eating in the office cafeteria.

If it's not possible to bring children there during working hours, maybe you could do it on a weekend. If even that is against the rules, get someone to take pictures of you in your workplace so your children can relate to where you go every day.

Brenda Cooper's job often requires her to go to evening receptions. Occasionally she has taken one of her children along to see how she spends those evenings away from them. They found out that the parties can be dull instead of fun, and now they feel sorry for her instead of resenting her absence.

A pediatric surgeon we know takes her kids on rounds at the hospital so they can grasp why she sometimes has to leave home at night to be with other people's children. Parents who work in muse-ums, firehouses, libraries, or grocery stores sometimes arrange tours not only for their own child but for the child's entire class at school.

In April 1993, the Ms. Foundation began an annual program called "Take Our Daughters to Work Day," which encourages parents to expose their daughters to the workplace. But you don't have to wait until April or limit the visit to daughters only. It's especially important for sons to see their mothers at work. Boys who learn of the challenges faced by mothers in the workplace will grow up to have better understanding as employees or bosses.

TAKE YOUR WORK HOME?
While there's value in parents' taking their kids to work from time to time, it's not good to bring the job home very often. If your evenings and weekends are spent on paperwork, or if dinner-table conversation is consumed by your problems at the office, your kids will resent the way your job interferes with family life. When you do talk about your job in front of the kids, don't just focus on the horror stories of your day. Display the positive side, too, so your children won't be turned off by the work world.

CAREERS WITH FLEXIBILITY

HERE'S HELP ON:

Making the case for a flexible schedule, page 224

Working from home, page 229

Going part time, page 233

Job sharing, page 236

Finding a flexible new job, page 238

Slowing down on the fast track, page 238

Combining more family time with rewarding work, page 239

Evaluating a firm's "family-friendliness," page 240

Making the break to your own business, page 242

When we asked working parents what they want in their jobs, the most common response was "flexibility." Workers who are juggling jobs and kids want more choice in when, where, or even how many hours they work. Many men and women want to be able to work schedules other than 9 to 5, or work at home, or work part time, or share a job with someone else, or take a leave, or reduce their business travel, or step off the fast track for a couple of years without losing the chance to get back on later.

This is not to suggest that workers aren't serious about their work or don't want to give their employers a day's work for a day's pay. *The National Study of the Changing Work Force*, released by the Families and Work Institute in 1993, found employees are working hard and are willing to work harder when necessary to do their jobs well. But they are just as interested in the effect of the job on personal and family life as they are in money and advancement.

"American workers are at a turning point, and they're telling employers what they need to be more effective," says Ellen Galinsky, co-president of the institute. A supportive work environment that recognizes employees have a home life as well as a work life is what makes for committed and productive employees.

Work problems are more likely to spill over into the home than family problems are to encroach upon the workplace, the researchers found. Housework, personal time, and family time all give way to job demands. Parents aren't the only employees in this boat, either. Flexibility is important also to workers who care for elderly parents, who want to further their education, or who want time to pursue personal interests.

Employees express fear that the "downsizing" many companies have undergone in the last few years means those who are left should just be glad to have a job rather than be asking their employers for new benefits.

Not so, says Dana Friedman, the institute's other co-president. "We've really found a surge of employer involvement (in work/family issues) since the recession," she explains. "They have become survivor benefits. After a company downsizes, it has fewer people to rely on and needs maximum production from them. So it's in the best interests of the company to keep them from being demoralized. Options such as flexible schedules or job sharing send a message that the company still cares."

Making the Case for a Flexible Schedule

If you're seeking a flexible work arrangement, you're in good company. More than a fifth of the U.S. work force is employed on flexible, compressed, or reduced work schedules, according to Suzanne Smith, co-director of New Ways to Work, a San Francisco nonprofit group that advises businesses on flexible work arrangements.

No matter what you're asking for—flextime, job sharing, part-time work—your proposal must be framed in business terms to show how it will be beneficial to your boss as well as to you. At a minimum, you should be able to demonstrate that the arrangement would improve your productivity by eliminating or reducing the distraction of work/family conflicts.

Flexible work options also help businesses avoid losing qualified employees and incurring the expense of recruiting and training new ones. Each of the arrangements described in this section has additional advantages—and probably some disadvantages—for the boss. Your job is to highlight the positives and show how you could minimize the impact of the negatives.

> **TIP:** For more information on flexible work options, send a self-addressed, stamped business envelope to New Ways to Work, 785 Market Street, Suite 950, San Francisco, CA 94103, and request a publications list.
>
> Also contact the Association of Part-Time Professionals, a national membership group offering workshops, seminars, a newsletter, fact sheets, and several publications. Call 703-734-7975 or write 7700 Leesburg Pike, Suite 216, Falls Church, VA 22043.
>
> Another source is Catalyst, a nonprofit research organization that advises businesses on increasing options for working women. Write Catalyst at 250 Park Avenue South, New York, NY 10003-1459, and ask for a publications list.

DECIDING TO GO FOR IT

Susan Dynerman, co-author of *The Best Jobs in America for Parents Who Want Careers and Time for Children, Too* (Rawson, 1991), says parents should ask themselves the following questions if they are thinking of making a request for a change in their work arrangements:

- ❑ What would I lose by asking?
- ❑ Do I know all the players who must approve this, and do they know my work? Is it just my boss, or must higher-ups also be involved?
- ❑ What will be my fallback position if I don't get what I ask for?
- ❑ How's the timing? Does my family situation call for immediate action? Could my request be received more positively if I waited until the new budget year, for example?
- ❑ If I'm turned down, will I suffer any negative professional consequences from having raised the issue?

Be sure of what you want because you might get it, says Suzanne Smith, who co-authored the book *Creating a Flexible Workplace: How to Select and Manage Alternative Work Options* (AMACOM,

1989) with Barney Olmsted. Once you've gone forward with a plan to work part time, for example, it may not be possible to get back on full time if you change your mind. Or, if the company sets you up with a computer at home and you find you miss the office, you may not be able to reclaim your old desk.

PREPARE YOUR CASE

Dynerman successfully negotiated a job share in which she and Lynn Hayes managed a communications department for a large international hotel chain. Dynerman advises parents to prepare a well-thought-out plan before knocking on the boss' door.

"Don't do it the morning your babysitter failed to show and you've reached the breaking point," she cautions. "There has to be a strong business reason for an employer to accept a proposal for making a job flexible."

The first step is to break down the job's contents. Maybe part of it could be done by a lower-level employee. Maybe some functions could be eliminated. Perhaps some of your job could be done at home. If your plan could save your employer money, be sure to point that out.

NEGOTIATE YOUR SALARY AND BENEFITS PACKAGE

If you're negotiating to work fewer hours, include an equitable salary and continued benefits in your goals. Smith says workers often are so desperate for a reduced schedule that they will bargain away everything.

Check your company's policy to see how benefits are handled for part-timers. Some give full benefits, some prorate them, and some offer nothing. You might be able to keep full health coverage by offering to chip in a prorated share of the cost, Dynerman notes. And get a clear understanding of how overtime will be handled, especially when there is out-of-town travel that extends beyond the normal work schedule.

Be Persuasive

Point out others in your company whose flexible arrangements have been successful, Dynerman suggests, and provide the names and phone numbers of their supervisors. Also remind your boss of the good work you have done for the company as evidence of your value.

Give details of how the new arrangement would work, including everything from how your productivity will be measured to how you'll maintain communication with superiors and subordinates. Anticipate objections your boss might raise and prepare responses. Propose a trial period so either you or the boss could fine-tune or back out of the arrangement if it doesn't work the way you both thought it would.

If the boss doesn't accept your plan, have a fall-back position ready. She might be willing to compromise, if you are.

Protect Your Position

At some time during the negotiations, which likely will involve multiple meetings, let your boss know that you still want to move up in the organization. "An employer might assume you're not interested in advancement unless you say you are," Dynerman points out. "People with flexible jobs do get promoted, but maybe not as quickly."

When you've finished negotiating, put everything in writing. That protects you now as well as in the future, should you sometime find yourself with a new boss.

SAFETY IN NUMBERS

"I'd like to work a different schedule, but my company doesn't have a policy for flextime. I have co-workers who'd like that option, too. Would it be wise for us to approach the CEO together rather than for me to go as an individual?"

Yes. A company is more likely to respond if supervisors know that a problem is affecting a number of workers, not just one individual who is asking for special consideration. Dana Friedman of the Families and Work Institute suggests being prepared to tell the boss how many workers in your department have similar problems and need flexibility.

You can do your own informal poll of your immediate co-workers, or you might ask your personnel department to survey employees. You also could consider asking the company to form a task force to address the issue. If there is management resistance, "be prepared to suggest a pilot project," Friedman says.

Don't restrict your group to parents. Childless workers may need flexibility, too—to care for relatives or further their education, for example. The broader you make the workplace problem appear to be, the more likely you'll get action on it.

PRESENCE IS PERFORMANCE TO SOME BOSSES

"I'd like to work different hours so I'm home with my children when they return from school. My boss is concerned that if he lets me do it, everyone will want to."

Your boss's reluctance to allow widespread flexibility may be due to a view many managers still hold: that you have to be in the office with your supervisor to be productive. Enlightened bosses understand that employees should be judged by their work output rather than the number of hours they put in.

While researching the availability of flexible schedules in the federal government for a General Accounting Office study, Rosslyn Kleeman visited a manager new to his job who had a sign on his wall proclaiming "Presence Is Performance." She suggested to him this might not be the best way to build trust among his new subordinates.

But he was convinced that if he and the staff weren't in the office together at all times, the employees would goof off. Flextime was out because, if some workers started their day at 7 A.M. and others came later and didn't finish until 7 P.M., he'd have to work 12 hours to supervise them. Telecommuting was unthinkable.

Set Goals and Timetables, if Necessary

For a boss like this, your proposal must emphasize output and how it can be measured, according to Kleeman, who now is executive-in-residence at the George Washington University School of Business and Public Management. You have to set performance goals and timetables.

"If you want to start work at 6 A.M., you could say: 'By the time you arrive, I will have these tasks completed and on your desk,'" Kleeman explains. If you're in charge of a project, break it down into steps, write down the order in which each step will be done, and establish a timetable. "Some managers want to know how you are getting along, so you can build in milestones for reporting back on your progress," she adds. And be sure everything is in writing.

Rotating Schedules May Help

Unfortunately, there are some jobs in which presence is essential to performance. "If the phone needs to be answered at 9 A.M., somebody has to be there," says Suzanne Smith. She suggests that co-workers figure out together how they could rotate schedules to maximize flexibility while still making sure the phones are covered during the crucial hours. This plan can be presented to the boss with the suggestion that she allow a trial period for testing it.

If production slips, it's up to the group to take responsibility for getting things back on track. That takes the burden off the boss and gives the employees some autonomy in their work.

Working from Home

"My company is open to the idea of telecommuting, and the concept sounds great. But I wonder if I can make the adjustment to working at home away from my colleagues and with all the domestic distractions."

Home offices are becoming more popular due to technologies such as fax machines and computers with modems. Working at home—either self-employed or as a telecommuter for an employer—is an especially attractive option for parents because of the flexibility it affords them.

Companies that have gone into telecommuting in a big way save money by reducing the amount of office space they need. Firms also can increase productivity, especially when their telecommuting employees work varied schedules, thus extending the business day. Employees can opt to put in some time when the kids are in bed and business is going on in other time zones. And telecommuters aren't absent from work just because their child has the chicken pox or a snowstorm makes roads impassable.

The 1994 earthquake spurred telecommuting in the Los Angeles area. Collapsed bridges and damaged buildings forced people to work at home, many with computers and modems. Although unplanned, this taste of telecommuting will make converts of some L.A. employers and employees who hadn't seriously considered it before.

SATELLITE OFFICES

A growing number of firms and government agencies in large metropolitan areas are setting up satellite offices for telecommuters. That way, home-based workers can get to nearby satellites when necessary—for photocopying or meetings, for example—while avoiding lengthy commutes to downtown offices.

Some companies are giving their sales personnel portable fax machines and laptop computers and "kicking them out of the nest," Suzanne Smith says, because they want the salespeople on the road, not in the office. The salespeople can operate from home, going to the office for occasional meetings. And there's no need to provide big offices at headquarters for workers who are there only occasionally.

In the past, home-based workers were not held in high esteem because they were viewed as less serious about their work than full-timers. Now, home-based work is gaining respect—and, in some cases, envy—as workers show they can get the job done no matter where they do it. Not every job can be done from home, but many jobs have at least some components that are portable.

Technology has made it possible to serve clients or customers without their even being aware that you aren't sitting in a downtown office. To be sure, a client may not want to hear kids yelling or a vacuum cleaner humming in the background. You have to maintain professionalism—even if you're sitting at your desk in your bathrobe with the cat on your lap!

Despite the potential benefits, working at home is not for everyone. A lot depends on your capacity for self-discipline.

IS TELECOMMUTING RIGHT FOR YOU?

First, ask yourself whether you are a disciplined and organized person who needs little supervision. Can you be in your home office by a certain time every day, walking past the dirty dishes or piles of laundry without getting sidetracked? As Joyce Scall, a home-based legal research consultant, put it, "You have to build up the habit of compartmentalizing your work life and your home life."

Also consider whether you'd feel lonely working at home. Some people thrive on the solitude while others need co-workers around.

If you're in the latter category, consider working at home only one or two days each week and going into the office the rest of the time. (In fact, Suzanne Smith says, most telecommuting jobs require an em-

THE UPSIDE/DOWNSIDE OF WORKING FROM HOME

The Upside

- You're more accessible to your children. You can handle an emergency if it arises. You're there when they come home from school. You can offer advice on their homework or commiserate on their latest crises.
- You don't waste time commuting.
- You don't have to get dressed up.
- You cut work-related expenses (commuting costs, business wardrobe, eating out, and so forth).
- You can let in the plumber or sign for deliveries.
- You may be more productive away from office distractions such as colleagues dropping by to visit. You can get away from some of the office gossip, politics, or infighting.
- Your kids can learn from being exposed to the work side of your life.
- Older kids might be able to be involved in your work—helping out with such tasks as filing or stuffing envelopes.

The Downside

- Kids can be a distraction, even when you have a caregiver.
- Young children may be upset by seeing you at home but not receiving your attention.
- You may miss face-to-face interaction with your colleagues.
- Your career could suffer if being off site also means being out of your supervisors' minds.
- You may be tempted to let production slip by tending to household chores or minding personal business instead of doing your job.
- You have no support staff at hand.
- You may have even more interruptions than you had at the office—repairmen, door-to-door solicitors, nonbusiness phone calls, crying children.
- You can end up working more than full time if you let projects slip into nights and weekends. If you don't find it easier to spend time with your family, you've defeated the purpose of working at home.

ployee to be in the office at least part of the week.) If you're self-employed and feeling isolated, join a professional association or have lunch with other home-based workers in your neighborhood from time to time.

You can keep your work and home lives apart more easily if you can devote a room to office space. Use an answering machine or voice-mail service to take calls when your child is crying. Let friends know your work hours to minimize distracting phone calls or visits.

DEALING WITH CHILDREN WHILE WORKING AT HOME

Your kids may be the biggest factor in your decision. Don't even think about working at home without child care if your children are preschoolers. It can't be done effectively. Even children in the early elementary grades will have trouble leaving you uninterrupted. (They have this uncanny way of popping up right in the middle of a business call to ask where the peanut butter is!) But you can count on uninterrupted business time while they're in school.

If you have an in-home caregiver, working at home lets you keep an eye on the quality of care your child is getting. The downside is that your toddler may be upset that you're home and won't play with her. Joyce Scall solved that problem by making a big show of hugging her daughter good-bye in the morning. Then, while the sitter distracted the toddler, Scall sneaked upstairs to her third-floor office. She called it Suite 300, and for a long time her child never knew Mommy worked at home.

Others solve the child-distraction problem by taking their kids to daycare. A parent must handle those occasional days when a child is home sick, but has the rest of the business time free from the patter of little feet.

School-age children probably will appreciate having you there when they get home. If your employer doesn't care what schedule you work as long as you get the work done, you might knock off at 3 P.M. to be with your kids or to drive them to after-school activities. Then you can put in a couple of hours in the evening.

WHEN BOTH SPOUSES WORK FROM HOME

"I'd like to start working from home. But my husband is working there already, and I'm afraid that might be too much togetherness."

Increasing numbers of couples will be facing this dilemma as home-based work becomes more popular. And, if it's true that absence makes the heart grow fonder, being with your spouse 24 hours a day may be more of a strain than some relationships can handle.

Kate Petranech began working at home as a direct marketing consultant fifteen years ago. Two years later, her attorney husband, Barry Morewitz, started his own business combining legal work and securities trading.

"I always started my workday by going to the kitchen for a cup of coffee and would sit for a few minutes and collect my thoughts," Petranech recalls. But the first morning her husband began working at home, he walked in, flipped on the kitchen TV, and simultaneously started a conversation. "The rest of my working life flashed before my eyes," she says—and she didn't like what she saw. Fortunately, some frank communication led to an arrangement that suits them both.

Robert Frost said good fences make good neighbors, and that's the approach this at-home couple has taken. Her office is on the third floor, and his is in a converted garage, some distance from the house. She believes separate—and preferably distant—locations are critical for this arrangement to work. "Each person needs to have his own space, and ideally one that doesn't intrude on the family space," she says.

Petranech also suggests minimizing the need for frequent contact during the workday. "We have a 10- to 15-minute meeting every morning to clear away details," she says. "Then it's done. So we don't need to communicate later about who's going to put on the potatoes for dinner or pick up Risa [their daughter] at school."

To ease the loneliness of the home-based worker, the couple goes out to lunch together once a week. "It makes it seem as if I'm having a lunch date with someone whose office is not too far away!" says Petranech.

Going Part Time

"The stress of a full-time job and raising two small kids is driving me crazy. I'd like to cut back to part time, but I'm debating about whether we can handle it financially."

Going part time doesn't mean you have to cut your working hours—and income—in half. Even a small reduction in your work schedule can be a big stress reliever.

Take the example of Ann Hoenigswald. "One day I took vacation time on a Friday and went to a store to exchange something," she recalls. "I found spaces in the parking lot and no lines at the counter, and I realized how much more I could get done on a weekday than on the weekend." Coupled with the mounting stress she was feeling from having two sons whose after-school activities were rapidly increasing, the experience convinced her to reduce her hours at work.

By taking off Fridays, she reduced her workweeks to 32 hours, only a 20 percent decrease. Her salary and benefits were prorated. Because her husband continued to bring in his full-time salary, the impact on the couple's total income was fairly small. But it has made a world of difference to the family's quality of life. Weekends no longer evaporate in a swirl of errands. There's more time for the kids, and everyone is happier.

Hoenigswald thinks working 80 percent doesn't make her seem so much like a part-timer at work and hasn't hurt her career. She thinks that half-time employees, because they aren't around as much, aren't viewed as being very career-oriented. But, because Hoenigswald occasionally goes out of town on business trips and sometimes comes in on Fridays if she's needed, some of her co-workers don't even realize she's a part-timer.

The part-time option isn't available to everyone at the museum where Hoenigswald works as a conservationist. "You can't be a department head and work part time," she says. But she's not looking for upward mobility right now. "I enjoy the job I have, and other things in my life fulfill me besides my job."

Even a Small Cutback Can Ease the Stress

You might be surprised at how big an impact even a small reduction in hours can have on your home life. Going from 40 hours to 35 hours could put you at home an hour earlier each night and relieve some of the stress from evenings jammed with homework, meal preparation, or baby care.

The Financial Costs of Part-Time Work

The financial impact of switching to part-time work includes more than a drop in salary. On the plus side, note the savings you'll reap if you don't need as much child care or if you'll spend less on transportation, restaurant lunches, and other costs of working every day. On the minus side, don't forget to tote up any fringe benefits you'll lose as a part-time employee.

KEEPING PART-TIME HOURS FOR PART-TIME PAY

"I have a part-time job, but it feels more like full time without the paycheck. I often end up staying late, going in for meetings on my day off, and taking work home. How do I get out of this?"

It's your responsibility to see that the schedule is adhered to. Sometimes co-workers or bosses need friendly but firm reminders. It's okay, and probably a point in your favor, if you come in on your day off for a meeting once in a while or stay late to work on a project—as long as you don't let it become a habit. It's too easy to let the rest of your office ignore the fact that you're supposed to have a shortened schedule and that you have a smaller paycheck to go with it.

DEALING WITH JEALOUS COLLEAGUES

"My part-time job lets me leave the office every day at 2 P.M. to be with my kids after school. Some of my co-workers envy my schedule and occasionally make snide remarks. How should I handle this?"

Maybe with a snappy comeback like "I stop collecting my salary at 2 P.M., too." You have to educate colleagues that you're not getting some special luxury but have made a choice to forgo income to put in shorter workdays.

But consider the issue from your colleagues' point of view, also. Some may be jealous because they'd like to work part time, too, but can't afford it. In that case, you need to bring some sensitivity of your own to the situation.

Sometimes the childless co-workers feel the most resentment. Do they frequently have to cover for parents who are late for work or absent because of their kids? Does the company give workers who don't have children less opportunity for flexible schedules? Do employees without children get asked to stay late on crash projects when the parents leave at 5 P.M. to pick up their kids at the daycare center? All these may contribute to a feeling that you're part of a group that gets special treatment just because you have a family at home.

Make sure your colleagues know that, if they have to cover for you occasionally, you'll be there for them, too. You might also point out that your success in negotiating a part-time job can pave the way for your colleagues, including nonparents who might need that option someday to care for an elderly parent or ill spouse, for example.

Job Sharing

Although still not very common, job sharing makes part-time work possible in a job that requires full-time coverage. A secretarial job, for example, might require someone to answer the phone throughout the business day. But there's no reason two people couldn't split the job so each covers half the time.

Even management jobs can be shared, as Susan Dynerman and Lynn Hayes proved in directing their hotel chain's communications department. They split the job's functions—one taking media relations, the other, publications and speech writing. Hayes worked three days a week and Dynerman two and a half, so they overlapped in the office half of one day and had that time to keep each other informed. Each had subordinates to manage, and each was evaluated individually by the boss.

To show their own willingness to be flexible, they agreed to attend important meetings during their time off and to take occasional phone calls at home." The process of keeping in touch is critical," Dynerman stresses, both with each other and with the rest of the staff.

FINDING A JOB-SHARE PARTNER

"I'd like to share a job but I don't have a partner. Should I approach my boss with the idea and enlist her help in finding one?"

No, advises Suzanne Smith, who co-authored *The Job Sharing Handbook* (Ten Speed Press, 1983). "You have to find a partner and then show the boss how it will work."

Finding the right person is critical, Smith says. "We always say we've never found a job that couldn't be shared, but we've found people who couldn't share."

Dynerman and Hayes think the best partners are those who have the same work philosophy, a similar style, and complementary skills and experience. They should not be overly competitive. It's good to be friends, but not best friends, because it's unwise to

EVEN SKEPTICS SOMETIMES CAN BE CONVINCED THAT JOB SHARING WORKS

Some managers assume a job that involves working with clients or customers isn't a good candidate for job sharing, but that isn't always true. Cathy Crouch, a sales manager for an office equipment manufacturer, had two sales representatives who wanted to share a job. Crouch's superiors were skeptical. How would the customers react? The company decided to ask them.

"We interviewed twenty customers, and they were very favorable," Crouch says. "They said it reflected well on the company" to offer employees flexibility.

As a result, the company approved a plan under which the two sales reps would split a customer list, each taking half the accounts as her primary responsibility and pro-viding backup on the rest. Each customer had a primary representative plus a secondary one who knew the account and could handle matters that came up during the primary representative's time off. Each sales rep worked two and a half days, both working on Wednesday afternoon to keep each other informed.

"The way they structured their time, we had 100 percent coverage" without the gaps that occur when a full-time salesperson takes vacation, Crouch says. It also eliminated the burnout factor that sometimes hits full-time workers. And they "proved two heads are better than one. We got more productivity with two people in the assignment. It was win-win for the company."

mix too much personal and professional time.

Smith says that, although job sharers usually come from within, it may be possible for you to bring in one from outside. "Your partner doesn't have to be someone in the company, but the more the supervisor knows of the other person, the easier it is," she says.

Finding a Flexible New Job

"I'm about to launch a job search and I want to focus on family-friendly companies from the outset. Where can I find the ones with good reputations?"

A simple way to start is by asking other parents, especially those who are in a similar line of work. You might find them among the parents of your children's classmates or in your professional association.

Also watch for companies mentioned in the news for innovative programs, especially in the work/family area. A newspaper article about local telecommuters or corporate-sponsored child-care programs often yields the names of companies that have such benefits.

Another source is the annual list of one hundred best companies for working mothers, published each October by *Working Mother* magazine. Selection is made on the basis of pay, advancement opportunities, child care, and a host of family-friendly benefits. Competition for the recognition is keen. The magazine hears from hundreds of firms that want to be considered.

Because the selections change from year to year, you should check the last two or three lists in back issues at your library. A firm listed in the recent past is worth looking at and might be located near you.

Slowing Down on the Fast Track

"I think I'm about to be offered a promotion. Although I'd like to move up in the ranks in the future, I don't want to take on a job with more responsibilities and travel right now while I have two preschoolers. How can I turn down the promotion without throwing away my chance for future advancement?"

"The most honest thing to say is: 'I want it, but I want to postpone it for a couple of years,'" says Dana Friedman of the Families and Work Institute. She says to stress the word "postpone," so the boss knows

BUT WHAT ABOUT THE BOSS?

Even if the overall corporate climate seems supportive and there are good policies in place, you should try to psych out your prospective boss, too. Does he understand how family responsibilities affect workers? Is he coping with these issues, too?

In the Families and Work Institute's *National Study of the Changing Work Force* (1993), supervisors who have significant child-care responsibilities of their own were seen as more supportive than those who don't. So were supervisors with employed spouses.

This doesn't mean that an unmarried, childless man won't be a supportive boss. But a supervisor who has to cope with child-care crises, too, is likely to be more understanding when you have yours. A workplace may not be so sensitive to working parents if most of the managers are men whose wives stay home with their kids.

you'd like to move up in the future. "Continue to do your job well to prove you are still committed," Friedman says. "Make it clear you want to revisit this, and remind the boss in any way you can, maybe by establishing a time frame" for when you would like to be considered for promotion.

She also suggests thinking twice before turning down a promotion. It might be possible to revise the job to reduce its responsibility and travel load.

Remember, too, that temporarily slowing down on the fast track doesn't have to mean stepping off altogether. People who take parental leave or reduce their hours when their children are young can resume climbing the corporate ladder later if they are considered valued employees.

Combining More Family Time with Rewarding Work

"My job demands long hours, and I'm constantly torn by the lack of time left for my family. Sometimes I think about switching to a job with fewer hours and more flexibility, but I don't want to leave my profession. I'm afraid I won't find

EVALUATING A FIRM'S "FAMILY-FRIENDLINESS"

How can you make sure that your next employer isn't just using family-friendly benefits as window dressing?

Hal Morgan and Kerry Tucker recommend the following four steps in their book, *Companies That Care: The Most Family Friendly Companies in America—What They Offer and How They Got That Way* (Simon & Schuster/ Fireside, 1991):

1. Research the company. Read news articles about it and study its annual report, watching for mention of family benefits.

2. Ask safe questions at the first interview to get a sense of the company's attitudes toward employees. Inquire about common benefits, such as family health insurance and whether the employer contributes to a savings plan. If you are a woman, ask how women have progressed in the company.

3. Save tough questions for later interviews, when the company is close to offering or has offered you a job. Ask to see the employee handbook so you can review all the benefits offered. Ask how often employees are relocated and if the company will help your spouse find a job. Find out if the company offers personal absence days or paid leave when you have to stay home with a sick child, or if you have to use vacation days or take unpaid time off. Ask if you can take work home and if the company ever provides computer hookups to make working at home easier.

4. Before you accept the job, ask to talk with employees to assess the work climate. Ask them what hours are expected if you are moving up the career ladder, if reviews are based on how much time you put in or how much work you get done, and whether last-minute meetings are called early or late in the day. Notice, too, if family photos or children's artwork is on display. It's a good sign if employees are comfortable about touting their parenthood.

something with better hours that I'll also find rewarding as a career."

Fear of the unknown can be the main cause of inertia. People who find their current jobs fulfilling—even though they are overworked—are naturally reluctant to switch to a new position that they worry might not be as interesting or lucrative.

The fear is not unfounded. There very well may be trade-offs. Switching jobs might entail a pay cut, for example. But it is possible to find rewarding work that leaves more time for the family. You and your spouse have to weigh the costs and the benefits and identify your priorities for family and career.

Take the example of Jim Curtin (*see box*). He was an attorney with a big law firm who specialized in antitrust litigation. He switched to practicing environmental law for a government agency and found more time for his family and a more fulfilling career. Of course, many parents can't afford to take a big pay cut, even if they drive old cars, send their kids to public school, and have a medium-size mortgage. But that doesn't mean they couldn't find greater flexibility in another job. Even small changes in work hours can make a big difference in family life. Staying where you are, if there's no hope of reducing the time

FLEXIBILITY CAN BE WORTH THE TRADE-OFFS

As an attorney with a big law firm, Jim Curtin often worked nights and weekends, and he traveled regularly. "If it was Sunday night, my kids just accepted that Daddy had to fly to California," he recalls. In his new position, travel is infrequent and he can take advantage of a flexible work schedule.

"We can choose to work extra hours each day in exchange for a half or whole day off every two weeks," Curtin explains. Virtually everybody in his department works a compressed workweek, including the managers, so no one looks askance when he leaves at 4 P.M. to attend a school function, for example.

"People try to schedule meetings on Tuesday, Wednesday, or Thursday during the heart of the workday so the key players will be there," he says. On those occasions when an important meeting is scheduled for his day off, he'll change his personal plans to accommodate the job.

What Curtin lost in the job switch was a big chunk of pay. He advises parents considering such a move to look at their financial situation as well as their personal values. "A lot depends on your lifestyle," he says. "If you have a big mortgage, send your kids to private schools, and drive expensive cars, you might not be able to do it. Personally, I have not one regret."

spent on the job, will just lead to more frustration and stress.

DECIDING TO MAKE A JOB CHANGE

Contemplating a job change can be an emotionally wrenching experience. That's why it's a good idea to approach it systematically. The decision certainly should involve your spouse and maybe even your children if they are old enough.

With paper and pencil, list your goals, such as shorter hours, less travel, different responsibilities, and so forth. Then list the features a new job *must* have and those you *want* it to have. That helps you clarify what's really important to you.

Brainstorm places where your ideal job might be found. Talk with friends and acquaintances in your career field about what your prospects are. But be discreet if you don't want your boss to hear that you're looking around.

> **TIP:** Most libraries have directories with information on local companies. Some also keep notebooks with actual job listings such as those in local, state, or federal government offices.

Don't overlook the possibility of changing careers.

You probably have skills that could transfer to another line of work. For instance, if you're a computer programmer, you might consider becoming a computer instructor at a community college. Such a move could enable you to transfer your skills to a new job with a more flexible schedule.

When you have a specific job to consider, carefully analyze the details. If you would have to accept less pay, work out a family budget with the lower projected income. What would have to be cut? Are you and your spouse both willing? Does the new job mean moving to a smaller house or to another city? If your kids are old enough, they could be given the opportunity to express their opinions, too. You might be surprised by how much your children are willing to economize if it means they have more time with you.

Making the Break to Your Own Business

"I'd like to start my own business, but I hear lots of them fail, and my income is important to my

family. How do I assess my chances for success and get off to a good start?"

If your family needs two incomes, this move is not to be taken lightly. Most small businesses fail. Those that succeed often take years to turn profitable and require their owners to work long days, long weeks, and years without vacations. Your initial income probably will be less than you make now, and you will lose your employer-provided fringe benefits.

Some parents choose to work even though the family doesn't have to have a second full-time income, however. For those who want the psychic rewards of continuing a career while having more time for the kids, starting a business can be a fulfilling alternative to quitting altogether or switching to part-time work.

As your children demand less of your time, you can devote more to the business. The business could enable you to keep your professional skills sharp to ease your return to full-time employment later.

A common way to get started is to do what you do now and make your current employer your first client. Using the business contacts you already have, you can build up your client base.

Another approach is to start a business that fits your talents but does not resemble your current job very much, as Leora Hoffman and Robyn Quinter did (*see boxes on pages 244–245*).

> **TIP:** For information on starting your own business, contact the Small Business Administration, which has information on writing business plans, legal issues, licensing, financing, and many other issues. Check your phone book for the local office or call 800-827-5722.

TIPS FOR STARTING YOUR OWN BUSINESS

Susan has been operating a freelance writing business since shortly after our daughter was born in 1985. And she has experienced many of the joys and frustrations of other home-based-business owners. Here are some tips she can pass along:

- ❏ Don't quit your day job until you have at least one client. It's easier to get others when you can show what you are doing for the first one.
- ❏ Get business cards printed immediately so you can start making contacts. They don't have to have a fancy logo (unless maybe you are going into a business involving graphic design).

FROM LAWYER TO MATCHMAKER

Leora Hoffman of Washington, D.C., wanted more time with her children than her career as a criminal defense lawyer allowed. After the birth of her first child, she quit her law firm because court dates made it impossible to work a reduced schedule.

"In private practice, part time is 35 to 40 hours," she explains. "You get paid for part time and you're still working almost full time." The only part-time job in the legal profession she could find was with a government agency three days a week. It wasn't very interesting work, and on workdays she still "had to juggle two children and be gone from 8 A.M. to 6 P.M. I could only do it if I loved my work, and I didn't."

When her sister in New York City paid a hefty fee to a matchmaker, Hoffman hit on the idea of becoming one herself. She says matchmaking fits her interpersonal skills, and targeting lawyers and other professionals gave her a niche that wasn't being filled. In Washington, D.C., with its high proportion of workaholics, there are plenty of people who don't have time to meet others socially. Hoffman is essentially running a search firm, seeking someone's ideal companion.

"I spent six months researching the singles community," she recalls. "The more research I did, the more I realized there was a market." And she became convinced that her new profession would allow her more flexibility so that she could spend more time with her children.

She works around her children's school hours and often meets clients on evenings and weekends while the kids are with their father. For those client meetings, she sublets an office used by a psychologist during the day. The rest of the time she operates from a home office.

She advises other parents who want to start their own businesses to hold on to their jobs while they do the market research and develop a detailed business plan with short- and long-term goals. "It takes a long time to establish yourself and your reputation," she notes. So you don't want to give up a salary until you have to because you'll probably have little income when your business first opens.

FROM MARKETER TO PUBLICIST AND DESKTOP PUBLISHER

Robyn Quinter agrees with Leora Hoffman's advice. But she didn't have the luxury of advance preparation when she started her business. Having been laid off from a marketing job at a law firm, she decided it was time to try running a home-based business doing publicity and desktop publishing. It took her two months just to shop for a computer and get it up and running. Then there were business cards, stationery, and office supplies to be ordered—and, most important, clients to be found.

Quinter joined three organizations to make contacts with people who could advise her and who could be potential sources of business—the local chamber of commerce, a group of women business owners in her county, and an association of home-based businesses. She tapped the members of the home-based business group for tactics that had worked for them. "That's not something you can get out of a book," Quinter stresses.

Quinter loves the flexibility of being her own boss but still is adjusting to the biggest downside—an inconsistent income. "I have great months and lousy months," she says. In business less than a year, she expects her income to grow and become more consistent when she's had more time to establish herself.

If your office will be in your home, Quinter stresses the need for a self-contained space where you can shut the door on family distractions. Hers is an extension of the kitchen with no door, "not an ideal location to work in when other family members are around."

She thinks having a supportive spouse is a requirement for success. And, she adds, it is imperative to have some savings to fall back on initially.

Not only does the family bank account have to cover everyday living expenses, it also must pay business start-up costs, which can be as little as the price of business cards and stationery or a much larger capital outlay for office equipment and inventory. You also may have to pay for legal and tax advice.

- Get a fax machine and put the number on your business card. You won't be taken seriously without one.
- Don't waste time sending out blind letters to lots of potential clients. Use a personal approach. Contact everyone you ever knew, use all your networks, scatter your business cards, and follow up with the people you scatter them to. That is how you'll find your first clients.
- Join a professional association. Some people worry that, by sharing information with potential competitors, they run the risk of having clients stolen from them. Susan's experiences with her freelance writers' group is the opposite. When she's had more work than she could handle, she has passed jobs on to other writers she knows. When she thought she would have to turn down a job that was too many hours, she found a partner to split the work with, and they each got half the revenue from a job Susan stood to lose altogether. When members hear of jobs that aren't in their areas of expertise, they call someone else in the group who has the right skills. By sharing information about clients, they learn who is easy to work with, who's slow to pay, or who is expanding and will need more freelancers.
- Establish a routine so you are in your office by a certain time every day and work a regular schedule. But make that a flexible schedule that permits you to spend time with your children. Susan allows for volunteer time in Julie's school, and she tries to be with Julie when she comes home—even if that requires putting in a little extra time at night or on the weekends.
- Keep really good records. The IRS is fussy about home-office deductions, and you'll want to get the maximum tax benefit from your business expenses. You may want to consult an accountant to get your records set up and prepare your taxes, at least initially. We now have enough experience to do our own tax return by using a computer program that is updated each year to incorporate changes in the tax laws.
- Allow plenty of time to choose computer equipment and learn to use it to your best advantage. A computer can help you with many business chores from accounting to scheduling, but only

if you know how to use it. If you need help, ask colleagues in your professional association to recommend a computer consultant.

❑ Be professional. Don't tell a client you can't meet her on Monday because you're chaperoning the first grade's field trip. Just say you're already booked on Monday but are available on Tuesday.

PREPARING FOR THE FUTURE

T he stress and time pressures faced by families with two working parents are supposed to be compensated, at least in part, by the financial rewards flowing from two incomes. But financial benefits—now and later—are not automatic.

HERE'S HELP ON:

Saving dollars by pinching pennies, page 250
You don't have to be rich to save, page 250
Taking advantage of noncash benefits, page 252
Financing your child's education, page 253
Preparing for your retirement, page 257
Insuring your future—and your kids', page 259
Wills and guardians, page 263
What to do if you're incapacitated, page 267
Getting professional financial advice, page 267
Managing your own money, page 269
Raising money-savvy children, page 271

It's easy for two-income couples to spend a good deal of money on expenses related to work—transportation, clothing, lunches in restaurants, and child care, for example. Because time is scarce, some working couples are more inclined than one-income families to pay for housecleaning and home-maintenance services, less inclined to shop around for bargains or to clip money-saving grocery coupons, and more likely to eat out or to order home-delivered dinners.

However, if you manage your money well as you plan for the future, you'll be better prepared for your children's college bills and your own retirement. If your children are young today, saving and investing now could give you the financial cushion you need to create flexible work schedules, if you want to, when the kids are older. And your example will teach your children a valuable lesson.

Saving Dollars by Pinching Pennies

One key to sound money management is understanding that a penny saved is not a penny earned. Depending on your tax bracket, it could be one-and-a-half or even two pennies. That's because you aren't taxed on what you do for yourself—or what you don't get done at all.

For example, if you mow your own lawn, you may think you're saving the $10 you'd have paid the kid next door to mow it for you. In fact, you save the $10 plus the extra money you would have to earn to pay your tribute to Social Security, Medicare, and the federal, state, and local income-tax collectors. If you're making a purchase subject to sales tax, you've got to earn that much more, which, depending upon where you're making the purchase, could be 5, 7, or 9 percent.

The best way to prepare for your financial future,

therefore, is to cut back on expenditures now and to carefully invest what you've saved.

This advice may sound elementary, but we've found that even the most sophisticated people often overlook the simplest ways to improve their financial circumstances. None of us was born with an understanding of personal finance, and a lot of us didn't learn much about it in school. Many of today's parents grew up in families where Dad was the sole or main breadwinner, and he made the financial decisions without sharing much information with the children.

You Don't Have to Be Rich to Save

"We're just starting our family, and our incomes are low. It's tough enough making ends meet. How can we possibly think about saving?"

The benefits of good money management are not restricted to the affluent. *Parents* magazine (September 1993), for example, offered professional financial advice to a working couple who had two preschoolers and a below-average total annual income of $30,000. The parents were spending every penny they earned and then some, slipping ever more into debt rather than saving for the future.

Parents showed how the couple could reduce expenses by refinancing their mortgage, consolidating their credit card debt with a home equity loan, and trimming their spending on recreation, food, clothing, and other everyday items. For this family, important financial benefits could be gained simply from waiting longer between haircuts and spending less on holiday gifts.

Depending on how much of *Parents'* advice was followed, the family could save between $1,908 and $5,112 a year, the magazine estimated. By investing just the smaller figure each year in the 401(k) retirement plans offered by their employers, the couple would have more than half a million dollars at retirement age, assuming an 8 percent compounded growth rate.

MAKE SAVING A HABIT

Saving is easiest when you do it regularly, without thinking much about it. One way to make it a habit

---

ENFORCED SAVINGS

Here are some ways you can automatically save a portion of your earnings each pay period:

- ❑ If you have a credit union at work, arrange to have a portion of each paycheck deposited in a savings account there.
- ❑ Ask if your employer offers an automatic payroll deduction for purchase of U.S. savings bonds.
- ❑ If your employer will directly deposit your paycheck into your bank, ask him to allocate specific percentages to your checking account and your savings account.
- ❑ Ask if your bank will set up an automatic transfer of funds from checking to savings accounts at regular intervals.
- ❑ Ask a mutual fund to arrange for automatic periodic transfer of funds from your bank checking account.

is to adopt this rule: Always pay yourself first. Make a deposit in your savings plan before you pay bills or give yourself spending money.

Financial advisers suggest trying to save and invest at least 10 percent of your gross earnings. The Vanguard Group investment firm told its clients in 1994 that 10 percent savings would guarantee only "a very modest standard of living" in retirement. Yet the average American puts away just 4 percent, Vanguard says. If you have trouble disciplining yourself, use an enforced savings device. See the box on page 251 for some options.

Avoid using charge cards as if they were revolving loan funds. The cards are convenient for everyone and particularly handy for business travelers who don't like to carry large rolls of cash and who do like the automatic record of their expenditures. But make sure you pay them off every month, or you'll be socked with enormous interest charges. One of the most common ways families get into financial difficulty is by letting charge card debt get out of control.

> **TIP:** If you are having trouble with debt, or just need professional budgeting advice, you can get free counseling from the Consumer Credit Counseling Service, which has 700 locations around the country. Call 800-388-2227 to find the branch nearest you.

Taking Advantage of Noncash Benefits

"We've got friends who seem to take a nice vacation every year, once even to Hawaii. We don't think they make any more money than we do. Do they know some secret that we don't?"

Perhaps they do know about something that you don't: noncash benefits, like frequent traveler, telephone, and credit card programs that can save you travel money and upgrade your trips and vacations.

If your job requires travel, you should be signing up for every airline and hotel frequent-traveler program that you think you might someday use. And you should explore the affinity programs—tied to charge cards and telephone companies, for example—that can make your airline miles or hotel credits add up faster. Chosen and used wisely, they can be a good deal. (But, as we noted earlier, it's important to pay the credit card bills before they accumulate finance charges. And you don't want to buy more-expensive airplane tickets or hotel rooms just because they earn you some frequent-traveler points.)

You can benefit even if you don't travel very much. Some hotels offer free upgrades or reduced rates to members of their frequent-stayer programs, regardless of how many points a member has accumulated. If you use charge cards a lot—and most business travelers do—an affinity card will give you an airline mile for each dollar you charge. There also are interlocking relationships that earn you airline miles for hotel stays, hotel points for auto rentals, and so forth.

It amazes us how many people don't take advantage of these programs. On business trips, we often find ourselves staying in nicer accommodations for less money than our colleagues. We are not the most frequent of fliers. Yet, on a recent Price family vacation in the Southwest, airline miles eliminated all of our air fares, hotel points covered several nights' lodging, and our membership in a hotel plan got us upgraded to a suite.

Many of these airline miles were accumulated through our affinity credit cards, which we use to charge everything from groceries to pediatrician's bills. Our long-distance carrier gives us 5 frequent-flier miles for every dollar we spend on phone calls. We pay the phone bill with an affinity card. And we pay off the credit cards before finance charges show up. The only added cost is the charge card's annual fee, which usually is between $25 and $75—a lot less than the price of a single airline ticket.

Financing Your Child's Education

"We've seen projections of future college costs that make us think there's no way we'll be able to afford to send our children when they get out of high school. How do parents making an average income these days manage it? How can we?"

The College Board reported in 1994 that the average annual cost of attending a four-year college in 1993 was $17,846 at private schools and $8,562 at public institutions. Those figures include such expenses as room, board, transportation, and books as well as basic tuition and fees.

If your child will be attending college far in the future, inflation will push those costs much higher. According to calculations by the Ferris, Baker Watts investment firm in Washington, D.C., for example, a Maryland family with a 5-year-old child in 1993 would need nearly $125,000 to send that child to the public University of Maryland for four years beginning in 2006. Sending the same child through Boston College, a private school, would require nearly $230,000.

INVESTING NOW FOR COLLEGE

To have that kind of money available when it is needed, the family could start a monthly investment program or make one lump-sum investment. According to Ferris, Baker Watts' estimates, the family would have to invest $460 every month from 1993 until 2006 to cover the University of Maryland costs or $850 to pay for Boston College. If the family chose to make a lump-sum investment in 1993, they would have had to put down $36,000 for the state university or $66,000 for Boston College.

In the face of such staggering figures, many parents are tempted to throw up their hands and forget about saving for college altogether. But preparing for college is not an all-or-nothing deal. Even though you might not be able to save enough to cover all of the costs, you can save something.

The sooner you start saving, the more you'll have when you need it. And maybe costs won't soar so high. Using a different set of assumptions about rising costs, Certified Financial Planner Barbara Warner suggests that parents could save enough by putting away $100 each month from the moment a child is born.

It's likely that your family's income will increase over the years, making it easier for you to save more as time goes on. Your child might win a scholarship on merit or financial need. Your child could earn some of the money needed by working part time and during summers. You and/or your child could obtain loans. And there are likely to be government programs that provide financial aid in exchange for your child's performing some public service.

Financial aid is not limited to kids who come from low-income homes, who rank at the top of their classes, or who excel in athletics. A 1993 study by Peterson's Guides revealed that a majority of students at four-year institutions receive some financial assistance.

PRIVATE OR PUBLIC SCHOOLS FOR YOUNG STUDENTS?

"You read such horror stories about the public schools these days that we've been seriously think-

THE WORKING PARENTS HELP BOOK

ing about enrolling our children in private schools. But how can we send our kids to college if we've got to pay thousands of dollars a year first for private schools while they're young?"

One way to save money for college is to avoid spending it on elementary and secondary education. Many working couples believe they must send their young children to private schools to be certain they'll get a good education. But you shouldn't automatically assume that private schools are better than public schools or that—because you live in a big city, for instance—your public schools are bad.

In addition to avoiding the costs of private schools, you might also be able to save child-care expenses by using your public schools. Some public schools offer before- and after-school programs that are less expensive than private programs and that contain educational components as well.

Exploring All Your Public School Options

Before you decide on private education, take a good look at all your public school options. Don't rely on what you've heard; go see for yourself. A school district with a lousy overall reputation may have some excellent individual schools, and one may be in your neighborhood.

You also may have options beyond your neighborhood. School systems—particularly the larger ones—often have magnet schools that draw students from throughout the district. The magnets may specialize in particular subjects—the arts, say, or science. Or there may be magnet schools that follow different educational philosophies, from old-fashioned basics to cutting-edge innovation.

Evaluating Schools

"There's no science" to picking a school, says Chester Finn, Jr., an education professor at Vanderbilt University and a former assistant U.S. secretary of education. But there are objective and subjective criteria to consider.

"The objective data you want to get your hands on depend some on the age and grade level of the kid," Finn says. If you're picking a high school, you're going to want to know how many of its students go to college and where they go. "If it's a primary school, you're not going to care or be able to find out if the graduates got into Princeton."

You may be able to find out how a school's students score on standardized tests and if the student body and faculty are stable or experience a lot of turnover. You can obtain information about class size, curriculum, how the school is organized, and what kind of educational philosophy the teachers follow.

In some major metropolitan areas, local magazines rate schools. Newspapers often publish information about scores on standardized tests and awards of National Merit Scholarships. In some communities, there are books that rate schools and contain information about student test scores, student-teacher ratios, teachers' salaries, private school costs, and other matters. And some school districts publish profiles that contain basic information about individual schools.

Determining if a school really is right for your child also requires subjective analysis that entails "seeing it, smelling it, talking to people who work in it, and talking to parents of the kids in it," Finn adds.

You need to visit the schools you are considering, examine the facilities, talk to the principals and teachers, and sit in on some classes. A good school welcomes parents. If school officials don't encourage you to investigate the school ahead of time and to visit when your child is enrolled, look for another one.

Enrolling in Another School District

If you finally decide that your public schools don't meet your standards, consider nearby public school districts as well as private schools. Some public districts accept students from other jurisdictions and charge lower tuition than private schools do. And, of course, you could move to a different school district.

Financial Aid for Private Schools

Private schools often offer scholarships and other forms of financial aid. And schools affiliated with religious institutions sometimes offer discounts and preferential admission to members.

Private School for Upper Grades

Maybe you believe your neighborhood elementary school is good, but you're less comfortable with the quality of the middle school or high school. Some parents who feel this way enroll their kindergartners in private schools because they fear their children wouldn't be able to transfer from public to private schools later on. As a result, they may pay several years of tuition needlessly.

Even the most exclusive private schools have at least a few openings each year at every grade level. Some plan for transfers from the public schools in the upper grades.

If you're worried about transfers, check out the private schools you might want your child to attend when he's older. Ask how many transfers they accept from public schools. Ask the principal of your public elementary school how many of its graduates apply and are accepted at private schools. And remember that, when your kindergartner is ready for middle school, your public schools may have improved.

Each Child Is Different

Don't assume that what's best for your oldest child will be best for her younger siblings as well. Your neighborhood public school may be fine for a child who's a self-starter and works well independently, for example, but not good for another who needs tighter supervision.

Preparing for Your Retirement

"Both of our employers have suggested that we put some of our earnings into retirement plans that they sponsor. But we're young. Shouldn't we worry about paying for nursery school now and think about retirement when our kids are grown and we're older?"

Today's smart workers do not assume that their old-age needs will be met solely by their employers' pension plans. Financial advisers say workers need to put a plan of their own in place today for meeting those expenses when they arrive.

"It's important for them to understand that they need to make investments, and they need to educate themselves about investments, and they should never invest in anything they don't understand," says financial planner Barbara Warner.

A key to preparing for retirement is taking advantage of the benefits that are available to you. Many employers offer 401(k) plans, which allow employees to invest untaxed dollars in retirement accounts that grow tax-free. Many employers also match all or part of their employees' contributions to the plans.

The self-employed can invest in tax-sheltered retirement programs called Keogh or Simplified Employee Pension (SEP) plans. Everyone younger than 70 1/2 can invest his annual earnings, up to $2,000, in a tax-sheltered individual retirement arrangement (IRA). These three programs' earnings are not taxed until you withdraw them, which is a major financial benefit. In some cases, you can deduct the initial investment from your taxable income.

If two working parents invested $2,000 each in IRAs at age 25, and the investments grew at 8 percent a year, that $4,000 would be worth nearly $87,000 when they were ready to retire at age 65. If each put $2,000 in the IRAs every year, their retirement fund would be worth more than $1 million. Even if the investments returned just 6 percent a year, the fund would be worth $660,000 at retirement; at 10 percent a year, the couple would have nearly $2 million. If they could contribute to 401(k) plans with some employer match, their nest egg could be several times larger.

Financial advisers often use 10 percent as a figure for projecting anticipated returns on investments because the stock market has tended to return a bit more than that over the years. From 1934 through 1993, for example, the 500 stocks in the Standard & Poor's Index returned an average of 11.4 percent a year in appreciation and dividends. The consistency of that return is demonstrated when that sixty-year period is divided into two-decade intervals. From 1934 through 1953, the annual return was 10.7 percent. It was 10.8 percent for 1954-73 and 12.7 percent from 1974-93. And that last period included the crazy 1980s, which saw rapid market run-ups and a crash.

There is risk in the stock market. But if you diversify your investments and keep your eyes fixed on the long term, the risk is low.

You can avoid risk by putting your money into bank accounts that are insured up to $100,000 by the federal government. But your earnings are likely to be lower. From 1972 through 1991, for example, average interest paid on six-month certificates of deposit (CDs) bounced around from 5 percent in 1972 to 15.8 percent in 1981, with a two-decade average of 8.8 percent. In 1993 and 1994, six-month CDs fell below 4 percent.

Insuring Your Future—
And Your Kids'

"It seems that every week we get a phone call or letter from someone who wants to sell us insurance. We ignore the solicitations, but we're wondering if we have the right kinds of insurance and enough of it."

Everyone needs health insurance. Working parents need life and disability insurance as well, especially if both incomes are essential for paying current expenses, investing for retirement, and saving for the children's education.

> **TIP:** You can find a host of suggestions for making life-insurance decisions in *Consumer Reports'* July, August, and September issues of 1993. The exhaustive study is a typical example of why the magazine is an invaluable resource for any family that's trying to manage its money well. (*See the box* Financially Valuable Reading Matter *on page 270 for a list of useful personal finance publications.*)

There's a wide variety of opinions about how much life insurance you need. We've seen recommendations that you should have a policy worth anywhere from three to ten times your annual earnings.

"A good way to figure it is to look at what the wage earner who survives can pay for," says Jannet Carpien, a Ferris, Baker Watts vice president and a Certified Financial Planner (*see box* on page 260). Unfortunately, translating your income shortfall into a specific amount of insurance coverage is not a self-evident calculation. Inflation will increase your expenses. The surviving spouse's income probably will increase. You can't know for certain what return you will get when you invest the deceased spouse's insurance benefits.

Consumer Reports estimated insurance needs by assuming that earnings would increase with inflation, a conservative assumption. With that scenario, you would need insurance to match the income shortfall calculated in the box.

You could ask your insurance agent or financial planner to perform more complex calculations to try to estimate investment earnings more precisely; that probably would project a lower insurance need.

FIGURING LIFE INSURANCE NEEDS

To determine how much additional income would be needed by a surviving spouse, do these calculations for each parent:

❑ Total the surviving spouse and children's likely routine monthly expenses, including food, clothing, transportation, utilities, medical care, entertainment, charitable contributions, insurance, property taxes, rent or mortgage, debt retirement, saving for the children's education, and investing for the surviving parent's retirement.

❑ Figure the surviving family's monthly income by adding the surviving spouse's pay after taxes, post-tax earnings of savings and investments, and what the family would receive in Social Security survivors' benefits and from the deceased spouse's retirement programs. (Your employer and representatives of your retirement programs can help you figure the income these programs would provide. You can get a Personal Earnings and Benefit Estimate Statement from the Social Security Administration; call 800-772-1213 for an application.)

❑ Subtract income from expenses to determine how much additional monthly income the surviving spouse would need.

❑ Multiply by twelve to get an annual figure.

❑ Estimate how many years this level of expense is likely to continue—until your youngest child has graduated from college, for instance.

❑ Multiply the annual figure by the number of years.

❑ Add one-time expenses of the deceased spouse's death. *Consumer Reports* suggests estimating $7,000 to $8,000 for funeral costs.

❑ Subtract the value of investments that aren't dedicated to covering the surviving spouse's retirement needs.

❑ This total tells you how much additional income the surviving spouse would need until the children were self-sufficient and the spouse could afford to support herself.

WHOLE, UNIVERSAL, OR TERM INSURANCE?

Some insurance agents will try to sell you whole- or universal-life insurance, pointing out that it builds up a cash value that you can borrow against or spend in your old age. Term insurance, which costs less, has no value unless you die while the policy is in effect. And you stop buying it when you no longer need it—when your children are grown, for example, and each spouse could support himself on his own income.

Most financial advisers say that families usually are better off buying term insurance and investing the difference between its premiums and the cost of the more expensive policies. According to this theory, term usually is best unless you don't have the discipline to invest and need the automatic savings component of the insurance policy. Even if you need the discipline, advisers point out that there are other automatic investment options, such as a 401(k) plan (*see* Preparing for Your Retirement *on page 257*).

If you do buy term insurance, make sure you can renew it without reestablishing your physical fitness. You don't want to lose your insurance because you become ill.

OTHER INSURANCE

Financial advisers tend to agree that you should have disability insurance that would replace 60 to 80 percent of your income. They point out that your income is much more likely to be lost because you become disabled than because you die before you retire.

An extended liability policy, worth perhaps $1 million, also can be an advisable addition to your household insurance policy—in case you're sued because a child is hurt while playing at your home, for example.

DO SOME RESEARCH BEFORE YOU BUY

As with all major purchases, you should shop around for your insurance policies. Your employer may meet many of your insurance needs, but you will have to buy some insurance elsewhere. And you might find better deals than your employer offers.

You want to be sure to purchase your insurance from a financially sound corporation that's going to be around to pay your benefits when you need them. There are agencies that rate the financial strength of insurers, including A. M. Best, Duff & Phelps, Moody's, Standard & Poor's, and Weiss Research.

In its report on insurance, *Consumer Reports* compiled and averaged insurers' ratings. You can ask a broker or insurance agent for the current ratings of companies you're considering. Large libraries probably carry at least some of the ratings publications.

Be sure you get a definition of the rating and a list of all possible grades that the rating firm uses to report its assessment. You'll probably be surprised to find out that Standard & Poor's and Duff & Phelps each has five ratings higher than A, for instance, and that each firm's lowest rating is CCC.

When you get close to making an insurance decision, be sure you understand the details. You might think you could save money by dropping insurance you have through your employer, for instance. But would your new insurance company make it as easy for you to add a child or your spouse to the policy later? Is there some way the new policy might become less beneficial than your employer's at some time in the future? What counts is what's written in the policy, not what an agent tells you in conversation.

Those are questions you need to ask also if you consider changing jobs. You or a member of your family might have a medical condition that would not be covered under your prospective employer's insurance plan, for example.

Remember to review your insurance coverage from time to time. As your income changes and your children get older (or increase in number), your insurance needs will change as well.

EMERGENCY SAVINGS

Working parents should have one other piece of insurance—liquid savings that could be withdrawn with no or little penalty in an emergency. The amount needed depends on your disability insurance, your employer's sick-leave policy, and how you can draw down or borrow from your retirement plans if you are disabled.

You need enough in accessible savings to carry you between the time you lose your income because of disability and the time that your disability insurance or Social Security benefits kick in. Ask your employer's benefits department how much time that would be for you. If it's a month, you need a month's income in that savings pot.

In any case, financial planner Jannet Carpien advises that a working couple have at least $8,000 to $10,000 that can be tapped in case a car suddenly has to be replaced or a major home repair needs to be made on short notice.

Wills and Guardians

For some reason, many people have no problem buying life insurance yet feel extremely uncomfortable about writing a will. An estimated 70 percent of American adults haven't written one, according to *Kiplinger's Personal Finance Magazine* (April 1994), and more than half die without one.

But death is one of life's few certainties. You're doing your children a great disservice if you don't make a will and name a guardian. It is through your will that you dispose of your property. It's also how you instruct society to care for your children if they're not yet grown.

Some people think they don't need a will because they don't have a large estate. But if you own a house that is appreciating in value, have life insurance, and are contributing to a retirement plan, your estate could be worth a lot more than you think. If your death is caused by someone else—in an automobile accident, say—your heirs could be beneficiaries of substantial compensation.

One aspect of your will can be simple: You can leave everything to your spouse and name him or her to execute your will. But you also must prepare for the time when both of you are gone and for the possibility that that will occur before your children are grown.

Choosing an Executor, Guardian, and Trustee

You will need to name a guardian for your children, a trustee for your estate, and an executor of your will.

The same person can assume all three responsibilities, such as when you leave everything to your spouse, who will execute your will and maintain custody of your children. But that is not always best when you plan for the possibility of both parents dying before your children are grown.

To determine what is right for your family, you have to assess your own needs and the alternatives that are available to you. No single solution fits every family. "You need to understand the costs and the limitations as well as the expertise" of the individuals or institutions you consider for each responsibility, financial planner Jannet Carpien says.

Your choice for guardian might be a loving parent

but an inept money manager, for instance. You also can put a guardian in a conflict of interest by giving him custody of both your child and your estate. The guardian/trustee could benefit personally from spending your estate—on home improvements, vacations, a new car, and so forth—before your child matures. He would reap no personal financial benefit from conserving the estate for your child's use in adulthood.

The costs of managing your estate will be less if you have relatives or friends who are willing to perform the duties of executor and trustee with no charge and whom you trust to protect your children's interests.

Ideally, you will have confidence in the trustee's ability to manage your estate wisely. If you have a trusted financial adviser, you can instruct the trustee to consult with the adviser before making money-management decisions.

You also can turn to professional estate management, such as the trust department of a bank. Several advisers we consulted said that should be the choice of last resort, picked only if you do not have a trusted relative or friend who is able and willing to take on the responsibility. If you go that route, ask estate law-yers to recommend banks with good track records. And make sure you get a clear understanding of the fees the firm will charge for managing the trust.

MANAGEMENT OF YOUR ESTATE

Your will can contain detailed instructions for managing your estate. If you are leaving more than is needed to reimburse the guardian for reasonable costs of caring for your children, you can arrange for the trustee to provide for their higher education and for an inheritance when they reach adulthood. You also can impose limitations on distributions from the estate—providing your children with only minimal income until they pass the normal college years, for example, and giving them the bulk of their inheritance in parcels over time after that. It's probably not a good idea for an 18-year-old to suddenly come into possession of a substantial amount of money with no strings attached.

Once you have established these arrangements, you need to make sure that the rest of your financial documents are in sync. If you establish a trust for management of your estate, for instance, the trust should be the secondary beneficiary—after your spouse—on your insurance policies and retirement plans.

Keep Your Will Current

Remember that you will need to keep your will up-to-date. You might change your mind about a guardian, for example. You might have to change your will's financial provisions if your financial status changes significantly. If your spouse dies or you are divorced, many changes will have to be made and you will have a much more urgent need for a comprehensive, current will.

A married couple with children from previous marriages has some special circumstances to consider. If your former spouse has custody of your child from that marriage, for instance, you may want to establish a trust for the child that is outside the control of the former spouse. If you have custody of the child, you may want to leave a portion of your estate to the child rather than leaving it all to your surviving spouse.

If you do not make these decisions and express them in a will, and if your spouse does not survive you, you will be letting a court determine your children's future. Your estate will not be managed as you

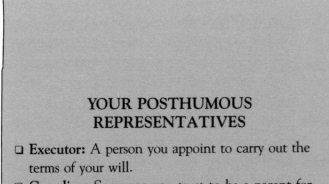

YOUR POSTHUMOUS REPRESENTATIVES

❑ **Executor:** A person you appoint to carry out the terms of your will.

❑ **Guardian:** Someone you trust to be a parent for your child in your place. He may be a relative or a close friend. You should have his agreement to assume the responsibility, and he should have a clear understanding of how you would want your children to be reared.

❑ **Trustee:** The person who will manage your estate.

Note: You should name one or more alternatives to each of these positions in case your first choice dies or is in some other way unable to assume the responsibility.

direct. Your children may not end up with the guardian you would have chosen. There's even a chance that your children could end up in a foster home or a child-care institution.

DO-IT-YOURSELF WILLS

The easiest and safest way to write a will is to retain an attorney who specializes in estate planning. For those who want to write a will without a lawyer, there are self-help books, fill-in-the-blank worksheets, and will-writing computer programs.

If you don't have children or your children are grown, there's a good chance you could write a simple will without a lawyer. The likelihood of needing legal help increases as you add children to the picture, accumulate a sizable estate, or want to establish trusts to manage your children's inheritance.

An Ohio lawyer told us, for instance, that he advises clients not to establish trusts in their wills in his state. He tells them to establish the trusts before they die and to use their wills only to instruct which portions of their estates are to go to the trusts. The reason is that under Ohio law, a trust established in a

will incurs probate court costs that a previously established trust does not.

Even those who publish self-help materials admit that they're not for everybody.

Nolo Press, which publishes a do-it-yourself book, kit, and computer program, includes information about "when you might consider a lawyer as opposed to doing it yourself," says Joanne Skinner, Nolo's publicity director. Some people use Nolo's products to prepare for conferring with a lawyer, she says. That way, she says, they may save some money by being able to use their time with the lawyer more efficiently.

Considering its importance, a will isn't very expensive. Fees vary around the country, but many lawyers will do a simple will for less than $150. Most parents wouldn't have to pay more than several hundred dollars.

"I think it's generally worth the cost of having an attorney do it," financial planner Barbara Warner says.

Before you decide to write a will on your own, you need to ask yourself how much time and effort you're willing to devote to doing the project right and how comfortable you are with risking a mistake.

WHAT IF YOU'RE INCAPACITATED?

You also should have a durable general power of attorney, a power of attorney for health care, and a living will. These documents assure that your wishes are followed should you become unable to manage your affairs while you're still alive. They can be prepared easily at the time you prepare your will.

If, like many people, you're not sure just what these legal terms mean, here are some definitions:

- ❑ **A durable general power of attorney** enables a representative whom you name—probably your spouse—to manage your finances and make other decisions should you be unable to.
- ❑ **A power of attorney for health care** enables your representative to consult with your doctors and to make health-care decisions for you if you can't.
- ❑ **A living will** tells how you wish to be treated should you be mentally incapacitated and suffering from a terminal illness or injury. Commonly, a living will explains the circumstances under which you would want life-support procedures to be withdrawn.

Getting Professional Financial Advice

"We're beginning to think we need a financial adviser to help us address specific needs we have, but that sounds like something for people with more money in the bank than we've got. Is a financial adviser appropriate for us middle-income families?"

To apply these general principles to your specific financial situation requires detailed advice that cannot be offered in a book. You don't have to be rich to benefit from such advice. Many working parents could profit from a session with a financial adviser who would review their economic situation and recommend how to manage their money better.

MAKING THE RIGHT CHOICE

Picking a financial adviser is much like picking a doctor. You won't find them evaluated in consumer magazines. You need to ask friends and colleagues for advice. You should check references. You should interview them to make sure that their expertise and philosophy match your needs. And you need to understand that they come in several varieties.

A financial planner will offer a wide range of advice. Some become Certified Financial Planners by meeting initial education and experience requirements and by participating in continuing education programs.

Broker/planners offer advice for free and earn commissions from the stocks and other financial instruments that they sell to you. Some insurance agents and sellers of other financial devices have earned certification. Banks also offer financial advice. Some people turn to accountants or lawyers for help.

Others choose a financial planner who charges a fee for her advice and does not sell financial instruments. The theory is that a fee-only planner's advice will be more objective because she's not earning a commission by selling you the stocks or insurance policies that she recommends.

Some planners will operate under either arrangement, depending upon each client's individual preference.

Before retaining a fee-only planner, ascertain her charges. The cost can be hefty, and some planners will take clients only if their assets exceed a certain level. But many will offer an initial consultation for free or at low cost.

If you use a fee-only planner, you may have to get a broker to make the investments that the planner suggests.

Know What You're Paying For

Whichever route you choose, it's important to be aware of your adviser's own financial interests and to evaluate her advice in light of those interests. Your broker makes money on your stock transactions. Your insurance agent makes money by selling you insurance. You should be skeptical of someone who suggests concentrating your money in one particular kind of investment.

Ideally, you'll have long-term relationships with your advisers, who will get to know you well, will keep an eye on your financial situation, will respond to your questions, and will make unsolicited recommendations for changes from time to time.

"I will not invest any capital until I know the investment objectives of the clients, understand their priorities and their risk-tolerance," financial planner Jannet Carpien says.

One way to pick a broker is to contact a reputable firm and talk with the manager about which of the firm's brokers would be a good match for you.

Managing Your Own Money

"Can't I make my own decisions and save on fees in the process?"

Money management is not a science like, say, mathematics. There are no universally accepted formulas for success, no handbooks guaranteed to make you affluent, no experts who always know the right time to make a specific investment and the right time to sell. If there were, it would be easy for everybody to become rich.

There are many financial experts who believe that a reasonably intelligent person can invest as successfully as the pros. But you have to devote time and effort to learn how investments work, to track how yours are performing, and to know when to make changes and what changes to make. It's easy to say that a young family trying to accumulate wealth should invest in mutual funds that buy stocks, for example. But it's not so easy to decide which specific mutual funds are best for you today.

If you don't want to hire an adviser, you can make yourself more knowledgeable about finances by reading business magazines and the business sections of newspapers and by keeping up with the general news. You can find books on personal finance in the library and bookstores. Some community colleges and other organizations offer courses on personal finance.

Becoming more knowledgeable will make you a better money manager even if you consult professional advisers. The more you know, the easier it is for you and your advisers to come up with the right decisions. As Carpien puts it: "No person can successfully lead you down the path to wealth if you don't participate."

A basic rule of investing is that your investments should be diversified. So should your information sources.

You can see why by taking a look at different financial magazines' periodic reports on mutual funds. "They survey the funds and evaluate the funds and they all come up with different evaluations," Barbara Warner notes, "which is why people need to take the advice with a grain of salt." The magazines

FINANCIALLY VALUABLE READING MATTER

Here are some periodicals and books that can help you learn to manage your money better. Don't rely on just one.

Periodicals

- ❑ *Consumer Reports*: Helps you to spend your money wisely by testing and evaluating everything from automobiles to yogurt. It also publishes periodic reports on such financial management topics as insurance and mutual funds.
- ❑ *Kiplinger's Personal Finance Magazine*: Gives advice on a wide range of personal finance matters from general economic forecasts to reports on specific bank accounts, mutual funds, and stocks.
- ❑ *Money*: Easy-to-read reporting and advice from the folks who bring you *Time*, *Life*, *Sports Illustrated*, and *People*.
- ❑ *Smart Money*: The *Wall Street Journal*'s personal finance magazine.
- ❑ Your nearest metropolitan newspaper's business section and general news pages: You can't make smart money-management decisions if you don't know what's going on in the world. The tables in major newspapers' financial pages will let you track your stock and mutual fund investments.
- ❑ The *Wall Street Journal*: If you want a lot more business news or if your local newspapers' business sections are inadequate.

Books

- ❑ *Dunn and Bradstreet's Guide to Your Investments* by Nancy Dunnan (Harper Collins, 1994): A basic guidebook that's updated annually.
- ❑ *Making the Most of Your Money* by Jane Bryant Quinn (Simon & Schuster, 1991): Advice from the syndicated columnist.
- ❑ *Your Financial Security* by Sylvia Porter (William Morrow, 1989): Advice from the late syndicated columnist.
- ❑ *The Only Other Investment Guide You'll Ever Need* by Andrew Tobias (Simon & Schuster, 1988): A witty financial education from the author of *The Only Investment Guide You'll Ever Need* and a lot of other books, magazine articles, and financial computer programs.

are "a good place to go to collect data," she says. "But don't blindly take the recommendations."

Raising Money-Savvy Children

If you're a capable money manager, you're not only securing your family's financial health, you're also serving as a good role model for your children. But the only way they will be exposed to your example is if you involve them in some basic understanding of the family's finances and teach them the importance of earning and saving.

We hear too many stories of parents who lavish designer-label presents on their children, never help the kids learn about delayed gratification, and keep them totally in the dark about the family finances. Is it any wonder that these kids grow up without developing the habit of saving money and spending it wisely?

Use shopping trips to help your children learn comparison shopping and how to judge the value of products. Let the kids participate in discussions about major family purchases. And don't keep them in the dark about the family's overall financial health. If things are tight, let them know, even if

ESTABLISHING A SAVINGS HABIT EARLY

When Julie was 5 and her friends started getting allowances, we wanted to teach her the benefits of saving. So, along with her $1-a-week allowance, she got a bank account in the computer program we use to track our family finances. The account earned 10-percent-a-month interest—a bit above the market rate, but we figured a measly 6 percent a year wouldn't inspire a 5-year-old to prodigious savings.

Julie saved so much that, in less than two years, the interest payments exceeded her allowance—a mark of a truly affluent person. We reduced the interest rate to 5 percent a month, explaining how real interest rates had been dropping, but that didn't deter her saving. She'd spend a small amount occasionally on a toy or a gift. But, mostly, she sat back and watched the dollars add up each week on the computer screen.

Eventually, she decided to spend $90 on an outrageously expensive doll that we never would have bought for her. But she didn't want to deplete her bank account. So she continued to save until she had about $150 before she bought the doll. If saving is a habit, she's acquired hers early.

Tom

you're afraid it may cause them anxiety. They'll be more anxious if they think you're hiding things from them and may imagine that problems are bigger than they are.

Allowances

A key to teaching a child about money is giving him an allowance. He won't learn to manage money if he doesn't have any. Help him set up a way to save some of it. Some banks have such high service charges that a child's allowance would be eaten up, but others have plans especially for kids.

TEACHING WITH ALLOWANCES

❑ Give the allowance weekly to kids in elementary school and always on the same day of the week.

❑ Start with a small amount, say 50 cents or a dollar for a first grader, and increase it gradually as the child gets older. Discuss the amount with your child so she can air her views.

❑ Though many parents do it, experts say allowances shouldn't be tied to chores. Kids' chores should be their contribution to the family. Don't tie the allowance to school grades either.

❑ The point is to give your child his own money to control. It's not whether he spends it on junk or saves it for something special; it's that he learns the value of money in the process.

APPENDIX: FURTHER READING

CHILD CARE

Berezin, Judith. *The Complete Guide to Choosing Child Care*. Random House, 1990, for the National Association of Child Care Resource and Referral Agencies. Thoroughly covers all aspects of selecting child care for infants through school-age children. Includes many helpful checklists and a state-by-state list of referral agencies.

Lusk, Diane, and Bruce McPherson. *Nothing But the Best: Making Day Care Work for You and Your Child*. Quill, 1992. Not about choosing child care but about living with it. Tips, presented in workbook style, for coping with arrivals, separations, toilet training, fighting, changing teachers, and many other issues for children in daycare.

Robinson, Bryan E., Bobbie H. Rowland, and Mick Coleman. *Home Alone Kids: The Working Parent's Complete Guide to Providing the Best Care for Your Child*. Lexington Books, 1989. Primarily for parents who must rely on self-care when their children aren't in school. Advice for preparing child for self-care, evaluating the arrangement, and finding alternatives if self-care isn't working.

Zigler, Edward F., and Mary E. Lang. *Child Care Choices: Balancing the Needs of Children, Families,* and Society. Free Press, 1991. A definitive look at child care in America and how it can be improved. Covers the specific care needs of infants, toddlers, and school-age children. Useful for parents, child-care professionals, policymakers, and corporate executives.

CHILD DEVELOPMENT

Brazelton, T. Berry. *Working and Caring*. Addison-Wesley, 1985. Using the examples of three families—a professional couple, a blue-collar couple, and a single working mother, the famed pediatrician offers advice on returning to work, coping with the lack of time, evaluating daycare, etc.

Galinsky, Ellen, and Judy David. *The Preschool Years*. Ballantine, 1988. Practical solutions for one hundred issues that arise when raising children ages 2 to 5. Includes a section on how work affects family life.

Greenspan, Stanley I. *Playground Politics: Understanding the Emotional Life of Your School-Age Child*. Addison-Wesley, 1993. A leading child development expert offers parents a road map to the stages of emotional development of children ages 5 to 12.

Helps parents support their children through these changes.

Kelly, Marguerite, and Elia Parsons. *The Mother's Almanac*. Doubleday, 1975; revised 1992. Packed with ideas to encourage and nurture children from birth to first grade. Explains behaviors at various stages and gives advice on handling them. Also includes fun things to do with children, including crafts, games, and cooking projects.

Kelly, Marguerite. *The Mother's Almanac II*. Doubleday, 1989. Similar to *The Mother's Almanac* but for parents of children ages 6 to 12.

PARENTS' ROLES

Crosby, Faye J. *Juggling: The Unexpected Advantages of Balancing Career and Home for Women and Their Families*. Free Press, 1991. A social psychologist draws on research to make a reassuring case for the ways husbands, children, and mothers benefit when mothers have both a work life and a home life.

Edelman, Marian Wright. *The Measure of Our Success: A Letter to My Children and Yours*. Beacon Press, 1992. The inspiring personal view of a parent's role by the famous child advocate and head of the Children's Defense Fund. Drawing on her own upbringing and her experiences raising her three sons, Edelman offers a compassionate message for parents trying to instill values in their children. Includes "Twenty-Five Lessons for Life."

Goldman, Katherine Wyse. *My Mother Worked and I Turned Out Okay.* Villard Books, 1993. Upbeat stories from adults raised by working mothers interwoven with Goldman's own experiences as the daughter of Lois Wyse, advertising executive and best-selling author.

Marshall, Melinda M. *Good Enough Mothers: Changing Expectations for Ourselves.* Peterson's, 1993. Offers comforting insights regarding the many trade-offs faced by working mothers and solutions to the problems they pose. Marshall contends that being "good enough" isn't tied to how many hours you spend at home but that it is a matter of choosing priorities and learning to live with compromise.

PARENTS AS SPOUSES

Byalick, Marcia, and Linda Saslow. *The Three-Career Couple.* Peterson's, 1993. Practical help for two-earner couples who have to juggle their individual careers with a third one—home and family.

Hochschild, Arlie. *The Second Shift.* Viking, 1989. A study of dual-earner families that points to the need for men to share more equally in child care and housework duties, which women continue to perform more often even though they, too, have jobs outside the home.

Sachs, Brad E. *Things Just Haven't Been the Same: Making the Transition from Marriage to Parenthood.* William Morrow, 1992. Takes a step back from the day-to-day trials of new parenthood to explain why the birth of a child can rock even the happiest marriage boat. Especially valuable for its discussion of fathers and their feelings about becoming parents.

THE WORKPLACE

Dynerman, Susan Bacon, and Lynn O'Rourke Hayes. *The Best Jobs in America for Parents Who Want Careers and Time for Children Too.* Rawson Associates, 1991. A comprehensive guide to locating, negotiating, and managing flexible careers. Includes information on 25 "flexible" companies. Invaluable for its negotiating tips.

Marzollo, Jean. *Your Maternity Leave: How to Leave Work, Have a Baby, and Go Back to Work Without Getting Lost, Trapped, or Sandbagged Along the Way.* Poseidon Press, 1989. Practical advice for anticipating and avoiding traps before the baby comes, during the leave, and upon returning to work.

Morgan, Hal, and Kerry Tucker. *Companies That Care: The Most Family-Friendly Companies in America—What They Offer and How They Got That Way.* Simon and Schuster/Fireside, 1991. Profiles firms that offer the best benefits, greatest job flexibility, and most support for working parents. Includes detailed case studies and an alphabetical directory.

INDEX

A

AAA (American Automobile Association), 136
Abuse
  drug and alcohol, by teenagers, 145, 148-51
  sexual, 63
Adolescents. *See* Teenagers
Adoption, 20
Affinity cards, 252, 253
Agreements. *See* Contracts and agreements
AIDS, 146
Airlines, savings programs from, 252-53
Alcohol abuse by teenagers, 145, 148
  prevention, 149-51
Allowances for children, 272
American Automobile Association, 135, 136
American Camping Association, 115, 116, 178
American Council of Nanny Schools, 47
Answering machines, 160
Anxiety. *See also* Guilt; Stress
  business trips and, 210-11
  daycare and, 87
  support groups for, 198
Association of Part-Time Professionals, 225
Au pairs, 36, 61–66
  arrangements, 64, 66
  costs, 61
  deciding on, 61-62
  definition, 46
  homesickness of, 62-63
  male, 63
  qualifications, 61
  yearly turnover, 63-64

Automobiles, teenagers and, 134-37

B

Babies. *See* Infants
Babysitters
  daycare staff as, 91
  definition, 46
  payments to, 68-70
  on vacations, 176-77
Babysitting, sharing, 197-98, 199
Bank accounts, 258, 271
Banking by phone, 161
Beepers, 161
Benefits
  negotiating, for flexible career, 226-27
  noncash, 252-53
  parental leave, 20-21
Berezin, Judith, 80
Book club for communication with teenagers, 146-47
Books
  financial, 270
  recorded on cassette, 161
Bosses. *See* Employers; Supervisors
Brazelton, T. Berry, 200
Breastfeeding, 35, 36
  pumps, 38, 39
  work and, 38-40
Buses, school, 109
Bush Center in Child Development and Social Policy, 101, 102
Business. *See also* Careers with flexibility; Companies; Employers; Workplace dilemmas
  associations, 246
  starting own, 242-47

C

Call waiting, 161
Camping, as family vacation, 176
Camps
  for family vacations, 178
  neighborhood informal, 113
  sleep-away, 116
  summer, 113-15
Career. *See also* Jobs; Workplace
  paternity leave and, 31-32
Careers with flexibility, 223-47
  deciding on, 239-42
  evaluating firms, 240
  finding, 238
  job sharing, 236-38
  making case for, 224-29
  parents' need for, 223-24
  part-time work (*see* Part-time work)
  postponing promotions, 238-39
  starting own business, 242-47
  trade-offs, 241
  working at home (*see* Working at home)
Caregivers. *See also* Au pairs; Babysitters; Daycare centers; Family daycare; Nannies
  arrangements with live-ins, 64, 66
  changing, 44
  desirable qualities, 44, 46
  getting along with, 58-61
  health, legal, and criminal checks, 52, 54, 57
  hiring process, 46-54
  options, 46
  pet peeves of, 59
  stories about, 55-56

taxes and immigration issues, 68-71
Car pools, 167, 196, 197
Cars, teenagers and, 134-37
Catalog shopping, 159
Catalyst, 225
CDs (certificates of deposit), retirement
  planning and, 258-59
Cellular phones, 161
Center for Early Adolescence, 133
Certificates of deposit, retirement planning
  and, 258-59
Charge cards, 252
Checklists
  child care
    daycare-center evaluation, 84, 86-87
    family daycare, 81
    in home, 45
    outside home, 75
    house rules for live-ins, 65
    interview questions, 50–51
    licensing standards for family daycare, 76
    nannies' pet peeves, 59
    nanny job description, 51
    placement agencies, 58
    references, 53
    relationship with daycare centers, 90, 91
    by relatives, 99
    school-age child-care program, 108
    self-care, 120
    written agreement, 58, 60
  children helping with chores, 193
  finances
    allowances for children, 272
    enforced savings, 251
    publications, 270
  life insurance needs, 260
  report card for parents, 218-19

shared vacations, 179
teenagers
  AAA teen driver's contract, 135
  book club for communication, 147
  depression, 153
work
  business trips and children, 212
  home-based work, 231
  job flexibility, 225
  parental leave, 19
  starting own business, 243, 246-47
Childbirth. See also Breastfeeding; Parental
leave
  classes, 26
  coping with, 41
  getting help after, 33-36, 37
  recovery period, 26-27
Child care. See also Caregivers; School-age
  child; Sharing responsibilities
  anxiety reduction over, 40
  changes in arrangements, 44
  employer assistance, 21
  in home, 43-71
  outside home, 73-102
  new parents' reactions to, 18
  time to search for, 36-37
Child Care Aware, 77, 87, 107
Child Care Connection, 85
Child Development Associate credentials, 86
Children. See also Child care; Infants;
  School-age child; Teenagers
  allowances for, 272
  business trips and, 210-13
  chores and, 164, 166, 191-92, 193
  custody after death, 263, 264, 265
  eating out and, 159
  financial education for, 271-72

relocation and, 213-14
time spent with, 168-71
understanding work demands, 220-21
vacations with, 174-79
work and, 205-6
working parents viewed by, 217
Children's Foundation, 75
Chores. See also Sharing responsibilities
  children and, 164, 166, 191-92, 193
  delegating, 164, 166
  free time and, 167-68
  organizing, 166-67
  sample chart for, 189
  sharing, 186-89
Cigarette smoking by teenagers, 145
Cleaning shortcuts, 162-66. See also
  Housekeeping
Clinton, Hillary, 156-57
Clothes, no-fuss, 162-63
Coaching, 203, 204
Cocaine, 145, 149
Colgate-Palmolive, 95
College education, financing, 253-57
College students supervising teenagers, 131
Communication
  for both spouses working at home, 233
  with caregivers, 57-61
  conflict resolution, 189-91
  with daycare center, 90-91
  negotiating maternity leave, 21, 24-25,
    27-30
  with other parents about teenagers, 141,
    143-44, 151, 152
  parent education classes, 203
  phone contact by children home alone after
    school, 122-24, 131, 133
  with relatives about child care, 97-99

THE WORKING PARENTS HELP BOOK

with schools and teachers, 129, 173-74
shared responsibilities and, 186
with teenagers, 128
time-saving technology, 160-62
working at home and, 221
Community daycare emergency network, 106
Community service by teenagers, 140-41, 142
Commuting time, 166
Companies. *See also* Careers with flexibility;
Employers
children and, 205-6. *See also* Workplace
dilemmas
fathers and, 208-9
job flexibility and, 229, 237, 240
support for nursing mothers, 39
support groups and, 202-3
year-round schools and, 118
Compromise, children and, 169
Computers
at home, 162
in self-owned business, 246-47
Conflict resolution, 189-91
with supervisors, 206-8
Consolidated Edison, 95
Consumer Credit Counseling Service, 252
Contracts and agreements. *See also* Law
AAA teen driver's contract, 135
with caregivers, 58, 60
for parental leave, 23
self-care after school, 122
for teen parties, 150-151
wills and guardians, 263-67
Cooking, 157, 158, 160
Co-ops
babysitting, 197-98, 199
daycare centers, 90
Cordless phones, 160

Costs. *See also* Finances
au pairs, 61
child care, 44
college education, 253-54
sick-child care, 95
summer camps, 114
wills, 266
Couples spending time together, 179-80
Credit cards, 252
Cruises, 177

D
David, Judy, 78
Daycare centers, 83-94. *See also* Family
daycare; School-age child
advantages and disadvantages, 84
choosing, 83, 85-89
drop-in, 93
emergency contacts form, 82
preschools, 99-101
relationship with, 90-92
school of 21st century, 101-2
separation anxiety and, 87
Debt, charge card, 25
Delegating chores, 164, 166
Depression in teenagers, 152-54
Disability insurance, 259, 261
parental leave and, 20
Doulas, 33-34, 35
Drinking, teenage, 145, 148
prevention, 149-51
Driving, teenage, 134-37
Drop-in daycare centers, 93
Drug abuse, teenage, 145, 148-49
increasing trend, 149
legal substances, 148-49
prevention of alcohol abuse, 149-51
signs, 148

Duties. *See* Chores; Sharing responsibilities
Dynerman, Susan, 225, 226, 236

E
Eating out with children, 159
Economics. *See* Costs; Finances
Education. *See also* Communication; Schools
financial, 269-71
financing, 253-57
parent education classes, 203
sex, 144-45, 146
Emergencies
daycare, 106
savings for, 262-63
self-care and, 120-21
Employers. *See also* Companies; Supervisors
child care assistance from, 77, 95
legal responsibilities for parental leave,
22-23
negotiating maternity leave with, 21, 24-25,
27
support groups and, 202-3
Errands. *See also* Chores
organizing, 166-67
Estate
executor, trustee, and guardian, 263-64, 265
management, 264-66
size, 263
Executor of estate, 263-64, 265
Exercise, 180-81
Expenses, reducing, 251

F
Family
cooking and, 158-59
fun with, 169
vacations for, 174-79
volunteering and, 172-73

Family and Medical Leave Act of 1993, 22-23
Family daycare, 74-81
  advantages and disadvantages, 75
  checklist, 81
  employer assistance, 77
  finding providers, 77, 80
  licensing, 74-76
  for older children, 104
  reasons for choosing, 78-79
  relatives caring for children, 95, 97-99
  resources and referral agencies, 76-77
Fathers
  guilt and, 217
  parental leave and, 18
  sharing responsibilities, 185-86
  workplace problems of, 208-9
Federal Child Care Income Tax Credit, 114
Federal Pregnancy Discrimination Act, 22, 23
Finances. *See also* Costs
  after-school program start-up, 111
  banking by phone, 161
  caregivers and, 68-70
  child's education, 253-57
  educating children, 271-72
  insurance, 259-63
  noncash benefits, 252-53
  part-time work and, 234-35
  paying relatives for child care, 99
  preparing for future, 249-72
  professional advice, 267-69
  publications, 270
  retirement planning, 257-59
  savings, 250-52, 271
  self-management, 269, 271
  wills and guardians, 263-67
Fire, children and, 119

Flexible jobs. *See* Careers with flexibility
Floor time, 170
401(k) plans, 257-58
Friends, 191-96
  childless, 194-95
  making, 193-94
  Mommy Wars prevention, 195-96
Future, preparing for, 249-72

G
Galinsky, Ellen, 78
Gifts for children after business trip, 210
Girl Scouts, 123, 172
Gleaning, 172
Goldman, Katherine Wyse, 216
Goodman, Ellen, 124
Grandparents
  child care by, 95, 97
  on family vacations, 177
Greenspan, Stanley, 170
Guardians, 263-64, 265
Guilt, working parents and, 215-20

H
Health of caregivers, 52
Hochschild, Arlie, 184
Home
  children alone at, after school, 118-25
  working at (*see* Working at home)
Home Box Office, 95
Honeywell, 95
Hotels
  family vacation packages from, 177
  savings programs, 252-53
Housekeeping
  childbirth and, 34, 36

  hiring help, 156-57, 167
  shortcuts, 162-66
  standards, 165

I
Illness
  child care and, 92, 94-95, 96
  disability insurance, 20, 259, 261
Immigration and Naturalization Service, 68-69, 71
Immigration of caregivers, 70-71
Individual retirement arrangements/accounts (IRAs), 258
Infants
  center-based care, 74
  morning routine with, 40-41
  nurses for, 34
  time management and, 19, 25, 30
Infections, childbirth recovery and, 28
Instincts about caregivers, 48
Insurance
  disability, 20, 259, 261
  emergency savings, 262-63
  life, 259-61
  research, 261-62
Internal Revenue Service, 70, 246
Interviews with caregivers, 47, 49-51
Investment decisions, 267-71
IRAs, 258
IRS, 70, 246

J
Jealousy
  of grandparents caring for children, 98
  part-time work and, 235-36
Job description for caregivers, 49, 51
Jobs. *See also* Careers with flexibility; Workplace

part-time, for teenagers, 137-39
protection of, parental leave and, 20
refusing promotions, 238-39
relocation, 213-14
Job sharing, 236-38

K
Kelly, Marguerite, 138, 151, 190
Keogh plans, 258
Keys, children and, 121
Kids Kab, 110
Kindercare, 112

L
Labor sharing, 184-89. *See also* Sharing responsibilities
Lactation. *See* Breastfeeding
La Leche League, 38, 40
Lateness for work, child care and, 220
Law(s). *See also* Contracts and agreements
  caregivers and, 68-70
  family daycare licensing, 74-76
  parental leave, 18, 22-23
  power of attorney, 267
  wills and guardians, 263-67
Layoffs, parental leave and, 20
Leadership, 203-4
Leave of absence. *See* Parental leave
Legal issues. *See* Law
Leisure time, 167, 168, 180-81
Life insurance, 259-61
Living will, 267
Loans for college education, 254

M
Marijuana, 149
Marshall, Melinda, 216

Marzollo, Jean, 24
Maternity leave. *See also* Parental leave
  negotiating, 21, 24-25, 27-30
McDonald's, 139
Mead, Margaret, 200
Meals, saving time and, 157-59
Mend 'n Tend, 96
Microwave ovens, 160
Mommy Wars prevention, 195-96
Money. *See* Costs; Finances
Moodiness in teenagers, 152-54
Morgan, Hal, 240
Mothers, working, labor burden for, 184-85
Mothers' centers, 202
Mother's helpers, 36
Moving for work, 213-14
Mrazek, David, 152, 153

N
Nannies, 44, 46. *See also* Caregivers
  getting along with, 58-61
  interview questions for, 50
  job description for, 51
  pet peeves of, 59
  stories about, 55-56
National Association for Family Child Care, 80
National Association for the Education of Young Children, 60, 86, 87, 88
National Association of Mothers' Centers, 202
National Association of Postpartum Care Services, 33, 34
National Center for Service Learning in Early Adolescence, 142
National Mental Health Association, 154
National PTA, 174

Negotiating
  maternity leave, 21, 24-25, 27-30
  salary and benefits for flexible career, 226-27
Neighborhood cooking, 158
Neighborhood daycare emergency network, 106
New Ways to Work, 224, 225
Night walks with children, 169
Nurses, baby, 34
Nursing. *See* Breastfeeding

O
Olmsted, Barney, 226
Overtime work, 209-10

P
Parent Action, 200, 214
Parental leave, 17-41
  arrangements with employer, 21, 28-30
  benefits, 20-21
  childcare search and, 36-37
  consecutive vs. simultaneous leaves, 33
  getting help after birth, 33-36
  laws, 22-23
  length of, 24-25, 27-28
  negotiating maternity leave, 21, 24-25, 27-30
  part-time work and, 24, 28-29
  pitfalls of early return to work, 25
  planning for, 17-21
  recovery period and, 26-27
  returning to work after, 37-41
  setting departure and return dates, 25, 27
  working at home and, 24, 30
  workplace accommodations, 18
Parent Connection, 67
Parent education classes, 203

Parenting Publications of America, 176
Parent-teacher organizations, 173-74
Parties for teenagers, 150, 151-52
Part-time work, 233-36. *See also* Job sharing
  childbirth and, 24, 28-29
  finances and, 234-35
  jealous colleagues and, 235-36
  for teenagers, 137-39
Paternity leave, 22, 30-32. *See also* Parental
  leave
Pediatrician, office location of, 166
Periodicals, financial, 270
Personal time, 167, 168, 180-81
Phone bills, affinity cards and, 252, 253
Phone contact
  business trips and, 211
  self-care by children and, 122-24, 131, 133
  with teachers, 174
Phone numbers, children and, 121
Phones, 160, 161
Placement agencies for caregivers, 54, 57, 58
Planned Parenthood Association of America,
  145
Play groups, 198, 201
Power of attorney, 267
Pregnancy. *See also* Parental leave
  complications, parental leave and, 25
Pregnancy Discrimination Act of 1978, 22,
  23
Prenatal benefits from employer, 20
Preparing for future, 249-72
Preschools, 99-101
Presents for children after business trip, 210
Private schools, 255-57
Procrastination, 164
Professional associations, 246
Promotions, refusing, 238-39

Proms, parties after, 152
PTA (Parent-Teacher Association), 173-74
Publications, financial, 270
Public schools, 254-56
  sponsoring preschools, 100-101

Q
Quality time with children, redefining,
  168-69, 171

R
Reading with children, 169, 171
Recorded books on cassette, 161
References for caregivers, 49, 52-54, 57, 77
Relationships. *See also* Family; Friends;
  Grandparents; Spouses
  cultivating, 193-95
  Mommy Wars prevention, 195-96
Relatives, child care by, 95, 97-99
Relocation for work, 213-14
Report card for parents, 218-19
Respiratory infections, childbirth recovery
  and, 28
Responsibilities. *See* Chores; Sharing
  responsibilities
Restaurants, children in, 19
Reston Children's Center, 123
Rest rooms, young children and, 185
Retirement planning, 257-59

S
Sachs, Brad, 209, 217, 220
Salary negotiation for flexible career, 226-27
Satellite offices, 230
Savings, 250-52. *See also* Finances
  airline and hotel programs, 252-53
  for child's education, 253-57
  emergency, 262-63

habit of, 271
  retirement, 257-59
Scales, Peter, 130, 138, 139, 140
Schedules for flexible work, 228-29
School-age child, 103-25. *See also* Teenagers
  care for, 103-4
  care programs, 104-7
  neighborhood emergency network for
    daycare, 106
  parental involvement with school, 173-74
  self-care after school, 118-25
  summer care, 112-16
  transportation for, 107, 109, 110
  year-round school for, 116-18
School-Age Child Care Project, 111
School buses, 109
Schools
  child care at, 104-5
  child care in 21st century, 101-2
  choosing new, 214
  driver education, 135, 136
  financing child's education, 253-57
  for nannies, 47
  parental involvement with, 129, 173-74
  parent peer groups in, 143-44
  preschools, 99-101
  private vs. public, for young students,
    254-57
  teenage volunteerism and, 140
  year-round, 116-18
Self-esteem, teen depression and, 153
Separation anxiety
  business trips and, 210-11
  daycare and, 87
SEP plans, 258
Sex education, 144-45, 146

Sex Information and Education Council of the United States, 145
Sexual abuse, 63
Sharing responsibilities, 183-204
  babysitting, 197-98, 199
  car pools, 196
  conflict resolution, 189-91
  fair shares, 187-89
  family action trends, 200
  fathers' involvement, 185-86
  friends' help, 191-96
  support groups, 198, 201-4
  trading responsibilities, 186-87
  on weekends, 187
  working mothers' burden, 184-85
Shopping, saving time and, 159-60
Siblings, child care by, 125
Sick-child care, 92, 94-95, 96, 189
Simplified Employee Pension plans, 258
Sleep-away camps, 116
Smith, Suzanne, 225, 230, 236, 238
Smoking by teenagers, 145
Socializing, 193-95
Social Security taxes, caregivers and, 68, 69-70
Spock, Benjamin, 47
Spouses
  both working at home, 232-33
  sharing responsibilities, 186-89
  spending time together, 179-80
Starting own business, 242-47
State parental leave laws, 23
Stocks, retirement planning and, 258
Strangers, children and, 121
Stress. See also Anxiety; Guilt
  part-time work and, 234
  teen depression and, 153

Summer camps, 113-15
Summer care for children, 112-16
Supervisors
  conflict resolution with, 206-8
  fathers' family concerns and, 208-9
  job flexibility viewed by, 239
  negotiating maternity leave with, 21, 24-25, 27
Support groups, 198
  leadership and, 203-4
  mothers' centers, 202
  parent education classes, 203
  play groups, 198, 201
  at work, 202-3

T
Tape recorders, 161-62
Taxes
  child care and, 68-69
  purchases and, 250
  in self-owned business, 246
Teachers, keeping in touch with, 174
Technology for saving time, 160-62
Teenagers, 127-54
  book club for communication with, 146-47
  cars and, 134-37
  child care by, 125
  depression in, 152-54
  drinking and drug use by, 145, 148-49
  parenting difficulties with, 128-29
  parent peer groups, 141, 143-44
  parties for, 150, 151-52
  part-time jobs for, 137-39
  problems of, 127-28
  risky behavior by, 144-54
  self-care after school, 119-25
  sex and, 144-45, 146
  supervised from distance, 129-34

volunteering by, 140-41, 142
Telecommuting. See Working at home
Telephones, 160, 161. See also Phone entries
Time management, 155-81. See also Careers with flexibility
  calendar for busy families with teenagers, 132
  challenge of, 155-56
  couples sharing time, 179-80
  family vacations, 174-79
  free time, 167-68, 180-81
  hiring help, 156-57, 167
  housekeeping shortcuts, 162-66
  infants and, 19, 25, 30
  involvement with children's school, 173-74
  mealtime, 157-59
  paternity leave and, 32
  setting priorities, 156
  shopping, 159-60
  spending time with children, 168-71
  technology for, 160-62
  transportation, 166-67
  volunteering, 171-73
Time Warner, 95
Tobacco use by teenagers, 145
Transportation
  car pools, 167, 196, 197
  cars for teenagers, 134-37
  saving time and, 166-67
  for school-age child, 107, 109, 110
Travel. See also Vacations
  airline and hotel savings programs, 252-53
  work requirements, 210-13
Trustee of estate, 263-64, 265
Tucker, Kerry, 240

U
Union contracts, parental leave and, 23

V

Vacations, 174-79
  babysitters on, 176-77
  camping, 176
  kid sharing, 178-79
  packages, 177
  shared with others, 178, 179
  year-round school and, 117
Van services for children, 110
Videocassette recorders (VCRs), 161
Volunteers/volunteering, 171-73
  for after-school child care, 111
  teenagers, 140-41, 142

W

Walks at night with children, 169
Waymon, Lynne, 206-7
Weekends, child care on, 187
Wills, 263

do-it-yourself, 266-67
keeping current, 265-66
living, 267
Work
  flexible hours, supervising teenagers and, 130-31
  part-time, for teenagers, 137-39
Working at home, 166, 229. *See also* Starting own business
  both spouses, 232-33
  childbirth and, 24, 30
  communicating with children and, 221
  dealing with children while, 232
  deciding on, 230-32
  satellite offices, 230
Work permits for foreign caregivers, 70-71
Workplace
  breastfeeding and, 38-40

support groups in, 202-3
teenagers helping parents at, 131

Workplace dilemmas, 205-21
  conflict resolution with supervisors, 206-8
  fathers' problems, 208-9
  guilt, 215-20
  helping children understand work, 220-21
  lateness for work, 220
  overtime trap, 209-10
  relocation, 213-14
  report card for parents, 218-19
  travel requirements, 210-13

Y

YMCA, child care and, 106-7
YWCA, child care and, 105, 112

Z

Zigler, Edward, 101-2

ABOUT THE AUTHORS

Susan Crites Price is a writer specializing in women's and family issues. Her articles have appeared in numerous publications, including the *Washington Post* and *Washingtonian* magazine. She was formerly an editor and manager with the Mead Corporation and was on the staff of Ohio University, where she chaired the President's Committee on Women.

Tom Price is the *Dayton Daily News* correspondent in the Cox Newspapers Washington bureau. His freelance writing has appeared in *Time*, *Rolling Stone*, the *New York Times*, *Harper's Weekly*, and the *Washington Post*.

The Prices live in Washington, D.C., with their nine-year-old daughter, Julie.